Chad Carter

Microsoft® XNA™ Game Studio 3.0

UNLEASHED

SAMS | 800 East 96th Street, Indianapolis, Indiana 46240 USA

Microsoft® XNA™ Game Studio 3.0 Unleashed

ISBN-13: 978-0-672-33022-3

ISBN-10: 0-672-33022-9

Library of Congress Cataloging-in-Publication Data:

Carter, Chad.

  Microsoft XNA game studio 3.0 unleashed / Chad Carter.

    p. cm.

  ISBN 978-0-672-33022-3

  1. Microsoft XNA (Computer file) 2. Computer games—Programming. 3. Video games. I. Title.

  QA76.76.C672C425 2009

  794.8'1536—dc22

                        2008054527

Printed in the United States of America

First Printing April 2009

Trademarks

Warning and Disclaimer

Bulk Sales

Sams Publishing offers excellent discounts on this book when ordered in quantity for bulk purchases or special sales. For more information, please contact

U.S. Corporate and Government Sales

1-800-382-3419

corpsales@pearsontechgroup.com

For sales outside of the U.S., please contact

International Sales

international@pearson.com

Editor-in-Chief
Karen Gettman

Executive Editor
Neil Rowe

Development Editor
Mark Renfrow

Technical Editor
Chris Williams

Managing Editor
Kristy Hart

Project Editor
Anne Goebel

Copy Editor
Bart Reed

Indexer
Lisa Stumpf

Proofreader
Language Logistics

Publishing Coordinator
Cindy Teeters

Multimedia Developer
Dan Scherf

Cover Designer
Gary Adair

Compositor
Jake McFarland

Contents at a Glance

Table of Contents

About the Author

Chad Carter authored the previous edition of this book, *Microsoft XNA Unleashed: Graphics and Game Programming for Xbox 360 and Windows*. He is the Chief Technology Officer at Robertson Marketing Group. He has been creating DirectX applications since 1996 and has developed games using Managed DirectX. Chad wrote a 3D locomotive simulator for Norfolk Southern that is used to teach children to obey railroad crossing signals. Chad's website devoted to the XNA Framework can be found online at www.xnaessentials.com.

Dedication

To the most beautiful woman in the world, my wife Christy.
To my precious daughter Caleigh and my second daughter,
whom I will meet very soon.

Acknowledgments

Just like the first book, a host of people were responsible for making this book a reality. My wife was extremely supportive this time around as well. Writing this book took much longer than the original book. Even though I spent much more time on the book than I originally anticipated, she was patient with the hours I put in. There is absolutely no way this book could have been completed if it were not for her support. Christy, I love you more than ever! With Caleigh being older, it was a little more difficult for her this time around. Caleigh, thank you for being patient with your daddy for the past few months! I love you very much, and I'm very proud of how much you have learned over the last year.

Next, I want to give praise to my Lord, God Almighty, who sustained me during these past few months while I completed this book. I also need to thank my pastor, Dr. Roy Carter, and the prayer partners for their prayers for me as I took on this task.

Next, I'd like to thank Neil Rowe, an executive editor at Sams Publishing. He agreed to work with me on this project and was my main point of contact at Sams. I'd also like to thank the rest of the Sams team with whom I had direct contact on this project—Mark Renfrow, Cindy Teeters, Anne Goebel, and Bart Reed. I'd also like to thank the rest of the Sams team with whom I did not have any communication but were behind the scenes making this book a reality. I'm looking forward to seeing those names on the first page.

Shawn Hargreaves, an XNA Framework developer at Microsoft, was the technical editor of the first edition of this book. His blog can be found at http://blogs.msdn.com/shawnhar/. His blog and his forum answers helped me tremendously in learning this technology. I'd like to thank all the XNA Framework developers and Microsoft in general for making this great technology. XNA Game Studio is truly awesome!

Chris Williams was the technical editor of this book. He was a huge help in making sure I didn't just gloss over a topic. He also made sure things flowed in a manner that would help those just starting out. He was very quick to turn around completed chapters and was a tremendous help in getting this book done. He also helped me test the networking chapters over Xbox LIVE.

I'd also like to thank my parents, John and Sandra Carter, for providing many things for me, including good education. Their support means the world to me. I'd also like to thank my wife's mom and dad, Wilson and Vicki Newsome, for helping our family with many of the duties that I would normally handle but abandoned to write this book. They also helped keep my family company while I was unavailable.

I'd also like to thank my Twitter Tribe. They have put up with my constant updates as to which chapter I was working on, what I was stuck on, and how far behind I was. If you are so inclined, you can follow me on Twitter at http://twitter.com/kewlniss.

Finally, I'd like to thank you for picking up this book. I hope that it serves its purpose and brings insight into some of the mysteries of writing games. This book does no good if it is not read, so thank you, and happy programming!

We Want to Hear from You!

As the reader of this book, *you* are our most important critic and commentator. We value your opinion and want to know what we're doing right, what we could do better, what areas you'd like to see us publish in, and any other words of wisdom you're willing to pass our way.

As an executive editor for Sams, I welcome your comments. You can fax, email, or write me directly to let me know what you did or didn't like about this book—as well as what we can do to make our books stronger.

Please note that I cannot help you with technical problems related to the topic of this book, and that due to the high volume of mail I receive, I might not be able to reply to every message.

When you write, please be sure to include this book's title and author as well as your name and phone or email address. I will carefully review your comments and share them with the author and editors who worked on the book.

Email: feedback@samspublishing.com

Fax: 317-428-3310

Mail: Neil Rowe, Executive Editor
Sams Publishing
800 East 96th Street
Indianapolis, IN 46240 USA

Reader Services

Visit our website and register this book at www.informit.com/title/9780672330223 for convenient access to any updates, downloads, or errata that might be available for this book.

Introduction

Many developers became interested in programming because they saw a video game and thought, "How did they do that?" This book helps demystify what is required to make video games. Being able to write games on a next-generation console such as the Xbox 360 has never been an option for the masses before. Now with the XNA Framework, games can be written for the console.

By the end of this book, you will have created four complete games and many demos along the way. This book takes a serious look at performance-related issues when writing games using XNA for Windows and the Xbox 360. Two chapters are devoted to the High Level Shader Language (HLSL), which is a necessity for writing great games. The book covers physics and artificial intelligence (AI). It also covers special effects, including explosions, transitions, and how to create a 3D particle system. It demonstrates how to create a sound project using the Microsoft Cross-Platform Audio Creation Tool (XACT) and how to directly access sound files in a game. Two chapters are devoted to programming games for the Zune. Saving and loading a high score list and creating a full menu system are also taught in this book. Five chapters are devoted to creating multiplayer games. Writing network games can be challenging, and this book covers networking in detail. The final two chapters are on best practices and provide tips on how to sell games on the Xbox LIVE Marketplace. In general, this book contains a great foundation for many topics that need to be learned to create and sell a full-featured single-player or multiplayer game.

Who Should Read This Book?

This book was written for developers. You should have a good understanding of programming in general. The book uses C#, but if you know any modern language, such as C++, Java, or VB.NET, you will have no problem understanding the code in this book. The book assumes some understanding of the Microsoft .NET Framework, which is what the XNA Framework runs on. Without prior experience writing code using the .NET Framework, you might have to do a little research now and then, but should not have trouble getting through this book.

This book was written with a few different audiences in mind. Business application developers who want to use their programming skill set to write computer games are one audience. Graphics and game developers who have been around the OpenGL and DirectX block should also find useful information in this book—especially in seeing how things are done "the XNA way." The book also targets readers who have some programming experience but have not done anything formal. The book teaches by example. It is written in such a way that if you are not in front of your computer, you can still get valuable information from the book because the code is presented as it is being discussed.

Hardware and Software Requirements

The code in this book is compiled with XNA Game Studio 3.0. In order to complete the games and demos in this book, the requirements that follow must be met.

Supported Operating Systems

The following operating systems are supported:

- ▶ Windows XP Home Edition
- ▶ Windows XP Professional Edition
- ▶ Windows XP Media Center Edition
- ▶ Windows XP Tablet Edition
- ▶ Windows Vista Home Basic Edition
- ▶ Windows Vista Home Premium Edition
- ▶ Windows Vista Business Edition
- ▶ Windows Vista Enterprise Edition
- ▶ Windows Vista Ultimate Edition

Windows XP requires Service Pack 2 or later.

Hardware Requirements

When you run XNA Framework games on Windows, a graphics card that supports Shader Model 1.1 is required. This book has samples that use Shader Model 2.0 and a couple that use Shader Model 3.0. To get the most from this book, you need a graphics card that supports Shader Model 3.0. The graphics card should have the most up-to-date drivers. Updated drivers can be found on the graphics card's hardware vendor website.

When you run XNA Framework games on the Xbox 360 console, a hard drive must be connected to the console.

Software Requirements

All the software required to utilize the XNA Framework on Windows is free:

- ▶ Microsoft Visual C# 2005 Express Edition
- ▶ Microsoft XNA Game Studio Express
- ▶ DirectX 9.0c

Instructions on installing the software can be found in Chapter 1, "Introducing the XNA Framework and XNA Game Studio."

Code Examples

The source code for the examples in this book can be found on the accompanying CD. Any updates to the code can be downloaded via www.samspublishing.com or www.xnaessentials.com.

How This Book Is Organized

This book is organized into 11 main parts, representing the information you need to understand to use XNA Game Studio effectively. Writing a book is an interesting challenge. There are basically two routes an author can go. One route is to create small bite-sized pieces that can be used as a reference. The other route is to take the reader on a journey from start to finish, covering important topics along the way but doing it in such a manner that the reader is gradually learning concepts. Then, once the entire book has been enjoyed, the reader can go back and reread certain sections for mastery.

I have tried to take the second approach in writing this book. The book is best read in order. The Internet has a wealth of information. Learning about a particular topic is not difficult. You can easily find information from many different sources on a particular topic. The problem is there is usually no place to see how a lot of different topics work together. With a book that is designed to be read from front to back, the main drawback is a larger time commitment. However, there is usually deeper understanding by the time the task is complete versus the same amount of time spent looking at particular topics on the subject from online tutorials and blog posts. Both are very important, but because a wealth of reference information is available online already, there was no need to make this a reference book.

There was some criticism concerning the order of the first book. This book is not organized in a manner similar to many other books. However, a lot of thought was put into the order of this book. I do believe this book's order is important, and I did not change it from the first edition. I start with a very basic chapter explaining the history of XNA and very detailed instructions on how to install XNA Game Studio. Most people will not need this, but it is there for those who do. The next chapter jumps right in to talking about the Xbox 360. Even though there are people who do not have an Xbox 360, it is important to put this chapter up front so you can be aware of certain things when creating games using XNA. It is always important to know what you are up against before you start. It is for this same reason that the very next chapter is on performance. Most books simply give a nod to performance in a later chapter or maybe an appendix, if at all. I personally believe that thinking about performance early on is crucial to making a good game. This does not mean we need to do micro-optimizations early in the process; instead, it is all about measurement. This is why performance is discussed so early in the book.

The first real game code that is presented in this book is written for 3D. Many people are shocked that 2D is not discussed until Chapter 9, "2D Basics." The reason for putting 3D before 2D in this book is because picking up 3D is not any harder than learning 2D. The early chapters are there to introduce you to the XNA Framework as well as the concepts behind a camera. It is my hope to tear down the mental block many people have that 3D is much harder than 2D. Granted, there are some complex topics surrounding 3D, and those are covered later in the book. However, by getting started by drawing models and responding to input, you'll see there is not a huge difference in the knowledge needed to write 3D games versus 2D games.

After discussing 3D and the Content Pipeline, the book discusses 2D and then moves into two chapters devoted to programming for the Zune. The next part of the book discusses the High Level Shader Language. Physics and artificial intelligence are discussed next. The code for those chapters uses the basic 3D information you will learn in earlier parts the book.

This is followed up by talking about more advanced 3D topics. A single-player 3D game is then built, thus allowing us to put into practice all you will learn in this book.

The next part of the book provides an intensive look at developing multiplayer games. Then the final part of the book discusses some best practices, most of which are done while creating the demos and games throughout the book. The last chapter explains the review process and getting your game into a condition to be sold on the Xbox LIVE Marketplace.

PART I

Get Up and Running with XNA Game Studio on Your PC and Xbox 360

CHAPTER 1

Introducing the XNA Framework and XNA Game Studio

Most developers I know decided to enter the computer field and specifically programming because of computer games. Game development can be one of the most challenging disciplines of software engineering—it can also be the most rewarding!

Never before has it been possible for the masses to create games for a game console, much less a next-generation game console. As a relatively new technology, XNA is going to experience tremendous growth. The sooner we get to know this technology, the better we will be able to understand the changes that will come in the future.

Microsoft is leading the way in how content will be created for game consoles. Soon other game console manufacturers will be jumping at a way to allow the public to create content for their machines. The great news for the Xbox 360 is that Microsoft has spent a lot time over the years creating productive and stable development environments for developers. We will be installing one of Microsoft's latest integrated development environments (IDEs) in this chapter. Before we get to that, though, let's take a look at the technology we discuss in this book—XNA.

What Is the XNA Framework?

You have probably heard the statement, "To know where you are going, you need to know where you have been." I am uncertain if that is entirely true, but I do believe it applies here. Before we dig into exactly what XNA is and what it can do for us, let's take a moment to look at DirectX because that is what the XNA Framework is built on.

The Foundation of the XNA Framework

Let's take a journey back to the days of DOS on the PC. When programming games, graphic demos, and the like in DOS, programmers typically had to write low-level code to talk directly to the sound card, graphics cards, and input devices. This was tedious, and the resulting code was error prone because different manufacturers would handle different BIOS interrupts, I/O ports, and memory banks differently. Therefore, the code would work on one system and not another.

Later, Microsoft released the Windows 95 operating system. Many game programmers were skeptical at writing games for Windows—and rightly so—because there was no way to get down to the hardware level to do things that required a lot of speed. Windows 95 had a protected memory model that kept developers from directly accessing the low-level interrupts of the hardware.

To solve this problem, Microsoft created a technology called DirectX. It was actually called Windows Game SDK to begin with, but the name was quickly switched after a reporter poked fun at the API names DirectDraw, DirectSound, and DirectPlay, calling the SDK "Direct 'X.'" Microsoft ran with the name, and DirectX 1.0 was born a few months after Windows 95 was released. I remember working with DirectDraw for a couple of demos back when this technology first came out.

Because of DirectX, developers had a way to write games with one source that would work on all PCs, regardless of their hardware. Hardware vendors were eager to work with Microsoft on standardizing an interface to access their hardware. They created device drivers to which DirectX would map its API, so all of the work that previously had to be done by game programmers was taken care of, and programmers could then spend their time doing what they wanted to—write games! Vendors called this a *hardware abstraction layer (HAL)*. They also developed a hardware emulation layer (HEL), which emulates hardware through software in case hardware isn't present. Of course, this was slower but it allowed certain games to be run on machines with no special hardware.

After a couple of years, Microsoft released DirectX 3.0, which ran on Windows NT 4 as well as Windows 95. As part of those upgrades, Microsoft introduced Direct3D. This allowed developers to create 3D objects inside of 3D worlds. DirectX 4 was never released, but DirectX 5 was released in 1997 and later had some upgrades to work under Windows 98.

When DirectX 8 came on the scene in 2000, some of the newly available graphics hardware had vertex and pixel shaders. As a result, Microsoft added in a way to pass custom program code to the hardware. Through assembly code, the game developer could manipulate the data the main game passed to the graphics card. This assembly code was consumed directly by the graphics hardware.

When there was no graphics hardware, games were slow, but they were very flexible. Later, as hardware rendering became prominent, the games were faster, but they were not very flexible in that all of the games really started to look the same. Now with shaders, the speed of the hardware is combined with the flexibility for each game to render and light its 3D content differently.

1

This brings us to present-day DirectX: We are up to DirectX 9 and 10. Before I talk about DirectX 9, I'll spend some time talking about DirectX 10. DirectX 10 was released at the same time as Microsoft Windows Vista. In fact, DirectX 10 only works on Vista. This is largely due to the fact that Microsoft has made major changes in the driver model for this operating system. DirectX 10 also requires a Shader Model 4.0 graphics card.

The Xbox 360 runs on DirectX 9 plus some additional partial support for Shader Model 3.0 functionality. DirectX 9 is the foundation for Managed DirectX, an API that exposed the core DirectX functionality to .NET Framework developers. There was a lot of concern about whether this "wrapper" could be as fast as the C++ counterparts. Fortunately, it was almost as fast—about 98% was the benchmark touted. I experienced these benchmark speeds first-hand while on the beta team for this technology. I fell in love with Managed DirectX.

The XNA Framework took the lessons learned from Managed DirectX and used that foundation as a launching pad. To be clear, XNA was built from the ground up and was not built on top of Managed DirectX. It doesn't use the same namespaces as Managed DirectX and is not simply pointing to the Managed DirectX methods in the background. Although XNA utilizes DirectX 9 in the background, there are no references to DirectX's API like there were in Managed DirectX.

XNA Today

XNA is actually a generic term, much like the term *.NET*. XNA really refers to anything that Microsoft produces that relates to game developers. The XNA Framework is the API we are discussing. The final piece to XNA is the XNA Game Studio application, which we discuss in detail later. This is the IDE we use to develop our XNA games.

> **TIP**
>
> In this book, whenever I use the term *XNA*, I am really referring to the XNA Framework, unless otherwise noted.

XNA allows us to do a lot of things. We have easy access to the input devices (keyboard, game pad or controller, mouse). XNA gives us easy access to the graphics hardware. We are able to easily control audio through XNA. XNA provides the ability for us to store information such as high scores and even saved games. XNA also has networking capabilities built in. This was introduced in version 2.0 of the product. Microsoft uses the Xbox LIVE technology for network support.

To get started using XNA, you have to install some software. You need to install the latest version of DirectX 9 as well as have a graphics card that supports DirectX 9.0c and Shader Model 1.1. (You should get a card that supports Shader Model 3.0 because some of the examples, including the starter kit we use in this chapter and the next one, will not run without it.) You also need to install Visual C# Express or one of the other Visual Studio SKUs, the DirectX 9 runtime, and finally XNA Game Studio. Fortunately, all of the software is free! If you don't have graphics hardware that can support Shader Model 2.0, you can pick up a card relatively inexpensively for about US$35. If possible, you should purchase a graphics card that can support Shader Model 3.0 because a couple of examples at the end of the book require it. Windows Vista machines have graphics cards that support Shader Model 4.0 and definitely meet the needs of our XNA games.

In the past, only subscribers to the XNA Creators Club could play the games made by other developers. Xbox LIVE Community Games, introduced in version 3.0 of XNA Game Studio, has changed that. Through a peer review process, games can be approved and put on Xbox LIVE for the world to download. Never before has there been such an easy way for a game to be seen by so many people.

Not only is XNA Game Studio great for the professional, it is great for the game hobbyist, the student, as well as someone just getting started because you do not have to shell out a lot of money to get up and running. One exception to this is if you actually want to deploy your games on your Xbox 360. To do that, you need to subscribe to the XNA Creators Club for US$99 a year (or US$49 for four months). Writing games for the PC using XNA is totally free! As an added benefit of paying for the Creators Club subscription, you are able to review other creators' games and are able to submit your own games to sell on Xbox LIVE Marketplace. This is discussed in Part XI, "Xbox LIVE Community Games."

Oh, in case you are wondering what XNA stands for, XNA's Not Acronymed (or so Microsoft says in the XNA FAQ).

Installing Visual C# 2008 Express

To get started, you must have the software installed. Let's start by installing Visual C# 2008 Express.

> **TIP**
>
> Any Visual Studio 2008 SKU works with XNA Game Studio 3.0.

XNA requires C# due to how the Content Pipeline is used. Some people have successfully created demos using other languages, such as VB.NET and even F#. However, this is not currently supported by Microsoft and won't be discussed in this book. This book assumes you have a good understanding of C#. If you know C++, Java, or VB.NET, you should be able to pick up C# pretty quickly.

I provide detailed steps to make sure anyone who has not worked with Visual C# Express will be able to get it installed with no issues. Feel free to skip this section if you already have a Visual Studio 2008 SKU installed.

TIP

Visit http://www.ILoveVB.net/ for some examples of using VB.NET to write XNA Game Studio games.

To install Visual C# 2008 Express, follow these steps:

1. You will need to be connected to the Internet to install the application. The application can be downloaded by browsing to http://www.microsoft.com/express/ download/ and clicking the Visual C# 2008 Express Edition Download link to download and run the vcssetup.exe setup program.

2. Optional. On the Welcome to Setup screen, select the check box to send data about your setup experience to Microsoft. This way, if something goes awry, Microsoft can get the data and try to make the experience better the next time around. This screen is shown in Figure 1.1.

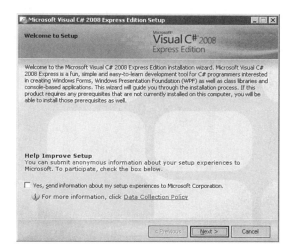

FIGURE 1.1   Select the check box if you want the system to provide feedback to Microsoft about your installation experience.

3. Click Next to continue.

4. The next screen is the End-User License Agreement. If you accept the terms, select the check box and click Next.

5. The following screen, shown in Figure 1.2, has two installation options you can check. Neither of these options is required to utilize XNA Game Studio.

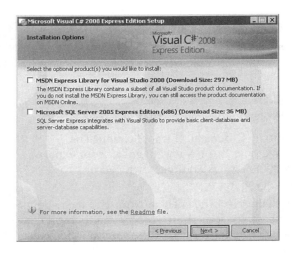

FIGURE 1.2   Neither of these options is required to utilize XNA Game Studio.

6. Click Next to continue.

7. The next screen, shown in Figure 1.3, asks where we would like to install Visual C# Express. Note that other required applications, including Microsoft .NET Framework 3.5, will be installed. This is required because C# runs on the .NET Framework. You will also notice it requires more than 300MB of space.

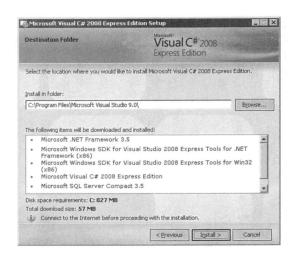

FIGURE 1.3   Specify in which directory you want Visual C# Express to be installed.

8. Click Next to continue.

9. Now you are looking at the Installation Progress screen, where you can monitor the progress of the installation.

10. On the Setup Complete screen, you can see the Microsoft Update link. Click it to get any of the latest service packs for Visual C# Express.

11. Click Exit to complete the installation.

TIP

After you install Visual C# 2008 Express, a reboot may be required.

You have now successfully installed the first piece of the pie to start creating excellent games with XNA! Before we continue to the next piece of software, you need to open up Visual C# Express. It might take a couple of minutes to launch the first time the application is loaded. Once the Visual C# Express is loaded, you should see the Start Page, shown in Figure 1.4.

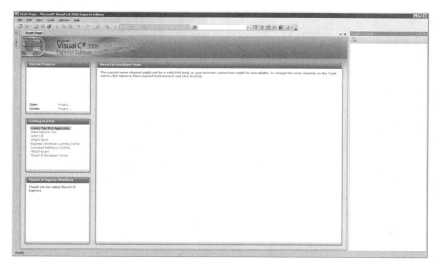

FIGURE 1.4   This is the Start Page inside of Visual C# Express.

The following procedure is optional, but it does ensure that everything is working correctly on your machine:

1. In the Recent Projects section, find Create Project and click the link. You can also create a new project under the File menu.

2. Visual C# Express installed several default templates that you can choose from. Select the Windows Application template, as displayed in Figure 1.5.

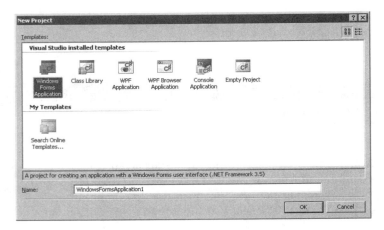

FIGURE 1.5   The New Project dialog box allows you to choose from the default templates to create an application.

3. You can leave the name set to WindowsFormsApplication1 because you will just be discarding this project when we are done.

4. Click OK to create the application.

5. At this point a new project should have been created, and you should be looking at a blank Windows Form called Form1.

6. Press Ctrl+F5 or click Start Without Debugging on the Debug menu.

If everything compiled correctly, the form you just saw in design mode should actually be running. Granted, it doesn't do anything, but it does prove that you can compile and run C# through Visual C# Express. The end result can be seen in Figure 1.6. Close down the application you just created as well as Visual C# Express. Feel free to discard the application.

FIGURE 1.6   A C# Windows Form application after the default template has been compiled and run.

Installing the DirectX Runtime

You also need the DirectX 9 runtime if it isn't already on your machine. To get started, follow these steps:

1. Run the dxwebsetup.exe file from Microsoft's website. This can be found by clicking the DirectX Runtime Web Installer link at the bottom of the XNA Creators Club Online – Downloads web page (http://creators.xna.com/en-US/downloads). This file contains the redistribution package of the February 2007 version of DirectX 9. You will need to be connected to the Internet so it can completely install the application.

2. You are greeted with the End-User License Agreement. Handle with care.

3. The next screen is a dialog box asking where you would like the installation files to be stored. You can pick any directory you want as long as you remember it so you can actually install the runtime—you are simply extracting the files needed to install the runtime.

4. Click OK to continue.

5. You will be prompted to create that directory if the directory entered doesn't exist. Click Yes to continue.

6. Wait for the dialog box with the progress bar to finish unpacking the files.

Now you can actually install the runtime by following these steps:

1. Browse to the folder where you installed the files and run the dxsetup.exe file to actually install DirectX 9 onto your machine.

2. The welcome screen you see includes the End-User License Agreement. Select the appropriate radio button to continue.

3. Following the agreement is a screen stating that it will install DirectX. Click Next.

4. Once it finishes installing (a progress bar will be visible while the files are being installed), you will be presented with the Installation Complete screen.

5. Simply click Finish to exit the setup.

Now we can move on to installing XNA Game Studio.

Installing XNA Game Studio

To use XNA Game Studio, you can use any of the Visual Studio SKUs, including Visual C# Express.

WARNING

You must run the Visual C# Express IDE at least one time before installing XNA Game Studio. If this is not done, not all the functionality will be installed. If XNA Game Studio was installed prematurely, you will need to uninstall XNA Game Studio, run Visual C# Express, and then exit the IDE. Then you will be able to reinstall XNA Game Studio. This is true for any of the Visual Studio SKUs.

To get started, complete the following steps:

1. Run the XNAGS30_setup.msi file from Microsoft's website. The file can be down-loaded by clicking the top link on the XNA Creators Club Online – Downloads website (http://creators.xna.com/en-US/downloads).

2. Click Next to get past the setup welcome screen.

3. The next screen is the End-User License Agreement. If you accept the terms, select the check box and click Next.

4. A notification dialog box opens that allows the Windows Firewall to have rules added to it. These rules allow communication between the computer and the Xbox 360, as well as allow for communication between network games. This can be seen in Figure 1.7.

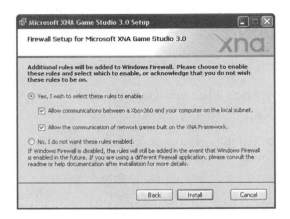

FIGURE 1.7   XNA Game Studio modifies the Windows Firewall so an Xbox 360 and the PC can talk to each other. It also allows network games created with XNA to communicate.

5. Click Install to continue. The next screen shows the progress of the installation.

6. Once all of the required files are installed, you are presented with a completion dia-log box. Simply click Finish to exit the setup.

After you have installed XNA Game Studio, you can go to the Start menu and see that it added a few more items than those contained in the IDE. Make sure to take the time and read through some of the XNA Game Studio documentation. There is also a Tools folder that contains a couple of tools we will be looking at later. We will discuss the XACT tool in Chapter 7, "Sound and Music," and the XNA Framework Remote Performance Monitor for Xbox 360 application in Chapter 3, "Performance Considerations." Go ahead and open the Visual C# Express or Visual Studio IDE.

TIP

Everything in this book works with all the Visual Studio 2008 SKUs as well as Visual C# 2008 Express. From this point on I will simply use the term Visual Studio, regardless of which SKU (including C# Express) is being used.

When you installed XNA Game Studio, it added properties to Visual Studio to allow it to behave differently under certain circumstances. Mainly it added some templates (which we will look at shortly) as well as the ability for Visual Studio to handle content via the XNA Content Pipeline. It also added a way for you to send data to your Xbox 360, as you will see in the next chapter.

Creating the Platformer Projects

With XNA Game Studio opened, once you create a new project, you should see a screen similar to Figure 1.8. Select the Platformer Starter Kit template and feel free to change the name of the project. Click OK to create the project.

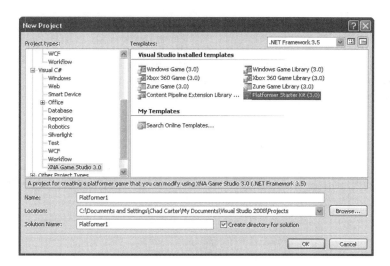

FIGURE 1.8   You can see that installing XNA Game Studio added eight more templates to Visual Studio.

Compiling and Running Platformer

At this point you have your software installed and have even created a starter template (created by Microsoft) that you can take for a spin. You need to make sure you can compile the code. To just compile without running, either press Ctrl+Shift+B, press F6, or click Build Solution on the Build menu. The code should have compiled without any issues. You can now press Ctrl+F5 to actually run the game. Have some fun playing the game. Feel free to look around the code and tweak it. Fortunately, you can always re-create the template if something gets really messed up!

> **TIP**
>
> When working with one solution file and multiple project files in Visual Studio, you can easily change which devices you are currently building and deploying to by changing the Solutions Platform dropdown box in the toolbar. If you select Mixed Platforms, you will compile for each platform every time. For the project you set as your startup project, XNA Game Studio will try to deploy the game to that device.

Summary

In this chapter, I laid the groundwork in getting all the software required installed so you can actually create games on your PC. We even compiled a game and played it. After getting a game session fix, join me in the next chapter, where we will get this project up and running on the Xbox 360!

XNA Game Studio and the Xbox 360

XNA Game Studio allows us to write games for the Xbox 360, but an Xbox 360 is not required to enjoy XNA. We can write games strictly for the PC. However, if we do want to write games that we can play on our Xbox 360 consoles and share with others to play on their consoles, we need to purchase the XNA Creators Club subscription. This will also allow us to play other community games (which other developers create) on our Xbox 360 consoles as well.

> **TIP**
>
> This chapter should be read even if you do not have an Xbox 360. Simply skim through the detailed steps and read the content to understand the concepts. The book is best when read in order.

Creating an Xbox 360 Project

With XNA Game Studio opened, we can follow these steps to create a new project that can run on the Xbox 360:

1. Create a new project. You should see a screen similar to Figure 2.1.
2. Select the Xbox 360 Game template and change the name of the project if desired.
3. Click OK to create the project.

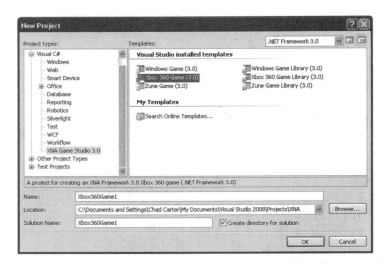

FIGURE 2.1   XNA Game Studio provides templates we can use to get up and running quickly.

Buying the XNA Creators Club Subscription

You need an Internet connection because you need to be connected to Xbox LIVE to deploy games from the PC to the Xbox 360 console. To purchase the subscription, you need to complete the following steps:

1. Select the Game Marketplace and then select Explore Game Content.
2. Select All Games and hold down the right trigger to page down to the end of the groupings. Select X because we are looking for the XNA Creators Club entry.
3. Toward the bottom you can see XNA Creators Club. Select this entry, as shown in Figure 2.2.

Can't Find the XNA Creators Club Game Entry?

If you do not see the XNA Creators Club entry, it is most likely because of the parental control setting. XNA Creators Club is unrated, which means you have to select Allow All Games. Fortunately, you can then change your parental controls to the setting you had before once you have subscribed and downloaded XNA Game Studio Connect. Then you will need to enter a valid passcode to actually run XNA Game Studio Connect.

---

4. Now select Memberships and pick a plan to purchase.
5. Follow the instructions to enter the appropriate billing information. The Xbox 360 supports any USB keyboard, which can make this data entry much less painful. After entering the billing information, confirm to purchase the plan selected.

FIGURE 2.2 XNA Creators Club can be purchased through the Xbox LIVE Marketplace.

TIP

If you are uncomfortable with providing your credit card information through the Xbox LIVE Marketplace, you can purchase Microsoft Points at many places, including Best Buy, Wal-Mart, and Target. These points can then be used to purchase the XNA Creators Club subscription.

6. Under XNA Creators Club, select and download the XNA Game Studio Connect application.
7. Once XNA Game Studio Connect is downloaded, go to Game Library under My Xbox, as shown in Figure 2.3.
8. Select the Collections list and then select Community Games.
9. Select XNA Game Studio Connect from the list and finally select Launch to run it.

Connecting the Xbox 360 to the PC

You have the subscription, but you also need to associate the Xbox 360 with the PC. To do this, follow these steps:

1. The first time the XNA Game Studio Connect application is launched, an encryption key that needs to be entered into XNA Game Studio is generated. The generated key is located at the bottom of the screen, as shown in Figure 2.4.
2. Inside of XNA Game Studio, go to the Tools menu and click the Launch XNA Game Studio Device Center menu item.
3. Click Add Device and then select the Xbox 360 option.

FIGURE 2.3   Game Library not only allows you to play demos and Xbox originals, but it also lets you navigate to XNA Game Studio Connect.

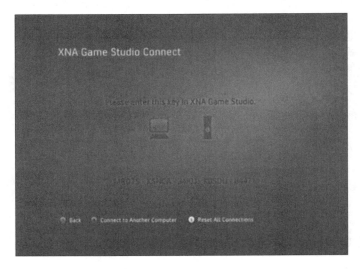

FIGURE 2.4   XNA Game Studio Connect generates an encryption key the first time it is run. This key is to be entered into XNA Game Studio.

4. Type the name of the Xbox 360 (this can be anything) and click Next.

5. Type the connection key in the space provided. An example of this screen is shown in Figure 2.5.

6. If everything is successful, XNA Game Studio will save the connection key. It is important that the Xbox 360 and the development and deployment PC are on the

same subnet. For example, if one is on a wireless router and the other on a wired router, connection issues will arise.

7. Close the XNA Game Studio Device Center application.

Now we are ready to deploy to the Xbox 360!

FIGURE 2.5   Associate the Xbox 360 with the PC by entering the connection key generated on the Xbox 360 into the XNA Game Studio Device Center.

Deploying on the Xbox 360

We need to either create another Platformer game or open up the solution we created in the last chapter. We also need to set the Xbox 360 project to the startup project so we can deploy it to the Xbox 360. To deploy on your Xbox 360, you need to perform the following steps:

1. Launch XNA Game Studio Connect on the Xbox 360. (If you're continuing from the previous step, the Xbox 360 is already in this waiting state.)

2. Go back inside of XNA Game Studio on the PC and select Deploy Solution from the Build menu.

3. The Xbox 360 will start receiving the files needed to run the application.

Deploying Content on the Xbox 360

Deploying on the Xbox 360 can take some time, depending on how much content needs to be sent over the wire. The good news is that if content does not change, it does not get sent over again, so you are only waiting on the items you actually changed.

There are a couple of times even after the first deployment that all content will be resent to the Xbox 360.

▶ During the deployment, if an error occurs or if the deployment is stopped for any reason, the next time the project is deployed it will be a complete deployment.

▶ If the configuration is different from the last deployment, a complete deployment will occur.

When the files have been fully deployed, the Xbox 360 will revert back to "Waiting for computer connection," as shown in Figure 2.6. Also, in XNA Game Studio you should see the message "Deploy Succeeded" in the status bar.

To actually play the game we just deployed on the Xbox 360, simply exit out of the connection. You should now see Platformer at the top of the Recent Games list as a game that is installed. Select it and then select Play Game and enjoy the game on the Xbox 360! You can find the game later by going to the Collections list and selecting Community Games and then selecting the game from that list.

Quitting Platformer

To exit the Platformer game, press the Back button on the game pad.

FIGURE 2.6   Before and after deploying a game to the Xbox 360, XNA Game Studio Connect shows that it is waiting for a computer connection.

Distributing Your Game

Not only can you deploy your games to your own Xbox 360, you can distribute them so that others can enjoy your games on their Xbox 360 console, Windows PC, or their Zune. You can distribute your assets and source code or you can package up your game and content and just distribute the package.

When consumers get the package, they will need an active XNA Creators Club subscription to use the game on their Xbox 360. For Windows, if they do not have XNA Game Studio installed, they will need the redistributable files that include the XNA Framework as well as certain DirectX 9 files. For more information, refer to the XNA Game Studio documentation. Information can be found in the "Sharing and Distributing Your Game" section under the "Using XNA Game Studio" section of the help.

Another way to distribute your Xbox 360 game is covered in detail in Part XI, "Xbox LIVE Community Games." The chapters discuss a peer review process to submitting games so that anyone can download and play your games!

Debugging on the Xbox 360

Without too much pain we were able to get a game running on the Xbox 360. Now comes this question: How hard is it to debug games deployed on the Xbox 360? Well, I answer that question in this section.

To get started, you need to run XNA Game Studio Connect and connect to your computer as previously described. Once the console is waiting on a connection, press F10 to step into the Platformer game.

> **NOTE**
>
> Make sure to set the active solution configuration to Debug to step through the code on the Xbox 360.

Follow these steps for this exercise:

1. Open the PlatformerGame.cs file.
2. Put a breakpoint in the first line of code under the constructor.
3. Press F5 to run the application in debug mode.

Visual Studio will do as expected and stop the code at the appropriate line. You can see that the console has a black screen because it hasn't been told to draw anything yet, because we are holding up the process with our breakpoint. Press F5 to let the game run. When you're finished with the game, close out the Platformer template.

Creating a Test Demo for the Xbox 360

We are going to create a simple application we can deploy and then debug on the Xbox 360. To begin, we need to create another project, but this time we will use the Xbox 360 Game template to start with.

The template creates a file called AssemblyInfo.cs. (It's hidden away under the Properties folder.) Once we open this file, we can see an attribute called `AssemblyTitle`. This attribute determines what is displayed under Community Games on the Xbox 360. Unless overridden by the `Windows.Title` property through code, this attribute is also used to populate the title of the window in Windows. Overriding `Windows.Title` has no effect on the Xbox 360 or the Zune.

Not only can we change the title attribute, but we can (and should) also change the description attribute `AssemblyDescription`. For Windows, this shows up if someone right-clicks the executable and looks at its properties. For the Xbox 360 it shows up on the side of the Community Games list as the game is highlighted in the list—very cool! There is a 300-character limit on the description. Anything over 300 characters will be truncated and not displayed.

Another thing to note in this code file is the attribute `Guid`. Although the source code comment above this attribute suggests that its only use is for COM, it is actually needed to deploy games to the Xbox 360 as well. Make sure you have a unique globally unique identifier (GUID) for each game you create. Fortunately, Visual Studio does this automatically when it creates the file. As long as our project contains the AssemblyInfo.cs source file, we will be able to deploy the application to the Xbox 360. The GUID is also used to match up games for networking game play. Only games with the same GUID can connect to each other.

After changing the assembly title and description, press F5 (we need to make sure the console is waiting for a computer connection) to run the demo on the Xbox 360. On the console, you should see a nice blank cornflower blue screen. To exit the demo, simply press the Back button on the controller. If you did not set the console to be waiting for a computer connection by running XNA Game Studio Connect, then Visual Studio will time out trying to deploy the game or demo.

It is easy to just gloss over how simple it is to create a graphics application and deploy it on the Xbox 360. This was not always the case, however. Just to get this screen up in a Windows environment was challenging in the days before XNA (even with Managed DirectX). You've just witnessed how easy it is to get a framework set up that talks to the graphics device, complete with a game loop.

Our game is now listed in the Community Games list under Game Library. Now you should see a list of the games we have deployed—Platformer and this demo. Figure 2.7 shows that XNA Game Studio Connect extracted the title and description from the assembly we deployed.

To start a debugging exercise, add the following member field to the top of our class:

```
private Texture2D spriteTexture;
```

Locate the `LoadContent` method and inside of the condition block add the following code:

```
spriteTexture = Content.Load<Texture2D>("texture");
```

2

FIGURE 2.7   XNA Game Studio Connect reads the title and description values entered in the AssemblyInfo.cs file of the XNA applications we deployed.

Find an image (.jpg, .bmp, or .tga) and add it into the project. Feel free to use a texture from the Platformer game folder we created. (The example on the CD uses the GameThumbnail.png file from the Platformer demo.) After the file is added into the Content subproject, change the Asset Name in the properties panel to "texture." We discuss all these items in detail in later chapters, so do not worry about them at this point.

Finally, add the following code inside of the Draw method under the TODO: Add your drawing code here comment:

```
spriteBatch.Begin();
spriteBatch.Draw(spriteTexture, Vector2.Zero, Color.White);
spriteBatch.End();
```

We simply added a texture that will be displayed at the top-left corner of our screen. Let's compile and deploy our changes. Once we have completed that task, we can put a breakpoint on spriteBatch.Begin() and run the project in debug mode. We need to make sure the Xbox 360 is waiting for a connection before we try to deploy.

When the application is finished deploying, we see the lovely black screen because we haven't let it get into the Draw method. Press F5 to let it process the Draw method once and then take a look at the Xbox 360 screen. We now have our blue screen with the texture we loaded at the top left. I won't labor the point of stepping through more code—we will have plenty of opportunity to debug our code as we progress in our game-writing journey. You can now remove the breakpoint and exit the demo.

The .NET Framework has a System.Diagnostics namespace that is also available on the Xbox 360. This namespace includes a Debug class that includes, among other things, the Write and WriteLine methods. Let's add the following code to the end of the condition inside of the LoadContent method:

```
System.Diagnostics.Debug.WriteLine("game content loaded");
```

While we are at it, we should add the following line of code inside of the UnloadContent method:

```
System.Diagnostics.Debug.WriteLine("game content unloaded");
```

This line of code can be put right after the call to unload our content.

You can now recompile, deploy, and run the changes on your Xbox 360. Notice that inside the output window of Visual Studio the text was printed out! Now we can capture data to our IDE if something is really puzzling us or if we just want to dump data during the game play—a manual log of sorts.

We can set breakpoints inside of our code and step through pieces of code even while it is running on the console. We can also write information to the output window inside of the IDE while the game is running on the Xbox 360. Wow!

Programming for Dual Platforms

There is something else we need to discuss as we continue our adventure of writing games for the Xbox 360. We need to share as much code as possible between our Xbox 360 game and our Windows PC game. Although it is perfectly acceptable to exclusively build applications for one platform or the other, with the XNA Framework it is not that much of a technical jump to use the same code base on both platforms.

TIP

Starting with XNA Game Studio 3.0, another platform is supported. The Zune is a third device that a developer can write games for using XNA Game Studio. Programming for the Zune device is covered in Part V, "XNA Game Studio and the Zune."

With that being said, there are valid reasons why certain developers only target one system or the other. Some developers do not own an Xbox 360 and that's a pretty good reason not to write games for it—it is difficult to debug on a platform without access to it. Some developers require additional components to be present with their game that cannot be installed on the Xbox 360. Some only want to fine-tune their game for the Xbox 360 hardware and not worry about the different graphic cards and other PC configurations that their games would need to support.

The goal of this section is to allow us to write one code base that we can easily maintain to work on both platforms. We could start the process by creating a Windows project and then creating an Xbox 360 project that shares the same files. Instead, we will start with the Xbox 360 demo we just created and add a Windows project to the solution. We cannot support both platforms inside of one project, but we can support both platforms inside of one solution. We could also create two different solutions and just link the files from one solution to the other. In this book we will have one solution with two projects that share the same source code location. The idea here is that we can quickly compile our changes in both solutions at the same time. We do this because we want to make sure we have not added calls to methods that do not exist in the platform we were not actively coding for. We discuss this in more detail in the next section.

Follow these steps to create our Windows Game project inside of the current solution that already contains our Xbox Game project:

1. Right-click the project and select Create Copy of Project for Windows from the context menu.

2. Read the information window and click OK.

3. Rename the newly created project to something more appropriate.

You can see that the solution platforms dropdown list box (located in the Visual Studio toolbar) now has Mixed Platforms as its selection. This allows us to quickly build, deploy, and run our projects at one time, or we can choose to only work on one platform at a time. Let's set the Windows project as our starting project. This can be done by right-clicking the WindowsGame1 project and selecting Set as StartUp Project. Change the solution platform to x86 if the machine is a 32-bit machine or x64 if the machine is a 64-bit machine. To make sure we have everything set up properly, run the application by pressing F5.

Visual Studio compiles and runs the Windows version of the demo and does not bother compiling the Xbox 360 version, which is what we were expecting. Expand the references tree node for both projects. You can see the two XNA references the templates provided us when we set up the projects. If you look at the paths in the properties panel, you will see that they are located in two different places. Appropriately, the Windows reference points to \Windows\x86\ (or \Windows\x64\ for 64-bit machines), and the console reference points to \Xbox360\. This is the reason we need to have two separate projects.

The solution platform dropdown list box tells Visual Studio which platforms to compile (and deploy). The project setting Set as StartUp Project tells the IDE which project to run. We cannot run both the executables for Windows and the Xbox 360 at the same time. This really would not be beneficial to us anyway because we could not tell the IDE which application we wanted to break into when debugging. When we create our multiplayer games, we will actually create two different solution files and run both at the same time. One will contain the Xbox 360 projects and the other will contain the Windows projects. Because the two projects have different references of the XNA Framework, we will run into the issue of having functionality in one system and not the other. An example of this is that the Xbox 360 does not have any support for the mouse. Fortunately, we do not have to create and maintain two separate code files for situations like this. Instead we can use a preprocessor directive to tell the compiler to ignore parts of our code if it is compiling for a certain platform. The following code shows an example of compiling functionality specific to the Xbox 360:

```
#if XBOX360
    //do Xbox 360 specific code here
#endif
```

The following code shows an example of compiling a Windows-specific functionality:

```
#if WINDOWS
    //do Windows specific code here
#endif
```

This means we can keep our code in one file and put a conditional preprocessor directive around the code we need to handle differently based on a particular platform. Of course, we can opt to create a totally separate file that would be included in one project but not the other. The key is that we have a choice, and it will make sense to do this both ways in a larger project. An example would be a large input handler class that might have its own Mouse source file that would be included in the Windows project and excluded from the Xbox 360 project. The main game loop that checks a particular input value might have the condition in place to ignore the mouse information unless it is being compiled for Windows.

The last thing we need to talk about in this section is the difference between PC monitors and television sets. On PC monitors, the developers have confidence that any objects they draw on the screen from the top-left corner to the bottom right will be seen by the gamer. When developing for a console such as the Xbox 360, developers have to account for the fact that not all TVs are created equal. When drawing to a television screen, we need to be aware of two items in particular: aspect ratio and the title safe area. We talk about the aspect ratio in Chapter 4, "Creating 3D Objects." The title safe area is the area of the screen that the user will definitely be able to see. This is the inner 80% or 90% area of the TV screen. It is beneficial to put any critical text (such as a title), game scores, timers, and the like inside of this title safe area while filling all the screen with our environment. Fortunately, the XNA Framework team has created the TitleSafeArea property, which we can access for either the graphics device's display mode or viewport properties. You can see what it takes to utilize the TitleSafeArea rectangle by modifying the demo we created. First, add the following private member field:

```
private Rectangle titleSafeArea;
```

Now assign a value to this rectangle by adding the following code to the top of the LoadContent method:

```
titleSafeArea = GraphicsDevice.Viewport.TitleSafeArea;
```

Now we can edit our code that draws the texture. We do not need to worry about the details of the graphic portion of this code because we will cover it later, but we do want to replace the spriteBatch.Draw line of code with the following line:

```
spriteBatch.Draw(spriteTexture, new Vector2(titleSafeArea.X, titleSafeArea.Y),
    Color.White);
```

Originally, we told the texture to render at coordinates 0, 0 (top left of the screen) by passing in Vector2.Zero. Instead of using Vector2.Zero, we use the x and y coordinates from the title safe rectangle retrieved at the beginning of the program. When we run this on Windows, the x and y coordinates will still be 0, but when we run it on the Xbox 360, it is offset to make up for televisions that do not display the entire screen. You can see an example of this in Figure 2.8.

FIGURE 2.8   Displaying a texture in the title safe area of the TV screen.

The .NET Compact Framework on the Xbox 360

We need to discuss another difference between developing for the Xbox 360 and developing for Windows—the version of the .NET Framework the two platforms are running. Windows runs on the full-blown .NET Framework (2.0 is required for XNA), whereas the Xbox 360 runs on the smaller .NET Compact Framework. The .NET Compact Framework is used in certain Windows CE–powered devices such as the Pocket PC, Pocket PC Phone Edition, Smartphone, and the Zune. As the name implies, it is compact—not only because the devices it typically runs on are compact, but also because the framework itself is a subset of what is available on the desktop. From an Xbox 360 development point of view, we need to make sure that if we are accessing functionality on the .NET Framework in our code that it also exists in the .NET Compact Framework. Fortunately, the two versions of the XNA Framework our projects have a reference to are utilizing the correct .NET Framework, so as long as we keep those references correctly set up, we will get compile errors in our Xbox 360 game if we try to access functionality that is not in the .NET Compact Framework.

The Xbox 360 version of the .NET Compact Framework actually includes items that are not in the other compact devices' framework. The console's .NET Compact Framework also includes a few things that the .NET Framework doesn't include. This is mainly due to the type of hardware that is inside the Xbox 360.

The XNA Game Studio team at Microsoft worked closely with the Visual Studio team to accomplish the tight integration with Visual Studio, but the team also worked very closely with the .NET Compact Framework team to make sure we could do what we want—make games for the Xbox 360! Without the .NET Compact Framework team, the XNA Framework would not work on the Xbox 360.

The .NET Compact Framework team had to add in floating-point support because the other devices the framework previously targeted did not have floating-point hardware. The team also added support for four of the six hardware threads that map to the Xbox 360's three cores—the other two threads (0 and 2) are reserved. This book does not cover multithreading on the Xbox 360, but the concepts from typical .NET programming will apply if you choose to tackle that task. In addition, information about the `Thread.SetProcessorAffinity` method will prove to be beneficial.

Summary

This chapter was all about the Xbox 360. We discussed how to buy an XNA Creators Club subscription through Xbox LIVE. You learned how to download and run XNA Game Studio Connect so you could deploy games on your console.

We created the Platformer project to run on the Xbox 360. We then deployed and debugged the project on the console. We also created a new Xbox 360 demo, starting with the most basic template, and we discussed important attributes in the AssemblyInfo.cs code file. You saw how to send text to the XNA Game Studio output window from inside the Xbox 360. You also learned about the `XBOX360` preprocessor compilation directive and how it can keep the compiler from compiling code for different platforms.

We discussed different ways to set up our projects so we can more easily use the same code base for both our Windows and Xbox 360 projects. Finally, we discussed the .NET Compact Framework that the XNA Framework utilizes on the Xbox 360.

Go play some games, and then we can continue our journey into the next chapter, where we discuss ways to make our XNA games perform well in Windows and on the Xbox 360.

CHAPTER 3

Performance Considerations

To be successful at writing games, we have to be very aware of the expense of the different tasks we want to perform. Before we write our code, we need to have an end goal we are striving to reach. As Stephen Covey stated in his book *The 7 Habits of Highly Effective People,* we need to "begin with the end in mind." This is crucial for personal growth, but it is also very important when thinking about performance. As software engineers we need to have goals and then continue to measure against those goals as we develop our code. The "end" can change, and we need to adjust accordingly.

In this chapter, we look at ways to measure how fast our code is running. We discuss key elements of performance tuning when running our code on the .NET Framework and also on the .NET Compact Framework that the Xbox 360 and the Zune uses.

Measure, Measure, Measure

The title of this section really says it all. In real estate they say what matters is location, location, location. In the performance realm, measuring is what really matters. How else can we know if we are meeting our goals if we do not take the time to measure along the way?

Before we start writing code, we need to take a benchmark measurement. Then we can see as we add functionality whether or not we are adversely affecting our performance goals.

So what is our goal? At the very least our goal should be to have our game run consistently at *n* number of frames per second (fps). *Frames per second* is the number of times a frame is drawn on the screen per second. The standard for today's games is 60 fps.

A *game loop* is a loop that updates objects and renders those objects to the screen while processing other elements, such as input, sound, artificial intelligence (AI), and physics. Each iteration of the render and draw loop is one frame, so we are stating that our goal is to consistently call the draw loop 60 times each second. XNA provides the game loop for us.

Shortly after Managed DirectX was released, there were several discussions regarding the best method to provide a game loop inside of the Windows environment. Fortunately, the XNA team has handled this for us, which most likely came from the discussions started with Managed DirectX. The XNA Framework game loop provides both an `Update` method and a `Draw` method we can override. When we create our game class, we inherit from the `Microsoft.Xna.Framework.Game` class, which provides these and other virtual methods.

The 80–20 Rule

More than 100 years ago, Vilfredo Pareto, an Italian economist, made the statement that 80% of Italy's wealth was distributed among only 20% of the people. He observed the same thing in other countries' economies as well. This has been called the 80–20 Rule. There have been other variations of this same principle. We've heard statements such as "20% of the people do 80% of the work." Successful leaders spend 80% of their time cultivating 20% of their people. It is hard to know exactly why this principle works, but it does work. The same is true when it comes to performance of our applications: 20% of the code will need optimization because it is the most critical to the overall performance of the application. Because 20% of our code will do 80% of the work, this makes sense.

As we discuss performance measurement in this chapter, it is key to keep in mind that we need to be concerned about performance as we write our code, but we should not get bogged down and try to perform micro-optimizations too early. Sir Tony Hoare is famous for the often quoted saying, "Premature optimization is the root of all evil." Most of the time when this quote is used, it is suggested that performance measurement is not important. However, it is very important. There is nothing worse than being at the end of a software development cycle and realizing that the application is not performing well.

When we develop any application—even games—we need to make sure we do not fall into the trap of thinking that optimization is the root of all evil. It is not. It is a lot like people misquoting the Bible, saying that "money is the root of all evil." Money is not the root of all evil; the *love* of money is the root of all evil. Likewise, in software development, it is not optimization that is the root of all evil; rather it is *premature* optimization that is the root of all evil.

So at what point in the development life cycle is it safe to be concerned about performance? There are those at one extreme who say premature is anything before the end of the development cycle. Then there are those who fall into the trap of doing micro-optimizations using micro-benchmark testing (which we discuss at the end of this chapter) before designing their application. Of course, the ideal time to optimize our code is somewhere between these two extremes.

The key to it all really is measurement. We do not know what needs to be optimized unless we measure. There is no reason to try and make a particular method blazing fast if it is only called one time when the application starts. Of course, if our load time is too long, then we would want to take a look at what is happening—and it might turn out to be that method we were not concerned about to begin with. The point is that we do not assume the method needs optimization until we measure and see it is causing a problem.

As we develop any application, we should do performance checks throughout the process just to see how we are doing in relation to our performance goals. If something is taking some time, but we are still within our performance goals, then we can just make a note of it and ignore it for the time being. It might be that there is no need to waste time optimizing that part of the code. If during measuring we do see that we need to make something perform faster, we can make the changes then.

When developing, if we are unsure of what our bottleneck is, we can use profiler tools to help us find the problem areas. I have used the ANTS Profiler from redgate software (http://www.red-gate.com/products/ants_profiler/index.htm) and have had great success with it. It costs a few hundred dollars, though, and is not in everyone's budget. A great open-source statistical profiler tool is available for Windows called NProf, which can be found at http://sourceforge.net/projects/nprof. The tool shows the amount of time each method in our application took to run, and sums up the total time. So when developing games we need to be aware of times when we are idling in our Start menu. Many resources on the Web discuss the different tools available and how to use them, so we will not dig into this here. The point is that tools are available for us to find bottlenecks in our code. Using these tools will help us find the 20% of our code that needs optimization.

Creating a Benchmark

To get a baseline for our game loop, we will start with a new Windows game project. We can call this project PerformanceBenchmark. We will add a frame rate counter and update our window title to show just how many frames per second we are getting "out of the box."

Now we can set the following properties inside of the constructor:

```
//Do not synch our Draw method with the Vertical Retrace of our monitor
graphics.SynchronizeWithVerticalRetrace = false;
//Do not call our Update method at the default rate of 1/60 of a second.
IsFixedTimeStep = false;
```

The template creates the GraphicsDeviceManager for us. We set the SynchronizeWithVerticalRetrace property of the manager to false. The default of this property is true. As the name suggests, this property synchronizes the call to the Draw method from inside of the XNA Framework's game loop to coincide with the monitor's refresh rate. If the monitor has a refresh rate of 60 Hz, it refreshes every 1/60th of a second, or 60 times every second. By default, XNA draws to the screen at the same time the monitor refreshes to keep the scene from appearing jerky. This is typically what we want. However, when measuring the change a piece of code has on our frame rate, it is difficult to determine how we are affecting it if we are always drawing 60 fps. We would not know anything was wrong until we did something that dropped us below that margin, keeping the XNA Framework from calling the Draw method fast enough.

We also set the fixed time step property (IsFixedTimeStep) to false. The default value of this property is true. This property lets XNA know if it should call the Update method immediately after drawing to the screen (false) or only after a fixed amount of time has passed (true). This fixed amount of time is 1/60th of a second and is stored in the property TargetElapsedTime, which we can change. At this point we need the framework to call Update as often as possible so that our Draw call will get called as soon as possible. The Draw call is executed after every call to Update.

Let's add the following private member fields to our Game1.cs file:

```
private float fps;
private float updateInterval = 1.0f;
private float timeSinceLastUpdate = 0.0f;
private float framecount = 0;
```

Finally, let's add the frame rate calculation inside of our Draw method:

```
float elapsed = (float)gameTime.ElapsedRealTime.TotalSeconds;
framecount++;
timeSinceLastUpdate += elapsed;
if (timeSinceLastUpdate > updateInterval)
{
    fps = framecount / timeSinceLastUpdate; //mean fps over updateIntrval
#if XBOX360
    System.Diagnostics.Debug.WriteLine("FPS: " + fps.ToString() + " - RT: " +
    gameTime.ElapsedRealTime.TotalSeconds.ToString() + " - GT: " +
    gameTime.ElapsedGameTime.TotalSeconds.ToString());
#else
    Window.Title = "FPS: " + fps.ToString() + " - RT: " +
        gameTime.ElapsedRealTime.TotalSeconds.ToString() + " - GT: " +
        gameTime.ElapsedGameTime.TotalSeconds.ToString();
#endif
    framecount = 0;
    timeSinceLastUpdate -= updateInterval;
}
```

The first thing we are doing with the code is storing the elapsed time since the last time the Draw method was executed. We then increment our frame count along with the variable that is keeping a running total of the time. We check to see if enough time has passed, at which point we update our frame rate. We have the updateInterval set at 1 second, but we can tweak that number if we would like. Once enough time has passed for us to recalculate our frame rate, we do just that by taking the number of frames and dividing it by the time it took us to get inside of this condition. We then update the title of the window with our fps. We also write out the ElapsedRealTime along with the

ElapsedGameTime. To calculate our fps, we used the real time. Play with the first two properties we set to see the effect it has on the time. Remember the SynchronizeWithVerticalRetrace property determines how often the Draw method gets called, and the IsFixedTimeStep property determines how often the Update method gets called. ElapsedRealTime is associated with the time it took to call our Draw method, whereas ElapsedGameTime is associated with the time it took to call our Update method.

Finally, we reset our frame count along with the timeSinceLastUpdate variable. Let's run the application so we can get our baseline for how our machine is performing.

Now that we have our base number, we want to make a note of it. This could be done in an Excel spreadsheet where we can easily track the changes in our performance. We should always try to run our performance tests under the same conditions. Ideally, nothing except the game should be run during all the benchmark testing.

As an example, let's add the following code inside of the Draw method:

```
//bad code that should not be replicated
Matrix m = Matrix.Identity;
Vector3 v2;
for (int i = 0; i < 1; i++)
{
    m = Matrix.CreateRotationX(MathHelper.PiOver4);
    m *= Matrix.CreateTranslation(new Vector3(5.0f));

    Vector3 v = m.Translation - Vector3.One;
    v2 = v + Vector3.One;
}
```

This does not do anything other than some 3D math that has absolutely no purpose. The reason we are going through this exercise is to see how our frame rate will drop as we increment the upper limit of our for loop. The point is that when we start writing real functionality inside the Draw method, we can measure how our frame rate is handling the addition of code. On the included CD, this example is called PerformanceTest1.

Monitoring Performance on the Xbox 360

Measuring performance on the Xbox 360 is relatively easy to do. To begin monitoring how the application is functioning on the Xbox 360, follow these steps:

1. Make sure your Xbox 360 is waiting for a computer connection (and not actually running the game we want to monitor).

2. Open the XNA Framework Remote Performance Monitor for Xbox 360 from the Tools group in the Microsoft XNA Game Studio group under All Programs.

3. Select your Xbox 360 console from the Device dropdown list box (it will only show up if step 1 was performed).

4. Tell the tool which game to launch and monitor by entering the name that we stored in the AssemblyTitle attribute (discussed in Chapter 2, "XNA Game Studio

and the Xbox 360") into the Application text box. You can enter **Platformer** assuming that has been deployed as discussed in Chapter 1, "Introducing the XNA Framework and XNA Game Studio."

5. If the game allows any command-line arguments, enter those into the Arguments text box. You can leave it blank for Platformer.

6. Click Launch to start the game on the Xbox 360.

Now that you have the tool running, we can take a moment and look at some of the numbers being displayed. Although all are beneficial to watch, and we should try to keep the numbers from incrementing too much, the following are some of the important numbers:

Garbage Collections (GC)

Managed Bytes Allocated

Managed Objects Allocated

Bytes of String Objects Allocated

Managed String Objects Allocated

Objects Not Moved by Compactor

Boxed Value Types

GC Latency Time (ms)

Calls to GC.Collect

A good exercise is to run an empty Xbox 360 game and watch the numbers. Those values will be our baseline. As we add functionality, we can check the numbers to see if anything is getting out of sorts and then act appropriately. Doing this as we go will help us keep our code working in an optimal way and will keep us from having to come back and scour through the code to find out where the bottlenecks are. To determine the amount of time the garbage collector is taking to run, we can take the product of the number of garbage collections that occurred with latency time. This is a key number to be aware of when checking the performance of our garbage collector. We discuss the garbage collector in detail later in this chapter.

Managing Memory

The two types of objects in the .NET Framework are reference and value. Examples of value types are enums, integral types (byte, short, int, long), floating types (single, double, float), primitive types (bool, char), and structs. Examples of objects that are reference types are arrays, exceptions, attributes, delegates, and classes. Value types have their data stored on the current thread's stack, and the managed heap is where reference types find themselves.

By default, when we pass variables into methods, we pass them by value. This means for value types we are actually passing a copy of the data on the stack, so anything we do to that variable inside of the method does not affect the original memory. When we pass in a reference type, we are actually passing a copy of the reference to the data. The actual data is not copied, just the address of the memory. Because of this, we should pass large value types by reference instead of by value when appropriate. It is much faster to copy an address of a large value type than its actual data.

We use the `ref` keyword to pass the objects as references to our methods. We should not use this keyword on reference types because it will actually slow things down. We should use the keyword on value types (such as structs) that have a large amount of data to copy if passed by value.

The other thing to note is that even if we have a reference type and we pass it into a method that takes an object type and we box the object (implicitly or explicitly), then a copy of the data is actually created as well—not just the address to the original memory. For example, consider a class that takes a general `object` type (such as an ArrayList's `Add` method). We pass in a reference type, but instead of just the reference being passed across, a copy of the data is created, and then a reference to that copy of the data is passed across. This eats up memory and causes the garbage collector to run more often. To avoid this we need to use generics whenever possible.

Understanding the Garbage Collector

A big plus of writing managed code is the fact that we do not need to worry about memory leaks from the sense of losing pointers to referenced memory. We still have "memory leaks" in managed code, but whenever the term is used, it refers to not decommissioning variables in a timely fashion. We would have a memory leak if we kept a handle on a pointer that we should have set to null. It would remain in memory until the game exits.

We should use the `using` statement. An example of the `using` statement can be found in the program.cs file that is generated for us by the game template. The entry point of the program uses this `using` statement to create our game object and then to call its `Run` method. The `using` statement effectively puts a `try/finally` block around the code while putting a call to the object's `Dispose` method inside of the `finally` block.

Garbage collection concerns on Windows are not as large as those on the Xbox 360. However, if we optimize our code to run well on the Xbox 360 in regard to garbage collection, the game will also perform well on Windows.

On the .NET Framework (Windows)

As we create an object (when we use the `new` keyword), it is put into the managed heap. .NET then calculates the needed memory for the object and confirms there is enough memory available on the managed heap. The constructor of the object is called, and the executing code returns a reference to that object (a location in the managed heap). Memory is created in a contiguous manner, which means that objects are typically stored next to each other as they are created.

If memory cannot be allocated on the managed heap, the garbage collector is executed to free up any unused memory. There are assumptions the garbage collector makes to free up memory. One such assumption is that objects that have just been created will only be around for a short while. Another assumption is that objects that have been around for a while will continue to be around for a while. Because of these assumptions, the garbage collector has a notion of generations. There are a total of three generations in the .NET Framework. The .NET Compact Framework only has one generation, but we are getting ahead of ourselves (this is covered in the next section). The first generation (0) stores all the recently added memory, so memory is allocated when variables are created, Then memory is "marked" as inactive when the variables go out of scope, get explicitly set to null, and so on. By marking memory as inactive, .NET is actually setting the root (which is just a pointer to the location of memory) to null. At some point in time the memory heap gets full. When this happens, the garbage collector runs and sends all objects that are still active (roots are not null) into generation 1, freeing up all of the generation 0 space. If generation 1 gets full, it goes through the same process and pushes up active objects to generation 2. If this last generation is full, a full garbage collection is carried out, which is very expensive. If an object is large enough, it will actually skip generation 0 and jump straight into generation 2 so that it does not incur the performance hit of being put into generation 0, maxing out the memory, and repeating the process again in generation 1.

So what does this mean in regard to writing games for Windows? Well, it means we need to be careful how and when we create objects. We do not want to create very large objects, and we want the objects we do create to be short lived so they do not get promoted to generation 1. We also need to let go of objects when we are done with them. We need to create objects that are related close together so they can move through the process together. We also need to be careful and not associate a short-lived object with a long-lived object because the long-lived object will keep a reference to it, which causes the short-lived object not to be collected. Short-lived objects that require little memory do not cause performance issues. Long-lived objects (as long as they are not too large) do not cause performance issues. If the long-lived objects are too big, this will cause the generation 2 memory to become full, and full collections will happen more often than we want. We need to keep our objects to a decent size. Objects that are neither short-lived nor long-lived objects are where we run into performance issues. These midlife objects will get promoted to generation 1 and then become inactive. Although this is not a huge problem, it becomes a real concern when the object stays alive and then gets moved into generation 2 and then shortly thereafter dies. By having the object die in generation 2 instead of generation 1, we are paying a very large performance price because when the garbage collector does a full collection (collects data in generation 2), it has to look at each and every object on the managed heap to determine whether the object is alive or not. While it is inspecting the objects, it creates a large load on the CPU that reduces the overall throughput. Any objects with finalizers really hurt the performance of the application. We do not want to generate full collections.

On the .NET Compact Framework (Xbox 360 and Zune)

The .NET Compact Framework handles garbage collection differently than its desktop counterpart. However, if we try to optimize our code for the .NET Compact Framework, we should also realize the benefits on the desktop version of the .NET Framework. The

.NET Compact Framework does not have generations. We can think of it as only having generation 2 actually, in that every collection is a full collection.

The .NET Compact Framework's garbage collector will also compact the memory into a contiguous space when it determines that the memory heap is overly fragmented. If there is not enough memory, the garbage collector will also pitch the code that was compiled "just in time." The code that is compiled just in time is kept in memory to help performance, but if memory gets too low the memory will be released.

Finally, the garbage collector will go through any objects in the finalization queue. This queue also exists in the full .NET Framework and works the same way. As memory is marked as not needed, the garbage collector determines if the object has a `Finalize` method. If it does, the object is actually put into this separate queue before the memory is marked on the heap as inactive. Then the next time the garbage collector runs, it loops through the finalization queue and disposes of the objects. This is why it is very important to not utilize the `Finalize` method unless we are using unmanaged resources. When developing for the Xbox 360 or the Zune, we do not need to worry about unmanaged objects because we do not have the ability to access them.

Optimization Suggestions

We have discussed how to measure performance and discussed a common performance issue with the garbage collector. Now we are going to look at different optimizations we could make if we determine that a certain piece of code is not performing well. This is considered micro-optimization and should only be done after taking measurements to make sure that the code we are about to optimize really needs it! If we spend our time trying to save CPU cycles on a method that did not need it, we wasted our time. Worse, we probably made the code less readable. Even worse, we could have introduced bugs during the process that put us even further behind the eight ball.

Although performing micro-optimizations is important, it is really one of the last steps we do. Great places for this type of optimization are inside of nested loops. For example, our `Update` and `Draw` methods are inside of a tight game loop the XNA Framework runs, and we will have loops inside of there to update AI logic and check physics and such. Even those could have nested loops. It is at those points we will be doing most of the micro-optimizations, but we only do this after we have confirmed that a particular section of code is our bottleneck. Measure!

Creating a Micro-Benchmark Framework

When we are trying to make a particular piece of code run faster because we see that it is taking more time compared to everything else in our application, we will need to compare different implementations of completing the same task. This is where micro-benchmark testing can help.

Micro-benchmark testing allows us to take a close look at how fast small bits of code are performing. There are a couple of items to keep in mind as we use micro-benchmark testing, though. The first is that we cannot exactly determine best practices from a micro-benchmark test because it is such an isolated case. The second is that although a piece of code might perform faster in a micro-benchmark test, it might very well take up a lot more memory and therefore cause the garbage collector to collect its garbage more often. The point here is that although micro-benchmark testing is good and we should do it (which is why we are going to build a framework for it), we need to be careful of any assumptions we make solely on what we find out from our micro-benchmark tests.

XNA Game Studio not only lets us create game projects, but also allows us to create library projects. When the library projects are compiled, they can be used by other applications—a game, a Windows form, or even a console application.

We are going to create another application, but this time it is going to be a normal Windows Game Library project. We can name this project XNAPerformanceChecker. This class should be called CheckPerformance. We will be utilizing this library from a console application. The code for the CheckPerformance class can be found in Listing 3.1. The purpose of this class is to create methods that perform the same tasks different ways. We will then create a console application that calls the different methods and measure the amount of time it takes to process each method.

LISTING 3.1   The CheckPerformance Class Has Methods That Produce the Same Results Through Different Means

```
public class CheckPerformance
{
    private Vector3 cameraReference = new Vector3(0, 0, -1.0f);
    private Vector3 cameraPosition = new Vector3(0, 0, 3.0f);
    private Vector3 cameraTarget = Vector3.Zero;
    private Vector3 vectorUp = Vector3.Up;
    private Matrix projection;
    private Matrix view;
    private float cameraYaw = 0.0f;

    public CheckPerformance() { }

    public void TransformVectorByValue()
    {
        Matrix rotationMatrix = Matrix.CreateRotationY(
            MathHelper.ToRadians(45.0f));
        // Create a vector pointing the direction the camera is facing.
        Vector3 transformedReference = Vector3.Transform(cameraReference,
            rotationMatrix);
        // Calculate the position the camera is looking at.
        cameraTarget = cameraPosition + transformedReference;
    }

    public void TransformVectorByReference()
```

```
    {
        Matrix rotationMatrix = Matrix.CreateRotationY(
            MathHelper.ToRadians(45.0f));
        // Create a vector pointing the direction the camera is facing.
        Vector3 transformedReference;
        Vector3.Transform(ref cameraReference, ref rotationMatrix,
            out transformedReference);
        // Calculate the position the camera is looking at.
        Vector3.Add(ref cameraPosition, ref transformedReference,
            out cameraTarget);
    }

    public void TransformVectorByReferenceAndOut()>
    {
        Matrix rotationMatrix = Matrix.CreateRotationY(
            MathHelper.ToRadians(45.0f));
        // Create a vector pointing the direction the camera is facing.
        Vector3 transformedReference;
        Vector3.Transform(ref cameraReference, ref rotationMatrix,
            out transformedReference);
        // Calculate the position the camera is looking at.
        Vector3.Add(ref cameraPosition, ref transformedReference,
            out cameraTarget);
    }

    public void TransformVectorByReferenceAndOutVectorAdd()>
    {
        Matrix rotationMatrix;
        Matrix.CreateRotationY(MathHelper.ToRadians(45.0f),
            out rotationMatrix);
        // Create a vector pointing the direction the camera is facing.
        Vector3 transformedReference;
        Vector3.Transform(ref cameraReference, ref rotationMatrix,
            out transformedReference);
        // Calculate the position the camera is looking at.
        Vector3.Add(ref cameraPosition, ref transformedReference,
            out cameraTarget);
    }

    public void InitializeTransformWithCalculation()
    {
        float aspectRatio = (float)640 / (float)480;
        projection = Matrix.CreatePerspectiveFieldOfView(
            MathHelper.ToRadians(45.0f), aspectRatio, 0.0001f, 1000.0f);
        view = Matrix.CreateLookAt(cameraPosition, cameraTarget, Vector3.Up);
    }
```

3

```
public void InitializeTransformWithConstant()
{
    float aspectRatio = (float)640 / (float)480;
    projection = Matrix.CreatePerspectiveFieldOfView(
        MathHelper.PiOver4, aspectRatio, 0.0001f, 1000.0f);
    view = Matrix.CreateLookAt(cameraPosition, cameraTarget, Vector3.Up);
}

public void InitializeTransformWithDivision()
{
    float aspectRatio = (float)640 / (float)480;
    projection = Matrix.CreatePerspectiveFieldOfView(
        MathHelper.Pi / 4, aspectRatio, 0.0001f, 1000.0f);
    view = Matrix.CreateLookAt(cameraPosition, cameraTarget, Vector3.Up);
}

public void InitializeTransformWithConstantReferenceOut()>
{
    float aspectRatio = (float)640 / (float)480;
    Matrix.CreatePerspectiveFieldOfView(
        MathHelper.ToRadians(45.0f), aspectRatio, 0.0001f, 1000.0f,
        out projection);
    Matrix.CreateLookAt(
        ref cameraPosition, ref cameraTarget, ref vectorUp, out view);
}

public void InitializeTransformWithPreDeterminedAspectRatio()
{
    Matrix.CreatePerspectiveFieldOfView(
        MathHelper.ToRadians(45.0f), 1.33333f, 0.0001f, 1000.0f,
        out projection);
    Matrix.CreateLookAt(
        ref cameraPosition, ref cameraTarget, ref vectorUp, out view);
}

public void CreateCameraReferenceWithProperty()
{
    Vector3 cameraReference = Vector3.Forward;
    Matrix rotationMatrix;
    Matrix.CreateRotationY(
        MathHelper.ToRadians(45.0f), out rotationMatrix);
    // Create a vector pointing the direction the camera is facing.
    Vector3 transformedReference;
    Vector3.Transform(ref cameraReference, ref rotationMatrix,
        out transformedReference);
```

```
    // Calculate the position the camera is looking at.
    cameraTarget = cameraPosition + transformedReference;
}
public void CreateCameraReferenceWithValue()
{
    Vector3 cameraReference = new Vector3(0, 0, -1.0f);
    Matrix rotationMatrix;
    Matrix.CreateRotationY(
        MathHelper.ToRadians(45.0f), out rotationMatrix);
    // Create a vector pointing the direction the camera is facing.
    Vector3 transformedReference;
    Vector3.Transform(ref cameraReference, ref rotationMatrix,
        out transformedReference);
    // Calculate the position the camera is looking at.
    cameraTarget = cameraPosition + transformedReference;
}


public void RotateWithoutMod()
{
    cameraYaw += 2.0f;

    if (cameraYaw > 360)
        cameraYaw -= 360;
    if (cameraYaw < 0)
        cameraYaw += 360;

    float tmp = cameraYaw;
}


public void RotateWithMod()
{
    cameraYaw += 2.0f;

    cameraYaw %= 360;

    float tmp = cameraYaw;
}


public void RotateElseIf()
{
    cameraYaw += 2.0f;

    if (cameraYaw > 360)
        cameraYaw -= 360;
    else if (cameraYaw < 0)
        cameraYaw += 360;
```

```
        float tmp = cameraYaw;
    }
}
```

We do not need to be concerned with the actual contents of the different methods. The main concept you need to understand at this point is that we have different groups of methods that do the same task but are executed in different ways. We discuss the details of the Matrix in Chapter 4, "Creating 3D Objects." For now we can take a look at the last three methods in the listing and see they are all doing the same thing. All three methods are adding 2 to the variable cameraYaw and then making sure that the value is between 0 and 360. The idea is that this code would be inside of the game loop reading input from a device and updating the cameraYaw variable appropriately.

Now we can create the console application that will actually call that class. We need to add a new Console Application project to the solution and can call this project XNAPerfStarter. We need to add a reference to the XNAPerformanceChecker project. The code for Program.cs is given in Listing 3.2.

LISTING 3.2   The Program Measures the Amount of Time It Takes to Execute the Different
CheckPerformance Methods

```
class Program
{
    static int timesToLoop = 10000;

    static void Main(string[] args)
    {
        while (true)
        {
            XNAPerformanceChecker.CheckPerformance cp =
                new XNAPerformanceChecker.CheckPerformance();

            Stopwatch sw = new Stopwatch();

            //Call all methods once for any JIT-ing that needs to be done
            sw.Start();
            cp.InitializeTransformWithCalculation();
            cp.InitializeTransformWithConstant();
            cp.InitializeTransformWithDivision();
            cp.InitializeTransformWithConstantReferenceOut();
            cp.TransformVectorByReference();
            cp.TransformVectorByValue();
            cp.TransformVectorByReferenceAndOut();
            cp.TransformVectorByReferenceAndOutVectorAdd();
            cp.CreateCameraReferenceWithProperty();
```

```
cp.CreateCameraReferenceWithValue();
sw.Stop();
sw.Reset();
int i;
sw.Start();
for (i = 0; i < timesToLoop; i++)
    cp.InitializeTransformWithCalculation();
sw.Stop();

PrintPerformance("        Calculation", ref sw);
sw.Reset();

sw.Start();
for (i = 0; i < timesToLoop; i++)
    cp.InitializeTransformWithConstant();
sw.Stop();

PrintPerformance("          Constant", ref sw);
sw.Reset();

sw.Start();
for (i = 0; i < timesToLoop; i++)
    cp.InitializeTransformWithDivision();
sw.Stop();

PrintPerformance("          Division", ref sw);
sw.Reset();

sw.Start();
for (i = 0; i < timesToLoop; i++)
    cp.InitializeTransformWithConstantReferenceOut();
sw.Stop();

PrintPerformance("ConstantReferenceOut", ref sw);
sw.Reset();

sw.Start();
for (i = 0; i < timesToLoop; i++)
    cp.InitializeTransformWithPreDeterminedAspectRatio();
sw.Stop();

PrintPerformance("        AspectRatio", ref sw);
sw.Reset();

Console.WriteLine();
Console.WriteLine("— — — — — — — — — —");
```

```
Console.WriteLine();

sw.Start();
for (i = 0; i < timesToLoop; i++)
    cp.TransformVectorByReference();
sw.Stop();

PrintPerformance("      Reference", ref sw);
sw.Reset();

sw.Start();
for (i = 0; i < timesToLoop; i++)
    cp.TransformVectorByValue();
sw.Stop();

PrintPerformance("          Value", ref sw);
sw.Reset();

sw.Start();
for (i = 0; i < timesToLoop; i++)
    cp.TransformVectorByReferenceAndOut();
sw.Stop();

PrintPerformance("ReferenceAndOut", ref sw);
sw.Reset();

sw.Start();
for (i = 0; i < timesToLoop; i++)
    cp.TransformVectorByReferenceAndOutVectorAdd();
sw.Stop();

PrintPerformance("RefOutVectorAdd", ref sw);
sw.Reset();

Console.WriteLine();
Console.WriteLine("— — — — — — — — — —");
Console.WriteLine();

sw.Start();
for (i = 0; i < timesToLoop; i++)
    cp.CreateCameraReferenceWithProperty();
sw.Stop();

PrintPerformance("Property", ref sw);
sw.Reset();
```

```
        sw.Start();
        for (i = 0; i < timesToLoop; i++)
            cp.CreateCameraReferenceWithValue();
        sw.Stop();

        PrintPerformance("   Value", ref sw);
        sw.Reset();

        Console.WriteLine();
        Console.WriteLine("— — — — — — — — — —");
        Console.WriteLine();

        sw.Start();
        for (i = 0; i < timesToLoop; i++)
            cp.RotateWithMod();
        sw.Stop();

        PrintPerformance("   RotateWithMod", ref sw);
        sw.Reset();

        sw.Start();
        for (i = 0; i < timesToLoop; i++)
            cp.RotateWithoutMod();
        sw.Stop();

        PrintPerformance("RotateWithoutMod", ref sw);
        sw.Reset();

        sw.Start();
        for (i = 0; i < timesToLoop; i++)
            cp.RotateElseIf();
        sw.Stop();

        PrintPerformance("   RotateElseIf", ref sw);
        sw.Reset();

        string command = Console.ReadLine();

        if (command.ToUpper().StartsWith("E") ||
            command.ToUpper().StartsWith("Q"))
            break;
    }
}

static void PrintPerformance(string label, ref Stopwatch sw)
{
```

```
    Console.WriteLine(label + " - Avg: " +
        ((float)((float)(sw.Elapsed.Ticks * 100) /
        (float)timesToLoop)).ToString("F") +
        " Total: " + sw.Elapsed.TotalMilliseconds.ToString());
    }
}
```

We need also to add the following using clause to the top of our Program.cs file:

```
using System.Diagnostics;
```

The System.Diagnostics class gives us access to the Stopwatch we are using to keep track of the time it takes to process the different methods. After starting the timer, we then loop 100,000 times and call a method in the CheckPerformance class we created earlier. Once the loop finishes executing the method the specified number of times, we stop the stopwatch and print out our results to the console. When using the Stopwatch object, we must first call the Reset method if we want to start another test. This isn't built into the Stop method in case we just want to pause the timer and start it back up for some reason. We could also use the static StartNew method instead of the instance Start method. The StartNew method effectively resets the timer as it returns a new instance of the Stopwatch.

When we are trying to measure performance on pieces of code that perform very fast (even inside of a large loop), it is important to be able to track exactly how much time is taken, even down to the nanosecond level.

Typically timing things in seconds does not give us the granularity we need to see how long something is really taking, so the next unit of time we can measure against is milliseconds. There are 1,000 milliseconds in a second. Next comes the microsecond, and there are 1,000 microseconds in a millisecond. Next is the tick, which is what the TimeSpan object uses. There are 10 ticks in a microsecond. Finally, we come to the nanosecond. There are 100 nanoseconds in each tick. A nanosecond is one-billionth of a second. Table 3.1 shows the relationships between the different measurements of time.

TABLE 3.1   Time Measurement Relationships

Nanoseconds	Ticks	Microseconds	Milliseconds	Seconds
100	1	0.1	0.0001	0.0000001
10,000	100	10.0	0.0100	0.0000100
100,000	1,000	100.0	0.1000	0.0001000
1,000,000	10,000	1,000.0	1.0000	0.0010000
10,000,000	100,000	10,000.0	10.0000	0.0100000
100,000,000	1,000,000	100,000.0	100.0000	0.1000000
1,000,000,000	10,000,000	1,000,000.0	1,000.0000	1.0000000

`PrintPerformance`, our method to print out the performance measurements, takes in the label that describes what we are measuring along with a reference to the `Stopwatch` object. `TimeSpan` is the type the .NET Framework uses to measure time. The smallest unit of time measurement this type allows is a tick.

Because we want to measure our time in nanoseconds, we multiply the number of elapsed ticks by 100. Then we take the total number of nanoseconds and divide by the number of times we executed the method. Finally, we display the average number of nanoseconds along with total number of milliseconds the task took to execute.

When we print out our measurements, we want the average time it took to execute a method for the number of iterations we told it to loop. The reason we do this instead of just running it once is so that we can easily determine a more accurate number. In fact, we even run an outer loop (that we exit out of by entering text that starts with "E" or "Q") to account for anomalies in performance on the machine in general.

An additional item to note about this code is that we call each method of the `CheckPerformance` object once before we start measuring execution times. The reason we do this is so the compiler can perform any just-in-time compiling for the methods we will be calling so we are not taking that time into account.

After setting the new XNAPerfStarter as the StartUp project, we can run the benchmark tests.

Sealing Virtual Methods

Although having virtual methods and virtual classes is extremely beneficial for extensibility and object-oriented design, it also causes a performance hit because virtual methods keep certain runtime performance optimizations from happening. This is because virtual methods require a virtual table lookup to occur. If we are not extending a class or a method, we can actually seal it to help with the performance. This lets the compiler know that no one else will be allowed to override the method, and the jitter will generate a direct call to the method instead of the lookup.

Collections

If possible, we want to utilize regular arrays instead of collections. Of course, if we need to dynamically add or remove items from our list, a collection is the way to go.

Regardless of which we use, we always want to have our lists to store a specific type. C# has generics that allow us to use strong types so we do not need to box and unbox objects in our lists. If we cannot get by with a regular array of a specific type, we need to use generics. We should never use a "normal" collection (that is, one that does not use generics).

Whether we are using normal arrays or a full-fledged collection, we should always set the initial size of our list to be as close as possible to the number of items we expect the list will store. This way, the correct amount of memory can be allocated once instead of having to reallocate often due to a growing list.

There is a lot of speculation about `foreach` loops and the overhead they bring with the garbage collection they cause. When we loop through an array, we do not create garbage. When we loop through certain collections, we do not create garbage. The key is whether or not the enumerator returns a struct. If a struct is returned, the data is put on to the stack, and we are in good shape. Looping through a `Collection<T>` will definitely create overhead because the enumerator will box the value and put it on the heap. If we stick with straight arrays when we can, there is nothing to worry about. If we need to work with the list in a dynamic fashion, we just need to choose the type of collection we will create—Lists, Stacks, and Queues are all good candidates because their `GetEnumerator` returns a struct, and no extra memory is allocated.

Summary

You should walk away from this chapter with the sense that before any optimization takes place, you need to know what you are going to optimize. To determine what needs a performance boost, you need to measure. Measuring is the key, and it cannot be stressed enough.

We discussed how to measure the real frame per seconds rate at which our game is capable of running. We looked at the remote performance monitoring tool for the Xbox 360 and saw how we could look at critical pieces of information to see how our game performs on the console.

We discussed a typical bottleneck of memory management and how the garbage collector runs. We also created a micro-benchmarking framework that allows us to determine how fast or slow a particular method (or part of a method) is and how it compares to alternative methods to produce the same results.

We really just scratched the surface of performance considerations. Searching the Web for more information on increasing our performance would be extremely helpful. Something not even touched on was the fact that knowledge of MSIL can be beneficial in seeing what the .NET Framework is really doing with our C# code. We could look at the IL code for any reference to `newobj` to see when we created an object and look for `box` to find when we boxed and unboxed items (unknowingly).

The main idea of this chapter is that we must have an end goal. We have to know how well we want our game to perform so we can write our code in such a way to meet those goals. In the real world we have deadlines, and writing code fast and writing fast code are often at odds with each other. This is where it is extremely beneficial to know exactly what we are shooting for. We should measure often to determine which piece of new code is causing an adverse affect on performance.

PART II

Understanding XNA Framework Basics

CHAPTER 4

Creating 3D Objects

In this chapter, we examine 3D concepts and how the XNA Framework exposes different types and objects that allow us to easily create 3D worlds. We will create a couple 3D demos that explain the basics. We will also create 3D objects directly inside of our code. Finally, we will move these objects on the screen.

Vertices

Everything in a 3D game is represented by 3D points. We can use one of two ways to get 3D objects on the screen: We can plot the points ourselves, or we can load them from a 3D file (which has all the points stored already). Later, in Chapter 6, "Loading and Texturing 3D Objects," you will learn how to load 3D files to use in our games. For now, we are going to create the vertices ourselves.

We defined these vertices with an x, y, and z coordinate (x, y, z). In XNA we represent a vertex with a vector, which leads us to the next section.

Vectors

XNA provides three different vector structs for us—Vector2, Vector3, and Vector4. Vector2 only has an x and y component. We typically use this 2D vector in 2D games and when working with a texture. Vector3 adds in the z component. Not only do we store vertices as a vector, but we also store velocity as a vector. We discuss velocity in Chapter 16, "Physics Basics." The last vector struct that XNA provides for us is a 4D struct appropriately called Vector4. Later examples in this book will use this struct to pass color information around because it has four components.

We can perform different math operations on vectors, which prove to be very helpful. We do not discuss 3D math in detail in this book because there are many texts available that cover it. Fortunately, XNA allows us to use the built-in helper functions without needing a deep understanding of the inner workings of the code. With that said, it is extremely beneficial to understand the math behind the different functions.

Matrices

In XNA a matrix is a 4×4 table of data. It is a two-dimensional array. An identity matrix, also referred to as a *unit matrix*, is similar to the number 1 in that if we multiply any other number by 1, we always end up with the number we started out with (5 * 1 = 5). Multiplying a matrix by an identity matrix will produce a matrix with the same value as the original matrix. Although the identity matrix can be useful in and of itself, the key is the individual fields in the 4×4 array are structured so that we can combine many transformations into a single matrix. The XNA Framework provides a struct to hold matrix data—not surprisingly, it is called Matrix.

Transformations

The data a matrix contains is called a transformation. The three common types of transformations are translation, scaling, and rotation. These transformations do just that: They transform our 3D objects.

Translation

Translating an object simply means we are moving the object. We translate an object from one point to another point by moving each point inside of the object correctly.

Scaling

Scaling an object will make the object larger or smaller. This is done by actually moving the points in the object closer together or further apart, depending on whether we are scaling down or scaling up.

Rotation

Rotating an object will turn the object on one or more axes. By moving the points in 3D space, we can make our object spin.

Transformation versus Translation

A translation is a type of a transformation. Transformations include translations (movement), scaling (size), and rotation. A translation is one type of transformation, but they are not the same thing.

Transformations Reloaded

An object can have one transformation applied to it, or it can have many transformations applied to it. We might only want to translate (move) an object, so we can update the object's world matrix to move it around in the world. We might just want the object to spin around, so we apply a rotation transformation to the object over and over so it will rotate. We might need an object we created from a 3D editor to be smaller to fit better in our world. In that case we can apply a scaling transformation to the object. Of course, we might need to take this object we loaded in from the 3D editor and scale it down and rotate it 30 degrees to the left so it will face some object, and we might need to move it closer to the object it is facing. In this case, we would actually do all three types of transformations to get the desired results. We might even need to rotate it downward 5 degrees as well, and that is perfectly acceptable.

We can have many different transformations applied to an object. This is done by multiplying different matrices together. However, there is a catch—there is always a catch, right? The catch is that because we are doing these transformations using matrix math, we need to be aware of something very important. We are multiplying our transformation matrices together to get the results we want. Unlike multiplying normal integers, multiplying matrices is not commutative. This means that Matrix A * Matrix B != Matrix B * Matrix A. So in our earlier example where we want to scale our object and rotate it (two different times) and then move it, we need to be careful in which order we perform those operations. You will see how to do this a little later in the chapter.

Creating a Camera

That is enough theory for a bit. We are going to create a camera so we can view our world. Now we can create a new Windows game project to get started with this section. We'll name this project XNADemo. To begin, we need to create the following private member fields:

```
private Matrix projection;
private Matrix view;
```

We then need to add a call to InitializeCamera in the beginning of our LoadGraphicsContent method. The InitializeCamera method will have no parameters and no return value. We will begin to populate the method, which can be marked as private, in the next three sections.

Projection

The Matrix struct has a lot of helper functions built in that we can utilize. The Matrix.CreatePerspectiveFieldOfView is the method we want to look at now:

```
float aspectRatio = (float)graphics.GraphicsDevice.Viewport.Width /
    (float)graphics.GraphicsDevice.Viewport.Height;
Matrix.CreatePerspectiveFieldOfView(MathHelper.PiOver4, aspectRatio,
    0.0001f, 1000.0f, out projection);
```

First, we set up a local variable called aspectRatio. This is to store, you guessed it, the aspect ratio of our screen. For the Xbox 360 the aspect ratio of the back buffer will determine how the game is displayed on the gamer's TV. If we develop with a widescreen aspect ratio and the user has a standard TV, the game will have a letterbox look to it. Conversely, if we develop with a standard aspect ratio and the user has a widescreen TV, the Xbox 360 will stretch the display. To avoid this we should account for both situations and then adjust the value of our aspect ratio variable to the default values of the viewport of the graphics device, like in the preceding code. If we needed to find the default value to which the gamer has his or her Xbox 360 set, we can gather that information by querying the DisplayMode property of the graphics device during or after the Initialization method is called by the framework.

However, if we want to force a widescreen aspect ratio on the Xbox 360, we could set the PreferredBackBufferWidth and PreferredBackBufferHeight properties on the graphics object right after creating it. Many gamers do not care for the black bars, so we should use this with caution. Forcing a widescreen aspect ratio on Windows is a little more complicated, but the XNA Game Studio documentation has a great "How To" page explaining how to do it. Once in the documentation, look for "How to: Restrict Graphics Devices to Widescreen Aspect Ratios in Full Screen" under the Application Model in the Programming Guide.

Second, we create our field of view. The first parameter we pass in is 45 degrees. We could have used MathHelper.ToRadians(45.0f), but there is no need to do the math because the MathHelper class already has the value as a constant. The second parameter is the aspect ratio, which we already calculated. The third and fourth parameters are our near and far clipping planes, respectively. The plane values represent how far the plane is from our camera. It means anything past the far clipping plane will not be drawn onto the screen. It also means anything closer to us than the near clipping plane will not be drawn either. Only the points that fall in between those two planes and are within a 45-degree angle of where we are looking will be drawn on the screen. The last parameter is where we populate our projection matrix. This is an overloaded method. (One version actually returns the projection, but we will utilize the overload that has reference and out parameters, which is faster because it doesn't have to copy the value of the data.)

View

Now that we have our projection matrix set, we can set up our view matrix. Although our projection can be thought of as the camera's internals (like choosing a lens for the camera), our view can be thought of as what our camera sees. The view matrix contains which way is up for the camera, which way the camera is facing, and the actual position of the camera. To set up our view matrix, we are going to use another XNA matrix helper method. The Matrix.CreateLookAt method takes three parameters. Let's create and initialize these private member fields now.

```
private Vector3 cameraPosition = new Vector3(0.0f, 0.0f, 3.0f);
private Vector3 cameraTarget = Vector3.Zero;
private Vector3 cameraUpVector = Vector3.Up;
```

Now we can actually call the CreateLookAt method inside of our InitializeCamera method. We should add the following code at the end of the method:

```
Matrix.CreateLookAt(ref cameraPosition, ref cameraTarget,
    ref cameraUpVector, out view);
```

The first parameter we pass in is our camera position. We are passing in the coordinates (0,0,3) for our camera position to start with, so our camera position will remain at the origin of the x and y axis, but it will move backward from the origin 3 units. The second parameter of the CreateLookAt method is the target of where we are aiming the camera. In this example, we are aiming the camera at the origin of the world Vector3.Zero (0,0,0). Finally, we pass in the camera's up vector. For this we use the Up property on Vector3, which means (0,1,0). Notice we actually created a variable for this so we can pass it in by reference. This is also an overloaded method, and because we want this to be fast we will pass the variables in by reference instead of by value. Fortunately, we do not lose much readability with this performance gain.

World

At this point if we compiled and ran the demo we would still see the lovely blank cornflower blue screen because we have not set up our world matrix or put anything in the world to actually look at. Let's fix that now.

As you saw, the templates provide a lot of methods stubbed out for us. One of these very important methods is the Draw method. Find this method and add the following line of code right below the TODO: Add your drawing code here comment:

```
Matrix world = Matrix.Identity;
```

This simply sets our world matrix to an identity matrix, which means that there is no scaling, no rotating, and no translating (movement). The identity matrix has a translation of (0,0,0), so this will effectively set our world matrix to the origin of the world.

At this point we have our camera successfully set up, but we have not actually drawn anything. We are going to correct that starting with the next section.

Vertex Buffers

3D objects are made up of triangles. Every object is one triangle or more. For example, a sphere is just made up of triangles; the more triangles, the more rounded the sphere is. Take a look at Figure 4.1 to see how this works. Now that you know that every 3D object we render is made up of triangles and that a triangle is simply three vertices in 3D space, we can use vertex buffers to store a list of 3D points. As the name implies, a vertex buffer is simply memory (a buffer) that holds a list of vertices.

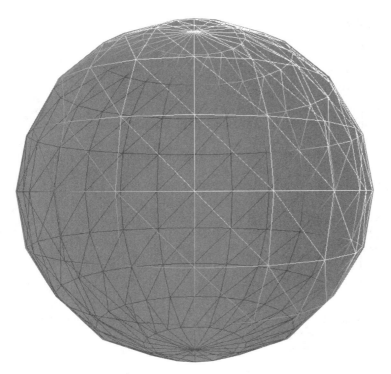

FIGURE 4.1   All 3D objects are made up of triangles.

XNA uses a right-handed coordinate system. This means that the x axis goes from left to right (left being negative, and right being positive), the y axis goes up and down (down being negative, and up being positive), and z goes forward and backward (forward being negative, and backward being positive). You can visualize this by extending your right arm out to your right and positioning your hand like you are holding a gun. Now rotate your wrist so your palm is facing the sky. At this point your pointer finger should be pointing to the right (this is our x axis going in a positive direction to the right). Your thumb should be pointing behind you (this is our z axis going in a positive direction backward). Now, uncurl your three fingers so they are pointing to the sky (this represents the y axis with a positive direction upward). Take a look at Figure 4.2 to help solidify how the right-handed coordinate system works.

Now that you know what the positive direction is for each axis, we are ready to start plotting our points. XNA uses counterclockwise culling. *Culling* is a performance measure graphic cards take to keep from rendering objects that are not facing the camera. XNA has three options for culling: `CullClockwiseFace`, `CullCounterClockwiseFace`, and `None`. The default culling mode for XNA is `CullCounterClockwiseFace`, so to see our objects we have to set up our points in the opposite order—clockwise.

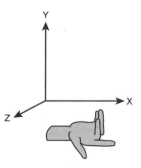

FIGURE 4.2   This demonstrates a right-handed coordinate system.

TIP

It is helpful to use some graph paper (or regular notebook paper for that matter) to plot out points. Simply put points where you want them and make sure when you put them into the code that you do it in a clockwise order.

Let's plot some points. Ultimately, we want to make a square. We know that all 3D objects can be made with triangles, and we can see that a square is made up of two triangles. We will position the first triangle at (-1,1,0); (1,-1,0); (-1,-1,0). That means the first point (-1,1,0) will be positioned on the x axis one unit to the left, and it will be one unit up the y axis and will stay at the origin on the z axis. The code needed to set up these points is as follows:

```
private void InitializeVertices(){
    Vector3 position;
    Vector2 textureCoordinates;

    vertices = new VertexPositionNormalTexture[3];

    //top left
    position = new Vector3(-1, 1, 0);
    textureCoordinates = new Vector2(0, 0);
    vertices[0] = new VertexPositionNormalTexture(position, Vector3.Forward,
        textureCoordinates);

    //bottom right
    position = new Vector3(1, -1, 0);
    textureCoordinates = new Vector2(1, 1);
    vertices[1] = new VertexPositionNormalTexture(position, Vector3.Forward,
        textureCoordinates);
```

```
    //bottom left
    position = new Vector3(-1, -1, 0);
    textureCoordinates = new Vector2(0, 1);
    vertices[2] = new VertexPositionNormalTexture(position, Vector3.Forward,
        textureCoordinates);
}
```

As you look at this function, notice that two variables have been created: `position` and `textureCoordinates`. XNA has different structs that describe the type of data a vertex will hold. In most cases, for 3D games we will need to store the position, normal, and texture coordinates. We discuss normals later, but for now it is sufficient to understand that they let the graphics device know how to reflect light off the face (triangle). The most important part of the vertex variable is the position of the point in 3D space. You saw earlier that XNA allows us to store that information in a `Vector3` struct. We can either set the data in the constructor as we did in this code, or we can explicitly set its X, Y, and Z properties.

I'll skip over explaining the texture coordinates momentarily, but notice they use the `Vector2` struct XNA provides for us. We need to add the following private member field to our class we have been using to store our vertices:

```
private VertexPositionNormalTexture[] vertices;
```

We need to call this method in our application. The appropriate place to call the `InitializeVertices` method is inside of the `LoadContent` method.

If we compile and run our application now we still do not see anything on the screen. This is because we have not actually told the program to *draw* our triangle! We will want to find our `Draw` method, and before the last call to the base class `base.Draw(gameTime)`, we need to add the following code:

```
graphics.GraphicsDevice.VertexDeclaration = new
    VertexDeclaration(graphics.GraphicsDevice,
    VertexPositionNormalTexture.VertexElements);

BasicEffect effect = new BasicEffect(graphics.GraphicsDevice, null);

effect.Projection = projection;
effect.View = view;

effect.EnableDefaultLighting();

world = Matrix.Identity;
effect.World = world;
effect.Begin();
```

```
foreach (EffectPass pass in effect.CurrentTechnique.Passes)
{
    pass.Begin();
    graphics.GraphicsDevice.DrawUserPrimitives(
        PrimitiveType.TriangleList, vertices, 0,
        vertices.Length / 3);

    pass.End();
}

effect.End();
```

You might think there is a lot of code here just to draw the points we have created on the screen. Well, there is, but it is all very straightforward, and we can plow on through. Before we do, though, let's take a minute and talk about effects.

Effects

Effects are used to get anything in our XNA 3D game to actually show up on the screen. They handle things such as lights, textures, and even the position of the points. We will talk about effects extensively in Part VI, "High Level Shader Language." For now, we can utilize the BasicEffect class that XNA provides. This keeps us from having to actually create an effect file, so we can get started quickly.

The first thing to notice is that we create a new variable to hold our effect. We do this by passing in the graphics device as our first parameter, and we are passing in null as the effect pool because we are only using one effect and don't need a pool to share among multiple effects. After creating our effect, we want to set some of the properties so we can use it. Notice we set the world, view, and projection matrices for the effect as well as tell the effect to turn on the default lighting. We discuss lighting in detail in the HLSL part of the book, but for now, this will light up the 3D scene so we can see our objects.

TIP

When working with 3D, it is a good idea to leave the background color set to Color.CornflowerBlue or some other nonblack color. The reason for this is if the lights are not set up correctly, the object will render in black (no light is shining on it). So if the background color is black, you might think that the object didn't render at all.

Now back to our code. Notice that we call the Begin method on our effect as well as the End method. Anything we draw on the screen in between these two calls will have that effect applied to them. The next section of code is our foreach loop. This loop iterates through all the passes of our effect. Effects will have one or more techniques.

A technique will have one or more passes. For this basic effect, we have only one technique and one pass. You will learn about techniques and passes in more detail in Part VI. At this point we have another begin and end pair, but this time it is for the pass of the current (only) technique in our effect. Inside of this pass is where we finally get to draw our triangle onto the screen. This is done using the DrawUserPrimitives method in the graphics device object:

```
graphics.GraphicsDevice.DrawUserPrimitives(
    PrimitiveType.TriangleList, vertices, 0, vertices.Length / 3);
```

We are passing in the type of primitive we will be rendering. The primitives we are drawing are triangles, so we are going to pass in a triangle list. This is the most common primitive type used in modern games. Refer to Table 4.1 for a list of different primitive types and how they can be used. The second parameter we pass in is the actual vertex data we created in our InitializeVertices method. The third parameter is the offset of the point data where we want to start drawing—in our case, we want to start with the first point, so that is 0. Finally, we need to pass in the number of triangles we are drawing on the screen. We can calculate this by taking the number of points we have stored and dividing it by 3 (because there are three points in a triangle). For our example, this will return one triangle. If we compile and run the code at this point we should see a triangle drawn on our screen. It is not very pretty because it is a dull shade of gray, but it is a triangle nonetheless (see Figure 4.3).

TABLE 4.1   PrimitiveType Enumeration from the XNA Documentation

Member Name	Description
LineList	Renders the vertices as a list of isolated straight-line segments.
LineStrip	Renders the vertices as a single polyline.
PointList	Renders the vertices as a collection of isolated points. This value is unsupported for indexed primitives.
TriangleFan	Renders the vertices as a triangle fan.
TriangleList	Renders the specified vertices as a sequence of isolated triangles. Each group of three vertices defines a separate triangle. Back-face culling is affected by the current winding-order render state.
TriangleStrip	Renders the vertices as a triangle strip. The back-face culling flag is flipped automatically on even-numbered triangles.

FIGURE 4.3   Drawing a triangle as our first demo.

Textures

We have a triangle finally drawn on the screen, but it does not look particularly good. We can fix that by adding a texture. Copy the texture from the Chapter4\XNADemo\ XNADemo folder on the CD (texture.jpg) and paste that into the Content project. This invokes the XNA Content Pipeline, which we discuss in Part III, "Content Pipeline." For now, you just need to know that the content pipeline makes the texture available as loadable content complete with a name by which we can access it. The asset will get the name "texture" (because that is the name of the file). We need to declare a private member field to store our texture:

```
private Texture2D texture;
```

We define our texture as a Texture2D object. This is another class that XNA provides for us. Texture2D inherits from the Texture class, which allows us to manipulate a texture resource. Now we need to actually load our texture into that variable. We do this in the LoadContent method by adding this line of code:

```
texture = Content.Load<Texture2D>("texture");
```

Now we have our texture added to our project and loaded into a variable (with very little code), but we have yet to associate that texture to the effect that we used to draw the triangle. We will do that now by adding the following two lines of code right before our call to effect.Begin inside of our Draw method:

```
effect.TextureEnabled = true;
effect.Texture = texture;
```

This simply tells the effect we are using that we want to use textures, and then we actually assign the texture to our effect. It is really that simple. Go ahead and compile and run the code to see our nicely textured triangle!

Index Buffers

We have covered a lot of ground so far, but we aren't done yet. We want to create a rectangle on the screen, and to do this we need another triangle. So that means we need three more vertices, or do we? Actually, we only need one more vertex to create our square because the second triangle we need to complete the square shares two of our existing points already. Feel free to review the sections earlier in this chapter where we talked about vertex buffers. We set up three points to make the triangle. To use the code as is, we would need to create another three points, but two of those points are redundant, and the amount of data it takes to represent the VertexPositionNormalTexture struct is not minimal, so we do not want to duplicate all that data if we do not need to. Fortunately, we do not. XNA provides us with index buffers.

Index buffers simply store indices that correspond to our vertex buffer. So to resolve our current dilemma of not wanting to duplicate our heavy vertex data, we will instead duplicate our index data, which is much smaller. Our vertex buffer will only store four points (instead of six), and our index buffer will store six indices that correspond to our vertices in the order we want them to be drawn. We need to increase our vertex array to hold four values instead of three. Make the following change in the InitializeVertices method:

```
vertices = new VertexPositionNormalTexture[4];
```

An index buffer simply describes the order in which we want the vertices in our vertex buffer to be drawn in our scene.

Find the InitializeVertices method in our code and add the last point we need for our rectangle. Try to do this before looking at the following code.

```
//top right
position = new Vector3(1, 1, 0);
textureCoordinates = new Vector2(1, 0);
vertices[3] = new VertexPositionNormalTexture(position, Vector3.Forward,
    textureCoordinates);
```

As you were writing the code, I imagine you were wondering about the texture coordinates for the points. We finally talked about textures, but not really how we mapped the texture to the vertices we created. We will take a moment and do that now before we continue our discussion of index buffers.

Texture coordinates start at the top left at (0,0) and end at the bottom right at (1,1). The bottom-left texture coordinate is (0,1), and the top right is (1,0). Take a look at Figure 4.4 to see an example.

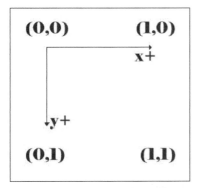

FIGURE 4.4   Texture coordinates start at the top left at (0,0) and end at the bottom right at (1,1).

If we wanted to map a vertex to the bottom-center pixel of a texture, what should the values be? The horizontal axis is our x axis, and the vertical axis is our y axis. We know we need a 1 in our y coordinate to get to the very bottom of the texture. To get to the middle of that bottom row, we would need to take the value in between 0 and 1, which is 0.5. So if we wanted to map a vertex to the bottom-center pixel of a texture, we would map it at (0.5, 1). Back to our demo: Because the vertex we just added was the top-right point of the rectangle, the texture coordinate we assigned to it was (1,0).

Now that you have a better understanding of why our texture mapped to our triangle correctly, we can get back to our index buffer. We have added a vertex to our code, and now we need to create an index buffer to reference these four points. We need to create another private member field called indices:

```
private short[] indices;
```

Notice that we declared this as an array of short. We could have used int, but short takes up less room, and we aren't going to have more than 65,535 indices in this demo. The next thing we need to do is actually create our method that will initialize our indices. We will name this InitializeIndices, and we will call this method from inside our

LoadContent method right after we make the call to InitializeVertices. Make sure that the vertex was added right before we initialized our vertex buffer and after we created all the other vertices. This way, the code for InitializeIndices shown next will work for us. It assumes the latest addition to our list of vertices is at the bottom of the list.

```
private void InitializeIndices()
{
    //6 vertices make up 2 triangles which make up our rectangle
    indices = new short[6];

    //triangle 1 (bottom portion)
    indices[0] = 0; // top left
    indices[1] = 1; // bottom right
    indices[2] = 2; // bottom left

    //triangle 2 (top portion)
    indices[3] = 0; // top left
    indices[4] = 3; // top right
    indices[5] = 1; // bottom right
}
```

In this method, we know we are going to create two triangles (with three points each), so we create enough space to hold all six indices. We then populate our indices. We took care to add our vertices in clockwise order when adding them to the vertex list, so we can simply set our first three indices to 0, 1, and 2. The second triangle, however, needs a little more thought. We know we have to add these in clockwise order, so we can start with any vertex and work our way around. Let's start with the top-left vertex (the first vertex we added to our list—index of 0). That means we need to set our next index to be the top-right vertex, which is the one we just added to the end of the list. We set that index to 3. Finally, we set the last point to the bottom-right vertex, which was added to the vertex buffer second and has the index of 1.

Now we have our vertices created, complete with textured coordinates and position and even normals. We have our indices set up to use the vertex buffer in a way that doesn't duplicate any of the complex vertex data. It may appear the data is duplicated, but only the indices are duplicated, not the actual vertex data. We further saved memory by using short instead of int because we will only have a few indices we need to store to represent our 3D object (our rectangle). Also, some older graphic cards do not support 32-bit (int) index buffers. The only thing left for us to do is to actually modify our code that draws the primitive to tell it we are now using an index buffer. To do that, find the Draw method and locate the call to DrawUserPrimitives. We will want to replace that line with the following line:

```
graphics.GraphicsDevice.DrawUserIndexedPrimitives(➥
    PrimitiveType.TriangleList, vertices, 0, vertices.Length,➥
    indices, 0, indices.Length / 3);
```

Notice that we changed the method we are calling on the graphics device. We are now passing in both vertex and index data. Let's break down the parameters we are passing in. We still pass in a triangle array as the first parameter and our array of vertices as the second parameter, and we are leaving our vertex offset at 0. The next parameter is new and simply needs the number of vertices that is in our vertex array. The fifth parameter is our array of indices (this method has an override that accepts an array of int as well). The sixth parameter is the offset we want for our index buffer. We want to use all the indices, so we passed in 0. The final parameter, primitive count, is the same as the final parameter in the method we just replaced. Because we only have four vertices, we needed to change that to our index array. Our indices array has six references to vertices in it, and we take that value and divide it by 3 to get the number of triangles in our triangle list. When we compile and run the code, we should see a rectangle that was created with our modified vertex buffer and our new index buffer!

As an exercise, modify the points in our vertex to have the rectangle slanted into the screen. This will require modifying a couple of our z values from 0 to something else. Give it a try!

XNA Game Components

Now that we have created this very exciting rectangle, let's take a look at what it did to our performance. In this section we are going to create an XNA GameComponent. A game component allows us to separate pieces of logic into their own file that will be called automatically by the XNA Framework. We will take the frame rate code we added in our PerformanceBenchmark project from the last chapter and create a game component out of it. To do this, we need to add another file to our project, which we can call FPS.cs. We need to pick GameComponent as the file type from inside the Add New File dialog box of XNA Game Studio.

With a blank fps.cs in front of us, we should see the class is inheriting from Microsoft.Xna.Framework.GameComponent. This is useful for components where we are only updating the internal data, typically through the Update method. For our frame rate calculation, however, we need to have our game component expose the Draw method because we want to know how many times a second we can draw our world on the screen. So we first need to change from which class we are inheriting. Instead of inheriting from GameComponent, we need to inherit from DrawableGameComponent so we can access the Draw method. We need to override the Draw method and use the same code we used in the PerformanceBenchmark project. To see the definition of the DrawableGameComponent to determine what is available for us to override, press F12 while the cursor is inside the DrawableGameComponent text.

Listing 4.1 contains the same code we used in the PerformanceBenchmark project. The difference is that it is inside of a drawable game component now. The biggest difference is our constructor, so let's take a minute to dissect that now. As you learned in the last chapter, to measure a true frame rate we need to get the screen to draw as many times as it can and not wait on the monitor to do a vertical refresh before updating the screen. We could put this code inside of our main game class, but for the projects in this book we typically let the game run at a fixed pace and only change it when we are trying to measure our true frame rate. Because of this assumption, the code is set up to take these values in via the constructor of the FPS game component. Typically a game component only requires passing in a game instance to the constructor, but we can require other parameters if we need to. For this game component, we are passing the values we initially set at the game level. We have a default constructor that will have the game render as fast as possible. These settings are per game, not per component.

LISTING 4.1   A Drawable Game Component That Calculates Our FPS

```
using System;
using System.Collections.Generic;
using Microsoft.Xna.Framework;

namespace XNADemo
{
    public sealed partial class FPS
        : Microsoft.Xna.Framework.DrawableGameComponent
    {
        private float fps;
        private float updateInterval = 1.0f;
        private float timeSinceLastUpdate = 0.0f;
        private float framecount = 0;

        public FPS(Game game)
           : this(game, false, false, game.TargetElapsedTime) { }

        public FPS(Game game, bool synchWithVerticalRetrace,
                   bool isFixedTimeStep, TimeSpan targetElapsedTime)
            : base(game)
        {
            GraphicsDeviceManager graphics =
                (GraphicsDeviceManager)Game.Services.GetService(
                typeof(IGraphicsDeviceManager));

            graphics.SynchronizeWithVerticalRetrace = synchWithVerticalRetrace;
            Game.IsFixedTimeStep = isFixedTimeStep;
            Game.TargetElapsedTime = targetElapsedTime;
        }
```

```
        public sealed override void Initialize()
        {
            // TODO: Add your initialization code here
            base.Initialize();
        }

        public sealed override void Update(GameTime gameTime)
        {
            // TODO: Add your update code here

            base.Update(gameTime);
        }

        public sealed override void Draw(GameTime gameTime)
        {
            float elapsed = (float)gameTime.ElapsedRealTime.TotalSeconds;
            framecount++;
            timeSinceLastUpdate += elapsed;
            if (timeSinceLastUpdate > updateInterval)
            {
                fps = framecount / timeSinceLastUpdate;

#if XBOX360
                System.Diagnostics.Debug.WriteLine("FPS: " + fps.ToString());
#else
                Game.Window.Title = "FPS: " + fps.ToString();
#endif

                framecount = 0;
                timeSinceLastUpdate -= updateInterval;
            }
            base.Draw(gameTime);
        }
    }
}
```

Now that we have the game component created and added to our project, we need to actually use it inside of the demo. To do this we need to create a private member field in our game class, as follows:

```
private FPS fps;
```

Then we can add the following code inside of our game constructor after we initialize our graphics variable:

```
#if DEBUG
    fps = new FPS(this);
#else
    fps = new FPS(this, true, true, this.TargetElapsedTime);
#endif
    Components.Add(fps);
```

We wrapped this with the DEBUG compiler directive, but we might want to run in debug mode without rendering the code as fast as possible. Either we can change how we are initializing our fps variable by passing in explicit values to the constructor, or we can create another configuration (that is, PROFILE). If we compiled in release or debug mode, the game is going to run at the normal pace but will still display the frame rate. This would allow us to see if the frame rate is dropping and we are falling behind, but in order to see how much room we have, we would want to run it under the new configuration (PROFILE). After initializing the fps object, we then add the component to our game's component collection. The XNA Framework will then call the component's Update and Draw methods (and other virtual methods) at the same time it calls the game's methods.

It can be very beneficial to separate logic and items we need to draw to the screen. It provides a nice clean way to separate our code, but it does have some overhead. It is definitely not wise to handle all the objects we want to draw as game components. Instead, if we want to separate our enemies from our player, it might be beneficial to have our player in its own game component and then have an "enemy manager" as its own game component. The enemy manager could then handle itself which enemies it needs to draw, move, and so on. This way, as enemies come and go, the manager is handling all that logic and not the core game class adding and removing a bunch of enemy components. Game components can really help, but we cannot go overboard with them or our performance will suffer.

Checking Performance

Now that we have our fps functionality inside of a game component, we can check out whether or not the code we wrote for the demo to display the rectangle is performing well. Fortunately, we recorded the frame rate we were getting in the last chapter, so we have a baseline from which to work.

We will need to set up an Xbox 360 game project for this solution as we discussed in Chapter 2, "XNA Game Studio and the Xbox 360." Once we have it set up, we can run our application on our machine and on the Xbox 360 to measure performance.

Machine A ran the benchmark code at about 280 fps. The Xbox 360 ran the same benchmark code at about 5,220 fps. With our new code, Machine A is running at 206 fps. The Xbox 360 is running at only 114 fps—ouch! What did we do wrong? Well, because we tested for performance right away, we know that it has to be an issue with our Draw method, so we should take a look at it again to see what is going on. We can also run the XNA Framework Remote Performance Monitor for the Xbox 360 and see what the garbage collector is doing. If a refresher is needed, you can find information on running this application in Chapter 2.

By launching our demo through the performance monitor tool, we can see that the "Objects Moved by Compactor" value is between 75,000 and 85,000 *every second*. We can see the "Objects not moved by Compactor" value is constantly growing with about 5,000 or more per second. This is obviously not good, and it is why we are thrashing our Xbox 360. Looking in the code we can see that we are creating a new instance of the BasicEffect class on every frame. That has got to be hurting us, so we can make that a member field of the game class because we are never changing it. We can break it out and actually initialize the effect inside our LoadContent method as follows:

```
effect = new BasicEffect(graphics.GraphicsDevice, null);
```

Now we can run our application again and look at the frame rate it is spitting out in our debug window. It is much better now—about 2,850 fps. However, that is still a far cry from our 5,220 fps. Checking the frame rate on Machine A reveals that we are running at 207 fps. So although the change really made a difference on the Xbox 360, it did not do much for us on the Windows side of things. Of course, this is expected because the issue we were having was with the garbage collector. Remember from the last chapter that each time we were creating a new BasicEffect object in Windows, the code was creating the effect object and destroying it all in the same frame, so when the garbage collector ran, it simply removed the dead objects. On the Xbox 360, however, the garbage collector has to go through the entire heap to determine what is dead as it starts to get full. So we have helped our situation on the console, but we are still only running at 53% of what we were at the baseline. Let's dig around some more. Notice the following lines of code at the top of our Draw method:

```
graphics.GraphicsDevice.VertexDeclaration = new
    VertexDeclaration(graphics.GraphicsDevice,
    VertexPositionNormalTexture.VertexElements);
```

This cannot be doing the garbage collector any favors. Although we need to set our vertex declaration on every frame, we do not need to create it every frame. We can create a private member field to hold our vertex declaration as follows:

```
private VertexDeclaration vertexDeclaration;
```

Now we can actually initialize that variable inside of the LoadContent method right after our BasicEffect initialization. The code for this is as follows:

```
vertexDeclaration = new VertexDeclaration(graphics.GraphicsDevice,
    VertexPositionNormalTexture.VertexElements);
```

Finally, we can change the original statement inside of Draw to set graphics device vertex declaration to the variable we just initialized:

```
graphics.GraphicsDevice.VertexDeclaration = vertexDeclaration;
```

Now we are only creating the vertex declaration once and setting it once instead of every frame. This is encouraging because we are now at about 3,230 fps on the Xbox 360 and the performance is still the same on Machine A at about 207 fps. So just with a little bit of effort we optimized our code from running at a mere 114 fps on the Xbox 360 to a more reasonable 3,230 fps.

What else can we do? Surely just displaying two triangles on the screen should not decrease our frame rate by 39%. As we go back to the performance monitoring tool, we can see that our "Objects Moved by Compactor" and "Objects Not Moved by Compactor" values are at a much better number—zero!

If we comment out the DrawUserIndexedPrimitives method, we see that our frame rate jumps back up to 5,220 fps. So it means the "problem" exists in this method. Is there anything that can be done with the code we have? Because our baseline code did not do anything and this code is actually drawing something (even if it is only two triangles), it might be that this is as good as it gets—after all, more than 3,000 fps is not that shabby! However, there has been some debate in regard to whether the DrawUser* methods are as fast as their Draw* counterparts. We are going to find out if that is the case.

DrawUserIndexedPrimitives versus DrawIndexedPrimitives

Make a copy of the solution folder we are working on and rename the new folder XNADemo–DIP. We can leave the solution file and everything else the same name. After opening this new project, we need to give it another title in the AssemblyInfo.cs file. We also need to change the GUID value so that when we deploy this, it will show up as a new entry in our XNA Game Launcher list. We can just replace any one digit with another digit for this example. This way, we can easily compare this demo with the one we just finished inside of the remote performance monitor for the Xbox 360. Once this has been done, we need to modify our game code by adding the following code to the end of the InitializeIndices method:

```
IndexBuffer ib = new IndexBuffer(graphics.GraphicsDevice,
    sizeof(short) * indices.Length, BufferUsage.WriteOnly,
    IndexElementSize.SixteenBits);
ib.SetData(indices);

graphics.GraphicsDevice.Indices = ib;
```

We are initializing the index buffer on our graphics device by telling it the size of our indices array. We use BufferUsage.WriteOnly because we will not be reading from the list (reading would fail with this setting) and it allows the graphics driver to determine the best location in memory to efficiently perform the rendering and write operations.

Finally, we tell it that we have an array of short by setting the IndexElementSize to 16 bits, the size of the short type (System.Int16). The second statement actually sets the array of indices inside of the graphic devices index buffer.

We needed to define our index buffer because the method we are replacing in the Draw method needs to have the data explicitly set on the graphics device. The following is the code we are going to replace our DrawUserIndexedPrimitives inside the Draw method with:

```
graphics.GraphicsDevice.DrawIndexedPrimitives(
    PrimitiveType.TriangleList, 0, 0, vertices.Length, 0, indices.Length / 3);
```

Finally, we need to set the source of our graphic devices vertex buffer. We do that with the following code, which should be placed at the end of the InitializeVertices method:

```
vertexBuffer = new VertexBuffer(graphics.GraphicsDevice,
    VertexPositionNormalTexture.SizeInBytes * vertices.Length,
    ResourceUsage.WriteOnly, ResourceManagementMode.Automatic);
vertexBuffer.SetData(vertices);

graphics.GraphicsDevice.Vertices[0].SetSource(vertexBuffer, 0,
    VertexPositionNormalTexture.SizeInBytes);
```

The first statement is used to populate our vertex buffer with the actual vertices we created. We pass in the graphics device followed by the size of the buffer. The size of the buffer is determined by taking the size of the struct we are using to represent our vertex (in this case it is VertexPositionNormalTexture) and multiplying that by the number of points we have. In this case it is three, but instead of hard-coding three, we grab the length property of our vertex array. The third parameter describes how we plan to use this vertex buffer. We can find all the different options for this enumeration by looking in the documentation that was installed with XNA Game Studio. We are setting the BufferUsage parameter just like we did before. The final parameter of this method tells XNA to handle our memory management automatically. For more information on this enumeration, take look at the documentation. The second statement takes our vertex data we set in our InitializeVertices method and sets our vertex buffer with it.

We can set up our vertexBuffer private member field next:

```
private VertexBuffer vertexBuffer;
```

After these changes, we can compile and run the code on the Xbox 360 and see that our frame rate has done nothing. The conclusion to draw here is that it does not make a difference if we use DrawUserPrimitives or DrawPrimitives methods. This was a good exercise, but for our example here it did not make a difference. Whichever version is more convenient for us as we develop our game is the one we should use. However, the results could change if we are drawing more vertices. Another performance test could be to add more vertices and indices to see if one scales better than the other. For example, instead of only rendering four vertices, you could render 10,000 and see how the two methods compare. Have fun finding the most efficient way to use these methods in your particular situation.

Transformations Revolutions

Just in case it is not clear where these transformation section titles come from, when dealing with matrices it is very hard not to think about *The Matrix* movies. What a great trilogy.

Anyway, the reason we are back yet again to discuss transformations is because you need to gain practical knowledge about transformations and not just the theory you learned about earlier. Therefore, we will look at some of the transformation functions that XNA has included in the framework.

In the earlier scenario we had a 3D object that we wanted to scale, rotate (twice), and then translate. We said that we had to do it in a particular order but did not take the discussion any further. Now that we know how to create a 3D object, we can run through the exercise of transforming the object the way we want.

We can make a copy of the first demo we created in this chapter (XNADemo) and call it Transformations. We need to rename the assembly title and the GUID again so we will not overwrite the demo with the same GUID on the Xbox 360. We can actually rename each project as well as the solution and change the namespaces if that is preferred.

In the earlier scenario, we wanted to move to a position and scale our object down and then rotate to the left and down some. This needs to be done in the correct order because matrix multiplication is not commutative. We are going to modify our code and move our existing rectangle into the distance. Then we will create another rectangle and transform it to get the desired effect.

To start, we need to refactor a section of code from our Draw method to create a new method called DrawRectangle. Cut all the code after we create the world matrix variable and before we call the Draw method on our base class. Now paste the code into the newly created DrawRectangle method, as follows:

```
private void DrawRectangle(ref Matrix world)
{
    effect.World = world;
    effect.Begin();

    //As we are doing a basic effect, there is no need to loop
    //basic effect will only have one pass on the technique
    effect.CurrentTechnique.Passes[0].Begin();

    graphics.GraphicsDevice.DrawUserIndexedPrimitives(
        PrimitiveType.TriangleList, vertices, 0, vertices.Length,
        indices, 0, indices.Length / 3);
```

```
effect.CurrentTechnique.Passes[0].End();

effect.End();
}
```

The method takes a matrix as a parameter. This is going to be the matrix we transform before sending it to the effect. To demonstrate another way of setting the passes on our `BasicEffect`, we can just grab the first pass on the current technique instead of doing a `foreach` loop because we know there is only one pass we can get by with this optimization.

Now we need to call this method inside of our `Draw` method where we just removed the code. So right above the call to `Draw` on our base class we can add the following code:

```
DrawRectangle(ref world);
```

If we run this, we should get the exact same results as before. We are still rendering one rectangle in the exact same position—the origin of the world. We can remove the member variable `world` and where we set it at the top of our `Draw` method because we are not using it in this example. Following is our new `Draw` method with the changes mentioned so far:

```
protected override void Draw(GameTime gameTime)
{
    graphics.GraphicsDevice.Clear(Color.CornflowerBlue);

    effect.Projection = projection;
    effect.View = view;

    effect.EnableDefaultLighting();

    effect.TextureEnabled = true;
    effect.Texture = texture;

    Matrix world = Matrix.Identity;
    DrawRectangle(ref world);

    base.Draw(gameTime);
}
```

Let's move our existing triangle into the distance. We can move it backward and to the right some. To do this we will need to use the built-in XNA matrix helper method `Matrix.CreateTranslation`. We know we are at the origin (0,0,0), and we want to move back and to the right. Remember that XNA uses a right-handed coordinate system, so this means that to move the rectangle backward we need to subtract from the z position. To move it right we need to add to the x position. `CreateTranslation` takes in `Vector3` as a parameter, so we can set our values into the vector before passing it into the helper function. Change where we set the world matrix to the following:

```
Matrix world = Matrix.CreateTranslation(new Vector3(3.0f, 0, -10.0f));
```

We moved the rectangle to the right by three units and to the back by 10 units. Now we need to add another rectangle. Let's add the code to do this immediately following the first rectangle. To do this we need to simply pass in `Matrix.Identity` as the following code shows:

```
world = Matrix.Identity;
DrawRectangle(ref world);
```

When we run the code we cannot see the rectangle we originally drew because it is further back, and this new rectangle is obstructing our view. Let's scale it down to about 75% of what it is currently. To do this we need to call the XNA matrix helper method `Matrix.CreateScale` as follows:

```
world = Matrix.CreateScale(0.75f);
```

By replacing the identity matrix with this `CreateScale` matrix, we can see our rectangle is now smaller, so we can partially see the one we moved toward the back. A screenshot of this can be seen in Figure 4.5.

FIGURE 4.5   A smaller rectangle is obstructing the view of a larger rectangle that is further away.

Let's move this rectangle back about five units, to the left three, and down one unit. We want to keep the scale that we have in place. We need to multiply our matrices together, as discussed earlier, so we change our world matrix again to look like the following code:

```
world = Matrix.CreateScale(0.75f) *
    Matrix.CreateTranslation(new Vector3(-3.0f, -1.0f, -5.0f));
```

We also want to rotate our object to one side and downward. We can do that using a couple other helper methods in the `Matrix` struct. There are three different helper functions, and each will rotate one of the three axes. These methods are called `Matrix.CreateRotationX`, `Matrix.CreateRotationY`, and `Matrix.CreateRotationZ`. To add rotation to make the object turn to the side, we need to rotate around the y axis. To visualize this, take a look at Figure 4.6.

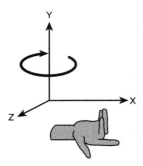

FIGURE 4.6   Rotating around the y axis.

Let's rotate around the y axis by 30 degrees. The rotation helper methods require a value in radians, but the `MathHelper` class allows us to easily convert degrees to radians. Thus, we can rotate 30 degrees around the y axis by using the following code:

```
world = Matrix.CreateScale(0.75f) *
    Matrix.CreateTranslation(new Vector3(-3.0f, -1.0f, -5.0f)) *
    Matrix.CreateRotationY(MathHelper.ToRadians(30.0f));
```

If we run this code, we do not see the rectangle. The reason is that we rotated the matrix after we translated it. By doing this, we effectively told it to rotate around the origin (where it was) instead of at its center. By rotating after translating, we are making it orbit around where it was. Instead, we want it to rotate around its own center, and to do this we need to replace the world matrix with the following code:

```
world = Matrix.CreateScale(0.75f) *
    Matrix.CreateRotationY(MathHelper.ToRadians(30.0f)) *
    Matrix.CreateTranslation(new Vector3(-3.0f, -1.0f, -5.0f));
```

Now when we run this, we have rotated around the center of our object to get the desired results. Finally, we want to throw in another rotation for good measure. This time we want to rotate downward, so we need to rotate on the x axis. Assuming we want to rotate it about 15 degrees, we can use the following code:

```
world = Matrix.CreateScale(0.75f) *
    Matrix.CreateRotationX(MathHelper.ToRadians(15.0f)) *
    Matrix.CreateRotationY(MathHelper.ToRadians(30.0f)) *
    Matrix.CreateTranslation(new Vector3(-3.0f, -1.0f, -5.0f));
```

The code scales our rectangle, rotates it around the x axis, rotates it around the y axis, and finally the code moves the rectangle. By multiplying the matrices in the right order, we were able to accomplish the desired effect (see Figure 4.7).

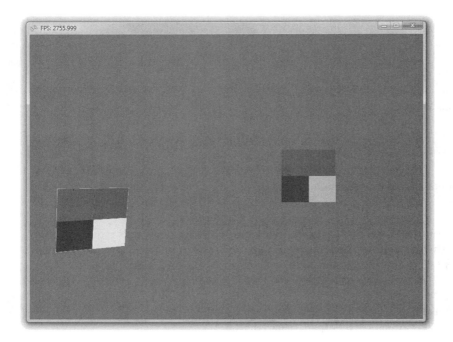

FIGURE 4.7   Applying matrix transformations in the correct order will produce the desired effect.

Summary

We covered a lot of ground in this chapter. We discussed the foundation of everything we will do in the 3D worlds we create. We set up a camera to view our 3D world. We discussed basic 3D terminology and how it correlates to XNA. We examined how to use different methods to create 3D objects on the screen with points we manually plotted inside of our code.

We spent quite a bit of time going through the performance-checking process to determine what things we could do to improve our code. We also put into practice what you learned in the last chapter.

We ended the chapter by actually performing matrix transformations, a concept you learned about at the beginning of the chapter. We applied multiple transformations to one of our objects and saw how important it was to get the multiplication order right when dealing with transformations.

This chapter is very important because the rest of the book will build on this foundation. Make sure to take time to let it sink in. Reread it, dwell on it, dream about it—OK, maybe that's a little bit too extreme.

4

Handling Input to Move Our Camera

We created a camera in the last chapter that does not move. We did not allow any input (other than exiting the demo with the GamePad's Back button, which the template provided for us). We are going to change that now. You are going to learn how to use input devices (keyboard, mouse, and game pad controller) by working with the camera. To accomplish this, we are going to start a game library that we can utilize in our demos and games. Let's get started!

Creating a Game Service

Instead of just throwing input and camera code inside of another demo, we are going to take the time to create a library (even if it is just a small one). Before we dig into that, however, we need to discuss game services and how they are used with game components. This will greatly simplify our library architecture.

We have a camera we have been using up to this point. The camera code is actually inside of the game object, which is perfectly acceptable for smaller demos. However, we're going to take the time in this chapter to move the camera into its own game component. We have already moved our FPS code into its own game component, and we will end up putting that game component into the library we are creating. In this chapter, we are also going to create an input handler that's a game service.

You learned how to create a game component in the last chapter using our FPS game component. Having a game component makes it easier to manage our code because items are broken out into logical pieces. However, we can run into a potential issue when multiple game components we create need to access the same piece of functionality (or each other). We can see this more easily when thinking about input.

We want to put our code that handles the input into its own game component—this is the XNA way after all. So let's assume we have our input game component done, and now we have a player game component that needs access to the input device so that the player game component can react to the gamer as he or she uses the input device. To enable our player game component (and any other future game component we make) to access the input handler game component, we will turn the input handler game component into a game service. A *game service* is simply a game component wrapped in a unique interface that allows other game components and services to interact with it.

> **NOTE**
>
> Remember what you learned from the last chapter: Too many game components can hurt performance. In such cases we can use a "manager" game component that handles its own objects. The example we discussed last chapter involved creating enemies. Some XNA beginners will create an enemy game component for every enemy they have on the screen (or even a bullet game component). They then try to add and remove or set visible and invisible each and every game component. This can bring a system to a crawl because of the overhead associated with the game components. They're just not meant to be used in that way. A better approach is to create an EnemyManager or BulletManager game component and allow the manager to handle which enemies or bullets are being displayed.

The Game object holds collections of services. We have actually been using one already. The GraphicsDevice is a game service built into XNA. When we created our FPS game component, we needed access to the GraphicsDevice. Therefore, we wrote the following code in the constructor for the FPS code:

```
GraphicsDeviceManager graphics =
    (GraphicsDeviceManager)Game.Services.GetService(
    typeof(IGraphicsDeviceManager));
```

Game components always have a Game object passed to them, so every game component can obtain access to any game service associated with the game. The preceding code does just that. It creates a reference to the game's GraphicsDeviceManager memory. When we create a new solution by selecting a game template, the code generated for us includes a variable called graphics that holds the graphics device manager. Although we could have made the graphics variable public and accessed the data that way, it is much more elegant to use a service. Otherwise, we would probably be creating many publicly accessible properties, which would hurt our game design.

Because the XNA Framework team used an interface for the graphics device manager object and because they added it to the services collection of the game object, we are able to access it from any piece of code that has access to the game object. You can see this if you look at the preceding code again. It calls out to the game object to which we have a reference and calls its `Services.GetService` method. This method takes in a type and returns an object. We pass in the type of the interface and get returned the graphics device object. We perform a cast on it so we have a strongly typed object that allows us to work with it intelligently.

You have seen how we used a game service that XNA created for us; now you'll learn how to create a game service. To get started, copy the Transformations project we created in the last chapter and name the new project InputDemo. Also rename the namespace in the projects and modify the GUID in the AssemblyInfo.cs file.

We will create the input game service now inside of this project and then move it along with our FPS game component when we create our library in the next section. We need to add a new game component file to our project, which we will call InputHandler. The first step to making this a game service is to create an interface.

The game services collection can only have one of any particular interface. This is how it knows which object to return when a request is made. This means that if we have more than one object of the same interface and need to access them all as a game service, we would need to create a different interface for each object. Fortunately, an interface can be empty. This means through inheritance we can quickly make our "duplicate" object inherit from the original object and from the new interface that does not require any additional implementation.

To add our interface we need to use the following code:

```
public interface IInputHandler { };
```

We can create a new code file to store this interface or we can put it directly in the input handler file. Currently, our input handler interface is blank, but we will be adding properties to it soon. Now we need our game component to inherit from this interface (as well as the `GameComponent` object it is already inheriting from). We do this by changing our class declaration to the following:

```
public class InputHandler
    : Microsoft.Xna.Framework.GameComponent, IInputHandler
```

We also need to make sure our input handler is using the XNA Framework's `Input` name-space:

```
using Microsoft.Xna.Framework.Input;
```

To finish making this game component into a game service, we need to add it to the game's services collection. We do this in the game component's constructor with the following code:

```
game.Services.AddService(typeof(IInputHandler), this);
```

Adding a service is much like getting a service. We pass in the type of the interface for the object and then we actually pass in our object. We always want to pass in the type of our interface and not the type of our actual class. This way, when other objects access the game service, they can simply do it through the interface without having to explicitly use the object. Of course if needed, we can cast to the actual object. We should be able to compile the code at this point. It currently does nothing differently than it did in the last chapter. However, we are laying a foundation so we can get started on our library. Let's do that now!

Starting a Library

We have two game components currently (well, one is a skeleton) and are planning on adding more. We should put these into a library that we can easily access from multiple demos and games. We are going to set up a library project to hold our FPS game component as well as the start of the input handler class we just created. To do this, we will create a new Windows Game Library project, which we'll call XELibrary.

Now that we have our solution set up with the two projects, we can start building our library. To begin, we add the FPS.cs file from our last project. Let's cut the actual FPS.cs and InputHandler.cs files from our InputDemo project and paste them into our XELibrary project (after saving InputHandler.cs of course). At this point we have started a library that contains our fully made FPS game component and a skeleton of our InputHandler game component. We can remove the Class1.cs file from our project. We should also make sure our namespace is consistent across the library and set it to XELibrary. We should be able to build the library project with no compilation errors.

> **NOTE**
>
> As we add items to one project (Windows), we need to add them to the other project (Xbox 360) as well (after we create the additional platform project like we did in Chapter 2, "XNA Game Studio and the Xbox 360"). From here on, it will be assumed that as we create a project we will create the other platform's counterpart, and as we add files to one project it will be assumed that they are added to the other project as well.

Before we start on our input handler code, we can go ahead and create another game component called Camera. We are going to move the initial camera code we have created to this game component. We will also talk to our input handler game service inside this game component. Let's go ahead and set up a private member field to hold an instance of the input handler because we know we will need it. We do this by adding the following code to our Camera.cs file:

```
private IInputHandler input;
```

Now that we have the field created, we can initialize it inside of our constructor as follows:

```
input = (IInputHandler)game.Services.GetService(typeof(IInputHandler));
```

Now we can move our `InitializeCamera` method from the `InputDemo` `Game1.cs` code into our `Camera` class. We need to cut the call to this method from the `Initialize` method inside our game project. Now we need to paste the call into our camera's `Initialize` method. The updated code in our camera class should look like the following:

```
public override void Initialize()
{
    base.Initialize();
    InitializeCamera();
}

private void InitializeCamera()
{
    float aspectRatio = (float)Game.GraphicsDevice.Viewport.Width /
        (float)Game.GraphicsDevice.Viewport.Height;
    Matrix.CreatePerspectiveFieldOfView(MathHelper.PiOver4, aspectRatio,
        1.0f, 10000.0f, out projection);

    Matrix.CreateLookAt(ref cameraPosition, ref cameraTarget,
        ref cameraUpVector, out view);
}
```

We did not modify this code; we simply moved it from our `InputDemo` game class into our XELibrary camera class. Notice we called `InitializeCamera` after calling `base.Initialize`. This is because we are utilizing the graphics device (from our component's `Game` object), and it is not available until the main game class finishes with its `Initialize` method.

Our `InitializeCamera` method is using some member fields we have not moved yet. We need to move the following code from our demo to our library:

```
private Matrix projection;
private Matrix view;
private Vector3 cameraPosition = new Vector3(0.0f, 0.0f, 3.0f);
private Vector3 cameraTarget = Vector3.Zero;
private Vector3 cameraUpVector = Vector3.Up;
```

Because we moved our view and projection fields from our demo, the demo will no longer compile until we change our demo's `Draw` method, where we set the effect's view and projection so it will display our objects correctly. We could leave these in the game class as public fields and have the Camera game component work with them there. A cleaner approach would be to leave the camera self-contained and access those properties from inside our demo. Let's create and initialize our Camera game component inside of our demo. We can use the following code:

```
camera = new Camera(this);
Components.Add(camera);
```

We also need to set up the member field as follows:

```
private Camera camera;
```

We need to reference our game library inside of our game project. This can be done by right-clicking the InputDemo's project References tree node in the Solution Explorer. Then click Add Reference and select the Projects tab. Selecting XELibrary and clicking Add will make XELibrary a dependency of InputDemo. We need to make sure to reference the Windows library in the Windows demo and the Xbox 360 library in the Xbox 360 demo.

> **NOTE**
>
> It is usually a good idea to create the Xbox 360 copy of the project early on and keep it up to date as new files are added. It is much better to know how the code is performing on another platform during the development cycle instead of at the end.

After loading the library projects inside our demo solution, we now need to add a using statement to the top of our Game1.cs file in the demo project. We need to use XELibrary, as shown here:

```
using XELibrary;
```

If we compile at this point, the only errors we should see are inside our demo's Draw method, stating that it has no idea what view and projection are. We are going to fix that now by changing the code to use our camera's view and projection properties. We do not have any properties yet in our Camera object. Well, let's change that. We need to add the following code to our Camera game component:

```
public Matrix View
{
    get { return view; }
}

public Matrix Projection
{
    get { return projection; }
}
```

Now we can access these properties inside of our demo's Draw method. Let's change the properties we set on our effect with the following code:

```
effect.Projection = camera.Projection;
effect.View = camera.View;
```

Now we can successfully compile our code again. Not only that, but we can run it and it will function just like before, but now we have started a library!

Working with Input Devices

We will be populating the stub we created for handling our input. We are going to create a stationary camera, a first-person camera, and a third-person camera. All these cameras will need to respond to user input. You'll learn how to handle input devices and utilize them to move our camera to fully see the worlds we create.

Keyboard

The first input device we will talk about is the keyboard. XNA provides helper classes that allow us to easily determine the state of our input devices. We determine the state of our keyboard by declaring a variable to store our keyboard state and then calling the GetState method on the Keyboard helper object. We can then query that variable to determine which key (or keys) is being pressed or released. We can start by adding a private member field to store our keyboard state. We do this via the following code inside of our InputHandler game component:

```
private KeyboardState keyboardState;
```

Then we can find the Update method that was stubbed out for us when the InputHandler game component was created:

```
keyboardState = Keyboard.GetState();
if (keyboardState.IsKeyDown(Keys.Escape))
    Game.Exit();
```

We can put this at the very beginning of the Update method. We are simply storing the state of the keyboard and then checking to see if the Escape key was pressed. If it was, we simply exit the program. It doesn't get much simpler than that! So now when we run the program we can exit by pressing the Escape key (instead of having to close the window with our mouse).

Although being able to exit our game easily is important, we still haven't done anything exciting. Let's set up our camera so we swivel back and forth if the left and right keys are pressed. To do this we need to add and initialize a new private member field called cameraReference inside our Camera game component:

```
private Vector3 cameraReference = new Vector3(0.0f, 0.0f, -1.0f);
```

This camera reference direction will not change throughout the game, but we will be passing it in as a reference. Therefore, we cannot declare it as a readonly variable. Typically this value will be either (0,0,1) or (0,0,-1). We chose to have a negative z value so we can continue to have our camera face the same way.

Now that we have our camera reference direction set up, we need to apply any movement and rotation to our view of the world. This way, if the player wants to look left and right, we can adjust our view matrix accordingly so that the view of the world is from a certain angle. To look left and right, we need to rotate around the y axis. We can add the following code to our Update method right before our call to the base object's Update method (we are still in our Camera class) :

```
Matrix rotationMatrix;
Matrix.CreateRotationY(MathHelper.ToRadians(cameraYaw), out rotationMatrix);
// Create a vector pointing the direction the camera is facing.
Vector3 transformedReference;
Vector3.Transform(ref cameraReference, ref rotationMatrix,
    out transformedReference);
// Calculate the position the camera is looking at.
Vector3.Add(ref cameraPosition, ref transformedReference, out cameraTarget);

Matrix.CreateLookAt(ref cameraPosition, ref cameraTarget, ref cameraUpVector,
    out view);
```

Because we know we will be rotating, we need to create a matrix to hold our rotation. With a helper function from XNA, we will create a matrix with the appropriate values to rotate our camera on the y axis by a certain number of degrees. We store that value in a variable we set with our input devices. You'll see how we set that value with our keyboard soon. Once we have our matrix with all the translations, scaling, and rotations that we need (in this case we are only rotating), we can create a transform vector that allows us to change the target of the camera. We get this transformed vector by using another XNA helper method, Vector3.Transform. We then add the transformed camera reference to our camera position, which will give us our new camera target. To do this, we could have used the plus (+) operator like in the following code:

```
cameraTarget = cameraPosition + transformedReference;
```

However, it is more efficient to use the built-in static Add method of the Vector3 struct because it allows us to pass our vectors by reference instead of having to copy the values to memory. Finally, we reset our view with our new camera target. We also need to set the following private member field that we used in the code:

```
private float cameraYaw = 0.0f;
```

Now we are to the point where we can compile the code, but our newly added code does not do anything for us. This is because we are never changing our rotation angle. It stays at 0 on every frame. Let's change that now with our keyboard. Inside our InputHandler class, we need to update our IInputHandler interface to expose the keyboard state we retrieved earlier. Let's add the following code inside our interface:

```
KeyboardState KeyboardState { get; }
```

Now we need to implement that property inside the class. An easy way to do this is to right-click IInputHandler where we derived it from and select Implement Interface. We will be doing this a couple times, and each time a region will be created. Therefore, we will have to clean up the code and remove the extra regions the IDE provides for us. Now we need to change the get value to retrieve our internal keyboardState value, as follows:

```
public KeyboardState KeyboardState
{
    get { return(keyboardState); }
}
```

Now that we have exposed our keyboard state, we can utilize it inside our Camera object. We need to add the following code to our Update method right above the previous code inside of our camera object:

```
if (input.KeyboardState.IsKeyDown(Keys.Left))
    cameraYaw += spinRate;
if (input.KeyboardState.IsKeyDown(Keys.Right))
    cameraYaw -= spinRate;

if (cameraYaw > 360)
    cameraYaw -= 360;
else if (cameraYaw < 0)
    cameraYaw += 360;
```

We also need to make sure camera is using the XNA Framework's Input namespace because we are accessing the Keys enumeration:

```
using Microsoft.Xna.Framework.Input;
```

Finally, we add this constant to the top of our camera class:

```
private const float spinRate = 2.0f;
```

In our Update code we utilized the current keyboard state we already captured and checked to see if either the left arrow or right arrow on the keyboard was pressed. If the player wants to rotate to the left, we add our spin rate constant to our current camera yaw angle. (*Yaw*, *pitch*, and *roll* are terms borrowed from flight dynamics. Because we are using a right-handed coordinate system, this means that yaw is rotation around the y axis, pitch is rotation around the x axis, and roll is rotation around the z axis.) If the player wants to rotate to the right, we subtract our spin rate constant from our current camera yaw angle. Finally, we just check to make sure we do not have an invalid rotation angle.

There is one last thing we need to do before we can run our code again. We need to add our input handler game component to our game's collection of components. We can declare our member field as follows:

```
private InputHandler input;
```

Now we can initialize that variable and add it to the collection inside our constructor with the following code:

```
input = new InputHandler(this);
Components.Add(input);
```

NOTE

The preceding code should be added before the camera component is processed. This is because the camera component uses the input component. Otherwise, you will get a null reference exception.

We can compile and run the code, and the left- and right-arrow keys will rotate the camera. When running the code, you can see that our objects are just flying by. They are turning so fast that they seem to be blinking. This is because we are calling our `Update` statement as fast as possible. We can modify the game code where we are initializing our `fps` variable to use a fixed time step:

```
fps = new FPS(this, false, true);
```

For the preceding code to work, we need to add another constructor to our FPS code. We are doing this so we don't need to actually pass in our target elapsed time value if we want it to be the default.

```
public FPS(Game game, bool synchWithVerticalRetrace, bool isFixedTimeStep)
    : this(game, synchWithVerticalRetrace, isFixedTimeStep,
          game.TargetElapsedTime) { }
```

Now when you run the code you should see the objects move by at a consistent and slower rate. This is because the `Update` method is now only getting called 60 times a second instead of whatever rate your machine was running at.

You will notice, however, as the rectangles are rendered that our screen is "choppy." The reason is that we are not letting XNA only draw during our monitor's vertical refresh. If we were to set the second parameter to true, we would see the screen rotate at a nice even pace with the screen drawing nicely. However, a better way to handle this is by utilizing the elapsed time between calls to our methods. We need to retrieve the elapsed time since the last time our `Update` method was called and then multiply our `spinRate` by this delta of the time between calls. Change the camera code snippet to match the following:

```
float timeDelta = (float)gameTime.ElapsedGameTime.TotalSeconds;
```

```
if (input.KeyboardState.IsKeyDown(Keys.Left))
    cameraYaw += (spinRate * timeDelta);
```

```
if (input.KeyboardState.IsKeyDown(Keys.Right))
    cameraYaw -= (spinRate * timeDelta);
```

We can modify our game code to call the default constructor again:

```
fps = new FPS(this);
```

Now we are just creeping along. This is because our spin rate is so low. We had it low because we were relying on the Update method to be called 60 times per frame, so we were basically rotating our camera 120 degrees per second. To get the same effect we simply set our spinRate to 120. The reason is we are now multiplying it by the time difference between calls. At this point we can safely set our units and know they will be used on a per-second basis. Now that we have our spinRate utilizing the delta of the time between calls, we are safe to run at any frame rate and have our objects drawn correctly based on the amount of time that has elapsed.

We can have it always run at 60 fps in release mode and run as fast as possible in debug mode by modifying our game code as follows:

```
#if DEBUG
    fps = new FPS(this);
#else
    fps = new FPS(this, true, false);
#endif
```

This allows us to run as fast as we can in debug mode while consistently moving our objects no matter the frame rate. It allows us to force XNA to only update the screen during the monitor's vertical retrace, which would drop us to 60 fps or whatever rate the monitor is refreshing at.

Making a game update itself consistently regardless of the frame rate can make the game more complex. We need to calculate the elapsed time (time delta) since the last frame and use that value in all our calculations. With the fixed step mode that XNA provides, we could cut down on development time and rely on the fact that the update code will be called 60 times a second. This is not sufficient if we are writing a library that can be plugged into games because those games might not run at a consistent frame rate.

Game Pad

The Microsoft Xbox 360 wired controller works on the PC. The wireless Xbox 360 controller will also work on the PC, but the Xbox 360 Wireless Gaming Receiver for Windows is required. The XNA Framework provides us with helper classes that make it very easy to determine the state of our game pad. The template already provided one call to the game pad helper class. This call is also in the Update method. Let's take a look at what is provided for us already.

```
if (GamePad.GetState(PlayerIndex.One).IsButtonDown(Buttons.Back))
    this.Exit();
```

The template is calling the built-in XNA class GamePad and calling its GetState method, passing in the specific player's controller to check. The template then checks the Back button on that controller to see if it has been pressed. If the controller's Back button has been pressed, the game exits. Now, that was pretty straightforward. To be consistent we can use our input class to check for the condition.

Before we can do that, we need to update our interface and add the appropriate property. We also need to get the game pad state just like we did for our keyboard. Let's jump to our input handler code and do some of these things. We can start by adding a property to get to our list of game pads in our interface:

```
GamePadState[] GamePads { get; }
```

Now we can create the member field and property to get that field, as in the following code:

```
private GamePadState[] gamePads = new GamePadState[4];
public GamePadState[] GamePads
{
    get { return(gamePads); }
}
```

We need to initialize each game pad state. We can do that in the Update method of the InputHandler object:

```
gamePads[0] = GamePad.GetState(PlayerIndex.One);
gamePads[1] = GamePad.GetState(PlayerIndex.Two);
gamePads[2] = GamePad.GetState(PlayerIndex.Three);
gamePads[3] = GamePad.GetState(PlayerIndex.Four);
```

Now, let's remove the code that checks to see if the Back button is pressed on player one's game pad from our demo. We can add this code in the Update method of our input handler game component to get the same effect:

```
if (gamePads[0].Buttons.Back == ButtonState.Pressed)
    Game.Exit();
```

Let's update our yaw rotation code inside the Camera game component so that we can get the same result with our controller. We can modify our existing code that checks for left and right to also handle input from our controller. Thus, we modify our two conditional statements that set the cameraYaw to also check the right thumb stick state of the game pad we are examining:

```
if (input.KeyboardState.IsKeyDown(Keys.Left) ||
    (input.GamePads[0].ThumbSticks.Right.X < 0))
{
    cameraYaw += (spinRate * timeDelta);
}
if (input.KeyboardState.IsKeyDown(Keys.Right) ||
```

```
    (input.GamePads[0].ThumbSticks.Right.X > 0))
{
    cameraYaw -= (spinRate * timeDelta);
}
```

The thumb stick x and y axes provide a float value between –1 and 1. A value of 0 means there is no movement. A value of –0.5 means the stick is pushed to the left halfway. A value of 0.9 means the stick is pushed to the right 90% of the way.

We did not change the keyboard code; instead, we simply added another "or" condition to handle our controller. You can see it is very simple—we only needed to check the ThumbSticks.Right property. We check the x axis of that joystick, and if it is less than zero the user is pushing the stick to the left. We check to see if it is positive (user pushing to the right) in the second condition. We leave our cameraYaw variable to be set by our spin rate (taking into account our time delta). At this point, regardless of whether the players are using the keyboard or the game pad, they will get the same result from the game: The camera will rotate around the y axis. Compile and run the program to try it out. You can also try the game on the Xbox 360 because we have hooked up our game pad code.

At this point you know how to get access to any of the buttons (they are treated the same way as the Back button) and either thumb stick, but we have not discussed the D-pad yet. The D-pad is actually treated like buttons. If we want to allow the player to rotate the camera left or right by using the D-pad, we could add the following as part of our condition:

```
input.GamePads[0].DPad.Left == ButtonState.Pressed
```

However, the XNA Framework has the helper methods IsButtonDown and IsButtonUp. We can get the same result by using the following condition:

```
input.GamePads[0].IsButtonDown(Buttons.DPadLeft)
```

We could replace the thumb stick condition by using IsButtonDown as well. Even though the movement on the thumb stick is not really a button, the XNA Framework can treat it like one and do the check for us. Therefore, the following condition to check whether the right thumb stick is pushed to the left is valid:

```
input.GamePads[0].IsButtonDown(Buttons.RightThumbStickLeft)
```

We can add those conditions to our code. Compile and run the code again and make sure the demo allows you to look left or right by using the keyboard, thumb stick, and D-pad. The code should now look like the following:

```
if (input.KeyboardState.IsKeyDown(Keys.Left) ||
    input.GamePads[0].IsButtonDown(Buttons.RightThumbstickLeft) ||
    input.GamePads[0].IsButtonDown(Buttons.DPadLeft))
{
    cameraYaw += (spinRate * timeDelta);
```

```
}
if (input.KeyboardState.IsKeyDown(Keys.Right) ||
    input.GamePads[0].IsButtonDown(Buttons.RightThumbstickRight) ||
    input.GamePads[0].IsButtonDown(Buttons.DPadRight))
{
    cameraYaw -= (spinRate * timeDelta);
}
```

The shoulder buttons are just that—buttons—and you know how to handle those already. We can determine when the left or right thumb stick is pressed down because both are also considered buttons. In fact, every input on a game pad is mapped to a button. However, the final item we'll discuss regarding our game pad controller is the triggers. Now, a good use of our triggers for this demo would be to turn on vibration!

Before we determine how to use the triggers, we can look at another property of the game pad state we have access to—whether or not the controller is actually connected. We can check this by getting the value of the IsConnected property.

Even though we can determine whether or not a trigger is pressed (just like we can determine whether the right thumb stick is pushed to the left), there are times we need more information. We may need to know how far in the trigger is pressed. All the way? Ten percent? Ninety percent? Fortunately, the trigger values return a float between 0 and 1 to signify how much the trigger is pressed (0 = not pressed; 1 = fully pressed). The Xbox 360 controller has two motors that create its vibration. The motor on the left is a low-frequency motor, whereas the motor on the right is a high-frequency motor. We can set the values on both motors in the same method call. We do this by calling the GamePad.SetVibration method. Because this is just something we are doing for our demo and not really a part of the library, we will put this code in our Game1.cs file inside the Update method:

```
if (input.GamePads[0].IsConnected)
{
    GamePad.SetVibration(PlayerIndex.One, input.GamePads[0].Triggers.Left,
        input.GamePads[0].Triggers.Right);
}
```

The first thing we are doing with this new code is checking to see whether the game pad is actually connected. If it is connected, we set the vibration of both the left and right motors based on how much the left and right triggers are being pressed. We'll call the GamePad's static SetVibration method. There is currently no benefit in wrapping that into a method inside of our input handler.

We can also change the information being displayed in our window title bar to include the left and right motor values. This can help you determine what values you should use as you implement vibration in your games! The following is the code to accomplish that task:

```
this.Window.Title = "left: " +
    input.GamePads[0].Triggers.Left.ToString() + "; right: " +
    input.GamePads[0].Triggers.Right.ToString();
```

Go ahead and add this debug line inside of the IsConnected condition and compile and run the code to check the progress. We will no longer be able to see our frame rate with this code, so we could just comment out the fps object until we are ready to check on our performance.

Mouse (Windows Only)

This input device is only available for Windows, so if you are deploying the game for the Xbox 360, you will need to put the XBOX360 compilation directive check around any code that references the mouse as an input device (refer to Chapter 2). Therefore, we will create a private member field with this preprocessor check inside our InputHandler class. We need to set up a private member field to hold our previous mouse state and another one to hold our current mouse state:

```
#if !XBOX360
    private MouseState mouseState;
    private MouseState prevMouseState;
#endif
```

Then in the constructor we tell XNA that we want the mouse icon visible in the window and we store the current mouse state:

```
#if !XBOX360
    Game.IsMouseVisible = true;
    prevMouseState = Mouse.GetState();
#endif
```

In our Update method of the input handler game component, we need to set the previous state to what our current state is and then reset our current state as follows:

```
#if !XBOX360
    prevMouseState = mouseState;
    mouseState = Mouse.GetState();
#endif
```

Now we need to expose these internal fields so our camera (and any other objects) can get their values. First we need to add the properties to our interface as follows:

```
#if !XBOX360
    MouseState MouseState { get; }
    MouseState PreviousMouseState { get; }
#endif
```

Now we can implement those properties in our class:

```
#if !XBOX360
    public MouseState MouseState
    {
```

5

```
        get { return(mouseState); }
    }

    public MouseState PreviousMouseState
    {
        get { return(prevMouseState); }
    }
#endif
```

In our camera's Update method, we want to get the latest state of our mouse and compare the current X value to the previous X value to determine whether we moved the mouse left or right. We also want to check whether the left mouse button is pushed before updating our cameraYaw variable. Of course, all this is wrapped in our compilation preprocessor condition, as follows:

```
#if !XBOX360
    if ((input.PreviousMouseState.X > input.MouseState.X) &&
        (input.MouseState.LeftButton == ButtonState.Pressed))
    {
        cameraYaw += (spinRate * timeDelta);
    }
    else if ((input.PreviousMouseState.X < input.MouseState.X) &&
        (input.MouseState.LeftButton == ButtonState.Pressed))
    {
        cameraYaw -= (spinRate * timeDelta);
    }
#endif
```

We can compile and run the code and test the latest functionality on Windows. If the preprocessor checks are in place correctly, we should be able to deploy this demo to the Xbox 360, although it will not do anything different than it did before we added the mouse support.

Creating a Stationary Camera

Now that you know how to utilize our input, we can get working on implementing our stationary camera. We actually have most of this done, but we need to add pitching in addition to the yaw. One use for a stationary camera is to look at an object and follow it by rotating as needed. This is commonly used in racing game replay mode.

Before we dig into the camera changes, though, let's add a few more rectangles to our world. We can do this by adding the following code to the end of our demo's Update method:

```
world = Matrix.CreateTranslation(new Vector3(8.0f, 0, -10.0f));
DrawRectangle(ref world);

world = Matrix.CreateTranslation(new Vector3(8.0f, 0, -6.0f));
```

```
DrawRectangle(ref world);

world = Matrix.CreateRotationY(MathHelper.ToRadians(180f)) *
    Matrix.CreateTranslation(new Vector3(3.0f, 0, 10.0f));DrawRectangle(ref world);
```

We should also change our cull mode to None so that as we rotate around, we will always see our rectangles. We can do that by calling the following code at the top of our game's Draw method:

```
graphics.GraphicsDevice.RenderState.CullMode = CullMode.None;
```

To get our camera updated, we need to modify our camera class a little bit. First we need to declare a private member field as follows:

```
private float cameraPitch = 0.0f;
```

Now we can modify the Update method to set our camera pitch. Remember, *pitching* refers to rotating around the x axis. To calculate this, we simply take the code we used for calculating the yaw and replace our reference to the y axis with the x axis. The following is the code to check our keyboard and game pad:

```
if (input.KeyboardState.IsKeyDown(Keys.Down) ||
    input.GamePads[playerIndex].IsButtonDown(Buttons.RightThumbstickDown) ||
    input.GamePads[playerIndex].IsButtonDown(Buttons.DPadDown))
{
    cameraPitch -= (spinRate * timeDelta);
}
if (input.KeyboardState.IsKeyDown(Keys.Up) ||
    input.GamePads[playerIndex].IsButtonDown(Buttons.RightThumbstickUp) ||
    input.GamePads[playerIndex].IsButtonDown(Buttons.DPadUp))
{
    cameraPitch += (spinRate * timeDelta);
}
```

No surprises there, and we need to do the same thing with our mouse code. Inside our #if !XBOX360 compilation directive, add the following code:

```
if ((input.PreviousMouseState.Y > input.MouseState.Y) &&
    (input.MouseState.LeftButton == ButtonState.Pressed))
{
    cameraPitch += (spinRate * timeDelta);
}
else if ((input.PreviousMouseState.Y < input.MouseState.Y) &&
    (input.MouseState.LeftButton == ButtonState.Pressed))
{
    cameraPitch -= (spinRate * timeDelta);
}
```

We want to clamp our values so we do not rotate over 90 degrees in either direction:

```
if (cameraPitch > 89)
    cameraPitch = 89;
if (cameraPitch < -89)
    cameraPitch = -89;
```

Finally, we need to update our rotation matrix to include our pitch value. Here is the updated calculation:

```
Matrix rotationMatrix;
Matrix.CreateRotationY(MathHelper.ToRadians(cameraYaw), out rotationMatrix);
//add in pitch to the rotation
rotationMatrix = Matrix.CreateRotationX(MathHelper.ToRadians(cameraPitch)) *
    rotationMatrix;
```

The last statement is the only thing we added. We just added our pitch to the rotation matrix that was already being used to transform our camera. The full Update code can be found in Listing 5.1.

LISTING 5.1   Our Stationary Camera's Update Method

```
public override void Update(GameTime gameTime)
{
    float timeDelta = (float)gameTime.ElapsedGameTime.TotalSeconds;

    if (input.KeyboardState.IsKeyDown(Keys.Left) ||
        input.GamePads[playerIndex].IsButtonDown(Buttons.RightThumbstickLeft) ||
        input.GamePads[playerIndex].IsButtonDown(Buttons.DPadLeft))
    {
        cameraYaw += (spinRate * timeDelta);
    }
    if (input.KeyboardState.IsKeyDown(Keys.Right) ||
        input.GamePads[playerIndex].IsButtonDown(Buttons.RightThumbstickRight) ||
        input.GamePads[playerIndex].IsButtonDown(Buttons.DPadRight))
    {
        cameraYaw -= (spinRate * timeDelta);
    }

    if (input.KeyboardState.IsKeyDown(Keys.Down) ||
        input.GamePads[playerIndex].IsButtonDown(Buttons.RightThumbstickDown) ||
        input.GamePads[playerIndex].IsButtonDown(Buttons.DPadDown))
    {
        cameraPitch -= (spinRate * timeDelta);
    }
    if (input.KeyboardState.IsKeyDown(Keys.Up) ||
        input.GamePads[playerIndex].IsButtonDown(Buttons.RightThumbstickUp) ||
```

```
            input.GamePads[playerIndex].IsButtonDown(Buttons.DPadUp))
    {
        cameraPitch += (spinRate * timeDelta);
    }


#if !XBOX360
    if ((input.PreviousMouseState.X > input.MouseState.X) &&
        (input.MouseState.LeftButton == ButtonState.Pressed))
    {
        cameraYaw += (spinRate * timeDelta);
    }
    else if ((input.PreviousMouseState.X < input.MouseState.X) &&
        (input.MouseState.LeftButton == ButtonState.Pressed))
    {
        cameraYaw -= (spinRate * timeDelta);
    }

    if ((input.PreviousMouseState.Y > input.MouseState.Y) &&
        (input.MouseState.LeftButton == ButtonState.Pressed))
    {
        cameraPitch += (spinRate * timeDelta);
    }
    else if ((input.PreviousMouseState.Y < input.MouseState.Y) &&
        (input.MouseState.LeftButton == ButtonState.Pressed))
    {
        cameraPitch -= (spinRate * timeDelta);
    }
#endif

    //reset camera angle if needed
    if (cameraYaw > 360)
        cameraYaw -= 360;
    else if (cameraYaw < 0)
        cameraYaw += 360;

    //keep camera from rotating a full 90 degrees in either direction
    if (cameraPitch > 89)
        cameraPitch = 89;
    if (cameraPitch < -89)
        cameraPitch = -89;

    Matrix rotationMatrix;
    Matrix.CreateRotationY(MathHelper.ToRadians(cameraYaw),
        out rotationMatrix);
    //add in pitch to the rotation
```

```
    rotationMatrix = Matrix.CreateRotationX(MathHelper.ToRadians(cameraPitch))
        * rotationMatrix;
    // Create a vector pointing the direction the camera is facing.
    Vector3 transformedReference;
    Vector3.Transform(ref cameraReference, ref rotationMatrix,
        out transformedReference);
    // Calculate the position the camera is looking at.
    Vector3.Add(ref cameraPosition, ref transformedReference, out cameraTarget);

    Matrix.CreateLookAt(ref cameraPosition, ref cameraTarget, ref cameraUpVector,
        out view);

    base.Update(gameTime);
}
```

Creating a First-person Camera

We can build on our stationary camera by adding a first-person camera. The main thing we want to do is to add in a way to move back and forth and to each side. Before we start, we should create a new camera class and inherit from the one we have. We can call this new class FirstPersonCamera. The following is the Update method for this new class:

```
public override void Update(GameTime gameTime)
{
    //reset movement vector
    movement = Vector3.Zero;

    if (input.KeyboardState.IsKeyDown(Keys.A) ||
        input.GamePads[playerIndex].IsButtonDown(Buttons.LeftThumbstickLeft))
    {
        movement.X--;
    }
    if (input.KeyboardState.IsKeyDown(Keys.D) ||
        input.GamePads[playerIndex].IsButtonDown(Buttons.LeftThumbstickRight))
    {
        movement.X++;
    }

    if (input.KeyboardState.IsKeyDown(Keys.S) ||
        input.GamePads[playerIndex].IsButtonDown(Buttons.LeftThumbstickDown))
    {
        movement.Z++;
    }
    if (input.KeyboardState.IsKeyDown(Keys.W) ||
```

```
         input.GamePads[playerIndex].IsButtonDown(Buttons.LeftThumbstickUp))
    {
        movement.Z--;
    }

    //make sure we don"t increase speed if pushing up and over (diagonal)
    if (movement.LengthSquared() != 0)
        movement.Normalize();

    base.Update(gameTime);
}
```

The conditional logic should look familiar. It is identical to our stationary camera, except we changed where we were reading the input and what values it updated. We are reading the A, S, W, D keys and the left thumb stick. We are not looking at the mouse for movement. The value we are setting is a movement vector. We are only setting the X (left and right) and Z (back and forth) values. At the end of the conditions we are normalizing our vector as long as the length squared of the vector is not zero. This makes sure that we are not allowing faster movement just because the user is moving diagonally. There is no more code in the FirstPersonCamera object. The rest of the changes were made back in our original Camera object.

We declared the movement as a protected member field of type Vector3 called movement inside our original Camera object. We also declared a constant value for our movement speed. Both of these are listed here:

```
protected Vector3 movement = Vector3.Zero;
private const float moveRate = 120.0f;
```

We also set the access modifier of our input field to protected so our FirstPersonCamera could access it:

```
protected IInputHandler input;
```

Finally, we updated the last part of our Update method to take the movement into account when transforming our camera:

```
//update movement (none for this base class)
movement *= (moveRate * timeDelta);

Matrix rotationMatrix;
Vector3 transformedReference;
Matrix.CreateRotationY(MathHelper.ToRadians(cameraYaw), out rotationMatrix);

if (movement != Vector3.Zero)
{
    Vector3.Transform(ref movement, ref rotationMatrix, out movement);
    cameraPosition += movement;
}
```

```
//add in pitch to the rotation
rotationMatrix = Matrix.CreateRotationX(MathHelper.ToRadians(cameraPitch)) *
    rotationMatrix;

// Create a vector pointing the direction the camera is facing.
Vector3.Transform(ref cameraReference, ref rotationMatrix,
    out transformedReference);
// Calculate the position the camera is looking at.
Vector3.Add(ref cameraPosition, ref transformedReference, out cameraTarget);

Matrix.CreateLookAt(ref cameraPosition, ref cameraTarget, ref cameraUpVector,
    out view);
```

Besides just moving our local variables closer together, the only things that changed are the items in bold type. We take our movement vector and apply our move rate to it (taking into account our time delta, of course). The second portion is the key. We transformed our movement vector by our rotation matrix. This keeps us from just looking in a direction but continuing to move straight ahead. By transforming our movement vector via our rotation matrix, we actually move in the direction we are looking! Well, the movement actually happens in the next statement when we add this movement vector to our current camera position. We wrapped all this in a condition to see if any movement happened because we do not want to take a performance hit to do the math if we did not move.

Another thing to note is that because we were creating a first-person camera, we only transformed our movement vector by the yaw portion of our rotation matrix. We did not include the pitch because that would have allowed us to "fly." If we did want to create a flying camera instead, we could simply move the following statement before the code in bold:

```
//add in pitch to the rotation
rotationMatrix = Matrix.CreateRotationX(MathHelper.ToRadians(cameraPitch)) *
    rotationMatrix;
```

In order to have our game actually use this new first-person camera, we need to replace the regular Camera component in our InputDemo class with the FirstPersonCamera component. Now when we compile and run the demo, we can use the left thumb stick or D-pad (or up and down arrows) to move through our world. Feel free to modify the moveRate value as desired.

Creating a Split Screen

Now that we know how to set up our camera and accept input, we can look into how our code will need to change to handle multiple players in a split-screen game. To start, we need to make a copy of the InputDemo project we just finished. We can rename the project SplitScreen. After we have our solution and projects renamed (complete with our assembly GUID and title), we can look at the code we will need to change to accomplish a split-screen mode of play.

To create a split screen, we need to two different viewports. We have only been using one up until now, and we actually retrieved it in our camera's Initialization method. We simply grabbed the GraphicsDevice.Viewport property to get our camera's viewport. Because we want to display two screens in one we need to define our two new viewports and then let the cameras (we will need two cameras) know about them so we can get the desired effect. To start we need to add the following private member fields to our Game1.cs code:

```
private Viewport defaultViewport;
private Viewport topViewport;
private Viewport bottomViewport;
private Viewport separatorViewport;
private bool twoPlayers = true;
private FirstPersonCamera camera2;
```

Then at the end of our LoadContent method we will need to define those viewports and create our cameras and pass the new values. We do this in the following code:

```
if (twoPlayers)
{
    defaultViewport = graphics.GraphicsDevice.Viewport;
    topViewport = defaultViewport;
    bottomViewport = defaultViewport;

    topViewport.Height = topViewport.Height / 2;

    separatorViewport.Y = topViewport.Height - 1;
    separatorViewport.Height = 3;

    bottomViewport.Y = topViewport.Height + 1;
    bottomViewport.Height = (bottomViewport.Height / 2) - 1;

    camera.Viewport = topViewport;

    camera2 = new FirstPersonCamera(this);
    camera2.Viewport = bottomViewport;
    camera2.Position = new Vector3(0.0f, 0.0f, -3.0f);
    camera2.Orientation = camera.Orientation;
    camera2.PlayerIndex = PlayerIndex.Two;
    Components.Add(camera2);
}
```

We discussed briefly that we would need more than one camera to pull this off. This is because we have our view and projection matrices associated with our camera class (which we should). It makes sense that we will have two cameras because the camera is showing what the player is seeing. Each player needs his or her own view into the game.

Our initial camera is still set up in our game's constructor, but our second camera will get added here. Our first camera gets the default viewport associated with it. The preceding code first checks to see if we are in a two-player game. For a real game, this should be determined by an options menu or something similar, but for now we have just initialized the value to true when we initialized the twoPlayer variable.

Inside the two-player condition the first thing we do is set our default viewport to what we are currently using (the graphic device's viewport). Then we set our top viewport to the same value. We also initialize our bottomViewport to our defaultViewport value. The final thing we do with our viewports is resize them to account for two players. We divide the height in two (we are making two horizontal viewports) on both. We then set our bottom viewport's Y property to be one more than the height of our top viewport. This effectively puts the bottom viewport right underneath our top viewport.

While still in the two-player condition, we change our first camera's viewport to use the top viewport. Then we set up our second camera by setting more properties. Not only do we set the viewport for this camera to the bottom viewport, but we also set a new camera position as well as the orientation of the camera. Finally, we set the player index.

None of these properties is exposed from our camera object, so we need to open our Camera.cs file and make some changes to account for this. First, we need to add a new private member field to hold our player index. We just assumed it was player 1 before. We can set up our protected index (so our FirstPersonCamera class can access it) as an integer, as follows:

```
protected int playerIndex = 0;
```

Now we can modify the input code that controls our camera to use this index instead of the hard-coded value 0 for the game pads. In the camera's Update method we can change any instance of input.GamePads[0] to input.GamePads[playerIndex]. We also need to do the same for the FirstPersonCamera object. We did not update the keyboard code and will not for the sake of time. However, to implement multiple users where both can use the keyboard, we should create a mapping for each player and check accordingly. In general, it is a good practice to have a keyboard mapping so that if the gamer does not like the controls we have defined in our games, he or she has a way to change the controls so they work more logically for him or her. The same can be said about creating a mapping for the game pads, but many games simply give a choice of a couple of layouts. Because the code does not implement a keyboard mapping, the only way for us to control the separate screens differently is by having two game pads hooked up to the PC or Xbox 360.

After we have changed our camera to take the player index into consideration before reading values from the game pad, we can add the following properties to our Camera.cs code file:

```
public PlayerIndex PlayerIndex
{
    get { return ((PlayerIndex)playerIndex); }
    set { playerIndex = (int)value; }
}

public Vector3 Position
{
    get { return (cameraPosition); }
    set { cameraPosition = value; }
}

public Vector3 Orientation
{
    get { return (cameraReference); }
    set { cameraReference = value; }
}

public Vector3 Target
{
    get { return (cameraTarget); }
    set { cameraTarget = value; }
}
public Viewport Viewport
{
    get
    {
        if (viewport == null)
            viewport = Game.GraphicsDevice.Viewport;

        return ((Viewport)viewport);
    }
    set
    {
        viewport = value;
        InitializeCamera();
    }
}
```

We are simply exposing the camera's position, orientation (reference), and target variables. We are casting the player index property to a PlayerIndex enumeration type. The final property is the Viewport property. We first check to see if our viewport variable is null. If it is, we set it to the graphics device's viewport. When we set our Viewport property, we also call our InitializeCamera method again so it can recalculate its view and projection matrices. We need to set up a private member field for our viewport. We allow it to have a default null value so we can declare it as follows:

```
private Viewport? viewport;
```

Because we are utilizing the `Viewport` type, we need to make sure the following using statement is in our code:

```
using Microsoft.Xna.Framework.Graphics;
```

The only thing left for us to do now is to update our game's drawing code to draw our scene twice. Because we have to draw our scene twice (once for each camera), we need to refactor our `Draw` code into a `DrawScene` method and pass in a camera reference. Our new code for the new `Draw` method is shown here:

```
protected override void Draw(GameTime gameTime)
{
    graphics.GraphicsDevice.Viewport = camera.Viewport;
    DrawScene(gameTime, camera);

    if (twoPlayers)
    {
        graphics.GraphicsDevice.Viewport = camera2.Viewport;
        DrawScene(gameTime, camera2);
        //now clear the thick horizontal line between the two screens
        graphics.GraphicsDevice.Viewport = separatorViewport;
        graphics.GraphicsDevice.Clear(Color.Black);
    }

    base.Draw(gameTime);
}
```

We took all the code that was inside this method and put it into a new method, `DrawScene(GameTime gameTime, Camera camera)`. The code we put into the `DrawScene` method did not change from how it looked when it resided inside of the `Draw` method.

The first thing we do with the preceding code is set our graphics device's viewport to be what our camera's viewport is. We then draw the scene passing in our camera. Then we check to see if we have two players; if so, we set the viewport appropriately and finally draw the scene for that camera. Run the application and see that it is using a split screen! The screenshot of this split-screen demo can be seen in Figure 5.1.

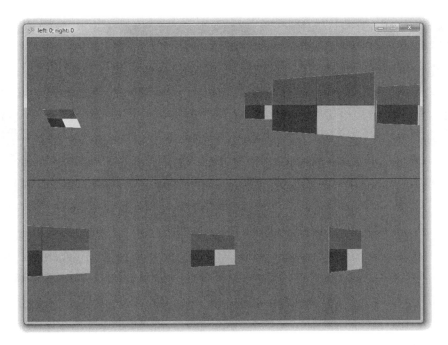

FIGURE 5.1   SplitScreen demo shows how you can create two cameras that can be controlled by two different game pads.

Summary

Another chapter is behind us. You have learned about XNA game services and how they, along with game components, can really add benefit to our overall game architecture. We started a small library that currently handles our camera (which we can currently switch between stationary and first-person), our input devices, and our frame rate counter component.

We discussed how to utilize the keyboard, game pad, and mouse to get input from our gamer to move our camera around. You learned specifically how to write a stationary camera that only rotates and created a functioning first-person camera.

We updated our camera functionality to handle two players. We added split-screen functionality by creating two different cameras and viewports the cameras could use.

In the next chapter, we are going to load 3D objects to the screen, which will allow us to move in a much better-looking world. Play some games, rest the mind, and come back strong as we jump right into working with the Content Pipeline.

PART III

Content Pipeline

Loading and Texturing 3D Objects

We are going to discuss the Content Pipeline in this part of the book. XNA provides out-of-the-box support for loading 3D objects, textures, effects, Extensible Markup Language (XML), sounds, music, and XACT projects. We discuss 3D objects and textures in this chapter. You will learn how to load 3D objects into our world and learn about different texturing techniques.

Understanding the Content Pipeline

The Content Pipeline can be used to solve a very real problem: The content we create for games is typically not game ready. For example, 3D content is usually stored in a proprietary format, and there is a need to convert the data before loading it into the game. This is where the Content Pipeline helps out. In general, it can take different files as input, massage them to get them into a type we can work with, and then compile them into a format that can easily be loaded when our game starts.

The XNA Framework Content Pipeline is made up of several components. First is the Content Importer, which is responsible for reading the data loaded into the solution. If there is data in the file the Content Importer does not know how to map to the Content Document Object Model (DOM), then the data is not stored. It only keeps the data it cares about. Once the importer is done reading in the data, it passes it along to the Content DOM, which stores the strongly typed data. The data is then passed from the Content DOM to a Content Processor, which then passes it to a Content Compiler. If the compilation fails, we get a nice message inside of the IDE that tells us what happened:

We do not have to wait and see if it is going to load at runtime, which is a huge improvement over how things used to work. The compiler actually builds files that are read in at runtime. These files typically have an .xnb file extension. Audio files create .xgs, .xwb, and .xsb files for the actual sound project, wave bank, and sound bank content. We discuss the sound and how it relates to the Content Pipeline in the next chapter. The Content Pipeline is smart enough not to recompile any content that has not changed since the last build. Finally, after all the content is compiled into files, they are read in via the Content Manager at runtime so our games can consume the content. We have been using the Content Manager since our very first application in Chapter 2, "XNA Game Studio and the Xbox 360." We used it to load the texture using the following code:

```
spriteTexture = Content.Load<Texture2D>("texture");
```

Fortunately, when we use the Content Manager, we do not need to actually dispose of our objects because it handles disposing of our content itself. The following method, which is always included in our new game projects, is available if we ever need to remove unmanaged objects such as files we haven't opened through the Content Pipeline:

```
protected override void UnloadContent()
{
    base.UnloadContent();
}
```

We discuss the counterpart of this method in the next section. The LoadContent method does the actual loading of the data.

As we add content to our project that is recognizable as XNA Framework content, it goes through the process just described. The Properties window inside the Visual C# Express IDE will show an asset name that we can modify. If we add content types that are not recognized, we can change the XNA Framework Content boolean value to true. We would then need to fill in the Content Importer and Content Processor properties, specifying how to turn the unknown content type into a format that XNA can recognize. This would require a custom importer and processor, which we discuss building in Chapter 8, "Extending the Content Pipeline."

Loading 3D Models

The XNA Framework's Content Pipeline handles loading .X and .FBX files automatically when they are pasted into the Solution Explorer (or included in the project). This is when the Content Pipeline goes through the process described in the previous section of importing, processing, and compiling the data. We then can use our game class and the Content Manager to read the model information.

We will start by creating a new project, which we can call Load3DObject. We can create both the Windows and Xbox 360 game projects. After getting our solution set up, we can then add an existing project to our solution—the XELibrary from last chapter. Once we import both the Windows and the Xbox 360 XELibrary projects, we need to reference them inside the game projects we created. We reference the XELibrary in our Windows project and the XELibrary_Xbox360 in our Xbox 360 game project.

After we have our initial setup of our solution file completed, we can jump right in and add a using statement at the top of our Game1.cs class to access our library:

```
using XELibrary;
```

We can set up our private member fields to access the game components in our library:

```
private FPS fps;
private FirstPersonCamera camera;
private InputHandler input;
```

The following is our constructor, where we initialize the variables we just set:

```
public Game1()
{
    graphics = new GraphicsDeviceManager(this);
    content = new ContentManager(Services);

    input = new InputHandler(this);
    Components.Add(input);
    camera = new FirstPersonCamera(this);
    Components.Add(camera);

#if DEBUG
    //draw 60 fps and update as often as possible
    fps = new FPS(this, true, false);
#else
    fps = new FPS(this, true, false);
#endif
    Components.Add(fps);
}
```

With just that little bit of coding (and setup), we now have access to all the code in our library. We automatically have a first-person camera now, and we can handle input as well as display our frame rate. Game components aren't too shabby.

The Content project is where we will add our content, but instead of just shoving all kinds of content in the root folder, we are going to add two subfolders—Models and Textures. This is not required, but it really helps keep the clutter minimal. Now with the preliminary work out of the way, we can actually get down to business and load a 3D object. Under the Contents\Models\ folder on this book's CD, copy the asteroid1.x file into the Content Project's Models folder. This model was created by Microsoft and is part of the Spacewar starter kit that is available to download from the XNA Creators Club website.

When you copy the 3D model from the CD and paste it into the Content project, XNA Game Studio flags it as XNA Framework Content. Now we can compile the code, which will also kick off the Content Pipeline. The Content Pipeline kicked off the Content Importer, shoved the data into the DOM, and then called the Content Processor, which passed it to the Content Compiler. So when we compile our game, it not only compiles our code, but also the content.

The Content Compiler throws an error, "Missing asset ... \Content\Textures\ asteroid1.tga," because the .X file we loaded has a reference to a texture inside of it. It references a sibling folder by the name of Textures. The following is a portion of the asteroid1.x file that references the texture in the texture's sibling folder:

```
Material phong1SG {
    1.0;1.0;1.0;1.000000;;
    18.000000;
    0.000000;0.000000;0.000000;;
    0.000000;0.000000;0.000000;;
    TextureFilename {
        "..\\textures\\asteroid1.tga";
    }
}
```

We have that folder, but we did not grab the .tga texture from the CD. Let's do that now and paste it into our Textures folder. Once we do this, we can compile again. The code should compile without issues. After it compiles successfully, browse to the /bin/x86/debug/content/models/ and /textures/ folders. Notice that a couple files were created at the time we compiled. The Content Compiler took the files and compiled them into the .xnb files shown here. The compiler gave us an error when it could not find the texture associated with the .X file. We have corrected that, and our code (and content) now compiles successfully.

We could run the code, but nothing would be on our screen because we have not actually told XNA to load and draw the object. We can get that ball rolling by creating a private member field in our Game1.cs class as follows:

```
private Model model;
```

Now we can initialize this variable by actually loading our model in our code. We do this inside the LoadContent method:

```
model = Content.Load<Model>(@"Models\asteroid1");
```

The LoadContent method is where we load all our content. This method as well as its counterpart, UnloadContent, gets called at the appropriate times. What are these appropriate times? This is a good place to discuss the logic flow of XNA.

The XNA Framework's logic flow works something like this:

1. The Main application calls the Game Constructor.
2. The Game Constructor creates any game components and calls their constructors.
3. The XNA Framework calls the game's Initialize method.

4. The XNA Framework calls each of the game component's `Initialize` methods.

5. The XNA Framework calls each of the `Drawable` game component's `LoadContent` methods.

6. The XNA Framework calls the game's `LoadContent` method.

7. The XNA Framework calls the game's `Update` method.

8. The XNA Framework calls each of the game component's `Update` methods.

9. The XNA Framework calls the game's `Draw` method.

10. The XNA Framework calls each of the drawable game component's `Draw` methods.

11. Steps 7 through 10 are repeated many times each second.

12. If the device is lost (the user moved the window to another monitor, the screen resolution is changed, the window is minimized, and so on), a call to `UnloadContent` is made.

13. If the device is reset, the logic flow starts at step 6 again.

14. The gamer exits the game.

15. The XNA Framework calls the game's `Dispose` method.

16. The game's `Dispose` method calls the base object's `Dispose` method, which causes the following two steps.

17. The XNA Framework calls each of the game component's `Dispose` methods.

18. The XNA Framework calls the game's `UnloadContent` method.

19. The game's `Dispose` method gets focus back, and the game exits.

Here's something to note about how the XNA Framework calls the game component's `Initialize` method (and `LoadContent` for drawable game components): It only happens once when the game's `Initialize` method is kicked off by the framework. If game components are added later, their `Initialize` (and `LoadContent`) methods will not be called. This is important to understand when managing game components.

At this point we have loaded our 3D content. We have created a private member field to store the model we added. We actually loaded our model in our code and initialized our variable. Now we just need to draw the model on the screen. Add the following method to draw the model:

```
private void DrawModel(ref Model m, ref Matrix world)
{
    Matrix[] transforms = new Matrix[m.Bones.Count];
    m.CopyAbsoluteBoneTransformsTo(transforms);

    foreach (ModelMesh mesh in m.Meshes)
    {
        foreach (BasicEffect be in mesh.Effects)
        {
            be.EnableDefaultLighting();
            be.Projection = camera.Projection;
```

```
            be.View = camera.View;
            be.World = world * mesh.ParentBone.Transform;
        }

        mesh.Draw();
    }
}
```

Our `DrawModel` method takes in a reference to our model as well as a reference to the world matrix we need to apply to our model. The first two statements get the transforms of each bone in the model. A model can have a parent bone with children bones associated with it. This is mainly used in animations, but even if a model does not have animations, it might still have bones. Therefore, our code should include this unless we know for certain that our model does not have any children. The transforms array will contain a transformation matrix of each mesh of the model that contains its position relative to the parent. By doing this, we can make sure that each `ModelMesh` of the parent `Model` will be drawn at the right location. This actually happens in the last statement inside of our inner `foreach` loop. We take the world matrix that the mesh is supposed to be transformed with and then multiply that transformation with the `ModelMesh`'s parent bone's transformation. This makes sure each `ModelMesh` is drawn correctly with the parent mesh.

We did not need to create our own `BasicEffect` object because XNA will apply one to a mesh we load. We can override this, which you'll see in Part VI, "High Level Shader Language," when we talk about the HLSL and make our own effect files. For now, we just ensure that the default lighting is enabled on the effect as well as set our projection and view matrices to what our Camera game component has updated them to be. Instead of having an effect that we are explicitly calling, we are tying into the one XNA applies to the `Model` when it loads it. This is also happening inside the inner `foreach` loop, so we could apply different effects to children meshes if we wanted to.

The other thing to notice is the fact that we did not reference our texture anywhere. Because it is inside the .X file and the Content Compiler stored that information, the Content Manager knew where to look for the texture and loaded it automatically. You will see how to override the texture through code a little later in this chapter. Let's just get it to draw with the normal texture for now! To do that, we need to call our `DrawModel` method inside our `Draw` method with the following code:

```
Matrix world = Matrix.CreateTranslation(new Vector3(0,0,-4000));
DrawModel(ref model, ref world);
```

The model we are loading is rather large, and as such we are going to push it way back into the world. In fact, we need to make a modification to our `Camera` class in our XELibrary. We originally had our near and far planes set up in the `Matrix.CreatePerspectiveFieldOfView` method as 0.0001 and 1000.0, respectively. The thing about the plane values is that they are floating points, which means there is a finite amount of precision we can have. We can either have the precision before the decimal point or after the decimal point, but not both. A lot of times programmers will set the far plane to a very high number, but then the depth buffer (also known as the *z buffer*) could have a hard time knowing which objects to draw first. As a result, during game play the screen will almost flicker as different vertices are fighting to be drawn first. The z buffer is confused because it cannot take into account the minor differences in the locations of those vertices. Of course, the .0001 near plane we originally had set was not exactly practical either. At this point having a near plane of 1 and a far plane of 10,000 should meet most of our needs without overly stressing our z buffer. We could have our far plane even further without causing an adverse effect on the depth buffer.

Now we can compile and run our code, and we should see our asteroid object sitting right in front of us. This is not extremely exciting, but we have just successfully drawn a .X model complete with a texture.

Texturing 3D Models

Now let's replace that texture with one we will load on the fly. We could just modify our texture resource if we wanted to, but let's assume that we want to keep that intact, and as we load different asteroids we want some to use that brownish texture and some to use our newly created texture, for which we will simply remove the color. So fire up your favorite paint program, open up the .tga file, and turn it into a grayscale image. If needed, the image asteroid1-grey.tga can be taken from the CD in this chapter's source code. Let's add our newly created image into our Content project inside the Solution Explorer (or you can just include it in your project if you saved the new version in the /Textures/ subfolder from your paint program).

Add the following code in the LoadContent method:

```
originalAsteroid = Content.Load<Texture2D>(@"Textures\asteroid1");
greyAsteroid = Content.Load<Texture2D>(@"Textures\asteroid1-grey");
```

Just like adding our model, we can add our texture asset very easily. Of course, now we have to actually declare our private member field:

```
private Texture2D originalAsteroid;
private Texture2D greyAsteroid;
```

Now we can make a couple changes to our DrawModel method. We need to add in another parameter of type Texture2D and call it texture. We also need to set our effect to use that texture if it is passed in, which can be seen in the following code:

```
if (texture != null)
    be.Texture = texture;
```

This code statement is inside of the inner foreach loop with the rest of the code that sets the properties of our basic effect that is being used by our model. We are simply checking to see if null is passed in; if it isn't, we are setting the texture of the effect. As you saw earlier, the effect is getting applied to the mesh of our model, so we only need to modify our call to our DrawModel to pass in the new texture. Go ahead and create another asteroid on the screen by replacing the current drawing code with the following:

```
Matrix world = Matrix.CreateTranslation(new Vector3(0, 0, -4000));
DrawModel(ref model, ref world, greyAsteroid);

world = Matrix.CreateTranslation(new Vector3(0, 0, 4000));
DrawModel(ref model, ref world, originalAsteroid);
```

The first line did not change, but it is added here for readability. The second statement we are passing in is our new texture. The last two statements place another asteroid behind us and reset the texture to the original one. We can run this program and spin the camera to see both asteroids being drawn.

Now let's apply some transformations to our asteroids. We can add some rotation to get them to do a little more than they are right now. To do this, replace the Draw code with the following:

```
Matrix world = Matrix.CreateRotationY(MathHelper.ToRadians(
        270.0f * (float)gameTime.TotalGameTime.TotalSeconds)) *
    Matrix.CreateTranslation(new Vector3(0, 0, -4000));
DrawModel(ref model, ref world, greyAsteroid);

world = Matrix.CreateRotationY(MathHelper.ToRadians(
        45.0f * (float)gameTime.TotalGameTime.TotalSeconds)) *
    Matrix.CreateRotationZ(MathHelper.ToRadians(
        45.0f * (float)gameTime.TotalGameTime.TotalSeconds)) *
    Matrix.CreateTranslation(new Vector3(0, 0, 4000));
DrawModel(ref model, ref world, originalAsteroid);
```

Even with the code wrapping to fit on the page, you can still see that we only have four statements, just like before. The only thing that changed is the code that modifies the world matrix. This makes sense because we want to rotate our asteroids. We start by looking at our first world transformation. You can see that we are simply rotating it around the y axis by 270 degrees, multiplied by the number of seconds our game has been running. This effectively makes it continuously render every frame. After the rotation, we still translate it like we did before, moving it 4,000 units into our world. The second world transformation is similar, except we are only rotating by 45 degrees instead of 270 degrees. We are also rotating around the x axis by the same amount. This should give us a decent wobble effect. Finally, we are translating 4,000 units behind us just like before. You can compile and run our program to see our asteroids are moving (well, rotating in place).

Summary

You were introduced to the Content Pipeline in this chapter. You saw just how easy it is to take content from the pipeline and load into our demo. We discussed how to organize our game content, especially in larger projects.

We loaded a 3D .X file into our demo. We discussed texturing techniques and how to override textures that are already set up in our 3D objects. You saw how to load the same 3D object more than once and apply different textures to each instance. Finally, we added some translation to our objects to get a better effect.

CHAPTER 7

Sound and Music

Stop and think for a moment what your favorite game would be like if it did not have sound. Music sets the atmosphere for our games, and sound effects add to the realism of our games. In this chapter, we discuss how to get music and sounds into our demos and games.

To do this, we will need two options. We can have direct access to sound and music files, or we can use the Microsoft Cross-Platform Audio Creation Tool (XACT), which Microsoft provides for us. We will discuss both options in this book, but the majority of this chapter is devoted to the Microsoft Cross-Platform Audio Creation Tool (XACT).

Direct Access to Sound Files

The way we directly access the files is by placing our raw wav or mp3 files into the Content project to be processed by the Content Pipeline directly. This is identical to how we have handled the 3D models and texture files.

Before XNA Game Studio 3.0, the only way to play sound files was by using the XACT tool. Although there's a lot of power and flexibility in using the tool, there are times when we simply want to play a sound or music file. For situations like these, the XNA Framework has the SoundEffect and MediaPlayer classes. We will discuss these in detail in Chapter 12, "Programming for the Zune," and Chapter 13, "Running the Game on the Zune."

Microsoft Cross-Platform Audio Creation Tool (XACT)

The Microsoft Cross-Platform Audio Creation Tool can be found in our Programs, Microsoft XNA Game Studio, Tools menu. Once you have the tool opened, we will create wave banks and sound banks and discuss global settings. We will then create a sound manager we can add to our library.

We use XACT to bundle raw wave files together and add effects to the different sounds. The XACT tool allows us to associate categories with our sounds. When we set a sound to have a category of music, it allows the Xbox 360 to ignore the game's custom music if the gamer has a playlist playing on his or her Xbox 360.

Before we open the actual tool, we need to open up the XACT Auditioning Utility, which is found in the same location as XACT itself. We do this to audition (listen to) the sounds we are making inside of XACT. This can, of course, be beneficial, especially when we want to add effects to the file. With that said, XACT is not a sound-editing software package. It takes completed wave files and puts them in a format that XNA can read and use. We can do simple effects such as change the pitch and volume, but the tool is not designed to be a wave file editor.

We first need to hook our XACT tool up to the launched Auditioning Utility. The Auditioning Utility must be run before the XACT tool is run. To play our sounds we need to tell XACT to connect to the Auditioning Utility by clicking the Audition menu item and then clicking the Connect to [machine] (local) item. After we have successfully connected, the Auditioning Utility will say "XACT tool is now connected...."

The XACT tool will not be able to connect to the Auditioning Utility if the there is a web server on the machine. If you are running IIS, you can run `iisreset/stop` to stop the service so it isn't listening on port 80.

When you open the tool, you will see an empty project to which we can add .wav files. After adding the files, we can then set them up as sounds and create cue names for them that we can kick off inside our code. We can modify properties to get different effects from the sounds.

Wave Banks

To get started, let's create a new wave bank from inside XACT. To create a wave bank, follow these steps:

1. Click File and select New Project. It does not matter what this project is named because it will be discarded.
2. Right-click Wave Banks and select New Wave Bank (see Figure 7.1).
3. Inside the Wave Bank empty pane, right-click and select Insert Wave File(s).
4. Find a wave file. You can use the Theme.wav file from this book's CD.

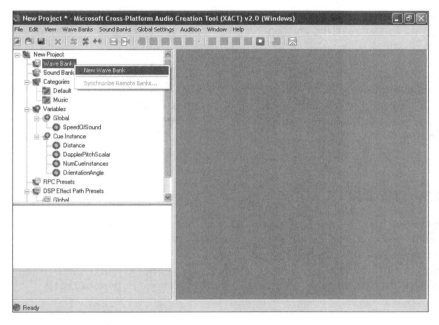

FIGURE 7.1   The XACT tool allows us to add wave banks to utilize the sounds in our games.

5. Because you have your Auditioning Tool set up and XACT connected to it, you can simply select the wave file and press the spacebar to hear it play. You can also right-click and select Play or click Play in the toolbar. As with most graphical user interfaces (GUIs), there are many ways to accomplish the same task. This book only lists one way in most cases.

Sound Banks

Even though we have the wave file loaded inside our XACT project, we still cannot use it in our game. We have to create a sound bank first. To create a sound bank, follow these steps:

1. Right-click Sound Banks and select New Sound Bank. As with the wave bank, we can also accomplish this through the toolbar or the main menu items.

2. Your work pane fills up with the Sound Bank window. You will need to work with the Wave Bank window as well as the Sound Bank window, so position them so you can see them both. One way to do this is to click Tile Horizontally inside the Window menu item.

3. Now that you can see both windows, drag the wave file from the wave bank into the sound bank, inside the top-left pane (sounds frame).

4. A cue for the sound needs to be created in order for our code to utilize it. Create a
   cue by dragging the sound from the top-left pane (sounds frame) into the bottom-
   left pane (cues frame).

This is the bare minimum we need to do to play sounds in our games when using the
XACT tool. To hear the sound, select it and press the spacebar. You can press Escape to
stop the sound. To get sound effects and music into our games, these steps will work. In
the next sections, we discuss more advanced ways to manipulate our sounds to get them
ready for our game.

Understanding Variations

To accomplish something more than just playing sounds, you need to understand variations. With variations we can assign many waves to a track, and we can create different
events for those tracks to create a sound. We can assign many sounds to a cue. We can
then set up how those sounds or waves are to be played. We will be utilizing XACT to
create different variations, and then we are going to write a library component that a
demo can use to play these cues.

Close out your existing XACT instance and open up a new one. We need to create a wave
bank and a sound bank to put our waves in. On this book's CD, under this chapter's folder
is a subfolder titled Sounds. You need to add all these waves into our wave bank. After
adding in the waves, we'll create some sounds. We are going to add the different sounds
and create different variations so you can learn how to use some of the XACT features by
example. Here are the steps to follow:

1. Drag the Attention and Explosion sounds directly into your cues frame (bottom left
   pane). We are going to play these sounds as is.

2. Drag the Axe_throw sound directly into your cues frame and rename the cue to
   Bullet. You can do this by right-clicking the name in the cues frame and selecting
   Rename. At this point, the screen should resemble Figure 7.2.

3. To start the more complicated tasks, drag the CoolLoop wave into your cues frame.

4. In the top-right pane (tracks frame) you can see that XACT created a track with a
   play event that includes our wave name. We want to make sure this sound loops, so
   click the Play Wave tree node of the Track 1 root to select it.

5. In the properties window you can see the Looping plane. The looping count default
   value is 0, but we can either loop it a certain number of times by changing the
   number of times to loop, or we can have it loop forever by selecting the Infinite
   check box. We are going to let this sound loop forever, so check the Infinite box (see
   Figure 7.3).

6. Because this loop is going to be music, click the CoolLoop's sound icon and drag it
   on top of the Music category on the left side of the window. When this is successful,
   you will see the category change from Default to Music.

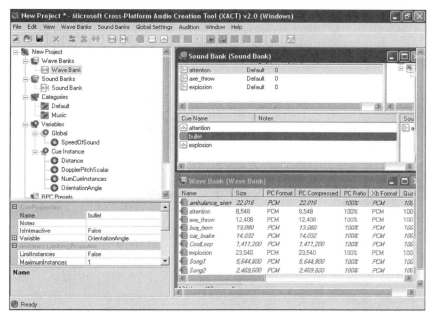

FIGURE 7.2   Wave files can be dragged directly into the cues frame.

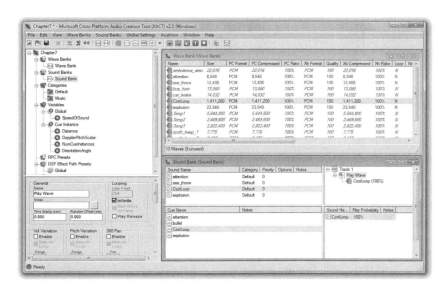

FIGURE 7.3   We can set our play event on a track to loop indefinitely.

7. Next up we are going to add multiple sounds into one cue. We will use Synth_beep_1 to start us off. Drag that wave into your cues frame.

8. Now make sure that the sound name is selected (in your sounds frame) so the track frame is showing the play event for track 1.

9. Drag the Synth_beep_2 and Synth_beep_3 waves and drop them on the play event inside track 1. Be careful to not drag over the sound or cue frames because this will make the tracks frame empty (it deselects the sound from the sound pane). You can see where you need to release the cursor in Figure 7.4. The final result after releasing the cursor and completing the drop operation can be seen in Figure 7.5.

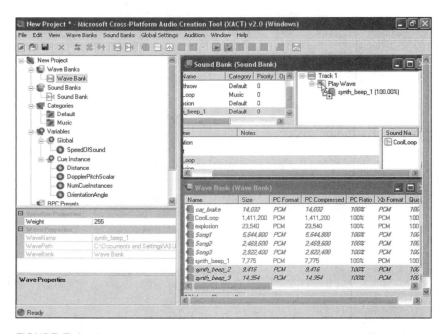

FIGURE 7.4   Drag the waves directly into a play event on a sound's track.

10. Rename the Synth_beep_1 cue to Hit.

11. With Hit as the active cue, press the spacebar to hear it play (assuming you are connected to the Auditioning Utility). Hit the spacebar several times in a row very fast. You can hear one sound being played every time you hit the spacebar regardless if the previous sound was played. You can see they are not played at the same time by "pressing play" once. By putting the different waves directly into a play event, we are giving XACT a list of waves to play from when we call play. It does not play them all at once (but you will see how to do that in a moment).

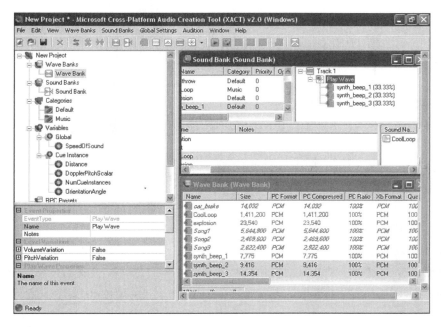

FIGURE 7.5   The waves show up underneath one play event inside of a track when you add them.

12. Because we do not want this particular cue to play more than one sound at a time, check the Limit Instances box in the Instance Limiting Properties section of the properties. You will need to have our cue name selected to do this. Now when you press the spacebar multiple times, it will not start playing until the last sound has finished.

13. You can hear the sounds are random, but we want them to play in the order we specified in the play event of our track. To do this, change the Playlist Type drop-down box in the Variation Playlist pane of the property frame. You need to do this when you have the cue selected. Changing this value to Ordered causes XACT to play the sounds in the order specified. If we wanted it to start with a random entry and then play them in order, we could have selected Ordered from Random.

14. Now when you play the sounds, they play in order and only play one at a time. However, we want the sounds to be queued up so that if you press the spacebar five times, it will play all of the waves in the sound, with each one starting as soon as the previous one finishes. To do this you need to change the Behavior At Max property to Queue instead of Fail To Play. This can be useful for queuing up voiceover audio, which we would never want to play simultaneously. This is shown in Figure 7.6.

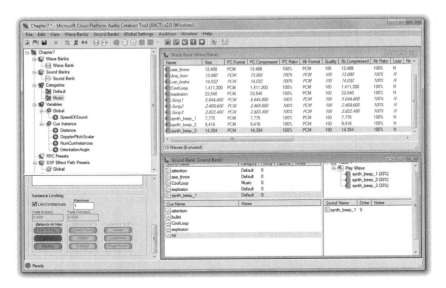

FIGURE 7.6   You can queue up calls to play your cues when you have Limit Instances checked.

15. Now we are going to make a crash cue. To start, drag Ambulance_siren from your waves into your cues and rename the cue Crash.

16. Inside the tracks frame, with the Ambulance_siren sound selected from the sound frame, right-click and add a new track.

17. Now you can add a play event to the track just added by right-clicking the track and selecting Add Event, Play Wave.

18. Drag the Car_brake wave into the play event of the track you just created. Remember not to drag across the sound or cue frame because the contents of the track frame will disappear.

19. Repeat steps 16 through 18 with the wave files Bus_horn and Explosion. When this step is completed, you should have a total of four tracks, each with its own play event that has a wave file associated with it. The Sound Banks window is expanded in Figure 7.7 so you can see the end result.

20. Now if you play the Crash cue, you will hear all four sounds at the same time. We want them to be spaced out so as to simulate an accident. You can delay the time at which different tracks start to play by setting the `Time Stamp (sec)` property in the Timing Properties section of the property frame when you have the play wave event selected. Our Car_brake wave can be left alone because it is a little longer of a sound file. Modify the rest of the values as follows:

Bus_horn: 0.300

Explosion: 1.000

Ambulance_siren: 1.600

FIGURE 7.7   You can create multiple tracks for a sound, each with one or more events in your tracks frame.

Now when you play the cue, you can hear something that resembles a car colliding with a bus, creating a large explosion, and the fastest EMT response time ever!

21. Now we want to make a variant of our explosion sound. We are going to make a gunshot sound without using an additional wave file. To do this, drag the Explosion wave bank file into the empty white space inside of the sound pane so it creates a copy of itself (named Explosion 2). Drag Explosion 2 from the sounds frame into the cues frame and rename the cue Gunshot.

22. When you play Gunshot, it does not sound any different from Explosion. Let's change that by adding a Pitch event to our only track for the Explosion 2 sound in our tracks frame. We add this event just like we added the play event earlier, by right-clicking the track and selecting Add Event, Pitch.

23. Now we need to modify the pitch to get the desired sound effect. To do this, we need to make sure our Pitch event is selected and then change the Value. You can find this value in the properties frame under the newly added Pitch pane. Let's change the pitch to 12.00, as shown in Figure 7.8. Now if you play the cue you will hear something that resembles a gunshot instead of an explosion. We did not have to add another large wave file to accomplish this effect.

24. We are now going to create a cue with multiple sounds. Right-click inside the cues frame and select New Cue. Name this cue Complex.

25. Drag the Explosion sound down on top of the Complex cue. Do the same thing with the Synth_beep_1 sound. Remember, this Synth_beep_1 sound has its own sound variations already because it plays three different waves in order.

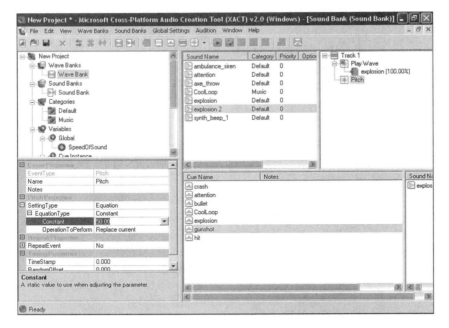

FIGURE 7.8   You can add a pitch event to the track and set the pitch value in the properties frame.

26. We need to change the Playlist Type for this Complex cue to Random. This way, it will just play a sound randomly even if the one it picks was just played.
27. The final thing we will do is add a music playlist. Unfortunately, XACT does not have a way to give us typical playlist functionality, so we will have to put that into our code. For now, though, we can at least add our songs to this playlist. Start by dragging the Song1, Song2, and Song3 waves into the sounds frame.
28. Also drag those sounds to the music category.
29. Now drag the Song1, Song2, and Song3 sounds from the sounds frame into the cues frame.
30. Save the project.

That was a long example, but it was worth going through because at this point you have a good idea of how to manipulate sound to prepare cues for our games. Our games will always reference the cue value.

There are other actions XACT allows us to do, such as setting local and global variables, setting up transitions through interactive audio settings, and setting up runtime parameter controls (RPCs).

We can create RPCs when a simple pitch or volume change across the board will not do. Perhaps we would like to add some reverb, or maybe we would like to modify the volume as a cue plays up and down. Doing any of these things requires setting up an RPC, which can be done by right-clicking the RPC tree node and selecting New RPC Preset, as shown in Figure 7.9.

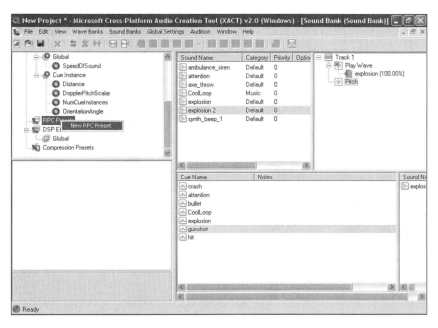

FIGURE 7.9   We can add runtime parameter controls and apply them to sounds to produce different effects.

Then we can drag that preset over to one of our sounds in the sounds frame. To test with, we can make a copy of our CoolLoop sound and then add our preset to this new sound by dragging the RPC on top of the new sound we just created. We can open the RPC preset by double-clicking it. Because there is only one sound associated with the RPC, it will play that one. The Attached Sounds pane displays all the sounds associated with this RPC. We can add a new curve by first choosing a variable from the dropdown list. Next, we can pick Sound as the object of this curve. Finally, for the parameter we can select Volume. After the final selection a curve will be added. We can move the points around, and then the vertical bar that is the same color as our curve can be moved left and right. The bar can be moved, or we can modify the Value of the curve declaration. As we play the sound and move the bar, we can see the value change and hear the effect it has on the sample being played. We can set that value in code for the variable to cause the sound to react exactly how we want. We might want to do this, for example, to dim the background music when dialogue is happening between characters. We can pass a value to the global variable that will produce the sound identical to what we are hearing as we audition the sound with our RPC added. We can add more curves (pitch and reverb) by selecting another variable from Variable dropdown list. We can add nodes to our curve by double-clicking the selected curve. A screenshot of this dialog box is shown in Figure 7.10. Have fun coming up with a totally different CoolLoop 2 sound!

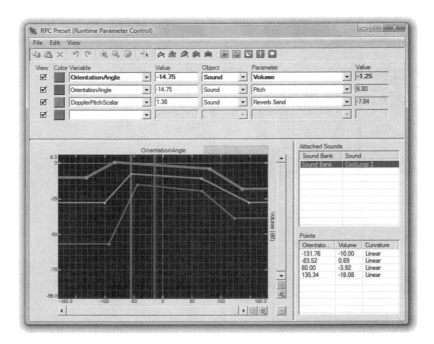

FIGURE 7.10   The RPC dialog box allows us to add new curves and nodes to manipulate the values.

We can pause and resume all sounds in a category. This means that we could organize our sounds in such a way that the sounds used in our playing state can all be assigned to a category we define. Then through the code we can pause that category, and it will pause all sounds that are playing. This way, we do not need to worry ourselves with making sure all the sounds stop when someone pauses the game. When we associate a sound with the Music category, the Xbox 360 can mute that sound and replace it with the playlist the gamer has his or her console playing at the time. This is a really nice feature because no matter how good our soundtrack is, at some point gamers will most likely want to play our games with their own music in the background.

Updating Our Input Handler

Before we dig into the code to utilize the XACT project we just created, let's back up a minute and take another look at our input handler. In particular we want to extend our keyboard and gamepad functionality. Currently, if we try to trigger any event with a key press or a button push, we will get the event kicked off several times. This is because for every frame we are checking in our Update method, if a key is pressed for a fraction of a second the method will return true for many frames. We already know how to solve the problem because we did it with our Mouse class. We stored the old state and compared it to the new state to see what has changed. We need to do the same thing here. With the mouse code, we did it inside the demo code. However, we want this to be done inside the library so our game and demo code do not need to be concerned with the gory details. We will not be updating the mouse code, but that would be an excellent exercise to go through once you are done with the chapter.

To get started, open up the InputHandler.cs code file inside of the XELibrary project. The code for our updated InputHandler.cs file is shown in Listing 7.1. We are not going to dive too deeply into the code in this chapter (this is devoted to sound after all), but we are going to quickly examine what has been modified.

LISTING 7.1   InputHandler.cs

```
using System;
using System.Collections.Generic;
using Microsoft.Xna.Framework;
using Microsoft.Xna.Framework.Input;

namespace XELibrary
{
    public interface IInputHandler
    {
        KeyboardHandler KeyboardState { get; }

        GamePadState[] GamePads { get; }
        ButtonHandler ButtonHandler { get; }

#if !XBOX360
        MouseState MouseState { get; }
        MouseState PreviousMouseState { get; }
#endif
    };

    public class InputHandler
        : Microsoft.Xna.Framework.GameComponent, IInputHandler
    {

        private KeyboardHandler keyboard;
        private ButtonHandler gamePadHandler = new ButtonHandler();

#if !XBOX360
        private MouseState mouseState;
        private MouseState prevMouseState;
#endif

        public InputHandler(Game game)
            : base(game)
```

```csharp
        {
            // TODO: Construct any child components here
            game.Services.AddService(typeof(IInputHandler), this);

            //initialize our member fields
            keyboard = new KeyboardHandler();

#if !XBOX360
            Game.IsMouseVisible = true;
            prevMouseState = Mouse.GetState();
#endif
        }

        public override void Initialize()
        {
            base.Initialize();
        }

        public override void Update(GameTime gameTime)
        {
            keyboard.Update();

            gamePadHandler.Update();

            if (keyboard.IsKeyDown(Keys.Escape))
                Game.Exit();

            if (gamePadHandler.WasButtonPressed(0, ButtonType.Back))
                Game.Exit();

#if !XBOX360
            //Set our previous state
            prevMouseState = mouseState;
            //Get our new state
            mouseState = Mouse.GetState();
#endif

            base.Update(gameTime);
        }

        #region IInputHandler Members
        public KeyboardHandler KeyboardState
        {
            get { return (keyboard); }
        }
```

```
        public ButtonHandler ButtonHandler
        {
            get { return (gamePadHandler); }
        }

        public GamePadState[] GamePads
        {
            get { return(gamePadHandler.GamePads); }
        }

#if !XBOX360
        public MouseState MouseState
        {
            get { return(mouseState); }
        }

        public MouseState PreviousMouseState
        {
            get { return(prevMouseState); }
        }
#endif
        #endregion
    }

    public class ButtonHandler
    {
        private GamePadState[] prevGamePadsState = new GamePadState[4];
        private GamePadState[] gamePadsState = new GamePadState[4];

        public GamePadState[] GamePads
        {
            get
            {
                return (gamePadsState);
            }
        }

        public ButtonHandler()
        {
            prevGamePadsState[0] = GamePad.GetState(PlayerIndex.One);
            prevGamePadsState[1] = GamePad.GetState(PlayerIndex.Two);
            prevGamePadsState[2] = GamePad.GetState(PlayerIndex.Three);
            prevGamePadsState[3] = GamePad.GetState(PlayerIndex.Four);
        }

        public void Update()
```

```
    {
        //set our previous state to our new state
        prevGamePadsState[0] = gamePadsState[0];
        prevGamePadsState[1] = gamePadsState[1];
        prevGamePadsState[2] = gamePadsState[2];
        prevGamePadsState[3] = gamePadsState[3];

        //get our new state
        //gamePadsState = GamePad.State .GetState();
        gamePadsState[0] = GamePad.GetState(PlayerIndex.One);
        gamePadsState[1] = GamePad.GetState(PlayerIndex.Two);
        gamePadsState[2] = GamePad.GetState(PlayerIndex.Three);
        gamePadsState[3] = GamePad.GetState(PlayerIndex.Four);
    }

    public bool WasButtonPressed(int playerIndex,
                                 Buttons button)
    {
        return (gamePadsState[playerIndex].IsButtonDown(button) &&
            prevGamePadsState[playerIndex].IsButtonUp(button));
    }
}

public class KeyboardHandler
{
    private KeyboardState prevKeyboardState;
    private KeyboardState keyboardState;

    public KeyboardHandler()
    {
        prevKeyboardState = Keyboard.GetState();
    }

    public bool IsKeyDown(Keys key)
    {
        return (keyboardState.IsKeyDown(key));
    }

    public bool IsHoldingKey(Keys key)
    {
        return(keyboardState.IsKeyDown(key) &&
            prevKeyboardState.IsKeyDown(key));
    }

    public bool WasKeyPressed(Keys key)
    {
```

```
        return(keyboardState.IsKeyDown(key) &&
            prevKeyboardState.IsKeyUp(key));
    }

    public bool HasReleasedKey(Keys key)
    {
        return(keyboardState.IsKeyUp(key) &&
            prevKeyboardState.IsKeyDown(key));
    }

    public void Update()
    {
        //set our previous state to our new state
        prevKeyboardState = keyboardState;

        //get our new state
        keyboardState = Keyboard.GetState();
    }
    }
}
```

The first thing to notice is that we added two more classes at the end of our file: KeyboardHandler and ButtonHandler. These objects each have an Update method that gets called by our main Update method inside InputHandler. The Update method stores the previous state and resets the new state. This is the key to it all. We simply check our new state against our old state to see if keys or buttons have been pressed or released. We have helper functions that our game code can call to check whether a key was pressed or a button was clicked. These helper functions just query the previous and new states of the appropriate input device and return a boolean value. With this implemented, we do not run into the issue of multiple events kicking off because the gamer is holding the button down. It also gives us a base from which to start working. We left our most current state available because we still need that for our triggers and D-pad. The D-pad could also be put into this handler because it is treated as a button, but that, along with wrapping up the mouse information, is not in the code. This should be a good starting point if either of these functions is needed, though.

Plugging In Our Sound Manager

Finally we can get to our sound manager code. We discussed XACT and how we can use it to create sound projects that our games can consume. We also extended our input handler code, and now we are ready to dive into the code that will allow us to play the sounds we set up in our XACT project.

To begin, we need to create a new game component code file inside our XELibrary called SoundManager.cs. The code for this class can be found in Listing 7.2.

LISTING 7.2   SoundManager.cs

```csharp
using System;
using System.Collections.Generic;
using Microsoft.Xna.Framework;
using Microsoft.Xna.Framework.Audio;

namespace XELibrary
{
    public class SoundManager : Microsoft.Xna.Framework.GameComponent
    {
        public bool RepeatPlayList = true;
        private AudioEngine engine;
        private WaveBank waveBank;
        private SoundBank soundBank;

        private Dictionary<string, Cue> cues = new Dictionary<string, Cue>();
        private Dictionary<string, AudioCategory> categories =
            new Dictionary<string, AudioCategory>();

        private string[] playList;
        private int currentSong;
        private Cue currentlyPlaying;
        public SoundManager(Game game, string xactProjectName)
            : this(game, xactProjectName, xactProjectName)
        { }

        public SoundManager(Game game, string xactProjectName,
                            string xactFileName)
            : this(game, xactProjectName, xactFileName,
                game.Content.RootDirectory + @"Sounds\")
        { }

        public SoundManager(Game game, string xactProjectName,
                            string xactFileName, string contentPath)
            : base(game)
        {
            xactFileName = xactFileName.Replace(".xap", "");

            engine = new AudioEngine(contentPath + xactFileName + ".xgs");
            waveBank = new WaveBank(engine, contentPath + "Wave Bank.xwb");
            soundBank = new SoundBank(engine, contentPath + "Sound Bank.xsb");
        }

        public override void Initialize()
        {
```

```
        base.Initialize();
    }

    public override void Update(GameTime gameTime)
    {
        engine.Update();

        if (currentlyPlaying != null) //are we playing a list?
        {
            //check current cue to see if it is playing
            //if not, go to next cue in list
            if (!currentlyPlaying.IsPlaying)
            {
                currentSong++;

                if (currentSong == playList.Length)
                {
                    if (RepeatPlayList)
                        currentSong = 0;
                    else
                        StopPlayList();
                }
                //may have been set to null, if we finished our list
                if (currentlyPlaying != null)
                {
                    currentlyPlaying = soundBank.GetCue(
                        playList[currentSong]);
                    currentlyPlaying.Play();
                }
            }
        }

        base.Update(gameTime);
    }

    protected override void Dispose(bool disposing)
    {
        soundBank.Dispose();
        waveBank.Dispose();
        engine.Dispose();

        playList = null;
        currentlyPlaying = null;
        cues = null;
        soundBank = null;
        waveBank = null;
```

7

```
        engine = null;
        base.Dispose(disposing);        }

    public void SetGlobalVariable(string name, float amount)
    {
        engine.SetGlobalVariable(name, amount);
    }

    private void CheckCategory(string categoryName)
    {
        if (!categories.ContainsKey(categoryName))
            categories.Add(categoryName, engine.GetCategory(categoryName));
    }

    public void SetVolume(string categoryName, float volumeAmount)
    {
        CheckCategory(categoryName);

        categories[categoryName].SetVolume(volumeAmount);        }

    public void PauseCategory(string categoryName)
    {
        CheckCategory(categoryName);

        categories[categoryName].Pause();
    }

    public void ResumeCategory(string categoryName)
    {
        CheckCategory(categoryName);

        categories[categoryName].Resume();
    }

    public bool IsPlaying(string cueName)
    {
        if (cues.ContainsKey(cueName))
            return (cues[cueName].IsPlaying);

        return (false);
    }

    public void Play(string cueName)
    {
        Cue prevCue = null;
```

```
    if (!cues.ContainsKey(cueName))
        cues.Add(cueName, soundBank.GetCue(cueName));
    else
    {
        //store our cue if we were playing
        if (cues[cueName].IsPlaying)
            prevCue = cues[cueName];

        cues[cueName] = soundBank.GetCue(cueName);
    }

    //if we weren't playing, set previous to our current cue name
    if (prevCue == null)
        prevCue = cues[cueName];
    try
    {
        cues[cueName].Play();
    }
    catch (InstancePlayLimitException)
    {
        //hit limit exception, set our cue to the previous
        //and let's stop it and then start it up again ...
        cues[cueName] = prevCue;

        if (cues[cueName].IsPlaying)
            cues[cueName].Stop(AudioStopOptions.AsAuthored);

        Toggle(cueName);
    }
}

public void Pause(string cueName)
{
    if (cues.ContainsKey(cueName))
        cues[cueName].Pause();
}

public void Resume(string cueName)
{
    if (cues.ContainsKey(cueName))
        cues[cueName].Resume();
}

public void Toggle(string cueName)          {
    if (cues.ContainsKey(cueName))
    {
```

```
            Cue cue = cues[cueName];

            if (cue.IsPaused)
            {
                cue.Resume();
            }
            else if (cue.IsPlaying)
            {
                cue.Pause();
            }
            else //played but stopped
            {
                //need to reget cue if stopped
                Play(cueName);
            }
        }
        else //never played, need to reget cue
            Play(cueName);
    }

    public void StopAll()
    {
        foreach (Cue cue in cues.Values)
            cue.Stop(AudioStopOptions.Immediate);
    }

    public void Stop(string cueName)
    {
        if (cues.ContainsKey(cueName))
            cues[cueName].Stop(AudioStopOptions.Immediate);
        cues.Remove(cueName);
    }

    public void StartPlayList(string[] playList)
    {
        StartPlayList(playList, 0);
    }

    public void StartPlayList(string[] playList, int startIndex)
    {
        if (playList.Length == 0)
            return;

        this.playList = playList;
        if (startIndex > playList.Length)
            startIndex = 0;
```

```
        StartPlayList(startIndex);
    }

    public void StartPlayList(int startIndex)
    {
        if (playList.Length == 0)
            return;

        currentSong = startIndex;
        currentlyPlaying = soundBank.GetCue(playList[currentSong]);
        currentlyPlaying.Play();
    }

    public void StopPlayList()
    {
        if (currentlyPlaying != null)
        {
            currentlyPlaying.Stop(AudioStopOptions.Immediate);
            currentlyPlaying = null;
        }
    }

    }
}
```

The sound manager can play playlists. The game can simply call a list of cues to be played, and the sound manager will continue to loop through the list until the game tells it not to. The sound manager allows us to set global variables so we can modify item cues that had an RPC associated with them. We can play, pause, and stop any cue in our sound manager as well.

This library component assumes that the name of the XACT project is the same name as the file. It also assumes that there is only one sound bank and one wave bank and that they keep their default names. This is handled in the constructor if there is a need to change the functionality. The library component assumes the location of the XACT project file is in the Sounds\ folder of the Content project, but that can be changed by calling the appropriate constructor.

During our Update method, we call the sound engine's Update method because it needs to perform tasks every so often, such as buffering sounds. During our Update call we also handle all the logic to determine whether we are playing a playlist and, if so, whether it is actually playing or we need to advance to the next song. Of course, a playlist does not need to be only music.

We expose functionality that allows us to process actions on categories. This way, we can set up our sound effects in one category (such as Default) and our music in another category (such as Music) and apply different sound volumes to each one differently through a user interface we display to gamers. Perhaps they do not like their music too loud but like the sound effects really loud. With the sounds associated with different categories, we can use the code in this class to pause, resume, stop, and even change the volume on an entire category at one time. This means all the sounds in that category can be altered with one call instead of many calls, one for each sound we had individually.

We store our list of categories and cues in a dictionary for easy access. This way, we are not constantly instantiating new objects. Most of the time sounds will last the entire life of the game (or at least the current level), so it makes sense to store the data this way.

Creating a Sound Demo

Now we need to add in another Windows game project to our XELibrary solution. We'll name this new project SoundDemo. We can also set up our solution for our Xbox 360 project if we want to test it on the console. Now we need to make sure our game is referencing the XELibrary project.

Once we have our XELibrary referenced correctly, we can start writing code to test out our new sound class (and updated input class). We need to use the library's namespace at the top of our game class as follows:

```
using XELibrary;
```

We should also add a Sounds folder to our demo's Content project. We can then paste our XACT project file into our Sounds folder. The wave files should be put in the folder but do not need to be included in the project. When we compile our code later, the Content Pipeline will find all the waves from the wave bank and wrap them into a wave bank .xwb file. It also creates a sound bank .xsb file, whereas the audio engine is stored in Chapter7.xgs (because that is what we had as our XACT project name).

We will now add in our Input Handler game component so we can kick off sound events based on our input. We need to declare our private member field to hold the component as well as add it to our game's components collection:

```
private InputHandler input;
private SoundManager sound;

public Game1()
{
    graphics = new GraphicsDeviceManager(this);
    Content.RootDirectory = "Content";

    input = new InputHandler(this);
    Components.Add(input);

    sound = new SoundManager(this, "Chapter7");
    Components.Add(sound);
}
```

We passed in "Chapter7" to our constructor because that is what we called our XACT project. Next we need to set up our playlist. We can do this inside our Initialize method because we added the sound component in our constructor:

```
string[] playList = { "Song1", "Song2", "Song3" };
sound.StartPlayList(playList);
```

The code tells our sound manager we will be playing three different songs. The library will keep checking to see if they are playing. The library will automatically play the next song and then loop back to the beginning song when it reaches the end of the list.

Now we can populate our Update method to check for our input to play all the sounds and songs we set up in XACT. We need to add the following code to our Update method:

```
if (input.KeyboardState.WasKeyPressed(Keys.D1) ||
        input.ButtonHandler.WasButtonPressed(0, InputHandler.ButtonType.A))
    sound.Play("gunshot");
if (input.KeyboardState.WasKeyPressed(Keys.D2) ||
        input.ButtonHandler.WasButtonPressed(0, InputHandler.ButtonType.B))
    sound.Play("hit");
if (input.KeyboardState.WasKeyPressed(Keys.D3) ||
        input.ButtonHandler.WasButtonPressed(0,
            InputHandler.ButtonType.LeftShoulder))
    sound.Play("attention");
if (input.KeyboardState.WasKeyPressed(Keys.D4) ||
        input.ButtonHandler.WasButtonPressed(0,
            InputHandler.ButtonType.LeftStick))
    sound.Play("explosion");
if (input.KeyboardState.WasKeyPressed(Keys.D5) ||
        input.ButtonHandler.WasButtonPressed(0,
            InputHandler.ButtonType.RightShoulder))
    sound.Play("bullet");
if (input.KeyboardState.WasKeyPressed(Keys.D6) ||
        input.ButtonHandler.WasButtonPressed(0,
            InputHandler.ButtonType.RightStick))
    sound.Play("crash");
if (input.KeyboardState.WasKeyPressed(Keys.D7) ||
        input.ButtonHandler.WasButtonPressed(0, InputHandler.ButtonType.X))
    sound.Play("complex");
if (input.KeyboardState.WasKeyPressed(Keys.D8) ||
        input.ButtonHandler.WasButtonPressed(0, InputHandler.ButtonType.Y))
    sound.Toggle("CoolLoop");
if (input.KeyboardState.WasKeyPressed(Keys.D9) ||
        input.ButtonHandler.WasButtonPressed(0,
```

7

```
            InputHandler.ButtonType.LeftShoulder))
    sound.Toggle("CoolLoop 2");

if (input.KeyboardState.WasKeyPressed(Keys.P) ¦¦
    input.ButtonHandler.WasButtonPressed(0, InputHandler.ButtonType.Start))
{
    sound.Toggle("CoolLoop");
}

if (input.KeyboardState.WasKeyPressed(Keys.S) ¦¦
        (input.GamePads[0].Triggers.Right > 0))
    sound.StopPlayList();
```

We are simply checking to see if different keys were pressed or different buttons were pushed. Based on those results, we play different cues that we set up in the XACT project. A good exercise would be to run the demo and then reread the section of this chapter where we set up all these sounds and see if they do what you expect when you press the appropriate key or button. In particular, you can press the B button or number 2 key repeatedly and see that the "hit" cue is queuing up, as we told it to limit itself to only playing once and to queue failed requests. You can also click down on the right thumb stick or press the number 6 key to hear our crash. If the playlist is hindering your hearing of the sounds, you can stop it by pressing the S key or pushing on the right trigger. The check to exit the game the template added should be removed from the Update method because that is already taken care of by our InputHandler.

The final piece of code for our sound demo is where we can set a global variable for the RPC we set up as well as the volume of our default category cues. To start, we need to add two more private member fields:

```
private float currentVolume = 0.5f;
private float value = 0;
```

Now we can finish up our Update method with the following code:

```
if (input.KeyboardState.IsHoldingKey(Keys.Up) ¦¦
        input.GamePads[0].DPad.Up == ButtonState.Pressed)
    currentVolume += 0.05f;
if (input.KeyboardState.IsHoldingKey(Keys.Down) ¦¦
        input.GamePads[0].DPad.Down == ButtonState.Pressed)
    currentVolume -= 0.05f;

currentVolume = MathHelper.Clamp(currentVolume, 0.0f, 1.0f);
sound.SetVolume("Default", currentVolume);

if (input.KeyboardState.WasKeyPressed(Keys.NumPad1))
```

```
        value = 5000;
    if (input.KeyboardState.WasKeyPressed(Keys.NumPad2))
        value = 25000;
    if (input.KeyboardState.WasKeyPressed(Keys.NumPad3))
        value = 30000;
    if (input.KeyboardState.WasKeyPressed(Keys.NumPad4))
        value = 40000;
    if (input.KeyboardState.WasKeyPressed(Keys.NumPad5))
        value = 50000; if (input.KeyboardState.WasKeyPressed(Keys.NumPad6))
        value = 60000;
    if (input.KeyboardState.WasKeyPressed(Keys.NumPad7))
        value = 70000;
    if (input.KeyboardState.WasKeyPressed(Keys.NumPad8))
        value = 80000;
    if (input.KeyboardState.WasKeyPressed(Keys.NumPad9))
        value = 90000;
    if (input.KeyboardState.WasKeyPressed(Keys.NumPad0))
        value = 100000;

    if (input.GamePads[0].Triggers.Left > 0)
        value = input.GamePads[0].Triggers.Left * 100000;

sound.SetGlobalVariable("SpeedOfSound", value);
```

This completes our sound demo code. Now if we run it and press the up- and down-arrow keys or the D-pad, we can hear the volume of the sounds associated with our "Default" category go up and down. We clamp our value between 0 and 1 because that is what the engine takes to set the volume. This is an example of how checking for the input state without considering the previous state can get us into trouble. The code will turn the volume up and down very quickly because it is getting back a true on every call every frame. Not only does this code let us test the volume settings, it also lets us set a global variable. In the XACT project, if we used SpeedOfSound as one of the parameters when setting up our curve, we can modify the way the cue sounds here at runtime. That is pretty powerful.

Summary

We covered a lot in this chapter. We discussed how to use the XACT tool. You saw that you could set up categories for sounds, and you learned to set up sounds by first adding waves to the project. We discussed variations at the sound level and the cue level. We went through several examples to set up those variants. We then used those variants in a demo we made, and we managed some of the sounds via our code.

We also fixed up our input handler code because we needed it to effectively write a demo to test our sounds. We discussed the new SoundManager class we added to our library. You saw how it handles the references to the cues so we can just pass in a string and not have to clutter up our game code.

You saw how the Content Pipeline can read in an XACT file to generate files that can be consumed on the Xbox 360 and Windows. The Content Pipeline is a great way to do things. In the next chapter, we will look at extending the pipeline so we can bring in our own file types or process existing file types in a different way.

CHAPTER 8

Extending the Content Pipeline

You have learned how to use the Content Pipeline out of the box and have seen how easy it is to load objects and consume them inside our game code. Sometimes, though, we need more. Sometimes we need to load in content that is custom to our game engine or content that we care about that others do not. We might just need to get a little more data about an object than the default processors obtain. In these cases, we need to extend the Content Pipeline to be able to access our content at runtime with ease. Running everything through the Content Pipeline makes our resources accessible on the Xbox 360 platform. We cannot simply copy files to read from onto the console because everything needs to be compiled up front. We spend this chapter discussing how to extend the pipeline.

Creating a Skybox

We want to add a skybox to our code. We are going to create a project that will contain the content, content processor, and content compiler. After creating this project, we will create another file inside our XELibrary to read the skybox data. Finally, we will create a demo that utilizes the XELibrary's Skybox Content Reader, which the Content Manager uses to consume the skybox.

Before we create the project, we should first examine a skybox and its purpose in games. A skybox keeps us from having to create complex geometry for objects that are very far away. For example, we do not need to create a sun or a moon or some distant city when we use a skybox. We create six textures that we put into our cube. Although there are skybox models we could use, for this chapter we are going to build our own skybox. It is simply a cube, and we already have the code in place to create a cube. You know how to create rectangles and how to position them where you want them. We can create six rectangles that we use as our skybox. When a texture is applied to each side of the skybox, we get the effect that our world is much bigger than it is. Plus, it looks much better than the cornflower blue backdrop we currently have!

Creating the Skybox Content Object

To start, let's create a new Content Pipeline Extension Library project called SkyboxPipeline. There is no need to create an Xbox 360 version of the project because this will only be run on the PC. This SkyboxPipeline project will have three files. The first file we need to add to this project is a new Class file called SkyboxContent.cs code file, shown in Listing 8.1.

LISTING 8.1   SkyboxContent.cs Holds the Design Time Class of Our Skybox

```
using System;
using Microsoft.Xna.Framework.Content.Pipeline.Processors;
using Microsoft.Xna.Framework.Content.Pipeline.Graphics;

namespace SkyboxPipeline
{
    public class SkyboxContent
    {
        public ModelContent Model;
        public Texture2DContent Texture;
    }
}
```

The SkyboxContent object holds our skybox data at design time. Because we created this project as a Content Pipeline extension, a reference to Microsoft.Xna.Framework. Content.Pipeline was added to our project.

Creating the Skybox Processor

The SkyboxContent object is utilized by the processor we will create next. When we created the project, the ContentProcessor1.cs file was added. We can rename the file SkyboxProcessor.cs. The code for this class is shown in Listing 8.2.

LISTING 8.2   SkyboxProcessor.cs Processes the Data It Gets as Input from the Content Pipeline

```
using System;
using System.Collections.Generic;
using Microsoft.Xna.Framework;
using Microsoft.Xna.Framework.Content.Pipeline;
using Microsoft.Xna.Framework.Content.Pipeline.Graphics;
```

```csharp
using Microsoft.Xna.Framework.Content.Pipeline.Processors;
using TInput = Microsoft.Xna.Framework.Content.Pipeline.Graphics.Texture2DContent;
using TOutput = SkyboxPipeline.SkyboxContent;

namespace SkyboxPipeline
{
    [ContentProcessor(DisplayName = "SkyboxProcessor")]
    public class SkyboxProcessor : ContentProcessor<TInput, TOutput>
    {
        private int width = 1024;
        private int height = 512;
        private int cellSize = 256;

        public override TOutput Process(TInput input,➥
        ContentProcessorContext context)
        {
            MeshBuilder builder = MeshBuilder.StartMesh("XESkybox");

            CreatePositions(ref builder);

            AddVerticesInformation(ref builder);

            // Finish making the mesh
            MeshContent skyboxMesh = builder.FinishMesh();

            // Create the output object.
            SkyboxContent skybox = new SkyboxContent();

            //Compile the mesh we just built through the default ModelProcessor
            skybox.Model = context.Convert<MeshContent, ModelContent>(
                skyboxMesh, "ModelProcessor");

            skybox.Texture = input;

            return skybox;
        }

        private void CreatePositions(ref MeshBuilder builder)
        {
            Vector3 position;

            //————near / back plane  (behind the camera)
            //top left
            position = new Vector3(-1, 1, 1);
            builder.CreatePosition(position); //0
```

```
        //bottom right
        position = new Vector3(1, -1, 1);
        builder.CreatePosition(position); //1

        //bottom left
        position = new Vector3(-1, -1, 1);
        builder.CreatePosition(position); //2

        //top right
        position = new Vector3(1, 1, 1);
        builder.CreatePosition(position); //3

        //————far / front plane (in front of camera)
        //top left
        position = new Vector3(-1, 1, -1); //4
        builder.CreatePosition(position);

        //bottom right
        position = new Vector3(1, -1, -1); //5
        builder.CreatePosition(position);

        //bottom left
        position = new Vector3(-1, -1, -1); //6
        builder.CreatePosition(position);

        //top right
        position = new Vector3(1, 1, -1); //7
        builder.CreatePosition(position);
    }

    private Vector2 UV(int u, int v, Vector2 cellIndex)
    {
        return(new Vector2((cellSize * (cellIndex.X + u) / width),
            (cellSize * (cellIndex.Y + v) / height)));
    }

    private void AddVerticesInformation(ref MeshBuilder builder)
    {
        //texture locations:
        //F,R,B,L
        //U,D

        //Front
        Vector2 fi = new Vector2(0, 0); //cell 0, row 0

        //Right
```

```
Vector2 ri = new Vector2(1, 0); //cell 1, row 0

//Back
Vector2 bi = new Vector2(2, 0); //cell 2, row 0

//Left
Vector2 li = new Vector2(3, 0); //cell 3, row 0

//Upward (Top)
Vector2 ui = new Vector2(0, 1); //cell 0, row 1

//Downward (Bottom)
Vector2 di = new Vector2(1, 1); //cell 1, row 1

int texCoordChannel = builder.CreateVertexChannel<Vector2>
    (VertexChannelNames.TextureCoordinate(0));

//————front plane first column, first row

//bottom triangle of front plane
builder.SetVertexChannelData(texCoordChannel, UV(0, 0, fi));
builder.AddTriangleVertex(4); //-1,1,-1
builder.SetVertexChannelData(texCoordChannel, UV(1, 1, fi));
builder.AddTriangleVertex(5); //1,-1,-1
builder.SetVertexChannelData(texCoordChannel, UV(0, 1, fi));
builder.AddTriangleVertex(6); //-1,-1,-1

//top triangle of front plane
builder.SetVertexChannelData(texCoordChannel, UV(0, 0, fi));
builder.AddTriangleVertex(4); //-1,1,-1
builder.SetVertexChannelData(texCoordChannel, UV(1, 0, fi));
builder.AddTriangleVertex(7); //1,1,-1
builder.SetVertexChannelData(texCoordChannel, UV(1, 1, fi));
builder.AddTriangleVertex(5); //1,-1,-1

//————right plane
builder.SetVertexChannelData(texCoordChannel, UV(1, 0, ri));
builder.AddTriangleVertex(3);
builder.SetVertexChannelData(texCoordChannel, UV(1, 1, ri));
builder.AddTriangleVertex(1);
builder.SetVertexChannelData(texCoordChannel, UV(0, 1, ri));
builder.AddTriangleVertex(5);

builder.SetVertexChannelData(texCoordChannel, UV(1, 0, ri));
builder.AddTriangleVertex(3);
builder.SetVertexChannelData(texCoordChannel, UV(0, 1, ri));
```

```
builder.AddTriangleVertex(5);
builder.SetVertexChannelData(texCoordChannel, UV(0, 0, ri));
builder.AddTriangleVertex(7);

//————back pane //3rd column, first row
//bottom triangle of back plane
builder.SetVertexChannelData(texCoordChannel, UV(1, 1, bi)); //1,1
builder.AddTriangleVertex(2); //-1,-1,1
builder.SetVertexChannelData(texCoordChannel, UV(0, 1, bi)); //0,1
builder.AddTriangleVertex(1); //1,-1,1
builder.SetVertexChannelData(texCoordChannel, UV(1, 0, bi)); //1,0
builder.AddTriangleVertex(0); //-1,1,1

//top triangle of back plane
builder.SetVertexChannelData(texCoordChannel, UV(0, 1, bi)); //0,1
builder.AddTriangleVertex(1); //1,-1,1
builder.SetVertexChannelData(texCoordChannel, UV(0, 0, bi)); //0,0
builder.AddTriangleVertex(3); //1,1,1
builder.SetVertexChannelData(texCoordChannel, UV(1, 0, bi)); //1,0
builder.AddTriangleVertex(0); //-1,1,1

//————left plane
builder.SetVertexChannelData(texCoordChannel, UV(1, 1, li));
builder.AddTriangleVertex(6);
builder.SetVertexChannelData(texCoordChannel, UV(0, 1, li));
builder.AddTriangleVertex(2);
builder.SetVertexChannelData(texCoordChannel, UV(0, 0, li));
builder.AddTriangleVertex(0);

builder.SetVertexChannelData(texCoordChannel, UV(1, 0, li));
builder.AddTriangleVertex(4);
builder.SetVertexChannelData(texCoordChannel, UV(1, 1, li));
builder.AddTriangleVertex(6);
builder.SetVertexChannelData(texCoordChannel, UV(0, 0, li));
builder.AddTriangleVertex(0);

//————upward (top) plane
builder.SetVertexChannelData(texCoordChannel, UV(1, 0, ui));
builder.AddTriangleVertex(3);
builder.SetVertexChannelData(texCoordChannel, UV(0, 1, ui));
builder.AddTriangleVertex(4);
builder.SetVertexChannelData(texCoordChannel, UV(0, 0, ui));
builder.AddTriangleVertex(0);

builder.SetVertexChannelData(texCoordChannel, UV(1, 0, ui));
builder.AddTriangleVertex(3);
```

```
      builder.SetVertexChannelData(texCoordChannel, UV(1, 1, ui));
      builder.AddTriangleVertex(7);
      builder.SetVertexChannelData(texCoordChannel, UV(0, 1, ui));
      builder.AddTriangleVertex(4);

      //————downward (bottom) plane
      builder.SetVertexChannelData(texCoordChannel, UV(1, 0, di));
      builder.AddTriangleVertex(2);
      builder.SetVertexChannelData(texCoordChannel, UV(1, 1, di));
      builder.AddTriangleVertex(6);
      builder.SetVertexChannelData(texCoordChannel, UV(0, 0, di));
      builder.AddTriangleVertex(1);

      builder.SetVertexChannelData(texCoordChannel, UV(1, 1, di));
      builder.AddTriangleVertex(6);
      builder.SetVertexChannelData(texCoordChannel, UV(0, 1, di));
      builder.AddTriangleVertex(5);
      builder.SetVertexChannelData(texCoordChannel, UV(0, 0, di));
      builder.AddTriangleVertex(1);
    }
  }
}
```

The SkyboxProcessor contains a lot of code, but the vast majority of it is building and texturing our skybox. We can go ahead and create this file in our pipeline project now.

To begin we used the [ContentProcessor] attribute for our class so the Content Pipeline could determine which class to call when it needs to process a resource with our type. We pass in SkyboxProcessor as the DisplayName parameter of the attribute. This will show up in the property window. We inherit from the ContentProcessor class and are going to be taking a Texture2D as input and outputting our skybox content type. We actually tell it we are using TInput and TOutput, but those are simply references to the actual types. The use of TInput and TOutput is definitely optional. They are simply added in the template to help us.

In the Process method we take in two parameters: input and context. To create our skybox we are going to pass in a single texture in our game projects. The processor creates a new MeshBuilder object, which is a helper class that allows us to quickly create a mesh with vertices in any order we wish and then apply different vertex information for those vertices that can contain texture coordinates, normals, colors, and so on. For our purposes we will be storing the texture. We create the actual eight vertices of our skybox cube in the CreatePositions method. We are simply passing a vertex position into the CreatePosition method of the MeshBuilder method.

Next up is our call to AddVerticesInformation. This method contains the bulk of the code, but it is not doing anything fancy. It is simply creating triangles in the mesh by passing the vertices index values to the AddTriangleVertex method of the MeshBuilder object. These vertices need to be called in the correct order. You can think of this as build-ing the indices of the mesh. The idea is that we created our unique vertices (in CreatePositions), and although we could have stored the value CreatePosition returned to us, we know that it will return the next number, starting with 0. Instead of using up memory for the index being passed back, we just made a note in the comment next to that vertex so we could build our triangles.

Before we actually add a vertex to a triangle of our mesh, we pass in our vertex channel information. We created a vertex channel before we started creating triangles with the following code:

```
int texCoordChannel = builder.CreateVertexChannel<Vector2>
    (VertexChannelNames.TextureCoordinate(0));
```

We can have multiple vertex channels. Although we are only storing texture coordinates, we could store normals, binormals, tangents, weights, and colors. Because we could store all these different pieces of information, we need to tell the vertex channel which type of data we are storing. We then store an index to that particular channel. Once we have that channel index, we can call the SetVertexChannelData method for each triangle vertex we add. In fact, we must set the channel data for the builder before adding the vertex. If we had more than one vertex channel to apply to a vertex, we would call all of them in succession before finally calling the AddTriangleVertex method. The following code shows the order in which this needs to take place:

```
builder.SetVertexChannelData(texCoordChannel, UV(0, 0, fi));
builder.AddTriangleVertex(4);
```

SetVertexChannelData takes in the vertex channel ID followed by the appropriate data for that channel. When we set up the vertex channel to handle texture coordinates, we did so by passing the generic Vector2 because texture coordinates have an x and a y component. This means that the SetVertexChannelData for our texture coordinate channel is expect-ing a type of Vector2.

For this texture mapping code to make sense, we need to discuss how the texture asset we are passing into our demo or game needs to be laid out. Instead of requiring six different textures to create a skybox, we are requiring only one with each plane of the cube having a specific location inside the texture. The texture size is 1024×512 to keep with the power-of-two restriction most graphic cards make us live by. We put four textures on the top row and two textures on the bottom row of our 1024×512 texture. The top row will have the cube faces Front, Right, Back, and Left (in that order). The bottom row will have Up (Top) and Down (Bottom). For this discussion, *Front* actually refers to the "far" plane, or the plane the camera sees. *Back*, on the other hand, refers to the "near" plane, or the plane behind the camera.

If we have skyboxes in other formats, we can use a paint program to get them in this format. We can also use tools to generate skybox images and output them into this format or one we can easily work with. The great thing about this being an extension of the

Content Pipeline is that we have free reign over how we want to read in data and create content that our games can easily use. If we stick with the current single texture, it leaves part of the texture unused. We could utilize these two spots for something else. For example, we could create one or two cloud layers for our skybox, so instead of just rendering a cube, it would render a cube with two additional layers that could prove to be a nice effect. We could use the unused part of the texture for terrain generation by reading in the values from a grayscaled image in one of those cells to create a nice ground layout. We do not discuss terrain generation in this book, but many excellent articles are available on the Web about generating terrains.

Now that you know how the texture is laid out, we can discuss some of the details of applying the texture to the different panels of the cube. In the following code, we declare a variable to hold the index of the right panel (R) in the texture:

```
//Right
Vector2 ri = new Vector2(1, 0); //cell 1, row 0
```

We are storing 1,0 in a vector, signifying that the right panel's portion of the large texture is in the first cell in row zero (this is zero-based). In Chapter 4, "Creating 3D Objects," we discussed how to texture our rectangle (quad) by applying different u and v coordinates to the different vertices of the rectangle. We are using the exact same concept here. The only difference is that we have to take into account the fact that we are extracting multiple textures from the one texture. For example, to texture the right panel of our skybox using just one texture, we could simply tell the top-left vertex to use texture coordinates 0,0 and the bottom-right vertex to use texture coordinates 1,1. However, our right panel's texture is not the entire texture we have in memory; instead, it is from pixels 256,0 to 512,256. You can see this in Figure 8.1, where the right panel(R) texture is not grayed out.

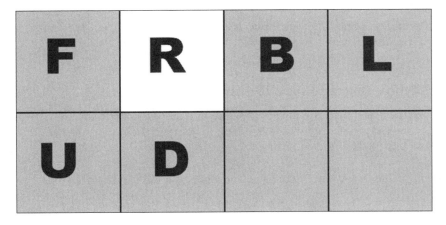

FIGURE 8.1   Our skybox texture is made up of six cells (Front, Right, Back, Left, Up, and Down).

To handle the offset issue, we create a UV method that takes in the typical 0 and 1 along with the index cell from which we need to get our updated u and v coordinates. The UV method that calculates our u and v values is shown here:

```
private Vector2 UV(int u, int v, Vector2 cellIndex)
{
    return(new Vector2((cellSize * (cellIndex.X + u) / width),
        (cellSize * (cellIndex.Y + v) / height)));
}
```

This method simply takes in the u and v coordinates we would normally map on a full texture along with the cell index we want to access in the texture. Then it returns the calculated u and v coordinates. Here, cellSize, width, and height are private member fields. We take the size of the cell, 256, and multiply that by the sum of the x value of our cell index and the u value passed in. We take that value and divide it by width to come up with the correct u position of the large texture. We do the same thing to get our v value. We pass those actual values to SetVertexChannelData so it will associate the right texture coordinates with that vertex.

After creating the Skybox vertices, setting up all the triangles needed, and applying our texture coordinates, we can finally save the mesh. We do this by calling the FinishMesh method on our MeshBuilder object, which returns a MeshContent type back to us. Conveniently, this is the type of object we need to pass to the default ModelProcessor to process our mesh (just as if we loaded a .X file through the Content Pipeline). This is done with the following code:

```
MeshContent skyboxMesh = builder.FinishMesh();
skybox.Model = context.Convert<MeshContent, ModelContent>(
    skyboxMesh, "ModelProcessor");
```

After setting our texture to the texture (our input) loaded to start this process, we return the skybox content and the compiler gets launched. We discuss the compiler in the next section.

Creating the Skybox Content Type Writer

This brings us to our third and final file for our pipeline project. We need to create another code file, named SkyboxContentTypeWriter.cs, to compile the skybox and write it to disk. The code for this file is found in Listing 8.3.

LISTING 8.3   SkyboxContentTypeWriter.cs Compiles and Writes Out the Content It Is Passed from the Processor

```
using System;
using System.Collections.Generic;
using Microsoft.Xna.Framework;
using Microsoft.Xna.Framework.Content.Pipeline.Graphics;
using Microsoft.Xna.Framework.Content.Pipeline.Processors;
```

```
using Microsoft.Xna.Framework.Content.Pipeline.Serialization.Compiler;

using TWrite = SkyboxPipeline.SkyboxContent;

namespace SkyboxPipeline
{
    [ContentTypeWriter]
    public class SkyboxWriter : ContentTypeWriter<TWrite>
    {
        protected override void Write(ContentWriter output, TWrite value)
        {
            output.WriteObject(value.Model);
            output.WriteObject(value.Texture);
        }

        public override string GetRuntimeType(TargetPlatform targetPlatform)
        {
            return "XELibrary.Skybox, " +
                "XELibrary, Version=1.0.0.0, Culture=neutral";
        }

        public override string GetRuntimeReader(TargetPlatform targetPlatform)
        {
            return "XELibrary.SkyboxReader, " +
                "XELibrary, Version=1.0.0.0, Culture=neutral";
        }
    }
}
```

We start off this class much like the last one in that we associate an attribute with it. This time we need to use the [ContentTypeWriter] attribute because it tells the Content Pipeline this is the compiler or writer class. We inherit from ContentTypeWriter with the generic type of SkyboxContent (which we created in the first file of this project). This way when the Content Pipeline gets the skybox content back from the processor, it knows where to send the data to be compiled.

We override the Write method and save our skybox as an .xnb file. The base class does all the heavy lifting, and all we need to do is write our object out. The next method, GetRuntimeType, tells the Content Pipeline the type of the skybox data that will be loaded at runtime. The last method, GetRuntimeReader, tells the Content Pipeline which object will be reading in and processing the .xnb data. The contents of these two methods are returning different classes inside of the same assembly. They do not need to reside in the same assembly, but it definitely makes sense in this case. We store the runtime type and runtime reader in a separate project. We do not add them to the pipeline project because the pipeline project is Windows-dependent, but our skybox type and reader object need to be platform-independent. We are going to set up these two classes (Skybox and

SkyboxReader) inside our XELibrary so our games and demos will already have access to our library. Plus, it makes sense to have our Skybox content reader in the same place.

Creating the Skybox Reader

Copy and open our Load3DObject project from Chapter 6, "Loading and Texturing 3D Objects." Then copy the latest XELibrary project from Chapter 7, "Sound and Music." When you open the Load3DObject solution, the XELibrary project should be inside this solution. We can now add a SkyboxReader.cs file to our XELibrary project. This file will contain both our Skybox type and our SkyboxReader type. We could have created separate files. If we had them in different assemblies, however, we would need to update the GetRuntimeType and GetRuntimeReader methods in our content writer. The code contained in SkyboxReader.cs can be found in Listing 8.4.

LISTING 8.4   SkyboxReader.cs Allows for Our Games to Read the Compiled .xnb Files Generated by the Content Pipeline

```
using System;
using System.Collections.Generic;
using Microsoft.Xna.Framework;
using Microsoft.Xna.Framework.Graphics;
using Microsoft.Xna.Framework.Content;

using TRead = XELibrary.Skybox;

namespace XELibrary
{
    public class SkyboxReader : ContentTypeReader<TRead>
    {
        protected override Skybox Read(ContentReader input, TRead existingInstance)
        {
            return new Skybox(input);
        }
    }

    public class Skybox
    {
        private Model skyboxModel;
        private Texture2D skyboxTexture;

        internal Skybox(ContentReader input)
        {
            skyboxModel = input.ReadObject<Model>();
            skyboxTexture = input.ReadObject<Texture2D>();
        }
```

```
public void Draw(Matrix view, Matrix projection, Matrix world)
{
    foreach (ModelMesh mesh in skyboxModel.Meshes)
    {
        foreach (BasicEffect be in mesh.Effects)
        {
            be.Projection = projection;
            be.View = view;
            be.World = world;
            be.Texture = skyboxTexture;
            be.TextureEnabled = true;
        }
        mesh.Draw(SaveStateMode.SaveState);
    }
}
}
}
```

Our SkyboxReader class is pretty small. It derives from the ContentTypeReader and uses a Skybox type that we will discuss in a moment. We override the Read method of this class, which gets passed in the skybox data as input as well as an existing instance of the object that we could write to if needed. We take the input and create an instance to our Skybox object by calling the internal constructor.

Inside the Skybox class we take the input that was just passed to us in our internal constructor and store the model embedded inside. We expose a Draw method that takes in view, projection, and world matrices as parameters. We then treat the model as if we loaded it from the pipeline (because we did) and set the basic effect on each mesh inside of the model to use the projection, view, and world matrices passed to the object. Finally, we actually draw the object onto the screen.

Using the Skybox

We have gone through a lot of work, but we are almost done. All we need to do now is actually use this Skybox object inside of our game. Let's open the Game1.cs file and add this private member field:

```
private Skybox skybox;
```

Now we need to add a skybox texture to our content folder. Let's create another subfolder under the Content project and call it Skyboxes. This is not required, but it might be helpful to remind us to change the processor type, which you will see how to do shortly. For now, we need to add an image to this Skyboxes subfolder. You can find one on this book's CD under the Load3DObject\Content\Skyboxes\skybox.tga inside of the Chapter 8 source code folder. Copy this texture and paste it into the Skyboxes folder through Solution Explorer. Inside the properties window we need to tell XNA Game Studio Express which importer and processor we want it to use when loading this content. We will leave the importer alone because it defaults to Texture – XNA Framework. See the sidebar "Creating a Custom Content Pipeline Importer."

We will change the `Content Processor` property, but before we do we need to tell our project about the custom processor. We do this by adding a reference to our Content project. We can browse to our pipeline project and then add the assembly located in the bin folder.

We will add this exact same assembly (under the x86 subfolder) to our Xbox 360 game project as well. This is because the assembly is only run on our PC when we are actually building our project. However, we do need to make sure our XELibrary_Xbox360 assembly has the same name as our Windows assembly. This is important because we have told the `SkyboxWriter` where to find the `Skybox` type and the `SkyboxReader` object. We told it XELibrary, not XELibrary_Xbox360.

Alternatively, we could have left the assembly names different and added a condition to our `GetRuntimeReader` method in our `SkyboxCompiler` class. We could have returned a different string depending on the target platform passed into that method.

Now that we have added our Content Pipeline extension to our game projects, we can select `SkyboxProcessor` from the list of content processors available in the property window when we have our skybox texture selected.

Creating a Custom Content Pipeline Importer

An example of setting up a custom importer follows:

```
[ContentImporterAttribute(".ext", DefaultProcessor = "SomeCustomProcessor")]
public class CustomImporter : ContentImporter<CustomType>
{
    public override CustomType Import(string filename,
        ContentImporterContext context)
    {
        byte[] data = File.ReadAllBytes(filename);

        return (new CustomType(data));
    }
}
```

This code is a theoretical importer that would be inside the pipeline project if we needed to import a type of file that the Content Pipeline could not handle. We could open up the file being loaded by the Content Pipeline and extract the data to our `CustomType` that could handle the data. This `CustomType` would also be used as the input inside our processor object (where we used `Texture2DContent`). We did not make our own importer because the XNA Framework's Content Pipeline can handle texture files automatically.

After declaring the private member field skybox, we need to load the skybox from our ContentManager by adding the following line inside of the `LoadContent` method:

```
skybox = Content.Load<Skybox>(@"Skyboxes\skybox");
```

Next we need to draw the skybox by adding the following two lines of code at the bottom of the `Draw` method, but right before the `base.Draw` call:

```
world = Matrix.CreateScale(5000.0f);
skybox.Draw(camera.View, camera.Projection, world);
```

We are finally ready to run our game. You should now see a star-filled background instead of the typical CornflowerBlue background. We have successfully built a Content Pipeline extension that takes a texture file and creates a skybox for us automatically. There is no limit to the things we can accomplish because of the Content Pipeline's opened architecture. We could create a level editor and save it in any format and then load it in at compile time to our game. We could write an importer for our favorite 3D model file type and work directly with the files. There are many opportunities to use the Content Pipeline. Taking a hit up front at build time instead of during runtime is always a good thing.

Content Pipeline Processor Parameters

A feature we did not discuss is the parameters for our pipeline processor. Parameters are simply properties in our processor class. These properties provide the ability to change the way the processor behaves at runtime (game or demo project's compile time).

For example, if we wanted to modify our Skybox processor to handle more than one type of texture, we could create a property with an enum type containing all the valid "types" of textures we allow. When the skybox pipeline is used in a project, the developer could decide which "type" of texture to use to generate his or her skybox. An XESkybox could signify the current layout we have coded for, like in Figure 8.1. More types could be created for textures that are created with other tools.

The Custom Model Effect example on the XNA Creators Club site (http://creators.xna. com/en-us/sample/custommodeleffect) includes a CubemapProcessor.cs file that takes a 2D texture and creates a cubemap from it. We do not discuss cubemaps in this book, but Shawn Hargreaves has a great article about cubemaps on his blog (http://blogs.msdn.com/ shawnhar/archive/2008/03/04/cubemaps-the-salt-of-computer-graphics.aspx).

So along with our XESkybox type, we could have a cubemap texture type. We will not walk through all the steps of doing this for the sake of time. However, we will look at the correct way to set up a property.

The Visual Studio IDE automatically picks up any public properties declared in the processor (unless they are decorated with the `Browsable` attribute with a false parameter). We can decorate our properties with other `System.ComponentModel` attributes, such as

`DisplayName`, `DefaultValue`, and `Description`. In order to set up our sample property, we could add the following code to the beginning of our `SkyboxProcessor` class:

```
public enum TextureType { XESkybox, Cubemap };


private TextureType type;

[DisplayName("Type of Skybox Texture")]
[DefaultValue(TextureType.XESkybox)]
[Description("Determines how to texture the skybox")]
public TextureType Type
{
    get { return (type); }
    set { type = value; }
}
```

The first thing we did was to create a new enum with our XESkybox and Cubemap values. We then created a private field and a public property to expose the field. We decorated the property with all three attributes we just discussed. The display name is what is shown in the properties window of the skybox texture asset. The description is displayed at the bottom of the properties window. The default value sets the initial value of the parameter in the properties window. This can be seen in Figure 8.2.

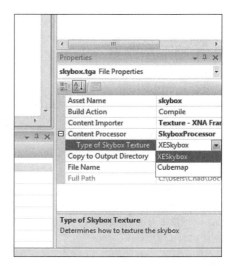

FIGURE 8.2   The property window displays the values set by the `System.ComponentModel` attributes: `DisplayName`, `DefaultValue`, and `Description`.

Not only can we add Content Pipeline processor parameters in our own pipeline extension, but also the standard Content Pipeline processors have their own parameters they expose. When working with a content asset, we simply need to expand the Content Processor node in the properties window to see the available parameters.

An excellent exercise would be to add the previous code and then modify the `AddVerticesInformation` and/or `UV` methods to handle multiple texture layouts for the skybox.

Debugging the Content Pipeline Extension

Extending the pipeline is excellent, but what happens when something goes awry? We can't exactly step through the code because this component is being loaded and run by the IDE...or can we? Fortunately, we can. We discuss how to do that in this section.

If you have the SkyboxPipeline solution opened, close it and then add the project to the Load3DDemo solution. This is not required to debug but does make it easier to ensure the IDE is using the latest changes to the pipeline processor. Alternatively, you could compile and change the standalone SkyboxPipeline solution and then compile the Load3DDemo. Again, it really is just personal preference.

The goal is to make sure our SkyboxPipeline code gets compiled before our game code. To do this we can either add the dependency directly to our game code or add it to our XELibrary, knowing that our game code already has a dependency on the XELibrary. We can right-click our XELibrary projects (one at a time) and select Project Dependencies. We can then add the check box to our SkyboxPipeline project. From now on, when we compile, the solution will compile the SkyboxPipeline first, followed by the XELibrary, and finally compile our Load3DObject project.

Now that the SkyboxPipeline project is open, we can add the following line of code at the top of the `Process` method inside of our `SkyboxProcessor` class:

```
System.Diagnostics.Debugger.Launch();
```

This will launch the debugger so we can step through the code to see what is happening. If we run our program with this line of coded added, the CLR debugger gets executed. We can then walk through the code like any other. We cannot edit and continue, just like on the Xbox 360. Regardless, being able to step through the code at runtime is very beneficial. We can set breakpoints wherever we need to. This is an excellent way to visualize exactly which pieces of code are calling other pieces and see the general flow of the Content Pipeline.

Summary

In this chapter, you learned how to extend the Content Pipeline to load data at design time or compile time instead of at runtime. You learned about skyboxes and actually created a pipeline component that makes a skybox based on a texture. We discussed the different components needed to extend the pipeline, including the content type of the object we are bringing into the Content Pipeline, the processor to process that object, the writer to compile that object, and finally (in a separate project) a reader to read the object and work with the content manager.

You also learned how to take this new skybox from our pipeline extension and use it in our demo. We discussed how to get the IDE to recognize the newly created Content Pipeline extension and how to set the content properties of our assets to use our importer and processor. We also discussed content pipeline processor parameters that are available in the standard processors as well as how we can create our own parameters for our content pipeline extensions. Finally, we discussed how to debug our Content Pipeline through the CLR debugger. There are many things we can do with a content processor that will make our job of writing games easier.

We take a break from 3D in the next part of the book, where we instead discuss how to use 2D in XNA. You will learn the basics of 2D, create some 2D effects, and then create a full 2D game.

PART IV

2D in XNA Game Studio

IN THIS PART

CHAPTER 9

2D Basics

The XNA Framework not only provides easy ways for us to utilize 3D objects, but it also provides excellent 2D support. We can achieve 2D inside of XNA in two ways. The first way is true 2D, which is sprite manipulation. We will discuss this kind of 2D. The other way involves setting up a 3D environment but locking the camera so that it is always looking at the same angle and cannot be moved—it is a 3D world with a stationary camera.

Whereas 3D uses models to display a scene, 2D uses images to create and animate a scene. The two dimensions are x and y—there is no z in 2D. It is very common to mix 2D and 3D into the same game. Scores, menus, and timers are examples of things that are typically 2D in a 3D world. Even if you are not interested in writing 2D games, the next three chapters will prove beneficial because we will discuss items that can be incorporated into your 3D masterpieces.

Sprite Batches

First you need to understand the term *sprite.* A sprite is an image. XNA represents sprites with a Texture2D object. We load them just like we load textures for our 3D applications because they are both images and get processed the same way. The difference is that in 3D we texture an object with the image, whereas in 2D we draw the image (or part of the image) on the screen. You saw an example of drawing part of an image in the last chapter. We applied different parts of an image to our skybox. The concept is the same, but the process is a little different. Really, we just pass in whole numbers instead of floats. Sprites are represented by x and y and, as such, have int values. It is impossible to draw something at pixel location 0.3, 0.3. If these types of values are passed in, XNA will perform some anti-aliasing to make it appear that the drawing is partially in the pixel area but the actual image location is rounded to a whole number.

We discussed the 3D coordinate system earlier, and now we'll discuss the 2D coordinate system. The top left of the screen is the origin of the screen (0,0). The x axis runs horizontally at the top of the screen, and the y axis runs vertically down the left side of the screen. The coordinate system is identical to how a texture's coordinate system is used. The difference is that instead of running from 0.0 to 1.0 like in a texture, the values run from 0 to the width and height of the screen. Therefore, if the resolution is 1024×768, the x values would run from 0,0 to 1023,0. The y values would run from 0,0 to 0,767. The x values run from left to right, and y runs from top to bottom. The bottom-right pixel of the screen would be 1023,767. This can be seen in Figure 9.1.

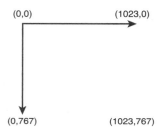

FIGURE 9.1   The 2D coordinate system origin is the top left of the screen.

Although the origin of the screen is 0,0, the origin of a sprite may or may not be. The default is 0,0, but the origin can be overridden if needed. When we draw sprites to the screen, we need to be aware of where the origin of the sprite is because when we pass in a coordinate (via a Vector2 type), XNA will draw the object to that location, starting with the origin of the sprite. Therefore, if we draw the sprite at location 100,200 and we do not touch the origin of the sprite, the top left of the sprite would get drawn in 100,200. If we wanted 100,200 to be the center, we would need to define the origin of our sprite, or we would need to offset our position manually. When we rotate our sprites, they will rotate around their origin. When we need to rotate our sprites, we will typically set the origin of the sprite to be its center. This way, the sprite will rotate around the center. Otherwise, the sprite would rotate around 0,0. The difference can be seen in Figure 9.2.

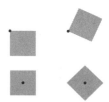

FIGURE 9.2   The origin of the sprite determines how the sprite will be rotated.

We can also scale a sprite. Scaling comes in three different flavors. We can give a number to scale the entire sprite by, or we can just scale one portion of the sprite. When we scale the entire sprite by a value, that value is stored as a float. The default scale used is 1.0, which does no scaling and displays the texture in its original size. The final way we can scale is to specify a source rectangle and then specify a destination rectangle. XNA can scale our source rectangle to fit into our destination rectangle.

Sprite batches are simply batches of sprites. Drawing a lot of sprites on the screen can put a load on the machine because we have to send a separate instruction to the graphics card each time we draw something to the screen. With a sprite batch, we have the ability to group our draw functions to occur within the same settings and send one draw call to the graphics card. When we create a `SpriteBatch` in our code, we can pass in the following values to its `Begin` method: `SpriteBlendMode`, `SpriteSortMode`, and `SaveStateMode`.

Sprite Blend Modes

The blend mode can be set to `AlphaBlend`, `Additive`, or `None`. The default blend mode is `AlphaBlend`. `AlphaBlend` does just that: It blends the sprite drawn (source) with the pixels it is being drawn on (destination) based on the alpha value of both. This includes transparency, but can be used to create different effects depending on the blend values we provide. We will cover overriding the blending values in the next chapter. `Additive` is another common blend mode that XNA provides support for automatically. It's used with our sprite batches. `Additive` will add the values of the colors together. This can be beneficial when dealing with fire and explosions. Finally, `None` simply does not set any blending modes. It just overwrites the destination area with the source sprite.

Alpha blending is used for normally translucent items such as glass, windows, water, and objects that fade in or out. Additive blending, on the other hand, is good to use when creating glowing objects such as explosions, sparks, and even magic effects. We will discuss these two blending modes and even more that are not directly supported by sprite batches in the next chapter.

Sprite Sort Modes

The sort mode determines how the different sprites that are drawn actually get displayed on the screen. In previous times, game developers had to take great care with how they displayed images to the screen to make sure the background did overwrite their foreground. They also needed to ensure that textures with alpha values rendered correctly. Although we still need to take care as we approach this task, a lot of the work has been done for us. We still need to be aware of how XNA handles this task for us so we can use it effectively and keep our frame rates high.

The sort mode can be set to `BackToFront`, `Deferred`, `FrontToBack`, `Immediate`, or `Texture`. The sort mode defaults to `Deferred` when we call `Begin` with no parameters. `Immediate` is faster than `Deferred`. `Immediate` works a little different from the rest of the sort modes. `Immediate` updates the graphics device settings immediately when the `Begin` method is called. Then as sprites are drawn to the screen, they immediately appear with no sorting. This is the fastest method available, but it requires us to sort the images the way we want them to be displayed. We draw the background images first and move up to the fore-ground. An interesting thing we can do with immediate mode is change our graphics device settings after Begin is called and before we actually draw our sprites to the screen. This will allow us to change how things are drawn dynamically. We will discuss this in more detail in the next chapter.

The rest of the sort modes will update the graphics device settings when End is called on the SpriteBatch instead of Begin. This means there is only one call out to the graphics device. The Deferred sort mode is like Immediate in that it does not do any sorting; it just defers talking to the graphics device until the end of the process.

The next two sort modes are BackToFront and FrontToBack. When we draw our sprites we can set the layer depth of those sprites. That value is a float between 0.0 and 1.0. The sprites will draw in this order for the two modes. BackToFront is typically used for trans-parent sprites, and FrontToBack is typically used for nontransparent (opaque) sprites.

Finally, we can pass in Texture as a sort mode to our sprite batch's Begin method. The Texture sort mode will check to see all the required draws and will sort them so that the graphics device does not need to change the texture for each draw, if possible. For example, if we have five sprites drawing and three of them use the same texture (could be different parts of the same texture), the graphics device is sent the texture and then the three draws. Then the other two draws occur with their textures. This can really help performance. However, we might need foreground and background images in the same texture. Sorting by texture alone is going to give us good performance, but we need to also sort by our layer depth. Fortunately, we can set up two sprite batches at the same time (as long as we are not using Immediate sort mode).

We could have our first batch sort by texture and our second batch sort by layer depth (BackToFront or FrontToBack). We can then draw our items, including the layer depth value. As long as we call End on our sprite batches in the appropriate order, our screen will display as we expect, and the performance will be good as well. Because the End method is what actually does the drawing, we need to make sure we call the sprites in order from background to foreground. It is best to draw our opaque sprites first in one batch and then our transparent sprites after that.

Save State Modes

As we complete different tasks inside of our Draw method, we might need to change settings on our graphics device. For example, we might want our depth buffer to be on when we are drawing certain items and off when drawing other items. When the sprite batch is executed (when Begin is called in Immediate sort mode; when End is called for all others), the graphics device will have the properties in Table 9.1 modified. We might want to save our properties so we can reset them when the sprite batch is done. This is impor-tant when mixing 2D and 3D. SaveStateMode.SaveState does exactly that. The other option is SaveStateMode.None, which is the default and does not save any state. It is quicker if we just reset the states ourselves, if needed, especially on the Xbox 360.

TABLE 9.1   The `SpriteBatch.Begin` Method Modifies These Graphics Device Properties

Property	Value
RenderState.CullMode	CullCounterClockwiseFace
RenderState.DepthBufferEnable	False
RenderState.AlphaBlendEnable	True
RenderState.AlphaTestEnable	True
RenderState.AlphaBlendOperation	Add
RenderState.SourceBlend	SourceAlpha
RenderState.DestinationBlend	InverseSourceAlpha
RenderState.SeparateAlphaBlendEnabled	False
RenderState.AlphaFunction	Greater
RenderState.ReferenceAlpha	0
SamplerStates[0].AddressU	Clamp
SamplerStates[0].AddressV	Clamp
SamplerStates[0].MagFilter	Linear
SamplerStates[0].MinFilter	Linear
SamplerStates[0].MipFilter	Linear
SamplerStates[0].MipMapLevelOfDetailBias	0
SamplerStates[0].MaxMipLevel	0

When we mix 2D and 3D together, we will definitely want to set the following properties before drawing our 3D content:

```
GraphicsDevice.RenderState.DepthBufferEnable = true;
GraphicsDevice.RenderState.AlphaBlendEnable = false;
GraphicsDevice.RenderState.AlphaTestEnable = false;
GraphicsDevice.SamplerStates[0].AddressU = TextureAddressMode.Wrap;
GraphicsDevice.SamplerStates[0].AddressV = TextureAddressMode.Wrap;
```

Practical Sprite Batches

Now that you have learned all about sprite batches, we can write some code to see how to make them work. We will make a splash screen we can display when our games load. We will create a demo that allows us retrieve multiple sprites stored in one texture. We will also write a small demo that allows us to quickly change the different blend modes as well as the sort modes so we can see what happens as we modify those settings. Finally, we will create a progress bar we can use later while we are waiting for our scenes to load.

Splash or Loading Screen Demo

We are going to create a demo called SplashScreenDemo, and we need to set up our solution to include our XELibrary project. We are going to make a small modification to our library in this demo, so we need to have the project opened as well. The purpose of this demo is to use our sprite batch knowledge to draw a sprite that covers the entire screen to simulate a splash or loading page.

Once we have our solution created we can jump right into our Game1.cs code. First, we want to define these private member fields:

```
private Texture2D splashScreen;
private Rectangle titleSafeArea;
private InputHandler input;
```

We need to make sure we have a using statement for our library and that we are referencing the library's assembly in our demo. Next up is our game's constructor, where we use the following code:

```
public Game1()
{
    graphics = new GraphicsDeviceManager(this);
    Content.RootDirectory = "Content";

    graphics.PreferredBackBufferWidth = 1280;
    graphics.PreferredBackBufferHeight = 720;

    input = new InputHandler(this);
    Components.Add(input);
}
```

We are setting the preferred backbuffer width and height. We are doing this because the image we are using for our splash screen is that size. This size is also considered to be HD (720p). "True HD" is 1920×1080 (1080p). Our Draw method allows the image to be put into any rectangle, but for this demo we will just force the aspect ratio to widescreen. We also add our input handler to our game's collection of game components.

Because we were just talking about the actual splash screen image, we should go ahead and add that to our project now. Let's create a Textures folder in the Content project for the sake of consistency. It is definitely not a requirement of XNA, and we could put all our assets in the Content project without any additional folders. We are trying to keep our solution tidy, though, and this is why we create these folders. You can find the image (called splashscreen.png) under this chapter's code folder on the CD in the SplashScreenDemo\Content\Textures folder.

After we have our image loaded, we can add the following code to our LoadContent method to initialize our title safe area and to load our splash screen:

```
titleSafeArea = GraphicsDevice.Viewport.TitleSafeArea;
splashScreen = Content.Load<Texture2D>(@"Textures\splashscreen");
```

After loading our sprite we can modify our Draw method with the following code over the TODO comment:

```
spriteBatch.Begin();
spriteBatch.Draw(splashScreen, titleSafeArea, Color.White);
spriteBatch.End();
```

We are simply calling the default Begin method on our sprite batch, which sets the blend mode to AlphaBlend, the sort mode to Deferred, and the save state mode to None. We pass in our texture asset, the rectangle on the screen we want to draw the sprite on, and the color we want to tint it with. We do not want to tint it, so we are passing in White. Finally, we call the End method of our sprite batch to actually draw our sprite on the screen. We can run the demo to see our splash screen.

Drawing Multiple Sprites from One Texture Demo

We need to set up another solution for this demo and do not need to reference the XELibrary this time. We can call this project MultiSpriteDemo. We are going to display multiple sprites from one texture.

Once we have our solution set up, we can open our game code file and add the following private member fields:

```
private Texture2D tiledSprite;
```

Once we have our sprite declared, we can initialize it inside of our LoadContent method:

```
tiledSprite = Content.Load<Texture2D>(@"Textures\shapes");
```

You can find the shapes.png file in the subfolder MultiSpriteDemo\Content\Textures of this chapter's folder on the CD. If we find ourselves always using the same content in different projects, we can add the asset files as links so we do not continue to eat up hard drive space. This also helps if multiple projects are accessing an asset that changes frequently. This is a 512×512 image that is broken up into four 256×256 cells (see Figure 9.3).

Finally, we need to add the following code to our Draw method to draw our sprites:

```
spriteBatch.Begin();
spriteBatch.Draw(tiledSprite, new Vector2(50, 50),
```

```
                              new Rectangle(0, 0, 256, 256), Color.White);
spriteBatch.Draw(tiledSprite, new Vector2(300, 50),
                              new Rectangle(256, 0, 256, 256), Color.White);
spriteBatch.Draw(tiledSprite, new Vector2(50, 300),
                              new Rectangle(0, 256, 256, 256), Color.White);
spriteBatch.Draw(tiledSprite, new Vector2(300, 300),
                              new Rectangle(256, 256, 256, 256), Color.White);
spriteBatch.Draw(tiledSprite, new Vector2(550, 50),
                              new Rectangle(0, 256, 256, 256), Color.White);
spriteBatch.Draw(tiledSprite, new Vector2(550, 300),
                              new Rectangle(0, 256, 256, 256), Color.White);
spriteBatch.End();
```

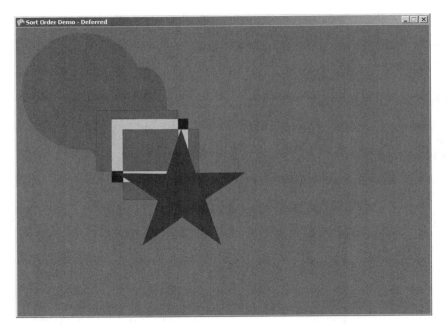

FIGURE 9.3   shapes.png.

We call Begin on our sprite batch to get started. After that we call the Draw method on our sprite batch six times. We could have just drawn each tile one time each, but we display one of the tiles (0, 256, 256, 256) three times. We can reuse the same source as many times as we want. We use the same tiledSprite texture in each call. The second parameter is where we want to draw our sprite on the screen. In the last demo we used a rectangle, but we are using a vector here. The third parameter is the rectangle we are going to use as our source from the texture we have loaded. In the past we have not used this parameter because we have used the entire image for our sprite. Because we are only using a portion of the image, we are telling the sprite batch which region we want to draw. Finally, we pass in Color.White again so there is no color modulation effect (tinting) in place.

The key to the preceding code is the third parameter, where we draw only a portion of our rectangle. We know each cell is a 256×256 block, so we pass in 0,0 for the first cell on the first row. We pass in 256,0 for the second cell on the first row. We pass in 0,256 for the first cell on the second row, and finally we pass in 256,256 for the second cell on the second row. We always pass in the same width and height of 256.

We drew each of the cells once and then the cell containing our star an additional two times. They are positioned on the screen based on the second parameter we passed in. Finally, we call the End method on the sprite batch so it will pass all the data to our graphics card. We can run the demo to see the different cells on our screen at the coordinates we specified as well as see the one texture split into multiple sprites on the screen.

Sprite Batch Blend and Sort Mode Demo

Now, we are going to update the project from the previous section (MultiSpriteDemo). We can just modify it or make a copy to modify. We will need to reference our XELibrary assembly. We do not need to include the project in the solution if we do not want to, and can just add a reference to our project. Of course, we need to add a using statement to the top of our code as well. The name of this project on the CD is SortOrderDemo.

We can start, as usual, by declaring the private member fields we will be using for this demo. In addition to what we already have, we need to declare the following:

```
private SpriteBlendMode blendMode = SpriteBlendMode.AlphaBlend;
private SpriteSortMode sortMode = SpriteSortMode.Deferred;
private InputHandler input;
```

We are using our input handler component in this demo, so we need to initialize that in our constructor and add it to our game's component collection:

```
input = new InputHandler(this);
Components.Add(input);
```

We created member fields earlier to hold our blend mode and our sort mode. We are going to set those modes based on input we get from our gamepad and keyboard. To do this, we will want to replace our Update method with the following code:

```
protected override void Update(GameTime gameTime)
{
    if (WasPressed(InputHandler.ButtonType.A, Keys.A))
        blendMode = SpriteBlendMode.AlphaBlend;
    if (WasPressed(InputHandler.ButtonType.B, Keys.B))
        blendMode = SpriteBlendMode.Additive;
    if (WasPressed(InputHandler.ButtonType.X, Keys.X))
        blendMode = SpriteBlendMode.None;

    if (WasPressed(InputHandler.ButtonType.LeftShoulder, Keys.D1))
        sortMode = SpriteSortMode.BackToFront;
```

```
    if (WasPressed(InputHandler.ButtonType.RightShoulder, Keys.D2))
        sortMode = SpriteSortMode.FrontToBack;
    if (WasPressed(InputHandler.ButtonType.LeftStick, Keys.D3))
        sortMode = SpriteSortMode.Deferred;
    if (WasPressed(InputHandler.ButtonType.RightStick, Keys.D4))
        sortMode = SpriteSortMode.Immediate;
    if (WasPressed(InputHandler.ButtonType.Y, Keys.D5))
        sortMode = SpriteSortMode.Texture;

    base.Update(gameTime);
}

private bool WasPressed(InputHandler.ButtonType buttonType, Keys keys)
{
    return(WasPressed(0, buttonType, keys));
}

private bool WasPressed(int playerIndex, InputHandler.ButtonType buttonType,
    Keys keys)
{
    if (input.ButtonHandler.WasButtonPressed(playerIndex, buttonType) ||
        input.KeyboardState.WasKeyPressed(keys))
        return (true);
    else
        return (false);
}
```

We added an overloaded method called WasPressed that takes in the player's index (or optionally defaults to 0 [player 1]) as well as the button we want to check along with the keys we want to check. The method simply calls our input handler to check if the buttons or keys were pressed. The Update method uses the WasPressed method to check for different buttons and keys and it sets our blend mode along with our sort mode as needed.

Finally, we can replace the contents of our Draw method with the following code:

```
graphics.GraphicsDevice.Clear(Color.CornflowerBlue);
spriteBatch.Begin(blendMode, sortMode, SaveStateMode.None);

//only affects the code if we are using the Immediate sort mode
graphics.GraphicsDevice.RenderState.DestinationBlend =
    Blend.InverseDestinationAlpha;

//draw heart
spriteBatch.Draw(tiledSprite, new Rectangle(64, 64, 256, 256),
    new Rectangle(256, 256, 256, 256), Color.White, 0, Vector2.Zero,
    SpriteEffects.None, .10f);
//draw circle
```

```
spriteBatch.Draw(tiledSprite, new Rectangle(0, 0, 256, 256),
    new Rectangle(256, 0, 256, 256), Color.White, 0, Vector2.Zero,
    SpriteEffects.None, .15f);

//draw shape
spriteBatch.Draw(tiledSprite, new Rectangle(128, 128, 256, 256),
    new Rectangle(0, 0, 256, 256), Color.White, 0, Vector2.Zero,
    SpriteEffects.None, .05f);

//draw star
spriteBatch.Draw(tiledSprite, new Rectangle(192, 192, 256, 256),
    new Rectangle(0, 256, 256, 256), Color.White, 0, Vector2.Zero,
    SpriteEffects.None, .01f);

Window.Title = "Sort Order Demo - " + blendMode.ToString() + " : " +
    sortMode.ToString();
spriteBatch.End();
base.Draw(gameTime);
```

The first thing we do in our Draw code after clearing our graphics device is call Begin on our sprite batch. We are passing in the member fields we used in our Update method. This way, we can control how our scene is rendered by pressing different buttons. We can see how the blending modes work and how the sorting mode works in real time.

After executing our Begin method, we call the sprite batch's Draw method to display our sprites. These draw methods are similar to our last demo. We used a different overload, which requires us to pass in a rectangle for our destination location instead of just a vector. We had to use this one because we wanted to set our layer depth value, which is the last value of the method. We could also choose a rotation angle and a point of origin, but we will discuss that in the next chapter.

Right after we call Begin on our sprite batch, we set the DestinationBlend value. We will talk more about this in the next chapter, but for now you can see that we can override the default blend mode when we are in Immediate sort mode. The reason is that the Begin method (for Immediate mode) calls the graphics device immediately, whereas the other sort modes do not call the graphics device until the End method is executed, which will override any of the properties we had set inside the sprite batch.

We can run the demo and push the appropriate buttons or keys to see the results. The demo will launch in deferred mode, and the sprites will be displayed in the order they are in the code: heart, circle, shape, and star, as shown in Figure 9.4. If we go into an immediate sort mode, we will see the different blend states we set. If we switch to the BackToFront sort mode, we can see it uses the layer depth values we created because the shapes are in the order of circle, heart, shape, and star. It drew the highest value on the screen first and ended with the lowest value (causing the lowest value to be "closer" than the largest value), as shown in Figure 9.5. Sorting FrontToBack does the opposite and outputs the star first and finishes up with the circle, as shown in Figure 9.6.

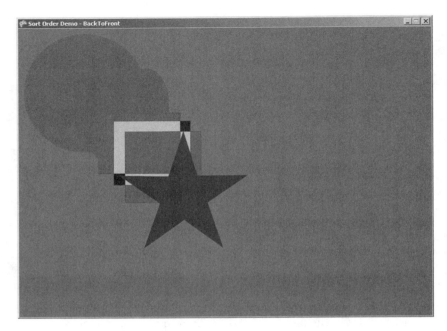

FIGURE 9.4 `SpriteSortMode.Deferred` does not sort the images drawn and displays them in the order they were drawn in the code.

FIGURE 9.5 `SpriteSortMode.BackToFront` sorts the images based on the layer depth values, with the highest number being farthest from the screen.

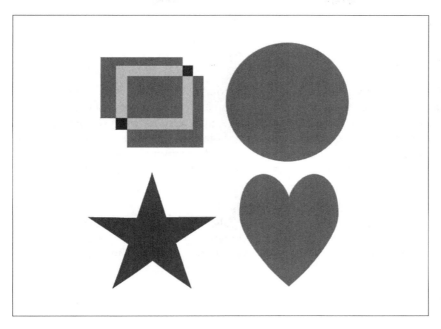

FIGURE 9.6 `SpriteSortMode.FrontToBack` sorts the images based on the layer depth values, with the lowest number being farthest from the screen.

We can also press the appropriate buttons and keys to change our blending state. If we select None, we get to see the full textures complete with black where they are transparent. If we select Additive, we see the pixels added together to create rather "bright" sprites. This demo should help you see exactly how the sort mode works inside of our sprite batch.

Progress Bar Demo

Now that you understand how to use the blend modes and sort modes and you have a firm grasp on drawing a portion of a texture on the screen, let's create a new project called ProgressBarDemo. We can open up our XELibrary project because we will be modifying our library. We are going to add a new game component to our library called ProgressBar.cs. We need to set up the following private member fields of our progress bar game component:

```
private Texture2D progressBar;
private readonly Vector2 initializationVector = new Vector2(-99, -99);
private Vector2 currentPosition;
private Vector2 originalPosition;
private Vector2 position;
//background area of our texture (256 - 63 = 193)
private Rectangle progressBarBackground = new Rectangle(63, 0, 193, 32);
//foreground of our texture
```

```
private Rectangle progressBarForeground = new Rectangle(0, 0, 63, 20);
// where we want our foreground to show up on our background
private Vector2 progressBarOffset = new Vector2(7, 6);
public float MoveRate = 90.0f;
```

The first variable we set up was our initialization vector. We do this so we can tell if our Draw method has ever been called before. We are going to create our own Draw method and will not be inheriting from DrawableGameComponent because we want to pass in an instance of our sprite batch and cannot change the signature of the Draw method inside of DrawableGameComponent. We will get to our Draw method in a moment, but for now we need to initialize our variables inside our constructor with the following statement:

```
Enabled = false;
```

We set the Enabled flag of our game component to false. We explicitly need the caller to enable this component when they want this component to draw the progress bar. This brings us to the next section of code, where we override the event that tells us that the Enabled property has changed:

```
protected override void OnEnabledChanged(object sender, EventArgs args)
{
    if (Enabled)
        currentPosition = originalPosition = initializationVector;

    base.OnEnabledChanged(sender, args);
}
```

When the game enables our game component, we initialize the original and current position of the actual progress bar foreground. Next up is the Load method, which will load the progress bar texture from the content manager:

```
public void Load(Vector2 position)
{
    progressBar = Game.Content.Load<Texture2D>(@"Textures\progressbar");
    this.position = position;
}
```

Fortunately, XNA allows us to load content inside our game components. We do not have to rely on our game to hold the resources because we can add the content directly inside our component project. We need to create a Textures folder in our Content project, as usual. We can then add the progressbar.png file to the Textures folder. This file can be found under the XELibrary project's Content\Textures folder on this book's CD for this chapter.

Our Load method loaded our progress bar texture, and it also stored the position where the component should be drawn. The game will pass in the position to this method, and we will use the value to draw the progress bar at the correct place on the screen.

When we set up our member fields, we created rectangles to specify where in our texture the progress bar background and foreground are. We also set up an offset of where we want to draw the foreground on our background. We will be using these values in our Draw method, as follows:

```
public void Draw(GameTime gameTime, SpriteBatch spriteBatch, Color color)
{
    if (!Enabled)
        return;

    if (progressBar == null)
        throw (new ApplicationException("You must call Load before calling Draw"));

    spriteBatch.Draw(progressBar, originalPosition, progressBarBackground,
        Color.White);
    spriteBatch.Draw(progressBar, currentPosition + progressBarOffset,
        progressBarForeground, color);
}
```

We pass in the game time, the sprite batch we are supposed to draw to, the top-left position of the screen where we want to draw our progress bar, and finally the color that we want to tint our progress bar's foreground. The first thing we check in this function is whether our component is enabled. If it is not, we simply return. The next thing we check for is to make sure our progressBar texture has been created. If it is has not, we throw an error letting the developer know he or she needs to call the component's Load method before calling the Draw method.

Now we draw our progress bar onto the screen. We have two different calls to the sprite batch passed in. One draws the background at the original position passed in, and the other draws the foreground at the current position. We store the original position just in case the game decides to change positions in the middle of our drawing. As we draw our foreground, we are using the color passed in to tint our white progress bar. This way our progress bar can be any color we want. We determine the position to draw our foreground by adding our offset vector to our current position vector. This way, we can center the foreground vertically and push it over a little so it is not flushed to the left when it starts out.

6

Our `Update` method will update the current position the `Draw` method is using. Our `Update` method is as follows:

```
public override void Update(GameTime gameTime)
{
    if (currentPosition == initializationVector) //first time in
        currentPosition = originalPosition = position;
    else
        currentPosition += new Vector2(MoveRate *
            (float)gameTime.ElapsedGameTime.TotalSeconds, 0);

    //have we reached the end (or the beginning) of our area?
    //If so reverse direction
    if (currentPosition.X > originalPosition.X +
            (progressBarBackground.Width - progressBarForeground.Width - 15)
        || currentPosition.X < position.X)
    {
        MoveRate = -MoveRate;
    }

    base.Update(gameTime);
}
```

We check to see if this is the first time our `Update` method has been called. We do this by checking our current position's value. If it is still set to the initialization value, then we know this is the first time this component has been called since it has been enabled. At this point we reset our current and original positions to match the position passed into the `Load` method.

If this is not the first time our `Update` method has been called, we update our `currentPosition` by the public member field `MoveRate` we declared. We set this up as public to allow our game to override how fast or slow the progress bar should move. To translate our foreground position, we are simply adding a vector that contains the product of our move rate and the elapsed total seconds of our game time. Remember, we do this so that when our frame rate changes we still get nice, even flow.

The last check we do in our `Update` method tests to see if our foreground is about to be moved outside the progress bar's background rectangle. If it is, we simply reverse the direction by changing the `MoveRate` value. This way, our progress bar foreground will simply bounce back and forth inside the background.

Now that we are done adding the component to our library, we can open our game code and add the following private member fields:

```
private Vector2 position = new Vector2(150, 150);
private ProgressBar progressBar;
private InputHandler input;
```

We start by setting up the position at which we want to draw our component on the screen. Next, we set up our sprite batch, our progress bar game component, and our input handler game component. Next, we need to set up our game components inside our constructor:

```
input = new InputHandler(this);
Components.Add(input);

progressBar = new ProgressBar(this);
Components.Add(progressBar);
```

This code should be very familiar to you by now—we are just adding our game components to our game's component collection. Now we can initialize our sprite batch by calling the following code inside our LoadContent method:

```
progressBar.Load(position);
progressBar.Enabled = true;
```

We load our progress bar so it can grab its asset and be ready to draw when we are. We next add the following to our Update code to enable (or disable) our progress bar when the Start button or spacebar is pressed:

```
if (input.ButtonHandler.WasButtonPressed(0, InputHandler.ButtonType.Start) ¦¦
    input.KeyboardState.WasKeyPressed(Keys.Space))
{
    progressBar.Enabled = !progressBar.Enabled;
}
```

We finish up our game class by adding the following to our Draw code:

```
spriteBatch.Begin();
progressBar.Draw(gameTime, spriteBatch, Color.Blue);
spriteBatch.End();
```

We are drawing our progress bar on the screen at position 50,50, and we are tinting the color of the foreground to blue. With just a little bit of code, we have a reusable progress bar we can now use in our games on our splash and load screens.

Using Sprite Fonts

The XNA Framework includes built-in font support. We can use any TrueType font in our games. It also allows the use of bitmaps, which can either be drawn by hand or be generated with the Bitmap Font Make Utility (ttf2bmp). This utility can be found on XNA Creators Club Online at http://creators.xna.com/en-us/utilities/bitmapfontmaker.

CAUTION

Most font files are licensed pieces of software. They are not typically sold. Most do not allow distribution of fonts in any applications, even games. This even includes distributing bitmap reproductions of the fonts and many of the fonts that are distributed with Microsoft Windows. Be careful not to distribute any copyrighted fonts with your game.

Importing TrueType Fonts

We want our library to handle fonts, so we will add a TrueType font to our XELibrary project. We need to create a Fonts folder under the Content project in the XELibrary project. You can import TrueType fonts by following these steps:

1. Right-click the Fonts subfolder and click Add.

2. Click New Item and choose Sprite Font. Name the file Arial.spritefont. This will open the newly created .spritefont XML file.

3. In the .spritefont XML file, change the `FontName` element to the friendly name of the font we want to load, Arial.

TIP

You can find the name of the font by looking in the Fonts folder in the Control Panel. You can use any TrueType font, but you cannot use bitmap (.fon) fonts.

4. (Optional) Change the `Size` element to be the point size we want the font to be. You can also scale the font, which you will see later.

5. (Optional) Change the `Spacing` element, which specifies the number of pixels there should be between each character in the font.

6. (Optional) Change the `Style` element, which specifies how the font should be styled. This value is case sensitive and can be one of the following values: Regular, Bold, Italic, or Bold Italic.

7. (Optional) Change the `CharacterRegions` element, which contains the start and end characters that should be generated and available for drawing. If we were only displaying specific characters, utilizing this can save on the font file size, which can help with loading times.

Now that we have added this spritefont file, when we compile our code, the compiler will generate the resource needed so we can utilize the font in our game. The XML file is simply a description to the compiler as to which TrueType font to grab and which characters to create in the .xnb file.

Creating Bitmap Fonts

Not only can we use TrueType font resources, we can make our own bitmap fonts to be used. To do this we need to create the bitmap. We can do it either by hand or by using the Bitmap Font Maker Utility mentioned at the beginning of this section. After getting the base bitmap generated, we can modify it in our favorite paint program.

The background of the image must be a fully opaque, pure magenta color (R: 255, G: 0, B: 255, A: 255). It needs to include an alpha channel that specifies which parts of the characters are visible. Once the image is created or modified, we can import the image into our Fonts subfolder. XNA Game Studio will think it is just a normal texture, so we need to modify the Content Processor value in our properties panel to be Sprite Font Texture.

Drawing 2D Text

Now that we have our font imported, we can actually use it. We are not going to create a demo for this. Instead, we are going to modify our ProgressBarDemo project and have it display the text "Loading..." right above the progress bar. We need to add the following private member fields to the Game1.cs file:

```
private Vector2 loadingPosition = new Vector2(150, 120);
private SpriteFont font;
```

We already added the actual SpriteFont to our XELibrary project. We could have added the asset to our game, but it's likely we will want to print text out on the screen in the future. However, we need to actually load the font in our game class. We do this just like any other content inside of our LoadContent method:

```
font = Content.Load<SpriteFont>(@"Fonts\Arial");
```

Finally, inside the Draw method, above our call to end our sprite batch, we need to add the following statement:

```
spriteBatch.DrawString(font, "Loading ...", loadingPosition, Color.White);
```

You can now run the ProgressBarDemo and see "Loading..." displayed above the progress bar. Things are shaping up nicely!

Summary

You were introduced to 2D concepts in this chapter. We spent the majority of the time covering sprites and sprite batches. You learned the importance of the blend modes and sort modes for our sprites when dealing with our sprite batch. You saw the different graphics device state changes that happen when we call a sprite batch. You learned how to have the sprite batch save the state and reset it automatically, and we discussed some common values we could reset manually if we were mixing 3D with 2D.

We spent a good a portion of this chapter creating demos to help firm up your understanding of these concepts. We created a splash screen that could also be used to create a loading screen, especially if we add the progress bar component. In addition to those two demos, you learned how to draw part of a texture as a sprite to save the amount of textures we have. We created a demo that allowed us to quickly see the changes the different blend and sort modes had on our scene. We finished the chapter by adding in the ability to draw fonts on the screen. With these 2D basics down, we can move on to writing 2D effects in the next chapter.

CHAPTER 10

2D Effects

Now that we've covered the basics of 2D, we can get into some more exciting 2D content creation—effects. In this chapter we are going to discuss cel animation, rotating and scaling our sprites, as well as the different blend modes available to use when dealing with sprite batches. You will learn how to fade to a particular color as well. We will finish out the chapter by discussing how to create fire and explosion effects.

Cel Animation

In the last chapter, you saw how to render portions of a texture into multiple sprites. In this section we are going to use the same principle to create cel animation. This involves taking a texture with multiple rows and columns and looping them to create an animation. This is typically done for characters in the game and really any objects that require animation in 2D. For example, we could have a texture that includes five cels of a stick figure jumping. Cel one could contain him right before he jumps, cel three would have him in the middle of the air, and the last cel would show him landing. We would want to display those cels in order in a rapid fashion to make it appear that our stick man just jumped.

To get started we are going to create a demo called CelAnimation. We will be including our XELibrary in this project because we will be creating a cel animation helper class. Once our solution is set up, we'll create a new game component called CelAnimationManager. The code for this new class is given in Listing 10.1.

LISTING 10.1   CelAnimationManager.cs

```csharp
using System;
using System.Collections.Generic;
using Microsoft.Xna.Framework;
using Microsoft.Xna.Framework.Graphics;
using Microsoft.Xna.Framework.Content;

namespace XELibrary
{
    public sealed class CelAnimationManager
        : Microsoft.Xna.Framework.GameComponent
    {
        private Dictionary<string, CelAnimation> animations =
            new Dictionary<string, CelAnimation>();
        private Dictionary<string, Texture2D> textures =
            new Dictionary<string, Texture2D>();
        private ContentManager content;

        public CelAnimationManager(Game game, string contentPath)
            : base(game)
        {
            this.contentPath = contentPath;

            if (this.contentPath.LastIndexOf('\\') <
                this.contentPath.Length - 1)
            {
                this.contentPath += "\\";
            }
        }

        public override void Initialize()
        {
            base.Initialize();
        }

        public void AddAnimation(string animationKey, string textureName,
                                 CelCount celCount, int framesPerSecond)
        {
            if (!textures.ContainsKey(textureName))
            {
                textures.Add(textureName, Game.Content.Load<Texture2D>(
                    contentPath + textureName));
            }

            int celWidth = (int)(textures[textureName].Width /
```

```
        celCount.NumberOfColumns);
    int celHeight = (int)(textures[textureName].Height /
        celCount.NumberOfRows);

    int numberOfCels = celCount.NumberOfColumns *
        celCount.NumberOfRows;

    //we create a cel range by passing in start location of 1,1
    //and end with number of column and rows
    //2,1  =   1,1,2,1  ;    4,2  =  1,1,4,2
    AddAnimation(animationKey, textureName,
        new CelRange(1, 1, celCount.NumberOfColumns,
        celCount.NumberOfRows), celWidth, celHeight,
        numberOfCels, framesPerSecond);
}

public void AddAnimation(string animationKey, string textureName,
    CelRange celRange, int celWidth, int celHeight,
    int numberOfCels, int framesPerSecond)
{
    CelAnimation ca = new CelAnimation(textureName, celRange,
        framesPerSecond);

    if (!textures.ContainsKey(textureName))
    {
        textures.Add(textureName, Game.Content.Load<Texture2D>(
            contentPath + textureName));
    }

    ca.CelWidth = celWidth;
    ca.CelHeight = celHeight;

    ca.NumberOfCels = numberOfCels;

    ca.CelsPerRow = textures[textureName].Width / celWidth;

    if (animations.ContainsKey(animationKey))
        animations[animationKey] = ca;
    else
        animations.Add(animationKey, ca);
}

public void ToggleAnimation(string animationKey)
{
    if (animations.ContainsKey(animationKey))
```

10

```
            animations[animationKey].Paused =
                !animations[animationKey].Paused;
        }
    }

    public override void Update(GameTime gameTime)
    {
        foreach(KeyValuePair<string,CelAnimation> animation in animations)
        {
            CelAnimation ca = animation.Value;

            if (ca.Paused)
                continue; //no need to update this animation,check next one

            ca.TotalElapsedTime +=
                (float)gameTime.ElapsedGameTime.TotalSeconds;
            if (ca.TotalElapsedTime > ca.TimePerFrame)
            {
                ca.Frame++;

                //min: 0, max: total cels
                ca.Frame = ca.Frame % (ca.NumberOfCels);

                //reset our timer
                ca.TotalElapsedTime -= ca.TimePerFrame;
            }
        }
        base.Update(gameTime);
    }

    public void Draw(GameTime gameTime, string animationKey,
        SpriteBatch batch, Vector2 position)
    {
        Draw(gameTime, animationKey, batch,
            position, Color.White);
    }

    public void Draw(GameTime gameTime, string animationKey,
        SpriteBatch batch, Vector2 position, Color color)
    {
        if (!animations.ContainsKey(animationKey))
            return;

        CelAnimation ca = animations[animationKey];

        //first get our x increase amount
```

```
            //(add our offset-1 to our current frame)
            int xincrease = (ca.Frame + ca.CelRange.FirstCelX - 1);
            //now we need to wrap the value so it will loop to the next row
            int xwrapped = xincrease % ca.CelsPerRow;
            //finally we need to take the product of our wrapped value
            //and a cel's width
            int x = xwrapped * ca.CelWidth;

            //to determine how much we should increase y, we need to look
            //at how much we increased x and do an integer divide
            int yincrease = xincrease / ca.CelsPerRow;
            //now we can take this increase and add it to
            //our Y offset-1 and multiply the sum by our cel height
            int y = (yincrease + ca.CelRange.FirstCelY - 1) * ca.CelHeight;

            Rectangle cel = new Rectangle(x, y, ca.CelWidth, ca.CelHeight);
            batch.Draw(textures[ca.TextureName], position, cel, color);
        }
    }

public class CelAnimation
{
    private string textureName;
    private CelRange celRange;
    private int framesPerSecond;
    private float timePerFrame;

    public float TotalElapsedTime = 0.0f;
    public int CelWidth;
    public int CelHeight;
    public int NumberOfCels;
    public int CelsPerRow;
    public int Frame;
    public bool Paused = false;

    public CelAnimation(string textureName, CelRange celRange,
        int framesPerSecond)
    {
        this.textureName = textureName;
        this.celRange = celRange;
        this.framesPerSecond = framesPerSecond;
        this.timePerFrame = 1.0f / (float)framesPerSecond;
        this.Frame = 0;
    }

    public string TextureName
```

10

```
        {
            get { return (textureName); }
        }

        public CelRange CelRange
        {
            get { return (celRange); }
        }

        public int FramesPerSecond
        {
            get { return (framesPerSecond); }
        }

        public float TimePerFrame
        {
            get { return (timePerFrame); }
        }
    }

    public struct CelCount
    {
        public int NumberOfColumns;
        public int NumberOfRows;

        public CelCount(int numberOfColumns, int numberOfRows)
        {
            NumberOfColumns = numberOfColumns;
            NumberOfRows = numberOfRows;
        }
    }

    public struct CelRange
    {
        public int FirstCelX;
        public int FirstCelY;
        public int LastCelX;
        public int LastCelY;

        public CelRange(int firstCelX, int firstCelY, int lastCelX,
            int lastCelY)
        {
            FirstCelX = firstCelX;
            FirstCelY = firstCelY;
            LastCelX = lastCelX;
            LastCelY = lastCelY;
```

```
        }
    }
}
```

The CelAnimationManager.cs file has two classes and two structs inside of it. Typically, we have one class per file, but we have them all listed here together so we can discuss them easily. Our game will talk to at least one of the two structs and the manager class. Our manager class exposes two different AddAnimations methods that our games can use to create animation textures. The first is the most simplistic to set up, but it requires that the texture contain only one animation. The signature for this method is shown here:

```
public void AddAnimation(string animationKey, string textureName,
    CelCount celCount, int framesPerSecond)
```

It allows us to pass in an animation key, along with a texture name, the number of rows and columns our texture contains, and finally the rate per second at which we would like our animation to be drawn. We store the animation key inside an animations dictionary. We do the same thing with the textures by storing them in their own dictionary. This way, we do not need to have multiple textures when we have multiple animations that share the same texture. This will be obvious as we get into the other overload of this method. By us passing in the number of columns and rows in our texture, the cel animation manager can determine how many cels are in the texture.

The second overload of our AddAnimation method is a little more complex. The parameters we pass into this method are shown here:

```
public void AddAnimation(string animationKey, string textureName,
    CelRange celRange, int celWidth, int celHeight, int numberOfCels,
    int framesPerSecond)
```

As with the other overload, we pass in the animation key, the texture name, and the frames per second we want our animation to play at. We do not pass in the CelCount struct (which tells us how many rows and columns are in the texture). Instead, we pass in the CelRange struct (which tells us which cel our animation starts with and which cels it ends with). We also need to tell the method our cel's width and height because it cannot determine that based on the texture size (because we are not using the entire texture). Finally, we need to tell the method exactly how many cels we are rendering. This could be computed, but it is not something difficult for the game to pass in. The CelCount is basically identical to Vector2. The properties have changed to make it more intuitive for our situation. Also the CelRange struct is basically identical to a Rectangle struct.

Our cel animation manager's constructor takes in the path to where the textures that contain the animation are located. The path should have a trailing backslash when it is passed in, but the code will append one if needed. It is assumed the texture content will be loaded inside the game.

The manager actually holds a collection of CelAnimation objects in a dictionary. This class stores all the relevant information about itself, so the manager does not need to. It keeps track of which frame it is currently on as well as how many cels it has, its texture name, how many frames a second it is supposed to be drawn, along with some other information. We can look at one of the AddAnimation methods to see how the manager adds a cel animation to its dictionary and prepares it to be drawn:

```
public void AddAnimation(string animationKey, string textureName,
    CelRange celRange, int celWidth, int celHeight, int numberOfCels,
    int framesPerSecond)
{
    CelAnimation ca = new CelAnimation(textureName, celRange,
        framesPerSecond);

    if (!textures.ContainsKey(textureName))
    {
        textures.Add(textureName, Game.Content.Load<Texture2D>(
            contentPath + textureName));
    }

    ca.CelWidth = celWidth;
    ca.CelHeight = celHeight;

    ca.NumberOfCels = numberOfCels;

    ca.CelsPerRow = textures[textureName].Width / celWidth;

    if (animations.ContainsKey(animationKey))
        animations[animationKey] = ca;
    else
        animations.Add(animationKey, ca);
}
```

First, we create an instance of our CelAnimation object, passing it the required information about the animation. Next, we check to see if the texture name this animation is using is already in our list before adding it. We then set some more properties on our cel animation object, and finally we either add the object to our dictionary or reset our dictionary with the new object.

Inside our Update method, we loop through our animation dictionary. As long as the animation is not paused, we add to our timer (much like we did for our FPS code). If enough time has elapsed, we add to our frame number. We make sure we do not exceed the number of cels we have in our animation. Finally, we reset our time.

The last piece of this cel animation manager object is the Draw method. It does not contain much code, but it does all the work of rendering the correct cel. First, it makes sure an animation by that key actually exists in the collection. If it does not, the method just returns, but it could just as easily throw an error. If the animation does exist, the manager obtains a reference to it. Next is the math to calculate which cel to display. The code to do this is as follows:

```
//first get our x increase amount (add our offset-1 to our current frame)
int xincrease = (ca.Frame + ca.CelRange.FirstCelX - 1);
//now we need to wrap the value so it will loop to the next row
int xwrapped = xincrease % ca.CelsPerRow;
//finally we need to take the product of our wrapped value and a cel's width
int x = xwrapped * ca.CelWidth;

//to determine how much we should increase y, we need to look at how much we
//increased x and do an integer divide
int yincrease = xincrease / ca.CelsPerRow;
//now we can take this increase and add it to our Y offset-1 and multiply
//the sum by our cel height
int y = (yincrease + ca.CelRange.FirstCelY - 1) * ca.CelHeight;

Rectangle cel = new Rectangle(x, y, ca.CelWidth, ca.CelHeight);
batch.Draw(textures[ca.TextureName], position, cel, color);
```

First, we determine how much our x index should increase by looking at our current frame and adding our first cel's x offset. It is zero-based, so we subtract one. Then we perform a mod function to make sure it will wrap around if needed. Then we can set the x location of our texture to what we just wrapped, multiplied by the width of our cels.

Next, we perform similar calculations to get our y value. Instead of performing a mod function on the increased value of x, we do an integer divide, giving us just the whole number available. This will return a zero for the first row, one for the next row, and so on. We take that value and add our first cel's y offset. Again, it is zero-based, so we subtract one. Finally, we multiply the value with the height of our cels.

We take the x and y values we just calculated and create a rectangle that we will pass to our sprite batches' Draw method as our source rectangle. We also pass in the position at which the game told us to draw this animation. The code also allows our game to tint the animations if needed because it allows us to pass in the color.

Now that we have discussed the cel animation manager, let's use it in our demo. Let's open the Game1.cs code and make sure we have all our references (as well as using clauses and such) set up. Once we do, we can add the following member fields to the top of our code:

```
private CelAnimationManager cam;
```

Then in our constructor, we need to add the cel animation manager to our collection of components and pass in the location of the animation textures we will be using:

```
cam = new CelAnimationManager(this, @"Textures\");
Components.Add(cam);
```

10

Let's go ahead and add the MrEye.png and the complex.png textures to our Content\Textures folder. The files can be found on the CD that accompanies the book under this project's folder. The next code we need to add goes into our `LoadContent` method. We will call the `AddAnimation` methods of our `CelAnimationManager`:

```
cam.AddAnimation("enemy1", "MrEye", new CelCount(4, 2), 8);
cam.AddAnimation("enemy2", "MrEye", new CelCount(4, 2), 12);
cam.AddAnimation("enemy3", "MrEye", new CelCount(4, 2), 6);

cam.AddAnimation("complex1","complex",new CelRange(1, 1, 2, 1), 64, 64, 2, 2);
cam.AddAnimation("complex2","complex",new CelRange(3, 1, 1, 3), 64, 64, 7, 8);
cam.AddAnimation("complex3","complex",new CelRange(2, 3, 1, 4), 64, 64, 4, 2);
cam.AddAnimation("complex4","complex",new CelRange(2, 4, 4, 4), 64, 64, 3, 5);
```

The enemy methods use the shorter signature of our overloaded `AddAnimation` method. MrEye uses an entire texture. It is a 1024×512 texture with a total of eight cels (four on two rows). Therefore, we can just pass in the number of columns (four) and the number of rows (two) through our `CelCount` struct into the `AddAnimation` method. We then simply pass in how fast we want our animation to run. The value is measured in fps. We could make `framesPerSecond` equal `numberOfCels` if we wanted all the animations to complete at the same time in one second. Instead, we use different values in this case for demonstration purposes.

TIP

Certain graphics cards require that textures be a power of two in size. For example, 512 is a power of two because we can keep dividing it by two and never end up with a fraction. On the other hand, 768 is not a power of two.

The complex methods use the larger signature and need more information. The complex methods allow us to have multiple animations in the same texture to save on space. The image we are loading can be seen in Figure 10.1.

We pass the `AddAnimation` method cel 1,1 to start and cel 2,1 to end for our first animation. We then pass in the cel width and height of our animation (in this case both are 64). We then pass in the total number of cels inside of our animation. Finally, we pass in how fast we want the animation to play, just like the other method.

The last task we need to perform is to actually draw the animations. The following code needs to be added to the `Draw` method:

```
spriteBatch.Begin();
cam.Draw(gameTime, "enemy1", spriteBatch, new Vector2(50, 50));
cam.Draw(gameTime, "enemy2", spriteBatch, new Vector2(150, 75));
cam.Draw(gameTime, "enemy3", spriteBatch, new Vector2(70, 130));
```

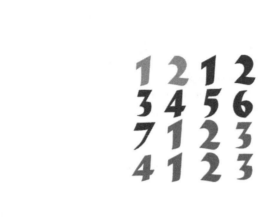

FIGURE 10.1   The `CelAnimationManager` allows us to utilize one texture to contain multiple animations.

```
cam.Draw(gameTime, "complex1", spriteBatch, new Vector2(400, 50));
cam.Draw(gameTime, "complex2", spriteBatch, new Vector2(400, 150));
cam.Draw(gameTime, "complex3", spriteBatch, new Vector2(400, 250));
cam.Draw(gameTime, "complex4", spriteBatch, new Vector2(400, 350));
spriteBatch.End();
```

We can run this code and see the animations.

Rotating and Scaling

We are going to create a small rotation and scaling demo as an example of what we talked about in the last chapter. We'll create a new solution and call it RotateAndScaleDemo. This is going to be a very simple program. First, we need a texture. You can load the texture called circular from the CD included with this book. Next, we need to set up our class variables, as follows:

```
private Texture2D circular;
private Rectangle destination;
private Rectangle source;
private float rotation;
private Vector2 origin;
private float scale;
```

We can then replace our LoadContent code with the following:

```
spriteBatch = new SpriteBatch(GraphicsDevice);
circular = Content.Load<Texture2D>(@"Textures\circular");

destination = new Rectangle(graphics.PreferredBackBufferWidth / 2,
    graphics.PreferredBackBufferHeight / 2, circular.Width, circular.Height);
origin = new Vector2(circular.Width / 2, circular.Height / 2);
source = new Rectangle(0, 0, circular.Width, circular.Height);

rotation = 1.0f;
scale = 0.5f;
```

We simply create our sprite batch and load a texture. Then we set up a destination where we will be placing our sprite on the screen. We are going to center it, so we take the dimensions of our preferred backbuffer and divide them by two. We set the width and height to match that of our texture so it does not stretch. Next, we declare an origin that we will use for our sprite. If we do not set an origin, it defaults to 0,0 (the top left of the texture). We set the origin to be the center of our texture by dividing the texture's width and height by two. We then need to set our source rectangle, which is used to grab a portion (or all) of the texture we are drawing. In this case we are grabbing the entire texture. Finally, we set our rotation to 1.0 and our scale to 0.5.

Inside our Update method we can add the following statement so that our rotation value will continually be updated:

```
rotation += .05f;
```

Finally, we can add the following code to our Draw method and run the demo:

```
spriteBatch.Begin();
spriteBatch.Draw(circular, destination, source, Color.White, rotation, origin,
    SpriteEffects.None, 0.0f);
spriteBatch.Draw(circular, new Vector2(100,600), null, Color.White, -rotation,
    new Vector2(256,256), scale, SpriteEffects.None, 0.0f);
spriteBatch.Draw(circular, new Vector2(600, 100), null, Color.White, -rotation,
    new Vector2(256, 256), scale, SpriteEffects.None, 0.0f);
spriteBatch.Draw(circular, new Vector2(300, 300), null, Color.White, rotation,
    new Vector2(0, 0), scale, SpriteEffects.None, 0.0f);
spriteBatch.End();
```

The code draws four sprites. The first one it draws is at its normal size (512,512) and passes in the rotation that is being updated. The origin is the one we set up earlier (center of the texture). The next two sprites are similar, except we explicitly set the origin. We can tweak these values to examine how XNA rotates our sprites. We also switched the rotation by negating the rotation value. The last sprite we drew with the origin set to the default 0,0 location. This looks like it is orbiting because it is rotating around the top left of the texture. We applied the scale of 0.5 for all the sprites except the first one. We can modify the scale variable to see the effect it has on our demo.

Blending Mode Example

We will use the preceding code and tweak it a little bit to show some interesting blending effects. Let's replace the contents of our previous Draw method with the following code:

```
spriteBatch.Begin(SpriteBlendMode.AlphaBlend, SpriteSortMode.Immediate,
    SaveStateMode.None);
graphics.GraphicsDevice.RenderState.SourceBlend = Blend.DestinationColor;
graphics.GraphicsDevice.RenderState.DestinationBlend = Blend.SourceColor;
spriteBatch.Draw(circular, destination, source, Color.White, rotation, origin,
    SpriteEffects.None, 0.0f);
spriteBatch.End();

spriteBatch.Begin(SpriteBlendMode.AlphaBlend, SpriteSortMode.Immediate,
    SaveStateMode.None);
graphics.GraphicsDevice.RenderState.SourceBlend = Blend.One;
graphics.GraphicsDevice.RenderState.DestinationBlend = Blend.One;
spriteBatch.Draw(circular, new Vector2(600, 100), null, Color.White, -rotation,
    new Vector2(256, 256), scale, SpriteEffects.None, 0.0f);
spriteBatch.End();

spriteBatch.Begin(SpriteBlendMode.AlphaBlend, SpriteSortMode.Immediate,
    SaveStateMode.None);
graphics.GraphicsDevice.RenderState.SourceBlend = Blend.DestinationColor;
graphics.GraphicsDevice.RenderState.DestinationBlend = Blend.SourceAlpha;
spriteBatch.Draw(circular, new Vector2(100,600), null, Color.White, -rotation,
    new Vector2(256,256), scale, SpriteEffects.None, 0.0f);
spriteBatch.End();

spriteBatch.Begin(SpriteBlendMode.AlphaBlend, SpriteSortMode.Immediate,
    SaveStateMode.None);
graphics.GraphicsDevice.RenderState.SourceBlend = Blend.InverseSourceColor;
graphics.GraphicsDevice.RenderState.DestinationBlend =
    Blend.InverseDestinationColor;
spriteBatch.Draw(circular, new Vector2(300, 300), null, Color.White, -rotation,
    new Vector2(0, 0), scale, SpriteEffects.None, 0.0f);
spriteBatch.End();
```

We wrapped each of the sprites we drew into its own immediate mode sprite batch calls. We did this so we could easily see some interesting effects by explicitly setting the source and destination blend modes of our render state. This way, we are not just limited to alpha blending or additive blending when dealing with sprite batches. We can play with the values to see the effects they have on our sprites.

Fade to Color

We are going to create another simple demo. In fact, we can continue to modify the code we have open. This demo will wait one second after the program launches and then start to fade to black, although we could fade to any color. First, we want to add the following member fields to our code:

```
private float fadeAmount;
private Texture2D fadeTexture;
```

Next, in our LoadContent method we want to create a texture that we can store in our fadeTexture variable. We can do this with the following code:

```
fadeTexture = CreateFadeTexture(GraphicsDevice.Viewport.Width,
    GraphicsDevice.Viewport.Height);
```

We are calling a method that requires us to pass in the width and height of the texture it will create. We are passing in the width and height of our viewport so the texture will fill the entire screen. Now we can look at this method to see how it creates a texture through code:

```
private Texture2D CreateFadeTexture(int width, int height)
{
    Texture2D texture = new Texture2D(
        GraphicsDevice, width, height, 1,
        TextureUsage.None,
        SurfaceFormat.Color);

    int pixelCount = width * height;
    Color[] pixelData = new Color[pixelCount];
    Random rnd = new Random();

    for (int i = 0; i < pixelCount; i++)
    {
        //could fade to a different color
        pixelData[i] = Color.Black;
    }

    texture.SetData(pixelData);

    return (texture);
}
```

The key to this code is the very first statement. XNA provides a constructor to the Texture2D object that allows us to create a texture on the fly! We simply pass in the graphics device, the width and the height of the texture, and the number of mipmaps we will have (we have set it to 1). We also have to pass how we will be using this texture (None).

We are not specifying any particular texture usage for this code. Most have to do with the Vertex Buffer, which we discussed earlier. The Xbox 360 has Linear and Tiled, which determine how the texture is stored in memory. We pass in Color as our surface format because it is available on all hardware.

After creating our texture, we can define it inside our code. In this case, we are simply going to set all the pixels to a single color, black. To do this, we add an array of unsigned integers. Unsigned types allow us to have very large numbers without needing to allocate memory for a long time because an unsigned type does not store negative numbers, effectively doubling the maximum positive number the type can hold. We initialize our array to be the width times height of our texture so we have enough room to store each pixel. Then inside the for loop, we simply set each pixel. In this case, we are setting them all to black. This could be any color. In fact, we could create a random color for each pixel. An easy way to get to a particular pixel in a texture is to use the following formula in our array:

```
Color pixelvalue = pixeldata[(y * width) + x];
```

Although we do not need that formula in this example, it is a very clean way of easily passing in an x and y value to get or set a particular pixel in a texture. The array starts at position 0,0 of our texture, and each pixel is stored consecutively from left to right. When the array gets to the end of the texture, it grabs the value from the first pixel in the next row and just continues down until it has stored all the values. This is the way developers used to access data on old graphics cards. In fact, we will be using this technique in the next section, where we create fire old-school style.

As we look back at the code, we see that the only thing left to do is to take the generated pixel data and apply it to our texture through the SetData method. There is a counterpart to this method called GetData. Both are generic methods that allow us to set and get, respectively, the data in multiple formats. Not only can we use unsigned integers, but we can also use the XNA Color type.

The next code we will update is in our Update method. Add the following code to the bottom of that method:

```
//start fading out after 2 seconds
if (gameTime.TotalGameTime.Seconds > 2)
    fadeAmount += (.0005f * gameTime.ElapsedGameTime.Milliseconds);

//reset fade amount after a short time to see the effect again
if (fadeAmount > 2.0f) //two seconds passed?
    fadeAmount = 0.0f;
```

10

We are simply updating a value holding our fade amount. Because we don't actually have anything to kick this off, we are just doing it after the game has been running for two seconds. Then we start to gradually add to this fade amount each frame. The next condition simply removes the fading amount after a couple seconds so we can see the effect again. We can create an interesting flicker effect by changing .0005f to 0.1f. This will make the fade happen very quickly (in about 10 frames) and get to the 2.0 value very quickly (in about 20 frames). The result is an interesting flashing screen effect.

Finally, we need to add the following code to the end of the Draw method:

```
spriteBatch.Begin();
spriteBatch.Draw(fadeTexture, Vector2.Zero,
    new Color(new Vector4(Color.White.ToVector3(), fadeAmount)));
spriteBatch.End();
```

This starts up a new batch (we can leave the origin sprite batch alone to draw like it was doing). This batch always draws our fadeTexture. In a real game, we would only call this code when we were actually going to fade our scene. We can use the texture we created just like any other texture and see it displayed on the screen with our specified tint value. We are still passing in Color.White, but in alpha we are sending in our fade amount. Because we are starting with a small number and making it larger, we are fading in our texture, which in effect fades out our scene. If we wanted to fade in our scene, we could reverse our fade amount to start at 1.0 and gradually work itself to 0. We could also use this fading code "as is" to fade in a particular sprite or something else. We do not need to create a sprite to cover the entire scene in that case. We can just fade in (or out) the sprite we are concerned with. With just a little code we can get a nice transition effect.

Making Fire, Old-School Style

Making fire in real life can be dangerous business, but making fire in games is excellent! The code we will be writing in this section is not optimal for use in a real game. It is more of a history lesson than anything else, especially when discussing Windows and Xbox 360 development. However, this code does well on the Zune platform, which makes sense because the Zune has inferior hardware compared to the other platforms. You will learn more about texture manipulation, which we touched on in the last section, but this actual implementation crawls on many machines and really does poorly on the Xbox 360. Fortunately, to get this type of effect with today's hardware is similar, but we just have to use effects, which we cover in Chapter 14, "HLSL Basics," and Chapter 15, "Advanced HLSL." With that disclaimer out of the way, let's get started by creating a new project called FireDemo. We can add a reference to our XELibrary. We will not be changing our library for this demo, so we can just create a reference if we do not want to include the actual project. You can create an Xbox 360 project, but it does not perform well at all.

We can get started with our code by declaring the following private member fields:

```
private Texture2D fire;
private InputHandler input;
```

```
private FPS fps;
private uint[] pixelData;
private uint[] firePalette;
private Dictionary<uint, uint> firePaletteData;
private Random rand = new Random();
```

We then need to update our constructor to use our game components and to force the backbuffer to a certain width and height:

```
graphics.PreferredBackBufferHeight = 256;
graphics.PreferredBackBufferWidth = 512;

fps = new FPS(this);
Components.Add(fps);

input = new InputHandler(this);
Components.Add(input);
```

Next is our LoadContent method, which will contain the following code:

```
//256x1 image
Texture2D fireTexture = Content.Load<Texture2D>(@"Textures\FireGrade");

//initialize our array to store the palette info
firePaletteData = new Dictionary<uint, uint>(fireTexture.Width *
fireTexture.Height);
firePalette = new uint[fireTexture.Width * fireTexture.Height];

//storing image data in our fireTexture
fireTexture.GetData<uint>(firePalette);

for (uint i = 0; i < firePalette.Length; i++)
{
    if (!firePaletteData.ContainsKey(firePalette[i]))
        firePaletteData.Add(firePalette[i], i);
}

//now we can create our fire texture
fire = CreateFireTexture(128, 128);
```

We are loading a 256×1 texture from our content. This texture can be found on the CD. It is simply a single-line image that has a gradient color strip ranging from black to red to orange to yellow to white, so we can easily get a "fire palette" instead of generating one in our code. We store the palette data in our firePalette variable, which we initialize to hold all the pixels of our texture. Then we call GetData from the fire palette texture, and each pixel is placed inside our array in the order we discussed in the last section. We populate the firePaletteData dictionary we created with the actual fire palette data and the

10

corresponding index. When we need this information later, it is much faster to store the information in a way we can quickly search. Finally, we create our own texture that we will be rendering to the screen. We are calling a method, much like we did in the last section, to create the texture for us. Let's look at that method now:

```
private Texture2D CreateFireTexture(int width, int height)
{
    Texture2D texture = new Texture2D(
        GraphicsDevice, width, height, 1,
        TextureUsage.None,
        SurfaceFormat.Color);

    int pixelCount = width * height;
    pixelData = new uint[pixelCount];

    for (uint i = 0; i < pixelCount; i++)
        pixelData[i] = Color.Black.PackedValue;

    //set bottom 16 rows to fiery colors
    for (int y = height - 1; y > height - 16; y--)
    {
        for (int x = 0; x < width; x++)
        {
            pixelData[(y * width) + x] = GetRandomFireColor();
        }
    }

    texture.SetData(pixelData);

    return (texture);
}
```

The first statement should be familiar to you because we just used it in the last section. We then set up our structure to hold the pixel data for the fire texture we are making. It needs to contain enough room for our texture's pixels. We loop through all the pixels, setting each one to black. We did this in the last section as well, but we did not discuss the PackedValue property on the Color struct. This property represents a color in an unsigned integer, which is really useful when we are working with textures this way, because they do not require a tremendous amount of memory. This is great considering how big our textures could be!

TIP

Textures that are sized 2048×2048 are the largest that work reliably across all shader-based Windows cards. Many can go up to 4096, and Xbox 360 supports textures up to 8192.

After initializing all our pixels, we then set the bottom 16 rows of our texture to fiery colors. We can look closely at these 16 rows to which we are assigning values. We are in a nested for loop, with the outer loop handling rows and the inner loop handling columns. You can see that the formula mentioned in the last section is being used here. We are setting a particular piece of texture to a color by taking the sum of our x value with the product of our y value and the width of the texture. This way, we can easily access our 2D image in a 1D array. After completing our loops, we set the texture's pixel data. We finish up by returning the texture to the calling method.

We are setting the color on those last 16 rows of pixels through a method called GetRandomFireColor, shown here:

```
private uint GetRandomFireColor()
{
    return (firePalette[rand.Next(0, 256)]);
}
```

This one line simply gets a random number from 0 to 255 and uses that as an index to our fire palette. The firePalette contains the uint color associated with the index of the palette.

Next, we want to add a call to the following method in our Update method:

```
UpdateFire();
```

This method does all of the work and is shown here:

```
private void UpdateFire()
{
    int height = fire.Height;
    int width = fire.Width;

    uint left, right, bottom, top;
    uint colorIndex;
    int xRight, xLeft, yBelow, yAbove;

    for (int y = 0; y < height; y++)
    {
        for (int x = 0; x < width; x++)
        {
            xRight = x + 1;
            yBelow = y + 1;
            xLeft = x - 1;
            yAbove = y - 1;

            //make sure our values are within range
            if (xRight >= width)
                xRight = 0;
```

```
        if (yBelow >= height)
            yBelow = height - 1;

        if (xLeft < 0)
            xLeft = width - 1;
        if (yAbove < 0)
            yAbove = 0;

        //we need to get uint value of each surrounding color
        right = pixelData[(y * width) + xRight];
        left = pixelData[(y * width) + xLeft];
        bottom = pixelData[(yBelow * height) + x];
        top = pixelData[(yAbove * height) + x];

        //we now have the uint value of the colors stored
        //we need to find our palette index for this color
        //and do an average and reset the color
        colorIndex = (firePaletteData[right] + firePaletteData[left] +
            firePaletteData[top] + firePaletteData[bottom]) / 4;
        colorIndex -= 3; //could make a random number

        if (colorIndex > 255) //went "negative" (unsigned)
            colorIndex = 0;

        //finally, we can set this pixel to our new color
        pixelData[(yAbove * width) + x] = firePalette[colorIndex];
    }
}


    //now, it is time to animate our fire
    AnimateFire(width, height);
}
```

The code is long but not really that complex. The overall concept is that we loop through each pixel and find its neighbors (to the right, left, top, and bottom). Then we average those colors together to come up with the new color for the pixel above the current one. We then keep the flame from rising too high by deducting the index of the pixel color a little bit. We finally set the color of the pixel above the current one to our new color.

To explain this method further, notice that we are calculating the pixel positions neighboring the current pixel in our for loops. We hold our left and right values beside the current pixel's x location and the above and below values around the current y pixel location. If we are on an edge, we wrap to the other side to get the value.

To obtain our new color value, we take each pixel location and obtain the color for each. We look up the palette index from our firePaletteData dictionary for each color. We take the average of these four indices and store it in the colorIndex variable. We then subtract 3 from our index (this could be a random number if we wanted to allow the flame to rise or fall in different ways) to find our final index. We make sure our index is in a valid range and finally set the color associated with that palette index to the pixel directly above the pixel we are processing.

After we have finished looping through all the pixels, we make a call to the AnimateFire method. At this point our code will animate the pixels on the texture; however, it will get to a point where nothing will update because everything will be averaged out. This is why we have the AnimateFire method at the bottom. This method takes all the pixels on the bottom row of the texture and changes them. This way, the main UpdateFire method actually has something to update. The AnimateFire method is shown here:

```
private void AnimateFire(int width, int height)
{
    int newColorIndex;

    //we could work with just one pixel at a time,
    //but we will work with five for a broader flame
    for (int x = 0; x < width - 5; x += 5)
    {
        // we are only going to modify the bottom row
        int y = height - 1;

        //we get our palette index for the color we just set on the
        //bottom row we then either add or subtract a substantial 64 to or from
        //that index
        newColorIndex = (int)firePaletteData[pixelData[(y * width) + x]] +
            (rand.Next(-64, 64));
        //now we make sure our palette index is within range
        if (newColorIndex > 255)
            newColorIndex = 255;
        if (newColorIndex < 0)
            newColorIndex = 0;

        //Because we are stepping through our loop by a factor of 5
        //we can set all adjacent rows from here and over 4 additional
        //space and set those pixels to the same color.
        //an interesting effect is to change line 4 (x + 2) with
        //Color.Navy.PackedValue; It makes it look like it has a
        //really hot blue center
        uint ci = (uint)newColorIndex;
        pixelData[(y * width) + x] = firePalette[ci];
        pixelData[(y * width) + x + 1] = firePalette[ci];
        pixelData[(y * width) + x + 2] = firePalette[ci];
        pixelData[(y * width) + x + 3] = firePalette[ci];
        pixelData[(y * width) + x + 4] = firePalette[ci];
    }
}
```

10

Fortunately, this code is very straightforward. You can see that we loop the entire width of our texture for the last row (y = height – 1) of our texture. We find the index in our palette of this color and then add or subtract 64 from that index, making sure we keep within the 0-to-255 range. This results in a new pseudo-random index that this pixel should now become.

When we loop through the bottom row, we are looking at every fifth pixel, so we are setting all five pixels: the one we are on as well as the four to the right of us. In this case, we are setting them all to the same color value. This produces nice wide flames. We could change this effect if we desire.

We now have code that creates a texture and then updates that texture on every frame. The creation consists of blacking out the entire texture and then setting the last 16 rows to some random colors in our fire palette. The update consists of reading in the pixel values of our texture and averaging the indices of the colors to come up with a new color for the pixel above the one we are reading in. We also reset the bottom row of our texture with new colors so the process can continue endlessly.

This brings us to the final piece of code in our fire demo. We have to draw our texture on the screen. Of course, this is the simplest piece because that is what we have been doing for the last two chapters! The Draw method code is shown here:

```
protected override void Draw(GameTime gameTime)
{
    graphics.GraphicsDevice.Clear(Color.Black);

    graphics.GraphicsDevice.Textures[0] = null;
    fire.SetData<uint>(pixelData);

    int h = graphics.GraphicsDevice.Viewport.Height - fire.Height;
    // TODO: Add your drawing code here
    sb.Begin(SpriteBlendMode.Additive);

    //bottom left
    sb.Draw(fire, new Vector2(0, 0), null, Color.White, 0, Vector2.Zero,
        2.0f, SpriteEffects.None, 0);

    //bottom right
    sb.Draw(fire, new Vector2(256, 0), null, Color.White, 0, Vector2.Zero,
        2.0f, SpriteEffects.FlipHorizontally, 0);

    //top left
    sb.Draw(fire, new Vector2(0, 0), null, Color.White, 0, Vector2.Zero,
        2.0f, SpriteEffects.FlipVertically, 0);

    //top right
    sb.Draw(fire, new Vector2(256, 0), null, Color.White, 0, Vector2.Zero,
```

```
        2.0f, SpriteEffects.FlipVertically ¦ SpriteEffects.FlipHorizontally,0);

    //left
    sb.Draw(fire, new Vector2(128,128), null, Color.White, MathHelper.PiOver2,
        new Vector2(64, 64), 2.0f, SpriteEffects.FlipHorizontally, 0);
    //right
    sb.Draw(fire, new Vector2(512-128, 128), null, Color.White,
        MathHelper.PiOver2, new Vector2(64, 64), 2.0f,
        SpriteEffects.FlipVertically, 0);

    sb.End();

    base.Draw(gameTime);
}
```

After clearing our device (to black because fire looks so much better on black than corn-flower blue), we clear the texture associated to the graphics device.

TIP

The `Texture2D.SetData` documentation warns of using the method inside the `Draw` method on the Xbox 360. Here's what it states:

"Do not use SetData when writing data to vertex buffers, index buffers, and textures. This method may lead to graphics corruption or crashes.

This is because, in cases where the size of the back buffer and depth-stencil buffer exceed the size of the Xbox 360 10 MB of embedded memory (EDRAM), predicated tiling is utilized on this platform to compensate for the additional memory require-ments. Predicated tiling is a process by which scene rendering is performed multiple times on subsections of the final render target dimensions.

When predicated tiling has been triggered, the drawing commands contained in the Draw function are not submitted until Present is called. (Note that Draw implicitly calls Present at the end of this method.) In this case, these resources are not available for modification until the GPU is finished with presenting the entire frame."

Because we are only creating a small amount of data, we can get by with it here, even on the Xbox 360. A much better way to handle the fire effect on the Xbox 360 (and even Windows) is to use HLSL. We will discuss this in Chapter 20, "Special Effects."

We then take the array of pixel colors and call `SetData` on the fire texture. We do the call here instead of in our `Update` method, so we only set it right before we draw it and not on every update. We are going to be repeating our small 128×128 texture on the screen for a total of six textures. We are basically going to make a frame of fire. Because our textures are going to be overlapping and we have cleared our background to black, we can easily set our blend mode to `Additive`. As we discussed earlier, this allows our images to draw on top of each other without interfering with each other. With additive blending, black is treated as transparent.

Now we will draw our texture six times. We will draw it twice (side-by-side) on the bottom, twice (side by side) on the top, and then once on the left and right. We will also scale the textures by two so they appear 256×256. If we tried to make the update method work with 256×256 pixels, it would be harder for the CPU to handle. We also rotate our left and right textures as needed.

For some of the textures we add a `SpriteEffect`. This enum simply allows us to flip a texture vertically, horizontally, both, or not at all. The enumeration does not have "both," but we can bit OR `FlipVertically` and `FlipHorizontally` together to get the desired result.

Now we have successfully created a fire effect, old-school style! Fortunately, there are now much faster ways of doing this. We can use pixel shaders to get much better results, which are discussed in detail in Part VI, "High Level Shader Language."

Explosions

What would a chapter on effects be without some explosions? We are going to create some explosion effects by animating more sprites. This means we need to have a texture that contains explosions. Fortunately, there is an application that Cliff Harris of Positech Games has provided free of charge that allows us to generate explosion textures. The application can be found at http://www.geocities.com/starlinesinc/. With this great tool and our cel animation library file, we are equipped to create great-looking explosions in our games.

We need to create a new solution named ExplosionDemo. We will need to reference our XELibrary project so we can use the cel animation class we built at the beginning of this chapter. We need to add our `using` clause and set up our Xbox 360 project as usual.

After we get our demo solution created, we can dive into our Game1.cs file and add the following private member fields to get started:

```
private InputHandler input;
private CelAnimationManager cam;
```

We can then add our input and cel animation management game components to our constructor. This should be engraved in your memory by now, so there is no need to display the code here. After we initialize our game components and add them to our game component collection, we can add the following code to our `LoadContent` method:

```
cam.AddAnimation("explosion", "explode_1", new CelCount(4,4), 16);
cam.AddAnimation("explosion2", "explode_1", new CelCount(4, 4), 16);
cam.AddAnimation("explosion3", "explode_3", new CelCount(4, 4), 12);
cam.AddAnimation("explosion4", "explode_4", new CelCount(4, 4), 20);
```

```
cam.AddAnimation("explosion5", "explode_3", new CelCount(4, 4), 12);
cam.AddAnimation("explosion6", "explode_4", new CelCount(4, 4), 20);

cam.AddAnimation("bigexplosion", "bigexplosion", new CelCount(4, 4), 18);
```

We are adding seven different animations to be drawn later. To refresh the animation code, we make the first parameter the name of the animation, which needs to be unique so we can easily access it later. The second parameter is the name of the texture. You can see that we use the same texture in some of these animations. The third parameter takes the size (in cel columns by cel rows) of our texture. The final parameter is the number of cels we want to render per second. These textures can be found on the CD. The Bigexplosion texture was made using Paint.NET by adding in the other three images and doubling their size and then using the additive blend method available in that program for each layer. Then it was saved as a .png file to be loaded here. The explosion generator is an excellent tool!

Finally, to get some great explosion effects, we only need to draw them on the screen. All the heavy lifting has been accomplished by the cel animation class we created earlier. Our Draw method is shown here:

```
protected override void Draw(GameTime gameTime)
{
    graphics.GraphicsDevice.Clear(Color.Black);

    spriteBatch.Begin(SpriteBlendMode.Additive, SpriteSortMode.Immediate,
        SaveStateMode.None);

    cam.Draw(gameTime, "explosion", spriteBatch, new Vector2(32, 32));
    cam.Draw(gameTime, "explosion2", spriteBatch, new Vector2(40, 40));
    cam.Draw(gameTime, "explosion3", spriteBatch, new Vector2(64, 32));
    cam.Draw(gameTime, "explosion4", spriteBatch, new Vector2(64, 64));
    cam.Draw(gameTime, "explosion5", spriteBatch, new Vector2(28, 40));
    cam.Draw(gameTime, "explosion6", spriteBatch, new Vector2(40, 64));

    cam.Draw(gameTime, "bigexplosion", spriteBatch, new Vector2(150, 150));
    spriteBatch.End();

    base.Draw(gameTime);
}
```

We clear the device to black and set our blend mode to Additive just like we did for our fire demo. We are doing this because we are going to draw multiple explosions in relatively the same spot to create the illusion of a massive explosion followed by a chain reaction of explosions. We are also going to display our larger explosion that was created by massaging the output of the generator in a paint program at a different location. Now we can have nice-looking explosions in our games by using this simple technique to create the effect.

Summary

We started this chapter by adding a very helpful class to our growing library, which was a class to handle animating a texture that is made up of cels. We used different ways to pass in data to create our animation, ranging from as simple as one animation in one texture to as complex as multiple animations in one texture. We send in a value that tells the animator how many cels per second it should draw on the screen.

After creating that class and testing it with a demo, we created another demo that showed how easy it is to rotate and scale sprites in XNA. You saw how to set the origin of our sprite and how that affects whether or not the sprite rotates around the center. We then discussed the different blending modes of XNA and modified our demo to display the objects in different blending modes. You saw how easy it is to change the blending modes on our render state after creating our sprite batch in immediate mode.

Fading to a particular color can be a nice transition effect, and we discussed a very easy way to accomplish that effect. We also discussed a technique to fade something into the scene. We could easily use the same code concept to fade that object in as a certain color.

We spent some time discussing an old technique for manipulating pixel data to create a fire effect. You saw the algorithm needed to pull off the effect and saw some modifications we could make. Although it was nice going down memory lane, there are better ways to create fire, which you learn about a little later in the book. We finished up this chapter by discussing how to make realistic-looking explosion effects in our games.

We touched on quite a few subjects through the different examples in this chapter. To make anything you've learned stick, it is beneficial to use it in examples and prototypes. This is what we are going to do in the next chapter. You will learn some new techniques, such as parallax scrolling, but will see how to implement the items you've already learned to create a nice, simple 2D game.

Creating a 2D Game

Y ou now have enough basics under your belt that we can actually create a small 2D game. In this chapter we use the knowledge you have gained so far and add a little bit more to create a parallax side-scrolling game, complete with collision detection.

Setting Up the Game Skeleton

To get started, we need to create our solution and project files as well as add the XELibrary project. We will call this game SimpleGame because it will be a rather basic (but complete) game.

After we have our environment set up, we can jump right into our Game1.cs code. To begin with, as usual, we create some member fields:

```
public enum GameState { StartMenu, Scene }
public GameState State = GameState.StartMenu;
private InputHandler input;
private Texture2D startMenu;
private Vector2 centerVector;
private int viewportWidth;
private int viewportHeight;
```

Because this is going to be slightly more complicated than a demo, in that we have to maintain our game state, we have set up an enum variable to define the different states for our game. For now, the game can only be in two states: StartMenu and Scene (or playing). We then declared a variable to hold the current game state and initialized it to the start menu state. We are going to use input in this game, so we set up that variable. We also declared a variable to hold our start menu texture. Finally, we create some reference variables so we do not have to continue to query our graphics device for the information.

We discuss states at length in Chapter 17, "Finite State Machines and Game State Management." For now, it is enough to know that our game can be in different states and we need to perform different tasks (draw certain items on the screen, update different objects, and so on) depending on which state our game is in.

After declaring our variables, we need to initialize and set up our input handler in our constructor.

```
input = new InputHandler(this);
Components.Add(input);
```

After that, we need to get our viewport's width and height values in our Initialize method, as follows:

```
viewportHeight = graphics.GraphicsDevice.Viewport.Height;
viewportWidth = graphics.GraphicsDevice.Viewport.Width;
```

Now we can load up our graphics content by adding the following code in our LoadContent:

```
startMenu = Content.Load<Texture2D>(@"Textures\startmenu");
centerVector = new Vector2((viewportWidth - startMenu.Width) / 2,
    (viewportHeight - startMenu.Height) / 2);
```

The first two lines should be very familiar—we are initializing our sprite batch and loading a texture called startMenu. The next line simply stores a vector so we will not have to calculate it every frame. It finds the position where we need to draw our start menu texture to center it inside the viewport. Next, we update our Update method with the following code:

```
switch (State)
{
    case GameState.Scene:
        {
            UpdateScene(gameTime);
            break;
        }
    case GameState.StartMenu:
        {
            UpdateStartMenu(;
            break;
        }
}
```

We are simply checking the state of our game to determine what we need to update. The starting point for these methods is shown here:

```
private bool WasPressed(int playerIndex,Buttons button, Keys keys)
{
    if (input.ButtonHandler.WasButtonPressed(playerIndex, button) ||
            input.KeyboardState.WasKeyPressed(keys))
        return (true);
    else
        return (false);
}

private void UpdateScene(GameTime gameTime)
{
    if (WasPressed(0,Buttons.Start, Keys.Enter))
    {
        State = GameState.StartMenu;
    }
}

private void UpdateStartMenu()
{
    if (WasPressed(0, Buttons.Start, Keys.Enter))
    {
        State = GameState.Scene;
    }
}
```

The first method is simply a helper method that allows us to easily determine if a button or key was pressed in the same call so we do not clutter up our code. The other two methods are doing the exact same thing at this point—that is, checking to see if Start has been pressed and, if so, changing the game state. Our Draw method will start out looking like this:

```
protected override void Draw(GameTime gameTime)
{
    graphics.GraphicsDevice.Clear(Color.Black);

    spriteBatch.Begin(SpriteBlendMode.Additive, SpriteSortMode.Immediate,
        SaveStateMode.None);

    if (State == GameState.StartMenu)
        DrawStartMenu();
```

```
        base.Draw(gameTime);

        spriteBatch.End();
}
```

We clear our backbuffer to black and start our sprite batch so we can draw to the screen. We then check to see if we should draw our start menu. We do not have a switch statement here because we will be drawing everything through our game components. We could turn the start menu into its own game component. However, there is not very much code, so we can live with it being directly inside our game class. The thing to notice about this method is the fact that we are calling our `base.Draw` method inside our sprite batch's `begin` and `end` methods. Thus, we can pass our sprite batch to our game components and they can draw using the same sprite batch object we have set up. We are going to be setting up this game using `Immediate` mode with `Additive` blending, and we are not going to be saving our render state.

Our `DrawStartMenu` method only has one line of code, which draws the start menu texture in the center of the screen:

```
spriteBatch.Draw(startMenu, centerVector, Color.White);
```

We need to add in a start menu asset to our Textures folder (which needs to be created) under the Content project. This should be old hat to you by now, but you can find the startmenu.png file on this book's CD under this chapter's folder. Once we have successfully added our asset, we should be able to compile and run our game skeleton. All the code does at this point is display the start menu and toggle between our two game states when Start (or Enter) is pressed. Our scene state (the state when the game is being played) does not have anything in it currently, so we just toggle between our start screen and a black screen.

Creating Parallax Scrolling

Let's make our `DrawScene` method do something—perhaps it could draw the scene. Our game is going to be a side scroller that looks 3D. The idea behind parallax scrolling is that we have a view of something (such as mountains or clouds) way off in the distance. This faraway plane scrolls at a pretty slow rate. Then we have one or more background planes that each scroll faster than the one before it. We then render our player, the enemies, and an immediate background, which all move at the same rate. Optionally, we could create a foreground plane that scrolls even faster than our main playing plane. The purpose of scrolling the planes at different rates is that it causes the illusion of those planes being off in the distance.

To start with, we are going make our `DrawScene` method draw our scrolling backgrounds. Then we create a `ScrollingBackgroundManager` game component to go inside our XELibrary project. The code for this new class can be found in Listing 11.1.

LISTING 11.1   ScrollingBackgroundManager.cs Goes Inside XELibrary to Handle Generic Parallax Scrolling Backgrounds

```csharp
using System;
using System.Collections.Generic;
using Microsoft.Xna.Framework;
using Microsoft.Xna.Framework.Graphics;
using Microsoft.Xna.Framework.Content;

namespace XELibrary
{
    public interface IScrollingBackgroundManager { }

    public class ScrollingBackgroundManager
        : Microsoft.Xna.Framework.GameComponent, IScrollingBackgroundManager
    {
        private Dictionary<string, ScrollingBackground> backgrounds =
            new Dictionary<string, ScrollingBackground>();
        private Dictionary<string, Texture2D> textures =
            new Dictionary<string, Texture2D>();
        private string contentPath;

        private int screenWidth;
        private int screenHeight;

        private float scrollRate;

        public ScrollingBackgroundManager(Game game, string contentPath)
            : base(game)
        {
            this.contentPath = contentPath;

            if (this.contentPath.LastIndexOf('\\') < this.contentPath.Length-1)
                this.contentPath += "\\";
            game.Services.AddService(
                typeof(IScrollingBackgroundManager), this);
        }

        public override void Initialize()
        {
            base.Initialize();

            GraphicsDeviceManager graphics =
                (GraphicsDeviceManager)Game.Services.GetService(
                typeof(IGraphicsDeviceManager));
```

```
        screenWidth = graphics.GraphicsDevice.Viewport.Width;
        screenHeight = graphics.GraphicsDevice.Viewport.Height;
    }
    public void AddBackground(string backgroundKey, string textureName,
        Vector2 position, float scrollRateRatio)
    {
        AddBackground(backgroundKey, textureName, position, null,
            scrollRateRatio, Color.White);
    }

    public void AddBackground(string backgroundKey, string textureName,
        Vector2 position, Rectangle? sourceRect, float scrollRateRatio,
        Color color)
    {
        ScrollingBackground background = new ScrollingBackground(
            textureName, position, sourceRect, scrollRateRatio, color);

        background.ScrollRate = scrollRate * scrollRateRatio;

        if (!textures.ContainsKey(textureName))
        {
            textures.Add(textureName, Game.Content.Load<Texture2D>(
                contentPath + textureName));
        }

        if (backgrounds.ContainsKey(backgroundKey))
            backgrounds[backgroundKey] = background;
        else
            backgrounds.Add(backgroundKey, background);
    }

    public override void  Update(GameTime gameTime)
    {
        foreach (KeyValuePair<string, ScrollingBackground> background
                                                    in backgrounds)
        {
            ScrollingBackground sb = background.Value;

            sb.Position.X += (sb.ScrollRate *
                (float)gameTime.ElapsedGameTime.TotalSeconds);
            sb.Position.X = sb.Position.X % textures[sb.TextureName].Width;
        }

        base.Update(gameTime);
    }
```

```csharp
    public void Draw(string backgroundKey,
        SpriteBatch batch)
    {
        ScrollingBackground sb = backgrounds[backgroundKey];
        Texture2D texture = textures[sb.TextureName];
        //Draw the main texture
        batch.Draw(texture, sb.Position, sb.SourceRect,
            sb.Color, 0, Vector2.Zero, 1.0f, SpriteEffects.None, 0f);

        //Determine if we need to scroll left or right
        Vector2 offset;
        if (sb.Positive)
            offset = sb.Position - (new Vector2(texture.Width, 0));
        else
            offset = new Vector2(texture.Width, 0) + sb.Position;
        //now draw the background again at the appropriate offset
        //NOTE: If our Width is larger than two times the size of our
        //texture then the code will need to be modified
        batch.Draw(texture, offset, sb.SourceRect,
            sb.Color, 0, Vector2.Zero, 1.0f, SpriteEffects.None, 0f);
    }

    public float ScrollRate
    {
        get { return(scrollRate); }
    }

    public void SetScrollRate(float scrollRate)
    {
        this.scrollRate = scrollRate;

      foreach (ScrollingBackground sb in backgrounds.Values)
          sb.ScrollRate = scrollRate * sb.ScrollRateRatio;
    }
}

public class ScrollingBackground
{
    public Rectangle? SourceRect;
    public string TextureName;
    public Vector2 Position;
    public float ScrollRateRatio;
    public float ScrollRate;
    public Color Color;
    public bool Positive
    {
```

11

```
            get { return (ScrollRate > 0); }
        }

        public ScrollingBackground(string textureName, Vector2 position,
            Rectangle? sourceRect, float scrollRateRatio, Color color)
        {
            TextureName = textureName;
            Position = position;
            SourceRect = sourceRect;
            ScrollRateRatio = scrollRateRatio;
            Color = color;
        }
    }
}
```

The scrolling background manager class works much like the cel animation manager class we created in the last chapter. We add backgrounds to a dictionary, and we add textures to a dictionary so we do not waste memory on the same texture. It could prove to be helpful to create a texture manager game service that our components could reference when adding textures. In this case, we will not be sharing textures between our cel animation manager and our scrolling background manager, but seeing patterns like this should make us consider it.

We derive from GameComponent so we have an Update method that gets called automatically. Inside that method we move our backgrounds based on each of their scroll rate values. Just like we had a cel animation object, we also have a scrolling background object. Each object contains information about itself that the manager has easy access to so it can manipulate each object as needed. We also set this game component up as a game service because we need to access it from other components as we write our game.

Some of the properties the scrolling background object include are the texture name, the position of the texture, how fast the texture should scroll, any color tinting values, and a source rectangle value that allows us to have multiple backgrounds inside one texture.

We did not inherit from DrawableGameComponent because we need to pass in specific information (backgroundKey and batch) to our Draw method. Our scrolling background manager will draw a scrolling background based on the background key it is given (again, much like our cel animation manager). The key piece of the code is the last part of our Draw method. After drawing our main texture, we then determine where to draw an additional texture to create our scrolling effect. We check to see if we are scrolling left or right, and based on that we put the next copy of the background we are drawing to one side or the other. Remember, the position of the background is set in our Update method.

Now that we have another class added to our library, we can plug it into our game code so that when we press Start we actually see something. However, before jumping to our game code, we want to create an additional game component to have the game handle our backgrounds. We are adding this game component to our actual game project and not our library because this is specific to our game. We are putting it inside a component so we can keep our game code separated in a logical place and maintain it easier.

We are going to create a game component called `Background`. We need to derive from `DrawableGameComponent`. Let's make sure we add a `using` statement for our XELibrary so we can access our `ScrollingBackgroundManager` class. Inside this file, we can create a member field to hold our scrolling background manager and a sprite batch:

```
private ScrollingBackgroundManager sbm;
private SpriteBatch spriteBatch;
```

We can also initialize our scrolling background manager object and add it to our components in our constructor. We can also cast our game object to our specific `SimpleGame` object type. This allows us to access the game state.

```
public Background(Game game, string contentPath)
    : base(game)
{
    sbm = new ScrollingBackgroundManager(game, contentPath);
    game.Components.Add(sbm);
}
```

Our constructor takes in the game instance like all game components do, but it also receives the content path so we can get to our textures as needed. We can load game components inside of game components like we are doing here. We also set the game component to be disabled because our game launches with the start menu active first, and we do not want any kind of update code to be running when it does not need to.

We will need to create a custom `Load` method that our game needs to call:

```
public void Load(SpriteBatch spriteBatch)
{
    this.spriteBatch = spriteBatch;
}
```

This method takes in a sprite batch as a parameter. This way, our components can all share the same sprite batch to draw on. This is better than creating many different sprite batches for each of our components. It also gives us more control because we can draw everything in immediate mode. We would have problems if we started up an `Immediate` mode batch in our game, created a different sprite batch, and then called `End` on that batch before we finished with our `Immediate` mode batch.

Next, we are going to look at the code we need to add inside our `LoadContent` method:

```
int viewportWidth = GraphicsDevice.Viewport.Width;
int viewportHeight = GraphicsDevice.Viewport.Height;
int textureWidth = 1024;
int cloudHeight = 512;
int cityHeight = 256;
```

```
int foregroundHeight = 128;
int streetHeight = 128;
int cloudY = 0;
int streetY = cloudHeight;
int foregroundY = streetY + streetHeight;
int cityY = foregroundY + foregroundHeight;

sbm.SetScrollRate(-75.0f); //75 pixels a second

sbm.AddBackground("clouds1", "background",
    Vector2.Zero,
    new Rectangle(0, cloudY, textureWidth, cloudHeight),
    0.4f, Color.White);

sbm.AddBackground("clouds2", "background",
    new Vector2(128, 0),
    new Rectangle(0, cloudY, textureWidth, cloudHeight),
    0.6f, new Color(255, 255, 255, 127));

sbm.AddBackground("street", "background",
    new Vector2(0, viewportHeight - streetHeight),
    new Rectangle(0, streetY, textureWidth, streetHeight),
    1.0f, Color.White);

sbm.AddBackground("foreground", "background",
    new Vector2(0, viewportHeight - foregroundHeight),
    new Rectangle(0, foregroundY, textureWidth, foregroundHeight),
    1.5f, Color.White);

sbm.AddBackground("city", "background",
    new Vector2(0, viewportHeight - cityHeight - streetHeight + 64),
    new Rectangle(0, cityY, textureWidth, cityHeight),
    0.8f, Color.White);
```

Dissecting this code, you can see that the first thing we do is create several variables storing height and y values. These values are the position of the background in our texture. We only have one 1024×1024 background texture and are creating a total of five backgrounds from that one texture. For these values to make sense, look at the background image in Figure 11.1. Let's go ahead and add the texture background.png into our Content project (under the Textures folder).

After initializing the variables that make it easier for us to work with our background coordinates, we add our backgrounds to our scrolling background manager. We add two different cloud backgrounds, but they are really accessing the same location from our texture. We pass in the initial position of 0,0 to draw one background, and then we offset the other cloud background by 128 pixels to the right. For the second cloud background, we set the alpha channel of our color modulation parameter to about halfway transparent.

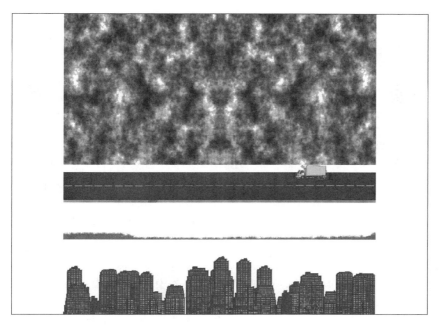

FIGURE 11.1   We are able to pack multiple backgrounds into one texture.

This way, we can get an interesting depth effect for our clouds. It would be even better if the two cloud textures were not the same. We could modify our manager to allow a SpriteEffect and flip it horizontally or vertically to get a nice effect. However, the example as is gets the point across. We also set different speeds for the cloud backgrounds. The one farthest away moves slower than the closer one. Everything is relative to the speed we set a couple statements earlier. The next three statements simply set more backgrounds at different speeds from different sources in our texture and place them in different locations in our scene.

Finally, to get our scrolling backgrounds to draw on our scene, we need to add the following code to our background game component's Draw method:

```
sbm.Draw("clouds1", spriteBatch);
sbm.Draw("clouds2", spriteBatch);

GraphicsDevice.RenderState.SourceBlend = Blend.SourceAlpha;
GraphicsDevice.RenderState.DestinationBlend = Blend.InverseSourceAlpha;
sbm.Draw("city", spriteBatch);
sbm.Draw("street", spriteBatch);
```

Remember, when we set up our sprite batch in our game's Draw method, we set the blend mode to additive, and we will set our sort mode to immediate, which means our objects draw in the order in which we send them. By using immediate mode, we can also switch blend modes in the middle of drawing our sprites. We do that here. We draw our two cloud backgrounds in additive blending mode (because they are being drawn on top of each other), but then we switch to normal alpha blending mode to draw the remaining pieces of our scene.

> **NOTE**
>
> Typically we would not use additive blending for our clouds because different cloud textures could produce unwanted results. The colors would be easily oversaturated. It would be better to use alpha blending and make sure our cloud textures include an alpha channel. However, for demonstration purposes we set our clouds up to be drawn with additive blending.

You saw that when the default `SpriteBatch.Begin` method is called, different render states get modified. These states were listed in Table 9.1 in Chapter 9, "2D Basics." In that table, you saw that the source blend state is set to `SourceAlpha`, and the destination blend state is set to `InverseSourceAlpha`. We set those values manually here because we are in immediate mode using additive blending and we want to get back into an alpha blending mode.

Finally, let's add the needed code to our game class. After we declare our variable to hold our background, we need to set up our background in our game's constructor method, as follows:

```
background = new Background(this, @"Textures\");
background.Enabled = background.Visible = false;
Components.Add(background);
```

When we start out, we disable the game component because we will be in our start menu mode to begin with. We need to call the background's `Load` method to pass it our sprite batch. We do this at the bottom of our `LoadContent` method:

```
background.Load(spriteBatch);
```

Let's add our foreground "background." We need to do this after everything else has drawn on the screen. Therefore, we cannot do it in our background's game component; instead, we will do it inside our `Draw` method in our game code after we call the `base.Draw` method:

```
//Display our foreground (after game components)
if (State == GameState.Scene)
    sbm.Draw("foreground", spriteBatch);
```

By calling the `Draw` method on our scrolling background manager after we call our `base.Draw` method, we ensure that this will be last thing drawn on the screen (unless a particular `DrawOrder` on a component is set). We need to add a variable to hold our `ScrollingBackgroundManager` game component. We have called it sbm. Next, we need to initialize this variable inside our constructor, but because our `Background` game component already created it, we just need to reference it. We can do that because it is a game service. We need to add this code to our game's `Initialize` method:

```
sbm = (ScrollingBackgroundManager)Services.GetService(
                           typeof(IScrollingBackgroundManager));
```

We added that statement after calling `base.Initialize` so that the background component has a chance to load it.

Switching States

Now we need to correctly switch out between our two states (`StartMenu` and `Scene`). We already have a stub created for our `UpdateStartMenu` method. We need to replace the contents of our `WasPressed` condition with the following code:

```
ActivateGame();
```

We can now create the method as follows:

```
private void ActivateGame()
{
    background.Visible = background.Enabled = true; //start updating scene
    State = GameState.Scene;
}
```

That is all there is to creating scrolling backgrounds. We took it a step further and created multiple scrolling backgrounds to create a parallax scroller. If we wanted to create a typical scrolling background, we would only need to modify our scroll rate based on our player's movement.

NOTE

Creating a large background that can repeat is not the only (or even the usual) way of creating side scrollers. Typically textures are broken down into tiles and drawn using level maps. Many resources online discuss tiles. The Role-Playing Game Starter Kit (http://creators.xna.com/en-us/starterkit/roleplayinggame) uses this tile-based approach.

At this point, if we run the code and press the Start button or Enter key, we will see our background scrolling. We want to be able to get back to our start menu, so we need to hook up the code to make that happen. To start, we need to replace the contents of the `WasPressed` condition inside the `UpdateScene` method:

```
ActivateStartMenu();
```

Now we can create this method:

```
public void ActivateStartMenu()
{
    //stop updating scene backgrounds
    background.Visible = background.Enabled = false;
    State = GameState.StartMenu;
}
```

We will be updating these two methods (`ActivateStartMenu` and `ActivateGame`) as we create more components our game will use. This is where we hide/show and disable/enable our different game components. Our background game component is just the first. We need to go ahead and call the `ActivateStartMenu` method at the end of our `LoadContent` method.

If we run our code now, we can see that we can toggle between our start menu and our scene as expected. The problem, though, is that even though we have changed our background component to be disabled and not visible, when we move from our scene into our start menu, the background is still scrolling. Looking at the truck and watching as we go in and out of our scene, we can see that it is still updating in the background. The reason is because even though we disabled our background component, the scrolling background manager component was not disabled. We need to hook into the `Enable` property of our background component so we can correctly set our scrolling background manager's `Enable` property using the following code:

```
protected override void OnEnabledChanged(object sender, EventArgs args)
{
    base.OnEnabledChanged(sender, args);
    sbm.Enabled = this.Enabled;
}
```

Game components allow us to tie into the `Enabled` and `Visible` properties. When they change, the changed event is kicked off. We can override the preceding method to set our scrolling backorder manager game component's `Enabled` property.

Drawing Our Hero

We have a game with simple state management that allows us to switch back and forth from a start screen to our game scene. The next step we need to take is to draw our main character on the screen. The code for the player game component we will be adding to our game is shown in Listing 11.2.

LISTING 11.2 Player.cs

```
using System;
using System.Collections.Generic;
using Microsoft.Xna.Framework;
```

```
using Microsoft.Xna.Framework.Input;
using Microsoft.Xna.Framework.Graphics;

using XELibrary; // for input handler

namespace SimpleGame
{
    public class Player : Microsoft.Xna.Framework.DrawableGameComponent
    {
        public string CurrentAnimation = "hero";
        public Vector2 Position;

        private float kickTime = 0.0f;
        private bool kicking = false;

        private InputHandler input;
        private CelAnimationManager cam;
        private SpriteBatch spriteBatch;

        public bool Attacking
        {
            // could OR ( ¦¦ ) a bunch of other actions if we had them
            get { return (kicking); }
        }

        public Player(Game game) : base(game)
        {
            input = (InputHandler)game.Services.GetService(
                typeof(IInputHandler));
            cam = (CelAnimationManager)game.Services.GetService(
                typeof(ICelAnimationManager));
            Visible = Enabled = false;
        }

        public void Load(SpriteBatch spriteBatch)
        {
            this.spriteBatch = spriteBatch;
        }

        public void SetPause(bool paused)
        {
            cam.ToggleAnimation(CurrentAnimation, paused);
        }

        public override void Update(Microsoft.Xna.Framework.GameTime gameTime)
        {
```

```
        if (WasPressed(0, Buttons.A, Keys.Space))
        {
            kickTime = 0;
            kicking = true;
        }

        if (kicking)
        {
            CurrentAnimation = "hero-kick";
            kickTime += (float)gameTime.ElapsedGameTime.TotalSeconds;
            if (kickTime > 0.5f)
                kicking = false;
        }
        else
            CurrentAnimation = "hero";

        base.Update(gameTime);
    }

    protected override void LoadContent()
    {
        cam.AddAnimation("hero", "hero", new CelCount(4, 4), 16);
        cam.AddAnimation("hero-kick", "hero-kick", new CelCount(4, 1), 8);

    }

    public override void Draw(GameTime gameTime)
    {
        float elapsedTime = (float)gameTime.ElapsedGameTime.TotalSeconds;

        cam.Draw(elapsedTime, CurrentAnimation, spriteBatch, Position);

        base.Draw(gameTime);
    }

    private bool WasPressed(int playerIndex,  Buttons button, Keys keys)
    {
        if (input.ButtonHandler.WasButtonPressed(playerIndex, button) ||
                input.KeyboardState.WasKeyPressed(keys))
            return (true);
        else
            return (false);
    }
    }
}
```

Our player game component has two public fields: CurrentAnimation and Position. Although in this game we will not be changing the player's position, it would be an easy modification. Therefore, we will leave it here in case we want to make that modification later. The CurrentAnimation string holds the cel animation key of the animation our player is displaying. We set up our cel animation in our LoadContent method.

We currently only have two different animations for our hero, which are him running and him kicking. A real game would have more, but this allows us to see how we can switch between the different animations. We have an Attacking property that tells us whether or not our player is attacking. This currently is only returning our kicking variable, but if we had other actions, such as punching, swinging a machete, and so on, we could just "OR" them all together with this one property. This will allow us to handle our collision detection appropriately. We discuss collision detection later in this chapter.

We modified our CelAnimationManager to be a game service so we could access it in multiple components. We access the InputHandler and the CelAnimationManager both in our constructor. This game component and most we will be creating for this game have their own Load methods that must be called manually. This Load method will be used to pass around our sprite batch.

To change our cel animation manager to a game service, we need to create an interface (it can be blank) and then inherit from the interface. Then inside of the constructor we need to add the interface to our game's Services collection. We did this for our scrolling background manager if you need a reference on how to set it up.

We have a helper method for checking input in our class called WasPressed. This method allows us to pass in a player index, the button we want to check, and the key we want to check. This helps make our code a little cleaner. We could actually add it directly to our InputHandler class because we also need to use it in our main game class.

Because this is a drawable game component, not only do we have the Update method, but we also have the Draw method. In our Update method we are checking to see whether the kick button or key is being pressed. If so, we change our animation to our kick texture and set up a timer so we know how long to play our animation. It would be more robust to update our cel animation manager to allow us to call it and tell it to render the animation one time only (or a certain number of times). Time and space do not allow us to do this here, so we just improvise with a timer in our game code. We do that here and also when we draw our explosions a little later. When we are finished with the kicking, we revert back to our main hero animation (which is the hero running full speed ahead). The Draw method simply calls our cel animation manager and tells it to draw our current animation at the position we specify. All our player code is nicely contained in one source file.

We need to create our player variable with our Player type. We also need to initialize it and add it to our components in the game's constructor, as follows:

```
player = new Player(this);
player.Position = playerPosition;
Components.Add(player);
```

It is important that the preceding code is placed after we initialize our background game component. This is because the Components collection is called in the order the items were added. We could override this with the DrawOrder property. The components that are drawn last (have highest draw order) will be on top of other items drawn on the screen.

We need to declare our playerPosition member field as Vector2 with the values 64,350. Instead of having numbers sprinkled all through our code, we can create constants or variables (whichever is more appropriate) at the top of our code files for easy access. Now, because our backgrounds are relatively small, we are hard-coding the width and height for this game to be 640×480. These are also set at the top of SimpleGame:

```
private Vector2 playerPosition = new Vector2(64, 350);
private int width = 640;
private int height = 480;
```

We use the width and height properties in our constructor to force our aspect ratio so we do not have to do any extra calculation for our character placement:

```
graphics.PreferredBackBufferWidth = width;
graphics.PreferredBackBufferHeight = height;
```

Before we can check how our player looks, we need to add the actual textures to our project. The textures hero.png and hero-kick.png can be found in the usual manner. We need to call the Load method in our player component so we can initialize the sprite batch. We do that inside our LoadContent method:

```
player.Load(spriteBatch);
```

Now we need to update our ActivateStartMenu method to enable our hero and make him visible:

```
player.Visible = player.Enabled = false;
player.SetPause(true);
```

We want to do the exact opposite in our ActivateGame method:

```
player.Visible = player.Enabled = true;
player.SetPause(false);
```

The SetPause method calls the ToggleAnimation method in our cel animation manager. However, we do not have that particular overloaded method, and we need to add it to our CelAnimationManager.cs file:

```
public void ToggleAnimation(string animationKey, bool paused)
{
    if (animations.ContainsKey(animationKey))
        animations[animationKey].Paused = paused;
}
```

Finally, we need to add a `CelAnimationManager` object to our `SimpleGame` class. We then need to initialize it inside our constructor. This should be done before initializing our player game component because our player game component relies on the cel animation manager. We now have our hero running on the screen. If we run the game at this point, we will see our player is moving and he is getting paused correctly. We can also press the spacebar or the A button to get him to kick.

Drawing Our Enemies

Our hero looks a little lonely, so we need to give him some competition. We can add in some enemies in this section. We are going to use an enemy manager that will control our enemies. `EnemyManager` is a game component that will have a collection of `Enemy` objects. The code for these two classes can be found in Listing 11.3.

LISTING 11.3   EnemyManager.cs

```
using System;
using System.Collections.Generic;
using Microsoft.Xna.Framework;
using Microsoft.Xna.Framework.Graphics;

using XELibrary; //for cel animation manager

namespace SimpleGame
{
    public class EnemyManager
        : Microsoft.Xna.Framework.DrawableGameComponent
    {
        private readonly int maxXPosition = 800;
        private readonly int minXPosition = 650;
        private readonly float collisionDistance = 64.0f;
        private int yPosition = 350;
        private int xPosition = 650;

        private Enemy[] enemies;
        private int totalEnemies;
        private int enemiesThisLevel;
        private int maxEnemies;
        private bool paused;
        private SpriteBatch spriteBatch;
        private Random rand;
        private CelAnimationManager cam;
        public bool EnemiesExist
        {
            get { return (totalEnemies < enemiesThisLevel); }
        }
```

```csharp
public EnemyManager(Game game)
    : base(game)
{
    // TODO: Construct any child components here
    rand = new Random();

    cam = (CelAnimationManager)game.Services.GetService(
        typeof(ICelAnimationManager));
}

public void Load(SpriteBatch spriteBatch, int maxEnemies,
    int enemiesThisLevel, float speed)
{
    this.spriteBatch = spriteBatch;

    this.enemiesThisLevel = enemiesThisLevel;
    this.totalEnemies = 0;
    this.maxEnemies = maxEnemies;

    Vector2 position = new Vector2();
    enemies = new Enemy[maxEnemies];
    for (int i = 0; i < maxEnemies; i++)
    {
        position.X = GetNextPosition(); //off screen
        position.Y = yPosition;

        enemies[i] = new Enemy();
        enemies[i].Active = true;
        enemies[i].Position = position;
        enemies[i].Velocity = new Vector2(-speed, 0.0f);
    }
}

public void SetPause(bool paused)
{
    cam.ToggleAnimation("robot", paused);
}
public void ToggleAnimation()
{
    cam.ToggleAnimation("robot");
}

private float GetNextPosition()
{
    xPosition += rand.Next(50, 100);
    if (xPosition > maxXPosition)
```

```
        xPosition = minXPosition;
    return (xPosition);
}

protected override void LoadContent()
{
    cam.AddAnimation("robot", "robot", new CelCount(4, 4), 16);
}

public int CollidedWithPlayer(Vector2 playerPosition)
{
    for (int i = 0; i < enemies.Length; i++)
    {
        Enemy enemy = enemies[i];
        if (enemy.Active)                    {
            float distance =(playerPosition - enemy.Position).Length();
            //within collision distance?
            if (distance < collisionDistance)
                return (i);
        }
    }
    return (-1);
}

public Vector2 Die(int enemyIndex)
{
    Enemy enemy = enemies[enemyIndex];
    enemy.Active = false;
    Vector2 oldPosition = enemy.Position;

    if (totalEnemies + maxEnemies < enemiesThisLevel)
    {
        Vector2 position = new Vector2();
        position.X = GetNextPosition(); //off screen
        position.Y = yPosition;
        enemy.Position = position;
        enemy.Active = true;
    }
    totalEnemies++;

    return (oldPosition);
}

public override void Update(GameTime gameTime)
{
    float elapsed = (float)gameTime.ElapsedGameTime.TotalSeconds;
```

```
            for (int i = 0; i < enemies.Length; i++)
            {
                Enemy enemy = enemies[i];
                if (enemy.Active)
                {                 .
                    enemy.Position += (enemy.Velocity * elapsed);
                }
            }
            base.Update(gameTime);
        }

        public override void Draw(GameTime gameTime)
        {
            for (int i = 0; i < enemies.Length; i++)
            {
                Enemy enemy = enemies[i];
                if (enemy.Active)
                    cam.Draw(gameTime, "robot", spriteBatch, enemy.Position);
            }

            base.Draw(gameTime);
        }
    }

    public class Enemy
    {
        public Vector2 Position;
        public Vector2 Velocity;
        public bool Active;
    }
}
```

We will first talk about our Enemy class. This is a very simple class that has three public fields: Position, Velocity, and Active. The Position field holds this particular enemy's position. The Velocity field holds the direction and speed of our enemy. Finally, the Active flag determines if any logic should be done on this enemy. Instead of creating and destroying a bunch of Enemy objects, we create a list and then just set them to not active when they die and reset them when they are created.

We have a Load method that not only allows us access to the game's sprite batch, but it also tells us how many enemies we need to create, the total enemies to generate, and the speed at which they move. This makes it ideal to set up these properties when we load levels. Although we will not be creating levels in this simple game, it would not be much of a challenge to create a level manager with the needed information that could then populate our enemy manager's Load method.

We allow pausing our enemy sprite animation much like we did with our player. We create our enemies either at the time our Load method is called or when a previous enemy dies and we have not reached the total number of enemies specified in the Load method. When we update our enemies, we just iterate through our array and set their positions. We set the enemy position by randomly finding their x position through our GetNextPosition method. We do not do anything sophisticated, so the current code allows our enemies to stack up on each other. We could add better logic to make sure we do not set an enemy's position to one that is already used.

During our Draw method, we set our render state to make sure we are in alpha blended mode, and we loop through our enemies and draw each one (assuming it is active). We have two other methods in our EnemyManager class: Die and CollidedWithPlayer. We discuss the CollidedWithPlayer method in the next section. The Die method will be called if the game determines that a collision has happened and the player was attacking. If that happens, the game will call the enemy manager's Die method, passing in the particular enemy that needs to die.

We always have the maximum number of enemies generated, so as soon as one dies, another one is created off screen. Before we generate a new one, we make sure we should by checking to see if there are more enemies to create based on the values passed into the Load method. The Die method first sets the enemy's Active flag to false. It then stores the enemy's position. If more enemies are needed, another enemy is generated. Finally, the total number of enemies that have died is increased. We use this value to determine if there are any more enemies around. Our property EnemiesExist returns the condition if the total numbers of enemies is less than the enemies created for this level.

Before we dig into the collision code and collision detection concepts in general, let's utilize our enemy manager game component inside our game. Of course we need to create a member variable (enemies) and then initialize it and add it to our game component collections inside of our constructor right after we add our player game component.

Inside the ActivateStartMenu method, we need to disable our enemies and keep them from drawing on our screen. We also pause their animation for good measure:

```
enemies.Visible = enemies.Enabled = false; //stop updating enemies
enemies.SetPause(true);
```

Inside the ActivateGame method, we need to activate the enemy manager again. In fact, if we are getting into our game state, we need to load our enemies, but it would be nice to allow our gamer to pause the game. This means we need a way to know whether the game is starting from a paused state or a new game state. Let's add the following code to handle this in our ActiveGame method:

```
if (!paused)
    enemies.Load(spriteBatch, 5, 20, 120.0f); //should be read by level
enemies.Visible = enemies.Enabled = true; // resume updating enemies
enemies.SetPause(false);
```

We are going to use a boolean variable to determine whether or not our game was paused. If it was not paused, we are going to call the Load method of our EnemyManager. In a real game we would create a level manager and pass in data based on our level information. For example, level 1 would have a total of five enemies on the screen at once, with a total of 20 enemies for the level, and the enemies would move at a rate of 120 pixels per second. We could have our levels store different values for these items, and each time we finish a level, the next level's data is sent to the enemy manager.

We need to declare and initialize the paused field to false. In our UpdateScene method inside the WasPressed condition, right before we call our ActivateStartMenu method we need to set the paused variable to true. We need to set it to false inside the UpdateStartMenu method, at the end of our WasPressed condition after the call to ActivateGame. Making these changes will pause our game when we press the Start button while playing and then resume the game when we are no longer looking at our start menu.

We need to load our enemy textures to our project. The texture is called robot.png and can be found on the CD. We can copy it to the same location as our other textures. We can run our game and see our enemies are drawing on the screen (five of them) and coming toward us. We have not spaced them out at all and let them generate their x position randomly, so they could be all over each other. For this example, though, it is good enough for us to test out our concepts. The problem is that they run right past us because we have not set up any kind of collision detection.

Handling Collision Detection

In general, *collision detection* is the process of checking certain objects to see if they have collided with other objects. Algorithms to do this can be very simplistic (like ours is for this game) or very complex. A collision-detection algorithm can really drop a game's frame rate. The algorithm consists of searching for objects and comparing them.

One possible algorithm is to loop through all objects and check whether they collide with each other. Another involves checking only certain portions of the screen (in 2D) or the world (in 3D) where the player is. There are many ways to store our scene objects. We can simply store them in a list, like this game, or put them into a tree structure that we can quickly scan using an algorithm to check only certain objects. The idea is that we could easily exclude certain objects to check based on their position in the tree.

One possibility is to split up the screen or world into quadrants and only check the quadrant we care about. This can break down if we have bullets flying everywhere and most of the world has objects that can react (glass shattering, metal denting, water cooler gushing water, and so on) to being hit by a bullet. In these cases, it is all about checking the immediate objects close to the bullet we are testing. We would iterate through all our bullets, checking for objects close by and handling the collision. There is no reason to test whether the bullet collided with an object across the room when the bullet is currently positioned on this side of the room.

Different methods are appropriate for different needs. There are many ways to store our game objects so we can quickly search them. Although we will not even begin to scratch the surface of possibilities, it will really pay off to do some research in this area.

The key to remember is that perfect is the enemy of good enough. This means that if your game can get by with a more simplistic collision-detection algorithm, by all means use it. If it needs more robust collision-detection capabilities, benchmarking different algorithms is key.

Not only are there different ways to search for objects to test for the collision, there is the actual testing that can cause a slowdown in frame rates. For our game we are simply getting a vector between our player and the enemy we are checking. We have both positions as vectors, and we can simply subtract those two vectors to determine how far away they are from each other. Think of this as a bounding sphere with a certain radius around our objects; if we get within a certain range, we flag that we have a collision. Sometimes this is good enough. Other times, we need per-pixel collision detection in 2D or vertex collision detection in 3D.

Any detection we perform can adversely affect performance, and we need to be aware of the cost and determine how well it scales. If we only will ever have 100 objects in our scene, then our algorithm only needs to be good enough to handle those 100. If that increases, our algorithm might need to change so we do not drop frames.

We only have five enemies on the screen at a time, and we are only checking for collision against one player, so we pass our player's position to our enemy manager, which loops through all the enemies and does a simple vector distance check to determine whether a collision has occurred. The code takes the difference between the player's position and the enemy's position and checks the length of that vector. In our case, if the length is less than 64 units (pixels in this case), we return that a collision has occurred, and in this implementation we return the index of the enemy collided with.

A Collision-Detection Optimization

An easy optimization we can perform immediately is to not calculate the length of the vector because that involves a medium-expensive square root computation. Instead, we can use the `Vector2.DistanceSquared` method, which bypasses the square root computation, and compare this value with the square of our collision radius. We could replace our `EnemyManager`'s `CollidedWithPlayer` method with the following:

```
public int CollidedWithPlayer(Vector2 playerPosition)
{
    for (int i = 0; i < enemies.Length; i++)
    {
        Enemy enemy = enemies[i];
        if (enemy.Active)
        {
            float distance = Vector2.DistanceSquared(playerPosition,
                enemy.Position);
            if (distance < collisionDistance * collisionDistance)
```

```
                    return (i);
                }
            }


        return (-1);
    }
```

Inside our game object, we check to see whether or not the player is attacking. If the player is not attacking, he loses because the enemy touched him. If the player is attacking, the enemy dies. We need to set up our collision test inside our game so we create the following method:

```
private void CheckForCollisions(GameTime gameTime)
{
    int enemyIndex = enemies.CollidedWithPlayer(player.Position);
    if (enemyIndex != -1)
    {
        if (player.Attacking)
        {
            //die robot
            Vector2 enemyPosition = enemies.Die(enemyIndex);
        }
        else
        {
            background.Enabled = false;
            enemies.SetPause(true);
            enemies.Enabled = false;
            player.SetPause(true);
            player.Enabled = false;
        }
    }
}
```

You can see that we call the CollidedWithPlayer method we set up in our enemy manager, which checks the distance between the two sprites' positions. If a collision occurs, we check to see if the player was attacking. If so, the robot is destroyed. If the player was not attacking when the collision took place, we disable the background, player, and enemies game components.

We need to call our CheckForCollisions method inside our UpdateScene method. Now on every update of our game while we are in the Scene state, we will see if the player has collided with an enemy.

At this point we are correctly detecting whether the player is colliding with any of the enemy robots. We have our enemies dying and disappearing when they are kicked. If there are more enemies to be created, they are created offscreen correctly. If the player collides with a robot and the player is not attacking, the game is stopped and must be restarted to continue.

Winning and Losing

Now that we have successfully detected our collisions, we need to do something when we successfully kill all the enemies or when we get destroyed. Let's set two more game states for these events. We will add `Lost` and `Won` to our `GameState` enum.

We need to add the following code to the false condition inside our `CheckForCollisions` method:

```
State = GameState.Lost;
```

Now we need to add the following code to the `UpdateScene` method under our call to `CheckForCollisions`:

```
if (!enemies.EnemiesExist)
{
    //Level over  (would advance level here and on last level state won game)
    enemies.SetPause(true);
    enemies.Enabled = false;
    player.SetPause(true);
    player.Enabled = false;
    background.Enabled = false;
    State = GameState.Won;
}
```

We check our property to see if any more enemies exist after checking for collisions. If no more exist, we are done with the level (and because this game only has one level, we are done with the game). We set our state to `Won` to signify that we won.

Adding Transitions

We are going to create a transition effect that fades our screen out when we win or lose. If we win, we will fade to black; if we lose, we will fade to red. Then our fading game component will manage its fading cycle. When this is complete, it will call our game's `ActivateStartMenu` to get us back into a playable state.

Let's add some more conditions to our game's `Update` switch. We currently only check for `Scene` and `StartMenu`, but now we can add `Won` and `Lost` to the list:

```
case GameState.Won:
    {
        //Game Over - You Won!
        if (!fade.Enabled)
```

```
            {
                fade.Color = Color.Black;
                fade.Enabled = true;
            }
            break;
    }
case GameState.Lost:
    {
            if (!fade.Enabled)
            {
                fade.Color = Color.Red;
                fade.Enabled = true;
            }
            break;
    }
```

The code is pretty simple. We have a fade game component that we enable if it is not already enabled, and we set a property of what color we want to fade to. You can see the code for our FadeOut game component in Listing 11.4.

LISTING 11.4   FadeOut.cs

```
using System;
using System.Collections.Generic;
using Microsoft.Xna.Framework;
using Microsoft.Xna.Framework.Graphics;

namespace SimpleGame
{
    public class FadeOut : Microsoft.Xna.Framework.DrawableGameComponent
    {
        private Texture2D fadeTexture;
        private float fadeAmount;
        private double fadeStartTime;
        private SimpleGame simpleGame;

        public Color Color;
        private SpriteBatch spriteBatch;

        public FadeOut(Game game)
            : base(game)
        {
            simpleGame = (SimpleGame)game;

            this.Enabled = false;
            this.Visible = false;
```

```
    DrawOrder = 999;
}

public void Load(SpriteBatch spriteBatch)
{
    this.spriteBatch = spriteBatch;
}

public override void Update(GameTime gameTime)
{
    // TODO: Add your update code here
    if (fadeStartTime == 0)
    {
        fadeStartTime = gameTime.TotalGameTime.TotalMilliseconds;
        Visible = true;
    }

    fadeAmount += (.25f *(float)gameTime.ElapsedGameTime.TotalSeconds);

    if(gameTime.TotalGameTime.TotalMilliseconds > fadeStartTime + 4000)
    {
        fadeAmount = 0;
        fadeStartTime = 0;
        Visible = Enabled = false;

        simpleGame.ActivateStartMenu();
    }

    base.Update(gameTime);
}

protected override void LoadContent()
{
    fadeTexture = CreateFadeTexture(
        GraphicsDevice.Viewport.Width, GraphicsDevice.Viewport.Height);
}

public override void Draw(GameTime gameTime)
{
    Vector4 color = Color.ToVector4();
    color.W = fadeAmount; //set transparency
    spriteBatch.Draw(fadeTexture, Vector2.Zero, new Color(color));

    base.Draw(gameTime);
}
```

```
private Texture2D CreateFadeTexture(int width, int height)
{
    Texture2D texture = new Texture2D(GraphicsDevice, width, height, 1,
    TextureUsage.None, SurfaceFormat.Color);

    int pixelCount = width * height;
    Color[] pixelData = new Color[pixelCount];
    Random rnd = new Random();

    for (int i = 0; i < pixelCount; i++)
    {
        pixelData[i] = Color.White;
    }

    texture.SetData(pixelData);

    return (texture);
    }
  }
}
```

Most of this code should look very familiar to you from the last chapter. Note two key points here: First, we set the DrawOrder of our component to a high number, 999. This will make the component draw last on our screen so we can get the effect we are looking for. Second, in our Update method, we fade our texture in 25% each second. Once four seconds have passed, we reset our fade variables and then activate our game's start menu, which gets us out of the current state and back to our start menu state.

We need to use the FadeOut component in our SimpleGame class. Let's create the fade member field and initialize it as normal in our constructor. We also need to call the Load method inside the LoadContent method, passing in the sprite batch. We can now run our game and see that we handle our lose state as well as our won state appropriately.

Adding Explosions

We have all our game logic in place and are correctly switching between our game states and handling our collision detection. Now, we need to add a little flare to the game. When we kick an enemy, it just disappears. It would be nice to make a little explosion effect. We are going to do that now.

You can see the code for our new ExplosionManager game component in Listing 11.5.

LISTING 11.5   ExplosionManager.cs

```
using System;
using System.Collections.Generic;
```

```
using Microsoft.Xna.Framework;
using Microsoft.Xna.Framework.Graphics;
using XELibrary;

namespace SimpleGame
{
    public class ExplosionManager
        : Microsoft.Xna.Framework.DrawableGameComponent
    {
        private Dictionary<int, Explosion> explosions =
            new Dictionary<int, Explosion>(5);
        private CelAnimationManager cam;
        private SpriteBatch spriteBatch;
        private SimpleGame simpleGame;

        public ExplosionManager(Game game) : this(game, 0) { }
        public ExplosionManager(Game game, int maxExplosions) : base(game)
        {
            simpleGame = (SimpleGame)game;

            cam = (CelAnimationManager)game.Services.GetService(
                                typeof(ICelAnimationManager));
            if (maxExplosions > 0)
                SetMaxNumberOfExplosions(maxExplosions);
        }

        public void Load(SpriteBatch spriteBatch)
        {
            this.spriteBatch = spriteBatch;
        }

        public override void Update(GameTime gameTime)
        {
            if (simpleGame.State == SimpleGame.GameState.Scene)
            {
                //Check For Explosions
                int markForDeletion = -1;
                foreach (KeyValuePair<int, Explosion> explosion in explosions)
                {
                    //have we been playing our explosion for over a second?
                    if (gameTime.TotalGameTime.TotalMilliseconds >
                        explosion.Value.TimeCreated + 100)
                    {
                        markForDeletion = explosion.Key;
                        break;
                    }
```

```
            }

        if (explosions.ContainsKey(markForDeletion))
            explosions.Remove(markForDeletion);
    }

    base.Update(gameTime);
}

protected override void LoadContent()
{
    //add our explosions
    cam.AddAnimation("explosion", "explode_1", new CelCount(4, 4), 16);
    cam.AddAnimation("explosion2", "explode_1", new CelCount(4, 4), 16);
    cam.AddAnimation("explosion3", "explode_3", new CelCount(4, 4), 12);
    cam.AddAnimation("explosion4", "explode_4", new CelCount(4, 4), 20);
    cam.AddAnimation("explosion5", "explode_3", new CelCount(4, 4), 12);
    cam.AddAnimation("explosion6", "explode_4", new CelCount(4, 4), 20);

    cam.AddAnimation("bigexplosion", "bigexplosion", new CelCount(4, 4), 18);
}

public override void Draw(GameTime gameTime)
{

    switch (simpleGame.State)
    {
        case SimpleGame.GameState.Scene:
            {
                foreach (Explosion explosion in explosions.Values)
                {
                    cam.Draw(gameTime, "explosion4", spriteBatch,
                        explosion.Position);
                }
                break;
            }
        case SimpleGame.GameState.StartMenu:
            {
                //we can add our explosions to make our title page pop
                cam.Draw(gameTime, "explosion", spriteBatch,
                    new Vector2(32, 32));
                cam.Draw(gameTime, "explosion2", spriteBatch,
                    new Vector2(40, 40));
                cam.Draw(gameTime, "explosion3", spriteBatch,
                    new Vector2(64, 32));
                cam.Draw(gameTime, "explosion4", spriteBatch,
```

```
                              new Vector2(64, 64));
                    cam.Draw(gameTime, "explosion5", spriteBatch,
                        new Vector2(28, 40));
                    cam.Draw(gameTime, "explosion6", spriteBatch,
                        new Vector2(40, 64));

                    cam.Draw(gameTime, "explosion", spriteBatch,
                        new Vector2(432, 32));
                    cam.Draw(gameTime, "explosion2", spriteBatch,
                        new Vector2(440, 40));
                    cam.Draw(gameTime, "explosion3", spriteBatch,
                        new Vector2(464, 32));
                    cam.Draw(gameTime, "explosion4", spriteBatch,
                        new Vector2(464, 64));
                    cam.Draw(gameTime, "explosion5", spriteBatch,
                        new Vector2(428, 40));
                    cam.Draw(gameTime, "explosion6", spriteBatch,
                        new Vector2(440, 64));

                    cam.Draw(gameTime, "bigexplosion", spriteBatch,
                        new Vector2(250, 330));
                    break;
            }
        }
        base.Draw(gameTime);
    }

    public void StartExplosion(int explosionKey, Vector2 position,
        double time)
    {
        explosions.Add(explosionKey, new Explosion(position, time));
    }

    public void SetMaxNumberOfExplosions(int maxExplosions)
    {
        explosions = new Dictionary<int, Explosion>(maxExplosions);
    }
}

public class Explosion
{
    public double TimeCreated;
    public Vector2 Position;

    public Explosion(Vector2 position, double timeCreated)
    {
```

```
            Position = position;
            TimeCreated = timeCreated;
        }
    }
}
```

Most of the code in our `ExplosionManager` should look familiar. We set up a dictionary to hold our collection of explosions. We load up our cel animation manager with our different explosion textures. We require the game to set our sprite batch through the `Load` method.

We have an `Explosion` class with two public fields that are set through its constructor. We store the time the explosion was created as well as the position of the explosion. This way, the explosion manager can handle the life span of our explosion and draw it on the screen in the appropriate position.

Our explosion manager checks our game state to determine whether it should draw the active explosions for our game scene or it should draw our start menu explosions. We want the start screen to have a little more pop than it currently does, so we are going to add a few explosions around the texture.

In our update code, we check the time our explosions were created and compare that to our current time to determine if we should continue to draw the explosions. If enough time has passed, we remove them from our collection. We could have set this code up exactly like we have our enemy manager code, but this way you can see different ways to handle the same task.

We need to update our game code to use the explosion manager. First, we need to declare a variable to hold our explosion manager, and then we need to add the game component to our component collection. We can call our variable `explosionManager`. We can use the default constructor when we initialize our game component. We also need to call `Load` on our explosion manager inside the `LoadContent` method and pass in our sprite batch.

Next, we need to add this statement to our "not paused" condition inside our `ActivateGame` method:

```
explosionManager.SetMaxNumberOfExplosions(5); //should be read by level
```

We are hard-coding a value of 5 here just like we did for the line before it when we set up our enemy manager. The idea is that we have a level and we pass in the number of enemies to be created at one time into this method. The reason is that every time we kill off an enemy, we create an explosion. We need to have as many explosions as we do enemies at any given point.

We can add the code for this inside the `player.Attacking` condition in the `CheckForCollisions` method:

```
explosionManager.StartExplosion(enemyIndex, enemyPosition,
    gameTime.TotalGameTime.TotalMilliseconds);
```

We call our explosion manager's start explosion method, which takes in the key of the explosion we are creating (in this case, it is the enemy's index), the position where we want the explosion to draw (in this case, it is the same position as our enemy), and finally the current game time in milliseconds. Now, when we collide with our enemy and are kicking, we will see an explosion on the screen when the enemy disappears.

Before we run our game again to see the progress, we need to add the explosion textures we referenced inside our project. You can find the following files on the CD: bigexplosion.png, explosion_1.png, explosion_3.png, and explosion_4.png.

Let's run the game to see the explosions we have set up. You can see that our start menu screen has the explosions we added. As you play the game and collide with enemies, you can see the explosions being created. An improvement would be to center the explosions to the center of the enemy position. They are currently being drawn at the top left (0,0) of the enemy.

Adding Sounds

We can add in some sounds to further improve the game. We already have our sound manager class from Chapter 7, "Sound and Music," so we do not need to write any new code for that. Instead of going through the hassle of creating another XACT project, we will simply copy the XACT project and sound files from our Chapter 7 Sound Demo project folder. Create a Sounds folder in the Content project to store the files. We only need to have the XACT project included in the project with the wave files just in the same directory, but not in the solution itself.

We need to declare our sound manager variable and then initialize it in our constructor like all our other game components:

```
sound = new SoundManager(this, "Chapter7");
Components.Add(sound);
```

Now we can create our playlist just like we did in the SoundDemo project by adding the following code to our Initialize method:

```
string[] playList = { "Song1", "Song2", "Song3" };
sound.StartPlayList(playList);
```

Finally, we should play the explosion sound we set up back in Chapter 7. We should do this right after we start the explosion when an enemy dies, so we need to add the following statement at the end of the player.Attacking condition inside the CheckForCollisions method:

```
sound.Play("explosion");
```

Now we have our songs playing, and when we kick a robot we not only see an explosion but we hear one too.

Summary

In this chapter, we created a simple but complete game. You learned how to scroll the background and even how to create parallax scrolling. We discussed different blending options again and saw examples of how we can use them together in a game. We looked at changing states at a high level. We had some simple collision detection to check to see if we collided with our enemies. We utilized the fading transition you learned about in the last chapter but modified it so we could fade to any color. We also incorporated explosions into our game. We finished out the chapter by hooking up our sound manager and using the sounds we created in Chapter 7.

PART V

XNA Game Studio and the Zune

IN THIS PART

CHAPTER 12

Programming for the Zune

Using XNA Game Studio 3.0, not only can we make games for Windows and the Xbox 360, but we can also create games that run on the Zune. When we create games for the Zune, we need to make sure we take several things into consideration. As we create demos in this chapter, we will make note of these items to make sure our games are performing well on the Zune.

We will be creating three demos in this chapter. First, we will create a demo to display album artwork. We could use very similar code to display the images in a picture collection. For the second demo we will be modifying the earlier Fire demo to run on the Zune. For the last demo we will create a very simple media player that provides a visual representation of the music playing.

Display Album Art Demo

In our first Zune demo we are going to display the artwork for the albums in our media collection. When the demo loads, we check to see if any songs are playing. If they are, we display the album art of the song playing if it is available. If a song is not playing, we launch a specific playlist from our collection. We will display the album art if it is available.

We need to create a new Zune game project called DisplayAlbumArtDemo and add a Fonts folder to the Content project. We can create a new Arial sprite font. We need to change the FontName inside the XML file as well.

Next, we can set up the fields we need for this demo:

```
private SpriteFont font;
private Texture2D art;
private ICollection<MediaSource> mediaSources;
private MediaLibrary mediaLib;
private AlbumCollection albumCollection;
private int numAlbumArts;
private int currentAlbum = -1;
private int prevAlbum;
```

We can then add the following lines to our LoadContent method:

```
font = Content.Load<SpriteFont>(@"Fonts\Arial");


mediaSources = MediaSource.GetAvailableMediaSources();
foreach (MediaSource ms in mediaSources)
{
    mediaLib = new MediaLibrary(ms);
    break;
}
albumCollection = mediaLib.Albums;
numAlbumArts = albumCollection.Count - 1;

do
{
    currentAlbum++;

    if (currentAlbum >= albumCollection.Count)
        break;
} while (!albumCollection[currentAlbum].HasArt);

if (currentAlbum >= albumCollection.Count)
{
    //went through all albums and none had art.
    //nothing for the program to do but exit.
    Exit();
}


prevAlbum = -1;
```

After loading our sprite font, we get the available media sources from the XNA Framework. The GetAvailableMediaSources method retrieves all the media sources associated with the device. For the Xbox 360, the method can return multiple sources, depending on the number of connected computers via Windows Media Connect. The method will only return one media source for Windows and the Zune.

We break out of the foreach loop as soon as we get the first media source and create a reference to a new media library. We now have access to all the albums in this library. We could also get the Artists, Genres, Pictures, Playlists, and Songs categories. For this demo, we store the album collection and the number of albums in the collection.

Currently, Windows will only return a null when the album art is requested. It is unclear if this will change with future versions. For the Zune and Xbox 360, if the album art is not present, a null is also returned, so this needs to be handled. This can be done by calling GetAlbumArt on an album and checking for null or by checking the HasArt property first.

To load up the first album, we launch into a do while loop and keep checking for an album that has art. As soon as we find an album with artwork, we exit the loop. We also exit the loop if we iterate all the way through the albums and none of them have art. We check to see if that is the case. If it is, we simply exit the program because there is no album art to display. If we try to run the program on Windows, it always exits because Windows does not return album art. Assuming we do have album art, we initialize our previous picture variable. We will use this to determine whether or not we should look up a new album art cover.

We can add the following method to display the album art:

```
protected void DisplayArt()
{
    spriteBatch.Begin();

    //only get new pic if needed
    if (currentAlbum != prevAlbum)
    {
        if (art != null)
            art.Dispose();

        art = albumCollection[currentAlbum].GetAlbumArt(this.Services);
    }

    spriteBatch.Draw(art, Vector2.Zero, Color.White);

    spriteBatch.DrawString(font, currentAlbum.ToString(),
        new Vector2(110, 300), Color.Black);
    spriteBatch.DrawString(font, currentAlbum.ToString(),
        new Vector2(111, 301), Color.White);

    spriteBatch.End();

    prevAlbum = currentAlbum;
}
```

This method is very straightforward. We check to see if the current album index is the same as the previous album index. If they do not match, it means we have changed album art, so we dispose of our current texture and then get the new texture based on the current album's index. On the Zune it is very important to manually dispose of textures because there is a very large potential of running out of memory.

We can add the call to the newly created `DisplayArt` method to our `Draw` method. Although we are not done with the demo yet, we can now compile and deploy the demo to our Zune.

Deploying to the Zune

Before deploying to the Zune, we need to connect the device to the computer. The Zune client software on the computer must be shut down if it is running. The device will need to be added to the XNA Game Studio Device Center application. If we try to deploy the demo before registering our Zune in the Device Center, we will get the following error:

> No devices are available to deploy project 'DisplayAlbumArtDemo'.

> Register a device using the XNA Game Studio Device Center.

To add the Zune to the XNA Game Studio Device center, click the plus sign in the toolbar beside the Launch XNA Game Studio Device Center icon. After XNA Game Studio is installed, this should be visible. If it is not visible, select "XNA Game Studio 3.0 Device Management" in the Toolbars submenu under the View menu.

After clicking the plus sign on the toolbar or clicking the Add Device button on the XNA Game Studio Device Center, select the Zune as the device to add and then click Next and Finish when it is done.

With the Zune device set up, we can run our demo in its current state to see the first album in our collection displayed on the Zune, along with the value of `currentAlbum`. The template for the Zune game we started with has the typical check for the Back button being pushed to exit the game. We can press the Back button on the Zune to exit the demo.

Updating the XELibrary

In order to complete this demo, we need to utilize the `InputHandler` from our XELibrary. We need to complete the following steps in order to make the XELibrary run on the Zune:

1. Copy the XELibrary folder from the previous chapter.
2. Add the XELibrary to our solution.
3. Copy XELibrary to a Zune project.
4. Change the name of the newly created project to XELibrary_Zune.
5. Remove the original XELibrary from the solution.

Now when we compile our solution, we will encounter a few errors. All the errors are coming from two files in the XELibrary—SoundManager.cs and the SkyboxReader.cs are causing the issues. The Zune device does not support 3D. It doesn't have any kind of 3D acceleration hardware. The XNA Framework API for the Zune platform doesn't include any of the XACT functionality. To get our demo to compile again, we can simply exclude both of these files from our XELibrary project because they won't be needed. We are going to add a new Zune-specific SoundManager in the next chapter.

Now we can compile our project successfully again. It is time to have our demo allow the user to scroll through the album art on the Zune. Therefore, we need to add the following code to the Update method:

```
if (input.ButtonHandler.WasButtonPressed(0,Buttons.DPadRight))
{
    do
    {
        if (currentAlbum == numAlbumArts)
        {
            currentAlbum = 0;
        }
        else
        {
            currentAlbum++;
        }
    } while (!albumCollection[currentAlbum].HasArt);
}
else if (input.ButtonHandler.WasButtonPressed(0,Buttons.DPadLeft))
{
    do
    {
        if (currentAlbum == 0)
        {
            currentAlbum = numAlbumArts;
        }
        else
        {
            currentAlbum--;
        }
    } while (!albumCollection[currentAlbum].HasArt);
}
```

This code simply checks to see if the user is pressing left or the right on the DPad and increments or decrements the currentAlbum index, rolling over if it goes out of bounds. It skips over any albums that do not have artwork.

We need to add a reference to our XELibrary project in our demo project. We need to add the using XELibrary statement to our demo. We also need to add the InputHandler game component to our demo.

The Zune device control pad maps to the game controllers D-pad. Pressing the control pad in the center is the same as pressing A on the controller. Pressing the control pad anywhere except the center will also register as pressing the Left Shoulder button. Pressing the Play/Pause button is the same as pressing the B button on the gamepad controller. In addition to those inputs, the second-generation and later Zunes (4, 8, 16, 80, 120, and so on) also have the Zune Pad, which maps to the left thumbstick of the gamepad controller.

Now that we have added in the XELibrary, which has its own Arial font, we can remove the Fonts folder from the Content project in our demo project. We can again compile and run our demo. Clicking the left or right side of the Zune device control pad allows us to iterate through the albums that have artwork.

Fire Demo Zune Edition

We are going to create another fire demo to run on the Zune. To start, we can copy the FireDemo folder from Chapter 10, "2D Effects." After opening the FireDemo solution, we can add the existing XELibrary_Zune project. Then we can right-click the Windows version of the FireDemo and select Create Copy of Project for Zune. After renaming the project to FireDemo_Zune, we can compile the solution.

We are presented with an error stating that the GraphicsDevice does not have the property Textures. This is a difference between the Zune device and the other platforms. In the Draw method we need to wrap the following line in a #if !ZUNE preprocessor condition:

```
graphics.GraphicsDevice.Textures[0] = null;
```

Let's modify this demo so it can be run on all platforms with very little code change. We can start by replacing the code that sets the PreferredBackBufferHeight and PreferredBackBufferWeight properties with the following code:

```
#if ZUNE
    graphics.PreferredBackBufferHeight = 320;
    graphics.PreferredBackBufferWidth = 240;

    // Frame rate is 30 fps by default for Zune.
    TargetElapsedTime = TimeSpan.FromSeconds(1 / 30.0);
#else
    graphics.PreferredBackBufferHeight = 256;
    graphics.PreferredBackBufferWidth = 512;
#endif
```

Next we need to replace the call to CreateFireTexture inside the LoadContent method with the following code:

```
#if ZUNE
    fire = CreateFireTexture(32, 32);
#else
    fire = CreateFireTexture(128, 128);
#endif
```

We are shrinking the size of the texture because the Zune has a smaller display. There is no need to waste processing cycles on a larger texture. The last thing we need to do to is modify the code between our sprite batch Begin and End calls in our Draw method. Replace the code with the following:

```
//left side
int y = 0;
for (int i = 0; i < graphics.PreferredBackBufferHeight;
                                    i += fire.Height * scale, y++)
{
    spriteBatch.Draw(fire, new Vector2(fire.Width * scale, i), null,
        Color.White, MathHelper.PiOver2, Vector2.Zero, scale,
        (y % 2 == 0) ?
            SpriteEffects.None
        :
            SpriteEffects.FlipHorizontally,
        0);
}

//right side
y = 0;
for (int i = 0; i < graphics.PreferredBackBufferHeight;
                                    i += fire.Height * scale, y++)
{
    spriteBatch.Draw(fire, new Vector2(graphics.PreferredBackBufferWidth, i),
        null, Color.White, MathHelper.PiOver2,
        Vector2.Zero, scale, (y % 2 == 0) ?
            SpriteEffects.FlipVertically
        :
            SpriteEffects.FlipVertically | SpriteEffects.FlipHorizontally,
        0);
}

//bottom row
int x = 0;
for (int i = 0; i < graphics.PreferredBackBufferWidth;
                                    i += fire.Width * scale, x++)
{
    spriteBatch.Draw(fire, new Vector2(
        i, graphics.PreferredBackBufferHeight - fire.Height * scale),
        null, Color.White, 0, Vector2.Zero, scale,
        (x % 2 == 0) ?
            SpriteEffects.None
        :
            SpriteEffects.FlipHorizontally,
        0);
}
```

```
//top row
x = 0;
for (int i = 0; i < graphics.PreferredBackBufferWidth;
                                    i += fire.Width * scale, x++)
{
    spriteBatch.Draw(fire, new Vector2(i, 0), null, Color.White, 0,
        Vector2.Zero, scale,
        (x % 2 == 0) ?
            SpriteEffects.FlipVertically | SpriteEffects.FlipHorizontally
        :
            SpriteEffects.FlipVertically,
        0);
}
```

We made this code a little more robust by not having values hard-coded to plot the fire textures. Instead, we loop through our borders and plot each texture exactly where it should go. As we continue down one side of the border, we flip the texture so it has a mirrored effect. This is done with the ternary operator (? :) to determine which SpriteEffect to pass into the Draw method. We also are using a variable called scale. This integer needs to be added to our private member fields. It can be set to 1 for no scale or 2 to double the value.

When we compile and run this code on the Zune, we get the desired result. We now have fire displayed on our Zune.

Creating a Visualization Demo

We are going to create a visualization demo that plays music, displays the album art (if it is available), and finally displays a visual representation of the music being played. To start, we can create a new Windows game project called VisualizationDemo. We need to add the existing XELibrary project to the solution. We also need to add a using statement for the XELibrary and add the project reference.

Even though we are starting out with a Windows game project, this is mainly to be run on the Zune. We are starting with Windows so we can easily develop and debug it. Even with incremental deployments, it can take a little bit of time to launch the game or demo on the Zune.

To set up our window, we create a couple constants for the width and height:

```
private const int width = 240;
private const int height = 320;
```

Then in our constructor we set the preferred backbuffer width and height:

```
graphics.PreferredBackBufferHeight = height;
graphics.PreferredBackBufferWidth = width;
```

We want this demo to display the art at the top of the Zune, much like it does in its native player. We will print the name of the song directly under the artwork, and we will print the name of the artist under the song. We will then create two different visualizations below the artist name at the bottom of the Zune display.

We know the `GetAlbumArt` method returns a null if there is no album art associated with the song (or if we are running the demo on Windows), so we need to make sure we have a default image to show. We can add the following fields:

```
private SpriteFont font;
private Texture2D art;
private Texture2D noArt;
```

Then we can load the font and our fallback texture (NoArt) in the `LoadContent` method:

```
noArt = Content.Load<Texture2D>(@"Textures\NoArt");
font = Content.Load<SpriteFont>(@"Fonts\Arial");
```

The Arial font is already in our XELibrary project, so we do not need to create the font in this demo. We do need to add the NoArt.jpg file from the CD included in the book to the Textures folder in the Content project of the demo.

We need to load our media library and iterate through the songs to obtain and display the album artwork, the song name, and the artist name. We need to add the following member fields:

```
private string songName = string.Empty;
private string artistName = string.Empty;
private Playlist playlist = null;

private Vector2 songPosShadow = new Vector2(0, 230);
private Vector2 songPos = new Vector2(1, 231);

private Vector2 artistPosShadow = Vector2.Zero;
private Vector2 artistPos = Vector2.Zero;
```

Now we need to discover what playlists we have available to us and grab a specific one. If we can't find it, we just grab the first playlist the system tells us about. We need to add the following code to the `LoadContent` method:

```
ICollection<MediaSource> mediaSources = MediaSource.GetAvailableMediaSources();
MediaLibrary mediaLib = null;

foreach (MediaSource ms in mediaSources)
{
    mediaLib = new MediaLibrary(ms);
    break;
}
```

```
if (mediaLib != null)
{
    for (int i = 0; i < mediaLib.Playlists.Count; i++)
    {
        if (mediaLib.Playlists[i].Name == "Zune Gems")
        {
            playlist = mediaLib.Playlists[i];
            break;
        }
    }

    if (playlist == null)
        playlist = mediaLib.Playlists[0]; // just grab first one
}

//If can't find the playlist, just exit.
if (playlist == null)
    Exit();

//Assumes at least one song is actually in the playlist
MediaPlayer.Play(playlist.Songs);
```

The first part of the code should look very familiar to you—this is the same way we retrieved the albums to get access to the album art in the first demo. This time instead of just grabbing all the albums, we are looping through all the playlists to look for the special "Zune Gems" that is preloaded on some of the Zune devices. After looping through all the playlists, if the demo can't find the one we want, it simply sets itself to the first playlist on the device. If there are no playlists, the demo just exists. If it did find a playlist, the demo will play it starting with the first song. The Play method can also take a single song, and it can take the playlist and the index of the song to start with.

We can compile and run the program. We are not drawing anything yet, but as soon as the window loads we will hear the first song in the playlist selected. We do not have any input controls to go to the next or previous songs. We can add our InputHandler game component to our demo now. While we are at it, we might as well add our FPS game component as well.

With our InputHandler game component added, we can now iterate the songs playing in our playlist. In our Update method, we can add the following code:

```
    if (input.ButtonHandler.WasButtonPressed(0, Buttons.DPadRight)
#if !ZUNE
        || input.KeyboardState.WasKeyPressed(Keys.Right)
```

```
#endif
        )
    {
        MediaPlayer.MoveNext();
    }
    else if (input.ButtonHandler.WasButtonPressed(0, Buttons.DPadLeft)
#if !ZUNE
        || input.KeyboardState.WasKeyPressed(Keys.Left)
#endif
        )
    {
        MediaPlayer.MovePrevious();
    }
```

The code is pretty straightforward—it checks to see if the left or right button was pressed on the D-pad or if the left or right key was pressed. The keyboard is not supported on the Zune, so we wrapped that part of the condition in a preprocessor directive. We are calling the MediaPlayer's MoveNext and MovePrevious methods. As the names suggest, these methods move us forward and backward, respectively, in the playlist. We can run the demo again and control which song is playing by moving through the list.

Now it is time to display the album art and to print out the song and artist name. In the Draw method, we can clear the device to black and then add in the following code:

```
spriteBatch.Begin();

if (art != null)
    spriteBatch.Draw(art, pos, Color.White);
else
    spriteBatch.Draw(noArt, pos, Color.White);

spriteBatch.DrawString(font, songName, songPosShadow, Color.Gray);
spriteBatch.DrawString(font, songName, songPos, Color.White);

artistPosShadow.Y = songPosShadow.Y + font.LineSpacing;
artistPos.Y = songPos.Y + font.LineSpacing;

spriteBatch.DrawString(font, artistName, artistPosShadow, Color.Gray);
spriteBatch.DrawString(font, artistName, artistPos, Color.White);

spriteBatch.End();
```

With this code, we are displaying the album art if it exist. If it doesn't exist, we display our default image. We then display the song name and artist name.

TIP

To make the code a little more robust, we can put checks around drawing the text of the song or artist name. For example, to make sure the song name doesn't have any invalid characters, we could write the following code:

```
try
{
    spriteBatch.DrawString(font, songName, songPosShadow, Color.Gray);
    spriteBatch.DrawString(font, songName, songPos, Color.White);
}
catch
{
    spriteBatch.DrawString(font, "Song name has unhandled characters",
        songPosShadow, Color.Gray);
    spriteBatch.DrawString(font, "Song name has unhandled characters",
        songPos, Color.White);
}
```

When we have full control over the text in our games, this is not an issue. But when we are reading in values, we need to take care when handling any input that is passed our way. The sprite font can have ranges of characters added to its XML file to help minimize the risk, but if we include too many characters, the size of the font asset will increase in size.

With our `Draw` method out of the way, we can populate the data we want to draw. We haven't actually obtained the album artwork or the artist's name or the song name. We are going to hook into an event that will get fired anytime the song changes. This way, we can grab the data we need inside this event. In the constructor, we can register for the event by adding the following statement:

```
MediaPlayer.ActiveSongChanged +=
    new EventHandler(MediaPlayer_ActiveSongChanged);
```

Then we can create this method:

```
private void MediaPlayer_ActiveSongChanged(object sender, EventArgs e)
{
    if (art != null)
        art.Dispose();

    art = MediaPlayer.Queue.ActiveSong.Album.GetAlbumArt(Services);
    if (art == null)
        art = MediaPlayer.Queue.ActiveSong.Album.GetThumbnail(Services);
```

```
    songName = MediaPlayer.Queue.ActiveSong.Name;
    artistName = MediaPlayer.Queue.ActiveSong.Artist.Name;

    if (MediaPlayer.State != MediaState.Playing)
        MediaPlayer.Play(playlist.Songs, MediaPlayer.Queue.ActiveSongIndex);
}
```

The first thing we do when the song changes is to dispose of the current artwork if it exists. We then obtain the artwork again. If we cannot obtain the artwork, we try to get the thumbnail. We then store the song name and the artist name. Finally, if the media player isn't currently playing, we pass in the current active songs index to start playing the song.

When we compile and run the demo, we see the default art because we are running the demo on Windows, but we can see the song name and artist name displayed toward the bottom of the window. Now would be a good time to create a copy of our demo to run on the Zune so we can make sure the album art is displayed correctly. Before creating the copy, we should add in our existing XELibrary_Zune project. Then we can create a copy of our demo project. We can rename the newly copied project to VisualizationDemo_Zune. We need to make sure the Zune demo is referencing the correct XELibrary project. If the solution created another copy of the XELibrary, we can remove that from the project. We can set the Zune project as our startup project.

As we run the demo, we can see the album art displayed along with the name of the song with the name of the artist underneath. If we did not put try/catch blocks around the code that prints the song name and artist name, then the first time a song or artist is displayed that has characters not inside of our sprite font resource, the application would fail. To help get a few more common characters (general punctuation), we can add the following character region to our XELibrary's Arial font XML:

```
<CharacterRegion>
  <Start>&#8208;</Start>
  <End>&#8231;</End>
</CharacterRegion>
```

We should also change the End value of the first character region section from 126 to 563. This will cause our font asset to be larger, but the change is worth it to correctly display the characters the demo may encounter.

It is rather rude to stop users' playlists and force them into the ones we pick. Instead we can check to see if the MediaPlayer is playing when the demo launches. If it is, we can just return after calling our method to set the appropriate values. The following code should be added to the LoadContent method right before we get the available media sources:

```
if (MediaPlayer.State == MediaState.Playing)
{
    //the user is playing their own music - don't reset it
```

```
    //just retrieve the current playing song and artist and art
    MediaPlayer_ActiveSongChanged(this, null);

    return;
}
```

Now when we run our demo with music playing, it will use the currently loaded playlist (even if that playlist is just one song). It will also set the album art, song name, and artist name.

Creating the Visualization

The Media API gives us access to the songs' visualization data. We can query the MediaPlayer for the data by calling the static GetVisualizationData method. We need to set up our private member field:

```
private VisualizationData visualizationData;
```

We can initialize this variable and make sure the MediaPlayer is obtaining the visualization data by adding the following the code in our LoadContent method before checking to see if the state is playing:

```
visualizationData = new VisualizationData();
MediaPlayer.IsVisualizationEnabled = true;
```

Next we need to populate our visualization data and draw a representation of the data. Inside our Draw method, we need to add the following code right before we call End on our sprite batch:

```
if (MediaPlayer.IsVisualizationEnabled && !MediaPlayer.IsMuted)
{
    CreateVisualizationTexture(ref visualization);

    spriteBatch.Draw(visualization, pos, Color.White);
}
```

We are checking to make sure that the visualization is enabled and the song is not muted. If that condition is true, we then call a method to create our visualization text and finally draw it on the screen. The CreateVisualizationTexture method is shown here:

```
private void CreateVisualizationTexture(ref Texture2D texture)
{
    MediaPlayer.GetVisualizationData(visualizationData);

    texture = new Texture2D(GraphicsDevice, width, height, 1,
        TextureUsage.None, SurfaceFormat.Color);
```

```
pixelData = new Color[width * height];

//there are 256 total frequency/sample values, but we only have 240 pixels
//so we are going to chop off 8 values on both ends
maxData = width;

//Display Sample (Volume) Data
//now overwrite the pixel data with the waveform / sample data
for (x = 0; x < maxData; x++)
{
    baseline = (height - 50);
    y = baseline + (int)(visualizationData.Samples[x + 8] * 25);

    //plot base line
    pixelData[(baseline * width) + x] = Color.DarkGray;

    //now plot actual wave
    pixelData[(y * width) + x] = Color.White;
}

texture.SetData(pixelData);
}
```

To start, we are just going to display the sample data. The very first call we make in this method is to GetVisualizationData. The VisualizationData class exposes two properties. Both properties are filled with a collection of 256 floats. The first property, Frequencies, stores the frequencies, which are perceived as pitch. The XNA Game Studio documentation states the following:

> "Each element corresponds to a frequency band, ranging from 20Hz to 20KHz. In the collection, the distribution of bands from 20Hz to 20KHz is logarithmic, not linear. This means that elements at the lower end of the spectrum represent a smaller frequency range than those at the upper end of the spectrum.
>
> Each value in the frequency collection is a normalized float value from 0.0f to 1.0f, and is the logarithmic scaled power level for that frequency band."

The second property, Samples, stores its own collection of floats. These values range from −1.0 to 1.0. This approximates the wave form of the sound. The documentation states that the "sample data equates to the volume of the sound."

To begin with, we are only going to work with the sample data to display the wave of the sound. This is done in CreateVisualizationTexture after we create a blank texture and clear out the pixel data we will use to populate the visualization texture.

We set the maxData variable to the width of our device. The sample and frequency collections actually return 256 values. However, our device is only 240 pixels wide, so we are going to exclude eight pieces of data on the very ends of the sample. We exclude the last eight values by setting maxData to our width. We exclude the first eight values by offset-ting our value to get the data by 8 pixels.

We are looping through 240 of the 256 values. We explicitly set the baseline of the sound wave to the height of our display area minus 50. This will put it right under the artist name displayed. We then set the y value by adding our baseline amount to the product of the data returned from the Samples collection (with the offset of 8) and 25. By multiply-ing the value by 25, we get values from –25 to 25. When we add that to our baseline value of 270 (height [320] – 50), we end up with values that range from 245 to 295. Therefore, we are going to plot our values from left to right with our x value starting at 0 and our y value ranging from 245 to 295. Assuming the data we get back is not too varied, we will get a nice wave plotted in our pixelData array. If the data is varied, there will be gaps as it is plotted, but that isn't a problem because it should accurately reflect the type of song being played.

Once all the values are plotted in our pixelData array, we set the data to our visualization texture. Now we can add in the variables this method uses:

```
private Color color = Color.Black;
private Color[] pixelData;
private Texture2D visualization;
private Vector2 pos = Vector2.Zero;
private int x, y;
private int maxData;
private int baseline;
```

Now we can run the demo and see the dark gray baseline along with the white wave as the song is playing. Pretty cool!

We can treat the frequency/pitch data the same way. Let's add the following code in the CreateVisualizationTexture method right under the "Display Frequency (Pitch) Data" comment:

```
for (x = 0; x < maxData; x++)
{
    freqencyValue = (int)(visualizationData.Frequencies[x + 8] * 60);
    for (y = height - 1; y > height - freqencyValue; y--)
    {
        color.R = (byte)(y);
        color.G = (byte)(y);
        color.B = (byte)(y);

        pixelData[(y * width) + x] = color;
    }
}
```

With this code, we are looping through our sample data (excluding the eight values at the beginning and end) and storing the product of the data and 60. We chose 60 because that is just a little more than the value we used for our baseline earlier (50). This way, if the frequency is a full 1.0, the pixels will be drawn above the baseline and even on top of the artist text. This is obviously a style preference and can be changed. We are going to be drawing pixels from the bottom of the display to the bottom of the display minus the frequency value we are storing. This can be seen in the for loop. Inside the for loop we set our color to a gradient gray. We do this by setting all color components to the same value. The value is the vertical position we are plotting. We are starting at the bottom left of the display and moving up the y axis, setting each pixel to its own gray color. Once it reaches the peak and finishes the inner y loop, it continues to the next column and repeats the process until all the frequency data is plotted. After adding our private variable frequencyValue as an integer, we can run the demo and see the gradient gray pixels representing the frequency data.

We can add some color to this by replacing the three lines that set the red, green, and blue components with the following code:

```
if (y > height - freqencyValue + 4)
{
    color.R = (byte)(55 + (height - y));
    color.G = (byte)(65 - (height - y));
    color.B = (byte)(155 - (height - y) * 2);
}
else
{
    color.R = (byte)(y);
    color.G = (byte)(y);
    color.B = (byte)(y);
}
```

We only display the gray color to the top four pixels in a given column. This makes a nice border that almost has a 3D shadow effect. We can set the rest of the pixels any color we like. Here we have the red component going from 56 at the bottom of the row to a max of 120, assuming the frequency is a full 1.0 (frequencyValue = 60). We have green ranging from 64 down to 0 (at it's peak). Finally, we have blue ranging from 153 down to 25, skipping two numbers each iteration of the loop.

When we run the demo, we see the album art (if available), song name, artist name, the sound wave produced from the Samples data, and the frequency data to display a spectrum analyzer.

Summary

In this chapter you were introduced to the Zune platform. We utilized the Media API in two of the demos. The Media API is also available on Windows and the Xbox 360. You saw how we can deploy to the Zune. It is very similar to how we deploy on the Xbox 360. We updated the fire demo to play nice on the Zune. We removed the SoundManager and SkyboxReader classes from our XELibrary. Because the Zune does not have 3D capabilities, we will not be adding in the SkyboxReader object. However, in the next chapter we will make a Zune-specific SoundManager class.

We ended the chapter by making a visualization demo. We saw what data was available to use and implemented one of many ways to show the data in a graphical representation. During this demo, we also created a simple media player that allows us to move back and forth between the songs in the playlist. A good exercise would be to add functionality to capture the Play/Pause button (B button) to actually pause and resume playback.

CHAPTER 13

Running the Game on the Zune

In this chapter we are going to modify the 2D game we made in Chapter 11, "Creating a 2D Game," so it will run on the Zune. In the last chapter we had to remove the `SoundManager` class because the Zune cannot handle the XACT files and does not have access to the associated API. We will be adding our new Zune-specific sound manager in this chapter.

Along with having separate code files for the projects, we will use preprocessor directives as well for many places where we only need to do a few things differently. We have a special content project for the Zune game that the other two platforms will not include. We finish up the chapter by looking at ways we can make the code perform better for the Zune.

Porting the Game to Run on the Zune

To get started, we copy the SimpleGame folder from Chapter 11 and copy the XELibrary folder from the last chapter. We can open the SimpleGame solution file and add the existing XELibrary_Zune project. Then we can create a copy of our Windows SimpleGame project for the Zune.

When we compile the program, we see the error "XACT is not supported by the Zune platform." If we just exclude the Chapter7.xap XACT project file from our Zune Content project's Sound folder, it will also be removed from the other two platforms. Instead, we need to create a new Content project under the SimpleGame_Zune project. We can call it ZuneContent. When we create this new content project, it will be added to the Windows and Xbox 360 projects as well. We need to remove them. Before removing the original Content project from our Zune project, we should copy the Textures folder. The ZuneContent project is in its own folder as a sibling of the existing Content project. So we now have two copies of the textures. This is actually a good thing because we need to make the textures about half their existing size. Because the Zune has a limited amount of memory and a small screen, there is no reason to waste memory on the large textures we have for the other platforms. Each texture can be opened up and resized to 50% or copied from the CD under the ZuneContent subfolder for this chapter.

The only sound effect the game uses is the explosion sound. The rest of the sounds were just included because of the demo we did in Chapter 7, "Sound and Music." The songs (Song1, Song2, and Song3) that were wave files have been converted to MP3 to save space. The MP3 files are on the CD and need to be copied to our newly created Sounds subfolder along with the explosion sound effect. The songs' content processor should default to Songs – XNA Framework in the properties window of the assets. The explosion sound effect can be left to its default SoundEffect content processor. Using the song content processor basically puts the songs into the "Music" category you learned about when we discussed XACT in Chapter 7. This way, if the gamer already has music playing on the device, the game's music will not play.

Now when we compile, we get an error stating that SoundManager cannot be found. Therefore, now would be a good time to create our Zune version of the SoundManager. In the XELibrary_Zune project, we can add a new code file called ZuneSoundManager.cs. The code for this file is shown in Listing 13.1.

LISTING 13.1   ZuneSoundManager.cs

```
using System;
using System.Collections.Generic;
using Microsoft.Xna.Framework;
using Microsoft.Xna.Framework.Audio;
using Microsoft.Xna.Framework.GamerServices;
using Microsoft.Xna.Framework.Graphics;
using Microsoft.Xna.Framework.Input;
using Microsoft.Xna.Framework.Storage;
using Microsoft.Xna.Framework.Content;

using Microsoft.Xna.Framework.Media;

namespace XELibrary
{
    public class SoundManager
    {
        public bool RepeatPlayList = true;

        private Song[] playList;
```

```csharp
private int currentSong;

public void Update()
{
    if (playList.Length > 0) //are we playing a list?
    {
        //check current cue to see if it is playing
        //if not, go to next cue in list
        if (MediaPlayer.State != MediaState.Playing)
        {
            currentSong++;

            if (currentSong == playList.Length)
            {
                if (RepeatPlayList)
                    currentSong = 0;
                else
                    return;
            }

            if (MediaPlayer.State != MediaState.Playing)
                MediaPlayer.Play(playList[currentSong]);

        }
    }
}

public void StartPlayList(Song[] playList)
{
    StartPlayList(playList, 0);
}

public void StartPlayList(Song[] playList, int startIndex)
{
    if (playList.Length == 0)
        return;

    this.playList = playList;

    if (startIndex > playList.Length)
        startIndex = 0;

    StartPlayList(startIndex);
}

public void StartPlayList(int startIndex)
```

```
        {
            if (playList.Length == 0)
                return;

            currentSong = startIndex;
            MediaPlayer.Play(playList[currentSong]);
            MediaPlayer.IsRepeating = false;
        }

        public void StopPlayList()
        {
            MediaPlayer.Stop();
        }
    }
}
```

When we added the ZuneSoundManager.cs code file to our XELibrary_Zune project, it is automatically added to our Windows and Xbox 360 projects. We can exclude it from those projects and compile our solution.

Now when we compile our solution, we see that the constructor is different for our SoundManager class in our ZuneSoundManager.cs file than it is in the original SoundManager.cs file. We need to replace the lines where we initialize the sound variable and add the component with the following code:

```
#if !ZUNE
    sound = new SoundManager(this, "Chapter7");
    Components.Add(sound);
#else
    sound = new SoundManager();
#endif
```

We also see an error about the fact that we do not have a StartPlayList method in our SoundManager. We can wrap the first statements in the Initialize method with a ZUNE preprocessor condition:

```
#if !ZUNE
    string[] playList = { "Song1", "Song2", "Song3" };
    sound.StartPlayList(playList);
#endif
```

The Draw method in our Background class is complaining about RenderState not existing. Because this is specific to 3D hardware, the Zune API does not have the property. The code is doing additive blending in the main game's Draw method. It then needs to switch to alpha blending. We can replace the two lines in the Background class with this condition:

```
#if ZUNE
    spriteBatch.End();

    spriteBatch.Begin();
#else
    GraphicsDevice.RenderState.SourceBlend = Blend.SourceAlpha;
    GraphicsDevice.RenderState.DestinationBlend = Blend.InverseSourceAlpha;
#endif
```

The else condition continues to perform as it did before, but if we are compiling for the Zune, we simply end the original batch and start up a new one with default alpha blending.

Next, we see the compiler did not like the fact that our new Zune SoundManager object does not have a Play method. Instead of creating a Play method, we are just going to load the explosion sound effect directly in our game class. We need to add the private member field to our game:

```
#if ZUNE
    private SoundEffect explosion;
#endif
```

Now we can replace the call to the Play method located in the CheckForCollisions method with the following code:

```
#if !ZUNE
    sound.Play("explosion");
#else
    explosion.Play();
#endif
```

We need to load the explosion, set up our playlist, and add the following code to the LoadContent method:

```
#if ZUNE
    explosion = Content.Load<SoundEffect>(@"Sounds\explosion");

    //the user isn't playing their own music, we can set it to our music
    if (MediaPlayer.State != MediaState.Playing)
    {
        Song[] playList = {
            Content.Load<Song>(@"Sounds\Song2"),
            Content.Load<Song>(@"Sounds\Song3")
        };

        sound.StartPlayList(playList);
    }
#endif
```

We also need to add the following using statement to our Game1.cs file:

```
using Microsoft.Xna.Framework.Media;
```

We need to add a call to sound.Update to our game's Update method because the ZuneSoundManager is not a game component. The call to this method should be wrapped in a ZUNE preprocessor directive. We will change where we call this later in the chapter.

Inside the UpdateStateMenu method we need to check for the Start button and Enter key as well as the A button and the Spacebar. Also in the UpdateScene method we need to check for the B button and the Escape key. Remember the B button maps to the Play/Pause button on the Zune device.

Now that we can compile the code and set up our input for the Zune, we can set it as our startup project and run the program.

As soon as we run the game, we can tell something is drastically wrong. Our main start menu graphic is being displayed, but it is chopped off. The real problem arises when we hit the "A button" (clicking the center of the Zune device control pad). The game goes into the playing state, and everything is a mess. The reason must be our background, which makes sense because our background class extracted out different regions of our background image. We modified the image to be 50% of its original size, so our values are not matching up any longer. We need to replace the variables in the LoadContent method of the Background class with the following code:

```
#if ZUNE
    //flipped flopped on purpose. Wanting to do landscape
    int viewportWidth = GraphicsDevice.Viewport.Height;
    int viewportHeight = GraphicsDevice.Viewport.Width;

    int textureWidth = 512;
    int cloudHeight = 256;
    int cityHeight = 128;
    int foregroundHeight = 64;
    int streetHeight = 64;
    int cloudY = 0;
    int streetY = cloudHeight;
    int foregroundY = streetY + streetHeight;
    int cityY = foregroundY + foregroundHeight;
#else
    int viewportWidth = GraphicsDevice.Viewport.Width;
    int viewportHeight = GraphicsDevice.Viewport.Height;

    int textureWidth = 1024;
    int cloudHeight = 512;
    int cityHeight = 256;
    int foregroundHeight = 128;
    int streetHeight = 128;
    int cloudY = 0;
```

```
    int streetY = cloudHeight;
    int foregroundY = streetY + streetHeight;
    int cityY = foregroundY + foregroundHeight;
#endif
```

This code simply takes all the values and divides them by half for the Zune. Remember, the textures we are using for the Zune are 50% of the size of the textures being used for Windows and the Xbox 360.

Inside the Draw method of the ExplosionManager we need to wrap the code inside the StartMenu case in the false condition of a ZUNE preprocessor directive condition and add the following code to the true condition:

```
//we can add our explosions to make our title page pop
cam.Draw(gameTime, "explosion", spriteBatch,
    new Vector2(16, 16));
cam.Draw(gameTime, "explosion2", spriteBatch,
    new Vector2(20, 20));
cam.Draw(gameTime, "explosion3", spriteBatch,
    new Vector2(32, 16));
cam.Draw(gameTime, "explosion4", spriteBatch,
    new Vector2(32, 32));
cam.Draw(gameTime, "explosion5", spriteBatch,
    new Vector2(14, 20));
cam.Draw(gameTime, "explosion6", spriteBatch,
    new Vector2(20, 32));

cam.Draw(gameTime, "explosion", spriteBatch,
    new Vector2(216, 16));
cam.Draw(gameTime, "explosion2", spriteBatch,
    new Vector2(220, 20));
cam.Draw(gameTime, "explosion3", spriteBatch,
    new Vector2(232, 16));
cam.Draw(gameTime, "explosion4", spriteBatch,
    new Vector2(232, 16));
cam.Draw(gameTime, "explosion5", spriteBatch,
    new Vector2(214, 20));
cam.Draw(gameTime, "explosion6", spriteBatch,
    new Vector2(220, 32));

cam.Draw(gameTime, "bigexplosion", spriteBatch,
    new Vector2(125, 165));
```

This simply divides all the positions in half so they line up correctly on the screen.

This game is going to be played while the Zune is in "landscape mode." The player will need to play the game with the Zune oriented horizontally instead of the typical vertical position. This is why we flipped the width and height values for the Zune.

13

We also need to modify the position of our player and the enemies being drawn. We start by replacing the first section of variables in the EnemyManager class with the following code:

```
#if ZUNE
    private readonly int maxXPosition = 400;
    private readonly int minXPosition = 325;
    private readonly float collisionDistance = 32.0f;
    private int yPosition = 175;
    private int xPosition = 325;
#else
    private readonly int maxXPosition = 800;
    private readonly int minXPosition = 650;
    private readonly float collisionDistance = 64.0f;
    private int yPosition = 350;
    private int xPosition = 650;
#endif
```

We use the same values as before, and if we are on the Zune device, we take half of those values. The same thing needs to be done for the player values. We need to replace the playerPosition, width, and height variables with the following code:

```
#if ZUNE
    private Vector2 playerPosition = new Vector2(32, 175);
    private int width = 320;
    private int height = 240;
#else
    private Vector2 playerPosition = new Vector2(64, 350);
    private int width = 640;
    private int height = 480;
#endif
```

We are leaving the original values for Windows and the Xbox 360, but we are dividing those values in half for the Zune. Because we are going to be using the Zune in landscape mode, we set the width to 320 and the height to 240.

Running the Game in Landscape Mode

If we run the demo at this point, we can see our player and the enemies on the screen. The scene doesn't fill up the space because we are still in "portrait mode." To rotate our scene we will need to create a render target, draw all our textures to the render target, and then rotate the render target and draw it to our display. Sometimes we want to render our scene to its own texture instead of directly to the screen. A render target allows us to do this. We will discuss more uses for render targets in Chapter 15, "Advanced HLSL," but here is a list of steps we will complete to draw our game to the render target:

1. Tell our device to draw to our render target instead of the backbuffer.

2. Clear our device.

3. Draw our scene as normal (it will draw to our render target).

4. Reset render target back to null (so we will draw on the backbuffer).

5. Get the generated texture.

6. Draw the generated texture with appropriate rotation.

In the ZUNE preprocessor condition where we declare the explosion sound effect, we should also declare our render target:

```
private RenderTarget2D zuneRenderTarget;
```

We can initialize the render target in the game's constructor right after we set the preferred backbuffer's width and the height:

```
    graphics.ApplyChanges();


#if ZUNE
    zuneRenderTarget = new RenderTarget2D(
        GraphicsDevice,
        width,
        height,
        0,
        SurfaceFormat.Color);
#endif
```

Before we create the render target, we made sure to apply the changes to the graphics device. Now we can move to the Draw method and add this preprocessor condition to the top of the method:

```
#if ZUNE
    GraphicsDevice.SetRenderTarget(0, zuneRenderTarget);
#endif
```

Then at the end of the Draw method we can add the following code to rotate and draw the render target:

```
#if ZUNE
    //resolve the target
    GraphicsDevice.SetRenderTarget(0, null);

    //draw the texture rotated
    spriteBatch.Begin();
    spriteBatch.Draw(
        zuneRenderTarget.GetTexture(),
        new Vector2(120, 160),
```

13

```
            null,
            Color.White,
            MathHelper.PiOver2,
            new Vector2(160, 120),
            1f,
            SpriteEffects.None,
            0);
    spriteBatch.End();
#endif
```

We rotate the render target texture 90 degrees by passing in `MathHelper.PiOver2`. We set the origin of the texture to half the width and height (160, 120).

The final piece of code we need to put into place to complete the horizontal rotation is to replace the existing preprocessor condition in the `Initialize` method with the following code:

```
#if ZUNE
    viewportHeight = graphics.GraphicsDevice.Viewport.Width;
    viewportWidth = graphics.GraphicsDevice.Viewport.Height;
#else
    viewportHeight = graphics.GraphicsDevice.Viewport.Height;
    viewportWidth = graphics.GraphicsDevice.Viewport.Width;

    string[] playList = { "Song1", "Song2", "Song3" };
    sound.StartPlayList(playList);
#endif
```

The width and height values are switched on purpose when compiling for the Zune. Those values are used when calculating the center vector in the `LoadContent` method.

We need to modify our `FadeOut` class as well to correctly handle the landscape mode by replacing the contents of the `LoadContent` method with the following code:

```
#if ZUNE
    fadeTexture = CreateFadeTexture(
        GraphicsDevice.Viewport.Height, GraphicsDevice.Viewport.Width);
#else
    fadeTexture = CreateFadeTexture(
        GraphicsDevice.Viewport.Width, GraphicsDevice.Viewport.Height);
#endif
```

We can now run the game and see it is working, although it is very choppy. We determine where our performance is suffering in the next section.

> **TIP**
>
> There are a couple of other ways to draw in landscape mode on our Zune. We could use the Matrix transformations in the `SpriteBatch.Begin` call. This works, but I have seen it skew text that had to be rotated. Another way to handle this would be to either modify all our textures and rotate them sideways or, better yet, create a content pipeline extension that will do it automatically for us. We could then create our own SpriteBatch class that takes the normal X and Y values passed in and swap them so X is passed into the base SpriteBatch Y value of the texture position. The new X value will be calculated by starting with 240 and subtracting out the texture width and subtracting the original Y value. Shawn Hargreaves has a great blog post about this at http://blogs.msdn.com/shawnhar/archive/2008/12/02/zune-landscape-mode.aspx.

Optimizing the Game to Run on the Zune

To start, we can check the frames per second by updating our FPS game component. This way, we can measure how fast our game is running and see if any changes we make increase the frame rate. We can replace the content of the Draw method with the following code:

```
float elapsed = (float)gameTime.ElapsedRealTime.TotalSeconds;
framecount++;
timeSinceLastUpdate += elapsed;
if (timeSinceLastUpdate > updateInterval)
{
    fps = framecount / timeSinceLastUpdate;

    fpsText = "FPS: " + fps.ToString();

    framecount = 0;
    timeSinceLastUpdate -= updateInterval;
}

if (!inSpriteBatch)
    spriteBatch.Begin();

spriteBatch.DrawString(font, fpsText, Vector2.Zero, Color.Yellow);

if (!inSpriteBatch)
    spriteBatch.End();

base.Draw(gameTime);
```

A new boolean property called InSpriteBatch needs to be added. We also need to add in the LoadContent method:

```
protected sealed override void LoadContent()
{
    spriteBatch = new SpriteBatch(GraphicsDevice);
    font = Game.Content.Load<SpriteFont>(@"Fonts\arial");

    base.LoadContent();
}
```

Create the following private member fields:

```
private bool inSpriteBatch = false;
private SpriteBatch spriteBatch;
private SpriteFont font;
private string fpsText = string.Empty;
```

We can set the DrawOrder to 1000 in the constructor. We can also add the following Load method:

```
public void Load(SpriteBatch spriteBatch)
{
    this.spriteBatch = spriteBatch;
}
```

We call the Load method from the game's LoadContent method passing in the newly created sprite batch. We also tell the FPS game component that we will be drawing it inside a sprite batch so it does not need to create its own:

```
fps.Load(spriteBatch);
fps.InSpriteBatch = true;
```

Now when we run this game again, we see that as the music loads, it stalls our game. This is because the thread is being blocked as it is trying to load the song from the Zune. Because there are no asynchronous methods, we will need to create our own thread.

First, we can remove the call to sound.Update in our game's Update method along with the ZUNE preprocessor directive. Next, we can add the following Zune-specific private member variable:

```
private Thread backgroundThread;
```

We can create our background thread by adding the following Zune-specific code to the SimpleGame constructor:

```
backgroundThread = new Thread(BackgroundMusicThread);
```

This thread kicks off the following method:

```
#if ZUNE
    private void BackgroundMusicThread()
    {
        if (MediaPlayer.State == MediaState.Playing)
        {
            //the user is playing their own music
            //just kill the thread by returning
            return;
        }

        //the user isn't playing their own music, we can set it to our music
        if (MediaPlayer.State != MediaState.Playing)
        {
            Song[] playList = {
                Content.Load<Song>(@"Sounds\Song2"),
                Content.Load<Song>(@"Sounds\Song3")
            };

            sound.StartPlayList(playList);
        }

        while (true)
        {
            sound.Update();

            Thread.Sleep(1000);
        }
    }
#endif
```

Because we are loading the songs at the beginning of our background thread, we no longer need to load them in our LoadContent method. We should replace the existing code with the following code:

```
backgroundThread.IsBackground = true;
backgroundThread.Start();
```

We set the IsBackground property to true so the thread will exit gracefully when the game exists. We also start the thread. So at this point, when the LoadContent method is called after we load our explosion sound, this background thread starts, which will load up all the sounds we want to use as well as continue to make sure a sound is playing.

Now when we run the game, we can see that the songs loading does not bring the system to a halt because they are running on their own thread.

We need to replace the content of the Draw method in the Background class with the following code:

```
#if ZUNE
    spriteBatch.End(); //Don't bother rendering clouds in additive mode
    spriteBatch.Begin();

    sbm.Draw("clouds1", spriteBatch);
#else
    sbm.Draw("clouds1", spriteBatch);
    sbm.Draw("clouds2", spriteBatch);

    GraphicsDevice.RenderState.SourceBlend = Blend.SourceAlpha;
    GraphicsDevice.RenderState.DestinationBlend = Blend.InverseSourceAlpha;
#endif

    sbm.Draw("city", spriteBatch);
    sbm.Draw("street", spriteBatch);

    base.Draw(gameTime);
```

For Windows and the Xbox 360, we were drawing the same cloud texture two different times while in additive mode. This was just for demonstration purposes, and it is causing our frame rate to hang around 13 fps. By immediately ending the sprite batch and starting a new one with the default alpha blending mode while only drawing one cloud texture, we can double the frame rate to about 26 fps when running in standalone release mode. This is good enough because the best frame rate we can get on the Zune is 30 frames per second. When we develop a game we want to run on the Zune, it's best to measure as we go. We did not have this luxury, however, because we were porting an existing game created before the Zune was supported. It is very important to measure as we develop so we can determine what is causing bottlenecks and what we can do to correct them.

Zune Limitations

The Zune is a great little device. It is pretty amazing how well it plays games. The maximum amount of data we can create per game is 2GB. That really is not much of a limitation. However, the Zune only has 16MB of memory. This means all the content (textures, sounds, music, and so on), the .NET Compact Framework, and our game code must fit within this limit. If we are not careful about cleaning up after ourselves, we can quickly run out of memory on the Zune.

Also there are a few differences between the first generation of the Zune (Zune 30, also known as V1) and the second generation of the Zune (Zune 4, 8, 16, 80, and 120, also known as V2). The big difference is that the refresh rate on the Zune 30 is 60 frames a second while it is set to 30 frames a second on the other Zunes. The processor speed is a little faster on the first generation as well (524 MHz vs. 399 MHz). The processor was scaled back on the second generation to save on battery life. Playing games on the Zune will definitely drain the battery. If we can keep everything in memory and not have to continually spin up the hard drive on the Zune 30, 80, and 120, the battery will last longer.

Summary

This chapter was all about taking an existing 2D game we wrote for Windows and the Xbox 360 and porting it so it will also compile and run on the Zune. We added in a new sound manager specifically for our Zune project. We modified the textures and sounds to be smaller so we could stay within the 16MB memory limit of the Zune.

We utilized the ZUNE preprocessor directives when sharing the same code file, and we changed which files were loaded in our projects when the entire code file was different. We created a content project that was exclusively used by the Zune project.

We finished the chapter by updating our FPS display. We created a background thread to handle the songs. We boosted performance by not drawing a second cloud texture. After all the changes, we now have the same game we created for the other platforms running on the Zune.

13

PART VI

High Level Shader Language

IN THIS PART

CHAPTER 14

HLSL Basics

Before 2001, the only way to talk to the graphics hardware was through the Fixed Function Pipeline (FFP) provided in DirectX. Graphics card manufacturers then started allowing access through assembly code directly to their hardware. This was needed because the graphics cards were so much more complex than they were when the DirectX application programming interface (API) originally came out. It used to be enough to have an API that allowed us to set different properties and settings to get the graphics cards to work the way we wanted. However, as the cards became more complex, the DirectX API, specifically the FFP, also had to become more complex.

Instead of continuing to add functions to the FFP, Microsoft provided a way through its API to execute assembly code on the graphics cards directly. This assembly code is called a *shader*. The graphics cards have vertex shader instructions as well as pixel shader instructions. Vertex shaders are executed on every vertex in the visible scene. Pixel shaders are executed on all of the visible geometry in the scene.

Vertex Shaders Versus Pixel Shaders

Vertex shaders are executed on every vertex of an object. When we draw a face (triangle) of a 3D object, the vertex shader will be executed for all three vertices that make up that triangle. When we draw a 2D sprite, the vertex shader will run four times for each vertex that makes up that sprite—one vertex in each corner to make the rectangle.

Pixel shaders, on the other hand, execute on every visible pixel of the geometry in the scene. If the triangle of a 3D object is close to the camera so that it takes up most of the screen, the pixel shader will be run for every pixel where the triangle is visible. On the other hand, if the 3D object is far away so that it does not even make up an entire pixel, the pixel shader will not be run at all—not even one time. For a 2D sprite, it will be run for every pixel that is visible on the screen. If the sprite is a full-screen sprite, then every single pixel on the screen will be run through the pixel shader. You will see several examples of this in the next chapter as we look at postprocessing effects that are done through pixel shaders.

Assembly language is great. It allows us to get down to the hardware level and move data on particular registers, and we have complete control over how it is processed. However, writing assembly code can be time consuming. NVIDIA, one of the graphics cards leaders, came out with a language called Cg (for C for Graphics). As the name implies, Cg is a higher level C-like language that developers can use for their games instead of using assembly language.

Microsoft created a standard high-level language called the High Level Shader Language (HLSL). The two languages are similar because they actually started out as the same language via a joint project between NVIDIA and Microsoft. For some reason the project ended up forking into two separate final products. The advantage of HLSL for XNA programmers is that the XNA Framework can load in the .fx files automatically because the Content Pipeline compiles it for us automatically.

HLSL is a language that allows us to talk at a high level to the graphics card so we do not need to use assembly code to access the hardware. However, on the Xbox 360 we can still use assembler directly inside the HLSL syntax if we want to.

HLSL is an integral part of XNA. The FFP no longer exists in XNA. We can only get data on the screen using HLSL. Of course, until now we have been able to get our demos and game on the screen by using the `BasicEffect` XNA helper class. To help developers get up to speed quicker, Microsoft added this helper class to XNA. It allows us to write to the graphics card without understanding HLSL. However, all the `BasicEffect` helper class is doing is passing the data through to an internal shader.

NOTE

The `BasicEffect` shader has been released by Microsoft and is available for download at http://creators.xna.com/en-us/utilities/basiceffectshader. Although it's called "BasicEffect," the actual shader code is far from basic. The `SpriteBatch` we have been using also just uses shader code, which is available for download at http://creators.xna.com/en-us/utilities/spritebatchshader.

Effects give us the ability to render the same geometry in different ways. For example, we can have the exact same content and display it differently depending on how far away the camera is or based on the gamer's hardware capabilities.

Understanding the Shader Process

Before we get into the details of how to pass application data from our XNA application to the graphics card, we need to discuss the process flow in general, which is shown in Figure 14.1. I will take a little time to explain the flow so you can understand what shaders provide for us.

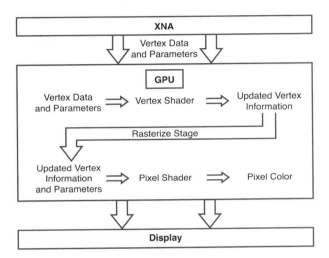

FIGURE 14.1   The flow of data from an XNA game to the graphics card and finally onto the rendering surface.

It helps to keep in mind that our end goal is to get our scene to display on the screen. We are trying to get pixels on the screen to look a certain way with different colors to form an image of our scene. We create our vertex information (either manually or by loading in a 3D file), and we texture the vertex. We then pass that vertex data (position, normals, textures, and so on) to the graphics card. Graphics cards have a graphics processing unit (GPU), sometimes referred to as a video processing unit (VPU). The GPU is just like a CPU, except it runs at a lower clock speed. It is able to process many vertices and pixels in parallel, which makes it much faster for doing graphics and rendering work.

After we pass our vertex data from our application to the GPU, the GPU can perform tasks on the data to get it to appear a certain way on the screen. This can be as simple as determining the colors from the texture being used, to as complex as translating vertices and doing multiple passes of the pixel shader to create very interesting effects.

The GPU processes our vertex information and displays our scene through the vertex and pixel shaders. (DirectX 10 has geometry shaders, but those are not supported under the current XNA Framework or on Xbox 360.) Once the GPU gets the vertex information and any parameters our XNA application passes to it, the vertex shader is executed. The vertex shader will "shade" the vertex and transform it to a format we specify using a transformation we specify. The rasterization process then occurs, which converts the primitives (triangles mainly) into the pixels that will need to be rendered on the screen. The pixel shader processes each pixel that is to be rendered on the screen and produces a color for that pixel. Finally, the pixels are sent to the frame buffer, which is sent to the display.

HLSL Syntax

Although I do not go into a lot of detail about the HLSL language syntax, I will touch on the high points and explain the mapping between the C# type and the HLSL type when appropriate. We not only discuss the types of data in HLSL, but also semantics, intrinsic functions, loops, and conditions.

Variable Types

Just like C#, HLSL allows us to declare variables of different types. Most use the same keyword as their C# counterpart. Examples of these are int, float, bool, struct, in, out, return, void, string, true, and false. There are more, of course, but those are the common ones we will be using.

Vectors can be defined several ways. Typically we see them listed as float3 for a vector with three components and float4 for a vector with four components. We could also declare a vector with the vector keyword. We can access the different components of the vector in different ways. We can access them like an array or through their component directly; for example, suppose we have a vector to hold a color value, such as this:

```
float4 color;
```

We could access the red portion of the color by writing either of the next two lines:

```
float red = color[0];
float samered = color.r;
```

Vectors have two component namespaces: r,g,b,a and x,y,z,w. We could also get the red value from our color by writing the following valid line of code:

```
float anotherred = color.x;
```

If we wanted the red and green components of our color to store them in a vector with two components, we could write the following code:

```
float2 something = color.xy;
float2 somethingelse = { color[0], color[1] };
```

When we access multiple components at the same time, like the first statement just shown, it is called *swizzling*. Although we can swizzle our components in the same namespace, the following is invalid code because we cannot combine component namespaces:

```
//bad code - we can't combine component namespaces
float2 wontcompile = color.xg;
```

We can set up matrices with the `matrix` keyword or by using `floatRxC` where R (rows) and C (columns) can be any values. To define a 4×4 matrix, we could use either of the following declarations:

```
float4x4 whatIsTheMatrix;
matrix <float, 4, 4> theMatrixHasYou;
```

The following code shows how we would access a particular row and column of a matrix:

```
float4x4 a = worldViewProjection;
float b = a._m11;
float c = a[0][0];
```

In HLSL, we have storage class modifiers that we can associate with our variables. These determine how the variables are used. The storage class modifiers are as follows:

```
extern

shared

static

uniform

volatile
```

The `extern` modifier allows our application to have access to our global variables. We can set and get those variables inside our XNA code. The default for global variables is `extern`. The `static` modifier, on the other hand, does not allow us access to the global variable. Local variables can also have the `static` storage class modifier, which means that the value it has persists while each vertex or pixel is being shaded. There is also a `shared` modifier that allows multiple effect files to share the value. The last two modifiers are `uniform` and `volatile`. The `volatile` storage class modifier lets the HLSL compiler know that the global variable data will change frequently. The `uniform` modifier does the opposite and lets the compiler know that the data will not change. This is the default of our global variables. This is important because if we did not mark our variables as uniform (again, this is the default), the shader would have many more instructions per vertex. Instead, the compiler does a preshader compilation and will execute those items to be executed once on the CPU and then do the per-vertex/pixel calculations on the GPU. This is very much the desired effect.

TIP

In practice, you will probably never need to use these modifiers because the defaults generally do the right thing.

Setting up variables in HLSL is very similar to setting up variables in C#. There is an additional step we need to take when setting up variables, though. HLSL has something known as *semantics*, which we discuss in the next section.

Semantics

Semantics are used to link our input with the output of the graphics pipeline function that was just executed. For example, semantics are used to link our output from our application to the vertex shader input. These are called *vertex input semantics*. After the vertex shader is done processing the vertices, it passes to the rasterization stage, which you saw in Figure 14.1. These are called *vertex output semantics*.

The pixel shader receives data from both the vertex shader and the rasterization stage. These are called *pixel input semantics*. After the pixel shader is done, it sends the data to the correct render target, and then the pixel shader output color is linked to the alpha blend stage. These are called *pixel output semantics*. A *semantic* is simply a label attached to the shader input or output. It conveys information about the intended use of the data. We discuss the syntax of semantics in the next section as we talk about structs.

Structs

We have to specify structs to hold our input and output data. For example, the vertex input struct that is populated from our XNA application could look something like this:

```
struct VertexInput //Application Data
{
    float4 Position : POSITION0;
    float3 Normal : NORMAL;
    float4 TextureCoords : TEXCOORD0;
};
```

We set up our structs much in the same way as we do in C#. The only difference is the semantics. We discussed semantics in the last section but didn't see their syntax. Our effect is expecting our game to pass in the position of the vertex, the normal of the vertex, and the texture coordinates of the vertex. It then maps all these types to a specific register so when it gets to the next stage in the pipeline it will be able to read in the appropriate values. A list of all the vertex input semantics can be found in Table 14.1.

TABLE 14.1   Vertex Input Semantic List

Vertex Shader Input Semantic	Description
BINORMAL[n]	Binormal
BLENDINDICES[n]	Blend indices
BLENDWEIGHT[n]	Blend weights
COLOR[n]	Diffuse and specular color
NORMAL[n]	Normal vector
POSITION[n]	Vertex position in object space
PSIZE[n]	Point size
TANGENT[n]	Tangent

TABLE 14.1   Vertex Input Semantic List

Vertex Shader Input Semantic	Description
TESSFACTOR[n]	Tessellation factor
TEXCOORD[n]	Texture coordinates

A struct that holds our vertex output data would look something like this:

```
struct VertexOutput
{
    float4  Position : POSITION0;
    float4  TexCoord : TEXCOORD0;
};
```

You can see it is set up the same as our input struct. The main thing to note about the vertex output is that it must return at least one vertex. All the vertex output semantics can be found in Table 14.2.

TABLE 14.2   Vertex Output Semantic List

Vertex Shader Output Semantic	Description
COLOR[n]	Diffuse or specular color. Any vertex shader prior to vs_3_0 should clamp a parameter that uses this semantic between 0 and 1, inclusive. A vs_3_0 vertex shader has no restriction on the data range.
	vs_1_1 through vs_1_3 only support two-color interpolators. vs_1_4 supports six and eight colors with subsequent versions.
FOG	Vertex fog. Not supported on Xbox 360 or with vs_3_0.
POSITION	Position of a vertex in homogenous space. Compute position in screen space by dividing (x,y,z) by w. Every vertex shader must write out a parameter with this semantic.
PSIZE	Point size.
TEXCOORD[n]	Texture coordinates. This is actually an all-purpose semantic, meaning that we can pass any data (not just texture coordinates) with this semantic.

The vertex output data is passed to the rasterization stage and then passed to the pixel shader. Our pixel shader also takes a struct as its input. An example of one follows:

```
struct PixelInput // Rasterization Data
{
    float4 Color : COLOR0;
};
```

A list of pixel shader input semantics can be found in Table 14.3.

TABLE 14.3   Pixel Input Semantic List

Pixel Shader Input Semantic	Description
COLOR[n]	Diffuse or specular color. For shaders prior to vs_3_0 and ps_3_0, this data ranges between 0 and 1, inclusive. Starting with ps_3_0, there is no restriction on the data range.
TEXCOORD[n]	Texture coordinates.
VFACE	Floating-point scalar that indicates a back-facing primitive. A negative value faces backward, whereas a positive value faces the camera. This is only valid with ps_3_0.
VPOS	Contains the current pixel (x,y) location. This is only valid with ps_3_0.

Here's an example of a pixel shader output struct:

```
struct PixelOutput // Pixel Output Data
{
    float4 Color : COLOR0;
    float Depth : DEPTH;
};
```

The pixel shader must return the color of the pixel at the very least. Both of the pixel shader output semantics can be found in Table 14.4.

TABLE 14.4   Pixel Output Semantic List

Pixel Shader Output Semantic	Description
COLOR[n]	Output color. Any pixel shader prior to ps_3_0 should clamp a parameter that uses this semantic between 0 and 1, inclusive. For ps_3_0 shaders, the data range is dependent on the render target format.
DEPTH[n]	Output depth.

You now have seen examples of the different structs we need to pass data around our shaders. You also saw the available semantics (description labels) listed for each of those structs.

Intrinsic Functions

We can define our own functions in HLSL much like we do in C#, but there are also a lot of built-in functions, which are called *intrinsic functions*. Table 14.5 lists all the intrinsic functions available in HLSL. These functions are listed here for easy reference in case the DirectX 9 SDK documentation is not handy. However, there is even more information about each function inside the documentation.

TABLE 14.5   Intrinsic Functions Available in HLSL

Syntax	Description
`value abs(value a)`	Absolute value (per component).
`acos(x)`	Returns the arccosine of each component of x. Each component should be in the range [–1, 1].
`all(x)`	Tests if all components of x are nonzero.
`any(x)`	Tests if any component of x is nonzero.
`asin(x)`	Returns the arcsine of each component of x. Each component should be in the range [–pi/2, pi/2].
`atan(x)`	Returns the arctangent of x. The return values are in the range [–pi/2, pi/2].
`atan2(y, x)`	Returns the arctangent of y/x. The signs of y and x are used to determine the quadrant of the return values in the range [–pi, pi]. atan2 is well defined for every point other than the origin, even if x equals 0 and y does not equal 0.
`ceil(x)`	Returns the smallest integer that is greater than or equal to x.
`clamp(x, min, max)`	Clamps x to the range [min, max].
`clip(x)`	Discards the current pixel, if any component of x is less than zero. This can be used to simulate clip planes, if each component of x represents the distance from a plane.
`cos(x)`	Returns the cosine of x.
`cosh(x)`	Returns the hyperbolic cosine of x.
`cross(a, b)`	Returns the cross-product of two 3D vectors, a and b.
`D3DCOLORtoUBYTE4(x)`	Swizzles and scales components of the 4D vector x to compensate for the lack of UBYTE4 support in some hardware.
`ddx(x)`	Returns the partial derivative of x with respect to the screen-space x coordinate.
`ddy(x)`	Returns the partial derivative of x with respect to the screen-space y coordinate.
`degrees(x)`	Converts x from radians to degrees.
`determinant(m)`	Returns the determinant of the square matrix m.
`distance(a, b)`	Returns the distance between two points, a and b.
`dot(a, b)`	Returns the · product of two vectors, a and b.
`exp(x)`	Returns the base-e exponent.
`exp2(value a)`	Base 2 Exp (per component).

14

TABLE 14.5   Intrinsic Functions Available in HLSL

Syntax	Description
faceforward(n, i, ng)	Returns –n * sign($\cdot$(i, ng)).
floor(x)	Returns the greatest integer that is less than or equal to x.
fmod(a, b)	Returns the floating point remainder f of a / b, such that a = i * b + f, where i is an integer, f has the same sign as x, and the absolute value of f is less than the absolute value of b.
frac(x)	Returns the fractional part f of x, such that f is a value greater than or equal to 0 and less than 1.
frexp(x, out exp)	Returns the mantissa and exponent of x. frexp returns the mantissa, and the exponent is stored in the output parameter exp. If x is 0, the function returns 0 for both the mantissa and the exponent.
fwidth(x)	Returns abs(ddx(x)) + abs(ddy(x)).
isfinite(x)	Returns true if x is finite; false otherwise.
isinf(x)	Returns true if x is +INF or –INF; false otherwise.
isnan(x)	Returns true if x is NAN or QNAN; false otherwise.
ldexp(x, exp)	Returns x * 2exp.
length(v)	Returns the length of the vector v.
lerp(a, b, s)	Returns a + s(b – a). This linearly interpolates between a and b, such that the return value is a when s is 0, and b when s is 1.
lit(n $\cdot$ l, n $\cdot$ h, m)	Returns a lighting vector (ambient, diffuse, specular, 1): ambient = 1; diffuse = (n $\cdot$ l < 0) ? 0 : n $\cdot$ l; specular = (n $\cdot$ l < 0) || (n $\cdot$ h < 0) ? 0 : (n $\cdot$ h * m).
log(x)	Returns the base-e logarithm of x. If x is negative, the function returns indefinite. If x is 0, the function returns +INF.
log10(x)	Returns the base-10 logarithm of x. If x is negative, the function returns indefinite. If x is 0, the function returns +INF.
log2(x)	Returns the base-2 logarithm of x. If x is negative, the function returns indefinite. If x is 0, the function returns +INF.
max(a, b)	Selects the greater of a and b.
min(a, b)	Selects the lesser of a and b.

TABLE 14.5   Intrinsic Functions Available in HLSL

Syntax	Description
modf(x, out ip)	Splits the value x into fractional and integer parts, each of which has the same sign as x. The signed fractional portion of x is returned. The integer portion is stored in the output parameter ip.
mul(a, b)	Performs matrix multiplication between a and b. If a is a vector, it is treated as a row vector. If b is a vector, it is treated as a column vector. The inner dimension acolumns and brows must be equal. The result has the dimension arrows × bcolumns.
noise(x)	Not yet implemented.
normalize(v)	Returns the normalized vector v / length(v). If the length of v is 0, the result is indefinite.
pow(x, y)	Returns xy.
radians(x)	Converts x from degrees to radians.
reflect(i, n)	Returns the reflection vector v, given the entering ray direction i, and the surface normal n, such that v = i - 2n * (i · n).
refract(i, n, R)	Returns the refraction vector v, given the entering ray direction i, the surface normal n, and the relative index of refraction R. If the angle between i and n is too great for a given R, refract returns (0,0,0).
round(x)	Rounds x to the nearest integer.
rsqrt(x)	Returns 1 / sqrt(x).
saturate(x)	Clamps x to the range [0, 1].
sign(x)	Computes the sign of x. Returns –1 if x is less than 0, 0 if x equals 0, and 1 if x is greater than zero.
sin(x)	Returns the sine of x.
sincos(x, out s, out c)	Returns the sine and cosine of x. sin(x) is stored in the output parameter s. cos(x) is stored in the output parameter c.
sinh(x)	Returns the hyperbolic sine of x.
smoothstep(min, max, x)	Returns 0 if x < min. Returns 1 if x > max. Returns a smooth Hermite interpolation between 0 and 1, if x is in the range [min, max].
value sqrt(value a)	Square root (per component).
step(a, x)	Returns (x >= a) ? 1 : 0.
tan(x)	Returns the tangent of x.
tanh(x)	Returns the hyperbolic tangent of x.

14

TABLE 14.5   Intrinsic Functions Available in HLSL

Syntax	Description
tex1D(s, t)	1D texture lookup. s is a sampler or a sampler1D object. t is a scalar.
tex1D(s, t, ddx, ddy)	1D texture lookup, with derivatives. s is a sampler or sampler1D object. t, ddx, and ddy are scalars.
tex1Dbias(s, t)	1D biased texture lookup. s is a sampler or sampler1D object. t is a 4D vector. The mip level is biased by t.w before the lookup takes place.
tex1Dgrad(s, t, ddx, ddy)	1D gradient texture lookup. s is a sampler or sampler1D object. t is a 4D vector. The gradient values (ddx, ddy) select the appropriate mipmap level of the texture for sampling.
tex1Dlod(s, t)	1D texture lookup with level of detail (LOD). s is a sampler or sampler1D object. t is a 4D vector. The mipmap LOD is specified in t.
tex1Dproj(s, t)	1D projective texture lookup. s is a sampler or sampler1D object. t is a 4D vector. t is divided by its last component before the lookup takes place.
tex2D(s, t)	2D texture lookup. s is a sampler or a sampler2D object. t is a 2D texture coordinate.
tex2D(s, t, ddx, ddy)	2D texture lookup, with derivatives. s is a sampler or sampler2D object. t, ddx, and ddy are 2D vectors.
tex2Dbias(s, t)	2D biased texture lookup. s is a sampler or sampler2D object. t is a 4D vector. The mip level is biased by t.w before the lookup takes place.
tex2Dgrad(s, t, ddx, ddy)	2D gradient texture lookup. s is a sampler or sampler2D object. t is a 4D vector. The gradient values (ddx, ddy) select the appropriate mipmap level of the texture for sampling.
tex2Dlod(s, t)	2D texture lookup with LOD. s is a sampler or sampler2D object. t is a 4D vector. The mipmap LOD is specified in t.
tex2Dproj(s, t)	2D projective texture lookup. s is a sampler or sampler2D object. t is a 4D vector. t is divided by its last component before the lookup takes place.
tex3D(s, t)	3D volume texture lookup. s is a sampler or a sampler3D object. t is a 3D texture coordinate.
tex3D(s, t, ddx, ddy)	3D volume texture lookup, with derivatives. s is a sampler or sampler3D object. t, ddx, and ddy are 3D vectors.

TABLE 14.5   Intrinsic Functions Available in HLSL

Syntax	Description
`tex3Dbias(s, t)`	3D biased texture lookup. s is a sampler or sampler3D object. t is a 4D vector. The mip level is biased by t.w before the lookup takes place.
`tex3Dgrad(s, t, ddx, ddy)`	3D gradient texture lookup. s is a sampler or sampler3D object. t is a 4D vector. The gradient values (ddx, ddy) select the appropriate mipmap level of the texture for sampling.
`tex3Dlod(s, t)`	3D texture lookup with LOD. s is a sampler or sampler3D object. t is a 4D vector. The mipmap LOD is specified in t.
`tex3Dproj(s, t)`	3D projective volume texture lookup. s is a sampler or sampler3D object. t is a 4D vector. t is divided by its last component before the lookup takes place.
`texCUBE(s, t)`	3D cube texture lookup. s is a sampler or a samplerCUBE object. t is a 3D texture coordinate.
`texCUBE(s, t, ddx, ddy)`	3D cube texture lookup, with derivatives. s is a sampler or samplerCUBE object. t, ddx, and ddy are 3D vectors.
`texCUBEbias(s, t)`	3D biased cube texture lookup. s is a sampler or samplerCUBE object. t is a 4D vector. The mip level is biased by t.w before the lookup takes place.
`texCUBEgrad(s, t, ddx, ddy)`	3D gradient cube texture lookup. s is a sampler or samplerCUBE object. t is a 4D vector. The gradient values (ddx, ddy) select the appropriate mipmap level of the texture for sampling.
`tex3Dlod(s, t)`	3D cube texture lookup with LOD. s is a sampler or samplerCUBE object. t is a 4D vector. The mipmap LOD is specified in t.
`texCUBEproj(s, t)`	3D projective cube texture lookup. s is a sampler or samplerCUBE object. t is a 4D vector. t is divided by its last component before the lookup takes place.
`transpose(m)`	Returns the transpose of the matrix m. If the source is dimension mrows × mcolumns, the result is dimension mcolumns × mrows.

14

In general, these methods are used identically to how C# methods are used. They have a return value and take in parameters. There are a lot of functions, and that is a good thing. Some of the more frequently used functions are `clamp`, which clamps a value within the range specified; `saturate`, which is identical to `clamp` with an implied value range of 0 and 1; dot, which computes the dot product of two vectors; `cross`, which computes the cross-product of two vectors; `normalize`, which returns the normalized vector; and `tex2D`, which allows us to get a color from a vertex by passing in a sampler and the position of the texture we want the color of. Samplers are required whenever we need to use textures. A sampler has a direct relation to the part of the hardware where the texture is stored.

Loops and Conditions

We are almost done hitting the highlights of the syntax, but we need to discuss loops and conditions—the shader's flow control. HLSL has many of the same flow controls that C# includes: `if`, `while`, `do`, and `for`. They are identical to their C# counterparts. When the `if` statement only has one line, the curly braces are optional, just like in C#. Fortunately, there is nothing new in regard to our loop and conditions inside of HLSL compared to how they are structured in C#.

Vertex Shaders

Now that we have discussed how vertex and pixel shaders are used and reviewed some of the syntax of the language, we can look at some real shader code. We start by looking at a simple vertex shader. Then we'll look at a pixel shader and finally we'll look at the techniques and passes needed to execute these shaders.

We can start by discussing an actual vertex shader. This shader is very simple because we are going to process our vertex position and texture coordinates:

```
VertexOutput vertexShader(VertexInput input)
{
    VertexOutput output;
    WorldViewProjection = mul(mul(World, View), Projection);
    output.Position = mul(input.Position, WorldViewProjection);
    output.TexCoord = input.TexCoord;
    return( output );
}
```

We take a parameter called `input` of type `VertexInput`. We return a `VertexOutput` value. Those structs look like this:

```
struct VertexInput
{
    float4 Position : POSITION;
    float2 TexCoord : TEXCOORD0;
};
```

```
struct VertexOutput
{
    float4 Position : POSITION;
    float2 TexCoord : TEXCOORD0;
};
```

Our `vertexShader` function calculates the world view projection matrix based on the world, view, and projection matrices being passed into the shader from our application.

After multiplying the matrices together, we then set the output position by transforming the position passed to us with our `worldviewprojection` matrix. Afterward, we simply do a passthrough of the texture coordinate information. The vertex information is then passed to the rasterization stage and then on to our pixel shader.

TIP

The position is being passed in as a `float4`, even though the C# code provides `Vector3` values. There is no need to "fix" the shader to input a `float3`. This is done on purpose, and the GPU automatically fills in the fourth component with the value 1 to make the projection work properly.

Pixel Shaders

Pixel shaders allow us to manipulate each and every pixel being rendered. This is very powerful. You can see an actual pixel shader here:

```
float4 pixelShader(PixelInput input) : COLOR
{
    return( tex2D(TextureSampler, input.TexCoord) * AmbientColor);
}
```

We are passed in our pixel input struct and return a color (a 4D vector). The single statement in this pixel shader gets the red, green, blue, and alpha values from the texture using the texture coordinates passed in. Here is the `PixelInput` struct (you can see we need the texture coordinates passed in):

```
struct PixelInput
{
    float2 TexCoord : TEXCOORD0;
};
```

After getting our color for that texture location, we multiply each component of our color with our ambient color passed in from our application. This produces a new color that we return. This color will ultimately be passed through to the buffer that gets put onto our screen.

Techniques

Now that we have our shaders created, we need to call them inside our effect file. When our game uses an effect, it passes in a technique. The technique can have one or more passes (we discuss passes in the next section). Effects can have multiple techniques. A technique is really just a name and a container of our pass (or passes).

```
technique Default
{
    ...
}
```

Techniques can have any name. This book will typically have one technique per effect file and call it `Default`.

Passes

Each pass in a technique will define which vertex and pixel shader should be used. The game typically will either loop through all the passes in a technique or will just call one directly. If more than one pass is contained in the technique, we can have our scenes go through a couple different changes before actually rendering to the screen by looping through the passes. We set up our passes in the following way:

```
pass P0
{
    VertexShader = compile vs_1_1 vertexShader();
    PixelShader = compile ps_1_1 pixelShader();
}
```

The preceding block is inside the technique code block. This is what kicks off our shaders. Our application specifies a technique and then specifies a pass. When the effect is processed, it searches for a vertex and pixel shader and processes them.

Inside of our pass we can also set render states. For example, we can set the following values:

```
CullMode = none;
AlphaBlendEnable = false;
FillMode = Wireframe;
```

These are just a few. Most render states we can set directly inside of XNA, we can also set in our HLSL code. If we set them directly in our HLSL code, the instruction is closer to the hardware.

Passing Application Data to the GPU

Our shaders need to have data passed to them to do any work. The main piece of information needed is our vertex data. Not only do we need to send in our vertex data, but we also need to send in some of the matrices. It could be our world, view, projection, or our world view projection matrix. We also can send in our textures and any other data we determine our shaders need from our game.

Before we can pass any information to our effect, we need to initialize a variable for it. We do this with the XNA `Effect` class as follows:

```
Effect effect;
```

Then we need to load our effect file. Fortunately, this is just as easy as loading our textures or any other resource because the Content Pipeline knows how to read them in. Therefore, the code to load our effect is as follows:

```
effect = Content.Load<Effect>(@"Effects\AmbientTexture");
```

It is very easy to load our effect, so let's see what hurdles we need to jump over to pass data to our actual effect file to use. We can jump straight into a code snippet to see the complexity:

```
effect.Parameters["Texture"].SetValue(texture);
effect.Parameters["Projection"].SetValue(camera.Projection);
effect.Parameters["View"].SetValue(camera.View);
effect.Parameters["World"].SetValue(world * mesh.ParentBone.Transform);
```

That is really not complex at all. We access our global variables from our effect file by accessing the Parameters collection of our effect. We pass in the name of our variable as the key to the collection and then call the SetValue method to set the value of the variable. We do not need to cast our value to any type—thanks to method overloading it just works.

HLSL Demo

Now we can create a demo using all this knowledge. To start with, we can load up our Load3DObject demo from Chapter 6, "Loading and Texturing 3D Objects." In the Draw method of our code, we are currently using the BasicEffect class that XNA provides for us. We are going to update the code to use an effect file we will create.

To start, we can create our HLSL effect file. Inside our project we need to create another folder under Content project called Effects. After we create that folder, we can add a new file. We can select an Effect file and call it AmbientTexture.fx. We can then clear out the code it created for us. Here is the code we need to enter into the file:

```
float4x4 World : WORLD;
float4x4 View;
float4x4 Projection;

float4 AmbientColor : COLOR0;

float4x4 WorldViewProjection : WORLDVIEWPROJECTION;
texture Texture;
sampler TextureSampler = sampler_state
{
    texture = <Texture>;
    magfilter = LINEAR;
    minfilter = LINEAR;
    mipfilter = LINEAR;
```

```
    AddressU = mirror;
    AddressV = mirror;
};

struct VertexInput
{
    float4 Position : POSITION;
    float2 TexCoord : TEXCOORD0;
};

struct VertexOutput
{
    float4 Position : POSITION;
    float2 TexCoord : TEXCOORD0;
};

VertexOutput vertexShader(VertexInput input)
{
    VertexOutput output;
    WorldViewProjection = mul(mul(World, View), Projection);
    output.Position = mul(input.Position, WorldViewProjection);
    output.TexCoord = input.TexCoord;
    return( output );
}

struct PixelInput
{
    float2 TexCoord : TEXCOORD0;
};

float4 pixelShader(PixelInput input) : COLOR
{
    return( tex2D(TextureSampler, input.TexCoord) * AmbientColor);
}

technique Default
{
    pass P0
    {
        VertexShader = compile vs_1_1 vertexShader();
        PixelShader = compile ps_1_1 pixelShader();
    }
}
```

We have already discussed most things in this shader. We will go over the items we did not discuss already. To start, we declare some variables to hold the matrices that our game will pass in. Then we declare our ambient color as a `float4`. When we process a texture from our scene, we need to set up a variable to hold our texture. We also need to set up a sampler so our HLSL code can sample that texture. We already discussed our vertex input and output structs as well as our pixel input structs. Instead of using a pixel output struct, we are just returning the color data because that is all that is required.

Now in our game code, we need to declare our effect:

```
private Effect effect;
```

Next, we need to load the effect into our content manager. We can do that inside of our `LoadContent` method, as follows:

```
effect = Content.Load<Effect>(@"Effects\AmbientTexture");
```

Now, we need to set our first parameter for this effect. We have an `AmbientColor` variable that we need to set, so we can do that now. We will not change our ambient light color every frame. In fact, we are just going to set it once, so we can set it up right after creating our effect. We need to add this line of code to set our variable:

```
effect.Parameters["AmbientColor"].SetValue(0.8f);
```

Finally, we need to replace the inner `foreach` loop in the `Draw` method. Before we had this:

```
foreach (BasicEffect be in mesh.Effects)
{
    be.EnableDefaultLighting();

    if (texture != null)
        be.Texture = texture;

    be.Projection = camera.Projection;
    be.View = camera.View;
    be.World = world * mesh.ParentBone.Transform;
}
```

Remember, XNA sets up a `BasicEffect` for each mesh we load, so we can simply set properties on the basic effect and be on our way. In this case, though, we want to replace that functionality with our own HLSL effect. You can see that we are setting the texture, the camera's projection, and view. We are also setting the world matrix on the mesh. We need to do all these things in our new effect as well, so let's replace the preceding code with the following code:

```
foreach (ModelMeshPart mp in mesh.MeshParts)
{
    if (texture != null)
        effect.Parameters["Texture"].SetValue(texture);
```

```
effect.Parameters["Projection"].SetValue(camera.Projection);
effect.Parameters["View"].SetValue(camera.View);
effect.Parameters["World"].SetValue(world * mesh.ParentBone.Transform);
mp.Effect = effect;
}
```

You can see this is very similar. The first thing to notice is that we are now looping through our mesh parts instead of our mesh effects. Our mesh part has an effect property that we need to set. We are using lights (a simple ambient light), and there is no need to set that value because our effect file is always using the ambient value. You can see we are setting our texture just like before, as well as our camera projection and view. After setting our world just like before, we set this mesh part's effect to our effect. We can now run the application and basically get the same results we got from the basic effect.

Actually, the basic effect has a little better lighting structure because it is using three directional lights, and a simple ambient light is used as well. Plenty of material is available on the Internet that shows how to set up directional lights, so we will not go into those details here. Instead, we will wrap up this chapter so we can cover some information in the next chapter that is not quite so abundant on the Web.

Summary

In this chapter, we discussed the purpose of shaders and went over the syntax needed to create a shader. We broke out each part of a shader and discussed what it is used for. We then created a full effect file, complete with a technique and pass. We modified an existing application to use our new effect we created in this chapter instead of the BasicEffect built in to XNA. At this point, you understand the basics of the HLSL syntax and how to structure a shader to use in our games. In the next chapter, we take things a step further and discuss vertex displacement as well as postprocessing effects.

CHAPTER 15

Advanced HLSL

In the last chapter, you learned the basics of HLSL. In this chapter, we take those concepts further by doing vertex displacement in our vertex shaders and by doing postprocessing techniques in our pixel shaders.

Vertex displacement is simply changing the position of our vertices through our vertex shader. *Postprocessing* is the process of taking a completed (or partial) scene and rendering that scene to a texture. It then takes that texture and processes it with a pixel shader to make some interesting effects.

Vertex Displacement

We are going to create an interesting effect that will allow us to move our vertices around. Shaders are not only used to texture and shade a scene, but they can actually transform it as well.

To begin, we are going to use the same Load3DObject code we left off with in the last chapter. Let's go ahead and load that solution. We are going to modify our effect file to modify the vertex position the file is passed in before passing it on to the rasterization stage.

We will be passing another value to our shader to accomplish this. We are going to pass in a timer based on our game time that we will scale down. Our vertex shader will combine this data with an offset to determine a new vertex location for the vertex it is shading. Let's set up our variable inside the effect file by adding the following declaration:

```
float Timer : TIME;
```

We are using the TIME semantic, which signifies we are passing in our game time in seconds to the shader. We also declare an offset of how far out we are going to move our vertex position. We are setting it to 100 because the objects are so large in this demo:

```
float Offset = 100.0f;
```

We are going to use simple sine and cosine functions to create our new vertex position. We need to add the following code at the top of our vertex shader:

```
float4 Pos = float4(input.Position.xyz,1);
float y = Pos.y * Offset + Timer;
float x = sin(y) * Offset;
Pos.x += x;
```

We set our position and then create an offset for our y position. We also add in the amount of time to create a variance of where that position is every frame. We then take that y position and calculate our real x position with the sine of the calculated y.

Because we modified the Pos variable, we need to make sure that is what we are using in our output calculation. Still inside the vertexShader function, we need to replace the line

```
output.Position = mul(input.Position, WorldViewProjection);
```

with this line:

```
output.Position = mul(Pos, WorldViewProjection);
```

Now, we can modify our game code to pass in our timer parameter. We need to add the following statement inside the inner foreach loop in the DrawModel method:

```
effect.Parameters["Timer"].SetValue(time);
```

To set the value of our time variable inside the Update method, we can add the following line of code:

```
time += (float)gameTime.ElapsedGameTime.TotalSeconds;
```

We can declare time as a private member field of type float. We are also going to modify the ambient color we are passing in. Of course we do not need to, but this shows that we can pass in a system-defined color as a Vector4. Also an asteroid fluctuating in shape looks cooler when it does not have a typical asteroid color. For this exercise, we are going set our asteroid color to red by just changing our ambient light color to red with the following code:

```
effect.Parameters["AmbientColor"].SetValue(Color.Red.ToVector4());
```

The preceding code should replace the existing statement where we set the color to a light gray inside the LoadContent method. The final change we make is to modify our first asteroid so it does not spin because it's harder to see our vertex displacement if it is spinning. We need to replace the first world variable initialization with the following statement, which simply removes the y rotation:

```
Matrix world =  Matrix.CreateTranslation(new Vector3(0, 0, -4000));
```

We can run the code and see our asteroid is doing a wavy effect. With some imagination and some decent algorithms, we could really make our models look different by changing vertex position through the vertex shader. Vertex displacement can also be used to deform objects when they collide. The options are endless with vertex displacement.

We could add in the following line to our shader code to also modify the y position of the vertex:

```
Pos.y += cos(y) * Offset;
```

This will effectively get each vertex to move in a circular motion.

To see the effects better, we can change our render states to turn off culling and set our scene to a wireframe. We could do this inside our XNA game, but we can also do it inside our shader. We can add the following code to the beginning of our pass to turn off culling and to render our objects in wireframe mode:

```
CullMode = None;
FillMode = Wireframe;
```

Postprocessing

Postprocessing is a great way to get excellent effects in our games to help them look polished. To set up our game to do postprocessing, we have to render our scene to a texture. We then draw that texture over the entire screen after running it through our pixel shader. As a result, our entire scene is generated as before, and then it appears as though we are running entire scene through a filter.

Setting Up Our Game Code

You can easily display a texture onscreen, as you learned in the 2D part of this book, but you do not yet know how to render a scene to a texture. We explore the code for doing that soon, but first we should look at the overall flow of the tasks we need to perform to handle postprocessing:

1. Declare our render target member field.
2. Initialize our render target inside the LoadContent method.

Inside of the Draw method, we do the following:

1. Tell our device to draw to our render target instead of the backbuffer.
2. Clear our device.
3. Draw our scene as normal (it will draw to our render target).

4. Reset the render target back to null (so we will draw on our backbuffer).

5. Clear the device.

6. Start the effect.

7. Start the sprite batch in immediate mode.

8. Start the effect pass.

9. Get the generated texture.

10. Draw the generated texture.

11. End the sprite batch.

12. End the effect pass.

13. End the effect.

Although this might seem like a lot of steps, it really is not that bad. We can look at steps we have not touched on previously in more detail. We can do postprocessing on our 2D or 3D scenes; it does not matter because we are ultimately processing a 2D texture anyway.

So that we can easily see our effects, we are going to copy our SimpleGame project from Chapter 11, "Creating a 2D Game." We are going to modify our game so that the game play will be run through a postprocessing filter. We will not be modifying our XELibrary, but we should copy it over so we do not need to modify our solution because it is using XELibrary as a project reference.

From the steps earlier, we know we need to declare our render target member field. We also know we will need an effect later on, so we might as well declare that now. We can declare those variables at the top of our game code:

```
private RenderTarget2D renderTarget;
private Effect effect;
```

We need to initialize our render target once we have a valid graphics device. We can also load up our effect file. Both of those tasks can be performed inside the LoadContent method, as follows:

```
renderTarget = new RenderTarget2D(GraphicsDevice,
    GraphicsDevice.Viewport.Width,
    GraphicsDevice.Viewport.Height, 1, GraphicsDevice.DisplayMode.Format,
    GraphicsDevice.PresentationParameters.MultiSampleType,
    GraphicsDevice.PresentationParameters.MultiSampleQuality);
effect = Content.Load<Effect>(@"Effects\NightTime");
```

The effect we added is called NightTime, so we can create an Effects folder in our Content project. We will create a new effect file in that folder and call it NightTime.fx later. We set up our render target by passing in our device as well as the width and height of our target (in this case, the whole screen, so we just use our viewport's width and height), along with the number of mip levels we want to create (one in our case). The format we will use is the current format of our device. We also pass in our device's multisample type and quality.

Next on our list is modifying the Draw method. We need to tell our device to draw to the render target we just created and initialized instead of rendering to the backbuffer like it does normally. To do this, we need to add the following statement at the top of the Draw code:

```
if (State != GameState.StartMenu)
    GraphicsDevice.SetRenderTarget(0, renderTarget);
GraphicsDevice.Clear(Color.Black);
```

We replaced the first line, graphics.GraphicsDevice.Clear(Color.Black);, with the preceding code to perform a couple tasks in one pass. We ensure we do our effect when we are not in the start menu screen. This is optional, of course. We let the device know that we are going to be rendering to our render target instead of the backbuffer by setting the render target on the device. Finally, we clear our device to black, which is actually the next step listed.

Now that we have our device rendering to our render target, we need to draw our scene. The remaining Draw code does not change because it is already drawing our scene. At this point, though, it is drawing the scene to our 2D render target and not our backbuffer, which will get put on the screen, so we need to do some things to get the scene to show up again. If we ran the code at this point and clicked Start, the screen would be a deep purple color. This is a debugging trick the XNA Framework team put into place to show that the render target had its contents discarded. Therefore, if you see purple, it means you discarded the render target but never drew anything on top of it.

TIP

Why purple? Tom Miller, who graciously wrote the foreword of my first book, had a blog post about why he chose that color. It can be found at http://blogs.msdn.com/tmiller/archive/2008/02/21/why-purple.aspx.

We need to get our scene rendering again, and to do that we need to complete the next step, which is resetting our render target to null. We can get the scene by calling renderTarget.GetTexture(). After we set our render target to null, we need to clear the device to make sure we do not have the default deep purple as our background. To do both of these things (discard our render target and clear our device), we add the following code at the end of the Draw method:

```
if (State != GameState.StartMenu)
```

```
{
    GraphicsDevice.SetRenderTarget(0, null);
    GraphicsDevice.Clear(Color.Black);
```

After clearing our device, we need to start our effect. We need to start our sprite batch in immediate mode so our effect can be applied as the texture is drawn. Then we need to begin our effect's pass. We can add that code now (still inside the State condition):

```
    effect.Begin();
    spriteBatch.Begin(SpriteBlendMode.None, SpriteSortMode.Immediate,
        SaveStateMode.None);
    EffectPass pass = effect.CurrentTechnique.Passes[0];
    pass.Begin();
```

Now we can actually draw our render target's texture on the screen. When we called SetRenderTarget earlier, it applied the surface it was drawing on into our 2D render target. We can get access to that texture by calling the GetTexture method. We do that as well as finish our effect's pass and close up our sprite batch and our effect in general:

```
    spriteBatch.Draw(renderTarget.GetTexture(), Vector2.Zero, Color.White);
    spriteBatch.End();
    pass.End();
    effect.End();
}
```

It did not take a lot of code to have our objects drawn onto a texture. We could use the same method to draw a rearview mirror in a racing game—there are plenty of uses for drawing a scene to a texture. In fact, we could use this technique for any mirror in a game. We could even apply the texture to a 3D object and render that on the screen. It is pretty cool to think of all the ways we could use this—and we have not even done our postprocessing effect yet. Let's do that now by creating our NightTime.fx file.

Setting Up Our Effect Code

Our NightTime effect file is actually pretty simple. It does not have a vertex shader because our sprite batch handles passing in a full-screen quad for us. All we need to do is create a pixel shader with our desired effect. As the name of the effect implies, we are going to create a nighttime effect. Really, we are just going to increase the blue color and decrease the red and green colors for each pixel. The entire code for this file is as follows:

```
sampler TextureSampler;


struct PixelInput
{
    float2 TexCoord : TEXCOORD0;
};
```

```
float4 pixelShader(PixelInput input) : COLOR
{
    float4 color = tex2D(TextureSampler, input.TexCoord);
    color.b = color.b + color.b * .25;
    color.rg *= .15;
    return( color );
}

technique Default
{
    pass P0
    {
        PixelShader = compile ps_2_0 pixelShader();
    }
}
```

This code is very simple. Replace the generated code in the effect file with preceding code. To start, we need a sampler so our sprite batch can pass in our texture. We use that texture inside our pixel shader function by using the intrinsic text2D function. You learned that we pass in the texture coordinate of the pixel we are wanting from our texture, and it will return the color of that pixel. We get the coordinates from our sprite batch as well, so it has saved us some work yet again.

The actual effect is only two lines of code:

```
color.b = color.b + color.b * .25;
color.rg *= .15;
```

We are adding 25% to the blue component of our pixel color, and we are decreasing our red and green values to 15% of what they originally were. This gives us a nice shade of blue that emulates nighttime. If you run the game, you'll see we are now running and kicking at night.

> **NOTE**
>
> The code on the CD for this chapter has all the different effect files we load commented out. Each effect file is a copy with only the pixel shader statements changing. As we go through more postprocessing examples, we will only discuss the code that is different for the pixel shader.

More Postprocessing Examples

Now that you see how easy it is to set up a postprocessing effect, we can take a little time and indulge ourselves by making some attractive effects for our games. Some of these will be practical to use, and others will just be fun to experiment with.

Negative Image

We can get the negative of an image by doing a simple inversion of our colors. This is very simple: We just subtract our color from 1. That's it. We just need to replace the code inside our pixel shader function with this code:

```
float4 color = 1.0f - tex2D(TextureSampler, input.TexCoord);
return( color );
```

We cast 1 as a `float4`. This effectively puts a 1 in the RGBA components. Thus, we are subtracting 1 from red, 1 from green, 1 from blue, and 1 from alpha, which does not affect our end result because our sprite batch is being rendered with a blend mode of `None`. If we were using alpha blending, we would want to set our alpha to a fully opaque value:

```
color.a = 1.0f;
```

Switching RGB Values

Another simple effect we can make is to switch out the red, green, and blue values. With the following effect, the hero's red shirt will become green:

```
float4 color = tex2D( TextureSampler, input.TexCoord);
return( color.brga );
```

Without using our swizzle, we would have had to create a temporary value to store one of the colors and then swap the rest around. With swizzling, we can just modify the order in which we are returning our components. Simply returning `color` is the same as returning `color.rgba`. Therefore, by returning `color.brga` we are passing blue as the first component, red as the second, and so on.

You can see that when our hero dies, the screen turns green now instead of red. The sky is red instead of blue, and the grass is red instead of green. This is not necessarily useful in a real game, but it could be—perhaps the goal of a level is to correctly fix the colors by solving some puzzles.

Sharpening the Image

We can sharpen our image, much like the paint programs do, by subtracting the color values of pixels surrounding our pixel and by adding other surrounding pixels' colors in. Before we look at the code, it is important to understand that we can do arithmetic on the x and y values of our texture coordinates in the same call. This means that `input.TexCoord + 1` is the same as `input.TexCoord.x + 1`, `input.TexCoord.y + 1`. Also we are not required to sample in pixel increments. In other words, we can use floats if appropriate to sample a part of a pixel. You can see how we do this in the following code to sharpen our image:

```
float sharpAmount = 15.0f;
float4 color = tex2D( TextureSampler, input.TexCoord);
```

```
color += tex2D( TextureSampler, input.TexCoord - 0.0001) * sharpAmount;
color -= tex2D( TextureSampler, input.TexCoord + 0.0001) * sharpAmount;
return( color );
```

We sample a small offset and increase the intensity of the color by multiplying it by 15. This is our sharpening amount. We can adjust this value to get different effects.

Blurring an Image

Next on the list of effects is blurring. We actually did this already in our sharpen effect. We just need to leave off our sharp amount and use an average of several samples around the pixel. The code for this is as follows:

```
float4 color = tex2D( TextureSampler,
    float2(input.TexCoord.x+0.0025, input.TexCoord.y+0.0025));
color += tex2D( TextureSampler,
    float2(input.TexCoord.x-0.0025, input.TexCoord.y-0.0025));
color += tex2D( TextureSampler,
    float2(input.TexCoord.x+0.0025, input.TexCoord.y-0.0025));
color += tex2D( TextureSampler,
    float2(input.TexCoord.x-0.0025, input.TexCoord.y+0.0025));
color = color / 4;
return( color );
```

Most of the time this is implemented by sampling only four surrounding colors. We can play with our numbers to get the desired effect we are looking for. In this case, as we are adding each color, we just need to make sure we take the average at the end. Otherwise, we would have a very bright image because the color values would be so high.

Embossing

We can create an embossed effect by slightly modifying our sharpen image code. Instead of initializing our color by sampling the pixel we are on, we just set the red, green, and blue values to .5 (gray). We also set the alpha channel to 1.0 for fully opaque. Then we basically do the same thing we did for our sharpening effect by sampling an offset and sharpening it by a particular weight amount, then subtracting the same weight amount from another sample. Finally, we take an average of our red, green, and blue components to keep a flat gray look. The end result is the embossed raised effect we were looking for. The code to create this effect is shown here:

```
float sharpAmount = 15.0f;
float4 color;
color.rgb = 0.5f;
color.a = 1.0f;
color -= tex2D( TextureSampler, input.TexCoord - 0.0001) * sharpAmount;
color += tex2D( TextureSampler, input.TexCoord + 0.0001) * sharpAmount;
color = (color.r+color.g+color.b) / 3.0f;
return( color );
```

Grayscale

After doing the embossing effect, it does not seem a stretch to do a grayscale effect. We can do that with the following code:

```
float4 color = tex2D( TextureSampler, input.TexCoord);
color.rgb = dot(color.rgb, float3(0.3, 0.59, 0.11));
return( color );
```

You might think we could just use the last line from the embossed effect by averaging our red, green, and blue values. Unfortunately, the human eye is more sensitive to green brightness than it is to blue, so a standard computation is used to convert colors to grayscale. It weights the colors differently. After processing the colors with the appropriate weights, our scene is in black and white.

What if we wanted one side to be gray and the other side to be color? We could use the following code:

```
float4 color = tex2D( TextureSampler, input.TexCoord);
if (input.TexCoord.x > 0.5)
    color.rgb = dot(color.rgb, float3(0.3, 0.59, 0.11));
return( color );
```

Thus, if our x texture coordinate is the middle of the screen or further out, we average out the colors. Otherwise, we leave the initial color of our texture on the left side of the screen.

What if we wanted to have a gradient effect? Let's say we want the left and right of our screen to be gray and the middle of our screen to be fully saturated. To do that, we would just need to use the following code:

```
float4 color = tex2D( TextureSampler, input.TexCoord);
float4 gs = dot(color.rgb, float3(0.3, 0.59, 0.11));
if (input.TexCoord.x > 0.5f)
    color = lerp(gs, color, (1 - input.TexCoord.x) * 2);
else
    color = lerp(gs, color, input.TexCoord.x * 2);

return( color );
```

The first two lines were discussed earlier. We get the color of the pixel based on the texture coordinates. We then calculate the grayscale value for that same pixel. We have the same if statement checking to see whether we are drawing pixels on the left side of the screen or the right side. If we are drawing on the left side of the screen, we "lerp" (check back to the last chapter for a definition of what this intrinsic function does) between our color value and our grayscale value. We double the x component of our texture coordinate because we want full color in the middle of the screen. We do the exact same thing on the right side of the screen, except we subtract our texture coordinate from 1 and multiply the result by 2.

Chalk

We are going to modify our sharpen effect again to produce something that looks like a chalk effect. Our sharpening amount will be 100, and our sampling offset will only be 1/1000 instead of 1/10000. The code for this is as follows:

```
float sharpAmount = 100.0f;
float4 color = tex2D( TextureSampler, input.TexCoord);
color += tex2D( TextureSampler, input.TexCoord - 0.001) * sharpAmount;
color -= tex2D( TextureSampler, input.TexCoord + 0.001) * sharpAmount;
return( color );
```

This looks like an artist is actively drawing the scene on a chalkboard with very colorful chalk.

Wavy

We can also modify the position we read from to set our color instead of modifying the color itself. A great way to show this off is to create an effect that makes it appear that our scene is underwater or that we are looking at it through the side of a fish tank. Subtle x and y movements occur that make the scene wavy. See the following code:

```
float y = input.TexCoord.y;
float x = input.TexCoord.x;
y = y + (sin(x*100)*0.001);
float4 color = tex2D(TextureSampler, float2(x,y));
return( color );
```

We get the x and y values passed to us from the application. We then modify our y value by adding in the sine of our x value multiplied by 100. We then divide this by 1,000 (* 0.001). This creates a small wavy effect. For some interesting results, modify the 100 and .001 numbers.

TIP

To make the hero look like he is running up a hill, change 100 to 1 and change .001 to 0.1.

Summary

In this chapter, you learned how to use vertex shaders to displace vertices to create some interesting effects, as well as how to use pixel shaders to do postprocessing. With very little code, we were able to modify our example to make our asteroid look like it was morphing. Shaders are very powerful.

We spent the majority of the chapter covering postprocessing effects and how they can be used on 2D and 3D scenes alike. We went through many examples of some of the more common effects. This should give you a good starting point to branch out and try even more complex things with shaders.

PART VII

Physics and Artificial Intelligence

Physics Basics

This chapter provides an overview of some important physics principles we can model in our games. We do not go through an exhaustive list by any means. Physics in general requires an understanding of calculus, but there will not be any explanation of the math involved to create the physics in our games. It is very important to understand matrix and vector math to write any code that simulates real-world physics in 2D and 3D games.

Kinematics

To start our discussion of physics, we will talk about motion dynamics, particularly *kinematics*—the study of moving objects. It does not take into consideration any forces applied to those objects (that made them move).

To understand the movement of objects, we need to first understand our objects themselves. For starters, objects have a position, velocity, and acceleration. Just like the position of an object, the velocity and acceleration are represented by vectors. We know that vectors have a magnitude (length) and a direction. The magnitude of the velocity vector contains our speed value.

Many physics formulas are based on time. Fortunately, we have access to our game time in our `Update` method, where we will be doing (or calling) all our physics calculations. We have already used velocity in our demos up to this point. We moved our enemies in Chapter 11, "Creating a 2D Game," a few pixels every second. Regardless of the frame rate at which our game was running, we always moved them the same distance every second by taking into account how long it took between our update calls by getting the change in time (delta) between each instance our method was executed.

Velocity

We have also already handled velocity—that is, how fast our object is moving. We used velocity by having our enemies move at the same pace. Their velocity is constant. If we wanted to vary it, we could add acceleration. Whereas velocity is the rate of change of the distance traveled, acceleration is the rate of change of our velocity. Both are measured by the change in time. In other words, at timestamp A (0 seconds), we are at position 0 meters, and at timestamp B (5 seconds) we are at position 25 meters. Our velocity is the rate of change between those two points for the amount of time between our two time-stamps; in this case it would be 25 meters per 5 seconds (25 m / 5 s) or 5 meters per second (5 m/s). The formula for our velocity can be seen here:

$v = \Delta s\ /\ \Delta t$

Δs (delta s) is our change in position between two points—in other words, our displacement. Δt is our change in time. Using those values we can compute our velocity. Of course, this also means we can determine how long it will take us to get somewhere if we know our velocity and our starting and ending points. For example, if we are going 5 m/s, our starting position is 0 m, and our ending position is 10 m, we know we will be at our destination in 2 seconds.

Acceleration

Acceleration, on the other hand, is the rate of change of our velocity for our change in time. So, if we are going 0 m/s at timestamp A (0 seconds) and 21 m/s at timestamp B (3 seconds), and 25 m/s at timestamp C (5 seconds), we can calculate our acceleration for those last two timestamps. Our formula for acceleration is as follows:

$a = \Delta v\ /\ \Delta t$

We can plug in our numbers:

$a\ =\ 21m/s\ \ /\ \ \ 3s\ \ =\ \ 21m\ /\ s\ *\ 1/3s\ \ =\ \ 21m/3s*s\ =\ 7m/s\ *\ s\ =\ 7m/s^2$
$a\ =\ 4m/s\ \ /\ \ 2s\ =\ 4m/s\ *\ 1/2s\ =\ 4m/2s*s\ =\ 2m/s\ *\ s\ =\ 2m/s^2$

Our first measurement shows our average acceleration is 7 m/s², and our second measure shows our average acceleration is 2 m/s².

We typically want to add acceleration to our objects. We will use the acceleration value to update the objects' velocity. This is as simple as adding our two values together to get a new velocity. Now if we are adding in acceleration, we are just changing the velocity each frame.

If our object is traveling at 50 miles per hour (mph), we know it is traveling at 80.45 kilometers per hour (km/h) because there are 1.609 kilometers in 1 mile. If our acceleration is 16.6 m/s², then every second we need to add that value, but we need to make sure we are using the same units of measure. Therefore, we need to convert the km/h values to m/s. We know there are 1,000 meters in a kilometer, so we first multiply that value, and the product is 80,450 m/h. However, we need to be in seconds. We know there are 60 seconds in a minute and 60 minutes in an hour, so 1 hour becomes 3,600 seconds. We are now in the right unit of measure, and our velocity is 80,450 m/3,600 s (or 22.35 m/s). If we are at position (50,0,0) and our velocity is only on the x dimension, when the next second rolls around we should be at position 72.35, and the next second at 94.70. This represents our change in velocity and does not include any acceleration because we are moving at a constant rate.

If we start to accelerate, we only need to add in that value. Using C#, the code would look something like this:

```
model.Velocity.X += model.Acceleration.X;
```

The code assumes we have an object called `model` that has two vectors, `Velocity` and `Acceleration`. We simply continue to increase our velocity by the amount we are accelerating. We also continue to update our position by our velocity, as the following statement shows:

```
model.Position.X += model.Velocity.X;
```

Thus, we are not only updating our object's position by the velocity amount, we are also modifying the velocity based on the acceleration value our object contains.

We are going to write a small acceleration demo to help you understand how these concepts look in code. Let's create a new solution and call it AccelerationDemo. We are going to load up a skybox, so we need to make sure our skybox pipeline assembly is close by so we can tell the IDE to use it. On the CD that accompanies this book, the skybox pipeline assembly can be found in the root of this chapter's folder. We need to add a reference to the skybox pipeline assembly to our Content project. We also need to add a reference to our XELibrary in our main project. We will not be adding any code to the library, so we can just reference the assembly. We also need to grab the skybox2.tga file from the CD and add it to a newly created Skyboxes folder of our Content project. We need to make sure we associate our Content Processor for the skybox image with our custom `SkyboxProcessor`. We will also need to grab the `sphere0.x` object and add that to our Models folder.

Next, we need to add the following private member fields to the top of our demo code:

```
private PhysicalObject sphere = new PhysicalObject();
private InputHandler input;
private FirstPersonCamera camera;
private Model model;
private Skybox skybox;
private float maxSpeed = 163.0f;
private float maxReverseSpeed = 25.0f;
private float constantAcceleration = .5f;
private float constantDeceleration = .85f;
```

We also need to make sure we have our using XELibrary; statement included.
PhysicalObject is a class we are going to create. We can keep this in the same file because
it is going to be a small class. Let's add the following class to our Game1.cs file:

```
class PhysicalObject
{
    public Vector3 Position;
    public Vector3 Velocity;
    public Vector3 Acceleration;
}
```

We are going to store our object's position, velocity, and acceleration. We need to set up
the game components we declared earlier. As usual, we do this in our constructor:

```
input = new InputHandler(this);
Components.Add(input);
camera = new FirstPersonCamera(this);
Components.Add(camera);
```

We need to add this method, and we need to call it from our Initialize method:

```
private void InitializeValues()
{
    sphere.Position = new Vector3(-15.0f, 0, -500);
    sphere.Velocity = Vector3.Zero;
    sphere.Acceleration = Vector3.Zero;
}
```

Now we need to load our model and skybox content in our LoadContent method:

```
model = Content.Load<Model>(@"Models\sphere0");
skybox = Content.Load<Skybox>(@"Skyboxes\skybox2");
```

Next, we need to draw our skybox and our sphere in the Draw method:

```
skybox.Draw(camera.View, camera.Projection, Matrix.CreateScale(2000.0f));
Matrix world = Matrix.CreateScale(10.0f) *
               Matrix.CreateTranslation(sphere.Position);
DrawModel(ref model, ref world);
```

We scaled our skybox by 2,000 units and our sphere by 10 units. Our skybox is a light-
colored cement texture, and our sphere has no color or texture. We now need to create a
DrawModel method, which is not new. However, so we can more easily see the ball, we will
change our ambient color on the basic effect to red so it will shade our ball a red color.

```
private void DrawModel(ref Model m, ref Matrix world)
{
    Matrix[] transforms = new Matrix[m.Bones.Count];
```

```
        m.CopyAbsoluteBoneTransformsTo(transforms);

        foreach (ModelMesh mesh in m.Meshes)
        {
            foreach (BasicEffect be in mesh.Effects)
            {
                be.EnableDefaultLighting();
                be.AmbientLightColor = Color.Red.ToVector3();

                be.Projection = camera.Projection;
                be.View = camera.View;
                be.World = world * mesh.ParentBone.Transform;
            }
            mesh.Draw();
        }
    }
```

Next is the update code that allows us to speed up and slow down our sphere. We need to add the following code to our Update method:

```
if (input.KeyboardState.WasKeyPressed(Keys.Enter))
    InitializeValues();

float elapsed = (float)gameTime.ElapsedGameTime.TotalSeconds;

//increase acceleration
if (input.KeyboardState.IsHoldingKey(Keys.Space))
{
    sphere.Acceleration.X += (constantAcceleration * elapsed);
}
//decrease acceleration (brake)
else if (input.KeyboardState.IsHoldingKey(Keys.B))
{
    sphere.Acceleration.X -= (constantDeceleration * elapsed);
}
else //coast
{
    sphere.Acceleration.X = 0;
}

sphere.Velocity.X += sphere.Acceleration.X;

if (sphere.Velocity.X > maxSpeed)
    sphere.Velocity.X = maxSpeed;
```

```
if (sphere.Velocity.X < -maxReverseSpeed)
    sphere.Velocity.X = -maxReverseSpeed;

sphere.Position = sphere.Position + (elapsed * sphere.Velocity);

Window.Title = "Acceleration: " + sphere.Acceleration.X.ToString() +
    " Position: " + sphere.Position.X.ToString() + " Velocity: " +
    sphere.Velocity.X.ToString();
```

We can press the Enter key to reinitialize our variables just in case our sphere goes far away and we lose it. Next, we check to see if the spacebar is being held down. If it is, we increase our acceleration. If the B key is being pressed, we apply the brakes to slow down the sphere—and actually let it go into reverse. If we are neither accelerating nor braking, we are coasting, so we set our acceleration value to zero.

We then add our acceleration value to our velocity value and make sure we have not increased our speed over the maximum speed we have set up. We also check to make sure we are not reversing the sphere any faster than we allowed.

Finally, we set our new position by adding the new velocity to our current position. We display the current values of our position, velocity, and acceleration in the window title so we can easily see the values.

We can run this demo and see that our sphere is sitting still. To make it move, we only need to press the spacebar or the B key. If we lose sight of our sphere, we can press the Enter key to reset the values. This demo shows how we can set acceleration based on input and modify velocity based on the acceleration we set.

Force

Force changes the acceleration of an object. For example, when you hit a baseball, the acceleration of the ball is changed because you applied force (in the form of swinging a bat) to the ball. If the ball was pitched to you, it had a positive acceleration coming toward you; when you hit it, you changed the acceleration to the negative direction.

Force is a very important concept in physics. This is understandable because it is constantly in effect. For example, even when you are sitting down there is the force of gravity keeping you in the chair. The first example with the baseball is considered *contact force*, as an object (the bat) made contact with the ball, thus changing its acceleration. Gravity is considered a *field force* (or a force-at-a-distance) because it does not have to have contact with the object to apply its force. Gravity causes items to be drawn to the Earth's core. This is why we can sit (and stand) and not float about. This is why we have weight. It is all because of gravity. An object on the floor sits there because of gravity. If you try to pick it up, you have to apply enough force to counteract the force that gravity is applying to it. In outer space, objects float around and are very light. Regardless of their mass (assuming they are not as large as a planet) they do not weigh much at all because there is no force pushing them down.

Mass is the amount of physical matter an object comprises. With the force of gravity, our mass has weight. The more mass an object has, the more it weighs on Earth. The larger the mass, the more force is applied against that object to bring it toward the Earth's core. When we try to move an object, we have to apply enough force to accelerate the object. If we do not apply as much force to lift the object upward as gravity is pulling it downward, the object will not move.

Newton's Second Law of Motion describes the relationship between an object's mass and acceleration with force applied to the object:

```
F = ma
```

We know that acceleration is a vector and that force is a vector as well. This makes sense: When you hit that baseball, it can go in multiple directions (pop fly, foul ball, and so on). This is because we are creating acceleration when we apply force to the object at different angles. Mass is a scalar value (one dimension) and not a vector (multiple dimensions). We could also write the preceding formula as follows:

```
a = F/m
```

In our previous code example, we had an invisible force acting on our sphere that was generating the acceleration of the sphere. Newton's First Law of Motion basically states that objects that are in motion stay in motion, and objects that are sitting still stay still. Our previous demo shows this as well—if we do not press any keys to accelerate our sphere, it stays at rest. Once we do apply some force to the object, it accelerates and stays in motion.

Collisions

This section is pretty detailed and is best read with a physics textbook handy to get the full effect. This is not required, though, and the actual code is easier to understand than the math involved. Regardless, it is very beneficial to understand the reason why the code works so we can do further research to determine the best way to model other important physics needed in our games.

Momentum

When an object stays in motion, it is because of momentum. Objects in motion have momentum. Momentum is used to measure an object's mass and velocity. The formula to calculate momentum is

```
p = mv
```

where, p is our object's momentum, m is our object's mass, and v is the velocity. We know about mass because of our force formula. We can substitute the formula for acceleration in our formula for force:

```
F = ma = m Δv / Δt
```

Now we can multiply the change in time on both sides, which produces the following:

F∆t = m ∆v

Impulse

Fδt is called an *impulse*. We can do some vector math and multiply the mass by the change in velocity (the right side of our equation) and see that it can be represented as follows:

F∆t = ∆(mv)

Therefore, we know that an impulse is equal to the change in momentum, which can be written as follows:

F∆t = ∆p

Conservation of Momentum

When objects collide, their momentum changes. To be more precise, the magnitude of the momentum remains the same, just in the opposite direction. This is how we can model our collision response. We can reflect our objects off each other, knowing that whatever their momentum was before they collided will remain, but their direction will be reversed. We just threw two objects into the mix but thus far have only been discussing momentum on a single object. How does this change our momentum formula? Fortunately, it does not. This is called the law of conservation of momentum, and it means the total momentum for the objects is constant and does not change. This is true because any momentum changes are equal in magnitude and opposite in direction. This is expressed with the following formula:

$p_1 + p_2 = p_1 + p_2$

Kinetic Energy

Now we can discuss Newton's Third Law of Motion, which basically says that for every action there is an equal and opposite reaction. Whatever momentum one object decreases, the other object increases. As momentum is transferred from one object to another, yet another physical property takes place—kinetic energy. *Kinetic energy* is energy associated with moving objects. It is the amount of energy needed to make an object that is sitting still move. It is also the amount of energy needed to make a moving object stop and sit still. The formula for kinetic energy is

$E_k = 1/2 \; m \; v_2$

When a collision occurs and the amount of kinetic energy is unchanged, this is considered to be an *elastic collision*. When kinetic energy is lost, it is considered to be an *inelastic collision.* Objects that collide in the real world will deform and cause a loss of kinetic energy. If the objects do not deform, no energy is lost.

Coefficient of Restitution

The coefficient of restitution is the measurement of how elastic or inelastic a collision is based on the types of object that are colliding. The formula for coefficient of restitution is

$e = (v_{2f} - v_{1f}) / (v_1 - v_2)$

The coefficient of restitution models the velocity before and after a collision takes place and the loss of kinetic energy happens. The typical value for e is between 0.0 and 1.0, inclusive. A value of 0.0 means the collision is inelastic, and 1.0 means the collision is elastic. The values in between will have a proportionate elastic collision effect. The subscripts in the preceding formula specify which vectors we are using: 1 and 2 are the two objects, and f is the final velocity of the vector after the impact of the collision.

Conservation of Kinetic Energy

We need to discuss the conservation of kinetic energy, which says that the sum of the kinetic energy of two objects before they collide will be equal to the sum of the kinetic energy of the two objects after they collide. The formula for the conservation of kinetic energy is

$E_{k1} + E_{k2} = E_{k1} + E_{k2}$

Broken down into its components, the formula becomes the following:

$1/2 \ m_1 \ v_1^2 + 1/2 \ m_2 \ v_2^2 = 1/2 \ m_1 \ v_{1f}^2 + 1/2 \ m_2 \ v_{2f}^2$

Solving Our Final Velocities

When we are modeling collisions, we need to determine our final velocities (which is what the *f* in the earlier formula represents). Before we can do that, we need to expand our conservation of momentum formula from earlier. We will break down the momentum, p, into its components, as follows:

$(m_1 \ v_1) + (m_2 \ v_2) = (m_1 \ v_{1f}) + (m_2 \ v_{2f})$

Now, we can solve for our final velocity by combining both of our earlier conservation formulas with our coefficient of restitution formula. Our final velocities will equate to the following:

$v_{1f} = (\ (e + 1) \ m_2 \ v_2 + v_1(m_1 - e \ m_2) \ ) / (m_1 + m_2)$
$v_{2f} = (\ (e + 1) \ m_1 \ v_1 - v_2(m_1 - e \ m_2) \ ) / (m_1 + m_2)$

This uses the conservation of kinetic energy formula with our conservation of momentum formula, along with our coefficient of restitution, which allows us to solve the final velocity for each object. That is all we need to start modeling realistic collisions.

16

Creating a Collision Response Demo

We have gone through a lot of formulas, but what does any of this look like in code? Let's take a look. We are going to create a new demo called CollisionDemo. We need to reference our XELibrary component and include our Using statement as well.

To start, we need to declare the following private member fields:

```
private Model sphere;
```

```
private PhysicalObject[] spheres = new PhysicalObject[5];
private float e; //coefficient of restitution
```

```
private InputHandler input;
private FirstPersonCamera camera;
private FPS fps;
```

We also need to set up our game components in our constructor, as usual:

```
input = new InputHandler(this);
Components.Add(input);
camera = new FirstPersonCamera(this);
Components.Add(camera);
fps = new FPS(this, false, true);
Components.Add(fps);
```

Our PhysicalObject class is pretty small, so we can just add this class to our same Game1.cs code:

```
class PhysicalObject
{
    public Vector3 Position;
    public Vector3 Velocity;
    public float Mass;
    public float Radius;
    public Matrix World;
    public Color Color;
}
```

Our physical object has a position, velocity, mass, and a radius. We need these properties to model the object in a real-world manner. The World matrix is the object's world matrix, so we can draw it inside our 3D world. The Color is the color our object will be when it is drawn in the scene.

Now, we need to initialize the array of physical objects that will be colliding. We currently have set this to 3, but we can have as many objects as we want. We need to add the following loop inside of our Initialize method:

```
for (int i = 0; i < spheres.Length; i++)
    spheres[i] = new PhysicalObject();
```

Now we need to add the sphere0.x file from our last demo to this solution. We also need to load that model, which we can do in our LoadContent method:

```
sphere = Content.Load<Model>(@"Models\sphere0");
```

We need to initialize the values of our objects. We can call the following method inside our Initialize method:

```
InitializeValues();
```

Our InitializeValues method is shown here:

```
private void InitializeValues()
{
    e = 0.95f;

    spheres[0].Position = new Vector3(-90.0f, 0, -300.0f);
    spheres[0].Velocity = new Vector3(60.0f, 0, 0);
    spheres[0].Mass = 1.0f;
    spheres[0].Color = Color.Silver;

    for (int i = 1; i < spheres.Length; i++)
    {
        spheres[i].Position = new Vector3(25.0f + (i * 25), 0, -300);
        spheres[i].Velocity = new Vector3(-5.0f, 0, 0);
        spheres[i].Mass = 4.0f;
        spheres[i].Color = Color.Red;
    }

    spheres[spheres.Length - 1].Velocity = Vector3.Zero;
    spheres[spheres.Length - 1].Mass = 6.0f;
    spheres[spheres.Length - 1].Color = Color.Black;
}
```

The variable holds our coefficient of restitution. A value of .85 means that the collision will be mainly elastic. Remember, 1.0 is totally elastic, and 0.0 is totally inelastic (objects would not bounce off each other; instead they would stick together).

The next three sections of code are all doing the same thing: setting the physical properties of our objects. We are setting the position, velocity, and mass. We also set the color just so it looks a little better on the screen. Inside the for loop, we space our objects 25 units apart. The last section just resets the last object our for loop set so we can easily change the last object in the chain. We can definitely modify this code to plot our objects all over the world, wherever we want. To be concise, we currently have them in a row along the x axis.

Our Draw method will also have a for loop to draw the objects in the right position. You can see this here:

```
for(int i=0; i<spheres.Length; i++)
    DrawModel(ref sphere, ref spheres[i].World, spheres[i].Color);
```

This is similar to our previous Draw methods, except we are storing our world matrix inside our sphere object so we do not have to do the translations here. We are also passing the color of this object to our DrawModel method. The code for our DrawModel method is as follows:

```
private void DrawModel(ref Model m, ref Matrix world, Color color)
{
    Matrix[] transforms = new Matrix[m.Bones.Count];
    m.CopyAbsoluteBoneTransformsTo(transforms);

    foreach (ModelMesh mesh in m.Meshes)
    {
        foreach (BasicEffect be in mesh.Effects)
        {
            be.EnableDefaultLighting();

            be.AmbientLightColor = color.ToVector3();
            be.Projection = camera.Projection;
            be.View = camera.View;
            be.World = world * mesh.ParentBone.Transform;
        }

        mesh.Draw();
    }
}
```

The only thing that really changed from the way we have used this method in the past is that we actually passed in a color.

Now we can get to the core of our code: the Update method where we model the physics we have been talking about in this section. Here is the Update method:

```
protected override void Update(GameTime gameTime)
{
    float elapsedTime = (float)gameTime.ElapsedGameTime.TotalSeconds;

    if (input.KeyboardState.WasKeyPressed(Keys.Enter))
        InitializeValues();
```

```
for (int i = 0; i < spheres.Length; i++)
{
    spheres[i].World = Matrix.CreateScale(spheres[i].Mass) *
        Matrix.CreateTranslation(spheres[i].Position);

    Vector3 trans, scale;
    Matrix rot;
    MatrixDecompose(spheres[i].World, out trans, out scale, out rot);
    spheres[i].Radius = scale.Length();
}

for (int a = 0; a < spheres.Length; a++)
{
    for (int b = a + 1; b < spheres.Length; b++)
    {
        if (a == b)
            continue; //don't check against yourself

        float distance = (spheres[a].Position -
                        spheres[b].Position).Length();
        float tmp = 1.0f / (spheres[a].Mass + spheres[b].Mass);

        float collisionDistance = distance - (spheres[a].Radius +
                                        spheres[b].Radius);
        if (collisionDistance <= 0)
        {
            Vector3 velocity1 = (
                (e + 1.0f) * spheres[b].Mass * spheres[b].Velocity +
                spheres[a].Velocity * (spheres[a].Mass - (e * spheres[b].Mass))
                ) * tmp;

            Vector3 velocity2 = (
                (e + 1.0f) * spheres[a].Mass * spheres[a].Velocity +
                spheres[b].Velocity * (spheres[b].Mass - (e * spheres[a].Mass))
                ) * tmp;

            spheres[a].Velocity = velocity1;
            spheres[b].Velocity = velocity2;
        }
    }
    spheres[a].Position = spheres[a].Position +
        (elapsedTime * (spheres[a].Velocity));
}
base.Update(gameTime);
}
```

16

As soon as we start the program, our simulation will run. To reset the scene to all the initial values, we just have to press the Enter key. The first `for` loop in our method updates our object's world matrix information. We are scaling our object by the amount of mass we have associated with it. This is not needed, but it adds a nice visual effect when we run the demo. We also make sure our position is set. We update our position later in this method. Although still inside the first `for` loop, we also set our object's radius for collision detection. We are really just using the same algorithm we used in our 2D game.

Then we loop through all our objects, checking each object to every other object each frame. Again, for a small number of objects, this method is perfectly acceptable. As we discussed while working on collision detection in our 2D game, there are other ways to manage our objects that can help optimize how we search for them to test against collisions. We make sure we are not checking for a collision against our object by just continuing to the next index in our `for` loop.

For every iteration through our `for` loop, we calculate the distance between the two objects we are checking by calculating the length of the vector between them. This is identical to the code in our 2D game. Our `tmp` variable is actually part of our velocity formula.

Next, we calculate collision distance between these two objects. We sum up the radii and take the difference of the distance between our two objects. This is shown in Figure 16.1. If our collision distance reaches zero, we have a collision and we do all the real work of everything we have been discussing this section.

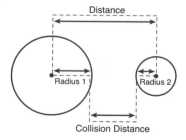

FIGURE 16.1   Calculating the collision distance.

The formulas we are using to determine the final velocity of our objects after they collide are listed again here for the sake of convenience:

$$v_{1f} = (\ (e + 1)\ m_2\ v_2 + v_1(m_1 - e\ m_2)\ )\ /\ (m_1 + m_2)$$
$$v_{2f} = (\ (e + 1)\ m_1\ v_1 - v_2(m_1 - e\ m_2)\ )\ /\ (m_1 + m_2\ )$$

And here's our code that represents these formulas:

```
float tmp = 1.0f / (spheres[a].Mass + spheres[b].Mass);


Vector3 velocity1 = (
    (e + 1.0f) * spheres[b].Mass * spheres[b].Velocity +
    spheres[a].Velocity * (spheres[a].Mass - (e * spheres[b].Mass))
    ) * tmp;

Vector3 velocity2 = (
    (e + 1.0f) * spheres[a].Mass * spheres[a].Velocity +
    spheres[b].Velocity * (spheres[b].Mass - (e * spheres[a].Mass))
    ) * tmp;
```

You can see this is a direct port. The only difference is that we are calculating the sum of our mass up front and storing the inverse in a tmp variable so we only need to do the division once and then multiply the value for our actual formulas inside our collision condition in our nested for loop. In the last statement inside this collision condition, we set the velocity of our objects to the new velocity just calculated. Finally, at the end of our outer loop, which iterates through each of the objects, we update the object's position based on its current velocity.

If we run our demo now, we can get a nice collision simulation. There is only one problem: The objects never stop moving! This is because while we labored so hard on the formulas to model the collision itself, we did not take friction into account. Friction, of course, is the force that is ever present on objects that resist their movement. As we slide an object on the ground, friction is generated that basically pushes back against it. A ball, for example, will roll for a while but will eventually stop because of the frictional force on it. Instead of going into the formulas to determine friction, we just jump straight to the code because it is very easy to plug in to our current demo.

Basically, we just need to subtract our friction amount from our positive velocity vector (or add to our negative vector) to create the new velocity. Of course, we do not want to actually reverse our velocity, so once we reach zero we stop applying the friction force (there will be none because the object is not moving). This is easy enough to do, so let's get to the code.

First, we need to create another private member field called friction:

```
private Vector3 friction;
```

Next, we need to initialize the value at the top of our InitializeValues method:

```
friction = new Vector3(-0.025f);
```

We can set our `friction` value to whatever is appropriate for our environment. We have set up `friction` as a vector to allow us to have friction in multiple dimensions. Now we need to apply the force on our velocity inside the `Update` method. Put the following code at the bottom of the first `for` loop in the `Update` method:

```
ApplyFriction(ref spheres[i].Velocity);
```

The code for that function is as follows:

```
private void ApplyFriction(ref Vector3 velocity)
{
    if (velocity.X < 0)
        velocity.X -= friction.X;
    if (velocity.X > 0)
        velocity.X += friction.X;

    if (velocity.Y < 0)
        velocity.Y -= friction.Y;
    if (velocity.Y > 0)
        velocity.Y += friction.Y;

    if (velocity.Z < 0)
        velocity.Z -= friction.Z;
    if (velocity.Z > 0)
        velocity.Z += friction.Z;
}
```

We are simply updating the velocity vector passed in to us by subtracting or adding our friction amount for that component (x, y, or z) of the vector. We do not update our velocity if we are at zero for that axis. When we initialize our friction vector, we set all components to be 0.025. However, we could definitely set different values for each component, depending on what we are trying to model. We are also using 3D here because this is a 3D demo, but if we wanted to do it in 2D, we could either just ignore the z component or rewrite the demo to use `Vector2`—we would also want to change our `friction` variable to a `Vector2` as well.

TIP

Applying friction can also be done by multiplying a constant slightly less than 1. Neither approach is fully accurate compared to a real physical model, but both will give realistic results in practice. Applying friction through multiplication involves less code because there is no need to worry about the sign of the velocity and no special handling for zero.

If we run our code, we will see our game is slowing down the objects and they stop after a while due to friction. The scene appears realistic.

A good exercise would be to plot some specific locations for some of these objects. We are only moving in one direction (along the x axis) in this demo, but the code allows for movement in any direction. It only takes us plotting our values correctly and setting our velocities so they will reach the other objects.

To get started, we could just modify our first sphere to have these values for a look at how our objects handle collisions when the velocity has a value in all three components:

```
spheres[0].Position = new Vector3(-25.0f, 5.0f, -430);
spheres[0].Velocity = new Vector3(70.0f, -8.0f, 70);
spheres[0].Mass = 6.0f;
spheres[0].Color = Color.Silver;
```

That ends a rather long section on collision response. This should get you well on your way to creating realistic collisions in your games.

Summary

This was a very technical chapter with lots of formulas and equations. Fortunately, we were able to model some nice real-world physics. We discussed acceleration and velocity in detail, as well as an object's position and how all three of these vectors have a relationship to each other. We discussed force and mass and several of Newton's laws.

We spent a good deal of time on our collision response theory and worked toward a very practical way to apply it in our code. We can now simulate multiple objects colliding in 3D space. We also simulated friction in our code so that our objects look realistic as they move through our scene. There are many more topics in physics related to game programming that we did not cover, but this chapter provided a good start.

16

CHAPTER 17

Finite State Machines and Game State Management

The next two chapters discuss artificial intelligence (AI). However, this chapter discusses our game engine structure as well. Using finite state machines (FSMs) is critical for believable objects. We discuss FSMs and how we can set up our game itself as an FSM as we structure our game.

Finite State Machine

A finite state machine (FSM) is a machine with a finite set of states. Maybe we should first talk about states. We discussed states some in Chapter 11, "Creating a 2D Game," where we created the SimpleGame. We had StartMenu, Scene, Won, and Lost as states the game could be in. The finite part simply means that there are a limited number of states. The machine, for our purposes, just means that the code is run in software. Therefore, an FSM is piece of software that has a finite number of states in and out of which it can be transitioned.

We had a very simplistic FSM in our 2D game. We just went from our StartMenu to our Scene (playing) state. Then we either went to a Lost or Won state, depending on whether or not we kicked all the enemies. Those states just had a timer to fade the screen. Finally, the game went back to the StartMenu state to start all over again. We also allowed pausing, which just toggled between our StartMenu state and our Scene state.

A little later in this chapter we will create a more advanced way to handle our game state, but for now we discuss how we can use this same concept to control our objects. Let's first consider our enemy objects because they will need to do some thinking. In our 2D game, our enemies only had one thought: Walk to the left. That was it. We just set their velocity and did not do anything else. It was a simple game, after all. In a real game, though, we would want to make our enemies think before acting. Perhaps they are not as strong as our hero and need to hide or attack from behind. Perhaps they need to run away when their health gets to a critical level. Perhaps they need to attack as much as possible but then will get tired and have to run away. All these actions are states. An enemy would have each of these states defined, and as the game progresses and an enemy is deployed, it "decides" which state it wants to be in.

We could even set up a probability table for our different states that would be set on a per-enemy basis. This means that some enemies would attack more, and others would retreat. We could assign these probabilities randomly, or we could actually create different enemy types (even if they looked the same on the screen), which would inherit from a base enemy object but would override its probability settings. This way, as it is deciding which state to be in, an enemy would use its own probability values to determine its state.

Object-Oriented Design

Once we start thinking about modeling our enemies as objects (which we did to a small degree in our SimpleGame), we can start seeing how we can create some really complex, thinking enemies. We can have a base enemy object from which all our other enemies inherit. Now, we do not want to go overboard with this because we can hurt performance with a lot of virtual methods that need to be overridden. However, we should not sacrifice design to save on performance. The key is balance. Because we are not creating a 3D engine to sell that needs to allow for all sorts of features our consumers might want, we can tighten up our design because we have full control over our code. While we are developing our game, if we decide we need to inherit from an enemy object, we can make just the methods we need to override virtual. We have that luxury. If we seal a class, but later realize that we should not have done that, we can easily modify the code to correct the problem. If we were releasing a library, however, this would not be appropriate unless breakable changes were clearly communicated. We do not need to worry about that, though, because we have full control over our game code and how our objects will interact with each other.

The main point of this section is to say that we should utilize XNA's game component and game services architecture, and when we write our code we should do so in an object-oriented way. It makes the code cleaner and easier to follow, and it makes a lot of sense because this is how we see the real world—in objects. Writing code this way really makes the code easier to maintain.

A Good Example of Object-Oriented Design: GTA III

One of the games with an AI that blew people away when it came out was *Grand Theft Auto III* from Rockstar Games. Of course, the successors of this game are also good, but this one was the first that just knocked people's socks off! The characters in the game are what caught players' eyes to begin with. Some would just walk around, and others would talk to each other. If someone died, a group of people would gather around gawking. An ambulance would soon arrive.

After getting on a gang's bad side, if the hero went into their territory, the gang would just start blasting away. The mob was ruthless with their shotguns! The game received a lot of press about its content, and although some of the content was a little much, users just could not get over how real the game felt. Good object-oriented design, along with each character having different properties associated with him or her, made this a very fun game. When characters were attacked, some would run away, and others would stay and fight. Road rage was also a fun item in the game. Accidentally (or not so accidentally) run into another person's car, and he or she might get out and wave a fist at you—or even chase you! Each character had his or her own probability (personality) of reaction in different situations. This allowed the gamer to be immersed in the game play. With decent AI and good object-oriented design, we can make (and maintain) a game with objects that think, which will result in very fun game play.

Managing Game States

When thinking about our overall game design, we should consider the different states our game will be in. When we made the SimpleGame in Chapter 11, we just used an enumerated type that we could pick from to change our game state. This was sufficient for that game, although the method we are going to discuss now would still fit the game well without adding a lot of complexity to the game code.

A common question from those starting out making games is, "How should I structure my game code?" This is a valid question with many different answers, each having its own merit. As with every other aspect of programming, tasks can be completed many different ways. For this discussion, we use a structure that is not very hard to implement and yields some very nice results in terms of flexibility.

Consider the following as a concrete example of the problem we are trying to solve:

1. Game is loaded, and the start or title screen is displayed.
2. The player presses A or Start, so the start or title screen is removed and the main menu screen appears.
3. The player selects a single-player game, the main menu is removed, and a submenu is displayed.
4. The game is a trial game, so a warning message is also displayed prompting the gamer to purchase the game or continue with limited play. The message is displayed on top of the submenu.

5. The player accepts the message, and the submenu no longer has the message obstructing his or her view.

6. The player selects Quick Game from the Single Player menu. The Single Player menu is removed, and the level starts, displaying a "start level" loading screen.

7. When the level finishes loading, the start level screen is removed, and the game's scene is loaded.

8. The player pauses the game, which brings up a paused screen that overlays the paused game play (this screen is a little blurred in the background).

Most of those state changes could be done with a simple enumerated type, but in some situations a simple enumerated type is not sufficient, such as when we display our message in a modal dialog box that does not allow the gamer to continue until he or she closes the box. However, we do not want to lose sight of the state the game was just in. We might use this same message dialog box at other times in our game for a tutorial or hints, and so on. Another example is when the gamer pauses the game. We could just switch the current state with the paused state and then return to the playing state when the pause button is toggled by the gamer, but then we could not display the current game's scene in a blurred (or grayscaled) manner behind the pause screen.

We are going to create a method that allows us to handle both of those situations and give us the flexibility of having access to the different states from within each state. We are going to create a game state manager class that will control a stack of our different game states. Instead of just switching between states, we are going to implement a stack.

What Is a Stack?

The typical real-world example computer scientists use to explain a stack is a stack of plates. We push and pop items on and off of the stack. In the plates example, we push a plate onto the top of the stack. We can then pop a plate off the top of a stack (but we need to be careful so we don't break it). It is a last in, first out (LIFO) method of processing. We do need to make sure we do not try to pop off a plate if the stack is empty, but that is easy enough to handle.

We are going to use a stack so we can easily handle situations such as adding a pause menu on top of our currently playing scene state. This way, we can continue to draw our scene even though the game is paused. We do not want to update our scene, though, because the enemies would keep coming, our timer would continue to count down, and so on. So when we pause, we really do want to pause our game play, but we still want to draw our game scene in its paused state. In fact, we might want to use some of the post-processing techniques you learned about to blur out, turn gray, or change our scene some other way when the game is in a paused state. By using a stack, we can accomplish any of these tasks.

Using a stack for game state management is also beneficial when trying to handle a dialog box because it effectively pauses the game to give players a hint, tell them the demo's time is up, and so on. Another benefit is multiple menus. We can push a menu state on top of our game play if the user backs out (or pauses) and then offer an options menu and sound or controller options under that. With a stack, we have the flexibility to leave our previous menus displayed or have our screen replace them. With a simple switch statement on an enumerated type, this would not be possible.

Fortunately, with all this flexibility we do not increase the complexity of our code very much. The principle is an easy one to grasp. We are going to have a game state manager that will manage the different states in our game. It will implement a stack to hold our states. Each state will contain logic that determines what happens next. The states themselves will drive the game flow.

Each state will inherit from a base game state abstract class. This abstract class will inherit from the DrawableGameComponent class. Each game state that inherits from our abstract state will be a game service. There are two reasons for this: One is that we want our state objects to be singleton objects because we do not want more than one instance of our state created. The second reason is because our game state manager will need access to the states.

Our game state manager also inherits from GameComponent because it is a game service that our states need a reference to. The game state manager will include an OnStateChange event. Normally, other objects would register for an event like this. Instead, we are going to expose the event handler in our game states and have our game manager manage the event registration process for our game states. The exposed event handler in our game states will be called StateChanged.

This StateChanged method in our game state class can be overridden but by default will simply check to see if the current state of the game is itself. If it is, the method will set its Enable and Visible properties to true; otherwise, it will set them to false. So by default, when a state is loaded, but not at the top of the stack, it will not update itself, nor will it draw itself. All active game states will have this event handler executed whenever the game changes state. Each state could also search the stack to see if it contains some other state and, if so, do some different processing. Because our StateChanged event handler will be protected, the actual game states can implement any functionality they want to as the game state changes. You can see that this system is pretty flexible.

Because we want our objects to use the singleton pattern and we want our states to be game services so that each state can access other states if needed, we can combine these two requirements because the game service collection can only have one object in its collection with a particular interface. Therefore, each one of our states will need its own interface, but you saw earlier that this can be a blank interface. In our situation, we are going to have an IGameState interface, but then each one of the states will have its own interface that implements the IGameState interface.

We need to be able to make comparisons between our game states. Mainly, we need to make comparisons between our game manager's current state and a particular game state. Enumerated types obviously lend themselves to comparisons easily, but what about actual game state objects? Fortunately, we can just as easily compare our object references, and this is why it is important that there is only one instance of the object—so our reference is always the same. We will create a property called `Value`, which is of type `GameState`. This property allows us to perform the comparisons we need.

Managing Game States Demo

So what exactly does this state game structure look like, and how do we actually implement it?

Figure 17.1 shows a partial diagram of our game state structure. We have several interfaces referenced in the diagram. `GameStateManager` has a private stack that holds all our states. It exposes methods that can change states permanently or temporarily by just pushing or popping them on and off the stack. It does not allow direct access to its stack. All the methods, the property, and the event we see to the side of `GameStateManager` are actually in the `IGameStateManager` interface. We have set up an interface so we can set up our `GameStateManager` as a game service. This is crucial because our individual game states will need access to our game state manager.

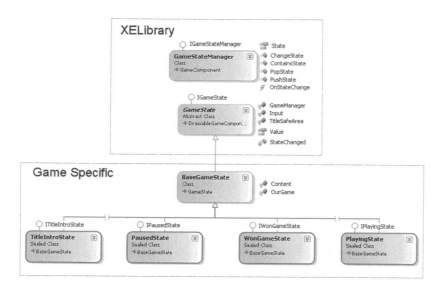

FIGURE 17.1   Our game state design diagram.

`GameState` is an abstract class that also implements an interface appropriately called `IGameState`. This interface allows us to use our states as a service, but we need to create individual interfaces for each game state we will have. You can see that at the bottom of Figure 17.1. The property and event handler are in the `IGameState` interface. The fields are declared inside the `GameState` abstract class itself. These fields are ones that all our states will need access to, and instead of making each one implement them, we let our abstract class do it for us.

Both the `GameStateManager` class and the `GameState` class are inside of XELibrary. The rest of the classes are in our game project. This brings us to `BaseGameState`, which is optional. The reason it is included here is to make our lives a little easier by exposing a field that most, if not all, of our game states will need: a reference to our specific game, not the `Microsoft.Xna.Framework.Game` type but our game type, such as `Game1` or `SimpleGame`. It is not in Figure 17.1, but our actual game class will be the class that declares each game state. Our game class will also expose its own `SpriteBatch`, which is typically private. For situations like this, it is beneficial to have a reference to our actual game, which will become clearer as we get into the code.

Each individual state will inherit from our `BaseGameState` (which inherits from the abstract `GameState` class). Each individual state will also implement its own interface. Each interface will inherit from the `IGameState` interface. All our individual state interfaces in this demo are empty except the `IFadingState` interface, which exposes a `Color` property that will allow another state to set the color to fade to before pushing it onto the stack.

To start with, we want to create a new project that we can call GameStateDemo. We also know we will be updating our XELibrary, so let's import that project as well. We can copy it from the last chapter. Once we have our solution set up, we can create a new file called interfaces.cs in our XELibrary project. Here's the code we will be entering into this file:

```
using System;
using Microsoft.Xna.Framework;
namespace XELibrary
{
    public interface IGameState
    {
        GameState Value { get; }
    }

    public interface IGameStateManager
    {
        event EventHandler OnStateChange;
        GameState State { get; }
        void PopState();
        void PushState(GameState state);
        bool ContainsState(GameState state);
        void ChangeState(GameState newState);
    }
}
```

You can see that this is just as we described before. For several of our `IGameStateManager` methods, we are passing around a reference to our abstract class `GameState`. The code for our `GameState` abstract class, which also needs to be added to our XELibrary project, is shown here:

```
using System;
using System.Collections.Generic;
using Microsoft.Xna.Framework;

namespace XELibrary
{
    public abstract partial class GameState : DrawableGameComponent, IGameState
    {
        protected IGameStateManager GameManager;
        protected IInputHandler Input;
        protected Rectangle TitleSafeArea;

        public GameState(Game game)
            : base(game)
        {
            GameManager = (IGameStateManager)game.Services.GetService(
                typeof(IGameStateManager));
            Input = (IInputHandler)game.Services.GetService(
                typeof(IInputHandler));
        }

        protected override void LoadContent()
        {
            TitleSafeArea = Utility.GetTitleSafeArea(GraphicsDevice, 0.85f);
        }

        internal protected virtual void StateChanged(object sender, EventArgs e)
        {
            if (GameManager.State == this.Value)
                Visible = Enabled = true;
            else
                Visible = Enabled = false;
        }

        #region IGameState Members
        public GameState Value
        {
            get { return (this); }
        }
        #endregion
    }
}
```

We create a reference to GameStateManager and InputHandler so our states can have easy access to those objects. We also set our TitleSafeArea property for the same reason. This is, of course, optional. If we determined that only one of our states really needed to be concerned with the title safe area of the screen, we could take it out and put it directly into the state that needed it. We only set the title safe area property after we know our device has been initialized.

Our GameState class also implements the event handler from the IGameState interface. This handler is here so we can be notified whenever the game state changes. We will see GameStateManager has an event that will kick off this code (or an overridden version from one of our specific states). By default, our game state will check to see if it is at the top of the stack when it is notified of a changed state event. If our game state is at the top, the state will make sure it is enabled and visible. If the state is not at the top of the stack, it will disable itself and make itself invisible. We have set both the internal and protected modifiers on this event handler method. The reason for the protected modifier is so our specific derived state classes can override this behavior if needed. The reason for the internal modifier is because we want our GameStateManager to handle whether or not the game state should be concerned about a state change. Marking the method as internal allows the GameStateManager to modify an internal variable of the GameState class.

Our GameState class inherits from the DrawableGameComponent class. We do not need to override the Update and Draw methods in this class, so we did not include them. Our individual states will most definitely override those methods to perform the tasks they need to.

Finally, our class implements the Value property from the interface so our objects can pass around the exact reference of the object. We are not strictly forcing a singleton pattern, but the game services collection does that for us by throwing an error if more than one object implementing the same interface is added to the collection. We know we will only have one instance of our state at any one time, so we can just compare on our value to determine whether we are on top on the stack. The Value property is the key to comparing our states.

Next, we can look at how our GameStateManager is implemented. Although this is not any more complex than our GameState class, we break it down into chunks to focus on the pieces that are important. To start, we need to set up our using statements:

```
using System;
using System.Collections.Generic;
using Microsoft.Xna.Framework;
using Microsoft.Xna.Framework.Content;
```

Now we can actually get into our class. We start with our private member fields and our constructor:

```
namespace XELibrary
{
    public class GameStateManager : GameComponent, IGameStateManager
    {
        private Stack<GameState> states = new Stack<GameState>();

        public event EventHandler OnStateChange;
```

```
    private int initialDrawOrder = 1000;
    private int drawOrder;

    public GameStateManager(Game game)
        : base(game)
    {
        game.Services.AddService(typeof(IGameStateManager), this);
        drawOrder = initialDrawOrder;
    }
```

We have our private stack that will store all the active states. We have also declared an event called OnStateChange. The initialDrawOrder and drawOrder fields are needed as we manage our states because each state is a game component, and we are tying into the built-in functionality of XNA. However, there is a problem. We have not specified a draw order. We need to set up our draw order and manage it in this class. The initial draw order value could be anything. We have it set as 1,000 and add or subtract 100 from the values. The idea is that we can have up to 10 states at any one time (which is definitely a stretch). Then, if we want to set the draw orders on the other components, that can be done as well. Most of the time this will not be needed, so we should be in good shape. An improvement would be to expose this field as a public property that could be set by our game. The constructor simply registers our object as a service and initializes our drawOrder with the initialDrawOrder value.

Next, we look at the methods that push and pop our temporary states onto our stack:

```
public void PopState()
{    RemoveState();
    drawOrder -= 100;

    //Let everyone know we just changed states
    if (OnStateChange != null)
        OnStateChange(this, null);
}

private void RemoveState()
{
    GameState oldState = (GameState)states.Peek();

    //Unregister the event for this state
    OnStateChange -= oldState.StateChanged;

    //remove the state from our game components
    Game.Components.Remove(oldState.Value);

    states.Pop();
}
```

The `PopState` method will pop a state from our internal stack. This is actually done by the private `RemoveState` method. The private method finds our current state and unregisters the `OnStateChange` event for that specific state. Finally, it removes the state from our game component collection. This might seem like we are breaking our rule of not over-utilizing game components, but in this situation we will not be changing states that often, and even so there will not be that many different states. The main thing we want to shy away from is creating game components for every enemy (or event bullet) in our games. We should have a manager for those.

After our `PopState` method calls the private `RemoveState` method that does all the tasks we just talked about, it subtracts 100 from the draw order so it will be ready to use the correct draw number when another state is pushed back onto the stack. To be more flexible, we could set that value up as a property that can be changed from within our game. We could at the very least set it as a constant. For now, this suffices. Finally, we fire off our `OnStateChange` event so that all the active game states can know that a state was removed and determine whether or not they should take control of the game.

Now we can discuss the counterpart of `PopState`—our `PushState` method. This method allows our individual game states (or even our game) to push a new state onto the stack:

```
public void PushState(GameState newState)
{
    drawOrder += 100;
    newState.DrawOrder = drawOrder;

    AddState(newState);

    //Let everyone know we just changed states
    if (OnStateChange != null)
        OnStateChange(this, null);
}
private void AddState(GameState state)
{
    states.Push(state);

    Game.Components.Add(state);

    //Register the event for this state
    OnStateChange += state.StateChanged;
}
```

When a game state is pushed onto the stack, we add our magic number of 100 to the draw order. `DrawableGameComponents` with the highest values get drawn last (which means they will obscure things drawn before them). After updating our draw order value, we set our game state's `DrawOrder` property so XNA will draw the game state in the order we want. Next, we call a private method `AddState` and pass in the state that is to be added to our stack. This method simply pushes the state onto our private stack and then adds the state (which is also a drawable game component) to our game component's collection. This method finishes up by registering the state for the OnStateChange event. The PushState method finishes up by actually firing the event, letting everyone know that the state was just changed.

Having the PopState and PushState methods is what we need, but we also need to replace the entire stack of states with a new state. This is done by the next method. Our ChangeState method allows us to do a permanent state change instead of a temporary one (of just pushing and popping states). You can see the ChangeState method here:

```
public void ChangeState(GameState newState)
{
    //We are changing states, so pop everything ...
    //if we don't want to really change states but just modify,
    //we should call PushState and PopState
    while (states.Count > 0)
        RemoveState();

    //changing state, reset our draw order
    newState.DrawOrder = drawOrder = initialDrawOrder;
    AddState(newState);

    //Let everyone know we just changed states
    if (OnStateChange != null)
        OnStateChange(this, null);
}
```

Because this is an all-out change state request, we pop everything off the stack. We already have a private method to handle this, so we simply call that while there are states in our stack. This is why we have the exposed methods firing our events instead of our private method. When we pop all these states off, we are not firing a bunch of needless events. Instead, we just pop them all off and reset our draw order to the initial value (as well as set the DrawOrder on the state we are adding) and finally add that state using our predefined method. After we have popped off all our states and added the one we changed to, we can fire off our OnStateChange to let the new state know that it is up to bat.

Because we do not expose the stack itself, we need to provide a method for our states to see if a certain state exists in the stack. This method can be helpful when a state needs to behave one way when another state is on the stack. It can query to see if the special case needs to be handled by determining whether or not the other state is in the stack. The following ContainsState method is very simple—it just exposes the Contains method from our stack:

```
public bool ContainsState(GameState state)
{
    return (states.Contains(state));
}
```

The final portion of our `GameStateManager` code is the property that returns the state that is on the top of the stack:

```
    public GameState State
    {
        get { return (states.Peek()); }
    }
  }
}
```

Those three files (Interfaces.cs, GameState.cs, and GameStateManager.cs) are all the files we will be adding to our XELibrary. We need to make another helper method in our InputHandler.cs file. Therefore, we add the following line to the top of our `IInputHandler` interface:

```
bool WasPressed(int playerIndex, Buttons button, Keys keys);
```

Then we implement the method in our `InputHandler` class, as follows:

```
public bool WasPressed(int playerIndex, Buttons button, Keys keys)
{
    if (keyboard.WasKeyPressed(keys) ||
                    gamePadHandler.WasButtonPressed(playerIndex, button))
        return (true);
    else
        return (false);
}
```

Now we can move to our actual game project and see what we need to do to start using this game state design. To begin with, we create a folder called GameStates. This is optional, but as our states grow it can be beneficial to have them tucked out of the way. Of course, it might be beneficial to have each state in its own folder, complete with its own game components and the logic it uses. This is a personal preference, of course. We can do whatever makes sense for the size of the project we are working on.

The first file we will add to our GameStates folder is the GameStateInterfaces.cs file. This file's contents are shown here:

```
using System;
using Microsoft.Xna.Framework.Graphics;
using XELibrary;

namespace GameStateDemo
{
    public interface ITitleIntroState : IGameState { }
    public interface IStartMenuState : IGameState { }
    public interface IOptionsMenuState : IGameState { }
    public interface IPlayingState : IGameState { }
```

```
public interface IPausedState : IGameState { }
public interface ILostGameState : IGameState { }
public interface IWonGameState : IGameState { }
public interface IStartLevelState : IGameState { }
public interface IYesNoDialogState : IGameState { }
public interface IFadingState : IGameState
{
    Color Color { get; set; }
}
}
```

We have simply set up a bunch of empty interfaces that all inherit from IGameState. This allows the game state objects we will create in a moment to all be accessed the same way, but it also allows them to be registered as a game service. A game service (and, therefore, our game states) must have a unique interface. Whenever we determine we need another game state, we need to add a new interface. Our demo will handle each one of these states. The last state, IFadingState, does expose a property: Color. This allows other states to specify the color to which the screen should fade when this state is loaded.

After setting up our interfaces for each state our game will be using, we can implement our BaseGameState. This class is optional because each individual state could simply inherit from the XELibrary's GameState class. However, this class is created so our states do not need to have the same code over and over again. The code for our BaseGameState is as follows:

```
using System;
using System.Collections.Generic;
using Microsoft.Xna.Framework;
using Microsoft.Xna.Framework.Content;
using XELibrary;

namespace GameStateDemo
{
    public partial class BaseGameState : GameState
    {
        protected Game1 OurGame;
        protected ContentManager Content;

        public BaseGameState(Game game)
            : base(game)
        {
            Content = new game.Content);
            OurGame = (Game1)game;
        }
    }
}
```

This is a very simple class that inherits from `GameState` and exposes two protected fields: `OurGame` and `Content`. We discussed how it is beneficial for our states to have access to our specific game instance. Having this hook in place can be good if we find ourselves needing to implement the same code for many of our game states.

Now we can take a look at the first state our game will push onto the stack—the `TitleIntroState`. The purpose of this state is to display all the title screens we want to show when our game starts. The demo will not be a game anyway. We are simply setting up a framework that allows us to easily move between the different game states. This is very beneficial to set up at the start. To demo this state, we are going to load a texture. We can add the Textures folder to our Content project and copy the titleIntro.png file from the CD included in this book. The code for this state is shown here:

```
using System;
using System.Collections.Generic;
using Microsoft.Xna.Framework;
using Microsoft.Xna.Framework.Content;
using Microsoft.Xna.Framework.Graphics;
using Microsoft.Xna.Framework.Input;
using XELibrary;

namespace GameStateDemo
{
    public sealed class TitleIntroState : BaseGameState, ITitleIntroState
    {
        private Texture2D texture;

        public TitleIntroState(Game game)
            : base(game)
        {
            game.Services.AddService(typeof(ITitleIntroState), this);
        }

        public override void Update(GameTime gameTime)
        {
            if (Input.WasPressed(0, Buttons.Back, Keys.Escape))
                OurGame.Exit();

            if (Input.WasPressed(0,Buttons.Start, Keys.Enter))
            {
                // push our start menu onto the stack
                GameManager.PushState(OurGame.StartMenuState.Value);
            }

            base.Update(gameTime);
        }
```

```
public override void Draw(GameTime gameTime)
{
    Vector2 pos = new Vector2(TitleSafeArea.Left, TitleSafeArea.Top);
    OurGame.SpriteBatch.Draw(texture, pos, Color.White);

    base.Draw(gameTime);
}

protected override void LoadContent()
{
    texture = Content.Load<Texture2D>(@"Textures\titleIntro");
}
    }
}
```

There is nothing special about the code; we are simply loading a texture and drawing it on the screen. We are using the SpriteBatch from our Game1 code (which we have not set up yet). We are also using the GameState's TitleSafeArea property to make sure we render the texture in a TV-friendly manner. Our update method checks to see whether the user is trying to exit the game or start the game. If the gamer presses Back (or Escape), the game exits. If the gamer presses Start (or Enter), the game is started by pushing StartMenuState onto the stack. We could have called the ChangedState method, but this allows us to have a small start menu pop up while the main intro and title are still being updated. We are not allowing our main intro and title screen to be updated, though, because we did not override the StateChanged event handler. You will see how to do that in another state we set up. For now, let's move on to our StartMenuState. You can copy the startMenu.png file from the CD included in this book. The code for this state is shown here:

```
using System;
using System.Collections.Generic;
using System.Text;
using Microsoft.Xna.Framework;
using Microsoft.Xna.Framework.Graphics;
using Microsoft.Xna.Framework.Input;
using XELibrary;

namespace GameStateDemo
{
    public sealed class StartMenuState : BaseGameState, IStartMenuState
    {
        private Texture2D texture;

        public StartMenuState(Game game)
            : base(game)
        {
```

```
        game.Services.AddService(typeof(IStartMenuState), this);
}

public override void Update(GameTime gameTime)
{
    if (Input.WasPressed(0, Buttons.Back, Keys.Escape))
    {
        //go back to title / intro screen
        GameManager.ChangeState(OurGame.TitleIntroState.Value);
    }

    if (Input.WasPressed(0, Buttons.Start, Keys.Enter))
    {
        //got here from our playing state,just pop myself off the stack
        if (GameManager.ContainsState(OurGame.PlayingState.Value))
            GameManager.PopState();
        else //starting game, queue first level
            GameManager.ChangeState(OurGame.StartLevelState.Value);
    }

    //options menu
    if (Input.WasPressed(0, Buttons.Y, Keys.O))
        GameManager.PushState(OurGame.OptionsMenuState.Value);

    base.Update(gameTime);
}

public override void Draw(GameTime gameTime)
{
    Vector2 pos = new Vector2(TitleSafeArea.Left, TitleSafeArea.Top);
    OurGame.SpriteBatch.Draw(texture, pos, Color.White);

    base.Draw(gameTime);
}

protected override void StateChanged(object sender, EventArgs e)
{
    base.StateChanged(sender, e);

    if (GameManager.State != this.Value)
        Visible = true;
}

protected override void LoadContent()
{
```

17

```
        texture = Content.Load<Texture2D>(@"Textures\startMenu");
    }
}
}
```

We seal all our states because we do not have any that need our functionality. Now, we do have a YesNoDialog class we will be creating, and it is feasible to think that we could have a DialogState with a YesNoDialog that inherits from the DialogState and some other ChooseWeaponState that might inherit from the DialogState. Therefore, we might not want every state to be sealed, but if we are pretty confident we will not be deriving other classes from it, we should seal this class for a slight performance gain.

We also register each state as a service in our constructor. This code should be pretty familiar to you by now. Besides our typical LoadContent, Draw, and Update methods, we have overridden the StateChange event handler method. We first call our base class so that it will do its normal tasks of enabling and making visible the state (if we are at the top of the stack) and disabling and making invisible the state otherwise. But then we reset our Visible property even if we aren't at the top of the stack. This way, other submenus such as our OptionsMenuState can be displayed on top of our main start menu.

Our Update method handles typical start menu actions. If the gamer escapes out of the start menu, we change states to our title menu. At this point, we could just pop; however, we will also allow getting to this start menu state from our playing state, and popping would not be enough.

You can see that we handle a special case if the user presses Enter (to start the game). We first check to see if the playing state is in our stack. If so, our start menu state was invoked by the playing state, and we should just pop off of the stack so the playing state will be at the top of the stack again. If the playing state is not on the stack, we are assuming the user got here from the title menu, so we do a permanent state change to go to our state-level state.

The next state we will look at is our Options menu. You can copy the optionsMenu.png file from the CD included in this book. The code for our OptionsMenuState.cs file is as follows:

```
using System;
using System.Collections.Generic;
using System.Text;
using Microsoft.Xna.Framework;
using Microsoft.Xna.Framework.Content;
using Microsoft.Xna.Framework.Graphics;
using Microsoft.Xna.Framework.Input;
using XELibrary;

namespace GameStateDemo
{
    public sealed class OptionsMenuState : BaseGameState, IOptionsMenuState
```

```
{
    Texture2D texture;

    public OptionsMenuState(Game game)
        : base(game)
    {
        game.Services.AddService(typeof(IOptionsMenuState), this);
    }

    public override void Update(GameTime gameTime)
    {
        if ((Input.WasPressed(0, Buttons.Back, Keys.Escape)
        || (Input.WasPressed(0, Buttons.Start, Keys.Enter))))
            GameManager.PopState();

        base.Update(gameTime);
    }

    public override void Draw(GameTime gameTime)
    {
        Vector2 pos = new Vector2(TitleSafeArea.Left + 50,
            TitleSafeArea.Top + 50);
        OurGame.SpriteBatch.Draw(texture, pos, Color.White);

        base.Draw(gameTime);
    }

    protected override void LoadContent()
    {
        texture = Content.Load<Texture2D>(
            @"Textures\optionsMenu");
    }
}
}
```

The only code of interest is the Update method. We determine whether we should exit the Options menu by checking for either the Escape key or the Enter key (or Back button or Start button). We could have multiple menus linked from here—perhaps an audio options menu or a controller options menu. We would handle them the same way. We would push on the new state and then let that state pop itself off. In the Web world, this is called *pogo sticking* because you have to perform so many "clicks" to get to where you want to be. Although this method of having multiple submenus would work and might be the only option in some situations, it's best to combine multiple menus so the gamer does not have to go so many levels deep.

Next is the StartLevelState code. This code is set up just like the rest you have seen and can be found here:

```csharp
using System;
using System.Collections.Generic;
using System.Text;
using Microsoft.Xna.Framework;
using Microsoft.Xna.Framework.Content;
using Microsoft.Xna.Framework.Graphics;
using Microsoft.Xna.Framework.Input;
using XELibrary;

namespace GameStateDemo
{
    public sealed class StartLevelState : BaseGameState, IStartLevelState
    {
        SpriteFont font;
        bool demoMode = true; //would be read in from some setting ...
        bool displayedDemoDialog = false;
        public StartLevelState(Game game)
            : base(game)
        {
            game.Services.AddService(typeof(IStartLevelState), this);
        }
        protected override void LoadContent()
        {
            font = Content.Load<SpriteFont>(@"Fonts\Arial");
        }
        public override void Update(GameTime gameTime)
        {
            if (Input.WasPressed(0, Buttons.Start, Keys.Enter))
                GameManager.ChangeState(OurGame.PlayingState.Value);
            base.Update(gameTime);
        }
        public override void Draw(GameTime gameTime)
        {
            OurGame.SpriteBatch.DrawString(font,
                "Starting Level ...", new Vector2(50, 50), Color.Black);
            base.Draw(gameTime);
        }
        protected override void StateChanged(object sender, EventArgs e)
        {
            base.StateChanged(sender, e);

          if (GameManager.State == this.Value)
           {
               if (demoMode && !displayedDemoDialog)
               {
                   GameManager.PushState(OurGame.YesNoDialogState.Value);
```

```
                    this.Visible = true;
                    displayedDemoDialog = true;
                }
            }
        }
    }
}
```

Our Update method is not doing anything special. We simply check for the Enter key (or Start button) and do a permanent change of state to our playing state. The overridden StateChanged method is a little more interesting. The idea here is that our game has not been purchased and is running in demo mode. As a result, we bring up a dialog box that the user must click through to start the game. As the game loads a new level, the user will be prompted to purchase the game. We call the base StateChanged method and then check to see if we are at the top of the stack. If we are, we are in demo mode, and we have not displayed the demo dialog box yet, so we push the YesNoDialogState (which simulates an annoying pop-up box) onto the stack. We do not do this with the code, but we could set properties to allow us to override the Yes and No captions as well as the message being displayed. This way, the YesNoDialogState can be used for multiple things.

The YesNoDialogState does not do anything special. It is simply popping itself off the stack when the gamer presses Enter or the A button. Its code including the Update method is as follows:

```
using System;
using Microsoft.Xna.Framework;
using Microsoft.Xna.Framework.Graphics;
using Microsoft.Xna.Framework.Input;
using XELibrary;

namespace GameStateDemo
{
    public sealed class YesNoDialogState : BaseGameState, IYesNoDialogState
    {
        SpriteFont font;

        public YesNoDialogState(Game game)
            : base(game)
        {
            game.Services.AddService(typeof(YesNoDialogState), this);
        }
        public override void Update(GameTime gameTime)
        {
            if (Input.WasPressed(0, Buttons.A, Keys.Enter))
                GameManager.PopState(); //we are done ...
            base.Update(gameTime);
        }
```

```
        public override void Draw(GameTime gameTime)
        {
            OurGame.SpriteBatch.DrawString(font,
                "Are you REALLY SURE you want to do THAT!?!?",
                new Vector2(50, 250), Color.Green);

            base.Draw(gameTime);
        }
        protected override void LoadContent()
        {
            font = Content.Load<SpriteFont>(@"Fonts\Arial");
        }
    }
}
```

Our PlayingState is as follows:

```
using System;
using System.Collections.Generic;
using System.Text;
using Microsoft.Xna.Framework;
using Microsoft.Xna.Framework.Content;
using Microsoft.Xna.Framework.Graphics;
using Microsoft.Xna.Framework.Input;
using XELibrary;

namespace GameStateDemo
{
    public sealed class PlayingState : BaseGameState, IPlayingState
    {
        SpriteFont font;
        Random rand;
        Color color;

        public PlayingState(Game game)
            : base(game)
        {
            game.Services.AddService(typeof(IPlayingState), this);
            rand = new Random();
        }

        public override void Update(GameTime gameTime)
        {
            if (Input.WasPressed(0, Buttons.Back, Keys.Escape))
                GameManager.PushState(OurGame.StartMenuState.Value);
```

```
        // push our paused state onto the stack
        if (Input.WasPressed(0, Buttons.Start, Keys.Enter))
            GameManager.PushState(OurGame.PausedState.Value);

        if (Input.WasPressed(0, Buttons.X, Keys.X))
        {
            //simulate game over
            //randomly pick if we win or lose
            if (rand.Next(2) < 1) //lose
                GameManager.PushState(OurGame.LostGameState.Value);
            else //win
                GameManager.PushState(OurGame.WonGameState.Value);
        }

        //simulate activity on the game
        //when updating ...
        if (color == Color.Black)
            color = Color.Purple;
        else
            color = Color.Black;

            base.Update(gameTime);
    }

public override void Draw(GameTime gameTime)
{
    OurGame.SpriteBatch.DrawString(font,
        "Playing the game ... playing the game",
        new Vector2(20, 20), color);
    OurGame.SpriteBatch.DrawString(font,
        "Playing the game ... playing the game",
        new Vector2(20, 120), Color.White);
    OurGame.SpriteBatch.DrawString(font,
        "Playing the game ... playing the game",
        new Vector2(20, 220), Color.Red);

    base.Draw(gameTime);
}

protected override void StateChanged(object sender, EventArgs e)
{
    base.StateChanged(sender, e);

    if (GameManager.State != this.Value)
    {
        Visible = true;
```

17

```
            Enabled = false;
        }
    }

    protected override void LoadContent()
    {
        font = Content.Load<SpriteFont>(@"Fonts\Arial");
    }
}
}
```

We start out by setting up a variable to hold a random number along with one to hold our color. We are going to use the random number to simulate winning or losing. We are using the color to "animate" our scene so we can easily tell that our Update method is being called (our state is enabled). We use that color in our Draw method to update the color of one of the lines we are drawing on the screen.

We override our StateChanged method by making sure we are still drawing on the screen but are not updating. As long as we are in the stack, we will draw our scene, but we will not update our game (enemies, timers, and so on) unless our state is at the top of the stack.

Our Update method will push the StartMenuState back on the stack if the gamer presses the Back button or the Escape key. That state will then either pop itself off (so the gamer can continue playing) or change back to the title screen state (if the user pressed Escape a second time). Our Update method will push the PausedState on the stack if the user paused the game by pressing Start or the Enter key. If the user presses the X button or the X key, we end the game and randomly pick whether the user wins or loses. Based on that random number, we either push LostGameState or WonGameState.

There are just a few more states to go over before we get to our game code. The next state we will look at is PausedState. The only thing of interest is the Update method. All it does is pop itself off the stack if the gamer presses the Enter key (or Start button):

```
using Microsoft.Xna.Framework;
using Microsoft.Xna.Framework.Graphics;
using Microsoft.Xna.Framework.Input;
using XELibrary;

namespace GameStateDemo
{
    public sealed class PausedState : BaseGameState, IPausedState
    {
        SpriteFont font;

        public PausedState(Game game)
            : base(game)
        {
            game.Services.AddService(typeof(IPausedState), this);
```

```
        }

        public override void Update(GameTime gameTime)
        {
            if (Input.WasPressed(0, Buttons.Start, Keys.Enter))
                GameManager.PopState(); //I am no longer paused ...

            base.Update(gameTime);
        }

        public override void Draw(GameTime gameTime)
        {
            OurGame.SpriteBatch.DrawString(font, "PAUSED",
                new Vector2(50, 20), Color.Yellow);
            base.Draw(gameTime);
        }

        protected override void LoadContent()
        {
            font = Content.Load<SpriteFont>(@"Fonts\Arial");
        }
    }
}
```

Next are WonGameState and LostGameState. The code for these states is basically identical. The WonGameState code is as follows:

```
using System;
using Microsoft.Xna.Framework;
using Microsoft.Xna.Framework.Graphics;

namespace GameStateDemo
{
    public sealed class WonGameState : BaseGameState, IWonGameState
    {
        SpriteFont font;

        public WonGameState(Game game)
            : base(game)
        {
            game.Services.AddService(typeof(IWonGameState), this);
        }

        public override void Update(GameTime gameTime)
        {
            base.Update(gameTime);
```

```
        }

        public override void Draw(GameTime gameTime)
        {
            OurGame.SpriteBatch.DrawString(font,
                "You Won!!!", new Vector2(50, 50),
                Color.White, 0, Vector2.Zero, 3.0f,
                SpriteEffects.None, 0);

            base.Draw(gameTime);
        }

        protected override void LoadContent()
        {
            font = Content.Load<SpriteFont>(@"Fonts\Arial");
        }

        protected override void StateChanged(object sender, EventArgs e)
        {
            if (GameManager.State == this.Value)
            {
                OurGame.FadingState.Color = Color.Black;
                GameManager.PushState(OurGame.FadingState.Value);
            }
        }
    }
}
```

The LostGameState class looks identical, except the Draw method displays "You Lost!!!" with Color.Firebrick. Also the StateChanged event handler changes the color to Red instead of Black.

We simply check to see if we are at the top of the stack and, if so, set a color (red for LostGameState, black for WonGameState) and then push the FadingState onto the stack. Alternatively, we could have kept our fading code as a drawable game component and not have an explicit state for it.

We will now look at our last state: FadingState. Our FadingState code is very similar to the previous FadeOut drawable game component. The code is listed here in its entirety:

```
using System;
using System.Collections.Generic;
using System.Text;
using Microsoft.Xna.Framework;
using Microsoft.Xna.Framework.Content;
using Microsoft.Xna.Framework.Graphics;
using Microsoft.Xna.Framework.Input;
```

```
using XELibrary;

namespace GameStateDemo
{
    public sealed class FadingState : BaseGameState, IFadingState
    {
        private Texture2D fadeTexture;
        private float fadeAmount;
        private double fadeStartTime;

        private Color color;

        public Color Color
        {
            get { return (color); }
            set { color = value; }
        }

        public FadingState(Game game)
            : base(game)
        {
            game.Services.AddService(typeof(IFadingState), this);
        }

        public override void Update(GameTime gameTime)
        {
            if (fadeStartTime == 0)
                fadeStartTime = gameTime.TotalGameTime.TotalMilliseconds;

            fadeAmount += (.25f *(float)gameTime.ElapsedGameTime.TotalSeconds);

            if (gameTime.TotalGameTime.TotalMilliseconds > fadeStartTime+4000)
            {
                //Once we are done fading, change back to title screen.
                GameManager.ChangeState(OurGame.TitleIntroState.Value);
            }
        }

        public override void Draw(GameTime gameTime)
        {
            GraphicsDevice.RenderState.SourceBlend = Blend.SourceAlpha;
            GraphicsDevice.RenderState.DestinationBlend =
                                            Blend.InverseSourceAlpha;
            Vector4 fadeColor = color.ToVector4();
            fadeColor.W = fadeAmount; //set transparency
            OurGame.SpriteBatch.Draw(fadeTexture, Vector2.Zero,
```

```
            new Color(fadeColor));

        base.Draw(gameTime);
    }


    protected override void StateChanged(object sender, EventArgs e)
    {
        //Set up our initial fading values
        if (GameManager.State == this.Value)
        {
            fadeAmount = 0;
            fadeStartTime = 0;
        }         }
    protected override void LoadContent()
    {
        fadeTexture = CreateFadeTexture(
            GraphicsDevice.Viewport.Width, GraphicsDevice.Viewport.Height);

        base.LoadContent();
    }


    private Texture2D CreateFadeTexture(int width, int height)
    {
        Texture2D texture = new Texture2D(GraphicsDevice, width, height, 1,
            TextureUsage.None, SurfaceFormat.Color);

        int pixelCount = width * height;
        Color[] pixelData = new Color[pixelCount];
        Random rnd = new Random();

        for (int i = 0; i < pixelCount; i++)
        {
            pixelData[i] = Color.White;
        }

        texture.SetData(pixelData);

        return (texture);
    }
  }
}


    protected override void LoadGraphicsContent(bool loadAllContent)
    {
        if (loadAllContent)
            fadeTexture = CreateFadeTexture(GraphicsDevice.Viewport.Width,
```

```
            GraphicsDevice.Viewport.Height);

        base.LoadGraphicsContent(loadAllContent);
    }

    private Texture2D CreateFadeTexture(int width, int height)
    {
        Texture2D texture = new Texture2D(GraphicsDevice, width, height, 1,
            ResourceUsage.None, SurfaceFormat.Color,
            ResourceManagementMode.Automatic);

        int pixelCount = width * height;
        Color[] pixelData = new Color[pixelCount];
        Random rnd = new Random();

        for (int i = 0; i < pixelCount; i++)
        {
            pixelData[i] = Color.White;
        }
        texture.SetData(pixelData);

        return (texture);
    }
  }
}
```

The logic of this class did not change at all. The only thing we need to focus on is our Update method and our StateChanged event handler. Our Update method is identical to before, except that in our condition once we have waited long enough for our screen to totally become opaque we change our state to our TitleIntroState. When the state changes and we get notified we are making the assumption that we will always be the last state in the list and we initialize fade amount and start time values. Again, this code really did not change much from before. We just plopped it in as a game state. It would have been perfectly acceptable to leave it as a game component, have it work similar to how it did before, and have our WonGameState and LostGameState code do a change state to the TitleIntroState.

One final thing we need to do in our XELibrary is to keep our input handler from just exiting our application. We want to add a flag so that when we create our input handler, we can let it know whether or not it should handle exiting our application. We will change the default behavior to not exit the game. If we are writing a demo, though, it might be beneficial to keep the code in place. We want to replace our current InputHandler's constructor signature with this:

```
private bool allowsExiting;

public InputHandler(Game game) : this(game, false) { }
```

17

```
public InputHandler(Game game, bool allowsExiting)
    : base(game)
        {
            this.allowsExiting = allowsExiting;
```

Then in our `Update` method we need to wrap our exit conditions with a check of that variable. The code for this is shown here:

```
if (allowsExiting)
{
    if (keyboard.IsKeyDown(Keys.Escape))
        Game.Exit();

    // Allows the default game to exit on Xbox 360 and Windows
    if (gamePadHandler.WasButtonPressed(0, Buttons.Back))
        Game.Exit();
}
```

We can finally take a look at our game code to see what we need to do to wrap this up. Here are the member fields we need to create:

```
private InputHandler input;
private Camera camera;
private GameStateManager gameManager;

public SpriteBatch SpriteBatch;

public ITitleIntroState TitleIntroState;
public IStartMenuState StartMenuState;
public IOptionsMenuState OptionsMenuState;
public IPlayingState PlayingState;
public IStartLevelState StartLevelState;
public ILostGameState LostGameState;
public IWonGameState WonGameState;
public IFadingState FadingState;
public IPausedState PausedState;
public IYesNoDialogState YesNoDialogState;
```

We have now created a way for our states to easily push other states onto the stack as well as change to states by making each state public. Notice we change `SpriteBatch` to a public field. We now initialize all the states in our constructor:

```
public Game1()
{
    graphics = new GraphicsDeviceManager(this);
    Content.RootDirectory = "Content";
```

```
    input = new InputHandler(this);
    Components.Add(input);

    camera = new Camera(this);
    Components.Add(camera);

    gameManager = new GameStateManager(this);
    Components.Add(gameManager);

    TitleIntroState = new TitleIntroState(this);
    StartMenuState = new StartMenuState(this);
    OptionsMenuState = new OptionsMenuState(this);
    PlayingState = new PlayingState(this);
    StartLevelState = new StartLevelState(this);
    FadingState = new FadingState(this);
    LostGameState = new LostGameState(this);
    WonGameState = new WonGameState(this);
    PausedState = new PausedState(this);
    YesNoDialogState = new YesNoDialogState(this);

    gameManager.ChangeState(TitleIntroState.Value);
}
```

The first part of this code should look very familiar to you. We are simply initializing our game components and adding them to the collection. This includes our GameStateManager. After that, we initialize each one of our states. Remember, each state registers itself as a game service in its constructor. Finally, we "change" our state to the TitleIntroState to kick things off. Things are shaping up nicely.

The only thing left is our Draw method, which really is not all that special. The main thing this shows is that we need to call Begin on our sprite batch and then call the base.Draw method before calling End on our sprite batch:

```
protected override void Draw(GameTime gameTime)
{
    graphics.GraphicsDevice.Clear(Color.CornflowerBlue);
    SpriteBatch.Begin();
    base.Draw(gameTime);
    SpriteBatch.End();
}
```

We now have a nice little demo that allows us to move in and out of the different game states. We should be able to use this as a starting point for our projects. A good exercise would be to plug this framework into the SimpleGame we created in Chapter 11.

17

Summary

We started the chapter discussing FSMs and their place within our games. We then took this concept and applied it to our actual game structure. We talked in detail about how we could use a stack-based system to manage our different game states to create a nice and clean process flow between states. This is key to a nice polished game. A lot of times, this aspect is left until the end, but that can have disastrous effects on the game because it might be hard to plug it in after the fact.

We finished out the chapter by looking at all the code needed to pull off our stack-based game state management system. Although there was good amount of code, it's definitely not difficult and is very easy to use once in place. Having a way to manage our game states effectively is huge. We are well on our way to creating excellent games!

CHAPTER 18

AI Algorithms

We discussed finite state machines (FSMs) in the previous chapter. In this chapter, as we look at common algorithms, we will put the knowledge into motion by having enemies that move randomly, chase, evade, and move in patterns.

Setting Up Our Demo

We need to create a new solution called AIDemo. We also need to reference our XELibrary but do not need to change it. We can either include it as a project or just add it as a reference.

We need to add the sphere0.x file to our Models folder in our Content project. We can create a private member field called sphere to hold our model:

```
private Model sphere;
```

We also need to add a skybox and add a reference to our skybox pipeline assembly in our Content project. We can use the same skybox texture from our acceleration demo and put the texture into the Skyboxes folder of our Content project. We need to create a private member to hold our skybox:

```
private Skybox skybox;
```

After making sure we have set our skybox2.tga asset's Content Processor property to SkyboxProcessor, we need to load our sphere and skybox in the LoadContent method:

```
sphere = Content.Load<Model>(@"Models\sphere0");
skybox = Content.Load<Skybox>(@"Skyboxes\skybox2");
```

We can set up our typical input and camera game components next. The camera we should use is our stationary `Camera` object. We need to set up the following private member fields:

```
private InputHandler input;
private Camera camera;
```

We then add them to our constructor:

```
input = new InputHandler(this, true);
Components.Add(input);
camera = new Camera(this);
Components.Add(camera);
```

We are allowing our `InputHandler` to exit the demo when the user presses the Back button or the Escape key. This is why we are passing true in as the second parameter of the constructor. We need to set up two new classes, and we can keep these inside our Game1.cs file because they are small:

```
class Player
{
    public Vector3 Position;
    public Vector3 Velocity;
    public Matrix World;
    public Color Color;
}


class Enemy
{
    public Vector3 Position;
    public Vector3 Velocity;
    public Matrix World;
    public Color Color;
}
```

We will add more properties to our `Enemy` class as we move through the chapter, but this is enough to get us started. We are going to be drawing multiple spheres on the screen. One represents our player, and the others represent the enemies. We need to add our faithful `DrawModel` method:

```
private void DrawModel(ref Model m, ref Matrix world, Color color)
{
    Matrix[] transforms = new Matrix[m.Bones.Count];
    m.CopyAbsoluteBoneTransformsTo(transforms);

    foreach (ModelMesh mesh in m.Meshes)
    {
```

```
        foreach (BasicEffect be in mesh.Effects)
        {
            be.EnableDefaultLighting();

            be.AmbientLightColor = color.ToVector3();
            be.Projection = camera.Projection;
            be.View = camera.View;
            be.World = world * mesh.ParentBone.Transform;
        }

        mesh.Draw();
    }
}
```

We can set up our variables to hold our player and enemies:

```
private const int MaxEnemies = 10;
private Player player;
private Enemy[] enemies = new Enemy[MaxEnemies];
```

We can initialize them in our Initialization method:

```
player = new Player();
player.Position = new Vector3(-100, 0, -300);
player.Velocity = Vector3.Zero;
player.World = Matrix.CreateTranslation(player.Position);
player.Color = Color.Black;

for (int i = 0; i < MaxEnemies; i++)
{
    enemies[i] = new Enemy();
    enemies[i].Position = new Vector3((i * 50) + 50, (i * 25) - 50, -300);
    enemies[i].Velocity = Vector3.Zero;
    enemies[i].World = Matrix.CreateTranslation(enemies[i].Position);
}
```

We are spacing our enemies out in a diagonal line. We can go ahead and draw our skybox and spheres by adding the following code in our Draw method:

```
skybox.Draw(camera.View, camera.Projection, Matrix.CreateScale(ArenaSize));
//Draw player
DrawModel(ref sphere, ref player.World, player.Color);

//Draw enemies
for (int i = 0; i < MaxEnemies; i++)
{
    Enemy enemy = enemies[i];
```

18

```
        DrawModel(ref sphere, ref enemy.World, enemy.Color);
}
```

ArenaSize is simply a float constant with a value of 500. If we run our demo at this point, we should see our skybox, our player sphere colored black, and our enemy spheres colored white. We set up our camera as a stationary camera, so we can rotate but not move it. We did this because we are going to hook our A, S, W, and D keys to moving the player sphere. We create a new method to do the update:

```
private void UpdatePlayer()
{
    player.Velocity = Vector3.Zero;

    if (input.KeyboardState.IsHoldingKey(Keys.W) ¦¦
        input.GamePads[0].ThumbSticks.Left.Y > 0)
    {
        player.Velocity.Y++;
    }
    else if (input.KeyboardState.IsHoldingKey(Keys.S) ¦¦
        input.GamePads[0].ThumbSticks.Left.Y < 0)
    {
        player.Velocity.Y--;
    }

    if (input.KeyboardState.IsHoldingKey(Keys.D) ¦¦
        input.GamePads[0].ThumbSticks.Left.X > 0)
    {
        player.Velocity.X++;
    }
    else if (input.KeyboardState.IsHoldingKey(Keys.A) ¦¦
        input.GamePads[0].ThumbSticks.Left.X < 0)
    {
        player.Velocity.X--;
    }

    //restrict to 2D?
    if (!restrictToXY)
    {
        if (input.KeyboardState.IsHoldingKey(Keys.RightShift) ¦¦
            input.GamePads[0].Triggers.Right > 0)
        {
            player.Velocity.Z--;
        }
        else if (input.KeyboardState.IsHoldingKey(Keys.RightControl) ¦¦
            input.GamePads[0].Triggers.Left > 0)
        {
            player.Velocity.Z++;
```

```
        }
    }

    //Normalize our vector so we don't go faster
    //when heading in multiple directions
    if (player.Velocity.LengthSquared() != 0)
        player.Velocity.Normalize();

    player.Velocity *= playerMoveUnit;
}
```

We need to add a private member boolean called restrictToXY, which we can set to true. This demo will only move on the x and y axes, so we can easily see how our enemies are thinking. We are including the z axis so that when we create a real world, we will be closer to the end goal of having thinking enemies that can move in 3D. This UpdatePlayer method needs to be called from our Update method. Not a lot is going on inside the method: We are checking whether the input is moving our player; if so, we update the velocity. We only do this on the z axis if we are supposed to. Finally, we normalize our vector so the player does not move faster when going in multiple directions. The last thing this method does is multiply the velocity by the playerMoveUnit value, which is a member field that needs to be set to 25. Let's call this method in our Update method and finish updating our player's position:

```
float elapsedTime = (float)gameTime.ElapsedGameTime.TotalSeconds;
UpdatePlayer();
player.Velocity *= elapsedTime;
player.Position += player.Velocity;
KeepWithinBounds(ref player.Position, ref player.Velocity);
player.World = Matrix.CreateTranslation(player.Position);
```

After calling the UpdatePlayer method, we factor in our calculated elapsed time so the player will move at a consistent rate no matter what the frame rate happens to be. We then update the player's position, taking into account the current velocity just calculated. We pass the position and velocity into a helper method that will keep the player within the boundaries of the arena. Finally, we update our world coordinates so the player will be drawn in the correct position. We can add in our helper method:

```
private void KeepWithinBounds(ref Vector3 position, ref Vector3 velocity)
{
    if ((position.X < -ArenaSize) || (position.X > ArenaSize))
        velocity.X = -velocity.X;
    if ((position.Y < -ArenaSize) || (position.Y > ArenaSize))
        velocity.Y = -velocity.Y;
    if ((position.Z < -ArenaSize) || (position.Z > ArenaSize))
        velocity.Z = -velocity.Z;
    position += velocity;
}
```

18

This method simply reverses velocity if the player hits the wall. We can run our code and move our player around the screen. The demo is almost 2D because the camera is fixed. It is definitely not going to win any awards for camera movement. However, we are interested in the AI code.

Chase Algorithm

To start, we are going to have the enemies target and try to catch the player. We can create a method called TrackPlayerStraightLine. This method will make the enemies do exactly that—track our player in the most direct path possible:

```
private void TrackPlayerStraightLine(Enemy enemy)
{
    if (player.Position.X > enemy.Position.X)
        enemy.Velocity.X = moveUnit;
    else if (player.Position.X < enemy.Position.X)
        enemy.Velocity.X = -moveUnit;
    else
        enemy.Velocity.X = 0;

    if (player.Position.Y > enemy.Position.Y)
        enemy.Velocity.Y = moveUnit;
    else if (player.Position.Y < enemy.Position.Y)
        enemy.Velocity.Y = -moveUnit;
    else
        enemy.Velocity.Y = 0;

    //restrict to 2D?
    if (!restrictToXY)
    {
        if (player.Position.Z > enemy.Position.Z)
            enemy.Velocity.Z = moveUnit;
        else if (player.Position.Z < enemy.Position.Z)
            enemy.Velocity.Z = -moveUnit;
        else
            enemy.Velocity.Z = 0;
    }

    enemy.Color = Color.Red;
}
```

The algorithm for tracking is very straightforward. We check to see if the enemy's position is less than the player's position. If it is, we add to the velocity appropriately. moveUnit is a float that needs to be set to 20 (just a little slower than the player's movement). If it is greater than the player's position, we subtract from the velocity. We do this for all the axes. We are also setting the color of the enemies to red so we can keep them straight later on when we have other types of enemies on the screen. We can call this method in our Update method:

```
foreach (Enemy enemy in enemies)
{
    TrackPlayerStraightLine(enemy);

    enemy.Velocity *= elapsedTime;
    enemy.Position += enemy.Velocity;
    KeepWithinBounds(ref enemy.Position, ref enemy.Velocity);
    enemy.World = Matrix.CreateTranslation(enemy.Position);
}
```

We track our player relentlessly and make sure we are moving according to the frame rate. We update the player's position based on the velocity and make sure the enemy stays within the walls of the arena. Finally, we update the enemies' world matrices. We can add the following code to our Draw method:

```
for (int i = 0; i < MaxEnemies; i++)
{
    Enemy enemy = enemies[i];
    DrawModel(ref sphere, ref enemy.World, enemy.Color);
}
```

We can run the code now.

A Better Chase Algorithm

Although the preceding algorithm gets the job done effectively, it is a little unrealistic because the enemies are moving in a very precise manner. We can modify how they turn to track the player, which slows them down a little but ultimately makes them look more realistic. We are going to create another method called TrackPlayer:

```
private void TrackPlayer(Enemy enemy)
{
    Vector3 tv = player.Position - enemy.Position;
    tv.Normalize();

    enemy.Velocity = tv * moveUnit;

    enemy.Color = Color.Red;
}
```

With this algorithm we are effectively doing the same thing, but this time we are utilizing some vector math to move the enemies in a more realistic manner. Of course, depending on the enemy, the first method we used might work. In this method, however, we are computing the vector between an enemy and the player. This is done by taking the difference of the two positions and then normalizing the resulting vector. We then set the velocity to the product of the resulting vector and the movement unit we have defined. We have a much better result with fewer lines of code. It did require a little bit of vector math, but even that is all done by XNA for us. We can replace the `TrackPlayerStraightLine` method with this updated `TrackPlayer` method and run our demo to see some nice results.

Evading Algorithm

Our evading algorithm is identical to our tracking algorithm. The only difference is that we change the resulting vector by switching the order in which we are subtracting the player and enemies' position vectors. The code is as follows:

```
private void EvadePlayer(Enemy enemy)
{
    Vector3 tv = enemy.Position - player.Position;
    tv.Normalize();

    enemy.Velocity = tv * moveUnit;

    enemy.Color = Color.Navy;
}
```

That's really all there is to it. We can replace the call to the `TrackPlayer` method in our `Update` method with this `EvadePlayer` method.

Because we are keeping our spheres within the arena, these evading bots will just move as far away as possible. The one that is on the same y axis will stay where it is, whereas those higher or lower will continue to move higher or lower while fleeing to the right. They do not want to come near the player, so they will basically end up in the corner.

Random Movement

Besides having the enemies chasing and evading, we can also have them move randomly. To do this, we need to add some more properties to the `Enemy` class. We want them to change directions every so often (each enemy should have a different timer it uses to determine when to switch directions). The direction should be random for each enemy (each enemy will need a random velocity). The properties we need to add to our `Enemy` class are as follows:

```
public float ChangeDirectionTimer;
public Vector3 RandomVelocity;
public int RandomSeconds;
```

We will create a method called MoveRandomly that contains the logic to move our enemies in a random motion:

```
private void MoveRandomly(Enemy enemy, GameTime gameTime)
{
    if (enemy.ChangeDirectionTimer == 0)
        enemy.ChangeDirectionTimer =
            (float)gameTime.TotalGameTime.TotalMilliseconds;

    //has the appropriate amount of time passed?
    if (gameTime.TotalGameTime.TotalMilliseconds >
        enemy.ChangeDirectionTimer + enemy.RandomSeconds * 1000)
    {
        enemy.RandomVelocity = Vector3.Zero;
        enemy.RandomVelocity.X = rand.Next(-1, 2);
        enemy.RandomVelocity.Y = rand.Next(-1, 2);
        //restrict to 2D?
        if (!restrictToXY)
            enemy.RandomVelocity.Z = rand.Next(-1, 2);

        enemy.ChangeDirectionTimer = 0;
    }

    enemy.Velocity = enemy.RandomVelocity;

    enemy.Velocity *= moveUnit;

    enemy.Color = Color.Orange;
}
```

Sometimes random movement can appear intelligent. Our method is utilizing the game time to keep track of how long the enemy should keep moving. It is very similar to the code we used for our fading method. This method checks to see if enough time has passed to change directions. Once enough time has elapsed, the enemy velocity vector is populated by random numbers ranging from –1 to 1. We need to add the following random number variable to our code:

```
private Random rand = new Random();
```

Random numbers are very important in AI work. We have taken care to not just have our enemies be jittery by changing directions every frame. As a result, we can have enemies that look like they are searching or patrolling. None of the code so far has been rocket science. All the algorithms are pretty simple but can provide great results.

We can replace our line in Update with the following:

```
MoveRandomly(enemy, gameTime);
```

18

Before we can run the code to see the results of our randomly moving enemies, we need to initialize our properties. We do this inside the enemy `for` loop in the `Initialize` method:

```
enemies[i].ChangeDirectionTimer = 0;
enemies[i].RandomVelocity = Vector3.Left;
enemies[i].RandomSeconds = (i + 2) / 2;
```

As we run the code, we can see that the enemies are moving around randomly. They are not moving in synchronization, and they definitely appear random.

Creating a Finite State Machine

We have three decent AI algorithms that we can apply to our enemies. However, it is likely that the enemies will want to perform each one of these behaviors at different times throughout their lives. This is where we can create an FSM and see how it can work in code. We discussed FSMs in the last chapter and really focused on game state. We can give our enemies a state machine that decides which state each enemy should be in. We will create an enumerated type with three states: Attack, Retreat, and Search. Each state will determine when it should change to another state. We will hook up the methods we have created to each state. We can start by creating the enumerated type in our `Enemy` class:

```
public enum AIState { Attack, Retreat, Search }
```

Next, we need to create a `State` property for the enemy by adding the following to our `Enemy` class:

```
public AIState State;
```

To help us know how to change states, we are going to add a `Health` property in which we will store a whole number from 1 to 10. The idea is that if the enemies have a lot of health, they will be more aggressive, but if they are low in health, they will run away. Of course, the enemies' personalities could be based on other things, so this is just an example. We can add a `Health` property to our `Enemy` class:

```
public int Health;
```

We can initialize these properties inside the enemy `for` loop in our `Initialize` method:

```
enemies[i].State = Enemy.AIState.Search;
//alternate every other enemy to either attack or evade (based on health)
if (i % 2 == 0)
    enemies[i].Health = 1;
else
    enemies[i].Health = 10;
```

We set each enemy to start out in a searching state. We also set every other enemy to have a high health or a low health. This will come into play soon as they decide whether they should attack or retreat.

Now we can set up our state machine in our Update method. We want to replace our call to the MoveRandomly method with the following switch statement:

```
switch (enemy.State)
{
    case Enemy.AIState.Search:
        {
            MoveRandomly(enemy, gameTime);
            break;
        }
    case Enemy.AIState.Attack:
        {
            TrackPlayer(enemy);
            break;
        }
    case Enemy.AIState.Retreat:
        {
            EvadePlayer(enemy);
            break;
        }
    default:
        {
            throw (new ApplicationException("Unknown State: " +
                enemy.State.ToString()));
        }
}
```

We are simply calling one of the methods we have set up based on the state the enemy is in. We have initialized our enemies to start in the Search state, which we have associated with the MoveRandomly method, but we have not created any way for them to actually change states. Each state will determine if a different state should be called. Our game states did the same thing. While the game was in a playing state, it would change to a paused state if the user pressed the Start button. Each state determines the next state. This means we need to modify the three methods being called every frame.

We are going to have the enemies continuously checking to see how close they are to the player. If they are close enough, they will change their state to either attacking or retreating, depending on how much health they have. We need to set up some constants to hold the radius in which the enemies will be looking for the player:

```
private const float SeekRadius = 75.0f;
private const float EvadeRadius = 75.0f;
```

We have set these to the same value, but we have the flexibility to modify them independently as we tweak the code. We can start modifying our methods by looking at the MoveRandomly method. This is our search method; as such, we need to do something if our search provides results. In other words, if the enemies stumble upon the player through their random movements, we need to change their state to either attack or retreat, depending on their health status. We can do that by adding the following code at the end of the MoveRandomly method:

```
float distance = (player.Position - enemy.Position).Length();


if (distance < EvadeRadius)
    if (enemy.Health < 5)
        enemy.State = Enemy.AIState.Retreat;

if (distance < SeekRadius)
    if (enemy.Health >= 5)
        enemy.State = Enemy.AIState.Attack;
```

We are simply getting the distance between the player and the enemy and checking to see if the distance is within the radius check. If it is, we check the enemy's health and change the state to attack or retreat, as appropriate.

Next, we can modify the EvadePlayer method by adding the following condition to the end of the method:

```
if (distance > EvadeRadius * 1.25f)
    enemy.State = Enemy.AIState.Search;
```

We are simply checking to see if the enemy is more than 25% further away than the evade radius. If it is, we can put the enemy back into random mode by setting the state to Search. We declare and set the local distance variable right after our first line and before we normalize our vector. We need to add the following line:

```
float distance = tv.Length();

```

We can update both TrackPlayer and TrackPlayerStraightLine by adding the following code to the end of the methods:

```
float distance = (enemy.Position - player.Position).Length();
if (distance > SeekRadius * 1.25f)
    enemy.State = Enemy.AIState.Search;
```

All of this code is doing the same thing: It is getting the length of the vector between the player and the enemy, and if the enemy is close enough we change its state back into search mode. We can run our code to see the enemies behaving differently.

We could also make a quick improvement by sending the retreating enemies back to the player's starting point if they are touched. We can also send the player to the origin if an enemy touches the player. Now if an enemy gets the player while at the origin, there is no way to get loose and the game is over.

To make this modification, we need to add the following conditions at the end of our enemy foreach loop in the Update method:

```
//reset player or enemy if collided
if ((enemy.Position - player.Position).Length() <
    (sphere.Meshes[0].BoundingSphere.Radius * 2))
{
    if (enemy.State == Enemy.AIState.Attack)
        player.Position.X = player.Position.Y = 0;
    else
        enemy.Position.X = enemy.Position.Y = 0;
}
```

This simply checks to see if an enemy has collided with the player. Depending on the state of the enemy, either the player is sent to its initial starting point or the enemy is. Now we can come up with different algorithms and have a test bed in which to try them out.

Summary

We have touched on only a few AI algorithms. The field is broad, and volumes of books have been written on the subject. This chapter's purpose was to introduce the concepts so you can research some more in-depth ways to make your game characters come to life. Other AI topics include path finding, fuzzy logic, minimap trees, and neural networks (having our AI creatures actually remember things). For example, "The last time the player did x and y, he did z right after, so let me get ready for that in the next frame."

We discussed how to create an enemy that tracks the player, evades the player, and moves randomly (or searches for the player). We put the concept of the FSM (which you learned about in the last chapter) into practice in this chapter. You saw how each state could determine which state the enemy should be in next. We finished up by making a small game with the player trying to catch the fleeing enemies without being caught by the attacking enemies.

The AI we add to our games can be very simplistic or very complex. Certain simplistic algorithms like the ones you saw in this chapter can be very effective in many games. When we are working on core opponents of the player, we definitely want to create an FSM with many states. For example, it might be that the enemy attacks in different ways based on the weapon the player has. It might be the enemies appear erratic in their movement, even as they are attacking, to keep the player on his or her toes. The sky is the limit with this material.

18

PART VIII

3D Effects

CHAPTER 19

Advanced Texturing Techniques

In this chapter, we are going to light our scene using more realistic lights. We also discuss some ways we can create better texturing effects to provide more realism in our games.

3D Lighting

Before we can really get down to business on some of the ways we can texture our objects to make them appear more realistic, we need to discuss lighting in more detail. The only way we can get a realistic effect on our textures is to have lights shining on them appropriately. Some of the common lighting algorithms include ambient lighting, directional lighting, point lights, spotlights, and specular lighting. We discuss the first two types of lights in this chapter.

Creating a Custom Vertex Format

To get started, we are going to create a demo that allows us to texture the rectangle we created in Chapter 4, "Creating 3D Objects." We need to create a new solution called AdvancedTexturingDemo. We are going to be modifying our XELibrary, so we need to add that project to our solution and reference it as a project.

We need to create a new struct for our XELibrary. We'll call our new code file VertexPositionNormalTexture.cs, which will hold our vertex declaration. When we created our first rectangle, we used the `VertexPositionNormalTexture` struct that XNA has built in. This struct describes the vertex data. It stores the position, texture coordinates, and normal of the vertex. Although we could get by with it for this lighting demo, the next section is going to need tangent information, so we will spend the time now to set up our own struct to handle all the data we need for this chapter. The code for our struct is shown in Listing 19.1.

LISTING 19.1   VertexPositionNormalTexture.cs

```csharp
using System;
using System.Collections.Generic;
using Microsoft.Xna.Framework;
using Microsoft.Xna.Framework.Graphics;

namespace XELibrary
{
    public struct VertexPositionNormalTangentTexture
    {
        public Vector3 Position;
        public Vector3 Normal;
        public Vector3 Tangent;
        public Vector2 TextureCoordinate;

        public VertexPositionNormalTangentTexture(
            Vector3 Position,
            Vector3 Normal,
            Vector3 Tangent,
            Vector2 TextureCoordinate)
        {
            this.Position = Position;
            this.Normal = Normal;
            this.Tangent = Tangent;
            this.TextureCoordinate = TextureCoordinate;
        }

        public static int SizeInBytes = 11 * sizeof(float);

        public static VertexElement[] VertexElements =
            {
                new VertexElement(0, 0,
            VertexElementFormat.Vector3,
                    VertexElementMethod.Default,
                    VertexElementUsage.Position, 0),
                new VertexElement(0, sizeof(float)*3,
                    VertexElementFormat.Vector3,
                    VertexElementMethod.Default,
                    VertexElementUsage.Normal, 0),
                new VertexElement(0, sizeof(float)*6,
```

```
                    VertexElementFormat.Vector3,
                    VertexElementMethod.Default,
                    VertexElementUsage.Tangent, 0),
                new VertexElement(0, sizeof(float)*9,
                    VertexElementFormat.Vector2,
                    VertexElementMethod.Default,
                    VertexElementUsage.TextureCoordinate, 0)
            };
    }
}
```

Our struct is going to store our vertex position, normal, tangent, and texture coordinates. The only new piece of data is our tangent. When loading models, we can store the tangent data with the model, so a vertex declaration would not be needed. Most likely the reading of the model data would be done in a custom content processor. An excellent example of this is the NormalMapSample, found on the XNA Creator's Club website (http://creators.xna.com/). This sample code uses an .fbx model that includes additional information extracted by the custom content processor. This way, it can be loaded just like any other asset, and the information will automatically be passed to our shaders.

However, we are not loading data from an outside source. Instead, we are using our sample rectangle, so we need to specify the type of data we are storing for each of our vertices. Our struct has a public static variable called SizeInBytes. This is to mimic the vertex declaration structs built in by XNA. We need to use this information when we set up our vertex buffer. The struct has three Vector3 types and one Vector2 type. That's a total of 11 floats. Therefore, we hard-code the SizeInBytes variable to return 11 times the size of our float value.

We need an array to store the vertex elements. This is what describes the properties we expose in our struct. When we initialize our vertex declaration in our game code, we have to pass in an array of vertex elements. We followed XNA's lead and called it VertexElements. We have four properties, so our array has four elements. The constructor for the VertexElement takes in the stream number to use. We will always use the first data stream. The second parameter is where we set the offset in the stream this element starts. Therefore, the first element in the first stream starts with no offset (zero). The next element's offset is at sizeof(float) * 3 because our first element was a Vector3 type (which holds three floats). Likewise, the next element bumps the total by another three floats. The next parameter we pass in is the actual type of data, and the next parameter we always pass in is VertexElementMethod.Default. This parameter rarely needs to be anything else. The purpose of the parameter is to tell the tessellator how to process the vertex data. We do not want it to do any additional calculations, so we leave it set to the default method. The other three options are LookUp, LookUpPresampled, and UV. More information on these methods can be found in the documentation. The next-to-last parameter tells XNA how the vertex element data is going to be used. The possible values are Position, BlendWeight, BlendIndices, Normal, PointSize, TextureCoordinate, Tangent,

`Binormal`, `TessellateFactor`, `Color`, `Fog`, `Depth`, and `Sample`. We are using `Position`, `Normal`, `Tangent`, and `TextureCoordinate` for our vertices. The final parameter is the usage index. This would be used if we wanted to store information in an additional usage type. For example, if we need to store information that did not have a specific usage type predefined, we could reuse the `TextureCoordinate` and pass in 1 as the usage index.

Creating the Demo

The demo we are creating allows us to easily switch between the different effects we are going to be discussing this chapter. We are going to start with ambient lighting because we discussed it in Chapter 15, "Advanced HLSL." Then we finish this 3D lighting section of the chapter with directional lighting. The next sections we add in different mapping techniques.

To begin with, we need to add our using XELibrary statement, and we need to add the following private member fields to our Game1.cs code:

```
private FirstPersonCamera camera;
private InputHandler input;

private VertexPositionNormalTangentTexture[] vertices;
private VertexBuffer vertexBuffer;
private VertexDeclaration vertexDeclaration;
private short[] indices;

private Effect ambientEffect;
private Effect currentEffect;
private Texture2D colorMap;
```

There is nothing surprising here. We have our favorite game components `FirstPersonCamera` and `InputHandler`. In Chapter 4, we used `VertexPositionNormalTexture`, but now we are using our custom `VertexPositionNormalTangentTexture` struct. We set up a field to reference our ambient effect and our texture (which we called color map).

Inside our constructor we need to set up our game components like normal:

```
input = new InputHandler(this, true);
Components.Add(input);
camera = new FirstPersonCamera(this);
Components.Add(camera);
```

Now we need to add in the same methods we created in Chapter 4 to set up the vertices that create our rectangle:

```
private void InitializeVertices()
{
    Vector3 position;
```

```
        Vector2 textureCoordinates;

        vertices = new VertexPositionNormalTangentTexture[4];

        //top left
        position = new Vector3(-1, 1, 0);
        textureCoordinates = new Vector2(0, 0);
        vertices[0] = new VertexPositionNormalTangentTexture(position,
            Vector3.Forward, Vector3.Left, textureCoordinates);
        //bottom right
        position = new Vector3(1, -1, 0);
        textureCoordinates = new Vector2(1, 1);
        vertices[1] = new VertexPositionNormalTangentTexture(position,
            Vector3.Forward, Vector3.Left, textureCoordinates);

        //bottom left
        position = new Vector3(-1, -1, 0);
        textureCoordinates = new Vector2(0, 1);
        vertices[2] = new VertexPositionNormalTangentTexture(position,
            Vector3.Forward, Vector3.Left, textureCoordinates);

        //top right
        position = new Vector3(1, 1, 0);
        textureCoordinates = new Vector2(1, 0);
        vertices[3] = new VertexPositionNormalTangentTexture(position,
            Vector3.Forward, Vector3.Left, textureCoordinates);

        vertexBuffer = new VertexBuffer(graphics.GraphicsDevice,
            VertexPositionNormalTangentTexture.SizeInBytes * vertices.Length,
            BufferUsage.WriteOnly);
        vertexBuffer.SetData<VertexPositionNormalTangentTexture>(vertices);
}

private void InitializeIndices()
{
        //six vertices make up two triangles, which make up our rectangle
        indices = new short[6];
        //triangle 1 (bottom portion)
        indices[0] = 0; // top left
        indices[1] = 1; // bottom right
        indices[2] = 2; // bottom left

        //triangle 2 (top portion)
        indices[3] = 0; // top left
        indices[4] = 3; // top right
```

19

```
    indices[5] = 1; // bottom right
}
```

These methods are identical to how we left them in Chapter 4, but the only difference is that we are now setting the tangent vector. We simply set it to Vector3.Left because our normal is set to Vector3.Up. Neither the normal nor tangent data is needed for ambient lighting. They are ignored in our current shader. We discuss the normal when we look at directional lighting. We discuss how the tangent vector relates to the normal vector later in this chapter. The InitializeIndices method did not change at all and is only listed here to avoid page flipping.

Inside our Initialize method, we need to call those two methods and set up our vertex declaration. The code to do that is as follows:

```
InitializeVertices();
InitializeIndices();

//Initialize our Vertex Declaration
vertexDeclaration = new VertexDeclaration(graphics.GraphicsDevice,
    VertexPositionNormalTangentTexture.VertexElements);
```

The only change is that we are now referencing our newly created custom vertex type.

Inside the LoadContent method, we need to load our content by adding the following code:

```
colorMap = Content.Load<Texture2D>(@"Textures\rockbump_color");
ambientEffect = Content.Load<Effect>(@"Effects\AmbientTexture");
currentEffect = ambientEffect;
```

We need to add our color map (texture) so we can apply the correct colors to the correct pixels. We also initialize our ambient effect. Finally, we set our currentEffect variable to our ambient light effect (which happens to be our only effect at this point).

Next, we need to draw our rectangle on the screen with our ambient light effect. The following code should be very familiar:

```
graphics.GraphicsDevice.RenderState.CullMode = CullMode.None;
graphics.GraphicsDevice.VertexDeclaration = vertexDeclaration;

Matrix world = Matrix.CreateScale(100.0f) * Matrix.CreateTranslation(
    new Vector3(0, 0, -450));
currentEffect.Parameters["World"].SetValue(world);
currentEffect.Parameters["View"].SetValue(camera.View);
currentEffect.Parameters["Projection"].SetValue(camera.Projection);

currentEffect.Parameters["AmbientColor"].SetValue(.8f);
```

```
currentEffect.Parameters["ColorMap"].SetValue(colorMap);

currentEffect.Begin();

foreach (EffectPass pass in currentEffect.CurrentTechnique.Passes)
{
    pass.Begin();

    graphics.GraphicsDevice.DrawUserIndexedPrimitives
        <VertexPositionNormalTangentTexture>(
        PrimitiveType.TriangleList, vertices, 0, vertices.Length,
        indices, 0, indices.Length / 3);

    pass.End();
}

currentEffect.End();
```

Because we are just drawing a rectangle, we have turned off culling. This way if we move behind the rectangle we will still be able to see it (although, depending on the effect, it might be black). We scale our rectangle and move it back in our world some, mainly so we can get an interesting lighting effect later on. The code is pretty much the same as it was in Chapter 4—the only difference is that we are using our new struct.

Ambient Lighting

Now that we have our demo set up, we need to create the ambient effect we referenced earlier. We can add our Effects folder to the Content project. We start with the previous AmbientTexture.fx file from Chapter 14, "HLSL Basics." You can find the starting code in Listing 19.2.

LISTING 19.2   AmbientTexture.fx

```
float4x4 World : WORLD;
float4x4 View;
float4x4 Projection;

float4 AmbientColor : COLOR0;

float4x4 WorldViewProjection : WORLDVIEWPROJECTION;
texture ColorMap;
sampler ColorMapSampler = sampler_state
{
    texture = < ColorMap >;
```

```
    magfilter = LINEAR;
    minfilter = LINEAR;
    mipfilter = LINEAR;
    addressU = mirror;
    addressV = mirror;
};

struct VertexInput
{
    float4 Position : POSITION0;
    float2 TexCoord : TEXCOORD0;
};

struct VertexOutput
{
    float4 Position : POSITION0;
    float2 TexCoord : TEXCOORD0;
};

VertexOutput vertexShader(VertexInput input)
{
    VertexOutput output = (VertexOutput)0;
    WorldViewProjection = mul(mul(World, View), Projection);
    output.Position = mul(input.Position, WorldViewProjection);
    output.TexCoord = input.TexCoord;

    return( output );
}

struct PixelInput
{
    float2 TexCoord : TEXCOORD0;
};

float4 pixelShader(PixelInput input) : COLOR
{
    return( tex2D(ColorMapSampler, input.TexCoord) * AmbientColor);
}

technique Default
{
    pass P0
    {
        VertexShader = compile vs_1_1 vertexShader();
```

```
        PixelShader = compile ps_1_1 pixelShader();
    }
}
```

This code is not exactly how we left it, but there are only two small modifications. The first is that we removed the vertex displacement; the second is that we renamed `Texture` to `ColorMap`. The purpose of the texture has not changed: It is there to provide the color pixels of our object. In later sections we are going to be adding more textures that have different purposes. They all map onto the 3D object, but do so for different reasons. We are just preparing for that now by calling our texture our color map. We need to put the rockbump_color.jpg file in our Textures folder. We can compile our demo and see the rectangle with our sample texture using the same ambient light from Chapter 15.

Directional Lighting

When we first created our 3D rectangle in Chapter 4, we set a normal vector for our vertex. I just briefly explained a normal, stating that it was used for lighting. Well, now you can see exactly how a vertex normal can help us light our objects better. This is going to require some vector and matrix math.

A *normal* is a vector that is perpendicular to the surface of a triangle. We know that every 3D object is made up of a bunch of vertices and that we use triangles that connect those points to create complex objects. Each triangle has a normal, which basically tells us in which direction the triangle is facing. This is very important when trying to calculate how well lit or how dark a triangle is. Triangles facing away (their normal vector is in the opposite direction of the light) will not be lit by that light, whereas triangles facing directly toward the light will be greatly lit. If the light source is close enough, the triangle will be white (or whatever color the light is).

The other piece to this is our light, of course. We know which direction our triangles are facing, and now we just need to know where our light source is. Where is it pointing, and how far away is it? We can specify both of those values with a vector. This is where the vector math comes in. We are going to take the dot product of both of those vectors to determine the angular relationship between them. This can be seen in Figure 19.1.

The larger the angle is between the two vectors, the darker the surface will be. The smaller the angle, the more lit the surface will be. We are only going to be talking about directional lighting in this section, but other lighting techniques do exist. The common light algorithms are ambient, directional, point, spot, and specular. Point, spot, and specular light algorithms can be found on the Web in many places, so we will not spend time on them in this book. The concepts are the same, but the algorithms change between them to better model the type of light they are mimicking.

Let's take a look at the code needed to create a directional light. We need to make a few changes to our game code. First, we need to add the following private member fields for our directional light:

```
private Vector3 LightPosition;
private Effect directionalEffect;
```

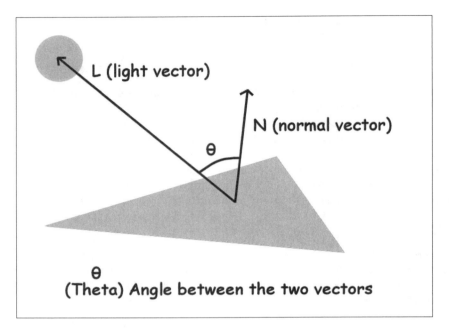

FIGURE 19.1 The normal vector is perpendicular to our triangle. The light vector is the line from our light vector to the origin of the normal vector.

We can initialize our light position in our `Initialize` method:

```
LightPosition = new Vector3(0, 0, -500);
```

We can initialize our directional light effect in our `LoadContent` method:

```
directionalEffect = Content.Load<Effect>(@"Effects\DirectionalLight");
```

We want to be able to switch between our different effects easily. We also want to be able to move the light we set up. Therefore, we add the following code to our `Update` method:

```
if (input.KeyboardState.IsHoldingKey(Keys.Z))
    LightPosition.Y++;
if (input.KeyboardState.IsHoldingKey(Keys.X))
    LightPosition.Y--;

Window.Title = "LightPosition: " + LightPosition.ToString();

if (input.KeyboardState.WasKeyPressed(Keys.D1))
    currentEffect = ambientEffect;
if (input.KeyboardState.WasKeyPressed(Keys.D2))
    currentEffect = directionalEffect;
```

There is nothing shocking here—we just update the position of our light if we press the Z or X key. We update our window title caption with our updated light position. We change our current effect by pressing the 1 and 2 keys.

In the Draw method, we need to add the light position to our effect's parameters:

```
if (currentEffect.Parameters["LightPosition"] != null)
    currentEffect.Parameters["LightPosition"].SetValue(LightPosition);
```

Now we just need to create our DirectionalLight.fx file. This file needs to be put into our Effects folder. The HLSL code can be found in Listing 19.3.

LISTING 19.3   DirectionalLight.fx

```
float4x4 World : WORLD;
float4x4 View;
float4x4 Projection;

float4 AmbientColor : COLOR0;
float3 LightPosition;

texture ColorMap;

sampler2D ColorMapSampler = sampler_state
{
    texture = <ColorMap>;
    magfilter = LINEAR;
    minfilter = LINEAR;
    mipfilter = LINEAR;
    addressU = mirror;
    addressV = mirror;
};

struct VertexInput
{
    float3 Position : POSITION;
    float3 Normal : NORMAL;
    float2 TexCoord : TEXCOORD0;
};

struct VertexOutput
{
    float4 Position : POSITION;
    float2 TexCoord : TEXCOORD0;
    float3 WorldSpacePosition : TEXCOORD1;
    float3 Normal : TEXCOORD2;
};
```

```
VertexOutput vertexShader(VertexInput input)
{
    VertexOutput output;
    output.WorldSpacePosition = mul(float4(input.Position, 1.0f), World);
    float4x4 worldViewProjection = mul(mul(World, View), Projection);
    output.Position = mul(float4(input.Position, 1.0f), worldViewProjection);
    output.TexCoord = input.TexCoord;
    output.Normal = normalize(mul(input.Normal, World));
    return output;
}


float4 pixelShader(VertexOutput input) : COLOR
{
    float3 LightDirection = normalize(LightPosition - input.WorldSpacePosition);
    float DiffuseLight = dot(LightDirection, input.Normal);

    return( tex2D(ColorMapSampler, input.TexCoord) * DiffuseLight + AmbientColor);
}


technique Default
{
    pass P0
    {
        VertexShader = compile vs_2_0 vertexShader();
        PixelShader = compile ps_2_0 pixelShader();
    }
}
```

Only the code shown in bold type changed from our ambient HLSL code. We added two variables to hold our light position and our diffuse light color. This is the color that is spread across the surfaces the light hits. Our vertex input struct takes in the normal passed in from our demo. We output the world position of our vertex along with the texture coordinates of our normal map texture and the diffuse color of our light.

Our vertex shader translates our vertex position into world space so our pixel shader can work with the position in world space. We calculate the inverse transpose of our world view projection matrix. This could be done inside our demo code instead of inside of HLSL.

In our pixel shader we calculate the light direction by normalizing the vector between our vertex position and our light position. Our diffuse light color is then calculated by taking the dot product of our light direction and our normal.

The key to this shader is that our normal is passed in as part of the vertex. It is then passed to the pixel shader so that all the pixels around the vertex can be shaded appropriately.

Each pixel in a triangle surface has the exact same normal—that is, the normal of the triangle itself. This might be sufficient in some scenarios, but we can actually set normal data per pixel. You will see how to do that in the next section of this chapter.

Bump Mapping

Bump mapping is a general term used to describe providing some kind of roughness to an object by texturing the object. The object will look complex on the screen with many divots, dimples, and bumps, but the actual 3D object is smooth. The object looks "bumpy" because of mapping our texture(s) onto it a little differently than we have so far.

Normal Mapping

Not only do we have our color map, but we will also have a normal map. This normal map is a texture that describes a normal for each and every pixel. Instead of using the vertex's normal for all the pixels on a triangle, we can declare each one individually. This is done with the RGB values of each pixel in the texture.

Normals pointing forward will have the RGB value 127,127,255. This is a purplish blue color. Normals pointing to the right will have the RGB value 255,127,255. This is a pink color. Normals pointing up will have an RGB value of 127,255,127. This is a greenish color.

Normal maps can be created by taking a grayscale of a color map (often called a bump map, height map, or depth map) and running it through a processor that converts it. NVIDIA has a plug-in that does this; it is available for PhotoShop. There is a free plug-in for Paint.NET as well. Of course, this can also be done through code. We could create a custom content processor to handle this. In fact, the SpriteEffects sample on the Creator's Club website (http://creators.xna.com/) contains a sample processor that does exactly that.

By having a normal map, our flat object can appear to have much more detail. This is because the light will modify the color of the pixel based on the normal associated with that pixel. Not only do we need to know the normal of our pixel, but we also need to know the tangent of our pixel as well as the binormal (also known as the *bitangent*) of the pixel. For our example, we are setting the binormals manually because we are creating our vertices by hand. The tangent will be perpendicular to our normal. The binormal can be calculated by taking the cross-product of our tangent vector and our normal vector. These vectors describe to the shader the way that the "up" direction has been mapped onto the geometry. This way, the shader will know how to transform the light direction from world space into the 2D coordinate system used by the normal map texture.

The HLSL code to produce this effect is in Listing 19.4.

LISTING 19.4   NormalMapping.fx

```
float4x4 World : WORLD;
float4x4 View;
float4x4 Projection;
```

```
float4 AmbientColor : COLOR0;
float3 LightPosition;
float4 LightDiffuseColor : COLOR1;

texture ColorMap;

sampler2D ColorMapSampler = sampler_state
{
    texture = <ColorMap>;
    magfilter = LINEAR;
    minfilter = LINEAR;
    mipfilter = LINEAR;
    addressU = mirror;
    addressV = mirror;
};


texture2D NormalMap;

sampler2D NormalMapSampler = sampler_state
{
    texture = <NormalMap>;
    minFilter = linear;
    magFilter = linear;
    mipFilter = linear;
};

struct VertexInput
{
    float3 Position : POSITION;
    float3 Normal : NORMAL;
    float3 Tangent : TANGENT;
    float2 TexCoord : TEXCOORD0;
};

struct VertexOutput
{
    float4 Position : POSITION;
    float2 TexCoord : TEXCOORD0;
    float3 LightDirection : TEXCOORD1;
    float2 Normal : TEXCOORD2;
};

VertexOutput vertexShader(VertexInput input)
{
```

```
    VertexOutput output;
    output.LightDirection = LightPosition - input.Position;

    float4x4 worldViewProjection = mul(mul(World, View), Projection);
    output.Position = mul(float4(input.Position, 1.0f), worldViewProjection);
    output.TexCoord = input.TexCoord;
    output.Normal = input.TexCoord;

    float3x3 tbnMatrix;
    tbnMatrix[0] = mul(input.Tangent, worldViewProjection);
    tbnMatrix[1] = mul(cross(input.Tangent, input.Normal),
        worldViewProjection);
    tbnMatrix[2] = mul(input.Normal, World);
    output.LightDirection = mul(tbnMatrix, output.LightDirection);
    return(output);
}

float4 pixelShader(VertexOutput input) : COLOR
{
    input.LightDirection = normalize(input.LightDirection);

    float3 Normal = 2.0f * (tex2D(NormalMapSampler, input.Normal).rgb - 0.5f);

    return( (LightDiffuseColor * saturate(dot(input.LightDirection, Normal)) +
        AmbientColor) * tex2D(ColorMapSampler, input.TexCoord));
}

technique Default
{
    pass P0
    {
        VertexShader = compile vs_2_0 vertexShader();
        PixelShader = compile ps_2_0 pixelShader();
    }
}
```

19

We can call this file NormalMapping.fx. We have added a global variable where we can set our light diffuse color. In our vertex input struct, we added a tangent vector. Instead of calculating our light direction inside the pixel shader, we are calculating it inside the vertex shader and passing it in with our new LightDirection vector in our VertexOutput struct.

To start the vertex shader, we calculate our light direction vector. We use this value a little later in the function. Our normal is not calculated like it was in the last effect. Instead, it is read in from our normal map. Next we transform our light vector into tangent space (sometimes this is called *texture space*). We need to do this transformation so that our math is being done in the right coordinate system. To do this, we create a matrix that is called a *tangent binormal normal (TBN)* matrix. We take the product of our tangent and our inverse transposed world matrix and store that in our first row. The second row gets the cross-product of our tangent and our normal. The third row gets the product of our normal and the inverse transposed world view projection matrix. After creating the TBN matrix, we can multiply that by our light direction vector to transform it into tangent space.

The pixel shader takes in this light direction and normalizes it for each pixel. The normal we have from our normal map has component values in the range of 0 to 1. We need them to be in the range of –1 to 1. To convert them we simply subtract .5 from our color and multiply that by 2. This changes the range like we need. The last thing the pixel shader does is calculate the diffuse color based on the dot product of our light direction vector and our normal. The saturate intrinsic function just clamps the value from 0 to 1. We factor in our light diffuse color along with the ambient color of our scene.

To see this effect in action, we need to modify our demo to load it. We need to add the following private member fields:

```
private Effect normalEffect;
private Texture2D normalMap;
```

Next, we need to initialize those variables inside our `LoadContent` method:

```
normalMap = Content.Load<Texture2D>(@"Textures\rockbump_normal");
normalEffect = Content.Load<Effect>(@"Effects\NormalMapping");
```

After adding our effect file to our Effects folder, we also need to add in our normal map to our Textures folder.

The `Update` method can be modified to allow us to easily switch between this effect and the other two by adding the following condition:

```
if (input.KeyboardState.WasKeyPressed(Keys.D3))
    currentEffect = normalEffect;
```

Finally, in our `Draw` method we need to add the two new parameters we added for this effect: our actual normal map and the diffuse color of the light. The code is shown here:

```
if (currentEffect.Parameters["LightDiffuseColor"] != null)
    currentEffect.Parameters["LightDiffuseColor"].SetValue(
        Color.White.ToVector4());

if (currentEffect.Parameters["NormalMap"] != null)
    currentEffect.Parameters["NormalMap"].SetValue(normalMap);
```

When we run the code, we can see a much better-looking texture. It has a lot more detail, which can easily be seen as we switch between effects by pressing 1, 2, or 3.

There is actually another type of normal mapping as well. We have been discussing tangent space normal mapping. Object space normal mapping is done by 3D modeling programs. We do not discuss it in this book, but the idea behind object space normal mapping is that two identical objects are made, one with a high polygon count with a lot of detail (one that could never make it in a game because of all the polygons) and another with a low polygon count (which is what we would use in our game). Inside the 3D modeling program the two objects are placed at the same point in the world. Then a special normal process is executed that creates normals from the low-polygon-count object to the high-polygon-count object. When used in a game, the end result is a 3D object with very little detail looking like it has a lot of detail because of the generated normal map.

Parallax Mapping

Although normal mapping gives us a lot of bang for our buck, there is another form of mapping that produces even nicer results. It takes a little more computation power, but it's worth it. This is the type of texture mapping that can be found in the game *Gears of War*. It is a variant of normal mapping. It adds another texture called a *depth map* (sometimes called a *height map*), so not only do we have our color map and our normal map, but we have a third map that specifies how high the pixels should be. Let's see how we implement this.

First, let's look at our new ParallaxMapping.fx file:

```
float4x4 World : WORLD;
float4x4 View;
float4x4 Projection;

float4 AmbientColor : COLOR0;
float3 LightPosition;
float4 LightDiffuseColor : COLOR1;

float2 ScaleAmount;
float3 CameraPosition;

texture ColorMap;

sampler2D ColorMapSampler = sampler_state
{
    texture = <ColorMap>;
    magfilter = LINEAR;
    minfilter = LINEAR;
    mipfilter = LINEAR;
```

```
        addressU = mirror;
        addressV = mirror;
};


texture2D NormalMap;

sampler2D NormalMapSampler = sampler_state
{
    texture = <NormalMap>;
    minFilter = linear;
    magFilter = linear;
    mipFilter = linear;
};


texture2D DepthMap;

sampler2D DepthMapSampler = sampler_state
{
    texture = <DepthMap>;
    minFilter = linear;
    magFilter = linear;
    mipFilter = linear;
};


struct VertexInput
{
    float3 Position : POSITION;
    float3 Normal : NORMAL;
    float3 Tangent : TANGENT;
    float2 TexCoord : TEXCOORD0;
};


struct VertexOutput
{
    float4 Position : POSITION;
    float2 TexCoord : TEXCOORD0;
    float3 LightDirection : TEXCOORD1;
    float2 Normal : TEXCOORD2;
    float3 ViewDirection : TEXCOORD3;
};
VertexOutput vertexShader(VertexInput input)
{
    VertexOutput output;

    output.LightDirection = LightPosition - input.Position;
```

```
    float3 worldPosition = mul(float4(input.Position, 1.0f), World).xyz;
    output.ViewDirection = worldPosition   - CameraPosition;

    float4x4 worldViewProjection = mul(mul(World, View), Projection);
    output.Position = mul(float4(input.Position, 1.0f), worldViewProjection);
    output.TexCoord = input.TexCoord;

    output.Normal = input.TexCoord;

    // Transform the light vector from object space into tangent space
    float3x3 tbnMatrix;
    tbnMatrix[0] = mul(input.Tangent, worldViewProjection);
    tbnMatrix[1] = mul(cross(input.Tangent, input.Normal),
        worldViewProjection);
    tbnMatrix[2] = mul(input.Normal, World);
    output.LightDirection = mul(tbnMatrix, output.LightDirection);
    output.ViewDirection = mul(tbnMatrix, output.ViewDirection);
    return(output);
}

float4 pixelShader(VertexOutput input) : COLOR
{
    float3 viewDirection = normalize(input.ViewDirection);
    float depth = ScaleAmount.x *
        (float)tex2D(DepthMapSampler, input.TexCoord) + ScaleAmount.y;
    input.TexCoord = depth * viewDirection + input.TexCoord;

    input.LightDirection = normalize(input.LightDirection);

    float3 Normal = 2.0f * (tex2D(NormalMapSampler, input.Normal).rgb - 0.5f);

    return( (LightDiffuseColor * saturate(dot(input.LightDirection, Normal)) +
        AmbientColor) * tex2D(ColorMapSampler, input.TexCoord));
}
technique Default
{
    pass P0
    {
        VertexShader = compile vs_2_0 vertexShader();
        PixelShader = compile ps_2_0 pixelShader();
    }
}
```

We discussed how we need an additional depth map for this effect. Not only did we add this new map, but we also added the camera position and the scale amount, which is simply the bias amount we are going to apply to our depth map.

In our vertex shader we calculate the view direction based on the camera position. We then transform it into tangent space, just like we did with our light direction vector.

In our pixel shader we normalize our view direction vector for each pixel. We then read in our depth value from our map and scale it based on the scale amount passed in. The last addition to the code is setting the color map texture coordinate, taking into account our view direction and the depth we just calculated. This stretches the color map a little to create a nice 3D effect on a 2D image. The rest of the pixel shader is unchanged from the normal mapping pixel shader.

We need to add the references to the effect and the depth map texture to our game code:

```
private Effect parallaxEffect;
private Texture2D depthMap;
```

We can initialize these variables in our LoadContent method:

```
depthMap = Content.Load<Texture2D>(@"Textures\rockbump_depth");
parallaxEffect = Content.Load<Effect>(@"Effects\ParallaxMapping");
```

We need to add our depth map texture to our solution. We also need to be able to switch to this effect in our demo. Therefore, we just need to add the following condition to our Update method:

```
if (input.KeyboardState.WasKeyPressed(Keys.D4))
    currentEffect = parallaxEffect;
```

Finally, we need to set this effect's parameters in our Draw method:

```
if (currentEffect.Parameters["DepthMap"] != null)
    currentEffect.Parameters["DepthMap"].SetValue(depthMap);
if (currentEffect.Parameters["ScaleAmount"] != null)
    currentEffect.Parameters["ScaleAmount"].SetValue(
        new Vector2(0.03f, -0.025f));
if (currentEffect.Parameters["CameraPosition"] != null)
    currentEffect.Parameters["CameraPosition"].SetValue(camera.Position);
```

The only value worth mentioning is our 2D vector that contains our scale bias amount. This is simply the amount the effect uses to add more depth by sampling an offset pixel. Parallax mapping can provide nice effects for our objects without having to actually create complex geometry.

Relief Mapping

The next advanced texturing technique we review is relief mapping. Relief mapping is similar to parallax mapping, but it does not require the additional depth map. The depth map is included in the normal map. It is in the alpha portion of the color for each pixel.

This keeps us from having to maintain and process another texture. We can call this HLSL code ReliefMapping.fx. The code for this shader is shown in Listing 19.5.

LISTING 19.5   ReliefMapping.fx

```
float4x4 World : WORLD;
float4x4 View;
float4x4 Projection;

float4 AmbientColor : COLOR0;
float3 LightPosition;
float4 LightDiffuseColor : COLOR1;

float2 ScaleAmount;
float3 CameraPosition;

texture ColorMap;
sampler2D ColorMapSampler = sampler_state
{
    texture = <ColorMap>;
    magfilter = LINEAR;
    minfilter = LINEAR;
    mipfilter = LINEAR;
    addressU = mirror;
    addressV = mirror;
};

texture2D ReliefMap;
sampler2D ReliefMapSampler = sampler_state
{
    texture = <ReliefMap>;
    minFilter = linear;
    magFilter = linear;
    mipFilter = linear;
};

struct VertexInput
{
    float3 Position : POSITION;
    float3 Normal : NORMAL;
    float3 Tangent : TANGENT;
    float2 TexCoord : TEXCOORD0;
};
```

```
struct VertexOutput
{
    float4 Position : POSITION;
    float2 TexCoord : TEXCOORD0;
    float3 LightDirection : TEXCOORD1;
    float3 ViewDirection : TEXCOORD3;
};

VertexOutput vertexShader(VertexInput input)
{
    VertexOutput output;
    output.LightDirection = LightPosition - input.Position;

    float3 worldPosition = mul(float4(input.Position, 1.0f), World).xyz;
    output.ViewDirection = worldPosition - CameraPosition;

    float4x4 worldViewProjection = mul(mul(World, View), Projection);
    output.Position = mul(float4(input.Position, 1.0f), worldViewProjection);
    output.TexCoord = input.TexCoord;

    float3x3 tbnMatrix;
    tbnMatrix[0] = mul(input.Tangent, worldViewProjection);
    tbnMatrix[1] = mul(cross(input.Tangent, input.Normal),
        worldViewProjection);
    tbnMatrix[2] = mul(input.Normal, World);
    output.LightDirection = mul(tbnMatrix, output.LightDirection);
    output.ViewDirection = mul(tbnMatrix, output.ViewDirection);

    return(output);
}

float4 pixelShader(VertexOutput input) : COLOR
{
    const int numStepsLinear = 15;   //linear search number of steps
    const int numStepsBinary = 6;    //binary search number of steps

    float3 position = float3(input.TexCoord,0);
    float3 viewDirection = normalize(input.ViewDirection);

    float depthBias = 1.0 - viewDirection.z;
    depthBias *= depthBias;
    depthBias *= depthBias;
    depthBias = 1.0 - depthBias * depthBias;
    viewDirection.xy *= depthBias;
    viewDirection.xy *= ScaleAmount;
```

```
// ray intersect depth map using linear and binary searches
// depth value stored in alpha channel (black at is object surface)
    viewDirection /= viewDirection.z * numStepsLinear;
    int i;
    for( i=0; i<numStepsLinear; i++ )
    {
        float4 tex = tex2D(ReliefMapSampler, position.xy);
        if (position.z < tex.w)
            position += viewDirection;
    }
    for( i=0; i<numStepsBinary; i++ )
    {
        viewDirection *= 0.5;
        float4 tex = tex2D(ReliefMapSampler, position.xy);
        if (position.z < tex.w)
            position += viewDirection;
        else
            position -= viewDirection;
    }

    input.TexCoord = position;
    //transform to tangent space
    viewDirection = normalize(input.ViewDirection);
    input.LightDirection = normalize(input.LightDirection);

    float3 Normal = 2.0f * (tex2D(ReliefMapSampler, input.TexCoord) - 0.5f);
    Normal.y = -Normal.y;
    Normal.z = sqrt(1.0 - Normal.x*Normal.x - Normal.y*Normal.y);

    return( (LightDiffuseColor * saturate(dot(input.LightDirection, Normal)) +
        AmbientColor) * tex2D(ColorMapSampler, input.TexCoord));
}

technique Default
{
    pass P0
    {
        VertexShader = compile vs_2_0 vertexShader();
        PixelShader = compile ps_2_a pixelShader();
    }
}
```

We removed the depth map sampler and changed the name of our normal map sampler to the relief map sampler. We also removed the normal from our VertexOutput and are no longer setting it in our vertex shader. That's all that changed in this part of the code. The biggest change is inside our pixel shader.

The pixel shader normalizes the viewing direction, just like we do for the parallax mapping pixel shader. After we modify a copy of the view direction vector to account for any additional depth bias we want, relief mapping does a linear search to find the first point inside the height-field surface that our viewing direction intersects. Once this is done, the binary search is carried out to narrow down the point of intersection. The reason the algorithm starts with a linear search instead of just using a binary search is because if the view ray intersects the height-field in more than one place, it could easily return the wrong intersection. By starting in a linear fashion, this is avoided. Another variation of this algorithm is called `IntervalMapping`. We do not discuss that variant, but it works the same way, except it uses a secondary linear search instead of a binary search. In some cases it can perform better because it does not take as long to find the intersection.

After the binary search is completed, we normalize our unmodified view direction from our input as well as our light direction. We then calculate the normal based on the calculated position. We use the same position to retrieve the color from our color map.

In our game code we need to add the following private member fields:

```
private Effect reliefEffect;
private Texture2D reliefMap;
```

As usual, we need to initialize these in the `LoadContent` method:

```
reliefMap = Content.Load<Texture2D>(@"Textures\rockbump_relief");
reliefEffect = Content.Load<Effect>(@"Effects\ReliefMapping");
```

In the `Update` method, we allow changing to this effect by pressing the 5 key:

```
if (input.KeyboardState.WasKeyPressed(Keys.D5))
    currentEffect = reliefEffect;
```

Finally, we need to set the relief map parameter in our effect:

```
if (currentEffect.Parameters["ReliefMap"] != null)
    currentEffect.Parameters["ReliefMap"].SetValue(reliefMap);
```

We can now run our demo and see the nice effect relief mapping gives us. We now have many different ways to map textures onto our 3D objects. Our relief mapping allows self-shadowing, which provides very nice results without the need for additional geometry.

Texture Animation

In this last section of the chapter, we discussed a relatively simple but effective texturing technique. We are now going to see how we can animate a texture. In this demo we will be texturing our rectangle, but we could easily do the same thing with a loaded 3D object such as our asteroid.

We need to set up a new solution, which we can call AnimateTextureDemo. We need to reference our XELibrary, but it is not necessary to actually include the project in the solution. We need to create the Textures and Effects folders in the Content project.

After our solution is created, we can create a new effect file called AnimateTexture.fx. This effect will be identical to the DirectionalLight.fx file we used in a previous section of this chapter. We only need to change one line of code and add the following variable:

```
float2 Offset;
```

We are changing our pixel shader's return value to include the offset that our demo will pass in. We need to replace the line

```
return( tex2D(ColorMapSampler, input.TexCoord) * DiffuseLight + AmbientColor);
```

with this line:

```
return( tex2D(ColorMapSampler, input.TexCoord + Offset) *
    DiffuseLight + AmbientColor);
```

We've simply added the offset 2D vector to our 2D texture coordinates.

Our Game1.cs file will need the InitializeVertices and InitializeIndices methods from the previous demo. All the vertex information needs to be added to the code. (I will not list it here because it is listed earlier in this chapter.) We need to set up a camera and our input handler. We also need to add the following private member fields to our demo:

```
private Effect effect;
private Texture2D colorMap;
private Vector3 LightPosition;
private Vector2 offset = Vector2.Zero;
```

We can initialize our light position inside of the Initialize method:

```
LightPosition = new Vector3(0, 0, -300);
```

We can set up our colorMap and our effect in the LoadContent method:

```
colorMap = Content.Load<Texture2D>(@"Textures\example");
effect = Content.Load<Effect>(@"Effects\AnimateTexture");
effect.Parameters["AmbientColor"].SetValue(.05f);
effect.Parameters["ColorMap"].SetValue(colorMap);
effect.Parameters["LightPosition"].SetValue(LightPosition);
```

Because those values are not going to change per frame, we just set them once when we set up our effect. We are going to animate our texture based on the game's timer. We want it to update every frame, so we can add the following lines to the Update method:

```
offset.X += (float)gameTime.ElapsedGameTime.TotalSeconds * 0.0333f;
offset.Y += (float)gameTime.ElapsedGameTime.TotalSeconds * 0.0033f;
```

We are simply adding a small amount to our offset value that will get passed to our shader. We are going to scroll horizontally faster than we will scroll vertically. Our Draw method will be similar to our previous project. The difference is that we do not need to set all the different values for the different mapping techniques. Also we are adding in our offset parameter. We need to insert the following code into the Draw method:

```
Matrix world = Matrix.CreateScale(100.0f) *
    Matrix.CreateTranslation(new Vector3(0, 0, -250));
effect.Parameters["World"].SetValue(world);
effect.Parameters["View"].SetValue(camera.View);
effect.Parameters["Projection"].SetValue(camera.Projection);
effect.Parameters["Offset"].SetValue(offset);
```

When we run the demo, we can see texture scrolling to the left and up. We would just need to subtract our values from the X and Y components of our offset to reverse the direction. Our shader has set the addressU and addressV values of our texture sampler to mirror. As a result, when our texture scrolls, it is a mirror image of itself. If we just wanted the texture to wrap without mirroring itself, we could change those values to wrap instead. Another option is clamp, which would result in our texture moving off the rectangle entirely. Of course, addressU and addressV can store different values. For example, we could set addressU to wrap and addressV to mirror.

TIP

A great example of how we could use the addressU and addressV values in a real application would be to create multiple layers of alpha blended textures scrolling in different directions. By doing this, we could create effects such as water, clouds, and even plasma fields.

Summary

In this chapter we discussed how to set up a directional light and reviewed our ambient light. We then discussed different types of bump mapping. We looked at normal mapping, which just uses a normal map (RGB values) to determine the normal of each pixel so that when lights shine on it, the object appears to have depth even though there is no extra geometry. Then we discussed parallax mapping, which takes in a depth (height) map in addition to the normal map. This extra data adds depth to objects. The last mapping technique we discussed was relief mapping. This also uses depth information, but it uses this information inside the alpha channel of the normal map. This way, there is no need to store and process an additional texture. It also allows self-shadowing for producing much more realistic results.

We finished up the chapter by discussing texture animation. You saw how easy it is to animate a texture on a 3D object by simply adding an offset to the texture coordinates. We updated that offset every frame with our game time. This allowed our texture to scroll left to right and up and down in a slow diagonal movement.

Special Effects

Creating special effects is a great way to polish games. Most of the time special effects are not absolutely critical to game play, but they really add the extra special touch our games need to stand out from the crowd. In this chapter we discuss transitions as well as the improved "new school" way of creating a procedural fire effect.

Transitions

We have already touched on one transition in this book—fading. We have faded to black, and we have faded to a specified color. This fade is simple and can help give our game that polished look. However, we can easily try a couple more transition techniques. One of these techniques builds on top of the knowledge you gained doing the fade-to-color transition.

Before we continue in this section, we need to create a new project called TransitionsDemo. We only need to reference the XELibrary because we will not be modifying the code in this chapter. There is no need to add the actual XELibrary project to our solution.

We need to add our private member fields:

```
private enum TransitionState { None, CrossFade, Wipe };


private FirstPersonCamera camera;
private InputHandler input;

private Model model;
private Texture2D texture;
```

```
private Effect effect;

private Texture2D splashScreen;

private RenderTarget2D renderTarget;

private TransitionState state = TransitionState.CrossFade;
```

We are going to be transitioning from a 3D scene to a 2D scene. We are simulating fading into the start menu. We have set up an enumerated type to store the different states in this demo. "None" could really be "playing" because it means no transitions are taking place. We are going to create the CrossFade and Wipe transitions after we get the framework set up for this demo.

Because we are transitioning from a 3D scene, we need to render our 3D scene into a 2D texture. This is where the render target comes in. Finally, we create our demo state field, which we also initialize to the cross-fade effect.

We do not want to break tradition, so we will look at the code we need to add to our constructor:

```
graphics.PreferredBackBufferWidth = 1280;
graphics.PreferredBackBufferHeight = 720;

input = new InputHandler(this, true);
Components.Add(input);

camera = new FirstPersonCamera(this);
Components.Add(camera);
```

We are going to be using the same splash screen we used in Chapter 9, "2D Basics." This texture is 1280×720, so we are asking our graphics device to use that resolution. We set up our input handler and our camera as usual.

We need to add the following code in the LoadContent method:

```
model = Content.Load<Model>(@"Models\asteroid1");
texture = Content.Load<Texture2D>(@"Textures\asteroid1");
effect = Content.Load<Effect>(@"Effects\AmbientTexture");
splashScreen = Content.Load<Texture2D>(@"Textures\splashscreen");

renderTarget = new RenderTarget2D(GraphicsDevice, GraphicsDevice.Viewport.Width,
    GraphicsDevice.Viewport.Height, 1, GraphicsDevice.DisplayMode.Format,
    GraphicsDevice.PresentationParameters.MultiSampleType,
    GraphicsDevice.PresentationParameters.MultiSampleQuality);
```

This code is simply a review of what we have done many times before. If you need a refresher on the render target, one can be found back in Chapter 15, "Advanced HLSL." We also want to make sure we dispose of our render target inside the UnloadContent method. We have to add the files we need for this demo as well. They can be found in the usual places.

Next, let's look at the framework for the Update method:

```
UpdateInput();


switch (state)
{
    case TransitionState.CrossFade:
        {
            UpdateFade(gameTime);
            break;
        }
    case TransitionState.Wipe:
        {
            UpdateWipe(gameTime);
            break;
        }
    default:
        {
            break;
        }
}


base.Update(gameTime);
```

Our UpdateInput method will simply check to see whether the A button or the spacebar has been pressed. If so, it will change the state. You can see that method here, along with UpdateFade and UpdateWipe stubbed out:

```
private void UpdateInput()
{
    if (input.KeyboardState.WasKeyPressed(Keys.Space) ||
        input.ButtonHandler.WasButtonPressed(0, InputHandler.ButtonType.A))
    {
        state--;

        if (state < TransitionState.None)
            state = TransitionState.Wipe;

        InitializeValues();
    }
}
```

20

```
private void UpdateFade(GameTime gameTime) { }

private void UpdateWipe(GameTime gameTime) { }
```

Every time we change the state, we also call the `InitializeValues` method, which can be created as an empty method for now. We need to also call the `InitializeValues` method inside the `Initialize` method. After creating that method, we can dig into the `Draw` methods:

```
protected override void Draw(GameTime gameTime)
{
    GraphicsDevice device = graphics.GraphicsDevice;

    //Set up our render target
    device.SetRenderTarget(0, renderTarget);
    //Clear out our render target
    device.Clear(Color.Black);

    //Draw Scene
    Matrix world = Matrix.CreateRotationY(
        MathHelper.ToRadians(45.0f *
            (float)gameTime.TotalGameTime.TotalSeconds)) *
        Matrix.CreateTranslation(new Vector3(0, 0, -4000));
    DrawModel(ref model, ref world, texture);

    //clear it out
    device.SetRenderTarget(0, null);
    Texture2D sceneTexture = renderTarget.GetTexture();

    //now, we can draw it for real ...
    //clear out our buffer
    device.Clear(Color.CornflowerBlue);

    spriteBatch.Begin(SpriteBlendMode.AlphaBlend, SpriteSortMode.Immediate,
        SaveStateMode.SaveState);

    //start transition
    switch (state)
    {
        case TransitionState.CrossFade:
            {
                break;
            }
        case TransitionState.Wipe:
            {
                break;
            }
```

```
        default:
            {
                spriteBatch.Draw(sceneTexture(), Vector2.Zero, Color.White);
                break;
            }
    }

    //close our batch
    spriteBatch.End();

    base.Draw(gameTime);
}


private void DrawModel(ref Model m, ref Matrix world, Texture2D texture)
{
    Matrix[] transforms = new Matrix[m.Bones.Count];
    m.CopyAbsoluteBoneTransformsTo(transforms);

    foreach (ModelMesh mesh in m.Meshes)
    {
        foreach (ModelMeshPart mp in mesh.MeshParts)
        {
            effect.Parameters["ColorMap"].SetValue(texture);
            effect.Parameters["Projection"].SetValue(camera.Projection);
            effect.Parameters["View"].SetValue(camera.View);
            effect.Parameters["World"].SetValue(world * mesh.ParentBone.Transform);
            mp.Effect = effect;
        }
        mesh.Draw();
    }
}
```

There is nothing new in the way we have set up this code. We have our faithful DrawModel method, which we call from within the default case in our Draw method. The other two cases do not draw anything at this point. We are simply putting the framework in place so in the next sections we can focus solely on what is needed for the transition.

The first part of our Draw method is where we draw our model like normal, except we are drawing it to our render target. Then we use our sprite batch to draw that texture on the screen. We save our state for this simple demo. Doing this once or twice per frame is not going to be total devastation, but any more than that would degrade performance. In Chapter 9, "2D Basics," we discussed the states that the sprite batch sets, and for optimal performance, these states should just be set back manually.

At this point we have our transition demo framework created. If we ran the code, we would need to press the spacebar (or the A button) a couple of times to see our asteroid because the two case statements for the other states do not actually draw anything on the screen. Now we can move to the actual transitions.

Cross-Fade (Dissolve)

The dissolve transition is a lot like the color fade. However, instead of fading to a color, we fade out of one scene and into another. It looks as though the scene dissolves as the next scene appears. Effectively, we will render one scene on top of the other. To start, both scenes will be fully opaque. This means we will need to draw the scene we are transitioning into under the current scene we are transitioning out of. Then during the transition period we just update the alpha component of our color. This is very similar to how we did the color fade.

To implement this effect in our demo, we need to add the following private member field:

```
private float fadeAmount;
```

We need to set this value to 0 in our InitializeValues method. We also need to add the following code to the UpdateFade method:

```
fadeAmount += (.0005f * gameTime.ElapsedGameTime.Milliseconds);


//reset fade amount after a short time to see the effect again
if (fadeAmount > 2.0f)
    fadeAmount = 0.0f;
```

This method is called from our demo's Update method, assuming we are in the CrossFade state. This is calculated just like the other fade-to-color demos we have done. The only other piece left for us to complete our dissolve (cross-fade) transition effect is to actually draw the effect. We do this inside the CrossFade case in the Draw method:

```
//Draw the screen we are transitioning to first
spriteBatch.Draw(splashScreen, Vector2.Zero, Color.White);

//Then draw the screen we are transitioning from
spriteBatch.Draw(renderTarget.GetTexture(), Vector2.Zero,
    new Color(new Vector4(Color.White.ToVector3(), 1.0f - fadeAmount)));
```

We are simply drawing the scene we are transitioning into first so it will be under the current scene. Then we draw the current scene, passing in our fade amount. We are actually subtracting our fade amount from 1 to start fully opaque and transition into a transparent image.

The UpdateFade method is letting the fadeAmount update for a little bit and then just resetting the fade amount back to zero so the transition can start over again. In a real game, instead of just resetting that value, the code would transition to a new state (for example, StartMenu). We are done with this transition effect. Once we put the framework in place, the actual transition is very simple and straightforward. Now if we run the demo we can see our asteroid fade out as our start menu fades in. Remember, the asteroid does not actually do any fading; the asteroid just appears because the texture being drawn on top of it is slowly becoming transparent.

Directional Wipes

Directional wipes are a great transitional effect. We see these a lot in movies, where one scene pushes the previous scene out of the way. We will be implementing four directional wipes: left, right, up, and down. A left directional wipe will have the new scene drawn starting on the left side of the screen. We can see the different stages of this in Figures 20.1 through 20.4.

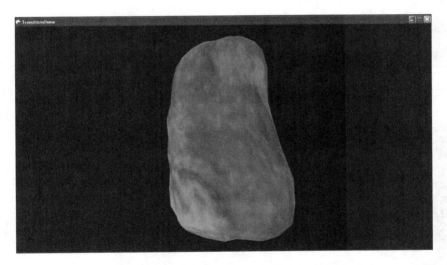

FIGURE 20.1   Our favorite asteroid represents the current playing scene that we will be transitioning from.

To implement this, we need to set up a few private member fields:

```
private Rectangle wipeInDestinationRectangle;
private Rectangle wipeInSourceRectangle;
private Rectangle wipeOutDestinationRectangle;
private Rectangle wipeOutSourceRectangle;
private enum WipeDirection { Left, Right, Up, Down };
private WipeDirection wipeDirection = WipeDirection.Left;
private int wipeX, wipeY, wipeWidth, wipeHeight;
private float wipeAmount;
```

We need to have several variables to manage our directional wipes. We are allowing four different wipes, and we have set up an enumeration type to handle them. We have also set up a wipeDirection state, which we have initialized to Left. We have a wipeAmount variable that we will use much like we did our fadeAmount. The four rectangle variables

FIGURE 20.2   Our start menu and splash page represents the scene we will be transitioning to.

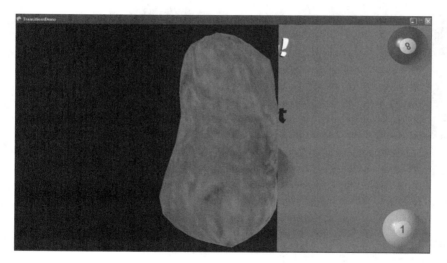

FIGURE 20.3   Using a left directional wipe, the splash screen starts to display on top of the current scene.

hold the source and destination rectangles of both the scene coming in and the scene going out. We need to initialize the wipeAmount variable to 0 inside the InitializeValues method.

Next, we are going to look at all the update methods to handle directional wipes:

```
private void UpdateWipe(GameTime gameTime)
{
```

FIGURE 20.4   Using a left directional wipe, the splash screen is 50% on top of the current scene.

```
Viewport viewport = graphics.GraphicsDevice.Viewport;

wipeAmount += (0.5f * (float)gameTime.ElapsedGameTime.Milliseconds);

switch (wipeDirection)
{
    case WipeDirection.Left:
        {
            WipeLeft(viewport);
            break;
        }
    case WipeDirection.Right:
        {
            WipeRight(viewport);
            break;
        }
    case WipeDirection.Up:
        {
            WipeUp(viewport);
            break;
        }
    case WipeDirection.Down:
        {
            WipeDown(viewport);
            break;
        }
}
```

```
    }

    private void WipeDown(Viewport viewport)
    {
        wipeY = 0;
        wipeX = 0;
        wipeWidth = viewport.Width;
        wipeHeight = Convert.ToInt32(wipeAmount);

        wipeInDestinationRectangle = new Rectangle(0, 0, wipeWidth, wipeHeight);
        wipeInSourceRectangle = new Rectangle(0, 0, wipeWidth, wipeHeight);
        wipeOutDestinationRectangle = new Rectangle(wipeX, wipeHeight, wipeWidth,
            viewport.Height - wipeHeight);
        wipeOutSourceRectangle = new Rectangle(wipeX, wipeHeight, wipeWidth,
            viewport.Height - wipeHeight);

        if (wipeAmount > viewport.Height)
            ChangeWipe();
    }

    private void WipeUp(Viewport viewport)
    {
        wipeY = Convert.ToInt32(viewport.Height - wipeAmount);
        wipeX = 0;
        wipeWidth = viewport.Width;
        wipeHeight = Convert.ToInt32(wipeAmount);

        wipeInDestinationRectangle = new Rectangle(wipeX, wipeY, wipeWidth,
            wipeHeight);
        wipeInSourceRectangle = new Rectangle(wipeX, wipeY, wipeWidth, wipeHeight);
        wipeOutDestinationRectangle = new Rectangle(0, 0, wipeWidth, wipeY);
        wipeOutSourceRectangle = new Rectangle(0, 0, wipeWidth, wipeY);

        if (wipeAmount > viewport.Height)
            ChangeWipe();
    }

    private void WipeRight(Viewport viewport)
    {
        wipeY = 0;
        wipeX = 0;
        wipeWidth = Convert.ToInt32(wipeAmount);
        wipeHeight = viewport.Height;

        wipeInDestinationRectangle = new Rectangle(0, 0, wipeWidth, wipeHeight);
        wipeInSourceRectangle = new Rectangle(0, 0, wipeWidth, wipeHeight);
```

```
    wipeOutDestinationRectangle = new Rectangle(wipeWidth, wipeY,
        viewport.Width - wipeWidth, wipeHeight);
    wipeOutSourceRectangle = new Rectangle(wipeWidth, wipeY,
        viewport.Width - wipeWidth, wipeHeight);

    if (wipeAmount > viewport.Width)
        ChangeWipe();
}

private void WipeLeft(Viewport viewport)
{
    wipeY = 0;
    wipeX = Convert.ToInt32 (viewport.Width - wipeAmount);
    wipeWidth = Convert.ToInt32(wipeAmount);
    wipeHeight = viewport.Height;

    wipeInDestinationRectangle = new Rectangle(wipeX, wipeY, wipeWidth,
        wipeHeight);
    wipeInSourceRectangle = new Rectangle(wipeX, wipeY, wipeWidth, wipeHeight);
    wipeOutDestinationRectangle = new Rectangle(0, 0, wipeX, wipeHeight);
    wipeOutSourceRectangle = new Rectangle(0, 0, wipeX, wipeHeight);

    if (wipeAmount > viewport.Width)
        ChangeWipe();
}

private void ChangeWipe()
{
    wipeAmount = 0.0f;
    wipeDirection--;
    if (wipeDirection < WipeDirection.Left)
        wipeDirection = WipeDirection.Down;
}
```

There is quite a bit of code here, but it is basically the same thing repeated four times. The actual UpdateWipe method is very straightforward. We update the wipeAmount and then, depending on the current wipe state, we call one of the directional wipes. We next look in detail at the WipeLeft method.

The first thing we do is set our wipeY, wipeX, wipeWidth, and wipeHeight variables. For our left wipe, we are not modifying our y value and are setting our x value to the width minus the wipe amount. The height is simply the same height as our viewport. With these values set, we can set up the four rectangles for this wipe.

We start with the rectangles associated with the scene being wiped in. The destination rectangle is the rectangle on the screen where we want to put the texture. The source rectangle is the rectangle of the texture we are pulling from. We used the source rectangles when we did cel animation. In this situation, we do not want to squish the entire texture onto the destination rectangle on the screen, so we specify which part of the scene being transitioned in we are going to display.

The rectangles we use to wipe out the current scene simply take up the other part of the screen, so in the case of this left wipe, they start on the right side of the screen and extend out to the wipeX value, which is being updated with the wipeAmount. You can see this in Figure 20.4.

After the rectangle values are set up, a final condition is checked to determine if the wipe amount has exceeded the width or the height of the viewport. Width is checked for the left and right wipes, and height is checked for the up and down wipes. If the threshold was exceeded, the ChangeWipe method is called, which just resets the wipeAmount value and changes the wipe direction state.

Now we need to draw the transition. In the Wipe case in the Draw method, we can add the following code, which simply draws both the sceneTexture and splashScreen textures in the appropriate places:

```
//Draw the screen we are transitioning from first
spriteBatch.Draw(sceneTexture, wipeOutDestinationRectangle,
    wipeOutSourceRectangle, Color.White);

//Then draw the screen we are transitioning into
spriteBatch.Draw(splashScreen, wipeInDestinationRectangle,
    wipeInSourceRectangle, Color.White);
```

We can run our demo and see that not only do we have a nice cross-fade transition, but we have an additional four directional wipe transitions. With these wipes under our belt, it would not be much of a stretch to tackle directional pushes (although we do not cover them in this book). With a left push, the new scene comes in from the left and pushes the old scene out to the right. The only values that need to change are the wipeOutDestinationRectangle and wipeOutSourceRectangle variables.

Making Fire

In Chapter 10, "2D Effects," we made a fire demo old-school style, but you need to know how to make a fire effect on today's 3D hardware using shaders. We will create a demo in this section that does just that. We need to create a demo called HLSLFireDemo. We will be referencing the XELibrary, but we will not be modifying it, so we do not need to add the actual project to our solution if we do not wish to.

Before we dig into the code, let's briefly discuss how we will do the fire effect in this chapter and how it differs from the one we did before. Before, all the calculations were done in software on the CPU. We modified a texture, pixel by pixel, and displayed that on the screen. In this demo, we will be using a pixel shader to do some of the heavy work. We will not be using a palette file in this demo. In fact, instead of the 256 colors we used in the earlier fire demo, we are only going to use six colors, after which the other color values will be computed inside the pixel shader. We are not going to be modifying a texture directly in our code; instead, we are going to render to a couple render targets to achieve this effect.

In each frame, we are going to animate the fire upward by drawing the previous render target onto the current one. We are going to offset our texture vertically and use a pixel shader to fade our fire. We are also going to create our hotspots across the bottom of the screen by using a bunch of 4×1 sprites with a sprite batch.

Here are the private member fields we need to add for this demo:

```
private InputHandler input;
private FPS fps;

private Effect fireEffect;
private Random rand = new Random();

private Texture2D hotSpotTexture;
private Texture2D fire;
private Rectangle tileSafeArea;

private RenderTarget2D renderTarget1;
private RenderTarget2D renderTarget2;

private int offset = -128;
private Color[] colors = {
    Color.Black,
    Color.Yellow,
    Color.White,
    Color.Red,
    Color.Orange,
    new Color(255,255,128) //yellowish white
};
```

You see the usual suspects, along with our two render targets, an offset value, and finally an array of six colors. We are going to use the offset to help us animate the fire upward. The color array is what we are going to use to generate the hotspots of the fire at the bottom of the screen.

We need to add the following lines to our constructor:

```
input = new InputHandler(this, true);
Components.Add(input);

fps = new FPS(this, true, true);
Components.Add(fps);
```

Our FPS component is set to draw at a consistent rate. We can check our frame rate when we want, but for the flames to move at a reasonable rate, we need the Draw method to be called at a consistent pace. Next, here's the code we need to add to the LoadContent method:

```
tileSafeArea = Utility.GetTitleSafeArea(GraphicsDevice, .8f);
hotSpotTexture = CreateTexture(4, 1);
fireEffect = Content.Load<Effect>(@"Effects\Fire");

renderTarget1 = new RenderTarget2D(GraphicsDevice,
    GraphicsDevice.Viewport.Width,
    GraphicsDevice.Viewport.Height, 1, GraphicsDevice.DisplayMode.Format,
    GraphicsDevice.PresentationParameters.MultiSampleType,
    GraphicsDevice.PresentationParameters.MultiSampleQuality);

renderTarget2 = new RenderTarget2D(GraphicsDevice,
    GraphicsDevice.Viewport.Width,
    GraphicsDevice.Viewport.Height, 1, GraphicsDevice.DisplayMode.Format,
    GraphicsDevice.PresentationParameters.MultiSampleType,
    GraphicsDevice.PresentationParameters.MultiSampleQuality);

fire = null;
```

We create our hotSpotTexture with the CreateTexture method, which we discuss in a moment. We are telling the method that we want the hotspot to be 4 pixels wide and 1 pixel tall. We load in our fire effect, which we will look at in a moment. Finally, we set up both our render targets and we set our fire texture to null. You will see why we do this here when we look at the Draw method a little later. For now, let's look at the CreateTexture method:

```
private Texture2D CreateTexture(int width, int height)
{
    Texture2D texture = new Texture2D(graphics.GraphicsDevice, width, height, 1,
        TextureUsage.None, SurfaceFormat.Color
);

    int pixelCount = width * height;
    Color[] pixelData = new Color[pixelCount];

    for (int i = 0; i < pixelCount; i++)
        pixelData[i] = Color.White;

    texture.SetData(pixelData);

    return (texture);
}
```

This method is no different from the other textures we have created. A new texture is created, and we loop through all the pixels, setting them to a particular color (white in this case). We save the pixel information on the texture and return it to the calling method.

It is important that when we create render targets, we dispose of them properly. We do this in the UnloadContent method:

```
protected override void UnloadContent()
{
    renderTarget1.Dispose();
    renderTarget2.Dispose();
}
```

The content of our Draw method is as follows:

```
GraphicsDevice device = graphics.GraphicsDevice;


//Draw hotspots on the first Render Target
device.SetRenderTarget(0, renderTarget1);
device.Clear(Color.Black);

spriteBatch.Begin();

//get last drawn screen -- if not first time in
//fire is null first time in, and when device is lost (LoadGraphicsContent)
if (fire != null) //render target have valid texture
    spriteBatch.Draw(fire, Vector2.Zero, Color.White);

//draw hotspots
for (int i = 0; i < device.Viewport.Width / hotSpotTexture.Width; i++)
{
    spriteBatch.Draw(hotSpotTexture,
        new Vector2(i * hotSpotTexture.Width,
            device.Viewport.Height - hotSpotTexture.Height),
        colors[rand.Next(colors.Length)]);
}

spriteBatch.End();

//resolve what we just drew to our render target
//clear it out
device.SetRenderTarget(0, null);

// Transfer from first to second render target
device.SetRenderTarget(0, renderTarget2);
```

20

```
fireEffect.Begin();
spriteBatch.Begin(SpriteBlendMode.None, SpriteSortMode.Immediate,
    SaveStateMode.None);

EffectPass pass = fireEffect.CurrentTechnique.Passes[0];
pass.Begin();
spriteBatch.Draw(renderTarget1.GetTexture(),
    new Rectangle(0, offset, device.Viewport.Width,
    device.Viewport.Height - offset), Color.White);
spriteBatch.End();
pass.End();
fireEffect.End();

//resolve what we just drew to our render target
//clear it out
device.SetRenderTarget(0, null);

device.Clear(Color.Black);

//set texture to render
fire = renderTarget2.GetTexture();

// Draw second render target onto the screen (back buffer)
spriteBatch.Begin(SpriteBlendMode.Additive);

//render texture three times (in additive mode) to saturate color
spriteBatch.Draw(fire, tileSafeArea, Color.White);
spriteBatch.Draw(fire, tileSafeArea, Color.White);
spriteBatch.Draw(fire, tileSafeArea, Color.White);

spriteBatch.End();

base.Draw(gameTime);
```

The Draw method is broken down into three sections. The first section draws the hotspots
of the fire onto the previous render target. The second section applies the post-processing
effect and animates the texture upward. The third and final section displays the final
result on the screen, which is used by the first section in the next frame, thus starting the
process all over again.

If this is the first time in, only the hotspots will be drawn. The hotspots are drawn across
the bottom of the screen, with each hotspot using one of the six colors in our array. If
this is not the first frame of the demo, the contents we last displayed on the screen are
drawn first.

Once we are done with the first render target, we start drawing to our second render target. We draw the texture from our first render target and send it through a post-processing pixel shader, which we have not yet discussed. We also use the offset value to animate our texture upward. Once the pixel shader is done, we start rendering to our backbuffer. We store the second render target's texture into our fire texture variable.

In the first section, we check this fire texture variable to make sure it is not null before trying to use it. It would be null on two occasions: when the demo first starts and when the device is lost. When the device is reset after it is lost, the LoadContent method is called. This is why we set the fire texture variable to null then. Otherwise, when Draw is called after the reset, it would not have a valid texture and would crash the demo.

The last section of the Draw method takes our final texture that is created after the post-processing, and we use additive blending mode to write the texture to the screen three times. The post-processing effect dulls the colors by blending them together. However, we need our fire to be bright. With additive blending we can easily achieve that effect by just drawing the same texture a few times. The end result is a nice-looking fire.

The only thing left is our effect file. We can call this effect Fire.fx. The code is shown here:

```
texture Fire;


sampler FireMapSampler = sampler_state
{
    texture = <Fire>;
    magfilter = LINEAR;
    minfilter = LINEAR;
    mipfilter = LINEAR;
    addressU = wrap;
    addressV = wrap;
};


struct PixelInput
{
    float2 TexCoord : TEXCOORD0;
};


float4 pixelShader(PixelInput input) : COLOR0
{
    float4 color;
    float2 Right, Left, Above, Below;
    //initialize all our values to be the texture coordinates
    Left = Right = Above = Below = input.TexCoord;

    Right.x += .001;
```

20

```
    Left.x -= .001;
    Above.y += .001;
    Below.y -= .001;

    //Sample the four texture positions
    color = tex2D(FireMapSampler, Left);
    color += tex2D(FireMapSampler, Right);
    color += tex2D(FireMapSampler, Above);
    color += tex2D(FireMapSampler, Below);

    //Get the average
    color *= 0.25; // divided by 4

    //Cool down flame
    color.rgb -= .035;

    return(color);
}


technique Default
{
    pass P0
    {
        PixelShader = compile ps_2_0 pixelShader();
    }
}
```

The pixel shader is not that bad. It does the blending of surrounding pixel colors. Just like in Chapter 10, we are grabbing the left, right, above, and below pixels and blending them together to get the final color of the current pixel. By doing this, we are dulling the color, though, and that is why we display the texture three times at the end of our Draw method. Just like we had a cool-down value in Chapter 10 (we used the value 3), we also have a cool-down value in our pixel shader of –.035. This allows the flame to fade out.

At this point we can run our demo and get much better frame rates than we did in Chapter 10, especially on the Xbox 360. An interesting challenge would be to make a progress bar that is populated with fire, much like the *Burnout* racing game series.

Summary

In this chapter, we discussed transitions and the way to handle procedural fire on today's hardware. During our discussion of transitions, we talked about the dissolve or cross-fade transition as well as wipes. You saw how to wipe the screen in four different directions. With these transitions, we can create some nice effects in our games. We finished up the chapter by creating another fire effect. We were able to create the effect with a lot less code that runs more efficiently. In the next chapter, we will be looking at particle systems; then we will move on to making a full 3D game in the last part of the book.

CHAPTER 21

Particle System

In this chapter we discuss how to create a particle system. Although this will be a modest particle system, it should be a good foundation on which to build. The main goal of this chapter is to provide you a good understanding of how to create a particle system. Once the basics have been nailed down, the sky is the limit in what we can do with particles.

Particle System Defined

Before we can dig into implementing a particle system, we need to determine exactly what one is. A particle system is simply a system of particles. Perhaps the better question is: What is a particle? A particle can be anything: dust, snow, rain, ants, sparks, smoke trails, debris, leaves, and so many more things. A particle is a single object. A particle system contains many particles and controls their properties. Some of the properties could control how long particles live, their velocity, acceleration, color, texture, and size.

A particle system controls the behavior of a group of particles. The idea is to have one flexible system that can be used for many different effects, just by adjusting some values. It could be that a rain effect and a snow effect share a lot of the same values: They both start on the same horizontal plane and fall downward, for example. Of course, other values would be different between the two particle systems. Rain would fall straight down and not be affected by the wind that much, whereas snow would fall downward but would be drastically affected by the wind.

The particle system we create in this chapter uses just one of many ways to create a particle system. It should be a great springboard to get us started. Hopefully it will serve our near future needs adequately. If not, we can take these concepts and modify our objects to better fit our needs.

Point Sprite Defined

Before we get into our engine, you need to have a firm understanding of the idea behind a point sprite. We use a point sprite to represent a particle in our 3D world. Prior to point sprites, game developers had to create a rectangle (quad) and apply a texture to it for each particle. This meant that there were four vertices for each and every particle. If we were rendering 5,000 particles, that would be 20,000 vertices, just on the special effect we were trying to produce!

Fortunately, when DirectX 8 came out, point sprites were added. With point sprites, the graphics card only needs one vertex (a point) for each particle. We can even tell the graphics card the size of that vertex. It can be as small as one pixel to as large as we want. By using a vertex shader, we can set each particle (vertex) to be a different size if we need to for our effect.

XNA automatically maps our texture to the vertex. It also makes sure that the texture is always facing the camera. A point sprite gets its name from being a point (vertex) and being a sprite (having a texture that is always facing the camera). If we wanted to create a 2D particle system, we could use the same concepts in this chapter, except we would use regular sprites instead of point sprites and keep our vectors to 2D.

Creating the Particle Class

I previously listed some of the values we need to store for each particle (see section "Particle System Defined." We are going to firm up that list and create a class that we can use to represent a particle our system can use. We will be creating this class in our XELibrary project. Let's create a new solution for this chapter called ParticleSystemDemo. We need to include our XELibrary project to our solution. Once our solution is set up, we can add a new code file to our XELibrary project called Particle.cs.

Here we will see the different values we want to store for our particle. These are the member fields of our Particle class:

```
private Vector3 velocity;
private Vector3 acceleration;
private float lifetime;
private Vector3 externalForce;

internal float Age;
internal bool IsAlive;
internal VertexPointSprite Vertex;
internal float ColorChangeRate;
```

```
internal float CurrentColorTime;
internal int CurrentColorIndex;
```

We are storing the particle's velocity and acceleration, which we have discussed in detail in past chapters. Next, we store a value to hold the amount of time this particle should live, in seconds. The last private field is a vector storing the external force that should be applied to the particle. This is where we model gravity and wind direction. Our wind will be in the x and z directions, and gravity will be in the y direction.

Next are our internal member fields. Our particle system will need to access each of these directly; there is no need for an outside source (for example, our game) to access these values. If we decide that our game does need read access to a value (such as Age), we could mark it as private and create a set method. You will see that in just a moment for the private fields we have set up.

The Age value is what we use to compare against the lifetime value to determine whether it is time for the particle to fade away. The IsAlive boolean flag just lets us easily know if this particle is being updated and drawn on the screen. Once the age is greater than the lifetime, the IsAlive flag is set to false. The last field holds our vertex data of type VertexPointSprite. This type is not an XNA type. We need to create that struct, which we'll do in the next section. For now, the main thing to know is that it stores the particle's position, color, and size.

The last three variables relate to the color of our point sprite (or rather how our texture is tinted). We discuss these in detail later when we use the point sprite in an example. For now, it is only important to know that we might want to have our particle change its color over time, and these variables allow that.

We will create the constructor for our class:

```
public Particle()
{
    Age = 0.0f;
    Vertex = new VertexPointSprite();
    CurrentColorIndex = 0;
    CurrentColorTime = 0;
}
```

Our default constructor simply sets the initial age of our particle and creates a new instance of its vertex. It also initializes the color fields we have created.

Our particle system needs an Update method. This will allow the particle to be updated every frame. The Update method for our Particle class is as follows:

```
internal void Update(float elapsedTime)
{
    Age += elapsedTime;
    CurrentColorTime += elapsedTime;
```

```
    if (Age >= lifetime)
        IsAlive = false;
    else
    {
        velocity += acceleration;
        velocity -= externalForce;
        Vertex.Position += velocity * elapsedTime;
    }
}
```

This method is very simple. Depending on what is needed, this could be complex enough to include some of the physics we saw in previous chapters or even state management so the particle would do different things at different states in its life. For our purposes, we are going to keep it simple and just update the velocity and position.

The first task the method performs is to add the amount of seconds that have passed since the last frame to the total age of our particle. It adds this same value to the total amount of time the particle has been tinted with the current color (Vertex.Color).

Then we check to see if the particle has lived past its lifetime. If so, we set the IsAlive flag to false. If it is still alive, we update the velocity with the current acceleration. We then subtract any external forces from the velocity. This does not take into account any kind of friction, but that would be trivial to add later if needed. Once the velocity has its final value, we update the position.

We need a way to initialize all of the particle's values. We are going to create an Initialize method. Actually, we are going to create two overloaded methods. These Initialize methods are as follows:

```
internal void Initialize(ParticleSystemSettings settings)
{
    Initialize(settings, true);
}

internal void Initialize(ParticleSystemSettings settings, bool makeAlive)
{
    Age = 0;
    IsAlive = makeAlive;

    Vector3 minPosition = (settings.EmitPosition - (settings.EmitRange * .5f));
    Vector3 maxPosition = (settings.EmitPosition + (settings.EmitRange * .5f));

    Vector3 position = Utility.GetRandomVector3(minPosition, maxPosition);

    Vertex.Position = position;

    if (settings.EmitRadius != Vector2.Zero)
    {
```

```
        float angle = Utility.GetRandomFloat(0, MathHelper.TwoPi);

        Vertex.Position = new Vector3(
            position.X + (float)Math.Sin(angle) * settings.EmitRadius.X,
            position.Y,
            position.Z + (float)Math.Cos(angle) * settings.EmitRadius.Y);
    }

    velocity = Utility.GetRandomVector3(
        settings.MinimumVelocity, settings.MaximumVelocity);

    acceleration = Utility.GetRandomVector3(
        settings.MinimumAcceleration, settings.MaximumAcceleration);

    lifetime = Utility.GetRandomFloat(
        settings.MinimumLifetime, settings.MaximumLifetime);

    if (settings.DisplayColorsInOrder)
    {
        Vertex.Color = settings.Colors[0];
        ColorChangeRate = lifetime / settings.Colors.Length;
    }
    else
    {
        Vertex.Color =
            settings.Colors[Utility.GetRandomInt(0, settings.Colors.Length)];
    }

    Vertex.PointSize = Utility.GetRandomFloat(
        settings.MinimumSize, settings.MaximumSize);

    externalForce = settings.ExternalForce;
}
```

The first overload simply passes true to our `makeAlive` parameter in the second overload, along with the values that were passed in. The values are being passed in with the `ParticleSystemSettings` class. You will see this class in a moment, but it really just contains the different values we need to successfully initialize our particle.

The main overload will do all the heavy lifting. Overall, this method is taking different settings and determining the initial values of our particle. Most settings have a minimum and a maximum value. We then set our particle variable equal to a random value using the minimum and maximum values as the valid range.

Before we dig into the method, let's look at the settings class we are passing in. We need to create another class in our XELibrary project called ParticleSystemSettings.cs. The code for this class is as follows:

```
public class ParticleSystemSettings
{
    public Texture2D Texture;

    public float RotateAmount;

    public bool RunOnce = false;
    public int Capacity;
    public int EmitPerSecond;

    public Vector3 ExternalForce;

    public Vector3 EmitPosition;
    public Vector2 EmitRadius = Vector2.Zero;
    public Vector3 EmitRange;

    public Vector3 MinimumVelocity;
    public Vector3 MaximumVelocity;

    public Vector3 MinimumAcceleration;
    public Vector3 MaximumAcceleration;

    public float MinimumLifetime;
    public float MaximumLifetime;

    public float MinimumSize;
    public float MaximumSize;

    public Color[] Colors;
    public bool DisplayColorsInOrder;
}
```

Although each particle will have a specific value, our particle system needs randomness. After all, it would look rather boring if every raindrop fell in the exact same position! To accommodate the randomness needed, we require the particle system to pass in minimum and maximum values for many of the particle properties. Our Initialize method takes these values and determines the initial value of our particle.

We will run through these fields as well as the particle's Initialize method at the same time. The first field is not actually used in our particle but is used in our particle system, as you will see later. If needed, the code could be modified to have an array of textures much like we have an array of colors. Each point sprite can be rotated, which is set with the RotateAmount setting. The RunOnce field is used to let the particle system know if it should just run the effect one time or continuously. Capacity lets the particle system know the maximum number of particles it will have at any one time. EmitPerSecond tells the system how many particles it should try to emit per second. It will not emit more than there is capacity for.

ExternalForce is used to apply forces such as gravity or wind. It is constant for every particle. EmitPosition, EmitRadius, and EmitRange are all used to set the initial position of the particle. Previously in the Initialize method, we first set our position to a random vector based on our calculated minimum and maximum positions. These values are determined by using the EmitRange vector. Next, we check to see if the particle system has specified a radius, which means that our particles should be emitted in a circular (or oval) pattern. We do this check so we do not need to take the hit of calculating the sine and cosine values if not needed. We factor in the calculated angle and radius to determine our real position.

TIP

For a performance boost, we could create a lookup table of common sine and cosine values. A method could then simply return the value from the lookup table when passed in the angle instead of doing the computation in real time.

We then store minimum and maximum values for the velocity, acceleration, lifetime, and size. In our Initialize method we calculate the initial values the particles will be assigned by retrieving random values between the minimum and maximum values.

We have an array of colors that we either pick from randomly or loop through in order (and in even intervals) for the life span of the particle. If DisplayColorsInOrder is true, the Initialize method calculates ColorChangeRate to determine how often the particle should change colors so that each color will be visible for the same amount of time. This is done by dividing the number of colors in the array by the particle's lifetime. If DisplayColorsInOrder is false, we simply pick a random index of our colors array and set the particle to that color for its entire lifetime.

We need to modify the Utility class in our XELibrary to add in the helper methods that return a random value based on a minimum and maximum value passed in:

```
private static Random rand = new Random();


public static int GetRandomInt(int min, int max)
{
    return (rand.Next(min, max));
}
public static float GetRandomFloat(float min, float max)
{
    return (((float)rand.NextDouble() * (max - min)) + min);
}
public static Vector2 GetRandomVector2(Vector2 min, Vector2 max)
{
    return (new Vector2(
        GetRandomFloat(min.X, max.X),
```

```
        GetRandomFloat(min.Y, max.Y)));
}
public static Vector3 GetRandomVector3(Vector3 min, Vector3 max)
{
    return (new Vector3(
        GetRandomFloat(min.X, max.X),
        GetRandomFloat(min.Y, max.Y),
        GetRandomFloat(min.Z, max.Z)));
}
```

The key to all these methods (except the random integer wrapper) is the `GetRandomFloat` method. This uses the `NextDouble` method, which returns a value between 0 and 1. We then multiply the difference of our maximum and minimum values passed in. Finally, we add in our minimum value to this total.

Creating the `VertexPointSprite` Struct

In Chapter 19, "Advanced Texturing Techniques," we created the `VertexPositionNormalTangent` vertex format. Because we are using a point sprite, we need to create another custom vertex format. This could actually be avoided if we did not want the flexibility to create particles of different sizes. If we only needed one size for all our particles, we could just use the `VertexPositionColor` struct already provided by XNA. We do want the flexibility of different-sized particles, however, so we will quickly create another custom vertex format. The `Vertex` field in our `Particle` class is declared as this type.

The code for this struct is as follows:

```
public struct VertexPointSprite
{
    public Vector3 Position;
    public float PointSize;
    public Color Color;

    public VertexPointSprite(
        Vector3 Position,
        Color Color,
        float PointSize)
    {
        this.Position = Position;
        this.Color = Color;
        this.PointSize = PointSize;
    }

    public static int SizeInBytes = 8 * sizeof(float);

    public static VertexElement[] VertexElements =
```

```
    {
        new VertexElement(0, 0, VertexElementFormat.Vector3,
            VertexElementMethod.Default, VertexElementUsage.Position, 0),
        new VertexElement(0, sizeof(float)*3, VertexElementFormat.Single,
            VertexElementMethod.Default, VertexElementUsage.PointSize, 0),
        new VertexElement(0, sizeof(float)*4, VertexElementFormat.Color,
            VertexElementMethod.Default, VertexElementUsage.Color, 0)
    };
}
```

There should not be anything surprising with this code. We have three properties that we need to set: `Position`, `PointSize`, and `Color`. We set up our vertex elements just like we did in Chapter 19.

Creating the Particle System Engine

Now that we have our particle created, along with the required custom vertex format struct, we can look into how we can implement our particle system. We can think of our particle system class like one of the other manager classes we have created in the past. It is simply a means to manage multiple objects of the same type. This class will be an abstract class that inherits from the `DrawableGameComponent` class. Each individual particle system we make (rain, bubbles, gas, and so on) will inherit from this base `ParticleSystem` class. We need to create the file for this class in our XELibrary project. We can declare our class as follows:

```
public abstract class ParticleSystem : DrawableGameComponent { }
```

As usual, we will start by declaring our private member fields:

```
private Particle[] particles;
private int lastParticleIndex = 0;
private int totalParticlesEmitted = 0;
private int numberOfActiveParticles;
private float rotateAngle = 0;

private Effect effect;
private VertexDeclaration vertexDeclaration;
private VertexPointSprite[] vertices;

private SpriteFont font;
private SpriteBatch spriteBatch;
private Rectangle titleSafeArea;
```

We have an array of particles that we are managing. We keep track of the number of particles we have emitted along with the number of active particles. We initialize our rotation angle to 0. This value will rotate the texture around our point sprite. You will see this in detail when we look at our effect file. Because our particles are point sprites, we need to create our vertices. Finally, we declare fields to hold our sprite batch, our sprite font, and the title safe area of the screen we can draw on. We are going to allow drawing some debug information, and this is why we need these variables.

Next are the protected and public member fields:

```
protected ParticleSystemSettings settings;
protected ContentManager content;


public Matrix View;
public Matrix Projection;
public bool DebugInfo = false;
```

Our specific particle system objects that inherit this class will need to initialize the settings that get passed to the particle's Initialize method. They might also need to load content, so we made both the settings and content protected variables. Our game needs to set these fields we have marked as public. The game will set the View and Projection fields during the Draw method so the particles will be displayed correctly. The game can set the debug information flag to display some particle information that can prove helpful while debugging a particular particle system effect.

Our constructor is very straightforward. We are just initializing our settings and content variables:

```
public ParticleSystem(Game game)
    : base(game)
{
    content = game.Content);
    settings = new ParticleSystemSettings();
}
```

Next, we can initialize our particle system with the following methods:

```
protected abstract ParticleSystemSettings InitializeSettings();


public override void Initialize()
{
    settings = InitializeSettings();

    particles = new Particle[settings.Capacity];

    vertices = new VertexPointSprite[settings.Capacity];

    for (int i = 0; i < settings.Capacity; i++)
    {
        particles[i] = new Particle();
        particles[i].Initialize(settings, false);
```

```
    }

    numberOfActiveParticles = 0;

    base.Initialize();
}
```

We populate our settings with a call to our abstract `InitializeSettings` method. When that is done, we will have all our settings populated, including the capacity value. We use the value to determine how big our particle array needs to be. We also create a vertex array of the same size. We loop through all the particles and initialize each one by calling the `Initialize` method on the particle itself. This is the method that created the values by getting random values based on the minimum and maximum values populated in the settings class. The `makeAlive` parameter is false because we do not want all the particles to be generated at once and show up on the screen. We want to ease into the effect.

Before we get to our `Update` method, let's look at the `LoadContent` method:

```
protected override void LoadContent()
{
    titleSafeArea = GraphicsDevice.Viewport.TitleSafeArea;

    effect = content.Load<Effect>(@"Effects\PointSprites");
    font = content.Load<SpriteFont>(@"Fonts\Arial");

    spriteBatch = new SpriteBatch(GraphicsDevice);

    vertexDeclaration = new VertexDeclaration(GraphicsDevice,
        VertexPointSprite.VertexElements);
    base.LoadContent();
}
```

Nothing too surprising here. We calculate our title safe area. We load our effect (which we talk about a little later) and our font. We create a new sprite batch and initialize our vertex declaration. Because we are going to allow debugging information to be drawn on the screen, we set our font variable. Besides loading the content and creating our sprite batch, we also set up our vertex declaration using the `VertexPointSprite` we created earlier. These are all straightforward tasks.

Now we are ready to jump into our `Update` method. The purpose of this method is to make sure our particles that are alive continue to move as needed and to create any new particles that should be created based on the emit rate. The following is the contents of our `Update` method:

```
float elapsedTime = (float)gameTime.ElapsedGameTime.TotalSeconds;

int particlesToEmitThisFrame =
    (int)(settings.EmitPerSecond * elapsedTime + .99);
int particlesEmitted = 0;
bool canCreateParticle;

for (int i = 0; i < particles.Length; i++)
{
    canCreateParticle = false;

    if (particles[i].IsAlive)
    {
        particles[i].Update(elapsedTime);
        if (!particles[i].IsAlive)
        {
            numberOfActiveParticles--;
            particles[i].CurrentColorTime = 0;
            particles[i].CurrentColorIndex = 0;

            canCreateParticle = ShouldCreateParticle(
                            particlesEmitted, particlesToEmitThisFrame);
        }
        else
        {
            if (settings.DisplayColorsInOrder)
            {
                if (particles[i].CurrentColorTime >
                    particles[i].ColorChangeRate)
                {
                    //due to rounding errors with floats we need to make sure
                    //we actually have another color
                    if (particles[i].CurrentColorIndex <
                        settings.Colors.Length - 1)
                    {
                        particles[i].CurrentColorIndex++;
                        particles[i].SetColor(
                            settings.Colors[particles[i].CurrentColorIndex]);
                        particles[i].CurrentColorTime = 0;
                    }
                }
            }
        }
    }
    else
    {
        canCreateParticle = ShouldCreateParticle(
```

```
                         particlesEmitted, particlesToEmitThisFrame);

    }

if (canCreateParticle)
    {
        particles[i] = CreateParticle();
        particlesEmitted++;
        numberOfActiveParticles++;
        totalParticlesEmitted++;
    }
}

if (settings.RotateAmount > 0)
{
    rotateAngle += settings.RotateAmount;
    if (rotateAngle > MathHelper.TwoPi)
        rotateAngle = 0;
}

base.Update(gameTime);
```

The first thing we do in this method is calculate the number of particles we should emit this frame. The calculation emits the same amount of particles every frame. We add the .99 at the end of the formula because we are truncating the value from a double to an integer. As a result we would not emit enough particles that frame. Better to emit one more particle than we can than to not emit enough particles. We then loop through each particle and check to determine whether or not the particle is alive.

> **TIP**
>
> A more accurate approach would be to store the fractional remainder and add that into the elapsed time during the next update. That way, frequencies such as 1.5 particles per frame will end up emitting either 1 or 2 particles on alternate frames, and we could specify emission rates even lower than the update frequency to get particles just emitted on some subset of frames.

If our particle is alive, we call the particle's Update method. Remember, this method actually determines if the particle has lived its entire life and, if so, sets the IsAlive flag to false. So after calling the Update method, we check that flag. If the particle died during that update cycle, we update our number of active particles counter as well as reset our color time and index. This is important for when we loop through our colors in order. We also check to see if we should immediately replace that particle with a new one. We will look at the condition inside the ShouldCreateParticle method in a moment.

If our particle is still alive even after calling the particle's Update method, we need to have our particle system manage which color our particle should be. This is only done if we are actually displaying our colors in order. Otherwise, there is nothing to do because the initial color of the particle will remain until the particle dies.

When we first came into our for loop checking each particle, we asked whether or not the particle was alive. We just discussed what happens when the particle is alive when we come into this Update method. Now you will see what we do with our particle if it is not alive.

If our particle is not alive, we need to determine whether we want to create another particle. We are using the ShouldCreateParticle method again, so now is a good time to see exactly what that method is doing:

```
private bool ShouldCreateParticle(
    int particlesEmitted, int particlesToEmitThisFrame)
{
    if (!settings.RunOnce || totalParticlesEmitted < settings.Capacity)
        return (particlesEmitted < particlesToEmitThisFrame);
    else
        return (false);
}
```

We determine whether we should create a new particle by looking at a few variables. As long as we are not running the particle system effect once, or if we are running the effect once but we have not reached our capacity yet, we continue to our next check; otherwise we return false, meaning that we should not create another particle. The next check we do is to see if we can still emit particles in this frame. We return that value.

This brings us to the canCreateParticle condition back in our Update method. If the preceding method told us we can create a particle, we do so by calling CreateParticle, and we update our counters. You will see that method in just a moment.

The last task we perform in our Update method is to update our rotation angle with the rotation amount supplied in the settings. If the rotation amount is set to zero, we do not update our rotation angle. By not setting the rotation amount or setting it to zero, we tell our particle system that we do not want our point sprite (or more accurately, our texture applied to our point sprite) to rotate. You will see how this value is used in our effect file in the next section.

The CreateParticle method is listed here:

```
private Particle CreateParticle()
{
    int index = lastParticleIndex;
    for (int i = 0; i < particles.Length; i++)
    {
        if (!particles[index].IsAlive)
            break;
        else
        {
```

```
            index++;
            if (index >= particles.Length)
                index = 0;
        }
    }

    //at this point index is the one we want ...
    particles[index].Initialize(settings);
    lastParticleIndex = index;

    return (particles[index]);
}
```

In this method we loop through our particles to find an empty slot (a particle that is not alive). Once we find this slot, we call the particle's Initialize method to set all the random values for this particle. We then update our index, stating where the last particle we created was located. This is done for performance reasons. The idea is that the particles are created in order and that if the lifetimes are relatively close, we might find an empty slot close to the last place where we found the empty slot. In a worst-case scenario, we would loop through the entire list this way. However, that should not happen anywhere near the amount of times it would if we always started with the first index.

The Update code called a SetColor method on the Particle object. We have not created that method yet. Let's add the following method to the Particle class:

```
internal void SetColor(Color color)
{
    Vertex.Color = color;
}
```

Now that we have updated our particles, we need to draw them. The content of our Draw method is shown here:

```
if (DebugInfo)
{
    spriteBatch.Begin(SpriteBlendMode.AlphaBlend, SpriteSortMode.Immediate,
        SaveStateMode.SaveState);
    spriteBatch.DrawString(font, "Particles Capacity: " +
        settings.Capacity.ToString(),
        new Vector2(titleSafeArea.Left, titleSafeArea.Top), Color.Black);
    spriteBatch.DrawString(font, "Active Particles: " +
        numberOfActiveParticles.ToString(),
        new Vector2(titleSafeArea.Left, titleSafeArea.Top + 20), Color.Black);
    spriteBatch.DrawString(font, "Free Particles: " +
        (particles.Length - numberOfActiveParticles).ToString(),
        new Vector2(titleSafeArea.Left, titleSafeArea.Top + 40), Color.Black);
    spriteBatch.End();
```

```
}

GraphicsDevice.RenderState.PointSpriteEnable = true;
GraphicsDevice.RenderState.DepthBufferWriteEnable = false;

SetBlendModes();

GraphicsDevice.VertexDeclaration = vertexDeclaration;

PopulatePointSprites();

if (numberOfActiveParticles > 0)
{
    effect.Parameters["View"].SetValue(View);
    effect.Parameters["Projection"].SetValue(Projection);
    effect.Parameters["ColorMap"].SetValue(settings.Texture);
    effect.Parameters["World"].SetValue(Matrix.Identity);

    effect.Parameters["RotateAngle"].SetValue(rotateAngle);

    effect.Begin();
    effect.CurrentTechnique.Passes[0].Begin();

    GraphicsDevice.DrawUserPrimitives(
        PrimitiveType.PointList, vertices, 0, numberOfActiveParticles);

    effect.CurrentTechnique.Passes[0].End();
    effect.End();
}

base.Draw(gameTime);
```

If we need to write out our debugging information, we display the counter information for our particles. Obviously, we could display anything we find helpful. We are taking a performance hit here by having our sprite batch save the state, but we will not be displaying the text in the game itself, so this is not a problem.

The next task we complete is to set our render state to handle our point sprites. We tell our graphics device that we are going to be rendering point sprites. We then have a method that will set our blend modes. This is done as a method so our derived particle systems can override it if they would like. This could be useful, for example, if we ever have a particle system that needs to appear to glow because we could set the blend modes to an additive blend mode. The code for the SetBlendModes method is as follows:

```
protected virtual void SetBlendModes()
{
```

```
    GraphicsDevice.RenderState.AlphaBlendEnable = true;
    GraphicsDevice.RenderState.SourceBlend = Blend.SourceAlpha;
    GraphicsDevice.RenderState.DestinationBlend = Blend.InverseSourceAlpha;
}
```

By default our particle system will use alpha blending. Our derived particle systems can override this method to change the blend mode.

Back in our `Draw` method, we set our graphics device vertex declaration so it will draw the point sprites correctly. We then populate our point sprites. The `PopulatePointSprites` method is shown here:

```
private void PopulatePointSprites()
{
    if (numberOfActiveParticles == 0)
        return;

    int currVertex = 0;
    for (int i = 0; i < particles.Length; i++)
    {
        if (particles[i].IsAlive)
        {
            vertices[currVertex] = particles[i].Vertex;
            currVertex++;
        }

        if (currVertex >= numberOfActiveParticles)
            break; //stop looping, we have found all active particles
    }
}
```

In this method we are setting each of the vertices that will be piped to the graphics card. We do this by looping through all the particles. If a particle is active, we set that vertex value to our particle's vertex value. We do not change the size of our vertices array. Instead, we just keep track of the number of active particles and make sure that the first part of our array contains all the valid values.

You can see back in our `Draw` method that we pass in this list of vertices along with the primitive count (the number of active particles). This tells the `DrawUserPrimitives` method to use the vertices from offset 0 to the number of active particles. By doing it this way, we are not constantly allocating and deallocating memory.

Before we actually call the `DrawUserPrimitives` method, we make sure we have active particles to draw. Assuming we have particles (vertices) to draw, we set the view, projection, world, texture, and rotation angle parameters of our effect file.

Before we look at our effect file, we need to round out our `ParticleSystem` class by adding in these methods that either our derived particle systems or our game will need:

```
protected void SetTexture(Texture2D texture)
{
    settings.Texture = texture;
}

public void SetPosition(Vector3 position)
{
    settings.EmitPosition = position;
}

public void ResetSystem()
{
    if (settings.RunOnce)
    {
        totalParticlesEmitted = 0;
    }
}
```

These methods are very straightforward. We allow the derived particle systems to set the texture. We could make this public if we also wanted our game to set the texture for the particle system. We do allow the game to set the initial emit position of our particle system. The last method we have here resets our system. Our game code can reset a particle system that only runs once. A good use for this would be for a fireworks particle system effect. Each time the game wants to kick off the fireworks, it could call this reset system. One caveat: The particle system would have to be completed because it only resets the total particles emitted counter. Of course, this could be modified to be more robust if needed.

Point Sprite Effect File

Finally we can look at the effect file we need to create to process our point sprites. We need to add a new effect file, called PointSprites.fx, to our Effects folder in our XELibrary's Content project. You can see the global variables here, which should be familiar to you by now:

```
float4x4 World : WORLD;
float4x4 View;
float4x4 Projection;

float RotateAngle = 0;

texture ColorMap;
sampler2D ColorMapSampler = sampler_state
{
    Texture = <ColorMap>;
```

```
        magfilter = LINEAR;
        minfilter = LINEAR;
        mipfilter = LINEAR;
        addressU = mirror;
        addressV = mirror;
};
```

Next, we have our vertex input and output structs:

```
struct VertexInput
{
    float4 Position    : POSITION0;
    float Size         : PSIZE0;
    float4 Color       : COLOR0;
};

struct VertexOutput
{
    float4 Position    : POSITION0;
    float Size         : PSIZE0;
    float4 Color       : COLOR0;
};
```

These are actually identical, and we could have used the same struct for both the input and the output. To avoid confusion, we left this as two different structs. Just like our VertexPointSprite custom vertex struct, we are expecting the Position, Size, and Color values from our application.

Our vertex shader is simple:

```
VertexOutput vertexShader (VertexInput input)
{
    VertexOutput output;
    float4x4 worldViewProjection = mul(mul(World, View), Projection);
    output.Position = mul(input.Position, worldViewProjection);
    output.Color = input.Color;
    output.Size = input.Size;

    return output;
}
```

We transform our position like normal; then we just set the output size and color to what we received as input.

Our pixel shader is not complex either, but the Xbox 360 has a different semantic for handling point sprite texture coordinates. Because of this, we need to declare our texture coordinates differently. We also need to extract those coordinates differently based on our platform. Let's take a look at the code before we get into the explanation:

```
struct PixelInput
{
    float3 Position : POSITION0;

    #ifdef XBOX360
        float4 TexCoords : SPRITETEXCOORD0;
    #else
        float2 TexCoords : TEXCOORD0;
    #endif
    float4 Color : COLOR0;
};

float4 pixelShader(PixelInput input) : COLOR0
{
    float2 texCoords;

    #ifdef XBOX360
        texCoords = abs(input.TexCoords.zw);
    #else
        texCoords = input.TexCoords.xy;
    #endif

    return ( saturate(tex2D(ColorMapSampler, texCoords) * input.Color) );
}
```

Our pixel input gets the position, texture coordinates, and the color. We have the XBOX360 preprocessor directive condition in place so that we use the appropriate semantic for the different platforms. In the actual pixel shader, we need to take the absolute value of the last two components of the texture coordinates for the Xbox 360. Because the values can be negative, it is very important for us to take the absolute value. For Windows, we take the typical x and y components of our 2D vector.

We actually have another section of code we need to add right before the return statement in our pixelShader function:

```
//only take the rotation penalty if we need to
if (RotateAngle > 0)
{
    texCoords -= .5f;

    float ca = cos(RotateAngle);
    float sa = sin(RotateAngle);
    float2 tempCoords;
    tempCoords.x = texCoords.x * ca - texCoords.y * sa;
```

```
    tempCoords.y = texCoords.x * sa + texCoords.y * ca;
    texCoords = tempCoords;
    texCoords *= 1.4142135623730951; //sqrt(2);

    texCoords += .5f;
}
```

Instead of cluttering the core of the pixel shader just given with our rotation code, I have listed it here. The great thing about this code is that we can simply ignore it if our particles should not rotate. If they do rotate, then we need to rotate our texture coordinates to simulate that the point sprite is rotating. We use the rotation angle that our game passes in to calculate the new texture coordinates that our pixel shader should sample. This is done with a little bit of trigonometry. When we complete this calculation, our texture coordinates have been changed based on the rotation angle.

Finally, we set up our default technique with the only pass that includes our pixel and vertex shaders:

```
technique Default
{
    pass P0
    {
        VertexShader = compile vs_1_1 vertexShader();
        PixelShader  = compile ps_2_0 pixelShader();
    }
}
```

Particle System Demo

Now that we have created our particle, custom point sprite vertex format, particle system, and effect file, we can finally create our demo to use our new particle system. We are just setting up the framework because we do not actually have any particle effects created yet. We will create several particle system effects in the next section.

As usual, we will begin with setting up our private member fields. We have all the usual suspects:

```
private FirstPersonCamera camera;
private InputHandler input;
private FPS fps;

private Model model;
private Texture2D texture;
private Effect effect;
private Skybox skybox;
```

We are going to using our FPS game component because the number of particles we have will directly affect performance. We will be using our skybox, and we can add the skybox2.tga file to the Skyboxes folder of the Content project. We need to add XELibrary as a reference to our game project and include the using statement. We also need to reference our SkyboxPipeline assembly in our Content project. Finally, we need to set the skybox2.tga texture to use the SkyboxProcessor in the properties window.

There are no surprises in our constructor:

```
public Game1()
{
    graphics = new GraphicsDeviceManager(this);
    Content.RootDirectory = "";

    input = new InputHandler(this, true);
    Components.Add(input);

    camera = new FirstPersonCamera(this);
    Components.Add(camera);

    fps = new FPS(this, false, true);
    Components.Add(fps);
}
```

When we set up our input handler, we let it know that it's possible to exit out of game by pressing the Back button or Escape. This is done by passing in true as the second parameter. We tell our FPS game component that we do not want to synchronize with our monitor's retrace but we do want our update method to run at a given rate.

TIP

An enhancement to our library would be to change the FPS and InputHandler game component's boolean values to enumerated types, which would not be so cumbersome to read as we look back over the code. It does not add that much clutter, but in order to keep the code a little cleaner, we left it out. It is usually not considered good design to simply have boolean values that signify whether or not something is supposed to happen. It requires memorization, extra documentation, or reliance on the IntelliSense of the IDE. Having a well-described enumerated type avoids confusion. Code is read a lot more than it is written, so it makes a lot of sense to create enumerated types for readability.

After setting up our constructor, the next thing we typically do is set up our LoadContent method:

```
protected override void LoadContent()
{
```

```
model = Content.Load<Model>(@"Models\asteroid1");
texture = Content.Load<Texture2D>(@"Textures\asteroid1");
effect = Content.Load<Effect>(@"Effects\AmbientTexture");
effect.Parameters["AmbientColor"].SetValue(
    Color.WhiteSmoke.ToVector4());

skybox = Content.Load<Skybox>(@"Skyboxes\skybox2");
}
```

We are going to display an asteroid model that will be surrounded by our particles.
Although this is not required, it helps us know that we are setting our render states properly. We will discuss this some more in a moment. For now, we are going load our content
like normal. We load our model and its texture. These can be added to our project as
usual. We are using the ambient texture effect file. We set the ambient color to XNA's
WhiteSmoke color. Our skybox is loaded next. Now that we have our content loaded, we
can take a look at the Draw method. Most of the code is actually drawing our asteroid:

```
protected override void Draw(GameTime gameTime)
{
    graphics.GraphicsDevice.Clear(Color.Black);

    graphics.GraphicsDevice.RenderState.AlphaBlendEnable = false;
    graphics.GraphicsDevice.RenderState.PointSpriteEnable = false;
    graphics.GraphicsDevice.RenderState.DepthBufferWriteEnable = true;

    skybox.Draw(camera.View, camera.Projection, Matrix.CreateScale(5000.0f));

    Matrix world = Matrix.CreateRotationY(
        MathHelper.ToRadians(45.0f * (float)gameTime.TotalGameTime.TotalSeconds)) *
        Matrix.CreateTranslation(new Vector3(0, 0, -4000));
    DrawModel(ref model, ref world, texture);

    base.Draw(gameTime);
}

private void DrawModel(ref Model m, ref Matrix world, Texture2D texture)
{
    Matrix[] transforms = new Matrix[m.Bones.Count];
    m.CopyAbsoluteBoneTransformsTo(transforms);

    foreach (ModelMesh mesh in m.Meshes)
    {
        foreach (ModelMeshPart mp in mesh.MeshParts)
        {
            if (texture != null)
                effect.Parameters["ColorMap"].SetValue(texture);
```

```
            effect.Parameters["Projection"].SetValue(camera.Projection);
            effect.Parameters["View"].SetValue(camera.View);
            effect.Parameters["World"].SetValue(world * mesh.ParentBone.Transform);
            mp.Effect = effect;
        }
        mesh.Draw();
    }
}
```

We clear our device and then set our render state before drawing our asteroid. Remember that we enable alpha blending and our point sprites as well as disable our depth buffer when we draw our particles. So we need to make sure we set the render state to the state we want it before we actually render our world. We then draw our skybox as we have in the past, as well as our loaded model.

We have not completed the code for our demo, but we have the framework in place. We could run the demo now, but we would only see our spinning asteroid in a room. In the next section we will dig into our specific particle system effects and incorporate them into our demo.

Creating Particle Effects

We are going to create actual particle systems that derive from our abstract particle system class. We will also add these to our demo so we can see them in action. Even with the basic particle system infrastructure we have set up, we can create a number of different effects. This section lists a few of them that show off some of the features. Because we will have a few particle systems, it might be beneficial to create a subfolder in our game solution called ParticleSystems.

Rain

To get started, we are going to create a rain effect. The first code file we create inside the ParticleSystems folder of our Game project is called Rain.cs.

Because this is the first particle system we are creating, the code is listed in its entirety in Listing 21.1.

LISTING 21.1   Rain.cs

```
using System;
using System.Collections.Generic;
using System.Text;
using Microsoft.Xna.Framework;
using Microsoft.Xna.Framework.Graphics;

using XELibrary;
```

```
namespace ParticleSystemDemo
{
    public class Rain : XELibrary.ParticleSystem
    {
        public Rain(Game game, int capacity, Vector3 externalForce)
            : base(game)
        {
            settings.Capacity = capacity;
            settings.ExternalForce = externalForce;
        }

        public Rain(Game game, int capacity)
            : this(game, capacity, new Vector3(0, 0, 0)) { }

        public Rain(Game game) : this(game, 5000) { }

        protected override ParticleSystemSettings InitializeSettings()
        {
            settings.EmitPerSecond = 1100;

            settings.EmitPosition = new Vector3(0, 4000, 0);
            settings.EmitRange = new Vector3(4000, 0, 4000);

            settings.MinimumVelocity = new Vector3(0, -10, 0);
            settings.MaximumVelocity = new Vector3(0, -50, 0);

            settings.MinimumAcceleration = new Vector3(0, -10, 0);
            settings.MaximumAcceleration = new Vector3(0, -10, 0);

            settings.MinimumLifetime = 5.0f;
            settings.MaximumLifetime = 5.0f;

            settings.MinimumSize = 5.0f;
            settings.MaximumSize = 15.0f;

            settings.Colors = new Color[] {
                Color.CornflowerBlue,
                Color.LightBlue
            };

            settings.DisplayColorsInOrder = false;

            return (settings);
        }
```

```
protected override void  LoadContent()
{
    SetTexture(
        content.Load<Texture2D>(@"Textures\raindrop"));
    }

        base.LoadContent();
    }
}
}
```

All the effects will have three constructors. The default constructor for our rain effect will set the capacity to 5,000 particles, which we need to allocate memory for, as well as an external force of 0 in all directions. We allow overriding any of those values with the main constructor. Remember, our abstract particle system class initializes our settings variable. In our main constructor we set the capacity and external forces. A particle system does not need to have three constructors. If they are needed, we could just have one constructor and not allow (or alternatively force) our game to set the different values. This provides a lot of flexibility.

The core of our particle system effect is in the InitializeSettings method. This is where we actually specify the minimum and maximum values of our particles. Specifically for our rain effect, we are saying we want to emit about 1,000 particles every second. This number was chosen because we are setting the minimum and maximum life value to 5 seconds and will only have a total of 5,000 particles available to us. Thus, we can basically emit 1,000 particles every second so there is no lull in the amount of particles we are creating.

We set the position and the range around the position where we will create the particles. In this case we are creating them 4,000 units above the origin. We are letting the particle system pick random positions within 4,000 units to the left or right (EmitRange.X) or 4,000 units ahead or behind (EmitRange.Z). We are not letting it pick random spots on the y axis because we want them to all start from the same plane above us.

We set the initial velocity of our raindrops to be between 10 and 100. They are supposed to fall downward, so we have made the Y values negative. We have forced the acceleration to be 10 by setting both the minimum and maximum values to the same value. We allow the size of our raindrops to vary in size from 5 to 10.

Finally, we set up the colors that our raindrops should be tinted. We have set the colors to light blue and—our favorite—cornflower blue. We want each raindrop to pick a random color and not change colors over time, so we set the DisplayColorsInOrder flag to false.

The last thing we do with this effect is set our raindrop texture. We do this in our LoadContent method, of course. There should not be any surprises with the code because we are just loading the content like normal. We do need to add the raindrop.png file to the Textures subfolder in our solution.

To see this particle system, we need to actually create it in our demo. We need to declare a private member field to hold our particle system in our game code:

```
private Rain rain;
```

Next, in our game's constructor we need to initialize the game component:

```
rain = new Rain(this);
Components.Add(rain);
```

If we want to display the debugging info on this particle system, we just need to set the DebugInfo property to true. Because this is a game component, if we did not want this information to be displayed or updated, we could set the Visible and Enabled properties to false.

In our game's Draw method we need to set the particle system's View and Projection properties. We do this by assigning them our camera's View and Projection properties:

```
rain.View = camera.View;
rain.Projection = camera.Projection;
```

That is it. It is very painless to plug in an effect to our demo. You can run the demo and see rain falling from the sky after you copy the raindrop.png file from the book's CD.

Bubbles

The next effect we create is one that looks like bubbles. We can copy our Rain.cs file and rename it Bubbles.cs. We will also rename the class to Bubbles. We need to change one of the constructors because we want our default external force to be different:

```
public Bubbles(Game game, int capacity)
    : this(game, capacity, new Vector3(0, .05f, 0)) { }
```

The texture we will be using is called bubble, so we can replace raindrop with bubble. We can add bubble.png to our Textures folder. This leaves the InitializeSettings method. Our new method is listed here:

```
protected override ParticleSystemSettings InitializeSettings()
{
    settings.EmitPerSecond = 1000;

    settings.EmitPosition = new Vector3(0, 0, -500);
    settings.EmitRange = new Vector3(50, 60, 50);

    settings.MinimumVelocity = new Vector3(-1, -1, -1);
    settings.MaximumVelocity = new Vector3(1, 20, 1);
```

```
settings.MinimumAcceleration = new Vector3(-0.1f, -0.1f, -0.1f);
settings.MaximumAcceleration = new Vector3(.1f, .1f, .1f);

settings.MinimumLifetime = 1.0f;
settings.MaximumLifetime = 25.0f;

settings.MinimumSize = 5.0f;
settings.MaximumSize = 15.0f;

settings.Colors = new Color[] {
    Color.WhiteSmoke,
    Color.White,
    Color.NavajoWhite,
    Color.Khaki};

settings.DisplayColorsInOrder = false;

return (settings);
}
```

We just modified our settings, but the concept is the same. We set the range to find a random position somewhere within 50 units in front of, behind, to the left, or to the right of the current position. It can place the particle within 60 units above or below the position as well. This is the same concept as our rain effect, except that we are allowing it to pick random Y values as well to plot our points. The lifetime of our particles is no longer a constant 5 seconds. We now have a minimum life span of 5 seconds with a maximum life span of 25 seconds. We are now using four colors instead of two but are still just setting them initially to random values.

We would add this effect to our game the same way we did our rain effect. We need to set up a variable and then initialize the variable in our game's constructor. We need to add the particle system to our game components, and finally we need to set its View and Projection properties in our Draw method.

Laser Shield

This effect produces a cylinder around our asteroid simulating a laser shield of sorts. We can copy our Rain.cs file and rename it LaserShield.cs and then rename the class to LaserShield. We start by replacing two of the constructors we had in our rain class:

```
public LaserShield(Game game, int capacity)
    : this(game, capacity, new Vector3(0, 0, 0)) { }
public LaserShield(Game game) : this(game, 2500) { }
```

We have no external force, and we are only creating 2,500 particles in this system. We need to add the texture 3dtubegray.png to the Textures folder in our solution and replace raindrop with 3dtubegray in our LoadContent method.

The heart of this particle system effect is in the `InitializeSettings` method:

```
protected override ParticleSystemSettings InitializeSettings()
{
    settings.EmitPosition = new Vector3(0, -1500, -4000);
    settings.EmitPerSecond = settings.Capacity;

    settings.EmitRadius = new Vector2(1200, 1200);

    settings.MinimumVelocity = new Vector3(0, 0, 0);
    settings.MaximumVelocity = new Vector3(0, 0, 0);

    settings.MinimumAcceleration = new Vector3(0, 100, 0);
    settings.MaximumAcceleration = new Vector3(0, 100, 0);

    settings.MinimumLifetime = 1.0f;
    settings.MaximumLifetime = 1.0f;

    settings.MinimumSize = 50.0f;
    settings.MaximumSize = 50.0f;

    settings.Colors = new Color[] {
        new Color(new Vector4(Color.SteelBlue.ToVector3(), .1f)),
        new Color(new Vector4(Color.Silver.ToVector3(), .1f))
    };
    settings.DisplayColorsInOrder = false;

    return (settings);
}
```

We set the lifetime of the particles to be 1 second. As a result we set our `EmitPerSecond` value to match our capacity (2,500). We are positioning our particle system at the same place as our asteroid: 4,000 units in front of us. However, we are starting the particle system under the asteroid, so we set the y value to –1,500. Our acceleration (both minimum and maximum values) is set to 100 units upward. In the 1-second life span of our particle, it travels to the top of our asteroid.

What makes this effect unique from the previous two is the fact that we are using the `EmitRadius` setting. Remember way back at the beginning of this chapter when we set up the `Initialize` method of our `Particle` class? We had a condition where we check whether or not the `EmitRadius` value was set to zero. If it was set to something other than its initial value, we calculated a random angle and used that angle in a calculation with our random position and the `EmitRadius`. That code is listed here for quick reference:

```
if (settings.EmitRadius != Vector2.Zero)
{
    float angle = Utility.GetRandomFloat(0, MathHelper.TwoPi);
```

```
Vertex.Position = new Vector3(
    position.X + (float)Math.Sin(angle) * settings.EmitRadius.X,
    position.Y,
    position.Z + (float)Math.Cos(angle) * settings.EmitRadius.Y);
}
```

An enhancement to this particle system would be to have a minimum and a maximum emit radius. This way, instead of having a constant circular or oval pattern, the particles could be all over the place.

After we set up the effect in our demo, we can run our demo and see a shield surround our asteroid.

Laser Scanner

Our laser scanner effect will actually inherit from the laser shield class in the previous section. Because of this, it is shown in its entirety in Listing 21.2.

LISTING 21.2   LaserScanner.cs

```
using System;
using System.Collections.Generic;
using System.Text;
using Microsoft.Xna.Framework;
using Microsoft.Xna.Framework.Graphics;
using XELibrary;

namespace ParticleSystemDemo
{
    public class LaserScanner : LaserShield
    {
        public LaserScanner(Game game, int capacity, Vector3 externalForce)
            : base(game, capacity, externalForce) { }

        public LaserScanner(Game game, int capacity)
            : base(game, capacity) { }

        public LaserScanner(Game game) : base(game) { }

        protected override ParticleSystemSettings InitializeSettings()
        {
            base.InitializeSettings();

            settings.EmitPerSecond = (int)(settings.Capacity * 4);

            settings.Colors = new Color[] {
```

```
                new Color(new Vector4(Color.Red.ToVector3(), .025f))
            };

            return (settings);
        }
    }
}
```

You can see that each constructor is simply passing the values to the base `LaserShield` class. If we wanted to change the capacity or external force, we could. However, we just left the majority of the code alone. In our `InitializeSettings` method, the first thing we do is call our base class `InitializeSettings`. By doing this, we only need to modify the settings that are truly unique in this scanner effect we are making.

We have changed our `EmitPerSecond` setting to be four times the capacity of our particle system. Because we cannot emit more particles than are within the capacity of the system, we can make the particles we want to emit do so faster. The result is an effect where the particles are more dense than normal, but there is a lull in the action because there are no more particles to create at the origin. In this effect, the 4 determines how wide the band is that is scanning the asteroid. The smaller the number, the more continuous the scanning will be. The higher the number, the smaller the band, causing a greater distance between the particles.

We can add the effect to our demo like normal by creating a variable and initializing it in our constructor and then adding it to our collection of game components. Running more than two of these effects at once can make most systems crawl, so be careful how many vertices you try to process at once.

TIP

An enhancement could be made to the particle system. There is a bottleneck in passing the data from our application to the graphics card. The graphics card is sitting idle while we generate our vertices to pass to it. Instead of building them all and sending them to the graphics card all at once, we could build them in chunks. A couple of options that come to mind are 10 chunks of 10% or three chunks of 33%. There is no hard-and-fast rule as to the best way to do this. However, the current code definitely produces a bottleneck when the particle count is very high. We will not be modifying the call in our `Draw` method, but it would be a good exercise to do if performance is suffering.

Poisonous Gas

The next effect we create is one that simulates a thick gas. The same effect could be used for smoke if we wanted. We will be using the `Rain` class as a starting point. We can call this class `PoisonGas`. Here are the constructors we replace:

```
public PoisonGas(Game game, int capacity)
    : this(game, capacity, new Vector3(0, 0, 0)) { }
```

```
public PoisonGas(Game game) : this(game, 5000) { }
```

We need to add the smoke.png file to our Textures folder. In our LoadContent method, we can replace raindrop with smoke. Finally, our InitializeSettings method is as follows:

```
protected override ParticleSystemSettings InitializeSettings()
{
    settings.EmitPosition = new Vector3(0, -2500, -4000);
    settings.EmitPerSecond = 500;

    settings.EmitRadius = new Vector2(10, 10);

    settings.MinimumVelocity = new Vector3(-.1f, 0, -.1f);
    settings.MaximumVelocity = new Vector3(.1f, 0, .1f);

    settings.MinimumAcceleration = new Vector3(-.5f, .6f, -.5f);
    settings.MaximumAcceleration = new Vector3(.5f, .6f, .5f);

    settings.MinimumLifetime = 5.0f;
    settings.MaximumLifetime = 20.0f;

    settings.MinimumSize = 50.0f;
    settings.MaximumSize = 50.0f;

    settings.Colors = new Color[] {
        new Color(new Vector4(Color.Green.ToVector3(), .05f))
    };

    settings.DisplayColorsInOrder = false;

    settings.RotateAmount = 0.025f;

    settings.RunOnce = true;

    return (settings);
}
```

The only thing new about this effect is the fact that we have told it to run only once. We also set the rotation amount so that each particle's texture will rotate. We can add the following code to our particle system demo's Update method so we can kick off the effect again:

```
if (input.ButtonHandler.WasButtonPressed(0, InputHandler.ButtonType.A) ||
    input.KeyboardState.WasKeyPressed(Keys.Space))
{
    gas.ResetSystem();
}
```

We simply check to see if the spacebar or the A button on the game pad has been pressed. If it has, we call the `ResetSystem` method on our gas particle system effect. This simply sets the `totalParticlesEmitted` variable to 0. Remember, this is checked when determining if we should create particles. So effectively, even if our particle system is only supposed to run one time, resetting this counter lets it continue to emit particles. The method does not actually kill off any existing particles; it just resets the counter for any particles that are being emitted.

The Colorful Effect

The last particle system effect we create is one that displays colors in order. We can start this effect by copying the bubble effect. We can call this new effect Colorful (that's creativity at its best). As usual, we start by replacing two of our constructors:

```
public Colorful(Game game, int capacity)
    : this(game, capacity, new Vector3(0, .05f, 0)) { }

public Colorful(Game game) : this(game, 2500) { }
```

We will be leaving the bubble texture for this effect, so nothing needs to change there. The following is our `InitializeSettings` method:

```
protected override ParticleSystemSettings InitializeSettings()
{
    settings.EmitPerSecond = 2500;

    settings.EmitPosition = new Vector3(0, 0, -1000);
    settings.EmitRange = new Vector3(50, 160, 50);
    settings.EmitRadius = new Vector2(100,100);

    settings.MinimumVelocity = new Vector3(-1, -1, -1);
    settings.MaximumVelocity = new Vector3(1, 20, 1);

    settings.MinimumAcceleration = new Vector3(-5, -10, -5);
    settings.MaximumAcceleration = new Vector3(5, 10, 5);

    settings.MinimumLifetime = 1.0f;
    settings.MaximumLifetime = 1.0f;

    settings.MinimumSize = 15.0f;
    settings.MaximumSize = 15.0f;

    settings.Colors = new Color[] {
        Color.Green,
        Color.Yellow,
```

```
        Color.Red,
        Color.Blue,
        Color.Purple};

    settings.DisplayColorsInOrder = true;

    settings.RunOnce = true;

    return (settings);
}
```

The main thing to notice in this effect is the fact that we set our `DisplayColorsInOrder` flag to true. This means that each particle will change its color as often as it needs to. It will display each color for the same amount of time, starting with the first color in the array.

We have also set this effect to run only once, so we will want to hook this up in our demo's `Update` class after we declare the variable and initialize it and then add it to our game component collection.

Summary

This was a rather long chapter, but hopefully you have gained a good grasp of particle systems. This implementation is not extremely robust, but you were able to see some examples of totally different effects by modifying just a few settings. The foundation is laid so that more complex particle systems can be created if needed. The main thing to keep in mind is that a particle system should only be as complex as needed.

We have covered a lot of ground in this book so far. We have a decent library we have been adding to, and we have several neat tricks under our belt. In the next part of the book we will take what we have covered so far and put it into practice by creating a 3D game.

PART IX

Putting It into Practice

Creating a 3D Game

We have covered a lot of ground in this book. Although there will be some new material in these next two chapters, most of it will be review as we take what you've learned and put it into practice. We are going to be creating a full 3D game, complete with sound effects, music, artificial intelligence, physics, a heads-up display (HUD), and scoring.

Creating the Tunnel Vision Game

The game is set in outer space. The tunnel to our space station is being attacked, so we need to defend the tunnel and not let our enemies breach the opening. We have missiles that we can fire. Fortunately, the enemies do not have any. They simply attack in swarms, which means we need to take swift action to destroy them.

Creating the Game States

To get started, we need to make a copy of our GameStateDemo from Chapter 17, "Finite State Machines and Game State Management." We want to use the latest XELibrary from the last chapter, and we need to add the project to our solution because we will be making a modification to it a little later.

Rename Game1.cs to TunnelVision.cs. We can also change the name of this class and the namespace to TunnelVision. Figure 22.1 shows how we can rename our namespace through the IDE. This will modify all our source files for us. We also need to rename our Game1 class to TunnelVision.

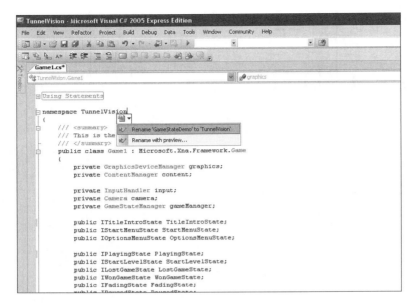

FIGURE 22.1   Visual Studio allows renaming the namespace through the IDE.

Adding a Skybox to Our Game

Let's add a skybox to our world. Find the skybox.tga file and add it to the Skyboxes folder in the Content project. We need to add a skybox content processor to our Content project as well as select SkyboxProcessor as the content processor for the skybox texture. Then we can add the following private member field to our game:

```
private Skybox skybox;
```

Next, we can load the skybox in our LoadContent method:

```
skybox = Content.Load<Skybox>(@"Skyboxes\skybox");
```

To finish up our skybox, we only need to draw it. We can add the following statement to the Draw method:

```
skybox.Draw(Camera.View, Camera.Projection, Matrix.CreateScale(1000));
```

Compiling the Game

While we are in our Draw method, we can remove the Begin and End methods for SpriteBatch because each game component will need to call its own. We need to leave the base.Draw method, of course.

Let's add a camera to our game. We are going to change this camera to one that is more suitable for our game, but for now we can just reference the normal `Camera` class. We need to change our private member field `camera` to the public member field `Camera`:

```
public Camera Camera;
```

We utilized the camera variable in the constructor (const). The variable will need to be changed from `camera` to `Camera` there as well. To get our game to run successfully, we need to modify our game states that utilize the sprite batch to call `Begin` and `End` because we removed it from the main `TunnelVision` game class. Once those methods are modified, we can compile and run our game.

Creating the Game Logic

After we successfully compile and run our game, we can start working on our game logic. Fortunately, we have the framework in place where we can easily put in our game code. We will first work on our game play by modifying the playing state code file (/GameStates/PlayingState.cs).

We need to remove `SpriteFont` from our member fields and add in the following fields:

```
private MissileManager missileManager;
private EnemyManager enemyManager;
private List<Level> Levels;
private int currentLevel;

private float totalCreatedEnemies;
public int TotalCollisions;

private BoundingSphere playerSphere;
```

We are going to manage our enemies and our missiles, so we have set up some variables for those. We also created a list to store our levels. Before we dig into our playing state any further, we can build out these classes. The code for our `Level` class, which can be added as Level.cs to our main game folder, is as follows:

```
public class Level
{
    public int Missiles;
    public int Enemies;
    public int Time;
    public float EnemySpeed;

    public Level(int missiles, int enemies, int time, float enemySpeed)
    {
    Missiles = missiles;
    Enemies = enemies;
```

```
    Time = time + 1;
    EnemySpeed = enemySpeed;
    }
}
```

The class is pretty straightforward—we are providing a way to store the number of missiles
that we are allowing on the screen at one time. One of the challenges of the game is to
not expend too many bullets at once. The next challenge is how many enemies this level
needs to generate before the level is over. We also have a timer that we will be using to
award bonus points if all the enemies are killed before it runs out. Finally, we store the
speed at which the enemy is moving in this level.

The enemy and missile managers do as their names imply and manage the missiles and
the enemies, respectively. These objects share a lot of the same properties. Therefore, we
are going to introduce a `SceneObject` and then have a `PhysicalObject` that inherits from
our `SceneObject`. Although everything in this game will really be a physical object, we
could have a trigger that, if reached, kicks off some animation; this would need to be a
scene object, not a physical object. You'll see that this makes more sense as we look at the
code, starting with the `SceneObject`:

```
public abstract class SceneObject
{
    public Matrix World;
    public BoundingSphere BoundingSphere;
}
```

This is a very simplistic abstract class that stores our world matrix for the object as well as
a bounding sphere. This allows us to place the object in the world and assign it a sphere
so that if something collides with it, we could kick off an event such as spawning enemies,
opening doors, doing a cut scene, or anything else we wanted. In our game, we will not be
using an object that is purely a scene object, but it is good to have it here for future
projects. The `Microsoft.Xna.Framework` namespace will need to be included because this
class uses `BoundingSphere`. Our physical object inherits from this and has more properties
for an actual drawable object. Here is the code for the `PhysicalObject` class:

```
public abstract class PhysicalObject : SceneObject
{
    public Vector3 Position;
    public Vector3 Velocity;
    public Vector3 Acceleration;
    public float Mass;
    public float Scale = 1.0f;
    public float Radius = 1.0f;
    public Color Color;
    public Matrix Rotation = Matrix.Identity;

    public virtual void Move(float elapsed)
```

```
    {
    //adjust velocity with our acceleration
    Velocity += Acceleration;

    //adjust position with our velocity
    Position += elapsed * Velocity;

    World = Matrix.CreateScale(Scale) * Rotation *
        Matrix.CreateTranslation(Position);

    BoundingSphere = new BoundingSphere(Position, Radius);
    }
}
```

We inherit from SceneObject so we get the bounding sphere and the world matrix, but we also add position, velocity, acceleration, mass, scale, radius, color, and rotation. This allows us to assign physical properties to our objects. We have a Move method that applies the physical forces we talked about in Chapter 16, "Physics Basics." This method adds the acceleration to our velocity and adds our velocity (taking the time delta into account) to our position. It then uses the scale, rotation, and position to update the world matrix for the object. Finally, it recalculates the bounding sphere based on the position and radius of the object. We need to add the following using statements:

```
using Microsoft.Xna.Framework;
using Microsoft.Xna.Framework.Graphics;
```

Now we are ready to look at our EnemyManager and MissileManager, which manage objects that inherit from our PhysicalObject. We will start with our MissileManager and our Missile class in particular:

```
class Missile : PhysicalObject
{
    public DateTime StartTime;
    public bool IsActive;
}
```

The missile object inherits all the properties from our physical object class and also includes the start time and a flag that states whether the missile is active. We will be treating this much like we did our particle system. We can jump right into our MissileManager to see how to manage these objects. Our MissileManager object will inherit from the DrawableGameComponent. As usual, we can start with our member fields and constructor:

```
public const int MISSILE_LIFE = 5; //5 seconds
private Model missile;
private Effect effect;

public Matrix View;
```

```
public Matrix Projection;

private Missile[] missiles;
private Texture2D missileTexture;

private int lastMissileIndex;
private float timer = 0;

public MissileManager(Game game)
    : base(game) { }
```

We have a constant that determines how long our missile should stay on the screen if it does not hit any enemies. One of the challenges we are presenting gamers is that only a certain number of missiles can be on the screen at any given time for each level. The more accurate the players are, the more frequently they can fire a missile. If they miss, the missile is active for 5 seconds, and if they have fired their allotment, players need to wait until the 5 seconds are up before they can fire another missile.

We also have fields that store the missile model and the effect we will be using for that model. We set our View and Projection properties (which our effect needs) inside of the game, so we set those fields with the public modifier. We have an array where we store and manage our missile objects and the texture we apply to those objects. Much like we did for our particle system, we are going to keep track of the last index in our array to which we added a missile so we know where to start when a new request is created to add a missile to our list.

Our constructor is empty and only passes the game object to the base DrawableGameComponent class. Next, we can look at the Load method that our game will call every time we start a new level. Each time a new level is started, we reset our array of missiles to handle the maximum amount the level allows the player to fire at one time. The code for the Load method is as follows:

```
public void Load(int capacity)
{
    missiles = new Missile[capacity];
    lastMissileIndex = 0;

    for (int i = 0; i < missiles.Length; i++)
    missiles[i] = new Missile();
}
```

At the beginning of the level, we reallocate our array and reset our last missile index. Finally, we loop through all the missiles and store an instance of each. Our LoadContent and UnloadContent methods are next:

```
protected override void LoadContent()
{
    missileTexture = Game.Content.Load<Texture2D>(
```

```
        @"Textures\FireGrade");
    missile = Game.Content.Load<Model>(@"Models\sphere");
    effect = Game.Content.Load<Effect>(
        @"Effects\VertexDisplacement");
    effect.Parameters["ColorMap"].SetValue(missileTexture);
    effect.Parameters["AmbientColor"].SetValue(0.8f);

    base.LoadContent();
}

protected override void UnloadContent()
{
    missiles = null;

    base.UnloadContent();
}
```

In our LoadContent method, we retrieve the texture from our TextureManager and the effect from our EffectManager. We then set the parameters on the effect. Our UnloadContent method sets our missiles array to null.

We need to add the FireGrade texture to our Content project. We also need to add the sphere model to our project. Both of these assets can be found on the accompanying CD in this chapter's code folder.

When the player fires a missile, we need to tell our MissileManager to add a missile to its array. Therefore, we provide a public method called AddMissile:

```
public bool AddMissile(Vector3 position, Vector3 direction, DateTime startTime)
{
    int index = lastMissileIndex;
    for (int i = 0; i < missiles.Length; i++)
    {
        if (!missiles[index].IsActive)
            break;
        else
        {
            index++;
            if (index >= missiles.Length)
                index = 0;
        }

        if (index == lastMissileIndex)
            return (false);
    }

    //at this point index is the one we want ...
```

```
        InitializeMissile(index, position, direction, startTime);

        missiles[index].IsActive = true;

        lastMissileIndex = index;

        return (true);
}
```

The AddMissile method loops through the entire array, finding the first empty slot it can initialize a missile into. If there are no free slots, the user has fired all the missiles allowed and the method returns false. The details of the InitializeMissile method are as follows:

```
private void InitializeMissile(int index, Vector3 position, Vector3 direction,
    DateTime startTime)
{
    missiles[index] = new Missile();
    missiles[index].Position = position;
    missiles[index].Acceleration = direction * 10f;
    missiles[index].Velocity = Vector3.Zero;
    missiles[index].StartTime = startTime;
}
```

The InitializeMissile method sets the values passed in from AddMissile, which gets the values from the game. Our MissileManager class also has a collision detection method. CheckCollision is used to determine if any of the missiles have collided with the bounding sphere passed in:

```
public bool CheckCollision(BoundingSphere check)
{
    for (int i = 0; i < missiles.Length; i++)
    {
        if ((missiles[i].IsActive) &&
            (missiles[i].BoundingSphere.Intersects(check)))
        {
            RemoveMissile(i);
            return (true);
        }
    }

    return (false);
}
```

If a collision is detected, we remove the missile from the list by setting its active flag to false. This is done in the RemoveMissile method:

```
private void RemoveMissile(int index)
{
```

```
        missiles[index].IsActive = false;
}
```

This leaves just the Update and Draw methods. The Update method simply loops through all the active missiles and checks to see how long they have lived. If they have lived too long, they are removed from the array. If they are still alive, they are moved by calling the Move method on the Missile object, which ultimately calls the Move method on the PhysicalObject class:

```
public override void Update(GameTime gameTime)
{
    float elapsed = (float)gameTime.ElapsedGameTime.TotalSeconds;

    timer += 0.655f;

    for (int mi = 0; mi < missiles.Length; mi++)
    {
        //we do not want to update any inactive missiles
        if (!missiles[mi].IsActive)
            continue;

        if ((DateTime.Now - missiles[mi].StartTime) > TimeSpan.FromSeconds(
            MissileManager.MISSILE_LIFE))
            RemoveMissile(mi);
        else
            missiles[mi].Move(elapsed);
    }

    base.Update(gameTime);
}
```

The Update method also adds a fixed amount to a timer, which is used for the effect of the missile. The Draw method is shown here:

```
public override void Draw(GameTime gameTime)
{
    GraphicsDevice.RenderState.DepthBufferEnable = true;
    GraphicsDevice.RenderState.AlphaBlendEnable = true;

    effect.Parameters["Timer"].SetValue(timer);

    effect.Parameters["View"].SetValue(View);
    effect.Parameters["Projection"].SetValue(Projection);

    for (int mi = 0; mi < missiles.Length; mi++)
    {
```

```
    if (!missiles[mi].IsActive)
        continue;

    effect.Parameters["World"].SetValue(missiles[mi].World);

    Matrix[] transforms = new Matrix[missile.Bones.Count];
    missile.CopyAbsoluteBoneTransformsTo(transforms);

    foreach (ModelMesh mesh in missile.Meshes)
    {
        for (int i = 0; i < mesh.MeshParts.Count; i++)
        {
            // Set this MeshParts effect to our RedWire effect
            mesh.MeshParts[i].Effect = effect;
        }

        mesh.Draw();

        missiles[mi].BoundingSphere = mesh.BoundingSphere;
        missiles[mi].BoundingSphere.Center += missiles[mi].World.Translation;
    }
    }

    base.Draw(gameTime);
}
```

The Draw method makes sure the render state is in the right state before drawing anything.
It sets the appropriate effect parameters; then it loops through all the missiles and applies
the effect to them. It also recalculates the bounding sphere of the missile.

Before we get back to the PlayingState, we need to add the enemy manager. The concept
is the same as our missile manager: Only a certain number of enemies can be displayed at
one time, determined by each level. The enemy object has tracking AI built in to it as
well. We start by creating the Enemy class, which inherits from PhysicalObject:

```
public class Enemy : PhysicalObject
{
    Random random = new Random(DateTime.Now.Millisecond);

    public Vector3 Target = Vector3.Zero;
    public Texture2D Texture;
    private float moveSpeed;
    private Vector3 Up, Forward;

    public Enemy(Texture2D texture, float moveSpeed)
    {
        Texture = texture;
```

```
        this.moveSpeed = moveSpeed;
        Scale = 0.01f;
        Radius = 5f;
        Position = XELibrary.Utility.GetRandomVector3(
            new Vector3(-300, -100, -100), new Vector3(300, 100, -100));

        Up = Vector3.Up;
        Forward = Vector3.Forward;
    }

    public override void Move(float elapsed)
    {
        Vector3 tv = Target - Position;
        tv.Normalize();

        Velocity = tv * moveSpeed;

        Forward = tv;

        Vector3 Right = Vector3.Normalize(Vector3.Cross(Forward, Vector3.Up));

        Up = Vector3.Normalize(Vector3.Cross(Right, Forward));

        Rotation = Matrix.Identity;
        Rotation.Forward = Forward;
        Rotation.Up = Up;
        Rotation.Right = Right;

        base.Move(elapsed);
    }
}
```

moveSpeed is the speed at which the enemies are moving toward the player. The Up and Forward vectors are stored so we can calculate the rotation. The position in which an enemy is generated is random. The Move method handles the AI for tracking the player as well as setting the rotation so the enemy is always facing the player. We define two vectors: Up and Forward. Then we calculate our Right vector by normalizing the cross-product of the Forward and Up vectors. Then we recalculate the Up vector again to make sure the vectors are truly perpendicular. Once we have all three vectors perfectly perpendicular to each other, we set our rotation matrix's vectors so we can use it inside our base class. After setting all the properties for our enemy, the base class is called to finish the move process.

Our EnemyManager class inherits from the DrawableGameComponent class, just like our MissileManager class. The member fields we need for this class are as follows:

```
public const int MAX_ENEMIES = 10;
private Texture2D[] enemyTextures;
private Model enemy;
private Effect effect;
private Random rand = new Random();

public Matrix View;
public Matrix Projection;

public List<Enemy> Enemies = new List<Enemy>(MAX_ENEMIES);
```

In our constructor, we need to store a reference to our game object:

```
public EnemyManager(Game game) : base(game) { }
```

`Microsoft.Xna.Framework`, `Microsoft.Xna.Framework.Graphics`, and
`System.Collections.Generic` will need to be added to the EnemyManager.cs file. The
`LoadContent` method of `EnemyManager` is as follows:

```
protected override void LoadContent()
{
    enemyTextures = new Texture2D[3];
    enemyTextures[0] = Game.Content.Load<Texture2D>(
        @"Textures\wedge_p2_diff_v1");
    enemyTextures[1] = Game.Content.Load<Texture2D>(
        @"Textures\wedge_p2_diff_v2");
    enemyTextures[2] = Game.Content.Load<Texture2D>(
        @"Textures\wedge_p2_diff_v3");
    enemy = Game.Content.Load<Model>(@"Models\p2_wedge");
    effect = Game.Content.Load<Effect>(
        @"Effects\AmbientTexture");

    effect.Parameters["AmbientColor"].SetValue(.8f);

    base.LoadContent();
}
```

We are loading three different textures that the model we are loading can use. This model
and these textures are taken from the Spacewar starter kit. They can also be found on the
accompanying CD in this chapter's code folder. The assets should be added to the appropriate folders in which the code is expecting to find them.

The `UnloadContent` method, which gets called by the XNA Framework whenever the
graphics device is reset or the game exits, simply clears out the list of enemies:

```
protected override void UnloadContent()
{
```

```
        Enemies.Clear();
        Enemies = null;

        base.UnloadContent();
}
```

The next method in our enemy manager class is the Draw method:

```
public override void Draw(GameTime gameTime)
{
        GraphicsDevice.RenderState.AlphaTestEnable = false;
        GraphicsDevice.RenderState.AlphaBlendEnable = false;
        GraphicsDevice.RenderState.PointSpriteEnable = false;
        GraphicsDevice.RenderState.DepthBufferWriteEnable = true;
        GraphicsDevice.RenderState.DepthBufferEnable = true;

        effect.Parameters["View"].SetValue(View);
        effect.Parameters["Projection"].SetValue(Projection);

        for (int ei = 0; ei < Enemies.Count; ei++)
        {
            effect.Parameters["World"].SetValue(Enemies[ei].World);
            effect.Parameters["ColorMap"].SetValue(Enemies[ei].Texture);

            Matrix[] transforms = new Matrix[enemy.Bones.Count];
            enemy.CopyAbsoluteBoneTransformsTo(transforms);

            foreach (ModelMesh mesh in enemy.Meshes)
            {
                foreach (ModelMeshPart mp in mesh.MeshParts)
                {
                    mp.Effect = effect;
                }

                mesh.Draw();
            }
        }

        base.Draw(gameTime);
}
```

First, we set our render state properties to the values we require. Then we set our effect's view and projection properties. Finally, we loop through all our enemies and draw each one with the appropriate texture and world matrix being passed into the effect.

The last method we need to add in our EnemyManager class is the AddEnemy method:

```
public void AddEnemy(float moveSpeed)
{
    Enemies.Add(new Enemy(enemyTextures[rand.Next(0, 3)], moveSpeed));
}
```

This is a public method the playing state code will use to tell the manager to add another enemy to the list. The enemy will be assigned one of the three textures we have specified, along with its movement speed.

Let's return to the playing state code and add the following to the constructor:

```
playerSphere = new BoundingSphere(OurGame.Camera.Position, 1.5f);


missileManager = new MissileManager(Game);
Game.Components.Add(missileManager);
missileManager.Enabled = false;
missileManager.Visible = false;

enemyManager = new EnemyManager(Game);
Game.Components.Add(enemyManager);
enemyManager.Enabled = false;
enemyManager.Visible = false;

Levels = new List<Level>(10);
Levels.Add(new Level(50, 10, 60, 9.0f));
Levels.Add(new Level(25, 10, 60, 9.0f));
Levels.Add(new Level(15, 15, 60, 9.0f));
Levels.Add(new Level(10, 15, 60, 9.0f));
Levels.Add(new Level(5, 15, 60, 9.0f));
Levels.Add(new Level(5, 20, 60, 9.0f));
Levels.Add(new Level(5, 25, 60, 9.0f));
Levels.Add(new Level(5, 30, 60, 10.0f));
Levels.Add(new Level(5, 40, 90, 10.0f));
Levels.Add(new Level(3, 50, 90, 10.0f));

currentLevel = 0;
enemyManager.Enemies = new List<Enemy>(Levels[CurrentLevel].Enemies);
```

In this game, we are using a stationary camera, so we are not going to continually update the player's bounding sphere. Instead, it is set once in the constructor. We add the missile manager and enemy manager game components and create all our levels.

Our PlayingState will start the game. The exposed method calls two private methods to prepare for the game and then to start the level. These methods are shown here:

```
public void StartGame()
{
    SetupGame();
```

```
    StartLevel();
}

private void SetupGame()
{
    TotalCollisions = 0;
    currentLevel = 0;
}

public void StartLevel()
{
    GamePad.SetVibration(0, 0, 0);
    enemyManager.Enemies.Clear();
    totalCreatedEnemies = 0;

    missileManager.Load(Levels[CurrentLevel].Missiles);

    GameManager.PushState(OurGame.StartLevelState.Value);
}
```

The only thing to point out in this code is that we push the StartLevelState onto the
stack inside the StartLevel method.

Next, we can look at the Update method in our PlayingGameState. We can replace the
contents of the existing Update method with the following:

```
float elapsed = (float)gameTime.ElapsedGameTime.TotalSeconds;

if (Input.WasPressed(0, Buttons.Back, Keys.Escape))
    GameManager.PushState(OurGame.StartMenuState.Value);

if (Input.WasPressed(0, Buttons.Start, Keys.Enter))
{
    // push our paused state onto the stack
    GameManager.PushState(OurGame.PausedState.Value);
}

if ((Input.WasPressed(0, Buttons.A, Keys.Space)) ||
    (Input.WasPressed(0, Buttons.RightShoulder,
        Keys.LeftControl)) ||
    Input.GamePads[0].Triggers.Right > 0
    )
{
    if (missileManager.AddMissile(new Vector3(
            OurGame.Camera.Position.X,
            OurGame.Camera.Position.Y - 1,
```

```
                OurGame.Camera.Position.Z + 1
        ), OurGame.Camera.Target - OurGame.Camera.Position,
        DateTime.Now))
    {
        //play sound
    }
}


if (enemyManager.Enabled)
{
    UpdateEnemies(elapsed);

    while (CheckCollisions())
    {
        //increase score if enemy was hit
    }

    //Are we finished with this level?
    if (TotalCollisions == Levels[CurrentLevel].Enemies)
    {
        TotalCollisions = 0;
        currentLevel++;

        //Are we finished with the game?
        if (CurrentLevel == Levels.Count)
        {
            //You won the game!!!
            GameManager.PushState(OurGame.WonGameState.Value);
            currentLevel--; //reset count back
        }
        else
        {
            StartLevel();
        }
    }
}


base.Update(gameTime);
```

We check our input and push on the start menu state or the paused state if it is appropriate. We check to see if the player has fired a missile and have a placeholder for playing a sound.

We update all the enemies that are on the screen and then check to see if any of the missiles have collided with them. We will review the CheckCollisions method next. If a collision did occur, we have a placeholder to increase the score. Now we check to see if any more enemies are left. If there aren't, we check to see if any more levels are left. If all the levels have been finished, the game is won. Otherwise, the game moves on to the next level. The CheckCollisions method is as follows:

```
private bool CheckCollisions()
{
    for (int ei = 0; ei < enemyManager.Enemies.Count; ei++)
    {
        //See if an enemy is too close first
        if (enemyManager.Enemies[ei].BoundingSphere.Intersects(playerSphere))
        {
            GameManager.PushState(OurGame.LostGameState.Value);
            return (false);
        }

        //if not, then we can check our missiles
        if (missileManager.CheckCollision(enemyManager.Enemies[ei].BoundingSphere))
        {
            enemyManager.Enemies.RemoveAt(ei);

            TotalCollisions++;

            return (true);
        }
    }

    return (false);
}
```

First, we check to see if an enemy has collided with the camera. If that happens, the game is over. Otherwise, we check to see if any of the missiles have collided with the enemies. Our Update method also calls the UpdateEnemies method, which is shown here:

```
private void UpdateEnemies(float elapsed)
{
    if (totalCreatedEnemies < Levels[CurrentLevel].Enemies)
    {
        if (enemyManager.Enemies.Count < EnemyManager.MAX_ENEMIES)
        {
            enemyManager.AddEnemy(Levels[CurrentLevel].EnemySpeed);
            totalCreatedEnemies++;
        }
    }

    for (int ei = 0; ei < enemyManager.Enemies.Count; ei++)
    {
```

```
        enemyManager.Enemies[ei].Target = OurGame.Camera.Position;
        enemyManager.Enemies[ei].Move(elapsed);
    }
}
```

The UpdateEnemies method checks to see if there are still enemies to be generated. We only allow MAX_ENEMIES on the screen at one time, so if a level has more than that, we wait until an enemy is destroyed before another one is spawned. The method then loops through all the enemies and updates their target based on the camera's position. For this game, this really isn't needed because we have a stationary camera. We then move each enemy.

For now our Draw method is very lightweight—it is only setting the view and projection properties for the missile manager and the enemy manager. We can replace the current contents of the Draw method with the following:

```
missileManager.View = OurGame.Camera.View;
missileManager.Projection = OurGame.Camera.Projection;

enemyManager.View = OurGame.Camera.View;
enemyManager.Projection = OurGame.Camera.Projection;

base.Draw(gameTime);
```

We need to clear out the contents of the LoadContent method. We will be adding code to that method a little later, but for now we just need to remove the old font we used in the previous demo.

We need to know which level we are on outside of our playing state, so we need to make a public property to expose it:

```
public int CurrentLevel
{
    get { return (currentLevel); }
}
```

We also need to modify our GameStateInterfaces code. Specifically, we need to modify the IPlayingState interface to include our StartGame method and this CurrentLevel property:

```
void StartGame();
int CurrentLevel { get; }
```

The final method we need to add to our PlayingState class is the StateChanged method. We override this method so we can turn on and off the appropriate game components:

```
protected override void StateChanged(object sender, EventArgs e)
{
    base.StateChanged(sender, e);

    if (GameManager.State != this.Value)
```

```
    {
        Visible = true;
        Enabled = false;
        missileManager.Enabled = false;
        missileManager.Visible = false;
        enemyManager.Enabled = false;
        enemyManager.Visible = false;
    }
    else
    {
        missileManager.Enabled = true;
        missileManager.Visible = true;
        enemyManager.Enabled = true;
        enemyManager.Visible = true;

    }
}
```

We specified an effect file for both the missile manager and the enemy manager. The enemy manager is using the AmbientTexture effect file from last chapter. The file needs to be added to our projects. The missile manager, however, is using a new effect file. The basis of the effect is the vertex deformation effect we created in Chapter 15, "Advanced HLSL." Here's the code for VertexDisplacement.fx:

```
float4x4 World : WORLD;
float4x4 View;
float4x4 Projection;

float4 AmbientColor : COLOR0;
float Timer : TIME;
float Offset = 1.0f;

texture ColorMap;
sampler ColorMapSampler = sampler_state
{
    texture = <ColorMap>;
    magfilter = LINEAR;
    minfilter = LINEAR;
    mipfilter = LINEAR;
    AddressU = Wrap;
    AddressV = Wrap;
};

struct VertexInput
{
    float4 Position : POSITION0;
```

```
      float2 TexCoord : TEXCOORD0;
};

struct VertexOutput
{
    float4 Position : POSITION0;
    float2 TexCoord : TEXCOORD0;
};

VertexOutput vertexShader(VertexInput input)
{
    VertexOutput output = (VertexOutput)0;
    float4x4 WorldViewProjection = mul(mul(World, View), Projection);
    output.TexCoord = input.TexCoord  + Timer * .005;

    float4 Pos = input.Position;
    float y = Pos.y * Offset + Timer;
    float x = sin(y) * Offset;
    Pos.x += x;

    output.Position = mul(Pos, WorldViewProjection);

    return( output );
}

struct PixelInput
{
    float2 TexCoord : TEXCOORD0;
};

float4 pixelShader(PixelInput input) : COLOR
{
    float4 color;
    color = tex2D(ColorMapSampler, input.TexCoord);
    return(color);
}

technique Default
{
    pass P0
    {
        VertexShader = compile vs_1_1 vertexShader();
        PixelShader = compile ps_1_4 pixelShader();
    }
}
```

This effect code is identical to the code we used in Chapter 15. The only difference is inside the vertex shader. Besides modifying the vertex position, we also modify the texture coordinates. When we shoot our missiles, they will wobble.

The next state we need to modify is our `StartLevelState`. We need to clear out the code inside the class and add the following private member fields:

```
private bool demoMode = true;
private bool displayedDemoDialog = false;

private DateTime levelLoadTime;
private readonly int loadSoundTime = 2500;

private string levelText = "LEVEL";
private string currentLevel;
bool startingLevel = false;

private Vector2 levelTextPosition;
private Vector2 levelTextShadowPosition;
private Vector2 levelNumberPosition;
private Vector2 levelNumberShadowPosition;
```

We are going to play a sound as we are loading the level. We want the actual game play to start as soon as the sound is over. There is no way to get notified of a sound being completed, so we put in our own timer. We will add the sound later but put the code into place now to handle the timing. The start level state will also display the number of the level we are starting. We store the level text once so we can use it multiple times. We also set up two sets of vectors to hold the locations of the level text (that is, LEVEL) as well as the level number (that is, 1) and their drop-shadow locations.

The constructor did not change but is listed here for completeness:

```
public StartLevelState(Game game)
    : base(game)
{
    game.Services.AddService(typeof(IStartLevelState), this);
}
```

The updated `StateChanged` method allows us to start the logic when we enter our start level state:

```
protected override void StateChanged(object sender, EventArgs e)
{
    base.StateChanged(sender, e);
```

```
if (GameManager.State == this.Value)
{
    startingLevel = true;

    if (demoMode && !displayedDemoDialog)
    {
        //We could set properties on our YesNoDialog
        //so it could have a custom message and custom
        //Yes / No buttons ...
        //YesNoDialogState.YesCaption = "Of course!";
        GameManager.PushState(OurGame.YesNoDialogState.Value);
        this.Visible = true;
        displayedDemoDialog = true;
        startingLevel = false;
    }
}

if (startingLevel)
{
    //play sound

    levelLoadTime = DateTime.Now;

    currentLevel = (OurGame.PlayingState.CurrentLevel + 1).ToString();

    Vector2 viewport = new Vector2(GraphicsDevice.Viewport.Width,
        GraphicsDevice.Viewport.Height);
    Vector2 levelTextLength = OurGame.Font.MeasureString(levelText);
    Vector2 levelNumberLength = OurGame.Font.MeasureString(currentLevel);
    levelTextShadowPosition = (viewport - levelTextLength * 3) / 2;
    levelNumberShadowPosition = (viewport - levelNumberLength * 3) / 2;
    levelNumberShadowPosition.Y += OurGame.Font.LineSpacing * 3;
    levelTextPosition.X = levelTextShadowPosition.X + 2;
    levelTextPosition.Y = levelTextShadowPosition.Y + 2;
    levelNumberPosition.X = levelNumberShadowPosition.X + 2;
    levelNumberPosition.Y = levelNumberShadowPosition.Y + 2;
}
}
```

The first part of the method is the same as it was in our previous game state demo. However, we also set the startingLevel flag with the initial value of true. We modify the demo condition to set the startingLevel flag to false. Assuming we are really starting the level, which will occur the first time if we are not in demo mode (or after the dialog box is closed if we are in demo mode), we begin playing our starting level sound. We have put a placeholder in to play that sound for now. We also initialize our level load time and set our current level variable. Finally, we initialize the vectors that store the position of the text we want to display when the level starts. The text will be centered on the screen.

The Update method for this state is as follows:

```
public override void Update(GameTime gameTime)
{
    if (DateTime.Now > levelLoadTime + new TimeSpan(0, 0, 0, 0, loadSoundTime))
    {
        //stop sound

        // change state to playing
        GameManager.ChangeState(OurGame.PlayingState.Value);
    }

    base.Update(gameTime);
}
```

Inside the Update method, we change to the PlayingState and stop the sound if enough time has passed. For now, we just have a placeholder where we will eventually stop the sound. The last method in this state is the Draw method:

```
public override void Draw(GameTime gameTime)
{
    if (startingLevel)
    {
        OurGame.SpriteBatch.Begin();
        OurGame.SpriteBatch.DrawString(OurGame.Font, levelText,
            levelTextShadowPosition, Color.Yellow, 0, Vector2.Zero, 3.0f,
            SpriteEffects.None, 0);
        OurGame.SpriteBatch.DrawString(OurGame.Font, levelText,
            levelTextPosition, Color.Red, 0, Vector2.Zero, 3.0f,
            SpriteEffects.None, 0);
        OurGame.SpriteBatch.DrawString(OurGame.Font, currentLevel,
            levelNumberShadowPosition, Color.Yellow, 0, Vector2.Zero, 3.0f,
            SpriteEffects.None, 0);
        OurGame.SpriteBatch.DrawString(OurGame.Font, currentLevel,
            levelNumberPosition, Color.Red, 0, Vector2.Zero, 3.0f,
            SpriteEffects.None, 0);
        OurGame.SpriteBatch.End();
    }

    base.Draw(gameTime);
}
```

The Draw method simply draws the level text and the level number in the right position, complete with a drop-shadow effect. It only draws this text if we are actually starting the level. If the YesNoDialog (Demo mode) is on the stack, we do not want to display the text.

We need to declare a font variable in our TunnelVision game class:

```
public SpriteFont Font;
```

Inside the LoadContent method we need to load our font:

```
Font = Content.Load<SpriteFont>(@"Fonts\Arial");
```

Before we compile and run our changes, we need to modify the StartMenuState class. Inside the Update method, we need to replace the contents of the condition where we check if either Start or Enter was pressed with the following code:

```
if (GameManager.ContainsState(OurGame.PlayingState.Value))
    GameManager.PopState();
else
{
    //starting game, queue first level
    GameManager.ChangeState(OurGame.PlayingState.Value);
    OurGame.PlayingState.StartGame();
}
```

We are still popping off our start menu state if our stack contains a playing state. However, instead of changing the state to the StartLevelState like in the previous demo, we are changing the state to PlayingState and calling its StartGame method.

At this point we can compile and run the game. The game logic is in place, but it is rather rough around the edges.

Creating the Crosshair

To allow better aiming, we need to add a crosshair to our screen. To start, we need to add the following texture to our member field list of the PlayingState class:

```
private Texture2D crossHair;
```

Inside our Draw method we need to add the following code:

```
OurGame.SpriteBatch.Begin();
if (OurGame.DisplayCrosshair)
{
    OurGame.SpriteBatch.Draw(crossHair, new Rectangle(
        (GraphicsDevice.Viewport.Width - crossHair.Width) / 2,
        (GraphicsDevice.Viewport.Height - crossHair.Height) / 2,
        crossHair.Width, crossHair.Height), Color.White);
```

```
    }
OurGame.SpriteBatch.End();
```

We actually populate the crosshair texture inside our `LoadContent` method:

```
protected override void LoadContent()
{
    crossHair = Content.Load<Texture2D>(@"Textures\crosshair");
    base.LoadContent();
}
```

The texture can be found in the usual place. Later, we are going to provide an option to turn on and off the crosshair, so we need to create the public boolean `DisplayCrosshair` field in our TunnelVision game code. It should be initialized to true. Now, we can more easily see where we are aiming!

Creating the Game-Specific Camera

Now we are going to add a new camera directly to our game. We are not going to add this to the XELibrary because it is a special camera that most likely will not be reused. The purpose of this new camera is to handle input a little differently and to restrict movement. The code for the new TunnelVisionCamera.cs file is as follows:

```
using System;
using System.Collections.Generic;
using Microsoft.Xna.Framework;
using Microsoft.Xna.Framework.Input;
using XELibrary;

namespace TunnelVision
{
    public partial class TunnelVisionCamera : Camera
    {
    private float spinLeft = 0;
    private float spinRight = 0;
    private float spinDown = 0;
    private float spinUp = 0;

    private float spinLeftChange = 0;
    private float spinRightChange = 0;
    private float spinDownChange = 0;
    private float spinUpChange = 0;

    public TunnelVisionCamera(Game game) : base(game) {}

    public override void Update(GameTime gameTime)
```

```
{
    if (!UpdateInput)
    return;

    float timeDelta = (float)gameTime.ElapsedGameTime.TotalSeconds;

    if (input.KeyboardState.IsKeyDown(Keys.Left))
        spinLeftChange += .1f;
    else
        spinLeftChange -= .1f;
    spinLeftChange = MathHelper.Clamp(spinLeftChange, 0, 1);
    spinLeft = spinLeftChange;
    if (input.GamePads[playerIndex].ThumbSticks.Left.X < 0)
        spinLeft = -input.GamePads[playerIndex].ThumbSticks.Left.X;
    if (spinLeft > 0)
        cameraYaw += (Utility.PowerCurve(spinLeft) * SpinRate *
            timeDelta);

    if (input.KeyboardState.IsKeyDown(Keys.Right))
        spinRightChange += .1f;
    else
        spinRightChange -= .1f;
    spinRightChange = MathHelper.Clamp(spinRightChange, 0, 1);
    spinRight = spinRightChange;
    if (input.GamePads[playerIndex].ThumbSticks.Left.X > 0)
        spinRight = input.GamePads[playerIndex].ThumbSticks.Left.X;
    if (spinRight > 0)
        cameraYaw -= (Utility.PowerCurve(spinRight) * SpinRate *
            timeDelta);

    if (input.KeyboardState.IsKeyDown(Keys.Down))
        spinDownChange += .1f;
    else
        spinDownChange -= .1f;
    spinDownChange = MathHelper.Clamp(spinDownChange, 0, 1);
    spinDown = spinDownChange;
    if (input.GamePads[playerIndex].ThumbSticks.Left.Y < 0)
        spinDown = -input.GamePads[playerIndex].ThumbSticks.Left.Y;
    if (spinDown > 0)
        cameraPitch -= (Utility.PowerCurve(spinDown) * SpinRate *
            timeDelta);

    if (input.KeyboardState.IsKeyDown(Keys.Up))
        spinUpChange += .1f;
    else
        spinUpChange -= .1f;
```

```
        spinUpChange = MathHelper.Clamp(spinUpChange, 0, 1);
        spinUp = spinUpChange;
        if (input.GamePads[playerIndex].ThumbSticks.Left.Y > 0)
            spinUp = input.GamePads[playerIndex].ThumbSticks.Left.Y;
        if (spinUp > 0)
            cameraPitch += (Utility.PowerCurve(spinUp) * SpinRate *
                timeDelta);

        //reset camera angle if needed
        if (cameraYaw > 80)
            cameraYaw = 80;
        else if (cameraYaw < -80)
            cameraYaw = -80;

        //keep camera from rotating a full 90 degrees in either direction
        if (cameraPitch > 89)
            cameraPitch = 89;
        if (cameraPitch < -89)
            cameraPitch = -89;

        Matrix rotationMatrix;
        Vector3 transformedReference;

        Matrix.CreateRotationY(MathHelper.ToRadians(cameraYaw),
            out rotationMatrix);

        //add in pitch to the rotation
        rotationMatrix = Matrix.CreateRotationX(
            MathHelper.ToRadians(cameraPitch)) * rotationMatrix;

        // Create a vector pointing the direction the camera is facing.
        Vector3.Transform(ref cameraReference, ref rotationMatrix,
            out transformedReference);
        // Calculate the position the camera is looking at.
        Vector3.Add(ref cameraPosition, ref transformedReference,
            out cameraTarget);

        Matrix.CreateLookAt(ref cameraPosition, ref cameraTarget,
            ref cameraUpVector, out view);
    }
  }
}
```

This is very similar to the base object's Update method, except that we are restricting movement. We only allow the camera to move 80 degrees left or right. The pitch did not change. Instead of going through the entire class, line by line, we'll just look at the section of code that handles if the user rotated to the left and infer how the rest of the movements work:

```
if (input.KeyboardState.IsKeyDown(Keys.Left))
    spinLeftChange += .1f;
else
    spinLeftChange -= .1f;
spinLeftChange = MathHelper.Clamp(spinLeftChange, 0, 1);
spinLeft = spinLeftChange;
if (input.GamePads[playerIndex].ThumbSticks.Left.X < 0)
    spinLeft = -input.GamePads[playerIndex].ThumbSticks.Left.X;
if (spinLeft > 0)
    cameraYaw += (Utility.PowerCurve(spinLeft) * SpinRate *
        timeDelta);
```

During game play, the keyboard movement was too fast and too jerky. To solve this, we build up our spin left value. In the base class, it simply gets set to 1. Here, we are adding 10% each frame and clamping the results to 1. Now we can tap the keyboard to have more precise control over targeting our enemies. If the game pad is used to rotate the camera, we use a new helper method to produce a curve in the movement. In the Utility.cs file in the XELibrary we can add the following code:

```
Private const float power = 3;
public static float PowerCurve(float value)
{
    return ((float)Math.Pow(Math.Abs(value), power) * Math.Sign(value));
}
```

The PowerCurve helper method provides a curve we can apply to the values our thumbstick produces. Instead of strictly using the value of the thumbstick, we are making the low values lower, which gives us more control. Now as we barely move the thumbstick, the camera will barely move. And when we move the controller to target our enemies, we have more precise control.

We need to modify our Camera object in the XELibrary. The following public member field needs to be created:

```
public bool UpdateInput = true;
```

The following condition needs to be added at the very top of the Update method:

```
if (!UpdateInput)
{
    base.Update(gameTime);
    return;
}
```

We also want to change the modifier for the cameraReference, cameraTarget, cameraUpVector, view, cameraYaw, and cameraPitch fields to be protected instead of private. The private const spinRate and moveRate should be changed to public and no longer be a const because we need to be able to set them anywhere.

To use this new camera, we need to change our TunnelVision game class to use TunnelVisionCamera instead of Camera. We also need to modify our PlayingState class to use the new UpdateMethod boolean property. Inside the StateChanged method we need to add the following code to the first branch of our condition:

```
OurGame.Camera.UpdateInput = false;
```

We need to do the opposite in the else of our if condition:

```
OurGame.Camera.UpdateInput = true;
```

Inside the constructor of PlayingState, we need to add the following code to set the move rate and spin rate of our camera:

```
OurGame.Camera.MoveRate = 10;
OurGame.Camera.SpinRate = 60;
```

We have improved our input handling and have restricted movement on our camera so we only rotate 80 degrees to the left or right instead of the full 360 degrees.

Summary

In this chapter, we have laid the foundation for creating our game. We have put into place all the game logic. There were not really any new concepts in this chapter, but by putting what you learned in previous chapters into practice, we should be well on our way to creating our own masterpieces. The next two chapters are spent updating our game states and UI enhancements.

CHAPTER 23

Improving the Game

In this chapter, we enhance the game by adding a 2D radar of the enemies. A level timer and scoring capability are also created and displayed on the screen. Finally, we will store and save high scores to a storage device.

Creating the Radar

As we play the game, it becomes difficult to know where the enemies are. We need to spin around often to see them. Although some prefer to play games this way, it makes the game much more difficult, and many gamers will get frustrated and not play if we do not give them a bird's-eye view of what is going on. Therefore, we are going to create a radar in this section that does just that.

Inside our playing state's Draw method, we need to add the following condition before we call SpriteBatch.End:

```
if (OurGame.DisplayRadar)
{
    if (enemyManager.Radar != null)
        OurGame.SpriteBatch.Draw(enemyManager.Radar,
            new Rectangle(
                TitleSafeArea.Left,
                TitleSafeArea.Bottom - 200,
                200, 200),
            new Color(new Vector4(1, 1, 1, .5f)));
}
```

We are checking to see if the Radar texture our enemy manager exposes is null. If it is not null, we display it at the bottom left of our screen. We can add the public boolean

DisplayRadar field to our TunnelVision game, initialized to true. Later, we provide an option where gamers can turn this feature on or off as they play.

We need to create this radar texture inside our enemy manager. To start, we need to add the following fields to our EnemyManager class:

```
private RenderTarget2D radarRenderTarget;
private Texture2D radarPlayerDot;
public Texture2D Radar;
```

Inside the LoadContent method, we need to add the following code:

```
radarPlayerDot = new Texture2D(GraphicsDevice, 1, 1, 1,
    TextureUsage.None, SurfaceFormat.Color);
radarPlayerDot.SetData(new Color[] { Color.White } );
```

In the center of our radar we are going to place a white dot that represents the player. This code simply creates the 1×1 white pixel. While we are inside this method, we can add the following code:

```
radarRenderTarget = new RenderTarget2D(GraphicsDevice, 200,
    200, 1, GraphicsDevice.DisplayMode.Format,
    GraphicsDevice.PresentationParameters.MultiSampleType,
    GraphicsDevice.PresentationParameters.MultiSampleQuality);
```

Because we are creating a texture that our game can use to display on the screen, we need to create a render target onto which we can render our enemies. We need to make sure we dispose of the render target in our UnloadContent method. The final piece we need to complete to have a radar in our game is to actually draw our enemies on our texture. We need to insert the following code at the beginning of the Draw method:

```
GraphicsDevice.SetRenderTarget(0, radarRenderTarget);
GraphicsDevice.Clear(Color.Green);

Matrix birdsEyeView = Matrix.CreateLookAt(new Vector3(ourGame.Camera.Position.X,
    250, ourGame.Camera.Position.Z), ourGame.Camera.Position, Vector3.Forward);

effect.Parameters["View"].SetValue(birdsEyeView);
effect.Parameters["Projection"].SetValue(ourGame.Camera.Projection);
```

We set our render target like we have done in the past and clear the device to green. This will make our radar a nice shade of green. We need to view our world (or at least the enemies in our world) from a bird's-eye view. To do this, we set up a new view. Instead of using our normal camera view, which looks straight at the enemies, we create a bird's-eye view by positioning our camera 250 units above the player (camera). Finally, we set the effect's view and projection parameters. We need to add the ourGame variable as a TunnelVision type and add the following line to our constructor:

```
ourGame = (TunnelVision)game;
```

Next, we need to draw our enemies. We are already doing this in our Draw method, so we should refactor the for loop code that draws our enemies and make another method called DrawEnemies. We then need to call this newly created method:

```
DrawEnemies();
```

After drawing our enemies on the render target, we can draw the player dot texture we created earlier:

```
ourGame.SpriteBatch.Begin();
ourGame.SpriteBatch.Draw(radarPlayerDot, new Vector2(100, 100), Color.White);
ourGame.SpriteBatch.End();
```

Next, we need to resolve our render target and set our Radar texture:

```
//clear out the render target
GraphicsDevice.SetRenderTarget(0, null);

Radar = radarRenderTarget.GetTexture();
```

When we set the render target at the beginning of our Draw method, we are erasing anything we previously drew to the screen (unless we immediately call the GetTexture method). We draw the skybox in the main TunnelVision game Draw method before this EnemyManager drawable game component gets called. We have not specified a particular order for the game components, so if the missiles get drawn first they will also disappear. To fix this, we have a couple options. We could set up a render target that our main game draws to, and then each game component could grab a snapshot of what was rendered to that target by calling GetTexture. Then we need to make sure we render that texture before adding anything else to the scene. This way is the most flexible because it allows us to have any number of render targets in our game components, and we don't have an issue of items "disappearing" on us. However, this approach takes more code in that we need to get the texture for the current render target and display that for each of our game states.

Because we are only using render targets in one of our game states (EnemyManager), we are going to set up the code with the second option. With this option, we will declare that we want this game component to draw first so that we don't lose any items that other game components would draw to the screen (such as missiles). We can set the DrawOrder property to –1 in the EnemyManager constructor.

If we were only rendering with game components, that would be enough. However, we are also using a Content Pipeline extension to render our skybox. Because this is not a game component, we cannot set a DrawOrder property. We also can't draw it after calling base.Draw in our TunnelVision game file because we would only see the skybox. So we are going to expose the Skybox so our game components can draw it. We can change the modifier to public:

```
public Skybox Skybox;
```

If we run the game now, we will lose the skybox as soon as the game goes to the playing state because we have cleared the buffer. In fact, the screen would be purple because the target had its content discarded. (See the note about the color purple in Chapter 15, "Advanced HLSL," for more information.)

In order to get our Skybox back, we can add the following code to the EnemyManager's Draw method after we set the RenderState properties:

```
GraphicsDevice.Clear(Color.CornflowerBlue);
ourGame.Skybox.Draw(ourGame.Camera.View,
    ourGame.Camera.Projection, Matrix.CreateScale(1000));
```

We cleared the device to our favorite color. Although this isn't needed because the skybox will fill up the screen, the Clear cost is very cheap. We are drawing the skybox just as we did in the main TunnelVision game class. We are now drawing the Skybox data twice for every frame we are in the playing state. For this game, this is acceptable. If we did not want to do that, we could write additional code to draw that skybox in the specific game states we wanted it to be displayed in and then remove it from the main game class. Alternatively, we could go with the first option and render the skybox to a render target and have all the game states display the captured texture.

We have successfully created a radar for our game. Now we can see our enemies when they come into range!

Creating the Tunnel

With a game named Tunnel Vision, it would be wise to actually add a tunnel to the game. We need to create a code file named Tunnel.cs for our projects. This file will have all the normal using statements. The class will inherit from the DrawableGameComponent. Here are the member fields we will need for the Tunnel class:

```
private VertexPositionNormalTangentTexture[] vertices;
private short[] indices;
private VertexDeclaration vertexDeclaration;

private Effect effect;
private Texture2D colorMap;
private Texture2D normalMap;

public Matrix View;
public Matrix Projection;

private TunnelVision ourGame;
```

We will be creating the four tunnel walls manually. We created the rectangle in the early chapters of this book. We will be using the same code and transforming it to make up our tunnel, and we will be using the normal mapping technique to texture our tunnel walls. We also expose two public fields the playing state can set for the view and projection matrices.

Now let's look at the constructor and initialize methods of our `Tunnel` class:

```
public Tunnel(Game game) : base(game)
{
    ourGame = (TunnelVision)game;
}

public override void Initialize()
{
    base.Initialize();

    InitializeVertices();
    InitializeIndices();
}
```

The `InitializeVertices` and `InitializeIndices` methods are not new, but are listed here for completeness:

```
private void InitializeVertices()
{
    Vector3 position;
    Vector2 textureCoordinates;

    vertices = new VertexPositionNormalTangentTexture[4];

    //top left
    position = new Vector3(-100, 100, 0);
    textureCoordinates = new Vector2(0, 0);
    vertices[0] = new VertexPositionNormalTangentTexture(
        position, Vector3.Forward, Vector3.Left, textureCoordinates);

    //bottom right
    position = new Vector3(100, -100, 0);
    textureCoordinates = new Vector2(1, 1);
    vertices[1] = new VertexPositionNormalTangentTexture(
        position, Vector3.Forward, Vector3.Left, textureCoordinates);

    //bottom left
    position = new Vector3(-100, -100, 0);
    textureCoordinates = new Vector2(0, 1);
    vertices[2] = new VertexPositionNormalTangentTexture(
        position, Vector3.Forward, Vector3.Left, textureCoordinates);
```

23

```
    //top right
    position = new Vector3(100, 100, 0);
    textureCoordinates = new Vector2(1, 0);
    vertices[3] = new VertexPositionNormalTangentTexture(
        position, Vector3.Forward, Vector3.Left, textureCoordinates);
}

private void InitializeIndices()
{
    //6 vertices make up 2 triangles which make up our rectangle
    indices = new short[6];

    //triangle 1 (bottom portion)
    indices[0] = 0; // top left
    indices[1] = 1; // bottom right
    indices[2] = 2; // bottom left

    //triangle 2 (top portion)
    indices[3] = 0; // top left
    indices[4] = 3; // top right
    indices[5] = 1; // bottom right
}
```

Next, we can look at the LoadContent method. We are simply setting up our vertex declaration as well as our effect and maps for the tunnel:

```
protected override void LoadContent()
{
    //Initialize our Vertex Declaration
    vertexDeclaration = new VertexDeclaration(GraphicsDevice,
        VertexPositionNormalTangentTexture.VertexElements);

    effect = ourGame.Content.Load<Effect>(
        @"Effects\NormalMapping");
    colorMap = ourGame.Content.Load<Texture2D>(
        @"Textures\rockbump_color");
    normalMap = ourGame.Content.Load<Texture2D>(
        @"Textures\rockbump_normal");

    base.LoadContent();
}
```

The NormalMapping effect file we used in Chapter 19, "Advanced Texturing Techniques," needs to be added to our project. The rockbump_color and rockbump_normal texture files also need to be added. The files can be found in this chapter's code folder on the accompanying CD.

The code for our Draw method is as follows:

```
public override void Draw(GameTime gameTime)
{
    GraphicsDevice.RenderState.AlphaTestEnable = false;
    GraphicsDevice.RenderState.AlphaBlendEnable = false;
    GraphicsDevice.RenderState.PointSpriteEnable = false;
    GraphicsDevice.RenderState.DepthBufferWriteEnable = true;
    GraphicsDevice.RenderState.DepthBufferEnable = true;

    GraphicsDevice.VertexDeclaration = vertexDeclaration;

    Matrix world = Matrix.Identity;
    effect.Parameters["World"].SetValue(world);
    effect.Parameters["View"].SetValue(View);
    effect.Parameters["Projection"].SetValue(Projection);
    effect.Parameters["AmbientColor"].SetValue(.05f);
    effect.Parameters["ColorMap"].SetValue(colorMap);
    effect.Parameters["NormalMap"].SetValue(normalMap);
    effect.Parameters["LightPosition"].SetValue(Vector3.Zero);
    effect.Parameters["LightDiffuseColor"].SetValue(Color.White.ToVector4());

    DrawRectangle(world * Matrix.CreateRotationY(
        MathHelper.ToRadians(-90)) *
        Matrix.CreateTranslation(60, 0, 100), effect); //right
    DrawRectangle(world * Matrix.CreateRotationY(
        MathHelper.ToRadians(90)) *
        Matrix.CreateTranslation(-60, 0, 100), effect); //left
    DrawRectangle(world * Matrix.CreateRotationX(
        MathHelper.ToRadians(90)) *
        Matrix.CreateTranslation(0, 60, 100), effect); //top
    DrawRectangle(world * Matrix.CreateRotationX(
        MathHelper.ToRadians(-90)) *
        Matrix.CreateTranslation(0, -60, 100), effect); //bottom

    base.Draw(gameTime);
}
```

We make sure the render state is set up the way we need it to be to render our tunnel. Then we set our vertex declaration and populate our effect. We then create four rectangles, passing in the transformation to position and rotate those rectangles to make a tunnel. We also pass in the effect to the method that creates the rectangle. The code for the DrawRectangle method is shown here:

```
private void DrawRectangle(Matrix world, Effect effect)
{
    effect.Parameters["World"].SetValue(world);
    effect.Begin();
    foreach (EffectPass pass in effect.CurrentTechnique.Passes)
    {
        pass.Begin();

        GraphicsDevice.DrawUserIndexedPrimitives(
            PrimitiveType.TriangleList, vertices, 0, vertices.Length,
            indices, 0, indices.Length / 3);

        pass.End();
    }
    effect.End();
}
```

The DrawRectangle method uses the DrawUserIndexedPrimitives method to create the rectangle. The world transformation that is passed in is applied to the effect that is used.

We need to modify our playing state to load the tunnel. The following private member field needs to be added:

```
private Tunnel tunnel;
```

In the constructor we need to add the following code:

```
tunnel = new Tunnel(Game);
Game.Components.Add(tunnel);
```

We need to set the tunnel's View and Projection properties inside the Draw method:

```
tunnel.View = OurGame.Camera.View;
tunnel.Projection = OurGame.Camera.Projection;
```

We can compile and run the code and see our tunnel on the edges of our screen.

Creating the Level Timer

Our game itself is looking better, but we need a sense of urgency added to the game play. Each level has a timer associated with it, but we have not implemented the timer yet. To start, we can add the following private member fields to PlayingState:

```
private TimeSpan? storedTime;
private TimeSpan currentLevelTime;
private DateTime currentLevelStopTime = DateTime.Now;
```

The storedTime field is a private field that allows a null value and will be used to handle us pausing the game. We do not want our timer to continue to count down while the game is paused. We also store our current time and the stop time of our level.

In the SetupGame method, we need to add this statement:

```
currentLevelTime = TimeSpan.Zero;
```

In our StartLevel method, we need to add this statement:

```
storedTime = null;
```

In our Update method, we need to add the following code:

```
currentLevelTime = currentLevelStopTime.Subtract(DateTime.Now);
if (currentLevelTime.Seconds < 0)
    currentLevelTime = TimeSpan.Zero;
```

We continually update our current level time, making sure our level time does not go negative. Next, we need to store our current time if we pause the game. The following conditions need to be modified inside the Update method:

```
if (Input.WasPressed(0, InputHandler.ButtonType.Back, Keys.Escape))
{
    storedTime = currentLevelTime;
    GameManager.PushState(OurGame.StartMenuState.Value);
}

if (Input.WasPressed(0, InputHandler.ButtonType.Start, Keys.Enter))
{
    storedTime = currentLevelTime;
    GameManager.PushState(OurGame.PausedState.Value);
}
```

At the bottom of the else condition inside the StateChanged method, we need to add the following code:

```
if (storedTime != null)
    currentLevelStopTime = DateTime.Now + (TimeSpan)storedTime;
else
    currentLevelStopTime = DateTime.Now +
        new TimeSpan(0, 0, Levels[CurrentLevel].Time);
```

When we come into our playing state, we set our current level stop time to the stored time (from where we paused the game). Alternatively, if this is the first time in the playing state, we use the current time, adding in the length of time we have for this level. We will next create a HUD where we can display the remaining time.

Creating the HUD

We have created some variables to store the level time, but we do not display it anywhere to the gamer. In this section we are going to display the current level, the number of enemies that remain, and the remaining amount of time. We will add the score in the next section. For now, we need to add in the following private member fields in our PlayingState class:

```
private string levelText = string.Empty;
private Vector2 levelTextShadowPosition;
private Vector2 levelTextPosition;

private string enemiesText = string.Empty;
private Vector2 enemiesTextShadowPosition;
private Vector2 enemiesTextPosition;

private string timeText = string.Empty;
private Vector2 timeTextShadowPosition;
private Vector2 timeTextPosition;
```

We are storing the actual text we will be displaying as well as the position of the text and the offset shadow position of the text. The text can be set inside our Update method:

```
levelText = "Level: " + ((int)(CurrentLevel + 1)).ToString();
timeText = "Time: " + ((int)currentLevelTime.TotalSeconds).ToString();
enemiesText = "Enemies: " +
    ((int)(Levels[CurrentLevel].Enemies - TotalCollisions)).ToString();
```

We calculate the number of enemies by subtracting the total number of collisions we have had by the number of enemies inside the current level.

Inside the Draw method we can actually draw our text on the screen. We need to add the following code to our Draw method:

```
OurGame.SpriteBatch.DrawString(OurGame.Font, levelText,
    levelTextShadowPosition, Color.Black);
OurGame.SpriteBatch.DrawString(OurGame.Font, levelText,
    levelTextPosition, Color.WhiteSmoke);

OurGame.SpriteBatch.DrawString(OurGame.Font, enemiesText,
    enemiesTextShadowPosition, Color.Black);
OurGame.SpriteBatch.DrawString(OurGame.Font, enemiesText,
    enemiesTextPosition, Color.Firebrick);

OurGame.SpriteBatch.DrawString(OurGame.Font, timeText,
    timeTextShadowPosition, Color.Black);
OurGame.SpriteBatch.DrawString(OurGame.Font, timeText,
    timeTextPosition, Color.Firebrick);
```

Finally, we need to initialize the positions of the text and their drop shadow counterparts. This is done inside of the LoadContent method right before we call End on the SpriteBatch:

```
levelTextShadowPosition = new Vector2(TitleSafeArea.X, TitleSafeArea.Y);
levelTextPosition = new Vector2(TitleSafeArea.X + 2.0f,TitleSafeArea.Y + 2.0f);

enemiesTextShadowPosition = new Vector2(TitleSafeArea.X, TitleSafeArea.Y +
    OurGame.Font.LineSpacing);
enemiesTextPosition = new Vector2(TitleSafeArea.X + 2.0f, TitleSafeArea.Y +
    OurGame.Font.LineSpacing + 2.0f);

timeTextShadowPosition = new Vector2(TitleSafeArea.X, TitleSafeArea.Y +
    OurGame.Font.LineSpacing * 2);
timeTextPosition = new Vector2(TitleSafeArea.X + 2.0f, TitleSafeArea.Y +
    OurGame.Font.LineSpacing * 2 + 2.0f);
```

The lines of text are positioned in the top-left part of the screen with the drop shadow having a two-pixel offset.

Adding Scoring

Our game play is shaping up, but it would be nice to actually be gaining points when we destroy the enemy ships. We will award points every time an enemy is destroyed, and we will give bonus points for every second that remains after all the enemy ships have been eliminated.

We start by listing the private member fields that need to be added to the PlayingState class:

```
private string scoreText = string.Empty;
private Vector2 scoreTextShadowPosition;
private Vector2 scoreTextPosition;
public int score;
```

We have created variables to store the text that will display our score as well as a variable to store the score itself. We want to initialize the score to zero when the game starts, so we need to add the following statement inside the SetupGame method:

```
score = 0;
```

We will award a point each time a missile collides with an enemy ship, so inside the while loop for CheckCollisions in the Update method, we can add this statement:

```
score += 100; //100 points for each enemy
```

Immediately following this `while` loop is a condition that checks to see if the level is over. To award the points when the level is over and time still remains, we need to add the following code to the top of that condition:

```
if (currentLevelTime.Seconds > 0)
    score += ((int)currentLevelTime.TotalSeconds * 500);
```

We can store the score text at the end of our `Update` method:

```
scoreText = "Score: " + score.ToString();
```

We will draw the score on the screen by adding the following code to the `Draw` method right after we draw the level time remaining:

```
OurGame.SpriteBatch.DrawString(OurGame.Font, scoreText,
    scoreTextShadowPosition, Color.Black);
OurGame.SpriteBatch.DrawString(OurGame.Font, scoreText,
    scoreTextPosition, Color.Firebrick);
```

We will initialize the position vectors for the text and the drop-shadow text in the `LoadContent` method:

```
scoreTextShadowPosition = new Vector2(TitleSafeArea.X, TitleSafeArea.Y +
    OurGame.Font.LineSpacing * 3);
scoreTextPosition = new Vector2(TitleSafeArea.X + 2.0f, TitleSafeArea.Y +
    OurGame.Font.LineSpacing * 3 + 2.0f);
```

We make sure that the score shows up under the remaining time in the top-left corner of our screen. We can compile and run the game and see all our new additions. A screenshot of the game in its current state can be seen in Figure 23.1.

Keeping Track of High Scores

After playing the game and seeing the score, the next logical step is to create a way to store our high score list. The XNA Framework exposes the gamer tag's profile name. It also exposes the built-in display keyboard. We are going to set the default value to the player's signed-in gamer tag.

This section describes what is needed to create an initial high score file as well as what is needed to save new names to the file.

We are creating another game state to handle the high scores. The goal is to have a self-contained game state that we can use in all our games where we need to store a high score list. To get started, we need to add an `IHighScoresState` interface to our GameStateInterfaces.cs file:

FIGURE 23.1   TunnelVision screenshot with crosshair, HUD, and scoring.

```
public interface IHighScoresState : IGameState
{
    void SaveHighScore();
    bool AlwaysDisplay { get; set;  }
 }
```

We discuss the method and property we added to the interface a little later. For now, we can add a HighScoresState.cs file to our GameStates folder. We need to make sure the namespace is simply TunnelVision. The sealed class needs to inherit from BaseGameState and IHighScoresState.

We can add the struct we will use to actually hold the high score data:

```
[Serializable]
public struct HighScoreData
{
    public string[] PlayerName;
    public int[] Score;
    public int[] Level;

    public int Count;

    public HighScoreData(int count)
    {
        PlayerName = new string[count];
        Score = new int[count];
```

```
    Level = new int[count];

    Count = count;
    }
}
```

We mark this struct as serializable so we can save the data to a file. We are simply storing a list of player names, their scores, and the levels they reached. The constructor requires a count parameter that determines how many player names will be stored in the high score list. We need to add the System.Xml.Serialization, System.IO, Microsoft.Xna.Framework.Storage, and Microsoft.Xna.Framework.GamerServices namespaces to our using statements.

The following private member fields need to be added to the HighScoresState class:

```
private readonly string highScoresFilename = "highscores.lst";
private readonly string containerName = "TunnelVision";

private StorageDevice storageDevice;
private HighScoreData entries;
private StorageContainer container;
private IAsyncResult result;
private bool signingIn = false;
private bool needToLoadHighScores = false;
private bool needToSaveHighScores = false;
private bool newHighScore = false;

private bool alwaysDisplay = false;
```

As with the rest of our game states, our constructor method needs to add itself to the game's services:

```
public HighScoresState(Game game)
    : base(game)
{
    game.Services.AddService(typeof(IHighScoresState), this);
}
```

The method we exposed in our interface is SaveHighScore. This method is what an outside state will call to save the score and other data if the score is high enough to be on the list. It is up to our high scores state to determine if the score is high enough. The calling state can just blindly call this when a game is over. The SaveHighScore method is shown here:

```
public void SaveHighScore()
{
    if (entries.PlayerName == null)
    {
```

```
        newHighScore = true;
        return;
    }

    int scoreIndex = -1;
    for (int i = 0; i < entries.Count; i++)
    {
        if (OurGame.PlayingState.Score > entries.Score[i])
        {
            scoreIndex = i;
            break;
        }
    }

    if (scoreIndex > -1)
    {
        AlwaysDisplay = true;   //if a high score was obtained, always display

        if (SignedInGamer.SignedInGamers.Count > 0)
        {
            //New high score found ... do swaps
            for (int i = entries.Count - 1; i > scoreIndex; i--)
            {
                entries.PlayerName[i] = entries.PlayerName[i - 1];
                entries.Score[i] = entries.Score[i - 1];
                entries.Level[i] = entries.Level[i - 1];
            }

            entries.PlayerName[scoreIndex] = Gamer.SignedInGamers[0].Gamertag;
            entries.Score[scoreIndex] = OurGame.PlayingState.Score;
            entries.Level[scoreIndex] = OurGame.PlayingState.CurrentLevel + 1;

            SaveHighScores();
        }
        else
        {
            //register to be notified when gamer signs in
            SignedInGamer.SignedIn +=
                new EventHandler<SignedInEventArgs>(SignedInGamer_SignedIn);

            signingIn = true;
            Guide.ShowSignIn(1, false);

            return;
        }
    }
}
```

```
    else
        newHighScore = false;

    //We no longer need to be notified
    SignedInGamer.SignedIn -=
        new EventHandler<SignedInEventArgs>(SignedInGamer_SignedIn);
}
```

We start the method by seeing whether or not we have loaded our high score file by checking the `PlayerName` collection for null. If we have not loaded any entries, we set the `newHighScore` flag to true and exit the method. If we have already loaded our high score entries, we then loop through each high score, checking to see if the score we ended the game with is higher than the one we are checking. We loop through the scores in order. They are saved highest to lowest, and if we find that the game score is greater than the stored score, we store the index.

If a new high score should be added, we set the `AlwaysDisplay` property to true so the high score list will be displayed. Then we loop through the current high scores and swap out as many as needed. We push the other scores down the list and then save our high score in the newly available spot. We set the `newHighScore` flag to true. This will be used in the next chapter to actually display the high scores if a new high score was obtained. We store the name of the player by getting the first signed-in player's `Gamertag`. Finally, we save the high score list again. We need to make sure the gamer is actually signed in, which is why we have this wrapped in the condition. If the gamer isn't signed in, we drop to the false part of the condition.

The first thing we do if the gamer is not signed in is to register for the event when he or she does sign in. We then set a flag indicating that the player is actually signing in. Then we display the built-in Sign In screen. Because this is a nonblocking call, we set the `signingIn` flag and return from this method. We do not want to exit from this fading state until the gamer has signed in and we have stored his or her high score. If the gamer did not receive a high score, he or she would not be in this condition because his or her `scoreIndex` would still be –1.

The XNA Framework provides the `SignedInGamers` collection for us. This is a way we can check to see who all is signed into the device. We want to make sure we are storing the player's name in the high scores file. Therefore, we are forcing the player to sign in. We could bring up the internal keyboard and let him or her type in a value, but for this game we are requiring a signed-in account. We are only checking for this when we bring up the high score list for the first time.

We need to add the following condition at the top of the `Update` method:

```
if (signingIn)
{
    if (!Guide.IsVisible)
        Guide.ShowSignIn(1, false);
```

```
      return;
}
```

We add the preceding code to make sure that if the player is signing in, the Sign In window is kept open. If the gamer closes the window without signing in, it simply opens up again on the next frame. While we are in the Update method, we should handle exiting from this game state when the user presses Continue:

```
//If high scores aren't being displayed, display them
//if they are being displayed, hide them
if (Input.WasPressed(0, Buttons.Back, Keys.Escape) ||
    (Input.WasPressed(0, Buttons.Start, Keys.Enter) ||
    (Input.WasPressed(0, Buttons.A, Keys.Space))))
{
    GameManager.PopState();
}
```

The event handler we registered for is as follows:

```
private void SignedInGamer_SignedIn(object sender, SignedInEventArgs e)
{
    SaveHighScore();
}
```

Once the gamer signs in, we simply call the SaveHighScore method again. This time the method actually stores the gamer's score and his or her gamer tag, as we discussed earlier. We could force the gamer to sign in when the game starts, but doing so at the time of entering a high score seems fitting because that is the only time it is needed. Requiring a user to set up a profile to enter a high score may not be desired. If the decision is made, the code could be modified to just set the player name to "Player1" and save the high score and exit the condition in the Update method instead of just displaying the Guide again.

The SaveHighScore method called the SaveHighScores method. The LoadHighScores method is very similar:

```
private void LoadHighScores()
{
    if ((result == null) || (result.IsCompleted))
    {
        result = Guide.BeginShowStorageDeviceSelector( null, null);
    }

    needToLoadHighScores = true;
}

private void SaveHighScores()
{
```

```
if ((result == null) || (result.IsCompleted))
{
    result = Guide.BeginShowStorageDeviceSelector(null, null);
}


needToSaveHighScores = true;
}
```

These methods are checking to see if `result` is null or if it has completed. If the condition is true, we need to ask the gamer where he or she wants to store the high score data file. We do this by calling the `BeginShowStorageDeviceSelector` method on the built-in `Guide` object. The method allows passing in a callback method, but we are passing in null and setting flags so we can make sure we are always on one thread. We can check for these flags by adding the following code to our `Update` method:

```
if ((result != null) && (result.IsCompleted))
{
    if (needToSaveHighScores)
    {
        needToSaveHighScores = false;
        FinishSavingHighScores();
    }

    if (needToLoadHighScores)
    {
        needToLoadHighScores = false;
        FinishLoadingHighScores();
    }
}

if (newHighScore && entries.PlayerName != null)
{
    SaveHighScore();
    newHighScore = false;
}
```

We make sure the result has completed and then check our flags. We reset our flags and call the appropriate method to finish the task of either loading the high scores or saving them. We will look at those methods in a moment. In the last condition we are making sure we have our high score entries loaded; the `SaveHighScore` method was called but did not complete because the high scores were not loaded yet. Therefore, we call the method again now that the high scores are loaded, and we reset the flag to false.

The `FinishSavingHighScore` method is shown here:

```
private void FinishSavingHighScores()
{
```

```
storageDevice = Guide.EndShowStorageDeviceSelector(result);
if (storageDevice.IsConnected)
{
    //storage device is connected, open container and finish
    //saving the high scores
    if (container == null)
        container = storageDevice.OpenContainer(containerName);

    // Get the path of the save game
    string fullpath = Path.Combine(container.Path, highScoresFilename);

    FileMode fileMode = FileMode.Truncate;
    if (!File.Exists(fullpath))
        fileMode = FileMode.Create;

    // Open the file, creating it if necessary
    FileStream stream = File.Open(fullpath, fileMode);
    try
    {
        // Convert the object to XML data and put it in the stream
        XmlSerializer serializer = new XmlSerializer(typeof(HighScoreData));
        serializer.Serialize(stream, entries);
    }
    finally
    {
        // Close the file
        stream.Close();

        //Since we saved, we will also dispose the container
        //so it will stick in case the console is turned off
        //before the game exits
        if (container != null)
        {
            container.Dispose();
            container = null;
        }
    }
}
else
    SaveHighScores();
}
```

The first thing we do is call the `Guide.EndShowStorageDeviceSelector` method, passing in the result we stored. We then check to see if the storage device is connected. It is possible the storage device was disconnected or the player cancelled out. If this happens, we simply call `SaveHighScores` again. Assuming our storage device is connected, we open up the container. The containerName we passed into the OpenContainer method should be a human readable string and be unique for each game we create.

Regardless of whether we are using the Xbox 360 or Windows, we use normal .NET Framework methods to load and save files. We use the Combine method from the Path class to combine the container path we retrieved from the storage device. We wrap the serialization code around a try/finally block in case something goes wrong. We do not want to leave the file stream open. We also dispose of the container so the high scores will actually be saved. Until we call Dispose, the data is not actually stored. If we lose power, we would lose the data.

Next, you can see how we load the high scores in the FinishLoadingHighScores method, which is very similar:

```
private void FinishLoadingHighScores()
{
    storageDevice = Guide.EndShowStorageDeviceSelector(result);
    if (storageDevice.IsConnected)
    {
        //storage device is connected, open container and finish
        //saving the high scores
        if (container == null)
            container = storageDevice.OpenContainer(containerName);

        // Get the path of the save game
        string fullpath = Path.Combine(container.Path, highScoresFilename);

        if (!File.Exists(fullpath))
        {
            InitializeDefaultHighScores();
            return;
        }

        // Open the file, creating it if necessary
        FileStream stream = File.Open(fullpath, FileMode.Open, FileAccess.Read);
        try
        {
            // Convert the object to XML data and put it in the stream
            XmlSerializer serializer = new XmlSerializer(typeof(HighScoreData));
            entries = (HighScoreData)serializer.Deserialize(stream);
        }
        finally
        {
            // Close the file
            stream.Close();
        }
    }
}
```

```
    else
        LoadHighScores();
}
```

The code is very similar to how we saved the data. The filename is passed in to the method, and we obtain the full path the same way. Then we check to see if the file exists. If the high score file does not exist, we create the entries by calling the InitializeDefaultHighScore method, which you will see shortly. We open the file for read-only access and then deserialize the high score data inside a try/finally block. We store the high score data in our entries variable. We close the stream in our finally clause so we do not leave the resource open in case an error occurs.

Now we can look at the InitializeDefaultHighScore method, which is called when the high score file is not on the storage device:

```
private void InitializeDefaultHighScores()
{
    // Create the data to save
    entries = new HighScoreData(5);
    entries.PlayerName[0] = "Neil";
    entries.Level[0] = 10;
    entries.Score[0] = 200500;

    entries.PlayerName[1] = "Chris";
    entries.Level[1] = 10;
    entries.Score[1] = 187000;

    entries.PlayerName[2] = "Mark";
    entries.Level[2] = 9;
    entries.Score[2] = 113300;

    entries.PlayerName[3] = "Cindy";
    entries.Level[3] = 7;
    entries.Score[3] = 95100;

    entries.PlayerName[4] = "Sam";
    entries.Level[4] = 1;
    entries.Score[4] = 1000;
}
```

The code simply populates some default high score values. We are not actually saving the data to the storage device at this point. It will only be saved if a high score is obtained. We need to implement the property in our interface. We will discuss this property more in the next chapter, but we have already set it:

```
public bool AlwaysDisplay
{
    get { return (alwaysDisplay); }
    set { alwaysDisplay = value; }
}
```

Because this is a game state, we should override the `StateChanged` event:

```
protected override void StateChanged(object sender, EventArgs e)
{
    base.StateChanged(sender, e);

    if (GameManager.State == this.Value)
    {
        signingIn = false;
        newHighScore = false;
        alwaysDisplay = false;

        //Load high scores
        //gets stored in entries
        if (entries.PlayerName == null)
            LoadHighScores();
    }
}
```

When our game changes to this state, we want to load the high scores. We also want to initialize the `signingIn` and `newHighScore` flags to false.

We need to create the `HighScoresState` in our game object and then call the exposed `SaveHighScore` method from the `Update` method in our `FadingState`. The `FadingState` will always be on the stack at the end of the game regardless of whether the player has won or lost. We need to replace the `ChangeState` line with our call to `SaveHighScore`:

```
if (gameTime.TotalGameTime.TotalMilliseconds > fadeStartTime2 + 24000)
{
    //We get here by winning or losing
    //Change State to Intro and push on HighScore
    //It is up to HighScore to show or not depending on
    //if a high score was achieved
    GameManager.ChangeState(OurGame.TitleIntroState.Value);
    GameManager.PushState(OurGame.HighScoresState.Value);
    OurGame.HighScoresState.SaveHighScore();
}
```

The last task we need to complete is to expose the `Score` field we have been using in the code. `PlayingState` does not currently expose that field. We need to create a property in both the class and the `IPlayingState` interface.

After playing the game on Windows, we can see the highscore.lst file in the bin folder. We are not displaying the values yet but will modify our game state for that purpose in the next chapter.

Summary

In this chapter, we improved the game by adding a radar to more easily see the enemies. We actually created the tunnel and added it to our world. We added a level timer and displayed the time along with the number of enemies we had left to clear the level on the screen. We also added scoring to our game.

You learned how to serialize high score data to save it to a file on Windows and the Xbox 360. You also saw how to deserialize the same data. Finally, you learned how to call up the built-in Sign In window from the Guide so we could obtain and store the player's gamer tag.

23

Finishing Touches

In this chapter, we are going to finish our 3D game. We are going to update the title screen, the start menu, and option menu. We are also going to create the high score screen. We are going to add a particle system that will be executed when an enemy is destroyed. Finally, we are going to create a sound project in XACT and add it to our game.

Updating the Title Screen

We are going to spice up the title screen some by adding in the same fire effect we used in Chapter 20, "Special Effects." We need to add the following private member fields to our TitleIntroState class:

```
private Effect fireEffect;
private Random rand = new Random();
private Texture2D hotSpotTexture;
private Texture2D fire; //gets render target's texture
private RenderTarget2D renderTarget1;
private RenderTarget2D renderTarget2;
private int offset = -128;
private Color[] colors = {
    Color.Black,
    Color.Yellow,
    Color.White,
    Color.Red,
    Color.Orange,
    new Color(255,255,128) //yellowish white
};
```

The code is listed here for completeness, but there is not much description because it was discussed in detail in

Chapter 20. The current position of our texture in the Draw method needs to be changed to the following so it will be centered on the screen:

```
Vector2 pos = new Vector2((GraphicsDevice.Viewport.Width - texture.Width) / 2,
    (GraphicsDevice.Viewport.Height - texture.Height) / 2);
```

After setting that variable and before calling Begin on the SpriteBatch, we need to add the following code:

```
GraphicsDevice device = GraphicsDevice;
//Draw hotspots on the first Render Target
device.SetRenderTarget(0, renderTarget1);
device.Clear(Color.Black);
```

After the call to Begin and before the call to SpriteBatch.Draw, we need to add the following code:

```
//get last drawn screen -- if not first time in
//fire is null first time in, and when device is lost (LoadContent)
if (fire != null) //render target has valid texture
    OurGame.SpriteBatch.Draw(fire, Vector2.Zero, Color.White);

//draw hotspots
for (int i = 0; i < device.Viewport.Width / hotSpotTexture.Width; i++)
{
    OurGame.SpriteBatch.Draw(hotSpotTexture,
        new Vector2(i * hotSpotTexture.Width,
        device.Viewport.Height - hotSpotTexture.Height),
        colors[rand.Next(colors.Length)]);
}

OurGame.SpriteBatch.End();

//resolve what we just drew to our render target
//and clear it out
device.SetRenderTarget(0, null);

// Transfer from first to second render target
device.SetRenderTarget(0, renderTarget2);

fireEffect.Begin();
OurGame.SpriteBatch.Begin(SpriteBlendMode.None, SpriteSortMode.Immediate,
    SaveStateMode.None);
EffectPass pass = fireEffect.CurrentTechnique.Passes[0];

pass.Begin();
OurGame.SpriteBatch.Draw(renderTarget1.GetTexture(), new Rectangle(0, offset,
```

```
        device.Viewport.Width, device.Viewport.Height - offset), Color.White);
OurGame.SpriteBatch.End();
pass.End();

fireEffect.End();

//resolve what we just drew to our render target
//and clear it out
device.SetRenderTarget(0, null);
device.Clear(Color.Black);

//set texture to render
fire = renderTarget2.GetTexture();

// Draw second render target onto the screen (back buffer)
OurGame.SpriteBatch.Begin(SpriteBlendMode.Additive);
```

None of the code changed from Chapter 20. After creating the fire and setting the texture, we set up our sprite batch in additive blending mode so we can add our texture. That code is already in the state. After the sprite batch call to draw the texture, we need to draw our fire texture:

```
OurGame.SpriteBatch.Draw(fire, Vector2.Zero, Color.White);
OurGame.SpriteBatch.Draw(fire, Vector2.Zero, Color.White);
OurGame.SpriteBatch.Draw(fire, Vector2.Zero, Color.White);
OurGame.SpriteBatch.Draw(fire, Vector2.Zero, null, Color.White, 0,
    Vector2.Zero, 1.0f, SpriteEffects.FlipVertically, 0);
OurGame.SpriteBatch.Draw(fire, Vector2.Zero, null, Color.White, 0,
    Vector2.Zero, 1.0f, SpriteEffects.FlipVertically, 0);
OurGame.SpriteBatch.Draw(fire, Vector2.Zero, null, Color.White, 0,
    Vector2.Zero, 1.0f, SpriteEffects.FlipVertically, 0);
```

The first three lines are identical to what appears in Chapter 20. We are drawing the fire texture three times to keep the color intensity we lost from the averaging of colors. The second set of three lines does the same thing, except it flips the texture vertically so the fire is coming from the top of the screen as well.

We now need to add the CreateTexture method to our class:

```
private Texture2D CreateTexture(int width, int height)
{
    Texture2D texture = new Texture2D(GraphicsDevice, width, height, 1,
    TextureUsage.None, SurfaceFormat.Color);
    int pixelCount = width * height;
    Color[] pixelData = new Color[pixelCount];

    for (int i = 0; i < pixelCount; i++)
```

```
        pixelData[i] = Color.White;

    texture.SetData(pixelData);
    return (texture);
}
```

Next, we can replace the entire contents of the `LoadContent` method with the following code:

```
GraphicsDevice device = GraphicsDevice;


hotSpotTexture = CreateTexture(4, 1);

OurGame.SpriteBatch = new SpriteBatch(device);
fireEffect = Content.Load<Effect>(@"Effects\Fire");
texture = Content.Load<Texture2D>(@"Textures\titleIntro");

renderTarget1 = new RenderTarget2D(device, device.Viewport.Width,
    device.Viewport.Height, 1, device.DisplayMode.Format,
    device.PresentationParameters.MultiSampleType,
    device.PresentationParameters.MultiSampleQuality);

renderTarget2 = new RenderTarget2D(device, device.Viewport.Width,
    device.Viewport.Height, 1, device.DisplayMode.Format,
    device.PresentationParameters.MultiSampleType,
    device.PresentationParameters.MultiSampleQuality);

fire = null;
base.LoadContent();
```

The titleIntro.png file has changed since the game state demo. The new titleIntro.png file can be found in this chapter's code folder on the accompanying CD. The Fire.fx file can be found in the same location. It did not change from Chapter 20. Most of this code should be reviewed. We incorporated the demo we made in the special effects chapter into our game. The title screen can be seen in Figure 24.1.

Updating the Start Menu

Our start menu is going to have a major overhaul. We create actual items that can be selected instead of the fake texture we have in place currently. Some of the code in this section is taken from Microsoft's GameStateManagementDemo, which can be found on the Creator's Club website (http://creators.xna.com/). To get started, we need to add the following private member fields to our `StartMenuState` class:

```
private SpriteFont font;
private GamePadState currentGamePadState;
```

FIGURE 24.1   The title screen consists of a texture and the fire effect.

```
private GamePadState previousGamePadState;
private int selected;
private string[] entries =
{
    "Play",
    "Options",
    "High Scores",
    "Exit Game"
};
```

We keep track of our game pad state so the selection between the menu items can be done effectively. The actual menu items are stored in an array.

In our Update method, we can leave the condition that checks for the Escape key or the Back button alone. However, we need to replace the next condition that checks for starting the game with the following:

```
if (Input.KeyboardState.WasKeyPressed(Keys.Up) ¦¦
    (currentGamePadState.DPad.Up == ButtonState.Pressed &&
     previousGamePadState.DPad.Up == ButtonState.Released) ¦¦
    (currentGamePadState.ThumbSticks.Left.Y > 0 &&
     previousGamePadState.ThumbSticks.Left.Y <= 0))
{
    selected--;
}
if (Input.KeyboardState.WasKeyPressed(Keys.Down) ¦¦
```

```
    (currentGamePadState.DPad.Down == ButtonState.Pressed &&
     previousGamePadState.DPad.Down == ButtonState.Released) ¦¦
    (currentGamePadState.ThumbSticks.Left.Y < 0 &&
     previousGamePadState.ThumbSticks.Left.Y >= 0))
{
    selected++;
}

if (selected < 0)
    selected = entries.Length - 1;
if (selected == entries.Length)
    selected = 0;

if (Input.WasPressed(0, InputHandler.ButtonType.Start, Keys.Enter) ¦¦
    (Input.WasPressed(0, InputHandler.ButtonType.A, Keys.Space)))
{
    switch (selected)
    {
        case 0: //Start Game
        {
            if (GameManager.ContainsState(OurGame.PlayingState.Value))
                GameManager.PopState();
            else
            {
                GameManager.ChangeState(OurGame.PlayingState.Value);
                OurGame.PlayingState.StartGame();
            }
            break;
        }
        case 1: //Options Menu
        {
            GameManager.PushState(OurGame.OptionsMenuState.Value);
            break;
        }
        case 2: //High Scores
        {
            break;
        }
        case 3: //Exit
        {
            GameManager.ChangeState(OurGame.TitleIntroState.Value);
            break;
        }
    }
}
```

```
previousGamePadState = currentGamePadState;
currentGamePadState = Input.GamePads[0];
```

The code checks to see if the player is pressing up or down and changes the selected index appropriately. The index is kept within the bounds of the array of menu items. Now, when the Enter key or the Start button is pressed, the case statement checks to see which menu item is selected and changes the state accordingly. We have put in a placeholder for the high score screen but will be adding that screen in the next section. The final condition in the Update method can be removed because it was bringing up the option menu before we had a way to select option menu from the main menu.

The contents of the Draw method can be replaced with the following:

```
Vector2 pos = new Vector2((GraphicsDevice.Viewport.Width - texture.Width) / 2,
(GraphicsDevice.Viewport.Height - texture.Height) / 2);
Vector2 position = new Vector2(pos.X + 140, pos.Y + texture.Height / 2);
OurGame.SpriteBatch.Begin();
OurGame.SpriteBatch.Draw(texture, pos, Color.White);
for (int i = 0; i < entries.Length; i++)
{
    Color color;
    float scale;

    if (i == selected)
    {
        // The selected entry is yellow, and has an animating size.
        double time = gameTime.TotalGameTime.TotalSeconds;
        float pulsate = (float)Math.Sin(time * 12) + 1;
        color = Color.White;
        scale = 1 + pulsate * 0.05f;
    }
    else
    {
        // Other entries are white.
        color = Color.Blue;
        scale = 1;
    }

    // Draw text, centered on the middle of each line.
    Vector2 origin = new Vector2(0, font.LineSpacing / 2);
    Vector2 shadowPosition = new Vector2(position.X - 2, position.Y - 2);

    //Draw Shadow
    OurGame.SpriteBatch.DrawString(font, entries[i],
    shadowPosition, Color.Black, 0, origin, scale, SpriteEffects.None, 0);

    //Draw Text
```

```
    OurGame.SpriteBatch.DrawString(font, entries[i],
    position, color, 0, origin, scale, SpriteEffects.None, 0);
    position.Y += font.LineSpacing;
}

OurGame.SpriteBatch.End();
base.Draw(gameTime);
```

The code calculates the center of the screen as well as the position to print the title on top of the texture. After beginning our sprite batch, we draw our screen texture. Next is the part of the code that uses techniques from the GameStateManagementSample demo from Microsoft. The code loops through all the menu items; when it finds the menu item that is selected, it sets its color to white and starts scaling the text in and out. The rest of the menu items are displayed in blue with no animation. The last section of the code in the for loop actually displays the menu items, spacing them vertically so they do not draw on top of each other.

The final piece is to update our LoadContent method. We need to replace the entire contents of the method with the following code:

```
texture = Content.Load<Texture2D>(@"Textures\startMenu");
font = Content.Load<SpriteFont>(@"Fonts\menu");

base.LoadContent();
```

The startMenu.png texture has changed from the game state demo we created. The file can be found on the accompanying CD in this chapter's code folder. We also use a new font to display these menu items. We can create a new font file inside of the Content project called menu.spritefont. We need to change the font name to Comic Sans MS and the size to 32. We can also set the demo flag at the top of our code to false so the demo message is not displayed.

Before we compile and run the code, we need to make a small modification to our TunnelVision game code. When we add the camera game component in the constructor, we need to add the following statement to keep the camera from accepting input:

```
Camera.UpdateInput = false;
```

Turning off the input to our camera keeps the background from moving when we select our menu items. We can now compile and run the code and see our improved start menu screen. The start menu screen can be seen in Figure 24.2.

Creating the High Score Screen

In the last chapter, we saved and loaded high scores but did not actually display them. In this section, we are going to modify our high scores state to display the high score list. This screen can be entered from the main start menu or after the game is over if the player has a high enough score to be entered into the high score list.

FIGURE 24.2   The TunnelVision start menu screen.

The following private member fields need to be added to the `HighScoresState` class:

```
private Texture2D texture;
private SpriteFont font;
```

The `LoadContent` method will load a new texture, which can be found in this chapter's code folder on the accompanying CD, and the menu font we added in the previous section:

```
protected override void LoadContent()
{
    texture = Content.Load<Texture2D>(@"Textures\highscores");
    font = Content.Load<SpriteFont>(@"Fonts\menu");

    base.LoadContent();
}
```

The highscores.png file, located on the accompanying CD, needs to be added to our projects. The `UnloadContent` also needs to be added to the class:

```
protected override void UnloadContent()
{
    texture = null;

    if (storageDevice != null)
    {
        //Save out our highscores to disk
```

```
    if (container != null)
        container.Dispose();
    }
    base.UnloadContent();
}
```

We also dispose of our container if we unload the game state. Because we are disposing the container when we save the high scores, we should not lose any data, but we should do it here as well to clean up after ourselves.

The last section of code we need in this class is the Draw method:

```
public override void Draw(GameTime gameTime)
{
    if (AlwaysDisplay || newHighScore)
    {
        Vector2 pos = new Vector2(
            (GraphicsDevice.Viewport.Width - texture.Width) / 2,
            (GraphicsDevice.Viewport.Height - texture.Height) / 2);
        Vector2 position =
            new Vector2(pos.X + 90, pos.Y + texture.Height / 2 - 50);
        OurGame.SpriteBatch.Begin();
        OurGame.SpriteBatch.Draw(texture, pos, Color.White);
        if (entries.PlayerName != null)
        {
            for (int i = 0; i < entries.Count; i++)
            {
                // Draw text, centered on the middle of each line.
                Vector2 origin = new Vector2(0, font.LineSpacing / 2);
                Vector2 scorePosition =
                new Vector2(position.X + 150, position.Y);
                Vector2 levelPosition =
                    new Vector2(scorePosition.X + 150, scorePosition.Y);
                Vector2 shadowPosition =
                    new Vector2(position.X - 1, position.Y - 1);
                Vector2 shadowScorePosition =
                    new Vector2(scorePosition.X - 1, scorePosition.Y - 1);
                Vector2 shadowLevelPosition =
                    new Vector2(levelPosition.X - 1, levelPosition.Y - 1);

                //Draw Name Shadow
                OurGame.SpriteBatch.DrawString(font, entries.PlayerName[i],
                    shadowPosition, Color.Black, 0, origin, .5f,
                    SpriteEffects.None, 0);

                //Draw Name
                OurGame.SpriteBatch.DrawString(font, entries.PlayerName[i],
```

```
                position, Color.Blue, 0, origin, 0.5f, SpriteEffects.None, 0);

                //Draw Score Shadow
                OurGame.SpriteBatch.DrawString(font, entries.Score[i].ToString(),
                    shadowScorePosition, Color.Black, 0, origin, .5f,
                    SpriteEffects.None, 0);

                //Draw Score
                OurGame.SpriteBatch.DrawString(font, entries.Score[i].ToString(),
                    scorePosition, Color.Blue, 0, origin, 0.5f,
                    SpriteEffects.None, 0);

                //Draw Level Shadow
                OurGame.SpriteBatch.DrawString(font, entries.Level[i].ToString(),
                    shadowLevelPosition, Color.Black, 0, origin, .5f,
                    SpriteEffects.None, 0);

                //Draw Level
                OurGame.SpriteBatch.DrawString(font, entries.Level[i].ToString(),
                    levelPosition, Color.Blue, 0, origin, 0.5f,
                    SpriteEffects.None, 0);
                position.Y += font.LineSpacing;
            }
        }
        else
        {
            Vector2 shadowPosition =
                new Vector2(position.X - 1, position.Y - 1);

            //Draw Name Shadow
            OurGame.SpriteBatch.DrawString(font, "Loading ...",
                shadowPosition, Color.Black, 0, origin, .5f,
                SpriteEffects.None, 0);

            //Draw Name
            OurGame.SpriteBatch.DrawString(font, "Loading ...",
                position, Color.Blue, 0, origin, 0.5f, SpriteEffects.None, 0);
        }
        OurGame.SpriteBatch.End();
    }
    else //No high score was saved, and AlwaysDisplay flag is false
    {
        //no high score was saved
        //no need to torture player that
        //they didn't get on high score list
        GameManager.PopState();
```

24

```
    }

    base.Draw(gameTime);
}
```

We first check to see if we have obtained a new high score or if we were told to always display the high scores. If either of those flags are set, we display the high scores. If they are both false, we remove this state from the stack. Currently, if the player does not get a high score, he or she is shown the high score data. If we wanted the player to always see the high score data, we could set the AlwaysDisplay property to true in our FadingState. In fact, we do set this property when we push this state on the stack from our start menu. You will see that in a moment.

After checking to see if we should draw the high scores, we calculate the position we need to place our high score texture in the center of the screen. Next, we calculate the position of the first high score we will be displaying on the screen. Then we display the texture and loop through all the high scores, displaying them on the screen with exact spacing between the name, the score, and the level. We also increment the y position for each line having the text drawn down the screen. The actual high score entries are wrapped in a condition to determine if we have actually loaded the high score data. If we have not, we display a loading message. This will happen the first time we come into this state because it needs to read the data from the storage device. If this is the very first time the game has been played, it will also need to write out the initial high scores before it can read them back in.

Now that we have the high scores being displayed, we can modify our StartMenuState code to execute this state when the player selects the high score list from the menu. Inside the switch statement in the Update method under the high score case, we can add the following statement:

```
GameManager.PushState(OurGame.HighScoresState.Value);
OurGame.HighScoresState.AlwaysDisplay = true;
```

We are forcing the high score state to draw the high scores by overriding the default value of the AlwaysDisplay property. Now we can compile and run the code and see the high scores displayed in the appropriate places. The high score screen can be seen in Figure 24.3.

Updating the Options Menu

The options menu is currently just a placeholder. We are going to add functionality that allows the player to turn the radar on or off as well as the crosshair. To begin, we need to add the following private member fields to our OptionsMenuState class:

```
private GamePadState currentGamePadState;
private GamePadState previousGamePadState;
private Texture2D select;
```

FIGURE 24.3   The TunnelVision high score screen.

```
private Texture2D check;
private int selected;
```

For both options we have two check boxes that signify whether or not the option is turned on. Instead of us using the menu entry like we did for the start menu state, the options are embedded directly in the texture. We only need to display which option is selected and then display an X when an option is turned on.

The Update method can be replaced with the following code:

```
public override void Update(GameTime gameTime)
{
    if (Input.WasPressed(0, Buttons.Back, Keys.Escape))
        GameManager.PopState();
    if (Input.KeyboardState.WasKeyPressed(Keys.Up) ||
        (currentGamePadState.IsButtonDown(Buttons.DPadUp) &&
         previousGamePadState.IsButtonUp(Buttons.DPadUp)) ||
        (currentGamePadState.ThumbSticks.Left.Y > 0 &&
         previousGamePadState.ThumbSticks.Left.Y <= 0))
    {
        selected--;
    }

    if (Input.KeyboardState.WasKeyPressed(Keys.Down) ||
```

```
        (currentGamePadState.IsButtonDown(Buttons.DPadDown) &&
         previousGamePadState.IsButtonUp(Buttons.DPadDown)) ||
        (currentGamePadState.ThumbSticks.Left.Y < 0 &&
         previousGamePadState.ThumbSticks.Left.Y >= 0))
    {
        selected++;
    }

if (selected < 0)
    selected = 1;
if (selected == 2)
    selected = 0;
if ((Input.WasPressed(0, Buttons.Start, Keys.Enter)) ||
    (Input.WasPressed(0, Buttons.A, Keys.Space)))
    {
        switch (selected)
        {
            case 0: //Display Crosshairs
            {
                OurGame.DisplayCrosshair = !OurGame.DisplayCrosshair;
                break;
            }
            case 1: //Display Radar
            {
                OurGame.DisplayRadar = !OurGame.DisplayRadar;
                break;
            }
        }
    }
    previousGamePadState = currentGamePadState;
    currentGamePadState = Input.GamePads[0];
    base.Update(gameTime);
}
```

The code simply allows the player to move up and down the options menu, and it stores the selected index. If the player presses the Start or A buttons or presses the Enter key or spacebar, the option that is selected is toggled.

In the Draw method we can replace the first statement, which calculates the position of the options menu texture, with the following code:

```
Vector2 pos = new Vector2((GraphicsDevice.Viewport.Width - texture.Width) / 2,
    (GraphicsDevice.Viewport.Height - texture.Height) / 2);
Vector2 crosshairCheckPos = new Vector2(pos.X + 142, pos.Y + 44);
Vector2 radarCheckPos = new Vector2(pos.X + 142, pos.Y + 136);
Vector2 crosshairSelectPos = new Vector2(pos.X + 145, pos.Y + 81);
Vector2 radarSelectPos = new Vector2(pos.X + 145, pos.Y + 173);
```

The previous code also sets the position of the option texture to be centered on the screen. The code also calculates the position of the selected texture and the checked texture for both options.

The rest of the Draw code, which simply draws the option menu texture, can remain. However, we do need to add the following code before we call the End method on the sprite batch:

```
if (OurGame.DisplayCrosshair)
    OurGame.SpriteBatch.Draw(check, crosshairCheckPos, Color.White);
if (OurGame.DisplayRadar)
    OurGame.SpriteBatch.Draw(check, radarCheckPos, Color.White);
switch (selected)
{
    case 0: //Display Crosshairs
    {
        OurGame.SpriteBatch.Draw(select, crosshairSelectPos, Color.White);
        break;
    }
    case 1: //Display Radar
    {
        OurGame.SpriteBatch.Draw(select, radarSelectPos, Color.White);
        break;
    }
}
```

The code determines whether the check should be displayed for either option. It then draws the selected texture for whichever option is currently selected. The last piece of code we need to add to our OptionsMenuState is actually loading the select and check textures inside our LoadContent method:

```
check = Content.Load<Texture2D>(@"Textures\x");
select = Content.Load<Texture2D>(@"Textures\select");
```

The x.png, select.png, and the new optionsMenu.png files can be found on the accompanying CD under this chapter's code folder. Compiling and running the code allows us to turn on and off the radar and crosshair. The options menu can be seen in Figure 24.4.

Updating the Remaining States

We need to tweak some of the game states a little more to make the game a little nicer. We will be modifying the won and lost game states. We can remove the LoadingContent method from the WonGameState, LostGameState, YesNoDialogState, and PausedState classes. We can also remove the font member field from all four classes. We need to add the following code to our won game state's Draw method:

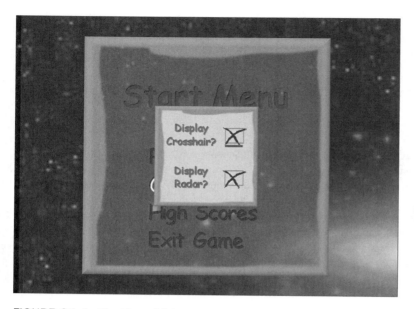

FIGURE 24.4   The TunnelVision options menu screen.

```
Vector2 viewport = new Vector2(GraphicsDevice.Viewport.Width,
    GraphicsDevice.Viewport.Height);
Vector2 fontLength = OurGame.Font.MeasureString("You Won!!!");
Vector2 pos = (viewport - fontLength * 3) / 2;
```

We are calculating the position to center the text on the screen. Similarly, we need to add the following code to the lost game state's Draw method:

```
Vector2 viewport = new Vector2(GraphicsDevice.Viewport.Width,
    GraphicsDevice.Viewport.Height);
Vector2 fontLength = OurGame.Font.MeasureString("You Lost!");
Vector2 pos = (viewport - fontLength * 3) / 2;
```

We need to do the same task for the PausedState:

```
Vector2 viewport = new Vector2(GraphicsDevice.Viewport.Width,
    GraphicsDevice.Viewport.Height);
Vector2 fontLength = OurGame.Font.MeasureString("PAUSED");
Vector2 pos = (viewport - fontLength) / 2;
```

We need do the exact same task for the YesNoDialogState:

```
Vector2 viewport = new Vector2(GraphicsDevice.Viewport.Width,
    GraphicsDevice.Viewport.Height);
```

```
Vector2 fontLength =
    OurGame.Font.MeasureString("Are you REALLY SURE you want to do THAT!?!?");
Vector2 pos = (viewport - fontLength) / 2;
```

On all four states, we need to replace the old private font the Draw method was using with the OurGame.Font. We also need to use the pos vector to position the text.

Using the Particle System

In this section, we are going to add some particles when an enemy ship is destroyed. We need to copy the Colorful.cs particle system file from Chapter 21, "Particle System." We need to add the private member field that holds a reference to our particle system inside our PlayingState:

```
private Colorful colorful;
```

We also need to add the particle system to our game components by adding the following to the constructor:

```
colorful = new Colorful(Game);
Game.Components.Add(colorful);
```

Inside the Draw method, we need to set the particle system's View and Projection properties:

```
colorful.View = OurGame.Camera.View;
colorful.Projection = OurGame.Camera.Projection;
```

Finally, when a collision occurs, we need to set the position of the particle system and call its ResetSystem method. The following code needs to be added to the top of the missileManager.CheckCollision condition inside the CheckCollisions method:

```
colorful.SetPosition(enemyManager.Enemies[ei].Position);
colorful.ResetSystem();
```

We need to add the bubble.png texture that the Colorful particle system uses to the Content project. The texture can be found in this chapter's code folder on the accompanying CD. We also need to copy the Colorful.cs code file from Chapter 21. There is no reason to create a ParticleSystems subfolder because this will be the only particle system in the game. The colorful particle system needs to be modified slightly to work well in the game. We need to change the namespace to TunnelVision. We can replace the last constructor and the InitializeSettings method of the Colorful particle system with the following code:

```
public Colorful(Game game) : this(game, 250) { }
protected override ParticleSystemSettings InitializeSettings()
{
```

```
    settings.EmitPerSecond = 250;
    settings.EmitPosition = new Vector3(0, 0, -1000);
    settings.EmitRange = new Vector3(2, 2, 2);
    settings.EmitRadius = new Vector2(3, 3);
    settings.MinimumVelocity = new Vector3(-1, -1, -1);
    settings.MaximumVelocity = new Vector3(1, 20, 1);
    settings.MinimumAcceleration = new Vector3(-5, -10, -5);
    settings.MaximumAcceleration = new Vector3(5, 10, 5);
    settings.MinimumLifetime = 0.2f;
    settings.MaximumLifetime = 0.2f;
    settings.MinimumSize = 3.0f;
    settings.MaximumSize = 3.0f;
    settings.Colors = new Color[] {
    Color.White,
    Color.Yellow,
    Color.Orange,
    Color.Red,
    Color.Black};
    settings.DisplayColorsInOrder = true;
    settings.RunOnce = true;
    return (settings);
}
```

After making those changes, we can run our game and see the particle effect when an enemy is destroyed.

Adding Sound

The last piece of the puzzle we need to put into place before completing the game is to add some sound effects and music. The wave files we need to add to our TunnelVision.xap project can be found on the accompanying CD in this chapter's code folder. We need to add the following wave files to the XACT project:

Robotic 4321

Doh

Death

Explosion

TunnelVisionMusic

TunnelVisionMenu

TunnelVisionTheme

If a refresher is needed on working with XACT, take time to look over Chapter 7, "Sound and Music." After adding the wave files to the wave bank, add the files to a new sound.

The three music files—TunnelVisionMusic, TunnelVisionMenu, and TunnelVisionTheme—need to be dragged over to the music category. Robotic 4321, Explosion, TunnelVisionMusic, TunnelVisionMenu, and TunnelVisionTheme can all be dragged into the cue pane as is. In the sound pane, we need to make a copy of Explosion for our gunshot. We can call this copy Explosion 2. We need to add a pitch event to this new explosion and set the equation type to constant and the value to 12. We did this in Chapter 7 as well. This is the sound we will play when we fire our missile. The regular explosion is what we will play when an enemy ship is destroyed. We also need to turn down the volume of the Explosion 2 sound. A good value is −16.4. After Explosion 2 is completely set up, we can drag it down to our cue pane and rename the cue to gunshot.

In the Death sound, we need to add an additional track and add a play event to that track. We then need to play the Doh wave inside the additional track's play event. We need to offset when it starts by changing the play event's TimeStamp to 1.25. This will make it wait 1.25 seconds before playing the second track. Finally, we can drag the Death sound to the cue folder and leave the cue name as Death. The detail of setting up the project was covered, but it was very lightweight. For reference, open the XACT project in this chapter's code folder on the accompanying CD.

We need to save the XACT project with the name TunnelVision; then we need to add the XACT project to our game projects. We also need to make sure the wave files are in the same Sounds folder, but they do not need to be included in the project. In our TunnelVision game code we need to add a reference to our sound manager:

```
public SoundManager Sound;
```

Inside the constructor of our TunnelVision game class, we need to initialize our sound manager:

```
Sound = new SoundManager(this, "TunnelVision");
```

Then, inside our Initialize method, we can create and start the playlist:

```
string[] playList =
    { "TunnelVisionMenu", "TunnelVisionMusic", "TunnelVisionTheme" };
Sound.StartPlayList(playList);
```

Finally, we need to make sure we call the sound manager's Update method inside our Update method:

```
Sound.Update(gameTime);
```

Inside our PlayingState class is where we will store most of our sound effects. Inside the Update method, where we add a missile, we have a placeholder. We need to add this line of code there:

```
OurGame.Sound.Play("gunshot");
```

When a collision occurs, we need to play the explosion sound. The following statement needs to be added to the `missileManager.CheckCollision` condition inside the `CheckCollisions` method:

```
OurGame.Sound.Play("explosion");
```

The next file we need to modify is our lost game state file. When we enter this state, we need to play the death sound because the gamer has lost the game. We need to add the following statement at the end of the condition inside the `StateChanged` method:

```
OurGame.Sound.Play("Death");
```

Now when the state is changed to the `LostGameState`, the death sound will be played. The last file we need to modify is the start level state file. When the level loads, we are going to play the Robotic 4321 countdown file. Inside the `StartLevelState` in the `StateChanged` method at the very beginning of the `startingLevel` condition, we add the following statement:

```
OurGame.Sound.Play("Robotic 4321");
```

We have finished adding all the sound effects and music to our game. We can compile and run our finished game. Have fun playing!

Suggested Improvements

We have completed a lot in these last three chapters. We have created a full game that we can play and share with others. However, some improvements could be made to make this game much better. To start with, better artwork would really add to the game. A more consistent look and feel throughout the game would also be beneficial. The fire on the title screen is cool, but does not really fit with the whole space theme. The options menu could be modified to have a submenu for sound. On that menu, there could be two slider bars: One to specify the level of the sound and the other to specify the level of music. There could be two more check boxes that turn off one or the other. Because the music is in its own category and the sound effects are all in a default category, this can be done easily.

Another way to improve the game is to have a transition between levels. It would be beneficial to improve the radar by creating a texture that actually looks like a radar screen, with circles surrounding the center. In fact, the texture could have an alpha channel to appear circular on the screen instead of the green square it is now. With very little effort, a post-processing effect could be applied to the radar texture that makes it appear to fade in and out or even have static.

We currently only allow one particle system at a time. When more than one enemy explodes, the particle system is abruptly ended and started again with the newly destroyed enemy. It might be beneficial to allow multiple particle systems. There's no provision to keep the enemies from jumbling up on each other. Another improvement would be to add AI logic that keeps them from occupying the same space.

A modification that could be made to the game is to remove the tunnel and the corresponding camera restriction. The player could move around freely in space, and the radar could rotate with the user. In fact, that could be another option. Gamers could decide if they want the radar to be static or to rotate with them. There are many more modifications that could make this game better. Have fun with it, or better yet, create your very own masterpiece!

Summary

In this chapter, we added a full-function menu system. We also added some detail to our title screen. You saw how to use sprite fonts in our menu system as well as how to use a premade texture in our option menu. We cleaned up the rest of the game states to fit better in our game framework, and we created a particle system. We created a sound project to bring our game to life. We also created a high score screen to display high scores. Finally, I listed some improvements that could make the game even better.

24

PART X

XNA Framework Networking

Networking Basics

Networking is an advanced topic. Writing single-player games can be tough, but writing multiplayer games can be downright rough. Fortunately, though, we can see some of the options we have when creating networked games using XNA Game Studio.

The XNA Game Studio team definitely helps us out by doing a lot of heavy lifting. Regardless, there is still a lot of thought we need to put into writing a multiplayer game. We will discuss the different types of multiplayer games as well as create a small demo that connects two machines together.

It is best to think about networking when first designing a game instead of trying to piece it in later. Although it can be done, it is definitely more work to factor in networking later.

Network Architecture

There are different approaches we can take when architecting our multiplayer games. We can use a client/server approach, where one machine sends all the information to the connected clients. We can use a peer-to-peer approach, where all the machines talk to all the other machines. We can also use a hybrid of the two approaches, where part of the game uses a client/server architecture while the rest of the game uses a peer-to-peer architecture.

Client/Server

The first approach we discuss involves using a client/server architecture. In this setup we have one machine (server) that acts as the host, and all the other machines (clients) connect to the host. All the data is passed to the server. The server then sends the messages to the individual clients. This scenario is common on Windows because cheating by modifying the packets is possible. The server can ignore any attempts at modifying the data because it knows exactly where all the players are and the status of each player.

Typically when trying to join a session, a particular machine needs to be the server so everyone who wants to join the game can find the game. Each client sends a ready command, and the host will start the game by sending a start command to each client.

Peer to Peer

The peer-to-peer approach broadcasts data from one peer to all the other peers. Or it can send a private message to one peer. The data can travel quicker in this environment because it does not have to be re-sent from a central location. The downside to this method is that each peer can modify the packet to cheat the game. Perhaps the third byte in the packet after the header is the health amount of the player. A hacker could modify the packet to always ensure byte 3 is at the maximum value, thus signifying full health and effectively making it so he can never die.

Fortunately, Xbox LIVE helps us with these concerns because the network traffic is secure. The data is encrypted, which makes it really difficult for anyone to decrypt a packet, modify it, encrypt it again, and then process it.

Hybrid

Most games actually use both approaches. The hybrid approach typically uses the client/server architecture for creating and joining a network session, and once the game play starts it moves into a peer-to-peer architecture, where each player is sending its data to the peers (or just the peers that are within range, on the team, and so on).

As with most things in life, programming multiplayer games is all about compromise. Writing a game that is both completely accurate and completely lag-free is not possible. It may make sense to be less accurate in order to have a more immediate response.

When determining which machines control what data, we need to keep in mind a few things. We need to ask ourselves, "Is it important that everyone actually be in synch on this particular piece of data?" It is easy to think that all data must be kept in synch, but actually there is a lot that doesn't need to be. Some data doesn't even need to be sent across at all, but we will get to that later. Here are some examples of data that absolutely must be kept in synch:

▶ Who won?

▶ Who just grabbed the flag?

▶ Did that player just score a goal?

The only way to keep these items in synch is by using a single authority machine (client/server approach) to decide the answers. Notice that there is nothing forcing us to have one machine to be the server for all data. We can split up the data that must be dictated to the other players on multiple machines. For example, if we wanted to make sure that only one person can carry the "flag" at any one point, then each machine (client) that is wanting to grab the flag will ask the authority machine (server), which is controlling who has the flag, whether it can have the flag. This way, if there is a race condition, the authority machine will allow one requesting machine to have the flag and tell the other requesting machines they cannot obtain the flag. It is not acceptable for more than one player to have the flag. So even if most of the game data is done with a peer-to-peer approach, this particular messaging is done in a client/server approach. This way, the game play is not ruined. For example, we don't want to be in a situation where we state that player 1 has won the game and then moments later have to say that player 2 actually won.

Then there is data that does not adversely affect game play, so while it still needs to be synchronized, having a delay is not the end of the world. Examples of data that does not require management by the server and is appropriate for individual machines to handle include the following:

- ▶ What is my position?

- ▶ Did I fire a bullet?

- ▶ In what direction am I moving?

Even though we definitely need to know if someone has fired a shot, we do not need to have the actual bullet managed from a central server. We can include enough information so the game can predict what will happen and where the bullet will land. If the player's position is off a little bit on each other player's machine, it is not completely consistent but does not really affect game play. Games should definitely not predict a player's death. Each peer can determine whether a bullet that was fired actually hit the player and then send out the appropriate message.

Remember that multiple machines can each have the authority over certain objects. Machine A could control who has the team flag while Machine B could control who is in each vehicle. Machine C could control when the session ends and track who has won. None of the machines will control how the bullets are flying. Each peer will simply send out data that contains its list of the bullet starting positions and velocities, and every machine can do its own physics calculations to determine where the bullets are in each frame. Even if a machine thinks a bullet might have hit a player, it does nothing unless that player is the machine's own gamer.

Here are some items that do not matter at all and should never be sent across the wire:

- ▶ Which way are the leaves on the tree blowing?

- ▶ Which way did that particle bounce?

- ▶ Which way did the bullet cartridge eject?

It does not matter to the gamers whether all the leaves are blowing the same way on all the machines. It does not matter which way a particular particle bounced. These types of data can simply stay on the local machines and be calculated locally.

System Link Versus LIVE

The actual machines playing the game can be either on the same local area network (LAN) or connected via the Internet. When games are being played on a LAN, latency is very low, and not too many packets should be lost. However, when we create games to be played over the Internet, we have to make sure we handle bandwidth constraints, latency issues, and packet loss. Fortunately, the XNA Framework gives us some tools to help simulate Internet conditions even when we are developing on a LAN. For example, to simulate the worst network conditions we are expected to handle, we can set two `NetworkSession` properties:

```
NetworkSession.SimulatedLatency = TimeSpan.FromMilliseconds(200);
NetworkSession.SimulatedPacketLoss = 0.2f;
```

Setting these values will help us make sure we are accounting for things that can go wrong when playing the game on the Internet. It is important, however, that we remove the simulation data when we are done with testing.

XNA Game Studio allows us to search for games regardless of whether they are being run on a LAN or on LIVE. The framework takes care of the heavy lifting for us. Natively these two connection methods have pretty different-looking code, but the API allows us to write a single code base for either option.

Actually enabling our game to be a network game requires only that we add the `GamerServicesComponent` to it. After we do this, we can press the Home key on the Windows keyboard or the Xbox button on the gamepad to bring up the Guide. We can test this out by creating a new Windows game project called NetworkTest. We can add the game component by supplying the following code in our constructor to initialize LIVE:

```
Components.Add(new GamerServicesComponent(this));
```

This one line of code is all that is needed to enable our game for multiplayer mode. Of course, we need to do a lot more work to actually get game data back and forth and do something intelligent with it, but this line of code will at least put the plumbing into place.

When we run the demo, we can press the Home key. We can sign in or create a profile if this is our first time using LIVE on the Windows machine. We could simply select Done instead of joining LIVE. By doing that, we create a local profile. We can create as many local profiles on as many computers as we would like. Having a LIVE membership is required for creating or joining LIVE network games, but we can do complete testing on a system link with local profiles.

XNA Requirements for Networked Games

To create a network game using the XNA Framework, we need to be aware of some requirements. There are membership requirements as well as hardware requirements when writing XNA multiplayer games.

Membership Requirements

When utilizing the network API of the XNA Framework, we must take note of a few things, depending on which platform the game will run on. Network games created for the Zune do not have any membership requirements. Those games are all ad-hoc local Wi-Fi networking.

Network games created for Windows using the XNA Framework's API do not require any memberships if the games are done over the LAN via a system link.

If the game needs to run over the Xbox LIVE services, then different requirements exist depending on which platform the game is running and whether the game is still in development. Both the Creators Club membership and the LIVE Gold membership are required. Table 25.1, which is taken from XNA Game Studio documentation, shows the different options available.

TABLE 25.1   Xbox LIVE Membership Requirements

	Xbox 360 Console	Windows-based Development Computer	Zune
Run an XNA Framework game	LIVE Silver membership + Premium XNA Creators Club membership	No memberships required	No memberships required
Use System Link for local area network game play	LIVE Silver membership + Premium XNA Creators Club membership	No memberships required	No memberships required
Sign on to Xbox LIVE and Games for Windows LIVE servers	LIVE Silver membership + Premium XNA Creators Club membership	LIVE Silver membership + Premium XNA Creators Club membership	Not available on Zune
Use LIVE to connect to other machines over the Internet while the game is in development	LIVE Gold membership + Premium XNA Creators Club membership	LIVE Silver membership + Premium XNA Creators Club membership	Not available on Zune
Use LIVE to connect to other machines over the Internet once the game is an XNA Community Game and has been downloaded from Xbox LIVE Marketplace	LIVE Gold membership + game purchase	LIVE Silver membership + game purchase	Not available on Zune

25

Developing and testing a networked game requires at least two machines, but you only need one Xbox 360 console and one Creators Club membership to test network code for the Xbox 360. This is because XNA Framework supports cross-platform system links so developers can run one instance of a game on an Xbox 360 and a second on a Windows-based computer. This functionality helps creators debug their titles without having to purchase a second console. It is also possible for more than one Windows-based development computer to connect several machines in a system link session without any memberships required.

CAUTION

An XNA Creators Club membership is required for any XNA Framework components that interact with Games for Windows LIVE. The game will not be able to connect to the LIVE service if a LIVE profile is set to auto sign-in on a Windows-based computer unless the profile has a Creators Club membership. In order to disable auto sign-in for a LIVE profile on a PC, you need to open the Guide after starting an XNA game while disconnected from the network.

Hardware Requirements

A minimum of two machines is needed to run a network game. Running multiple instances of a networked game simultaneously on a single development computer is not supported. It is recommended that you have multiple copies of the solution file opened on the different machines.

A multiplayer game can be created with one of the following hardware configurations:

▶ One PC and one Xbox 360—One instance of the game will be running on each machine.

▶ Two PCs—Each PC runs its own instance of the game.

▶ One PC and two Xbox 360 consoles—In this configuration, each console will run its own instance of the game. The deployment will be done from the PC.

Latency Issues

We have discussed latency already. It is affectionately known as *lag*. Latency is a physics issue. Data can only travel so fast. Network packets sent over the fiber travel at 65% the speed of light in a vacuum. One would think that is fast enough, but sadly it is not. Light is fast, but the world is really big. The speed of light in a vacuum is 299,792 km/s. So the speed of light over fiber travels at about 194,864 km/s. So how many kilometers do we need to travel? From New York City (NYC) to Los Angeles the distance is 3,961 km. So it would take 20ms—or (3,961 / 194,864) * 1000—for data to travel from NYC to LA. The distance from Tokyo, Japan to NYC is 10,878 km, so it would take about 56ms for the data to travel one way over fiber. The distance from Sydney, Australia to NYC is 15,988 km, and it would take about 82ms to travel that distance.

As if that weren't bad enough, there are delays in traveling over the Internet. Every router between the two destinations will add another 5ms to 50ms to the total time. Every DSL or cable modem will add another 10ms.

For commercial Xbox LIVE games, which target 99% of the Xbox LIVE users, the roundtrip latency between consoles can be as high as 500ms (or a half a second). This is a very large delay while playing an action-packed game.

It is worth mentioning again that the XNA Framework provides a way for us to mimic the delays of the Internet as we develop on our local LAN by allowing us to set the SimulatedLatency property on the NetworkSession object. This way, we can design our game to be tolerant of these delays. We do this with prediction and smoothing where appropriate. We discuss these topics in the "Prediction and Smoothing" section of this chapter.

Packet Loss

Besides the data taking a while to travel, sometimes we have the issue of the data not arriving at all! It is also possible that the data arrives in a different order than the order we sent it. Even the data that does arrive may have its contents corrupted. Networks are not reliable.

Another issue that people not using Xbox LIVE need to think about is people actually hacking the packets to cheat at the game. Fortunately, with the encryption Xbox LIVE has in place, it is impossible to ever receive data that has been modified.

The XNA Framework allows us to send our packets reliably and/or in order. The default is to fire and forget. This is done for speed and uses the User Datagram Protocol (UDP). To send a packet reliably and in order, the Transmission Control Protocol (TCP) needs to be used. We should very rarely use TCP (SendDataOptions.ReliableInOrder) in our games because it causes packets to be queued up and re-sent and will definitely add to our latency issues. Following is the workflow for sending data reliably and in order:

1. The sender sends the packet of data over the network.
2. The data is also stored in the sender's internal queue.
3. When the packet arrives at the recipient, the recipient sends an acknowledgement to the sender.
4. When the sender receives the acknowledgement, the data is removed from the internal queue.
5. If the sender does not receive an acknowledgement after a specific amount of time, the sender re-sends the packet.
6. If packets are received out of order, the receiver holds the newly sent packets in a queue while it waits for the one it missed.
7. Once the missing packet arrives, all the packets are processed, and the data is removed from the receiver's queue.

You can see that this just compounds latency issues. It is bad enough when the data actually gets there, but if we are sending the same packet multiple times, that just adds salt to the wound. Although TCP is great for many network applications, it just doesn't work for a fast-paced multiplayer game.

If we ask for unordered but reliable delivery of our packets and the first one is dropped, the game still gets the second packet right away. When the first one finally arrives (either because it was delayed or because it was re-sent), it is processed.

If we ask for unreliable but ordered delivery, a version number is included with each packet. As packets arrive, the version number is checked, and packets that have an older version number than the last one received are discarded.

Besides the `SendDataOptions` of `InOrder`, `Reliable`, and `ReliableInOrder` there are also `None` and `Chat`. `None` should be used whenever possible because there is no additional cost. However, for most game data `InOrder` should be used because most of the time we do not want old data changing our position or something. `Reliable` should only be used when it is really needed, and `ReliableInOrder` should be avoided if possible. The `Chat` option tells the XNA Framework to not encrypt the data being sent. It is very important that if the game is sending any player communication or chat data, it is sent with this option. It removes unneeded overhead, but it's also a legal requirement to send communication data over the Internet unencrypted.

To help us develop our code with packet loss in mind, the XNA Framework allows us to set the property `SimulatedPacketLoss` on the `NetworkSession` object. The typical case of packet loss will be about 2%, but worst case (and what the Xbox 360 commercial games account for) is up to 10%.

Bandwidth Constraints

As network programmers, we have latency issues and packet loss to deal with, but we also have bandwidth constraints to deal with. *Bandwidth* refers to the capacity we have to send data over a connection. Once we approach that capacity, we will see the amount of packet loss rise. If we exceed capacity, we will eventually be disconnected from our session.

So far the assumption has been we can send as much data as we would like. This is not the case. In fact, commercial Xbox 360 games cannot send any more than 8 kilobytes per second.

This is not a large amount of data. Assuming we only run at 30 frames per second in an eight-player game and we only are sending our `Position`, `Velocity`, and `Direction` (each a `Vector3`), that is still 7.56 kilobytes per second, as shown here:

8 players * 30 fps * (Position + Velocity + Direction) = 7 * 30 * (12 + 12 + 12) = 7,560 = 7.56KBps

---
NOTE

We use 7 for the number of players instead of 8 because we do not want to send data over the wire for ourselves.

Even with just this small amount of data, we are right at our limit. With so many limitations we need to make sure we measure our network performance. Fortunately, the XNA Framework exposes the `BytesPerSecondSent` and `BytesPerSecondReceived` properties on the `NetworkSession` object. We can monitor how much data we are sending and receiving. We should display this like we do our frame rate.

Voice

Unfortunately, the story does not end with our game data taking up the majority of our 8 kilobytes—there is also voice data. The XNA Framework compresses the voice stream to about 500 bytes. The data is only sent when a gamer is actually talking.

Voice is sent to all players by default. We can set who gets the voice data. This can be done by sending the data only to those players who are within a certain range or just to those players are on the same team or anything else we determine makes sense for our games. We can use the `EnableSendVoice` method on the `LocalNetworkGamer` object to implement this. It is important to note that we should not change who can talk very often because `EnableSendVoice` sends network data in order to coordinate the new settings. Changing it too often could cost us more than we have saved. Typically in the lobby we can let everyone talk because they most likely will not all talk at the same time, and even if they do there isn't any real game data being sent across the wire.

We can determine which players are allowed to send voice data by looking at the `AllowCommunication` property on the `GamerPrivileges` object. We can also check to see if another gamer has voice access by checking the `HasVoice` property on the `NetworkGamer` object. We can check to see if the player is currently talking by checking the `IsTalking` property, and we can see if they are muted by checking the `IsMutedByLocalUser` property.

Knowing that voice data can add up to about 500 bytes per player, our formula now becomes 7 * (30 * (12 + 12 + 12) + 500) = 11.06KBps.

As if that wasn't bad enough, we also have packet headers that get sent along with every packet. We will discuss these next.

Packet Headers

Every time we send data over the Internet, the packet is sent along with a packet header. Packet headers consist of the Internet Protocol (IP) header, which consists of 20 bytes. The UDP adds another 8 bytes. The LIVE data adds another 16 bytes, which is mainly for encryption and security. Finally, the XNA Framework data adds about 7 bytes, depending on what `SendDataOptions` are chosen. You can see that the packet header takes up 51 bytes. Our updated formula with this information is now

7 * (30 * (12 + 12 + 12 + 51) + 500) = 21.77KBps

We are well over double the recommended limit of 8KBps. What can we do? The first thing we need to do is send data less often. There is no reason to send data every frame. It is better to send more data less often than less data more often. The packet header size is not going to change, so we should make sure we get as much out of every packet as we can. It does not make sense to send a little bit of data and have the packet header take up the majority of the packet size. We should not send game data that is less than 50 bytes. Instead of sending a packet every frame, we can send about 15 to 20 packets a second. Therefore, if we are running at 60 fps, we can send a packet every three frames. This could be dynamic because we could send packets less often to the players they wouldn't effect. For example, we could save bandwidth by not sending packets to players who are not near us in the world if we can get by with it. Some games send even fewer packets a second, and they have really good prediction and smoothing algorithms to get by with sending so few packets.

Compression

Besides sending fewer packets, we can also compress the game data we are sending. Because the data being sent is very small, most compression algorithms will not work because they require a certain amount of data to actually compress.

One way we can compress the data is by simply sending less. For example, we do not ever want to send game data as strings over the network. They are too large. Instead it is better to have a lookup table and simply pass in an ID (byte, integer, or enum) to select the right text from the lookup table. A lookup table can also be used for things such as spawn points. For example, if the level always has weapons respawning at particular points, this is information that is known up front. It can be placed in a lookup table, and the only network data that needs to be sent is, for example, 34 in the SpawnWeapon event. Each machine knows that 34 for the current level means position X,Y,Z.

The size of the data matters. If we know an enumeration will never have more than 256 values, we should use a byte when setting up the enum. We can even store multiple low-value bytes in a single byte by shifting some bits. If we had two booleans, two integers, and one enum, we could combine all five of those pieces of data into 2 bytes. We would take 11 bytes—or (2 * 1) + (2 * 4) + 1—and compress them into 2 bytes. That's a pretty good compression ratio. This works by shifting the bits to the left. The integer values must be small enough to fit into 4 bits. This means the decimal value must be no smaller than 0 and no greater than 15. It is easier to cast the int as a byte if it is over 15 but less than 256.

We can create a new console application called BitShifter to see how this works. We are going demonstrate how to pack 11 bytes of data into 2 bytes. We start off our console app by adding in these member fields:

```
enum State
{
    Awake,
    Asleep,
    Random,
    Searching,
    Fleeing,
    Attacking
}
static bool isInventoryFull = true;
```

```
static bool isAbleToRun = false;
static State state = State.Random;

static int health = 15;
static int status = 1;

static byte firstByte = 0;
static byte secondByte = 0;
```

The first five fields are the sample data we are going to pack. firstByte and secondByte will hold the byte data as if we retrieved them from the sent network data (using PacketReader.ReadByte). We need to add the following two methods:

```
static void AddToBitfield(ref int bitfield, int bitCount, int value)
{
    bitfield <<= bitCount;
    bitfield |= value;
}

static int ReadFromBitfield(ref int bitfield, int bitCount)
{
    int value = bitfield & ((1 << bitCount) - 1);
    bitfield >>= bitCount;

    return value;
}
```

The first method will be used to pack the integer value into the bitfield. It knows how many bits to use based on the bitCount passed in. It shifts any existing bits to the left to make room for the new value. The left shift is done by the << operator. It then puts the value into newly opened bits by ORing the values together.

The second method does the exact opposite. It retrieves the value from the packed byte by extracting the bottom of the bitfield variable. It then shifts the values to the right (>>) to removed the data.

The following code can be added to our main method:

```
int bitfield = 0;
AddToBitfield(ref bitfield, 1, isInventoryFull ? 1 : 0);
AddToBitfield(ref bitfield, 1, isAbleToRun ? 1 : 0);
AddToBitfield(ref bitfield, 4, (int)state);

firstByte = (byte)bitfield; //packetWriter.Write((byte)bitfield);
Console.WriteLine("firstByte: " + Convert.ToString(firstByte, 2));
Console.WriteLine();
```

```
bitfield = 0;
AddToBitfield(ref bitfield, 4, health);
AddToBitfield(ref bitfield, 4, status);

secondByte = (byte)bitfield; //packetWriter.Write((byte)bitfield);
Console.WriteLine("secondByte: " + Convert.ToString(secondByte, 2));
Console.WriteLine();


bitfield = firstByte; //packetReader.ReadByte();
state = (State)ReadFromBitfield(ref bitfield, 4);
isAbleToRun = ReadFromBitfield(ref bitfield, 1) != 0;
isInventoryFull = ReadFromBitfield(ref bitfield, 1) != 0;

bitfield = secondByte; //packetReader.ReadByte();
status = ReadFromBitfield(ref bitfield, 4);
health = ReadFromBitfield(ref bitfield, 4);

Console.WriteLine("isInventoryFull: " + isInventoryFull.ToString());
Console.WriteLine("isAbleToRun: " + isAbleToRun.ToString());
Console.WriteLine("state: " + state.ToString());
Console.WriteLine("health: " + health.ToString());
Console.WriteLine("status: " + status.ToString());

Console.ReadLine();
```

We initialize the bitfield, which will hold our packed value. We then call our AddToBitfield method for the first three values we want to pack. For the boolean values we are storing 1 bit. The value of that bit will either be 1 or 0, depending on if the boolean value is true or false. The enum type will take up 4 bits. This is fine because our enum has fewer than 16 values.

Once we are done packing our byte, we simulate writing the byte by simply assigning it to our firstByte variable. We then print out the binary representation of the byte and then start packing our second byte. Because both of the values we are packing are integers (and they both have a value less than 15), we are passing in 4 bits to the AddToBitfield method. We then print out the secondByte after "writing" it.

Now we simulate reading the byte by setting our bitfield value to our firstByte value. Notice that we read the data out in the opposite order that we added it. We do the same thing for the second byte, and finally we print out all our values, which you can see are set to exactly what they started out with.

Not only can we utilize bitfields or store our integer values in a byte, but we can also utilize the Microsoft.Xna.Framework.Graphics.PackedVector namespace. This namespace contains functionality that was originally designed for packing vertex buffers and textures into a smaller format to be passed to the GPU. We can utilize this built-in functionality to pack our network data!

The best way to pack a float value if it ranges from 0 to 1 is to use `Alpha8`. Assuming we had a variable health that contained the value .85, we could write the following code to pack the value:

```
Alpha8 packedFloat = new Alpha8(health);
packetWriter.Write(packedFloat.PackedValue);
```

We discuss the `packetWriter` later in this chapter, but it is what allows us to write values so we can send them over the network. The point here is that we create a new `Alpha8` type and pass in our float value. We then pass the `.PackedValue` property of the newly populated `packedFloat` value. This compresses the value down to 25% of its original size.

If the float value does not range between 0 and 1, we can use `HalfSingle` instead of `Alpha8`. This would compress the value by 50%. If we wanted to pack a `Vector2`, we could use the `HalfVector2`. For `Vector4` we can use `HalfVector4`. For a `Quaternion`, we can use `NormalizedByte4`. For `Color`, we do not need to do anything because it already exposes the `PackedValue` property.

When packing `Vector3`, we have a couple options. We can use `Normalized101010` if it is a normalized vector. Otherwise, we can use three separate `HalfSingle` structs to hold the X, Y, and Z values.

In order to read the data on the other side, we would have the following code to handle our original health example:

```
Alpha8 packedFloat = new Alpha8();
packedFloat.PackedValue = packetReader.ReadByte();
float health = packedFloat.ToAlpha();
```

The last thing to mention about compressing data is compressing matrices. Most likely we do not need to pass in the full matrix data, which is a whopping 64 bytes. A matrix can store a lot of data, including scale and skew information. If we know a matrix will only combine rotation and translation and will never contain any scaling, shear, or projection, we can send just those two values instead of the entire matrix. We would send `Matrix.Translation`, which is a 12-byte `Vector3`. You just saw how we could compress that even further by using three `HalfSingle` structs. For the rotation we would use a 16-byte quaternion by calling `Quaternion.CreateFromRotationMatrix(matrix)`.

Do Not Send Unneeded Data

All the compression we just discussed is great, but sometimes we do not need to send the data at all. We need to make sure the data we are sending actually needs to stay in synch between machines. Only things that matter to game play need to be synchronized. Many things in our games do not actually matter to game play.

For example, animations and sounds usually do not need to be synchronized. Each machine can determine which animation to run based on the player data sent. There is no need to explicitly state the machine should play the "kick" animation if the input passed in includes the input of the player kicking.

Prediction and Smoothing

The key for network games is that each gamer's universe is actually a parallel universe. The universes are not identical. They cannot be identical because of latency. As long as the parallel universes are close enough, everyone can still experience great game play.

Typically for turn-based games, such as a card game, it will not matter if players have to wait a quarter of a second to see the last card played. For twitch-based (real-time) games, we will want to incorporate some prediction algorithms to try and hide the delay. There is no way we can ever know the exact state of a remote object, but if we know where that object was 250 milliseconds before and how fast it was moving, along with other input information (speeding up, turning, slowing down, and so on), we can make an educated guess as to where it should be on the frame we are drawing. Sometimes we guess right; other times we are wrong.

The key to handling prediction is to separate the physics state from the rest of the states of the objects. Set apart the pieces that the physics simulation needs to know about (position, velocity, orientation). Make this into a nested helper structure; we can have many of these inside the main actor class. It is useful to have multiple copies of the following data:

- ▶ Where am I drawing on the screen?

- ▶ Where was it for sure the last time I received a network packet?

- ▶ Where do I currently predict it is going to be, based on my updated version of the data I received from the network?

- ▶ What is the previous condition I made before making this prediction? (So I can smooth from the previous condition to this correct version.)

Once these are separated, we can run our current physics engine locally with the data. This is why it is so important to design our network games early on. It is not something that can easily be plugged in later. With our key network data in its own struct, our physics engine can process the data as many times as we need to predict where you will be. "If you were here and the controller was updating to the right, where would you be if I updated you five times?" We can simply pass in the information and call our physics Update method five times to get the answer.

No matter how good our prediction algorithm is, there are times when we will be wrong. When we are wrong we need to smoothly interpolate from the current (wrong) position to the correct position. This will keep the action from being too jerky. If we do not interpolate the data, the object will move smoothly until it gets a new network packet, and then it will abruptly jump to the new position. Instead, we want to target that new position in and smoothly move there.

Besides moving the character, there are other pieces of data we need to handle correctly. For example, if you are shooting in a game, you do not just want to say, "I'm at this location, and I am firing in this direction." Although it may seem that is what you want, the problem is that because universes are not identical across machines, you may think you hit another player, but on the other machine you missed entirely. Instead, it is better to say, "I'm shooting at gamer B but I missed 5 degrees to the left." With this type of information, each machine can determine the appropriate physics, sounds, and displays so that the player shooting will see he needs to adjust his aim to the right, and the person who was just shot at needs to get out of the way as a bullet whizzes by her head on the left.

Determining which data is important and then sending that data in such a way that it allows us to make correct predictions really helps us create believable game play and helps the gamers believe they really are in the same world.

How do we handle passing in all this data given everything you learned about bandwidth issues, latency issues, and packet loss? Basically, we need to pass around a lot of data to do predictions, but our bandwidth is limited. We can pass in position, velocity, and controller input. With these pieces of information, we can handle prediction better. With better prediction, we can send packets less frequently. Because the packet header takes up a lot of room, it is beneficial to send larger packets less often because this brings down the ratio of packet header information to actual game data.

Inviting Others to Join the Game

On Xbox LIVE, gamers can see what games their friends are playing. They can then join their friends' current network session pretty easily. Gamers can also receive invitations from other gamers to join a session.

This is supported in XNA Game Studio. To make this work, we first need to subscribe to the `InviteAccepted` event in our game constructor:

```
NetworkSession.InviteAccepted += OnInviteAccepted;
```

By hooking up the event, we enable the "Join Session In Progress" and "Invite to Game" options on the Guide. The actual `OnInviteAccepted` method is as follows:

```
private void OnInviteAccepted(object sender, InviteAcceptedEventArgs args)
{
    // Quit the current session
    if (session != null)
    {
        session.Dispose();
        session = null;
    }
    // Join the new session
    session = NetworkSession.JoinInvited(maxLocalGamers);
}
```

This event is kicked off regardless of whether a player accepts an invite or selects the "Join Session In Progress" option from his or her Friends List. XNA Game Studio handles making sure the player has the game being played on his or her Xbox 360. It launches the game or prompts the player to download. If the game is still in development, the gamer will see a message stating the invite could not be delivered because the game was not found.

For Windows, XNA Game Studio does not have a good way to automatically determine whether the correct game is installed. Therefore, a message box is displayed telling the player to launch the game.

Summary

We discussed networking in general and how to handle network games using XNA Game Studio. We talked about the different network architectures—client/server, peer to peer, and hybrid. We talked about the differences between System Link and LIVE. We discussed what memberships are required to play network games using XNA. We also discussed the hardware required for us to develop network games. We talked about latency, packet loss, and bandwidth constraints in detail. We created a demo where we compressed the data via bit shifting. We talked about other compression techniques to help us save bandwidth. We discussed using voice in our games and ways we can limit who is getting the voice data. We talked about prediction and smoothing so that our games can function efficiently and not appear jerky, even during the worst of latency issues. We finished up this chapter discussing game invites. You saw how easy it is to allow someone to join a game through an invite.

In the next chapter, we will put the things you learned into practice by creating a network demo that runs on Windows and the Xbox 360. We will then modify the demo so it can run on wirelessly connected Zune devices.

CHAPTER 26

Creating Multiplayer Demos

You learned about the basics of creating network games in the last chapter. Now it is time to take that knowledge and create a network demo that will not only run on Windows and the Xbox 360 but also on the Zune. We will start by creating a network game that runs on Windows and the Xbox 360. After we are done with that demo, we will port it so it runs on the Zune.

Creating a Network Demo for Windows and the Xbox 360

We are going to create a simple network demo. To start, we create a new Windows project called SimpleNetworkDemo. We can add in the following private member fields:

```
private Texture2D blankProfilePicture;
private SpriteFont font;

private NetworkSession networkSession;
private PacketReader packetReader = new PacketReader();
private PacketWriter packetWriter = new PacketWriter();

const int maxGamers = 16;
const int maxLocalGamers = 4;

private InputHandler input;

const int screenWidth = 1024;
const int screenHeight = 768;

private string errorMessage;
```

This demo simply displays the gamer picture (if the gamer is signed onto Xbox LIVE) so we have a field to hold that texture. We set up our network-specific variables as well as the screen width and height. We are using the `InputHandler`, so we need to include our latest XELibrary project. We also have an `errorMessage` variable in which we store any errors that occur so we can display them to the player.

In our game's constructor we add the following code:

```
graphics.PreferredBackBufferWidth = screenWidth;
graphics.PreferredBackBufferHeight = screenHeight;

input = new InputHandler(this, true);
Components.Add(input);

Components.Add(new GamerServicesComponent(this));
```

We need to load our content by adding the following statements to our `LoadContent` method:

```
blankProfilePicture = Content.Load<Texture2D>(@"Textures\noprofile");
font = Content.Load<SpriteFont>(@"Fonts\arial");
```

We are using the font from our XELibrary. The noprofile.bmp file can be added from the CD included in this book. Next, we jump right into our `Update` method by adding the following code:

```
if (networkSession == null)
{
    // If we are not in a network session, update the
    // menu screen that will let us create or join one.
    UpdateMenuScreen();
}
else
{
    // If we are in a network session, update it.
    UpdateNetworkSession();
}
```

We check to see whether or not our network session has been created. If it has not, we want to display a menu that lets the player choose whether he or she wants to host a game or join a game. For this demo we are forcing System Link, but the menu item would typically allow for a single player game, a network game over LIVE, or a System Link game. If the player is in a network session, we make sure we update the session. This could be a lobby or the actual game play. We are just going to put the player right into a game. The code for the `UpdateMenuScreen` is as follows:

```
private void UpdateMenuScreen()
{
```

```
    if (IsActive)
    {
        if (Gamer.SignedInGamers.Count == 0)
        {
            // If there are no profiles signed in, we cannot proceed.
            // Show the Guide so the user can sign in.
            Guide.ShowSignIn(maxLocalGamers, false);
        }
        else if (input.WasPressed(0, InputHandler.ButtonType.A, Keys.A))
        {
            // Create a new session?
            CreateSession();
        }
        else if (input.WasPressed(0, InputHandler.ButtonType.B, Keys.B))
        {
            // Join an existing session?
            JoinSession();
        }
    }
}
```

We only execute the code in this method if our game is active. This property returns true on Windows if the game is not minimized and has the current input focus. For the Xbox 360, the game is active if the user is not using the Guide.

Once we confirm the game is indeed active, we check for any signed-in gamers. If there aren't any, we bring up the Guide's sign-in screen. We pass in the maximum number of panes to display at sign-in. Windows only allows one pane, so it does not matter what we pass in. The Xbox 360 needs to be 1, 2, or 4. We set this value to 4 because that is the maximum the Xbox 360 allows. The second parameter determines the types that can be displayed. Passing in false means we want to see online and offline profiles. Passing in true will only show online profiles.

If there are signed-in gamers, the code checks to see if the A button or key was pressed. If it was, the code makes a call to CreateSession. Typically this would be a nice menu we could move up and down the list, but in an effort to keep the code small we are just looking for a particular key or button being pressed. The same thing is true to join a session. We are looking for the B button or key, and if either have been pressed we call JoinSession. Let's look at those methods next:

```
private void CreateSession()
{
    DrawMessage("Creating session...");

    try
    {
        networkSession = NetworkSession.Create(NetworkSessionType.SystemLink,
```

```
                maxLocalGamers, maxGamers);

        HookSessionEvents();
    }
    catch (Exception e)
    {
        errorMessage = e.Message;
        if (networkSession != null)
        {
            networkSession.Dispose();
            networkSession = null;
        }
    }
}
```

We are displaying a message on the screen before we go into a network-blocking call. This could be a nice generated graphic instead of just text. We will look at the DrawMessage method shortly.

We try to create a network session of type System Link. This could be read from a nicer menu to determine whether this session should be a LIVE session instead. The next two parameters are the maximum number of local gamers allowed on the session and the maximum number of total gamers allowed in the session. No more than 31 total gamers are allowed in a session. An overload to the method allows us to specify the number of private slots this session holds. It must be between 0 and whatever we passed in as the maximum number of total gamers. The overloaded method allows us to create a session with specific properties. It takes a NetworkSessionProperties type and can be used to supply custom values to distinguish this session from others. Then those searching for sessions can select different options to find a session that meets their needs. This would include the type of game (capture the flag, death match, co-op story mode, and so on), weapons available, and anything else we want to use to differentiate the sessions.

After creating the session, we make a call to our HookSessionEvents method, which simply hooks up the events we are interested in. We will look at the details of this method shortly. If creating the session fails, we store the error message in the string variable we declared earlier and clear out our session so the exception will be displayed on the screen.

Following is the code for the DrawMessage method:

```
private void DrawMessage(string message)
{
    if (!BeginDraw())
        return;

    GraphicsDevice.Clear(Color.CornflowerBlue);

    spriteBatch.Begin();
```

```
    spriteBatch.DrawString(font, message, new Vector2(6, 6), Color.Black);
    spriteBatch.DrawString(font, message, new Vector2(5, 5), Color.White);

    spriteBatch.End();

    EndDraw();
}
```

The `BeginDraw` method is built in to the XNA Framework. It allows us to draw to the screen outside of the typical `Draw` method. It must be followed up with the call to `EndDraw`, which you can see at the end of the method. The `BeginDraw` method can return false, which means the frame should not be drawn. We simply clear our device and draw our message with a shadow.

The `CreateSession` hooked into the events. It did this by calling the following `HookSessionEvents` method:

```
private void HookSessionEvents()
{
    networkSession.GamerJoined += GamerJoinedEventHandler;
    networkSession.SessionEnded += SessionEndedEventHandler;
}
```

The `GamerJoinedEventHandler` method, which handles gamers joining the session, is shown here:

```
private void GamerJoinedEventHandler(object sender, GamerJoinedEventArgs e)
{
    int gamerIndex = networkSession.AllGamers.IndexOf(e.Gamer);

    Texture2D gamerProfilePic = blankProfilePicture;

    foreach(SignedInGamer signedInGamer in SignedInGamer.SignedInGamers)
    {
        if (signedInGamer.Gamertag == e.Gamer.Gamertag &&
            signedInGamer.IsSignedInToLive)
        {
            GamerProfile gp = e.Gamer.GetProfile();
            gamerProfilePic = gp.GamerPicture;
        }
    }

    e.Gamer.Tag = new GamerObject(gamerIndex, gamerProfilePic,
        screenWidth, screenHeight);
}
```

We store the index of the gamer who just joined. The gamer is passed in via the `GamerJoinedEventArgs` parameter. We then need to set up a gamer object and associate it with the gamer. This gamer object could be a car in a racing game, a human, or anything else that describes what the player is as he or she is playing the game. For our demo purposes, we are calling it a general GamerObject. We will see this class a little later, but for now you can see that the constructor takes in the gamer index, the profile picture, and the screen width and height. We default the profile picture to the blank texture in our project. Then we check to see if the player is signed in to LIVE and assign his or her true profile picture. Finally, we store the gamer object we create in the Tag object property of our Gamer object. This way, we can retrieve it later.

> **NOTE**
>
> We can get by with checking to see whether the Gamertag is equal here because we are only looking at gamers signed in to LIVE. It is possible for local players to have the exact same Gamertag, so this check would not be sufficient. Also because we are not actually passing the gamer profile picture over the network, the remote player will never see this player's profile picture. The point of this exercise is to show a very simple networking demo, but for more robust functionality we would definitely want to pass the actual texture image to the other players.

The other event we hooked up was the "session ended" event with the SessionEndedEventHandler method:

```
private void SessionEndedEventHandler(object sender,
    NetworkSessionEndedEventArgs e)
{
    errorMessage = e.EndReason.ToString();

    networkSession.Dispose();
    networkSession = null;
}
```

The passed-in NetworkSessionEndedEventArgs parameter provides us with a reason why the session ended. We set our errorMessage string to that value. We then dispose of the network session and set it to null so our Update method will work properly.

The last method we called in the UpdateMenuScreen method was the JoinSession method, shown here:

```
private void JoinSession()
{
    DrawMessage("Joining session...");

    try
    {
        // Search for sessions.
        using (AvailableNetworkSessionCollection availableSessions =
```

```
                    NetworkSession.Find(NetworkSessionType.SystemLink,
                                        maxLocalGamers, null))
        {
            if (availableSessions.Count == 0)
            {
                errorMessage = "No network sessions found.";
                return;
            }

            // Join the first session we found.
            networkSession = NetworkSession.Join(availableSessions[0]);

            HookSessionEvents();
        }
    }
    catch (Exception e)
    {
        errorMessage = e.Message;
        if (networkSession != null)
        {
            networkSession.Dispose();
            networkSession = null;
        }
    }
}
```

The method starts out by drawing the status of "Joining Session." It then searches for the available sessions, passing in the type of session we are looking for (System Link) as well the maximum number of local players on this machine and the custom session properties we have set. (Because we did not set any when we created the session, we simply pass in null.)

If no sessions are found, the error message is updated, and we exit. If sessions are found, the code simply joins the very first one. This code may be okay for a quick match, but most of the time we would want to list the different sessions for the gamer to pick from. We finish up by hooking in the events we just created. We capture any errors that may have occurred in our variable and clear out the networkSession so we can display the error message.

Back in our Update method, we also called the UpdateNetworkSession method if a session was active (not null). The code for the UpdateNetworkSession method is as follows:

```
private void UpdateNetworkSession()
{
    //Update our locally controlled player and
    //send their latest position to everyone else
    foreach (LocalNetworkGamer gamer in networkSession.LocalGamers)
    {
```

```
        UpdateLocalGamer(gamer);
    }

    //Need to call Update on every frame
    networkSession.Update();

    //Make sure the session has not ended
    if (networkSession == null)
        return;

    //Get packets that contain positions of remote players
    foreach (LocalNetworkGamer gamer in networkSession.LocalGamers)
    {
        ReadIncomingPackets(gamer);
    }
}
```

We start updating our network session by looping through all the local gamers connected to the machine and calling the UpdateLocalGamer method, passing in the gamer from the list. We then call Update on the network session object to keep the XNA Framework sending and receiving packets. Finally, we loop through the same list of local gamers to receive any incoming packets from other players.

We can add the UpdateLocalGamer method to our class:

```
private void UpdateLocalGamer(LocalNetworkGamer gamer)
{
    // Look up what gamerObject is associated with this local player.
    //could be a car, ship, person object, anything we wanted
    //we are generically calling it a gamerObject
    GamerObject gamerObject = gamer.Tag as GamerObject;

    //Update the object
    ReadInputs(gamerObject, gamer.SignedInGamer.PlayerIndex);

    gamerObject.Update();

    //Write the player state into a network packet
    packetWriter.Write(gamerObject.Position);

    // Send the data to everyone in the session.
    gamer.SendData(packetWriter, SendDataOptions.InOrder);
}
```

The first thing we do in this method is retrieve the GamerObject we stored in the Tag property. We then call the method ReadInputs, passing in the gamer object and the player index. We call the Update method on the gamer object. We then write our packets. We are simply writing a `Vector2` value to the packets, but we could write more things. Also remember for optimal performance we could have used a `HalfVector2`. Once we have written our data to the packet writer, we actually send the data. We are using the `SendDataOptions` of `InOrder` so we can make sure the packets arrive in order. Some packets may be dropped, but that does not concern us for this demo.

The `ReadInputs` method called from the `UpdateLocalGamer` method contains the following code:

```
private void ReadInputs(GamerObject gamerObject, PlayerIndex playerIndex)
{
    //Handle the gamepad
    Vector2 gamerObjectInput = input.GamePads[(int)playerIndex].ThumbSticks.Left;

    //Handle the keyboard
    if (input.KeyboardState.IsKeyDown(Keys.Left))
        gamerObjectInput.X = -1;
    else if (input.KeyboardState.IsKeyDown(Keys.Right))
        gamerObjectInput.X = 1;

    if (input.KeyboardState.IsKeyDown(Keys.Up))
        gamerObjectInput.Y = 1;
    else if (input.KeyboardState.IsKeyDown(Keys.Down))
        gamerObjectInput.Y = -1;

    gamerObjectInput.Y *= -1;

    //Normalize
    if (gamerObjectInput.Length() > 1)
        gamerObjectInput.Normalize();

    //Store the input values into the gamer object
    gamerObject.Input = gamerObjectInput;
}
```

We use our input handler to get the game pad's left thumbstick state for the `playerIndex` passed in. We then use our input handler to get the keyboard state, checking to see if the left, right, up, or down key was pressed. Once we have our `gamerObjectInput` vector populated, we invert the Y axis by multiplying it by –1. This is so the texture will go down the screen when the down key is pressed. Finally, we normalize our vector and store the input in our gamer object's `Input` property.

At the end of the `UpdateNetworkSession` method we called the following `ReadIncomingPackets` method:

```
private void ReadIncomingPackets(LocalNetworkGamer gamer)
{
    //As long as incoming packets are available
    //keep reading them
    while (gamer.IsDataAvailable)
    {
        NetworkGamer sender;

        //Read a single network packet
        gamer.ReceiveData(packetReader, out sender);

        //Ignore packets sent by local gamers
        //since we already know their state
        if (sender.IsLocal)
            continue;

        //Look up the player associated with whoever sent this packet
        GamerObject remoteGamerObject = sender.Tag as GamerObject;

        //Read the state of this gamer object from the network
        remoteGamerObject.Position = packetReader.ReadVector2();
    }
}
```

As long as the incoming packets are available, we keep reading them from the network. We retrieve a single network packet from the gamer but ignore data from any player on the local machine because we already know what state they are in. We then store our remote gamer object by getting it from the Tag property where we stored it originally. Once we have that, we can set the position of our copy of the remote gamer object. We would set any additional information we wanted to store here as well. For this demo we are only concerned with the position.

We are done with our Update method and all the methods associated with it. Now we can dig into the GamerObject class we created:

```
public Vector2 Input;
public Vector2 Velocity;
public Vector2 Position;
private Vector2 screenSize;
public Texture2D GamerPicture;

public GamerObject(int gamerIndex, Texture2D gamerPicture,
    int screenWidth, int screenHeight)
{
    Position.X = screenWidth * 0.25f + (gamerIndex % 5) * screenWidth * 0.125f;
    Position.Y = screenHeight * 0.25f + (gamerIndex * .20f) * screenHeight * .20f;
```

```
    screenSize = new Vector2(screenWidth, screenHeight);

    GamerPicture = gamerPicture;
}

public void Update()
{
    Velocity = Input * 2.0f;

    //Update the position
    Position += Velocity;

    //Clamp so the pic won't go off the screen
    Position = Vector2.Clamp(Position, Vector2.Zero, screenSize);
}

public void Draw(SpriteBatch spriteBatch)
{
    spriteBatch.Draw(GamerPicture, Position, Color.White);
}
```

This class is pretty simple. The constructor does some math to space out the players so they are not on top of each other. We then store the size of the screen based on the width and height passed in. We finally set the gamer picture texture passed in.

The Update method sets the Velocity property to the Input property, which we just set in our game class. The input could be used for other things to help with prediction, but for this simple demo we are just storing the direction as a Vector2. We multiply this value by 2 to make the object move a little faster. We then add the velocity to the position of the object. We also make sure the position stays within the screen's width and height. We finish up the class with our Draw method, which simply displays the texture at the correct position.

We have not actually set up our Draw method in the game itself. We can do that now by adding the following code to the contents of the Draw method:

```
if (networkSession == null)
{
    // If we are not in a network session, draw the
    // menu screen that will let us create or join one.
    DrawMenuScreen();
}
else
{
    // If we are in a network session, draw it.
    DrawNetworkSession();
}
```

26

We are doing the same types of game state checks we did in the Update method. If we do not have a network session, we draw the simple menu where the gamer can select to join a game or create his or her own. The DrawMenuScreen is as follows:

```
private void DrawMenuScreen()
{
    string message = string.Empty;

    if (!string.IsNullOrEmpty(errorMessage))
        message += "Error:\n" + errorMessage.Replace(". ", ".\n") + "\n\n";

    message += "A = create session\n" +
               "B = join session";

    spriteBatch.Begin();

    spriteBatch.DrawString(font, message, new Vector2(6, 6), Color.Black);
    spriteBatch.DrawString(font, message, new Vector2(5, 5), Color.White);

    spriteBatch.End();
}
```

This initializes our message and then adds an error message (if one exists) to the message. We also add the actual menu options to the message. Finally, we draw the message, complete with a shadow, on the screen.

If we are in a network session, instead of drawing the menu we call the following DrawNetworkSession method:

```
private void DrawNetworkSession()
{
    spriteBatch.Begin();

    // For each person in the session...
    foreach (NetworkGamer gamer in networkSession.AllGamers)
    {
        //Look up the gamer object associated to this network gamer
        GamerObject gamerObject = gamer.Tag as GamerObject;

        //Draw the gamer object
        gamerObject.Draw(spriteBatch);
```

```
    //Draw a gamertag label
    string label = gamer.Gamertag;
    Color labelColor = Color.Black;
    Vector2 labelOffset = new Vector2(75, 40);

    if (gamer.IsHost)
        label += " (host)";

    //Flash the gamertag to yellow when the player is talking.
    if (gamer.IsTalking)
        labelColor = Color.Yellow;

    spriteBatch.DrawString(font, label, gamerObject.Position, labelColor, 0,
                         labelOffset, 0.6f, SpriteEffects.None, 0);
    }

    spriteBatch.End();
}
```

We start off by beginning our sprite batch as normal. We then loop through all the gamers in this network game, storing the gamer object (as stored in the `Tag` property.) We then call the `Draw` method of our gamer object, which we set up earlier. This method simply draws the profile picture stored in the object. We then store the player's gamer tag in a label we display above the picture. We set the label color to black and set the offset. If the player is the host, we append " (host)" to the label as well. Because voice chat is built in and works, we can check to see if the player is talking by looking at the `IsTalking` property. If the player is talking, we just change the label color to yellow to signal that player is the one speaking. Then we draw the label at the same location as the player's position with the offset in place. We also scale down the text a little bit so it does not overpower the picture being displayed. Finally, we call `End` on our sprite batch.

We have finished creating a simple networking demo that runs on Windows. In order to test this out, we need to copy our project to an Xbox 360 project. We can right-click the Windows project in the Solution Explorer and select Create Copy of Project for Xbox 360. Once this is done, we can save the solution, remove the newly created Xbox 360 project from our solution, and then save our solution again. Now we need to open up a new instance of Visual Studio and load in our newly created Xbox 360 SimpleNetworkDemo project. We can also add in the XELibrary_Xbox360 project and then save this solution using a name different from the solution with our Windows project. We can now run the projects for both solutions, and as long as the Xbox 360 is waiting for a computer connection, we can play the game between the two machines. This could have also been done with two Window PCs, but each solution would need to run its own PC or have just the executable copied over (assuming all the required components are installed).

Local Ad-Hoc Wi-Fi Gaming on the Zune

Now we are going to take our SimpleNetworkDemo and create a Zune networking demo. In order to get this to work, we need to have access to two Zunes. Currently there is no support for linking a game that runs on the Zune with a game that runs on Windows or the Xbox 360.

We can have a maximum of eight Zunes join in to a single game. To get started with this demo, we begin with one of the solutions we just finished and then add an existing project and select the XELibrary_Zune project. We can then make a copy of the demo project into a Zune project. We can set the Zune project as our startup project and make sure we are compiling for the Zune by selecting Zune from the Solution Platforms dropdown menu.

Now we can compile and see what all we need to change to get the game to run on the Zune. We see two errors. The first is that we cannot find the XELibrary assembly. This is because of the second error that caused the XELibrary_Zune project to fail to build. We have copied the project, along with each chapter, but we have not modified it. We need to remove the PointEffect file. The problem, though, is that if we just remove the file from the project, it will be removed from the Content project associated with the Windows and Xbox 360 XELibrary projects, too. We could create a Zune-specific content project like we did in some of the demos in the earlier chapters, but then we would duplicate assets in two different content projects. For the SimpleGame we did before, all the assets were different. The sound and the textures changed, so it was okay to just make a new copy. This time, however, we do not want to change the Arial font or the progress bar. We obviously could. We could make the font smaller and decrease the size of the progress bar. However, to show how we can have shared resources, we will use the same files for all the projects.

We first want to change the name of the current Content project to SharedContent. We could just assume everything in Content is shared and not do the renaming, but explicitly stating everything is shared leaves no room for confusion later. We cannot actually rename the project inside of Visual Studio, so we need to exclude the Content project from our XELibrary projects. We then will need to exit Visual Studio and rename the actual folder and .contentproj file. Once we have renamed these to SharedContent, we can reopen our solution and add in the existing SharedContent project. At this point we still have not solved our compiler problem, so we need to create a new Content project. We can call this 3DContent and then cut the Effects folder from the SharedContent project and paste the folder to this project. We want to remove the 3DContent project from our XELibrary_Zune project, which will solve our compiler error. The last thing we need to do is change the Content Root Folder property of both our content projects to be "Content" instead of "SharedContent" and "3DContent." This way our existing code will work as intended—everything is under a common folder called Content.

Creating Multiple Content Projects

XNA Game Studio allows us to create multiple content projects. We can give these projects meaningful names to help keep our content separated. If we have shared content across multiple platforms, we can have a content project called SharedContent. We could then have another content project called HighResolutionTextures or LowResolutionTextures and include the project we want in the particular platform. We would want our high-resolution textures in our Windows and Xbox 360 platform projects and our low-resolution textures loaded in our Zune platform project. We could create a special 3DContent project to hold all our 3D assets that we would not include in the Zune content project but would in the other platforms.

When we recompile, we see another compiler error concerning the System.Xml.Serialization namespace. We manually need to add a reference to System.Xml in our XELibrary_Zune project. Now when we compile we get an error with our actual network demo code.

We see that the Zune has no idea what the Guide is. Therefore, we can ignore that part of the condition because the gamer does not need to sign on to LIVE. Right after the IsActive condition inside the UpdateMenuScreen method, we can wrap the first if statement down to the else (but before the if) in a !ZUNE preprocessor directive. The portion of code should now look like this:

```
#if !ZUNE
    if (Gamer.SignedInGamers.Count == 0)
    {
        // If there are no profiles signed in, we cannot proceed.
        // Show the Guide so the user can sign in.
        Guide.ShowSignIn(maxLocalGamers, false);
    }
    else
#endif
    if (input.WasPressed(0, InputHandler.ButtonType.A, Keys.A))
```

Now we can compile the demo with no problems. If we run the demo on the Zune, we can create a session. However, we get an error that we cannot read because the text is cut off the screen. It states something about invalid parameters, but instead of guessing what that says we can change our Zune to landscape mode by adding the same code we did in our SimpleGame in Chapter 13, "Running the Game on the Zune." We start by adding in the private member field for our Zune render target:

```
#if ZUNE
    private RenderTarget2D zuneRenderTarget;
#endif
```

Then we need to initialize the render target in our constructor:

```
#if ZUNE
    zuneRenderTarget = new RenderTarget2D(
        GraphicsDevice,
        screenWidth,
        screenHeight,
        0,
        SurfaceFormat.Color);
#endif
```

Because we do not want our render target to be 1024×768, which is what our current screenWidth and screenHeight values are set to, we need to replace those constants with the following code:

```
#if !ZUNE
    const int screenWidth = 1024;
    const int screenHeight = 768;
#else
    const int screenWidth = 320;
    const int screenHeight = 240;
#endif
```

Then at the beginning of our Draw method and at the beginning of our DrawMessage method (right after we call BeginDraw), we can tell the device to render to this render target:

```
#if ZUNE
    GraphicsDevice.SetRenderTarget(0, zuneRenderTarget);
#endif
```

And finally at the end of our Draw method and at the end of our DrawMessage method (right before we call EndDraw), we can display on the screen the contents of our render target:

```
DrawRenderTarget();
```

The code for this new method is as follows:

```
private void DrawRenderTarget()
{
#if ZUNE
    //resolve the target
    GraphicsDevice.SetRenderTarget(0, null);

    //draw the texture rotated
```

```
    spriteBatch.Begin();
    spriteBatch.Draw(
        zuneRenderTarget.GetTexture(),
        new Vector2(120, 160),
        null,
        Color.White,
        MathHelper.PiOver2,
        new Vector2(160, 120),
        1f,
        SpriteEffects.None,
        0);
    spriteBatch.End();
#endif
}
```

So now if we run the network demo on the Zune, it will be in landscape mode. When we choose to create a session, we can see the majority of the error message telling us that the parameter `maxGamers` is out of range. We could clean this up by either using a smaller font or scaling down the font. For this demo, however, we are going to ignore it.

In order to fix the runtime error, we need to replace the constant where we set `maxGamers` to the following:

```
#if !ZUNE
    const int maxGamers = 16;
#else
    const int maxGamers = 8;
#endif
```

Because the maximum number of players we can have in a single Zune game is eight, we have set it to that value. The last thing we need to do is fix our input. Because we displayed our scene in landscape mode, we need to check our inputs with that in mind. In our `ReadInputs` method, we can replace the line of code where we inverse the y axis of the `gamerObjectInput` with the following code:

```
#if !ZUNE
    gamerObjectInput.Y *= -1;
#else
    float tmp = -gamerObjectInput.X;
    gamerObjectInput.X = -gamerObjectInput.Y;
    gamerObjectInput.Y = tmp;

    if (input.GamePads[(int)playerIndex].DPad.Up == ButtonState.Pressed)
        gamerObjectInput.X = -1;
    else if (input.GamePads[(int)playerIndex].DPad.Down == ButtonState.Pressed)
        gamerObjectInput.X = 1;
```

```
    if (input.GamePads[(int)playerIndex].DPad.Left == ButtonState.Pressed)
        gamerObjectInput.Y = 1;
    else if (input.GamePads[(int)playerIndex].DPad.Right == ButtonState.Pressed)
        gamerObjectInput.Y = -1;
#endif
```

With those final changes in place, we can now run the code and create our own session and move our texture around. Because there is no profile picture associated to the Zune device, we get the default blank gamer profile picture. We could customize the code to allow the gamer to pick a picture from his or her picture collection. We could then store which picture the gamer picked (like we stored the high score data) to be displayed the next time he or she plays the game.

Now it is time to bring our second Zune into the mix so we can actually play the multiplayer demo on both devices. First, we need to hook up the other Zune to our machine. If the Zune software comes up, we can exit it. Then we can add this Zune to our list of devices by bringing up the XNA Game Studio Device Center. After we add the Zune to the Device Center, we change the Zune we are deploying to by selecting it from the dropdown box next to the Device Center icon on our toolbar. We can bring up a new Visual Studio window and load the same solution and leave the device set to Default. This way, we can deploy and run the games on both Zune devices from the same computer. You can see that the same network code with just a couple of tweaks works on the Zune. Now you know how to write networking code for Windows, the Xbox 360, and the Zune.

Summary

We have just scratched the surface as to what it takes to create a full-scale multiplayer game, but there is enough information here to help us get started making an absolutely awesome network game. You saw the steps it takes to get the basics of a network game to run. You also saw that very little had to change with the networking code to get the demo to run on the Zune.

In the next two chapters, we will create two multiplayer games. We will create a turn-based game first and then create a real-time game.

CHAPTER 27

Creating a Networking Game Skeleton

In the last chapter we got our feet wet by creating a simple demo that allowed us to get two machines to talk to each other. In this chapter we are going to create a networking game template with multiple menu states that allow us to jump into a single player game, a local multiplayer game, a multiplayer game over a system link, and a multiplayer game over LIVE.

When we are finished with this chapter, you will be able to see all the code needed to create and join network sessions and to pass between the various game states correctly.

Creating the Template

To get started, we need to create a new Windows game project called NetworkGameTemplate. We are going to be using (and modifying) the latest game states we used in Chapter 24, "Finishing Touches." We need to create a GameStates folder and copy all the code from Chapter 24's TunnelVision/GameStates folder. We can also copy the latest XELibrary project from Chapter 26, "Creating Multiplayer Demos." We need to open the XELibrary project in our solution and a project reference to our NetworkGameTemplate game.

We are not going to need YesNoDialogState.cs and StartLevelState.cs, so remove both those files from the project. All our game states are using the old TunnelVision namespace. We need to change this to NetworkGameTemplate (our current project's namespace). The easiest way to do this is to open up BaseGameState.cs (or any file from the GameStates folder) and change the namespace. Then, using Visual Studio we can right-click the recently changed namespace and have Visual Studio replace all instances. We also need to change our Game1 class to NetworkGameTemplate.

When we try to compile our project, we should be greeted with five error messages in our PlayingState class. These were specific items our TunnelVision game used that we do not use in this game.

We are going to be stripping out a lot of code from the PlayingState that is no longer needed—the code is very game-dependent. We are going to modify the IPlayingState interface in the GameStateInterfaces.cs class under the GameStates folder of the game project:

```
public interface IPlayingState : IGameState
{
    void StartGame(int numberOfPlayers);
    int Score { get; }
}
```

We removed the CurrentLevel property and added a parameter containing the number of players our game has in our StartGame method. The updated PlayingState.cs file can be seen in Listing 27.1.

LISTING 27.1   PlayingState.cs

```
using System;
using Microsoft.Xna.Framework;
using Microsoft.Xna.Framework.Graphics;
using Microsoft.Xna.Framework.Input;

namespace NetworkGameTemplate
{
    public sealed class PlayingState : BaseGameState, IPlayingState
    {
        private const int CountdownTimer = 120;

        private TimeSpan? storedTime;
        private TimeSpan currentTime;
        private DateTime currentStopTime = DateTime.Now;

        private string timeText = string.Empty;
        private Vector2 timeTextShadowPosition;
        private Vector2 timeTextPosition;

        private string scoreText = string.Empty;
        private Vector2 scoreTextShadowPosition;
        private Vector2 scoreTextPosition;
        public int singlePlayerScore;
```

```csharp
private int numberOfPlayers;

public PlayingState(Game game)
    : base(game)
{
    game.Services.AddService(typeof(IPlayingState), this);
}

public override void Update(GameTime gameTime)
{
    float elapsed = (float)gameTime.ElapsedGameTime.TotalSeconds;

    currentTime = currentStopTime.Subtract(DateTime.Now);
    if (currentTime.Seconds < 0)
        currentTime = TimeSpan.Zero;

    if (Input.WasPressed(0, Buttons.Back, Keys.Escape))
    {
        storedTime = currentTime;
        GameManager.PushState(OurGame.StartMenuState.Value);
    }

    if (Input.WasPressed(0, Buttons.Start, Keys.Enter))
    {
        storedTime = currentTime;
        GameManager.PushState(OurGame.PausedState.Value);
    }

    base.Update(gameTime);

}


public void StartGame(int numberOfPlayers)
{
    this.numberOfPlayers = numberOfPlayers;

    SetupGame();
}

private void SetupGame()
{
    singlePlayerScore = 0;
    storedTime = null;
    singlePlayerScore = 0;
```

```
    }

    public override void Draw(GameTime gameTime)
    {
        OurGame.SpriteBatch.Begin();

        OurGame.SpriteBatch.DrawString(OurGame.Font, timeText,
            timeTextShadowPosition, Color.Black);
        OurGame.SpriteBatch.DrawString(OurGame.Font, timeText,
            timeTextPosition, Color.Firebrick);

        OurGame.SpriteBatch.DrawString(OurGame.Font, scoreText,
            scoreTextShadowPosition, Color.Black);
        OurGame.SpriteBatch.DrawString(OurGame.Font, scoreText,
            scoreTextPosition, Color.Firebrick);

        OurGame.SpriteBatch.End();

        base.Draw(gameTime);
    }

    protected override void StateChanged(object sender, EventArgs e)
    {
        base.StateChanged(sender, e);

        if (GameManager.State != this.Value)
        {
            Visible = true;
            Enabled = false;
        }
        else
        {
            if (storedTime != null)
                currentStopTime = DateTime.Now + (TimeSpan)storedTime;
            else
                currentStopTime = DateTime.Now +
                    new TimeSpan(0, 0, CountdownTimer);
        }
    }

    protected override void LoadContent()
    {
        timeTextShadowPosition = new Vector2(TitleSafeArea.X,
            TitleSafeArea.Y + OurGame.Font.LineSpacing * 2);
        timeTextPosition = new Vector2(TitleSafeArea.X + 1.0f,
            TitleSafeArea.Y + OurGame.Font.LineSpacing * 2 + 1.0f);
```

```
            scoreTextShadowPosition = new Vector2(TitleSafeArea.X,
                TitleSafeArea.Y + OurGame.Font.LineSpacing * 3);
            scoreTextPosition = new Vector2(TitleSafeArea.X + 2.0f,
                TitleSafeArea.Y + OurGame.Font.LineSpacing * 3 + 2.0f);

            base.LoadContent();
        }

        public int Score
        {
            get { return (singlePlayerScore); }
        }
    }
}
```

We renamed a couple variables to remove any notion of levels. For example, we changed
currentLevelTime to currentTime. Because this is going to be a multiplayer game and we
are only keeping track of scores (for high score purposes) if it is a single player game, we
renamed the private score member field to singlePlayerScore. The majority of the
changes involved stripping out code specific to the TunnelVision game.

In our Game1.cs file, we need change spriteBatch to SpriteBatch and change the modifier to public so our game states can access it. We need to add a public sprite font called
Font and then load it in our LoadContent method:

```
Font = Content.Load<SpriteFont>(@"Fonts\Arial");
```

Now we need to add our states to our NetworkGameTemplate class so the other states can
access them as needed. We can add the following member fields:

```
public ITitleIntroState TitleIntroState;
public IStartMenuState StartMenuState;
public IOptionsMenuState OptionsMenuState;
public IPlayingState PlayingState;
public ILostGameState LostGameState;
public IWonGameState WonGameState;
public IFadingState FadingState;
public IPausedState PausedState;
public IHighScoresState HighScoresState;
```

Now when we compile our solution, we are greeted with nine errors. The first ones we are
going to tackle are those surrounding the HighScoreState. We no longer are storing level
information in our high score data. Therefore, we can remove all instances of Level and
CurrentLevel. While we are in this file we can also change the containerName value to
NetworkGameTemplate. This needs to change to the actual game name when we create a

game from this template. We can also set the default high score values to more appropriate values for this game by changing the InitializeDefaultHighScores method:

```
private void InitializeDefaultHighScores()
{
    // Create the data to save
    entries = new HighScoreData(5);
    entries.PlayerName[0] = "Neil";
    entries.Score[0] = 1500;

    entries.PlayerName[1] = "Chris";
    entries.Score[1] = 1000;

    entries.PlayerName[2] = "Mark";
    entries.Score[2] = 700;

    entries.PlayerName[3] = "Cindy";
    entries.Score[3] = 400;

    entries.PlayerName[4] = "Sam";
    entries.Score[4] = 100;
}
```

Next, we are going to modify our OptionsMenuState. For now, we are simply going to remove all the game-specific code in the Update and Draw methods. We need to remove all references to Radar and Crosshairs. We can remove all references to the check and select textures but not the selected integer. We should also change the way we are exiting our states to look for the B button being pressed instead of the Back button. This is a best practice for Xbox LIVE Community Games.

We need to remove the death sound from the LostGameState. Also because we changed the StartGame method signature in our PlayingState interface, we need to modify the Start Game menu item in the StartMenuState class. In the Update method, we need to pass in 1 to the OurGame.PlayingState.StartGame method. Now we should be able to successfully compile the solution.

In our main game class, we need to add a using statement for our XELibrary project, and we need to add in the input handler and game state manager component variables:

```
private InputHandler input;
private GameStateManager gameManager;
```

We can clear out background color to Black instead of CornflowerBlue in our Draw method. In our Update method, we can remove the check to exit the game if the Back button is pressed because we will be handling exiting through our game states.

We need to set our preferred backbuffer height and width values. We can add in the following constants:

```
private const int screenWidth = 1280;
private const int screenHeight = 720;
```

Then in our constructor we can set the values on our graphics device:

```
graphics.PreferredBackBufferHeight = screenHeight;
graphics.PreferredBackBufferWidth = screenWidth;
```

We need to add in the InputHandler component:

```
input = new InputHandler(this);
Components.Add(input);
```

We also need to add in our GameStateManager component:

```
gameManager = new GameStateManager(this);
Components.Add(gameManager);
```

We need to add in network support by adding the GamerServicesComponent:

```
Components.Add(new GamerServicesComponent(this));
```

We need to initialize our game states in our constructor:

```
TitleIntroState = new TitleIntroState(this);
StartMenuState = new StartMenuState(this);
OptionsMenuState = new OptionsMenuState(this);
HighScoresState = new HighScoresState(this);
PlayingState = new PlayingState(this);
FadingState = new FadingState(this);
LostGameState = new LostGameState(this);
WonGameState = new WonGameState(this);
PausedState = new PausedState(this);
```

We need to change our game state to the TitleIntroState:

```
gameManager.ChangeState(TitleIntroState.Value);
```

We should remove the fire effect from TitleIntroState. The only member field that should remain is the Texture2D texture field. The rest should be removed. We can remove the CreateTexture method, and we can replace the Draw and the LoadContent methods with the following code:

```
public override void Draw(GameTime gameTime)
{
```

27

```
    Vector2 pos = new Vector2((GraphicsDevice.Viewport.Width - texture.Width) / 2,
        (GraphicsDevice.Viewport.Height - texture.Height) / 2);

    GraphicsDevice device = GraphicsDevice;

    device.Clear(Color.Black);

    OurGame.SpriteBatch.Begin();
    OurGame.SpriteBatch.Draw(texture, pos, Color.White);
    OurGame.SpriteBatch.End();

    base.Draw(gameTime);
}

protected override void LoadContent()
{
    texture = Content.Load<Texture2D>(@"Textures\titleIntro");

    base.LoadContent();
}
```

We need to add the titleIntro.png and optionsMenu.png files from the CD included in the book to our Content project in the Textures folder. We also need to add the menu.spritefont file to our Fonts folder.

Understanding the New Menu Layout

Our game will have a start menu with the following options:

Single Player Game

Multiplayer

Options

Help

Exit

The Single Player Game option will simply start the game without any additional menus to load. The next menu in the stack will be our multiplayer menu. When the gamer picks Multiplayer, a new menu will be displayed that has the following options:

Local Multiplayer

System Link

LIVE

Back

If the player picks Local Multiplayer, the game will start (assuming there are enough controllers hooked into the console). The next menu will be the network menu, assuming the player chose System Link or LIVE. This menu has the following options:

Create Session

Join Session

Back

The Join Session option allows the player to pick from the list of sessions. The Create Session option takes the gamer to the session lobby, where the gamer is allowed to set the player to "ready up." This menu is a little different from the others, but it still shares a lot of the same requirements.

Refactoring Our Menu States

With all these menus it makes sense for us to refactor our menu code. We are going to create a base class that our current `StartMenu` will inherit from. As we create the new menu states, they will inherit from this new class as well. We will call the new menu state `BaseMenuState`. You can see our new `BaseMenuState` class in Listing 27.2.

LISTING 27.2   BaseMenuState.cs

```
using System;
using Microsoft.Xna.Framework;
using Microsoft.Xna.Framework.Graphics;
using Microsoft.Xna.Framework.Input;

namespace NetworkGameTemplate
{
    public abstract class BaseMenuState : BaseGameState, IStartMenuState
    {
        protected SpriteFont font;
        private GamePadState currentGamePadState;
        private GamePadState previousGamePadState;
        protected int selected;

        protected Texture2D texture;
        protected Point menuSize = new Point(800, 600);

        public string[] Entries;

        public BaseMenuState(Game game)
            : base(game)
        {
        }
```

27

```
protected abstract void CancelMenu();

public override void Update(GameTime gameTime)
{
    PlayerIndex playerIndex;
    if (Input.WasPressed(PlayerIndexInControl, Buttons.Back, Keys.Escape,
            out playerIndex) ¦¦
        Input.WasPressed(PlayerIndexInControl, Buttons.B, Keys.Back,
            out playerIndex))
    {
        CancelMenu();
    }

    if (Input.KeyboardState.WasKeyPressed(Keys.Up) ¦¦
        (currentGamePadState.DPad.Up == ButtonState.Pressed &&
         previousGamePadState.DPad.Up == ButtonState.Released) ¦¦
        (currentGamePadState.ThumbSticks.Left.Y > 0 &&
         previousGamePadState.ThumbSticks.Left.Y <= 0))
    {
        selected--;
    }
    if (Input.KeyboardState.WasKeyPressed(Keys.Down) ¦¦
        (currentGamePadState.DPad.Down == ButtonState.Pressed &&
         previousGamePadState.DPad.Down == ButtonState.Released) ¦¦
        (currentGamePadState.ThumbSticks.Left.Y < 0 &&
         previousGamePadState.ThumbSticks.Left.Y >= 0))
    {
        selected++;
    }

    if (selected < 0)
        selected = Entries.Length - 1;
    if (selected == Entries.Length)
        selected = 0;

    if (Input.WasPressed(PlayerIndexInControl, Buttons.Start, Keys.Enter,
            out playerIndex) ¦¦
        (Input.WasPressed(PlayerIndexInControl, Buttons.A, Keys.Space,
            out playerIndex)))
    {
        PlayerIndexInControl = playerIndex;
        MenuSelected(playerIndex, selected);
    }

    previousGamePadState = currentGamePadState;
    currentGamePadState = Input.GamePads[(int)playerIndex];
```

```csharp
        base.Update(gameTime);
    }

    public abstract void MenuSelected(PlayerIndex playerIndex, int selected);

    public override void Draw(GameTime gameTime)
    {
        Vector2 pos = new Vector2(
            (GraphicsDevice.Viewport.Width - texture.Width) / 2,
            (GraphicsDevice.Viewport.Height - texture.Height) / 2);

        Vector2 position = new Vector2(pos.X + 240, pos.Y + 150);

        OurGame.SpriteBatch.Begin();
        OurGame.SpriteBatch.Draw(texture, pos, Color.White);

        if (Entries != null)
        {
            for (int i = 0; i < Entries.Length; i++)
            {
                DrawMenuItem(gameTime, ref position, i, Entries[i]);
            }
        }
        OurGame.SpriteBatch.End();

        base.Draw(gameTime);
    }

    protected void DrawMenuItem(GameTime gameTime, ref Vector2 position,
        int i, string text)
    {
        Color color;
        float scale;

        if (i == selected)
        {
            // The selected entry is yellow, and has an animating size.
            double time = gameTime.TotalGameTime.TotalSeconds;

            float pulsate = 0;
            //turn on pulsating if enabled
            if (Enabled)
                pulsate = (float)Math.Sin(time * 12) + 1;

            color = Color.Firebrick;
```

27

```
            scale = 1 + pulsate * 0.05f;
        }
        else
        {
            color = Color.WhiteSmoke;
            scale = 1;
        }
        // Draw text, centered on the middle of each line.
        Vector2 origin = new Vector2(0, font.LineSpacing / 2);
        Vector2 shadowPosition = new Vector2(position.X - 2, position.Y);

        //Draw Shadow
        OurGame.SpriteBatch.DrawString(font, text,
            shadowPosition, Color.DarkSlateGray, 0, origin, scale,
            SpriteEffects.None, 0);
        //Draw Text
        OurGame.SpriteBatch.DrawString(font, text,
            position, color, 0, origin, scale, SpriteEffects.None, 0);

        position.Y += font.LineSpacing;
    }

    protected override void LoadContent()
    {
        font = Content.Load<SpriteFont>(@"Fonts\menu");

        if (texture == null)
        {
            texture = new Texture2D(GraphicsDevice, menuSize.X, menuSize.Y,
                1, TextureUsage.None, SurfaceFormat.Color);

            uint[] pixelData = new uint[menuSize.X * menuSize.Y];
            for (int i = 0; i < pixelData.Length; i++)
            {
                pixelData[i] = new Color(0, 0, 0, 0.90f).PackedValue;
            }

            texture.SetData<uint>(pixelData);
        }

        base.LoadContent();
    }
}
}
```

We load the font at the base menu state level and expose the background texture but actually load the texture on each menu. This is in case we want different textures for the different menus. If a texture isn't specified by the derived class, we create a mostly opaque texture and use the menuSize field with a default size of 800×600. This can be modified by the derived class if the texture needs to be a different size.

We created an abstract method called MenuSelected that accepts the playerIndex. This method must be implemented by the derived classes. Currently, our menu states have their own Update and Draw methods that display the menu items and determine which item is selected. Now they can be replaced with this new MenuSelected method that will get called whenever the based menu state determines a menu item has been selected. The actual menu entries are still populated with the Entries collection. Each derived state can set those in the constructor. The base menu state class also exposes an abstract CancelMenu method that needs to be implemented. This will fire if the user presses the B button (or Escape) while in a menu state. You can see how this works in the updated StartMenuState, which now inherits from the BaseMenuState class, in Listing 27.3.

LISTING 27.3   StartMenuState.cs

```
using System;
using Microsoft.Xna.Framework;
using Microsoft.Xna.Framework.GamerServices;

namespace NetworkGameTemplate
{
    public sealed class StartMenuState : BaseMenuState, IStartMenuState
    {
        private string[] entries =
        {
            "Play Single Player Game",
            "Multiplayer",
            "Options",
            "High Scores",
            "Help",
            "Credits",
            "Exit Game"
        };

        public StartMenuState(Game game)
            : base(game)
        {
            game.Services.AddService(typeof(IStartMenuState), this);

            base.Entries = entries;
        }
```

27

```
public override void MenuSelected(PlayerIndex playerIndex, int selected)
{
    PlayerIndexInControl = playerIndex;

    switch (selected)
    {
        case 0: //Play Single Player Game
            {
                if (GameManager.ContainsState(OurGame.PlayingState.Value))
                    GameManager.PopState();
                else
                {
                    //clear out any network session
                    //TODO: Clear out network session

                    GameManager.ChangeState(OurGame.PlayingState.Value,
                        PlayerIndexInControl);

                    OurGame.PlayingState.StartGame(1);
                }
                break;
            }
        case 1: //Multiplayer Menu
            {
                GameManager.PushState(OurGame.MultiplayerMenuState.Value,
                    PlayerIndexInControl);
                break;
            }
        case 2: //Options Menu
            {
                GameManager.PushState(OurGame.OptionsMenuState.Value,
                    PlayerIndexInControl);
                break;
            }
        case 3: //High Scores Menu
            {
                GameManager.PushState(OurGame.HighScoresState.Value,
                    PlayerIndexInControl);
                OurGame.HighScoresState.AlwaysDisplay = true;
                break;
            }
        case 4: //Help
            {
                GameManager.PushState(OurGame.HelpState.Value,
                    PlayerIndexInControl);
```

```
                    break;
                }
        case 5: //Credits
            {
                GameManager.PushState(OurGame.CreditsState.Value,
                    PlayerIndexInControl);
                break;
            }
        case 6: //Exit
            {
                CancelMenu();
                break;
            }
    }
}

protected override void CancelMenu()
{
    GameManager.ChangeState(OurGame.TitleIntroState.Value, null);
}

protected override void StateChanged(object sender, EventArgs e)
{
    base.StateChanged(sender, e);

    if (GameManager.State != this.Value)
    {
        Visible = true;
    }
    else
    {
      foreach (SignedInGamer signedInGamer in SignedInGamer.SignedInGamers)
        {
            if (GameManager.ContainsState(OurGame.PlayingState.Value))
              signedInGamer.Presence.PresenceMode = GamerPresenceMode.Paused;
            else
              signedInGamer.Presence.PresenceMode = GamerPresenceMode.AtMenu;
        }
    }
}
}
}
```

We need to take into account that we are now allowing multiple players on the same local machine. This means that we should probably only allow input on some of our menus from only one player. It may be wise to do this for certain game states as well. For example, it may be that we allow anyone to pause the game, but as soon as that person pauses the game, only his or her controller can unpause the game. To do this, we need to keep track of which player is in control.

We need to add following variable to the XELibrary's GameState class:

```
public PlayerIndex? PlayerIndexInControl { get; set; }
```

Our InputHandler class and IInputHandler interface expose the WasPressed method. This method and the signature need to be modified. We need to change the WasPressed method signature of the IInputHandler interface to the following:

```
bool WasPressed(PlayerIndex? playerIndexInControl, Buttons button, Keys keys,
    out PlayerIndex playerIndex);
```

We need to change InputHandler's WasPressed method to this:

```
public bool WasPressed(PlayerIndex? playerIndexInControl, Buttons button,
    Keys keys, out PlayerIndex playerIndex)
{
    if (playerIndexInControl.HasValue)
    {
        playerIndex = playerIndexInControl.Value;

        if (keyboard.WasKeyPressed(keys) ||
            gamePadHandler.WasButtonPressed(playerIndexInControl, button,
                out playerIndex))
        {
            return (true);
        }
        else
        {
            return (false);
        }
    }
    else
    {
        // Accept input from any player.
        return (WasPressed(PlayerIndex.One, button, keys, out playerIndex) ||
                WasPressed(PlayerIndex.Two, button, keys, out playerIndex) ||
                WasPressed(PlayerIndex.Three, button, keys, out playerIndex) ||
                WasPressed(PlayerIndex.Four, button, keys, out playerIndex));
    }
}
```

Before this method was simply checking the keyboard and gamePadHandler states, passing in a player index, but it did not have a way to handle looking for any controller input. We changed this by making the PlayerIndex nullable (we used the ? on the end of the PlayerIndex type). This means that we can either pass in a PlayerIndex value or a null. If we pass in null, we are checking all four controllers. This is done in the false part of the condition where we check if the playerIndexInControl has a value. We have the out parameter because we want to know who pressed the button. Sometimes this out value will be ignored, but other times it will help us set the player index in control to the correct value so that the game only accepts input from that controller.

This method is really just calling the keyboard and gamePadHandler objects' own "was pressed" methods. We are not modifying the keyboard object, but we should if we wanted to handle the chat pad for multiple players. This would require passing in the PlayerIndex to the keyboard GetState method in the InputHandler. However, we do need to modify the ButtonHandler's WasButtonPressed method to accept the new values:

```
public bool WasButtonPressed(PlayerIndex? playerIndexInControl, Buttons button,
    out PlayerIndex playerIndex)
{
    if (playerIndexInControl.HasValue)
    {
        //Read input from specified player index
        playerIndex = playerIndexInControl.Value;

        int i = (int)playerIndex;

        return (gamePadsState[i].IsButtonDown(button) &&
            prevGamePadsState[i].IsButtonUp(button));
    }
    else
    {
        // Accept input from any player.
        return (WasButtonPressed(PlayerIndex.One, button, out playerIndex) ||
                WasButtonPressed(PlayerIndex.Two, button, out playerIndex) ||
                WasButtonPressed(PlayerIndex.Three, button, out playerIndex) ||
                WasButtonPressed(PlayerIndex.Four, button, out playerIndex));
    }
}
```

The functionality here is similar to the WasPressed method call in the InputHandler class. If we have a value in the player index, we check to see if a button was pressed. If we do not have a value, we check all the game pads connected to see if any of them had the button pressed. In both cases, we return back the player index of the controller with the button that was actually pressed. The Update method in our InputHandler class checks to see if the Back button was pressed and exits the game. However, it is currently hard-coded to 0 (the first player index). We want to change the condition to the following code:

```
PlayerIndex playerIndex;
// Allows the default game to exit on Xbox 360 and Windows
if (gamePadHandler.WasButtonPressed(null, Buttons.Back, out playerIndex))
    Game.Exit();
```

Making the changes to our InputHandler helps the newly added BaseMenuState and the updated StartMenuState, but it leaves other states in a mess. Not only did we change the way our input is handled, but we also made an assumption that we changed our game state manager's state-changing methods to accept a player index so it can let the new state know whom it should listen to input from. We need to update the GameStateManager in the XELibrary to use this new player index. We first need to update the IGameStateManager interface in the interfaces.cs code file by changing the PushState and ChangeState signatures to the following signatures:

```
void PushState(GameState state, PlayerIndex? playerIndexInControl);
void ChangeState(GameState newState, PlayerIndex? playerIndexInControl);
```

Then we need to replace the PushState, AddState, and ChangeState methods with the following code:

```
public void PushState(GameState newState, PlayerIndex? playerIndexInControl)
{
    drawOrder += 100;
    newState.DrawOrder = drawOrder;

    AddState(newState, playerIndexInControl);

    //Let everyone know we just changed states
    if (OnStateChange != null)
        OnStateChange(this, null);
}

private void AddState(GameState state, PlayerIndex? playerIndexInControl)
{
    state.PlayerIndexInControl = playerIndexInControl;
    states.Push(state);

    Game.Components.Add(state);

    //Register the event for this state
    OnStateChange += state.StateChanged;
}

public void ChangeState(GameState newState, PlayerIndex? playerIndexInControl)
{
    //We are changing states, so pop everything ...
    //if we don't want to really change states but just modify,
```

```
//we should call PushState and PopState
while (states.Count > 0)
    RemoveState();

//changing state, reset our draw order
newState.DrawOrder = drawOrder = initialDrawOrder;
AddState(newState, playerIndexInControl);

//Let everyone know we just changed states
if (OnStateChange != null)
    OnStateChange(this, null);
}
```

The only thing that changed in these methods is that we are now taking in a nullable `PlayerIndex`. This is because when we call `AddState` (which `PushState` and `ChangeState` also call), we set the state's `PlayerIndexInControl`. We added in that value to our `GameState` class in the XELibrary earlier in this chapter. This is what tells each state to whom it should listen for any input.

By changing that, we caused even more compile errors. The majority of them have to do with the fact that we changed the method signatures on our `WasButtonPressed` method as well as the `PushState`, `AddState`, and `ChangeState` methods we just modified.

Because we broke the XELibrary project, it is a good idea to select just that project from the Solution Explorer and build it. This way, we can know that our game project is looking at all the latest methods. Now we can compile the entire solution again and see over 20 compile errors.

We can go through each `WasPressed` compile error individually and add the `PlayIndexInControl` parameter to the beginning of the method. We also need to create a local variable wherever we are calling the `WasPressed` methods. We can call this variable `newPlayerIndex`. Here is the updated `Update` method for `PausedState` with our changes:

```
public override void Update(GameTime gameTime)
{
    PlayerIndex newPlayerIndex;
    if (Input.WasPressed(PlayerIndexInControl, Buttons.Start, Keys.Enter,
            out newPlayerIndex))
        GameManager.PopState(); //I am no longer paused ...

    base.Update(gameTime);
}
```

If we wanted to keep track of which player index was just passed to us via the `newPlayerIndex` parameter, we could set the `GameState.PlayerIndexInControl` property. We do this in the title intro state's `Update` method as follows:

```
public override void Update(GameTime gameTime)
{
    PlayerIndex newPlayerIndex;
    if (Input.WasPressed(PlayerIndexInControl, Buttons.Back, Keys.Escape,
            out newPlayerIndex))
        OurGame.Exit();

    if (Input.WasPressed(PlayerIndexInControl, Buttons.Start, Keys.Enter,
        out newPlayerIndex))
    {
        //We know which controller hit "Start",
        //so set them as the player in control
        PlayerIndexInControl = newPlayerIndex;

        // push our start menu onto the stack
        GameManager.PushState(OurGame.StartMenuState.Value, PlayerIndexInControl);
    }

    base.Update(gameTime);
}
```

If we are exiting the game, we do not bother storing the index for the player who pressed the Back button. However, if someone presses Start, we store that player's index in the PlayerIndexInControl property. While we were here, we also updated the GameManager.PushState method. We passed in the PlayerIndexInControl property to the method. We should open up the Game1.cs file and in the constructor change the call to ChangeState to the following:

```
gameManager.ChangeState(TitleIntroState.Value, null);
```

We are simply passing in null to let the TitleIntroState know that it can accept input from any controller. We need to go through all the game states giving us compiler errors and update any WasPressed, ChangeState, and PushState methods. We should only have three compile errors once we are done modifying the following game states:

HighScoreState

WonGameState

OptionsMenuState

LostGameState

FadingState

PlayingState

For the Update method of PlayingState where we checked for the Back or Start button, we want to make sure we set the PlayerIndexInControl to the out parameter for newPlayerIndex. This is because we do not want the StartMenuState or the PausedState to accept input from any other controller than the player who caused this state. With those updates, the two conditions are as follows:

```
PlayerIndex newPlayerIndex;


if (Input.WasPressed(PlayerIndexInControl, Buttons.Back, Keys.Escape,
    out newPlayerIndex))
{
    PlayerIndexInControl = newPlayerIndex;
    storedTime = currentTime;
    GameManager.PushState(OurGame.StartMenuState.Value, PlayerIndexInControl);
}

if (Input.WasPressed(PlayerIndexInControl, Buttons.Start, Keys.Enter,
    out newPlayerIndex))
{
    PlayerIndexInControl = newPlayerIndex;
    storedTime = currentTime;
    GameManager.PushState(OurGame.PausedState.Value, PlayerIndexInControl);
}
```

At this point, we should only have three compile errors where our updated StartMenuState is complaining about missing states. In Listing 27.3, we changed the menu items. We added in Multiplayer, Help, and Credits to the menu entries. We also referenced the corresponding game states, but they do not exist yet. We can create these now. We can start with HelpState. The code for HelpState.cs can be found in Listing 27.4.

LISTING 27.4   HelpState.cs

```
using Microsoft.Xna.Framework;
using Microsoft.Xna.Framework.Graphics;
using Microsoft.Xna.Framework.Input;

namespace NetworkGameTemplate
{
    public sealed class HelpState : BaseGameState, IHelpState
    {
        private Texture2D texture;

        public HelpState(Game game)
            : base(game)
        {
            game.Services.AddService(typeof(IHelpState), this);
        }
```

27

```
public override void Update(GameTime gameTime)
{
    PlayerIndex playerIndex;

    if (Input.WasPressed(PlayerIndexInControl, Buttons.B, Keys.Escape,
            out playerIndex))
        GameManager.PopState();

    base.Update(gameTime);
}

public override void Draw(GameTime gameTime)
{
    Vector2 pos = new Vector2(
        (GraphicsDevice.Viewport.Width - texture.Width) / 2,
        (GraphicsDevice.Viewport.Height - texture.Height) / 2);

    OurGame.SpriteBatch.Begin();
    OurGame.SpriteBatch.Draw(texture, pos, Color.White);
    OurGame.SpriteBatch.End();

    base.Draw(gameTime);
}

protected override void LoadContent()
{
    texture = Content.Load<Texture2D>(@"Textures\help");
}
    }
}
```

This game state is very straightforward. We initialize it as a game service like we do all our game states. We need to add the new IHelpState, ICreditsState, and IMultiplayerMenuState interfaces to our GameStateInterfaces.cs code file. While we are there we can remove the IYesNoDialogState and IStartLevelState interfaces because we are not using them.

We are loading in a texture by the name of help. You can find the help.png file on this book's CD. We can add the texture to our Textures folder under our game's Content project.

We add the following public fields to our Game class:

```
public IHelpState HelpState;
public ICreditsState CreditsState;
public IMultiplayerMenuState MultiplayerMenuState;
```

We initialize them in our game's constructor method:

```
HelpState = new HelpState(this);
CreditsState = new CreditsState(this);
MultiplayerMenuState = new MultiplayerMenuState(this);
```

Next, we can add in our `CreditsState`. We are not going to actually implement this state but will instead create a placeholder. A great exercise to complete at the end of the chapter would be to populate this state so that the text scrolls from the bottom of the screen to the top of the screen. For now we can just copy the HelpState.cs file we just created and rename the copy CreditsState.cs.

Creating the Network-Specific Game States

The initial MultiplayerMenuState.cs code can be found in Listing 27.5.

LISTING 27.5   MultiplayerMenuState.cs

```
using System;
using Microsoft.Xna.Framework;
using Microsoft.Xna.Framework.Net;
using Microsoft.Xna.Framework.GamerServices;

namespace NetworkGameTemplate
{
    public sealed class MultiplayerMenuState
        : BaseMenuState, IMultiplayerMenuState
    {
        private string[] entries =
        {
            "Play Local Multiplayer Game",
            "Play System Link Game",
            "Play LIVE Game",
            "Back"
        };

        public MultiplayerMenuState(Game game)
            : base(game)
        {
            game.Services.AddService(typeof(IMultiplayerMenuState), this);

            base.Entries = entries;
        }
        private bool startingLocalMultiplayer = false;
```

27

```
public override void MenuSelected(PlayerIndex playerIndex, int selected)
{
    PlayerIndexInControl = playerIndex;

    switch (selected)
    {
        case 0: //Play Local Multiplayer Game
            {
                //more than one controller active?
                int connectedControllers = 0;
                if (Input.GamePads[0].IsConnected)
                    connectedControllers++;
                if (Input.GamePads[1].IsConnected)
                    connectedControllers++;
                if (Input.GamePads[2].IsConnected)
                    connectedControllers++;
                if (Input.GamePads[3].IsConnected)
                    connectedControllers++;

                if (connectedControllers < 2)
                {
                    OurGame.MessageDialogState.Message =
                        "In order to play a multiplayer game " +
                        "locally you must have more than one " +
                        "controller connected.";
                    OurGame.MessageDialogState.IsError = true;
                    GameManager.PushState(
                        OurGame.MessageDialogState.Value,
                        PlayerIndexInControl);
                }
                else
                {
                    if (LocalNetworkGamer.SignedInGamers.Count < 2)
                    {
                        //Bring up "Press Start" screen with
                        //multiple panes?
                        if (connectedControllers > 2)
                            Guide.ShowSignIn(4, false);
                        else
                            Guide.ShowSignIn(2, false);

                        startingLocalMultiplayer = true;
                        SignedInGamer.SignedIn += new
                            EventHandler<SignedInEventArgs>(
                                SignedInGamer_SignedIn);
                    }
```

```
                    StartLocalMultiplayerGame();
                }
                break;
        }
        case 1: //Play System Link Game
            {
                OurGame.NetworkMenuState.NetworkSessionType =
                    NetworkSessionType.SystemLink;
                GameManager.PushState(OurGame.NetworkMenuState.Value,
                    PlayerIndexInControl);

                break;
            }
        case 2: //Play LIVE Game
            {
                OurGame.NetworkMenuState.NetworkSessionType =
                    NetworkSessionType.PlayerMatch;
                GameManager.PushState(OurGame.NetworkMenuState.Value,
                    PlayerIndexInControl);

                break;
            }
        case 3: //Back
            {
                CancelMenu();
                break;
            }
    }
}


private void StartLocalMultiplayerGame()
{
    if (LocalNetworkGamer.SignedInGamers.Count > 1)
    {
        OurGame.NetworkSession = NetworkSession.Create(
            NetworkSessionType.Local,
            OurGame.MaxLocalGamers, OurGame.MaxGamers);

        if (GameManager.ContainsState(OurGame.PlayingState.Value))
        {
            GameManager.PopState();
        }
        else
        {
            GameManager.ChangeState(OurGame.PlayingState.Value,
```

27

```
                        PlayerIndexInControl);
                OurGame.PlayingState.StartGame(
                    LocalNetworkGamer.SignedInGamers.Count);
            }
        }
    }

    private void SignedInGamer_SignedIn(object sender, SignedInEventArgs e)
    {
        if (startingLocalMultiplayer)
        {
            StartLocalMultiplayerGame();

            //unregister for event
            SignedInGamer.SignedIn -= new
                EventHandler<SignedInEventArgs>(
                    SignedInGamer_SignedIn);
        }
    }

    protected override void CancelMenu()
    {
        GameManager.PopState();
    }

    protected override void StateChanged(object sender, EventArgs e)
    {
        base.StateChanged(sender, e);

        if (GameManager.State != this.Value)
            Visible = true;
        else
        {
            if (OurGame.NetworkSession != null)
            {
                OurGame.NetworkSession.Dispose();
                OurGame.NetworkSession = null;
            }
        }
    }
}
}
```

The MultiplayerMenuState introduces a few pieces. First, this state introduces a new state we do not have. We need to create a new MessageDialogState game state. This state will always be pushed on the stack. It is used to display messages that the user needs to see. We are setting this up like a modal MessageBox. We need to add the following interface to our GameStateInterfaces.cs code file:

```
public interface IMessageDialogState : IGameState
{
    string Message { get; set; }
    bool IsError { get; set; }
}
```

We need to add this game state to our game class as well. The code for this game state can be seen in Listing 27.6.

LISTING 27.6   MessageDialogState.cs

```
using System;
using Microsoft.Xna.Framework;
using Microsoft.Xna.Framework.Graphics;
using Microsoft.Xna.Framework.Input;

namespace NetworkGameTemplate
{
    public sealed class MessageDialogState : BaseGameState, IMessageDialogState
    {
        private Texture2D backgroundTexture;
        private string message;
        private bool isError;

        public MessageDialogState(Game game)
            : base(game)
        {
            game.Services.AddService(typeof(MessageDialogState), this);
        }

        protected override void LoadContent()
        {
            backgroundTexture = new Texture2D(GraphicsDevice,
                GraphicsDevice.Viewport.Width, 150, 1,
                TextureUsage.None, SurfaceFormat.Color);
            uint[] pixelData = new uint[GraphicsDevice.Viewport.Width * 150];
            for (int i = 0; i < pixelData.Length; i++)
            {
```

27

```
                pixelData[i] = new Color(0, 0, 0, 0.9f).PackedValue;
        }

        backgroundTexture.SetData<uint>(pixelData);

        base.LoadContent();
    }

    public override void Update(GameTime gameTime)
    {
        if (isError)
        {
            PlayerIndex playerIndex;
            if (Input.WasPressed(
                    PlayerIndexInControl, Buttons.A, Keys.Enter, out playerIndex) ||
                Input.WasPressed(
                    PlayerIndexInControl, Buttons.B, Keys.Escape, out playerIndex))
            {
                GameManager.PopState(); //we are done ...

                //reset properties
                isError = false;
                message = string.Empty;
            }
        }

        base.Update(gameTime);
    }

    public override void Draw(GameTime gameTime)
    {
        Vector2 viewport = new Vector2(GraphicsDevice.Viewport.Width,
            GraphicsDevice.Viewport.Height);
        Vector2 fontLength =
            OurGame.Font.MeasureString(Message);
        Vector2 pos = (viewport - fontLength) / 2;

        OurGame.SpriteBatch.Begin();
        OurGame.SpriteBatch.Draw(backgroundTexture,
            new Vector2(0, pos.Y - (OurGame.Font.LineSpacing * 2)),
            Color.White);
        OurGame.SpriteBatch.DrawString(OurGame.Font,
            Message,
            pos, MessageColor, 0, Vector2.Zero, 1.2f, SpriteEffects.None, 0);
        OurGame.SpriteBatch.End();
```

```
            base.Draw(gameTime);
        }

        private Color MessageColor
        {
            get
            {
                if (isError)
                    return (Color.Red);
                else
                    return (Color.Blue);
            }
        }

        public string Message
        {
            get { return (message); }
            set { message = value; }
        }

        public bool IsError
        {
            get { return (isError); }
            set { isError = value; }
        }
    }
}
```

We create a mostly opaque text that is 150 pixels high and extends the entire width of the screen. We allow the state to be popped off if the A or B button is pressed. We also reset the properties when we pop off the state. The message set in the property is displayed in either blue or red, depending on if IsError was set to true. If it is marked as an error, the message is set to red. We could add in textures to signify whether this was an error message or just an information message. This also does not handle any kind of text wrapping. If the message is too long, it will simply be centered, and we will not see the first part or the last part of the message.

Now that we have the MessageDialogState created, we can get back to our MultiplayerMenuState from Listing 27.5. The first menu item is "Play Local Multiplayer Game." In our MenuSelected method we count how many controllers are connected. We can check the IsConnected property of our game pad to see whether or not the controller is connected. After we add up the connected controllers, we make sure we have at least two. If we do not, we push the newly created MessageDialogState on the screen with the appropriate error message. Notice we set the IsError property to true so the message we passed in will show up in red.

Assuming enough controllers are connected, we check to see how many local network gamers are signed in. If there are at least two, we call the StartLocalMultiplayerGame method. Otherwise, we tell the Guide to show the Sign In screen. If the number of controllers connected is more than two, we show the four-pane view; otherwise, we show the two-pane view. We also hook into the SignedInGamer.SignedIn event so we can kick off the local multiplayer game.

The StartLocalMultiplayerGame actually creates a network session. It passes in NetworkSessionType.Local. This is beneficial because it allows us to use the same game logic for multiplayer games regardless of whether the game is a system link, LIVE, or local multiplayer game. The NetworkSession.Create method also takes in the maximum number of local gamers our game allows as well as the total gamers our game allows. We need to add the MaxLocalGamers and MaxGamers fields to our game class:

```
public readonly int MaxGamers = 4;
public readonly int MaxLocalGamers = 2;
```

For this game, we are saying that we can have a maximum number of four players, but only two can be on one console. In the StartLocalMultiplayerGame method, we call the Create method on NetworkSession and store the session in our game's NetworkSession field. We can add that to our game code:

```
public NetworkSession NetworkSession;
```

We put this inside our Game1.cs code file so it can be accessible by different game states. We will be accessing the network session from different states, making it easy to get to.

At this point the compiler should only be complaining about the fact that we do not have the NetworkMenuState we referenced in our MultiplayerMenuState. We have the same code regardless of whether the player selected a system link game or a LIVE game. The only difference is what NetworkSessionType we use. You saw for the local multiplayer we use Local. For a system link game we use SystemLink, and for LIVE we use PlayerMatch. Ranked is available in the XNA Framework, but it is only for use for commercial games that pass LIVE certification. This would be used for games to be released on Xbox LIVE Arcade that are developed using XNA Game Studio.

We need to add the INetworkMenuState interface to our GameStateInterfaces.cs file:

```
public interface INetworkMenuState : IGameState
{
    NetworkSessionType NetworkSessionType { get; set;  }
}
```

We also need to add a using statement for Microsoft.Xna.Framework.Net because we are using XNA's networking code. We need to add the game state to our game class and initialize it in our constructor. Finally, we can add the code in Listing 27.7 to a blank file called NetworkMenuState.

LISTING 27.7   NetworkMenuState.cs

```
using System;
using Microsoft.Xna.Framework;
using Microsoft.Xna.Framework.GamerServices;
using Microsoft.Xna.Framework.Net;

namespace NetworkGameTemplate
{
    public sealed class NetworkMenuState : BaseMenuState, INetworkMenuState
    {
        private NetworkSessionType networkSessionType;

        private string[] entries =
            {
                "Create a Session",
                "Join a Session",
                "Cancel"
            };


        public NetworkMenuState(Game game)
            : base(game)
        {
            game.Services.AddService(typeof(INetworkMenuState), this);

            base.Entries = entries;
        }

        public override void MenuSelected(PlayerIndex playerIndex, int selected)
        {
            PlayerIndexInControl = playerIndex;

            switch (selected)
            {
                case 0: //Create a Session
                    {
                        try
                        {
                            OurGame.NetworkSession =
                                NetworkSession.Create(
                                    NetworkSessionType, OurGame.MaxLocalGamers,
                                    OurGame.MaxGamers, 0, null);
                            OurGame.NetworkSession.AllowJoinInProgress = true;
```

```
                            OurGame.NetworkSession.AllowHostMigration = true;

                            OurGame.SetSimulatedValues();
                    }
                    catch (GamerPrivilegeException exc)
                    {
                        //Change the game states to the previous state
                        CancelMenu();

                        OurGame.MessageDialogState.Message = exc.Message;
                        OurGame.MessageDialogState.IsError = true;
                        GameManager.PushState(
                            OurGame.MessageDialogState.Value,
                            PlayerIndexInControl);

                        return;
                    }

                    //Go to lobby
                    GameManager.ChangeState(OurGame.SessionLobbyState.Value,
                        PlayerIndexInControl);
                    break;
            }
        case 1: //Join a Session
            {
                OurGame.SessionListState.NetworkSessionType =
                    NetworkSessionType;
                GameManager.ChangeState(OurGame.SessionListState.Value,
                    PlayerIndexInControl);

                break;
            }
        case 2: //Cancel
            {
                CancelMenu();

                break;
            }
    }
}

protected override void CancelMenu()
{
    GameManager.PopState();

    if (OurGame.NetworkSession != null)
```

```
            {
                OurGame.NetworkSession.Dispose();
                OurGame.NetworkSession = null;
            }
        }

        protected override void StateChanged(object sender, EventArgs e)
        {
            base.StateChanged(sender, e);

            if (GameManager.State != this.Value)
                Visible = true;
        }

        public NetworkSessionType NetworkSessionType
        {
            get { return(networkSessionType); }
            set { networkSessionType = value; }
        }
    }
}
```

The menu items we set up are Create a Session, Join a Session, and Cancel. This is the state that gets called if a system link or a LIVE game is being played. The local multiplayer game created a network session, but for system link and LIVE we need to give gamers a choice whether they want to create a session or join one. Because we are nice, we also let gamers back out of this menu.

We are storing the NetworkSessionType, which the MultiplayerMenuState set before changing to this NetworkMenuState state. We pass this value to the NetworkSession.Create method if Create a Session was selected. We pass in the maximum local gamer and maximum total gamer values again. This time we also have two additional properties we are setting: 0 specifies that there are no private slots for this game. The XNA Framework allows us to create private sessions that can only be joined by invitation. If we want an invitation-only session, we can set the private slot value to match the maximum total gamer value. The last parameter passed into the Create method is the session properties. We are only setting up one type of game, but we could set up different game types, different maps, or anything else that distinguishes the type of game session we are creating. These NetworkSession properties can then be used to search for network sessions with specific criteria.

After we create the session, we tell it two things: that we allow gamers to join the session even if it is already in progress and that we are handling host migration. This means if the current host leaves the game, the game continues on, and any important host information is passed to the next player. Finally, after we create the session, we call a new method on our game object called SetSimulatedValues. This method is where we set our debugging network session information for latency and packet loss. We can add the following SetSimulatedValues method to our game object:

```
internal void SetSimulatedValues()
{
    NetworkSession.SimulatedLatency = TimeSpan.FromMilliseconds(200);
    NetworkSession.SimulatedPacketLoss = .2f;
}
```

We wrapped the call to create the session in a try/catch block. We are specifically checking to see if the gamer has enough privileges to run this game over LIVE. An Xbox LIVE Silver member does not have enough privileges to run a game over LIVE—a Gold membership is required. Parental controls can also cause this to throw an exception, even if a Gold membership is present. If that specific exception occurs, we back out of this menu state and display the error message. When we back out of this menu state for any reason, we also check to see whether or not our NetworkSession is null. If it is not null, we dispose of the network session and then set it to null. We cannot create another network session if we already have one created. If we successfully create a session, we change the state to SessionLobbyState. We will create this state a little later in the chapter. It is simply where the players wait until all players have joined and marked themselves as "ready."

If instead of creating a session, the player decides to join a session, we pass the NetworkSessionType value to the new SessionListState. We then change the state to SessionListState. The SessionListState lists all the available sessions and lets the gamer select which one he or she wants to join.

The ISessionListState interface also has the NetworkSessionType property so it can determine whether it is looking for a system link game or a LIVE game. We can set up the interface in the GameStateInterfaces.cs file:

```
public interface ISessionListState : IGameState
{
    NetworkSessionType NetworkSessionType { get; set; }
}
```

We need to add this state to our game and initialize it just like the rest. The code for SessionListState.cs can be found in Listing 27.8.

LISTING 27.8   SessionListState.cs

```
using System;
using Microsoft.Xna.Framework;
using Microsoft.Xna.Framework.Graphics;
using Microsoft.Xna.Framework.GamerServices;
using Microsoft.Xna.Framework.Net;

namespace NetworkGameTemplate
{
```

```
public sealed class SessionListState : BaseMenuState, ISessionListState
{
    private NetworkSessionType networkSessionType;
    private AvailableNetworkSessionCollection availableSessions;

    public SessionListState(Game game)
        : base(game)
    {
        game.Services.AddService(typeof(ISessionListState), this);
    }

    protected override void LoadContent()
    {
        texture = Content.Load<Texture2D>(@"Textures\SessionList");
        base.LoadContent();
    }

    protected override void UnloadContent()
    {
        texture.Dispose();
        texture = null;
        base.UnloadContent();
    }

    protected override void StateChanged(object sender, EventArgs e)
    {
        base.StateChanged(sender, e);

        if (GameManager.State == this.Value)
        {
            //set presence to looking for games since we are picking a session
            foreach (SignedInGamer signedInGamer in
                                            SignedInGamer.SignedInGamers)
                signedInGamer.Presence.PresenceMode =
                    GamerPresenceMode.LookingForGames;

            string errorMessage = string.Empty;

            try
            {
                availableSessions =
                        NetworkSession.Find(networkSessionType,
                                    OurGame.MaxLocalGamers, null);
            }
            catch (GamerPrivilegeException exc)
            {
```

27

```
                    //it's possible someone tried to join a
                    //LIVE game without enough privs
                    errorMessage = exc.Message;
                }

                if (errorMessage != string.Empty || availableSessions.Count == 0)
                {
                    //Change the game states to the previous state
                    CancelMenu();

                    if (errorMessage == string.Empty)
                        errorMessage = "No network sessions found.";

                    OurGame.MessageDialogState.Message = errorMessage;
                    OurGame.MessageDialogState.IsError = true;
                    GameManager.PushState(OurGame.MessageDialogState.Value,
                        PlayerIndexInControl);

                    if (availableSessions != null)
                    {
                        availableSessions.Dispose();
                        availableSessions = null;
                    }
                    return;
                }
                else
                {
                    int numberOfSessions = Math.Min(7, availableSessions.Count);
                    Entries = new string[numberOfSessions + 1];
                    for (int i = 0; i < numberOfSessions; i++)
                    {
                        if (availableSessions[i].HostGamertag.ToLower()
                                .EndsWith("s"))
                            Entries[i] = "Join " +
                                availableSessions[i].HostGamertag + "' Game";
                        else
                            Entries[i] = "Join " +
                                availableSessions[i].HostGamertag + "'s Game";
                    }

                    Entries[numberOfSessions] = "Cancel";
                }
            }
        }

public override void MenuSelected(PlayerIndex playerIndex, int selected)
```

```
    {
        PlayerIndexInControl = playerIndex;

        if (selected < availableSessions.Count)
        {
            //pick correct session
            OurGame.NetworkSession = NetworkSession.Join(
                availableSessions[selected]);

            GameManager.ChangeState(OurGame.SessionLobbyState.Value,
                PlayerIndexInControl);
        }
        else //Cancel
            CancelMenu();
    }

    protected override void CancelMenu()
    {
        GameManager.ChangeState(OurGame.StartMenuState.Value,
            PlayerIndexInControl);
        GameManager.PushState(OurGame.MultiplayerMenuState.Value,
            PlayerIndexInControl);
        GameManager.PushState(OurGame.NetworkMenuState.Value,
            PlayerIndexInControl);
    }

    public NetworkSessionType NetworkSessionType
    {
        get { return (networkSessionType); }
        set { networkSessionType = value; }
    }
    }
}
```

This state actually uses its own texture. You can find the SessionList.png file on this book's CD. We need to add this texture to our Textures folder. We dispose of the texture and set the variable to null when we unload the content.

Our StateChanged method has the majority of the code for this state. As soon as this state is active, we set our presence. This is the second time we have seen presence code in action. The first time was at the end of the StartMenuState, but we did not discuss it then. We simply set our presence depending on if we are in the middle of playing the game when we go into the start menu state.

In this SessionListState, we loop through all the signed-in gamers, and we set their presence to the predefined value of GamerPresenceMode.LookingForGames. This is optional, but it is a great idea to set the values so other gamers can see what their friends are up to. It may even encourage them to try out or buy our game.

After setting the presence information, we try to find available sessions. Just like the create session method, this code can throw a `GamerPrivilegeException`. If sessions are found, they are stored in the `availableSessions` variable. If they are not found or if an error has occurred, we call `cancel` for this menu state and set the appropriate error message. We then push the `MessageDialogState` onto the stack. Finally, we dispose of our `availableSession` variable and set it to null if it is not already null.

If `availableSessions` actually contains sessions, we dynamically populate our menu entries with the host of the session's gamer tag. We check to see whether or not the gamer tag ends with *s* to determine where to put the apostrophe. After we add each found session, we also add the cancel menu item. Because we are inheriting from our `BaseMenuState`, we get the functionality of scrolling through the sessions and selecting the session automatically. The `MenuSelected` method we set actually sets the `PlayerIndexInControl` value. It is important that each state does this at the very top of the `MenuSelected` method. We then check to see if an actual session was selected. If a session was selected, we call `NetworkSession.Join`. We pass in the session from our list. We store the network session that the `Join` method returns in our game's `NetworkSession` field. We then change the state to `SessionLobbyState`. If a session was not selected, we call the `CancelMenu` method.

The `CancelMenu` method changes the state and then pushes additional states to simulate us backing out of the current menu. It changes the state to the start menu and then pushes the multiplayer menu and network menu onto the stack. Finally, in the `CancelMenu` method we set the presence mode to `None` because we are no longer "looking for games." This clears out the presence text.

This state and the `NetworkMenuState` both can change the game state to `SessionLobbyState`. We are going to add that state next. The session lobby state is simply the lobby for all the gamers waiting for a particular game session to start.

The `ISessionLobbyState` interface also does not expose any methods or properties. The interface needs to be added to the GameStateInterfaces.cs code file:

```
public interface ISessionLobbyState : IGameState { }
```

The `SessionLobbyState` needs to be added and initialized in our game class. The code for the SessionLobbyState.cs is shown in Listing 27.9.

LISTING 27.9   SessionLobbyState.cs

```
using System;
using Microsoft.Xna.Framework;
using Microsoft.Xna.Framework.Graphics;
using Microsoft.Xna.Framework.Input;
using Microsoft.Xna.Framework.GamerServices;
using Microsoft.Xna.Framework.Net;
```

```
namespace NetworkGameTemplate
{
    public sealed class SessionLobbyState : BaseMenuState, ISessionLobbyState
    {
        private string[] statuses;

        public SessionLobbyState(Game game)
            : base(game)
        {
            game.Services.AddService(typeof(ISessionLobbyState), this);
        }

        protected override void LoadContent()
        {
            texture = Content.Load<Texture2D>(@"Textures\SessionLobby");
            base.LoadContent();
        }

        protected override void UnloadContent()
        {
            texture.Dispose();
            texture = null;
            base.UnloadContent();
        }

        protected override void StateChanged(object sender, EventArgs e)
        {
            base.StateChanged(sender, e);

            if (GameManager.State == this.Value)
            {
                if (OurGame.NetworkSession == null)
                    return;

                HookSessionEvents();

                foreach (SignedInGamer signedInGamer in
                                        SignedInGamer.SignedInGamers)
                    signedInGamer.Presence.PresenceMode =
                        GamerPresenceMode.WaitingInLobby;
            }
        }

        public override void Update(GameTime gameTime)
```

27

```
{
    PlayerIndex playerIndex;

    //Press X to set yourself as Ready
    if (Input.WasPressed(null, Buttons.X, Keys.X, out playerIndex))
    {
        PlayerIndexInControl = playerIndex;
        foreach (LocalNetworkGamer gamer in
                                OurGame.NetworkSession.LocalGamers)
        {
            if (gamer.SignedInGamer.PlayerIndex == playerIndex)
                gamer.IsReady = !gamer.IsReady;
        }
    }

    if (OurGame.NetworkSession == null)
        return;

    // The host checks if everyone is ready, & moves to game play if true.
    if (OurGame.NetworkSession.IsHost)
    {
        if (OurGame.NetworkSession.IsEveryoneReady &&
            OurGame.NetworkSession.SessionState ==
                NetworkSessionState.Lobby)
        {
            //Now that all people have come and gone & we are starting
            //our game, we reset playerindex & associate a single
            //id to each gamer object
            byte gamerIndex = 0;
            foreach (NetworkGamer gamer in
                                OurGame.NetworkSession.AllGamers)
                gamer.Tag = gamerIndex++;

            OurGame.NetworkSession.StartGame();
        }
    }

    //Update the session object
    OurGame.NetworkSession.Update();

    //Reset entries to get most recent ready state
    int gamerCount = OurGame.NetworkSession.AllGamers.Count;
    Entries = new string[gamerCount + 1];
    statuses = new string[gamerCount];

    for (int i = 0; i < gamerCount; i++)
```

```
        {
            Entries[i] = OurGame.NetworkSession.AllGamers[i].Gamertag;
            statuses[i] = OurGame.NetworkSession.AllGamers[i]
                .IsReady.ToString();
        }

        Entries[gamerCount] = "Cancel";

        base.Update(gameTime);
    }

    public override void Draw(GameTime gameTime)
    {
        base.Draw(gameTime);

        if ((statuses == null) ||
            (statuses.Length != OurGame.NetworkSession.AllGamers.Count))
            return;

        Vector2 pos = new Vector2(
            (GraphicsDevice.Viewport.Width - texture.Width) / 2,
            (GraphicsDevice.Viewport.Height - texture.Height) / 2);
        //offset the ready status further to the right
        Vector2 position = new Vector2(pos.X + 780, pos.Y + 150);

        OurGame.SpriteBatch.Begin();
        for (int i = 0; i < OurGame.NetworkSession.AllGamers.Count; i++)
        {
            base.DrawMenuItem(gameTime, ref position, i, statuses[i]);
        }

        OurGame.SpriteBatch.End();
    }

    public override void MenuSelected(PlayerIndex playerIndex, int selected)
    {
        PlayerIndexInControl = playerIndex;

        //Could bring up gamer info on selecting the name

        if (selected == OurGame.NetworkSession.AllGamers.Count)
            CancelMenu();
    }

    protected override void CancelMenu()
    {
```

27

```
        GameManager.ChangeState(OurGame.StartMenuState.Value,
            PlayerIndexInControl);
        GameManager.PushState(OurGame.MultiplayerMenuState.Value,
            PlayerIndexInControl);
        GameManager.PushState(OurGame.NetworkMenuState.Value,
            PlayerIndexInControl);
    }

    private void HookSessionEvents()
    {
        if (OurGame.NetworkSession != null)
        {
            OurGame.NetworkSession.GameStarted += new
                EventHandler<GameStartedEventArgs>(GameStartedEventHandler);
            OurGame.NetworkSession.GamerJoined += new
                EventHandler<GamerJoinedEventArgs>(GamerJoinedEventHandler);
            OurGame.NetworkSession.GamerLeft += new
                EventHandler<GamerLeftEventArgs>(GamerLeftEventHandler);
            OurGame.NetworkSession.SessionEnded += new
                EventHandler<NetworkSessionEndedEventArgs>(
                    OurGame.SessionEndedEventHandler);
        }
    }

    public void InviteAcceptedEventHandler(object sender,
        InviteAcceptedEventArgs e)
    {
        // Leave the current network session.
        if (OurGame.NetworkSession != null)
        {
            OurGame.NetworkSession.Dispose();
            OurGame.NetworkSession = null;
        }

        try
        {
            // Join a new session in response to the invite.
            OurGame.NetworkSession =
                NetworkSession.JoinInvited(OurGame.MaxLocalGamers);

            HookSessionEvents();
        }
        catch (Exception error)
        {
            OurGame.MessageDialogState.Message = error.Message;
            OurGame.MessageDialogState.IsError = true;
```

```
            GameManager.PushState(OurGame.MessageDialogState.Value,
                PlayerIndexInControl);
        }
    }

    private void GamerLeftEventHandler(object sender, GamerLeftEventArgs e)
    {
        OurGame.PlayingState.PlayerLeft(e.Gamer.Id);
    }

    private void GameStartedEventHandler(object sender,
        GameStartedEventArgs e)
    {
        GameManager.ChangeState(OurGame.PlayingState.Value,
            PlayerIndexInControl);

        OurGame.PlayingState.StartGame(
            OurGame.NetworkSession.AllGamers.Count);
    }

    private void GamerJoinedEventHandler(object sender, GamerJoinedEventArgs e)
    {
        //grab index and associate it to the gamer tag
        int gamerIndex = OurGame.NetworkSession.AllGamers.IndexOf(e.Gamer);
        e.Gamer.Tag = (byte)gamerIndex;

        //if we are playing
        //(if we are still in the lobby, then no need for this)
        if (OurGame.NetworkSession.SessionState ==
                                        NetworkSessionState.Playing)
        {
            //if we are already playing the game,
            //we don't want to change our state again
            if (!GameManager.ContainsState(OurGame.PlayingState.Value))
            {
                GameManager.ChangeState(OurGame.PlayingState.Value,
                    PlayerIndexInControl);
            }

            //All games need to be notified of the new player
            OurGame.PlayingState.JoinInProgressGame(e.Gamer,
                OurGame.NetworkSession.AllGamers.Count);
        }
    }
}
}
```

27

Just like the last state, `SessionLobbyState` has its own texture. You can find the SessionLobby.png file on this book's CD and add it to our Textures folder.

In the `StateChanged` method, we check to see if the network session is null. If it is, we simply return. Assuming we do have a valid network session, we call the private method `HookSessionEvents`. Finally, we set the presence on each signed-in gamer to `GamerPresenceMode.WaitingInLobby`.

In the `HookSessionEvents` method, we hook into the `GameStartedEvent`, the `GamerJoinedEvent`, the `GamerLeftEvent`, and finally the `SessionEndedEvent`. All these event handlers except `SessionEndedEventHandler` are in the current `SessionLobbyState`.

We can add the `SessionEndedEventHandler` method to our game class. The method is shown here:

```
public void SessionEndedEventHandler(object sender,
    NetworkSessionEndedEventArgs e)
{
    NetworkSession.Dispose();
    NetworkSession = null;

    gameManager.ChangeState(TitleIntroState.Value, null);

    MessageDialogState.Message = e.EndReason.ToString();
    MessageDialogState.IsError = true;
    gameManager.PushState(MessageDialogState.Value, null);
}
```

When the session ends, we dispose of the network session and set the variable to null. We then change the state to `TitleIntroState`. Finally, we add the `MessageDialogState` to our stack, passing in the reason why the session ended.

The `GameStartedEventHandler` method is kicked off when `OurGame.NetworkSession.SessionState` changes to `NetworkSessionState.Playing`. When we create a network session, passing in the `NetworkSessionProperties` (even null), the network session state is set to `Lobby`. If we call the other overload, passing in neither the private slots or the network session properties, the session state is set to `Playing`.

For the `SessionLobbyState` we are in a `Lobby` state, but as soon as everyone is ready we call the `OurGame.NetworkSession.StartGame` method inside the `Update` method. This changes the network state from `Lobby` to `Playing` and in turn kicks off the `GameStartedEvent`.

Inside the `GameStartedEventHandler` we change the state to `PlayingState` and call the playing state's `StartGame` method, passing in the number of players for this game.

The GamerLeftEventHandler method is kicked off when the network session realizes a gamer is no longer present. Inside this method we call the playing state's PlayerLeft method. We pass in the gamer's Id. We will modify the playing state after we go through the rest of the session lobby state.

The GamerJoinedEventHandler grabs the index of the gamer who just joined and stores it in the Tag property. In the SimpleNetworkDemo from the last chapter, we created a generic GamerObject we stored in the Tag property. For this demo we really only need the gamer's index because the host will be doing a lot of the heavy lifting. Because we are only allowing four players, we know the value will fit into a byte easily. If the network session state is set to Playing, we change to our playing state if the PlayingState is not in the stack; if it is in the state stack, we call the playing state's JoinInProgressGame method. We pass in the gamer and the number of players in the game. We will look at this method a little later.

The last event we need to hook up is the InviteAcceptedEvent. We have our event handler, InviteAcceptedEventHandler, which makes sure there is no current network session. If there is, we destroy it. Then we call the JoinInvited method on the NetworkSession object, passing in the maximum number of local gamers. Finally, we call the HookSessionEvents. If joining the session fails, we display the error message using our MessageDialogState.

This event gets kicked off when we invite a friend to join our game or when a friend tries to join our game without an invitation. We do not have to code anything special because both scenarios work the exact same way. In order to be notified we do need to register for this event. We do this in the constructor of our game class:

```
NetworkSession.InviteAccepted += SessionLobbyState.InviteAcceptedEventHandler;
```

This one line of code is needed to register for the InviteAccepted event. We are hooking into the session lobby state's InviteAcceptedEventHandler, which we just looked at. While we are in our game's constructor, we can also initialize our presence mode:

```
foreach (SignedInGamer signedInGamer in SignedInGamer.SignedInGamers)
    signedInGamer.Presence.PresenceMode = GamerPresenceMode.WastingTime;
```

We have simply set the mode to WastingTime, but we could set it to any of the valid values in the GamerPresenceMode enum. We need to add the InviteAcceptedEventHandler method to our ISessionLobbyState interface:

```
void InviteAcceptedEventHandler(object sender, InviteAcceptedEventArgs e);
```

Now that we have handled all the different events associated with handling a network game, we can look at the rest of our session lobby state. Because we are inheriting the BaseMenuState, we get the built-in functionality of drawing our menu entries and being able to select them. However, for this state we want to set the entries to each gamer in the session. We also want to set a flag beside their Gamertag to signify whether or not they are ready for the game to start. Because the A button is already being used to select the menu item, we look for the X button to be pressed to toggle our ready state. You can see this in the Update method. Once everyone is ready, we reset all the Tag properties with the correct gamer index and then we start the game.

At the end of the Update method we reset the menu Entries and the statuses array, which holds the ready status of each player. We will draw their ready status in the Draw method. After setting all the gamer tags in our Entries array and setting all the statuses, we add a final Cancel menu entry.

Our Draw method calls base.Draw immediately. This draws each of the gamer tags populated in the menu Entries array. After drawing the gamer tags, it does not draw anything until all the statuses have been set. We make sure the array is not null. We also make sure all the statuses have been populated. After that, we use the same code we set up in our BaseMenuState to draw the statuses. We set the X offset to 780 so it will line up under the "Ready?" text in our texture. Because we are calling the base class DrawMenuItem, we get all the pulsating draw logic for free.

We are done with SessionLobbyState, and now we can add in the methods we are expecting to be in PlayingState. The PlayerLeft method is as follows:

```
public void PlayerLeft(byte gamerId)
{
    if (OurGame.NetworkSession != null)
    {
        NetworkGamer gamer = OurGame.NetworkSession.FindGamerById(gamerId);
        //possible to return null if gamer was there,
        //but isn't by the time we call this
        if (gamer == null)
            return;

        //Handle the player leaving our game
        //TODO: Handle player leaving the game
    }
}
```

We set up the skeleton for this method but will leave the core of it for our game to implement. We need to add this method signature to the IPlayingState interface as well:

```
void PlayerLeft(byte gamerId);
```

The second method we need to add is the JoinInProgressGame method. The signature for this method, which needs to be added to the interface, is as follows:

```
void JoinInProgressGame(NetworkGamer gamer, int numberOfPlayers);
```

We need to add the actual JoinInProgressGame method to our PlayingState:

```
public void JoinInProgressGame(NetworkGamer gamer, int numberOfPlayers)
{
    this.numberOfPlayers = numberOfPlayers;

    if (gamer.IsLocal)
    {
        SetupGame();

        //Handle local player joining
        //TODO: Handle local player joining
    }
    else
    {
        //Handle remote player joining
        //TODO: Handle remote player joining
    }

    SetPresenceInformation();
}

private void SetPresenceInformation()
{
    //Determine what to set out online presence to
    foreach (SignedInGamer signedInGamer in SignedInGamer.SignedInGamers)
    {
        if (OurGame.NetworkSession != null)
        {
            if (OurGame.NetworkSession.SessionType == NetworkSessionType.Local ||
              OurGame.NetworkSession.SessionType == NetworkSessionType.SystemLink)
            {    //Local Multiplayer or System Link Multiplayer
              signedInGamer.Presence.PresenceMode = GamerPresenceMode.LocalVersus;
            }
            else if (numberOfPlayers > 1)
            {    //Network Multiplayer
              signedInGamer.Presence.PresenceMode = GamerPresenceMode.Multiplayer;
            }
            else
            {    // network session is not null, and single player
              signedInGamer.Presence.PresenceMode =
                    GamerPresenceMode.WaitingForPlayers;
            }
        }
        else if (numberOfPlayers == 1)
        {    //network session is null, so single player
```

27

```
            signedInGamer.Presence.PresenceMode = GamerPresenceMode.SinglePlayer;
    }
    else
    { //should not get here, non single player game always has network session
            signedInGamer.Presence.PresenceMode = GamerPresenceMode.CornflowerBlue;
    }


    }
}
```

Not only did we create the skeleton for the JoinInProgressGame method, but we also
created a generic presence mode method. For most games the values here should work well.
The main one that may need to be changed is LocalVersus. Any can be changed, but at
least they are all valid for many games that allow all the different game modes we have set
up in this networking template (Single Player, Local Multiplayer, System Link, and LIVE).

We can include the Xbox 360 XELibrary project in our solution and then create a copy of
our Windows NetworkGameTemplate project. Once all four projects are in one solution,
we can save this solution as NetworkGameTemplate_Xbox360 and then remove the
Windows-specific projects. We then need to modify our Windows solution so the only two
projects it includes are the Windows-specific projects. This way, we can easily test the
template on the Xbox 360 and a Windows machine using two different solutions.

We now have a template that we can use for our networking games. We have our menus
created and all the plumbing in place to create network sessions and join network sessions
as well as kick off single-player and local multiplayer games. We can run this template, but
there is no actual game play. You can see how we move in and out of the different menu
states and check out the session list and session lobby states. You can see that selecting a
local multiplayer game without having at least two controllers hooked into the console
will cause the error message to be displayed using the MessageDialogState.

Summary

This was a very long chapter. We took what we have covered about networking and
created a reusable template. We can now move back and forth between our different game
states, making sure we have a valid network session where we need one. We will use this
starting-point template for the next two chapters, where we will create a turn-based 2D
card game and a real-time 3D game.

CHAPTER 28

Creating a Turn-based Multiplayer Game

In this chapter, we are going to take the networking skeleton we created in the last chapter and create a turn-based multiplayer game. A turn-based game is one where each player goes after the other. Nothing can be done until the current player has completed his or her turn. Card games are a good example of turn-based games, as are most board games.

Game Design

To start, we need to think about what the game will do. We need to map this out so we can determine where we should use which networking strategies. Where should we use a peer-to-peer strategy versus a client/server strategy? We need to determine when we will have one computer controlling the objects versus letting each machine handle its own objects.

For this demo, we are making the classic Concentration (Memory Match) card game. The game is simplistic enough, but it allows us to utilize the networking template we created and illustrates the different strategies we can use for a turn-based game.

We can map out the game play for this turn-based game in the following steps:

1. Tell everyone the game has started (client/server).

   a. The server shuffles the cards.

   b. The server sends the cards to the clients.

    c. The server determines whose turn it is (who goes first).

    d. The server sends a "Go" command to the first player.

2. The player takes his or her turn (peer to peer).

    a. Highlight a card.

    b. Send highlighted index to other players.

    c. Flip selected card.

    d. Send selected card index to other players.

    e. Flip second selected card—start counter.

    f. Send second selected card index—start counter.

    g. After time reaches "display time," each peer calls its own CheckCards method.

    h. Determine whether match is made.

    i. If no more cards are face down, peer sends "Win" command along with all winners (there can be a tie).

    j. Current player is allowed to "Go" again.

    k. Otherwise, if no match is made, the server tells next player to "Go."

You can see we are using client/server and peer-to-peer strategies when sending and receiving game play data. This game could be completely client/server or completely peer to peer. However, we will use the hybrid method to showcase how to use both approaches in the same game.

Starting with the Network Template

With the multiplayer skeleton framework we created in the last chapter, we can get to the actual game play of our Concentration game. We can copy over the NetworkGameTemplate and XELibrary folders from the last chapter, as well as change the name of the folders, projects, solutions from NetworkGameTemplate to Concentration.

We can open up the Windows solution and rename the namespace from NetworkGameTemplate to Concentration. We also need to open the Game1.cs file and change the class name to Concentration. As we rename both the namespace and the class, we can let Visual Studio replace all instances for us by right-clicking the newly changed name and selecting Replace All Instances. We can also change AssemblyName and Default Namespace in the project properties to Concentration. Double-clicking the Properties node in the Solution Explorer window is a quick way to bring up the properties window.

We need to open up the AssemblyInfo.cs file and change the Guid so the games can find each other during network play. We can also change the AssemblyTitle so it will show up correctly on the Xbox 360. At this point, we should be able to compile our newly created Concentration game successfully. It still does not have any core game code, but we are going to correct that shortly.

We need to replace the TitleIntro.png file with the one from the CD. If we want to change any of the other default textures (session list, session lobby, and so on), we can do that as well. For this game we can use the same textures we used for the networking game template.

Adding in Game-Specific Functionality

The majority of the code in this chapter will be in our PlayingState.cs file. This makes sense because this is where all our game-specific code resides. We can start by adding the variables we need for this game:

```
private const int NumberOfCards = 20;
private const int MaxCardsAcross = 5;
private const int HorizontalCardSpacing = 100;
private const int VerticalCardSpacing = 170;
private const int HorizontalCardOffset = 400;
private const int VerticalCardOffset = 30;

public const int cardWidth = 96;
public const int cardHeight = 136;

public Card[] Cards = new Card[NumberOfCards];
private byte[] selectedCards;
private bool selectionChanged = false;
private byte prevHighlightedCard;
private double waitTime;
private int millisecondsToShowCards = 2000;

private List<Player> players;
private byte prevPlayer;
private byte currentPlayer;

private CelAnimationManager cam;

private PacketWriter packetWriter = new PacketWriter();
private PacketReader packetReader = new PacketReader();
```

Our game simply displays 20 cards on the screen—five cards across and four down. The first two constants hold these values. The next group of constants holds the actual spacing of our cards on the screen. Our cards will start in the top center of the screen. The final two constants hold the size of our cards. The width is set to 96 pixels, and the height it set to 136 pixels. With this data we will be able to set up the locations of the cards on the screen so they are five across and four down.

The next group of variables handles the different pieces we need to manage our cards. We will create a Card type, and we have an array that holds the 20 cards. We have another array (of bytes) that holds the two selected cards. Concentration allows the player to pick two cards. We store the card selection in the selected cards array. As the player scrolls through the cards to select one, we highlight that card. In order to know if the selection has changed, we store the previous card that was highlighted in the prevHighlightedCard field. Once the cards are actually selected, we display them to all the gamers. We want to make sure that each gamer has enough time to view the cards, so we set up a timer. waitTime holds the milliseconds the game has been running. As soon as the last card is selected, we reset our waitTime to 0. Then when the time hits 2,000 milliseconds (2 seconds), we make the call to check the cards.

The next section of variables refers to our player data. Just like we have a list of cards, we are storing the full list of our players. So every instance of our game will store a collection of players. We also store the previous and current player indices so the host can determine who should go next.

The actual card texture file we use has all the cards in one texture. Because of this, we will utilize the CelAnimationManager we created earlier in Chapter 10, "2D Effects." Although the cards do not have any animation, we can tie into this game component so we do not have to write any additional code. We need to add a using statement for our XELibrary:

```
using XELibrary;
```

The final fields we just created are packetWriter and packetReader. We will use these just like we did when we created the SimpleNetworkDemo in Chapter 26, "Creating Multiplayer Demos." We will write out bytes and send them to the other gamers, and we will receive the bytes sent by the other gamers.

We now need to create our Card class. We can add a new code file, called Card.cs, to our project. The code for Card.cs can be found in Listing 28.1.

LISTING 28.1   Card.cs

```
using System;
using Microsoft.Xna.Framework;
using Microsoft.Xna.Framework.Graphics.PackedVector;

namespace Concentration
{
    public class Card
    {
        public byte Value;
        public bool IsFaceUp = false;
        public bool IsVisible = true;
        public HalfVector2 Location;
    }
}
```

You can see this is a very simple class. It stores the actual value of the card. This is what we will use to determine whether or not two cards match. This class also stores whether the card should be drawn face up or face down. The cards will default to all face down. We also store whether the card is visible. As matches are made, we will hide the matching cards. Finally, we store the location of the card. This could have been done using a Vector2 instead of a HalfVector2, but we want to make sure we are not sending any extra information over the wire.

We need to add a using statement to our PlayingState.cs file to utilize a generic collection (list of players):

```
using System.Collections.Generic;
```

Next we can create our Player class, which can be found in Listing 28.2.

LISTING 28.2   Player.cs

```
using System;
using Microsoft.Xna.Framework;
using Microsoft.Xna.Framework.Graphics;
using Microsoft.Xna.Framework.Input;

using XELibrary;

namespace Concentration
{
    public class Player
    {
        private PlayerIndex playerIndex;
        private bool visible = true;
        private bool enabled = true;

        private Concentration ourGame;
        private InputHandler input;
        private PlayingState playingState;

        private Texture2D highlightCard;
        private byte highlightedCard = 0;

        public int Score = 0;

        public byte HighlightedCard
        {
            get { return (highlightedCard); }
            set
```

28

```
            {
                highlightedCard = value;
            }
        }

    public Player(Game game)
        : base()
    {
        input = (InputHandler)game.Services.GetService(
            typeof(IInputHandler));

        playingState = (PlayingState)game.Services.GetService(
            typeof(IPlayingState));

        ourGame = (Concentration)game;

        LoadContent();
        Visible = false;
        Enabled = false;
    }

    public byte HandleInput()
    {
        PlayerIndex throwAway;
        if (input.ButtonHandler.WasButtonPressed(playerIndex,
                Buttons.LeftThumbstickLeft, out throwAway))
            HighlightLeft();

        if (input.GamePads[(int)playerIndex].Triggers.Left > 0)
            HighlightLeft();

        if (input.ButtonHandler.WasButtonPressed(playerIndex,
                Buttons.LeftThumbstickRight, out throwAway))
            HighlightRight();

        if (input.GamePads[(int)playerIndex].Triggers.Right > 0)
            HighlightRight();

        if (input.ButtonHandler.WasButtonPressed(playerIndex, Buttons.A,
            out throwAway))
        {
            playingState.SelectCard(this, highlightedCard);
        }

        return (highlightedCard);
    }
```

```csharp
private void HighlightRight()
{
    do
    {
        highlightedCard++;

        if (highlightedCard >= playingState.Cards.Length)
            highlightedCard = 0;

    } while (!playingState.Cards[highlightedCard].IsVisible);
}

private void HighlightLeft()
{
    do
    {
        highlightedCard--;

        if (highlightedCard == 255)
            highlightedCard = (byte)(playingState.Cards.Length - 1);

    } while (!playingState.Cards[highlightedCard].IsVisible);
}

public void DrawHighlightedCard()
{
    if (visible)
    {
        ourGame.SpriteBatch.Draw(highlightCard,
            playingState.Cards[highlightedCard].Location.ToVector2(),
            Color.Yellow);
    }
}

public void LoadContent()
{
    highlightCard =
        ourGame.Content.Load<Texture2D>(@"Textures\highlightCard");
}

public PlayerIndex PlayerIndex
{
    get { return (playerIndex); }
    set { playerIndex = value; }
}
```

28

```
    public bool Visible
    {
        get { return (visible); }
        set { visible = value; }
    }

    public bool Enabled
    {
        get { return (enabled); }
        set { enabled = value; }
    }
  }
}
```

Our `Player` class stores the player index, which signifies the controller the player is using. The class also has flags to store if it is enabled and visible. If the player is not enabled, no input from the controller will be processed. If the player is not visible, the highlighted card texture (which you will see in a moment) will not be displayed.

We store our specific Concentration game object so we can have access to the `Font` and `SpriteBatch` in our game class. We are handling input in our `Player` class, so we will be creating the `InputHandler` game component. We also need to talk directly to the playing state, so we have a place to store a reference to that state as well. We also store a `Texture2D` of our `highlightCard` texture and a byte to store the actual card index that should be highlighted. Finally, we store the individual player's score.

We need to include the highlightCard.png file that we load in the `LoadContent` method. You can find the texture on the CD for this book. Our `Draw` method draws the highlighted card over the correct card location if the player is visible. We tint the highlighted texture to yellow.

The rest of the `Player` class handles the input. It has the main `HandleInput` method, which checks to see if the player has moved left or right either by moving the left thumbstick or by holding one of the triggers. Holding the triggers cause the player to quickly scroll left or right, depending on which trigger is being pressed. The thumbstick allows the player to move left and right one card at a time. An improvement would be to modify the code to allow vertical movement in addition to the horizontal movement.

Because cards are made invisible when they were part of a match, we simply keep incrementing our `highlightedCard` counter past any cards that are not visible. This is done in the individual `HighlightRight` and `HighlightLeft` methods. The `HandleInput` method returns the `highlightedCard` index.

Now we can move to our `PlayingState`. In this state, we can add a enum called `MessageType` that will include our game-specific messages:

```
private enum MessageType : byte { StartGame, RequestToJoinInProgressGame,
    JoinedInProgressGame, HighlightedCard, SelectedCards, StartCheckCardsTimer,
    Go, DeclareWinner };
```

This enum provides a way for us to pass in a single byte at the top of all our network data. Our code can then check this byte to determine what it is supposed to do with the data just passed in. As the name of the enum suggests, we can use this as the type of message we are sending or receiving. Most of our games will have the StartGame, RequestToJoinInProgressGame, and JoinedInProgressGame messages, so we could include those in the NetworkingGameTemplate project if we wanted to. The HighlightedCard, SelectedCards, StartCheckCardsTimer, Go, and DeclareWinner messages are specific to our game. You will see the actual data we pass along with the message types as we build out our playing state.

We need to add the following Initialize method to our playing state:

```
public override void Initialize()
{
    for (int i = 0; i < NumberOfCards; i++)
    {
        Cards[i] = new Card();
        Cards[i].Value = (byte)((i + 2) / 2);
        Cards[i].IsFaceUp = false;

        Cards[i].Location = new HalfVector2(
            HorizontalCardOffset + (i % MaxCardsAcross) * HorizontalCardSpacing,
            VerticalCardOffset + (i / MaxCardsAcross) * VerticalCardSpacing);
    }

    base.Initialize();
}
```

Every instance of the game, regardless of whether it is the "client" or the "server," will have all its cards initialized. We are setting each card location using the constants we set up earlier. This will space the cards out evenly. Even though 20 cards are being displayed, there are only 10 unique values. We have 10 pair of cards, so the value we are setting is the index i, with an offset of two, and that value divided by two. Therefore, when i is equal to 0 or 1, the value it gets is

$$0 + 2 = 2 / 2 = 1$$

or

$$1 + 2 = 3 / 2 = 1$$

Thus, both cards 0 and 1 get the value 1. Similarly, cards 2 and 3 will get the value 2. We will then check to see if the selected cards' values match up. If they do, we know we have a match. We also use this value to display the cards from our texture. You can copy the ConcentrationCards.png file from the CD included in this book. You can see the ConcentrationCards.png texture in Figure 28.1.

28

FIGURE 28.1   ConcentrationCards.png

In order to read the cards from the texture, we add the following code to the beginning of the LoadContent method:

```
cam.AddAnimation("1", "ConcentrationCards", new CelRange(1, 1, 1, 1),
    cardWidth, cardHeight, 1, 1);
cam.AddAnimation("2", "ConcentrationCards", new CelRange(2, 1, 2, 1),
    cardWidth, cardHeight, 1, 1);
cam.AddAnimation("3", "ConcentrationCards", new CelRange(3, 1, 3, 1),
    cardWidth, cardHeight, 1, 1);
cam.AddAnimation("4", "ConcentrationCards", new CelRange(4, 1, 4, 1),
    cardWidth, cardHeight, 1, 1);
cam.AddAnimation("5", "ConcentrationCards", new CelRange(5, 1, 5, 1),
    cardWidth, cardHeight, 1, 1);

cam.AddAnimation("6", "ConcentrationCards", new CelRange(1, 2, 1, 2),
    cardWidth, cardHeight, 1, 1);
cam.AddAnimation("7", "ConcentrationCards", new CelRange(2, 2, 2, 2),
    cardWidth, cardHeight, 1, 1);
cam.AddAnimation("8", "ConcentrationCards", new CelRange(3, 2, 3, 2),
    cardWidth, cardHeight, 1, 1);
cam.AddAnimation("9", "ConcentrationCards", new CelRange(4, 2, 4, 2),
    cardWidth, cardHeight, 1, 1);
cam.AddAnimation("10", "ConcentrationCards", new CelRange(5, 2, 5, 2),
    cardWidth, cardHeight, 1, 1);

cam.AddAnimation("d1", "ConcentrationCards", new CelRange(1, 3, 1, 3),
    cardWidth, cardHeight, 1, 1);
```

```
cam.AddAnimation("d2", "ConcentrationCards", new CelRange(2, 3, 2, 3),
    cardWidth, cardHeight, 1, 1);
cam.AddAnimation("d3", "ConcentrationCards", new CelRange(3, 3, 3, 3),
    cardWidth, cardHeight, 1, 1);

//No real animations so turn off Update method
cam.Enabled = false;
```

The `CelAnimationManager` allows us to specify `animationKey` (which we are setting as the card value [1–10,d1–d3]) and the texture asset we are loading (`ConcentrationCards`) as well as the cel range, cel width, cel height, and the number of cels that makes up the animation, in addition to the cel frames per second we should display.

If a refresher is needed, refer back to Chapter 10. Our cards do not have animation, so we pass in 1 for the number of cels that make up the animation, and we simply pass in 1 for the frames per second. We actually set the `enabled` flag to false for this game component so the `Update` method will not get called. This is because we do not have any animation and there is no reason to waste cycles trying to animate the cards. The `CelRange` values take in the first Cel X and Y and the last Cel X and Y. Because there is only one cel for each of our cards, the X and Y pairs will always match.

The last three animations we add are our deck card designs. This is where we could add more deck card designs and build out an options menu to allow the player to select the deck he or she wants to use.

We need to initialize the `CelAnimationManager` in our constructor:

```
cam = new CelAnimationManager(game, @"Textures\");
game.Components.Add(cam);
```

Now we can take a look at our `StartGame` method, which gets called either from the `StartMenuState` (if a single-player game is chosen), from the `MultiplayerMenuState` (if a local multiplayer game is chosen), or from the `SessionLobbyState` (if a regular multiplayer game is chosen). We need to add the following code to the end of the `StartGame` method in our playing state:

```
if (numberOfPlayers == 1)
{
    ShuffleCards();

    players[0].Enabled = true;
    players[0].Visible = true;
}
else
{
    foreach (LocalNetworkGamer gamer in OurGame.NetworkSession.LocalGamers)
    {
        if (gamer.IsHost)
```

28

```
        {
            ShuffleCards();

            packetWriter.Write((byte)MessageType.StartGame);
            for (int p = 0; p < NumberOfCards; p++)
            {
                packetWriter.Write(Cards[p].Value);
                packetWriter.Write(Cards[p].Location.PackedValue);
            }

            //Determine who goes first
            //For now, Host always goes first
            prevPlayer = 0;
            currentPlayer = 0;
            packetWriter.Write(currentPlayer);
            gamer.SendData(packetWriter, SendDataOptions.ReliableInOrder);

            players[currentPlayer].Enabled = true;
            players[currentPlayer].Visible = true;

            break;
        }
    }
}

SetPresenceInformation();
```

This method has already set the number of players and called the SetupGame method. We added a check to see whether we only have one player or more than one player. If we only have one player, we call ShuffleCards and set the first (only) player in our player collection to both visible and enabled. Setting the player to visible will cause the highlighted card to be displayed. Setting the player to enabled will allow input to read from the controller associated with that player.

If there is more than one player, we loop through all the local gamers in the network session. If the gamer is the host, we go through the same process we just went through for a single-player game of shuffling the cards, but before we set the current player to visible and enabled, we send all the cards to the other players. The host also determines which player will go first and passes the current (first) player to the other players. The host controls the location of all the cards as well as which ones are visible. Finally, we end the method by calling the SetPresenceInformation method we created in the last chapter.

We can now add the ShuffleCards method, which simply performs an in-place replacement of the cards in the array:

```
 private void ShuffleCards()
{
    Random r = new Random();
```

```
    byte tmp; //place holder
    int ri; //random index
    for (int t = 0; t < 10; t++) //shuffle 10 times
    {
        for (int i = 0; i < NumberOfCards; i++)
        {
            ri = r.Next(NumberOfCards);
            tmp = Cards[ri].Value; //store value
            Cards[ri].Value = Cards[i].Value; //swap
            Cards[i].Value = tmp; //get stored value
        }
    }
}
```

We also need to modify the SetupGame method by adding our game-specific code to the bottom of the private method:

```
currentPlayer = 0;
selectionChanged = false;
selectedCards = new byte[2] { 255, 255 };

if (OurGame.NetworkSession == null) //single player mode
{
    players = new List<Player>(1);
    players.Add(new Player(Game));
    players[0].PlayerIndex = PlayerIndexInControl.Value;
}
else
{
    //set capacity to the max gamers we can possibly have
    players = new List<Player>(OurGame.NetworkSession.MaxGamers);

    byte playerIndex = 255;
    //Initialize the player's collection
    foreach (NetworkGamer gamer in OurGame.NetworkSession.AllGamers)
    {
        if (gamer.Tag != null)
        {
            playerIndex = (byte)gamer.Tag;
        }
        else
        {
            playerIndex++;
            gamer.Tag = playerIndex;
        }
```

28

```
        players.Add(new Player(Game));
        players[playerIndex].Enabled = false;
        players[playerIndex].Visible = false;
        //We need to set the player's controller index if they are local
        if (gamer.IsLocal)
        {
            players[playerIndex].PlayerIndex =
                ((LocalNetworkGamer)gamer).SignedInGamer.PlayerIndex;
        }
    }
}
```

We make sure our variables are initialized for this new game. We then check to see whether we have a network session or are in single-player mode. Local multiplayer mode will create a network session, but it will not send network data across the wire because all the players are local. If our network session is null, we initialize our collection of players by adding a single player to it. We then set the player index to the player index in control. This tells the `Player` class from which controller it should be listening for input.

If we have a multiplayer game, we initialize the collection of players. We pass in the maximum number of gamers for the capacity value. We set the initial value of `playerIndex` to 255. Because this is a byte, it is similar to setting it to –1. This way, we can easily tell it is not a valid value. We then loop through all the gamers in the network session. If the gamer tag is not null, we set our `playerIndex` to the value in the `Tag` property. If it is null, we increment the `playerIndex` (which will increase 255 to 0) and then set the `Tag` property to the newly set `playerIndex`. This can happen when a gamer joins a session already in progress.

While we are still in our loop and after we have a valid `playerIndex`, we add the player to the collection. We then initialize the `Enabled` and `Visible` property flags to false. If the player is a local player, we set the player index to the player index associated with the signed-in gamer. This lets our `Player` class know from which controller to look for input.

In our `Player` class we were expecting to call the `PlayingState.SelectCard` method. Let's create this method now:

```
public void SelectCard(Player p, byte cardIndex)
{
    if (Cards[cardIndex].IsFaceUp)
        return; //don't do anything

    if (selectedCards[0] == 255)
    {
        selectedCards[0] = cardIndex;
        Cards[cardIndex].IsFaceUp = true;
    }
    else
```

```
    {
        selectedCards[1] = cardIndex;
        Cards[cardIndex].IsFaceUp = true;

        //don't let the player do anything while cards
        //are being displayed
        p.Enabled = false;
        //also remove highlighted texture
        p.Visible = false;

        waitTime = 0;
    }

    selectionChanged = true;
}
```

This method is called when a player who has control selects a card. The method takes in the player who selects the card as well as the actual card index selected. First, it checks to make sure the card is not already face up. If it is, the method simply returns. The method then checks the selectedCards array to see if the first value has been set yet. We are using the same value (255) to determine whether a card has been selected. If this has not been set, the method sets the value and turns the card face up. If the first card in the selected array was already set, then we set the second card, and we also set the player's Visible and Enabled flags to false. This will hide the highlighted card texture as well keep the player object from checking for any input. If the last card is selected, we also reset the waitTime millisecond counter to 0. Regardless of whether this is the first or second card in the selectedCards array, we always set the selectionChanged flag to true. We will use this to send out a network packet to the other players so that their cards can be updated appropriately.

We now need to modify the beginning of the Update method by adding the following code:

```
if (OurGame.NetworkSession == null)
{
    if (waitTime == 0 && readyToCheckCards)
        waitTime = gameTime.TotalGameTime.TotalMilliseconds;

    if (ReadyToCheckCards && gameTime.TotalGameTime.TotalMilliseconds >
                                        waitTime + millisecondsToShowCards)
        CheckCards();

    if (players[currentPlayer].Enabled)
    {
        players[currentPlayer].PlayerIndex = PlayerIndexInControl.Value;
        players[currentPlayer].HandleInput();
    }
}
```

The first thing we do is check to see if we have a network session. If we do not have a network session, we process the single-player logic. We check the waitTime flag and ReadyToCheckCards property to determine if we need to set the waitTime to the current total milliseconds. Therefore, if we land in our Update method as soon as the second card is selected (in a single-player game), we will execute that line of code. The next check is determining if 2,000 milliseconds (2 seconds) have passed. If so, we call out to the CheckCards method. We will look at this method shortly. Finally, we check to see if the player is enabled. If so, we set the player index and then call the HandleInput method on the Player object.

The ReadyToCheckCards property simply checks to see whether either card is set to the default value of 255:

```
private bool ReadyToCheckCards
{
    get { return (selectedCards[0] != 255 && selectedCards[1] != 255); }
}
```

We can add the following CheckCards method:

```
private void CheckCards()
{
    bool gameIsFinished = false;

    if (Cards[selectedCards[0]].Value == Cards[selectedCards[1]].Value)
    {
        //match
        Cards[selectedCards[0]].IsVisible = false;
        Cards[selectedCards[1]].IsVisible = false;

        //Score based off single player or multiplayer
        if (OurGame.NetworkSession == null)
        {
            singlePlayerScore += 100;

            //Set the single player's score
            foreach (SignedInGamer signedInGamer in SignedInGamer.SignedInGamers)
            {
                if (signedInGamer.PlayerIndex ==
                    players[currentPlayer].PlayerIndex)
                {
                    signedInGamer.Presence.PresenceMode = GamerPresenceMode.Score;
                    signedInGamer.Presence.PresenceValue = singlePlayerScore;
                }
            }
        }
    }
```

```
        else
        {
            players[currentPlayer].Score += 1;
        }

        //input was disabled while the cards were checked ...
        //re-enable it if we aren't done with the game
        gameIsFinished = IsGameFinished;
        if (!gameIsFinished)
            players[currentPlayer].Enabled = true;
    }
    else
    {
        //No match
        Cards[selectedCards[0]].IsFaceUp = false;
        Cards[selectedCards[1]].IsFaceUp = false;

        GetNextPlayer();
    }

    selectedCards[0] = selectedCards[1] = 255;

    //Make sure highlight texture is visible
    if (!gameIsFinished)
        players[currentPlayer].Visible = true;

    if (OurGame.NetworkSession == null && gameIsFinished)
    {
        if (currentTime.Seconds > 0) //add 100 for every positive second
            singlePlayerScore += ((int)currentTime.TotalSeconds * 100);
        else //subtract 10 for every negative second
            singlePlayerScore += ((int)currentTime.TotalSeconds * 10);

        GameManager.PushState(OurGame.WonGameState.Value, PlayerIndexInControl);
    }
    else if (gameIsFinished) //network session isn't null, and game is over
    {
        //Find Winner and End Game
    }
}
```

Not only does this method check to see if the cards match, it also checks to see if the game is over. The method compares the values of both the selected cards. If they are equal, we have a match. We set both cards to not be visible. We then check to see if the game is in single-player mode. If it is, we increment the singlePlayerScore by 100. We then loop through all the signed-in gamers and find the one that matches the player index of the current player. We can get by with just checking the index of the controller the player is using because the game is in single-player mode. We cannot just set it to the first signed-in gamer, however, because even though only one gamer is playing, we could have multiple gamers signed in to the console. Once we know we have the right signed-in gamer, we then set the presence mode to `Score`, which is one of the `GamerPresenceModes` that allow us to set a numeric value in the `PresenceValue` property. We set the value to our single-player score.

If we are in a multiplayer game, we simply add one to the score associated with the player. The high score state looks at the `Score` property from our `PlayingState`. This is not a problem for our multiplayer game because we do not store high scores for multiplayer games. The multiplayer score is only important to determine who won and lost.

Finally, after a match is made, we enable the current player so he or she can go again, assuming the game is not over. We will review the `IsGameFinished` property shortly.

If there is no match, we set both cards to be face down and then call `GetNextPlayer`, which has the logic to determine who the next player should be. `GetNextPlayer` will set the previous player's `Enabled` and `Visible` flags to false and the new player's flags to true. We will review this method in a moment.

Regardless of whether or not there is a match, we set the current player to be visible so his or her highlight texture card will be displayed, assuming the game is not over. We then clear out the `selectedCard` array. If we are in single-player mode (network session is null) and the game is over, we add up the single-player score. We add 100 points for every second that remains on the timer. We deduct 10 points for every second over the time limit. We then change the game state to the `WonGameState`.

We have a placeholder for when the game is over, but we are not in a single-player game. For now we are just concentrating on getting the game logic created for the single-player game. We will come back and find a winner in a multiplayer game in the "Adding in Multiplayer Game Play" section later in this chapter.

Here's the `GetNextPlayer` method that was called by the `CheckCards` method:

```
private void GetNextPlayer()
{
    //End this players Turn
    players[currentPlayer].Enabled = false;
    players[currentPlayer].Visible = false;

    if (numberOfPlayers > 1)
    {

        currentPlayer++;
        if (currentPlayer >= OurGame.NetworkSession.AllGamers.Count)
            currentPlayer = 0;
    }
```

```
    //Start next players Turn
    players[currentPlayer].Enabled = true;
    players[currentPlayer].Visible = true;
}
```

GetNextPlayer checks to see if we have more than one player. If so, we end this player's turn by setting the Enabled and Visible properties to false. We then add one to the index and reset the index to zero if we have passed the total number of gamers. Finally, we set the new currentPlayer's Enabled and Visible properties to true.

The IsGameFinished property, which was called by the CheckCards method, checks all the cards to determine whether any are left visible on the table:

```
private bool IsGameFinished
{
    get
    {
        bool gameIsFinished = true;
        for (int i = 0; i < Cards.Length; i++)
        {
            //auto skip if the cards we are checking are still visible
            if (selectedCards[0] == i || selectedCards[1] == i)
                continue;

            //see if this card is visible
            if (Cards[i].IsVisible)
            {
                //if any card is visible then we
                //are still playing the game.
                gameIsFinished = false;
                break;
            }
        }
        return gameIsFinished;
    }
}
```

We set a local gameIsFinished flag to determine if we have found all the matches. We loop through all the cards, and if any of them are visible we clear the gameIsFinished flag and exit from the loop. We also make sure we do not check the current selection of cards because they could still be visible.

Now we need to actually draw the cards on the screen. We can replace the contents of our Draw method with the following code:

```
//Draw Cards
OurGame.SpriteBatch.Begin();
```

28

```
OurGame.SpriteBatch.Draw(background, Vector2.Zero, Color.White);

for (int i = 0; i < NumberOfCards; i++)
{
    if (Cards[i].IsVisible)
    {
        if (Cards[i].IsFaceUp)
        {
            cam.Draw(gameTime,
                Cards[i].Value.ToString(), //get texture value from card
                OurGame.SpriteBatch,
                //position the cards in center of screen, 5 across
                Cards[i].Location.ToVector2());
        }
        else
        {
            cam.Draw(gameTime,
                "d3", //deck card texture
                OurGame.SpriteBatch,
                //position the cards in center of screen, 5 across
                Cards[i].Location.ToVector2());
        }
    }
}

players[currentPlayer].DrawHighlightedCard();

int y = 0;
if (OurGame.NetworkSession == null)
{
    //Single player, show individual score
    OurGame.SpriteBatch.DrawString(OurGame.Font, "Score: " + Score.ToString(),
        new Vector2(TitleSafeArea.X, TitleSafeArea.Y), Color.White);

    //And show the timer
    string timeText;
    if (currentTime.Seconds < 0)  //show negative total seconds
        timeText = "Time: " + currentTime.TotalSeconds.ToString("00");
    else  //show time in minute : seconds when positive
        timeText = "Time: " + currentTime.Minutes.ToString("0") + ":" +
            currentTime.Seconds.ToString("00");

    OurGame.SpriteBatch.DrawString(OurGame.Font, timeText,
        timeTextShadowPosition, Color.Black);
    OurGame.SpriteBatch.DrawString(OurGame.Font, timeText,
```

```
            timeTextPosition, Color.Firebrick);
}
else
{
    foreach (NetworkGamer gamer in OurGame.NetworkSession.AllGamers)
    {
        Player p = players[(byte)gamer.Tag];
        Color color = Color.White;
        if ((byte)gamer.Tag == currentPlayer)
            color = Color.Yellow;
        OurGame.SpriteBatch.DrawString(OurGame.Font, gamer.Gamertag + ": " +
            p.Score.ToString(), new Vector2(TitleSafeArea.X, 200 + (y * 60)),
            color, 0, Vector2.Zero, 2.0f, SpriteEffects.None, 0);
        y++;
    }
}

OurGame.SpriteBatch.End();

base.Draw(gameTime);
```

We start off by drawing a background texture. You can find the PlayingBackground.png file on the CD for this book. We need to create that `Texture2D` private member field and then initialize it in our `LoadContent` method:

```
background = Content.Load<Texture2D>(@"Textures\PlayingBackground");
```

After drawing our background texture, we loop through all the cards and draw each one that is still visible. We either draw the card face up or face down, depending on its current state. If the card is face down, we have hardcoded "d3" as the deck we are using. We could utilize a value returned from the `OptionMenuState` if we were to add code to allow the player to select the playing deck. After drawing the cards, we call the current player's `DrawHighlightedCard` method. If the player is visible, the card will be drawn.

If the game is in single-player mode, we display the single-player score on the screen. We also display the timer in different formats, depending on if we have counted down past zero. If the game is not in single-player mode, we display each gamer tag along with that player's score. We do this by iterating through the `AllGamers` collection on the `NetworkSession` object. We set the color of the current player to `Yellow` while the rest of the players are set to `White`.

At this point we can run the game and play the single-player version. After you get your fill of playing Concentration against the clock, we can start writing code to handle multiplayer game play.

28

Adding in Multiplayer Game Play

We have added different items to our game to prepare for multiplayer game play, but we have not actually handled any game play. To start, we can update the Update method in our playing state. The very first condition in our Update method is checking to see if the network session is null. We want to create a false portion to that condition to handle when we do have a network session and therefore are in a multiplayer (local, system link, or LIVE) game. We need to add the following false condition:

```
else
    UpdateNetworkSession(gameTime);
```

When our Update method is called and we are in a multiplayer game, we will call the following UpdateNetworkSession method:

```
private void UpdateNetworkSession(GameTime gameTime)
{
    bool sendPacketThisFrame = false;

    framesSinceLastSend++;
    if (framesSinceLastSend >= framesBetweenPackets)
    {
        sendPacketThisFrame = true;
        framesSinceLastSend = 0;
    }

    //Update our locally controlled player, and
    //send their latest position to everyone else
    foreach (LocalNetworkGamer gamer in OurGame.NetworkSession.LocalGamers)
    {
        UpdateLocalGamer(gamer, gameTime);
    }

    //We Do actual sending and receiving of network packets
    try
    {
        if (sendPacketThisFrame)
            OurGame.NetworkSession.Update();
    }
    catch (Exception e)
    {
        OurGame.MessageDialogState.Message = e.Message;
        OurGame.MessageDialogState.IsError = true;
        GameManager.PushState(OurGame.MessageDialogState.Value,
            PlayerIndexInControl);
```

```
        OurGame.NetworkSession.Dispose();
        OurGame.NetworkSession = null;
    }

    //Make sure the session has not ended
    if (OurGame.NetworkSession == null)
        return;

    //Get packets that contain data of remote players
    foreach (LocalNetworkGamer gamer in OurGame.NetworkSession.LocalGamers)
    {
        ReadIncomingPackets(gamer, gameTime);
    }
}
```

Before we dig into this method, we need to create two private member fields to help us determine if we should send network data:

```
private int framesBetweenPackets = 6;
private int framesSinceLastSend;
```

By setting framesBetweenPackets to 6, we are saying we want to send network data every six frames, or 10 "network sends" a second. If we set this to 1, we would send data every frame. If we set it to 3, we would send data every three frames, which would equal 20 "network sends" a second.

In our UpdateNetworkSession we set a local flag, sendPacketThisFrame, to false, so we will not send a network packet this frame. We then check the values of the two variables we just created to determine whether or not we should send the network data on this frame. If enough frames have passed, we set sendPacketThisFrame to true and reset the framesSinceLastSend variable.

We iterate through all the local gamers in this network session. These are the gamers on the console. We call the UpdateLocalGamer method and then call the NetworkSession.Update method, which allows the XNA Framework to send and receive messages. This method should be called several times a second. We are calling it every 10 frames. We have wrapped this call in a try/catch block because it is possible for errors to occur here. It could be that we just cannot send data fast enough or that some other critical error has occurred. We catch the error and display it using our message dialog state. We then dispose of our network session and set it to null.

Assuming we successfully called Update on our network session object, we then check to make sure it is not null. It is possible the session ended. If the session did not end, we iterate through all the local gamers and then call the ReadIncomingPackets method, passing in the local gamer object and the game time populated from our Update method.

The UpdateLocalGamer method contains a lot of the logic that determines which network messages we need to send. We need to add the following UpdateLocalGamer method to our playing state:

28

```
private void UpdateLocalGamer(LocalNetworkGamer gamer, GameTime gameTime)
{
    //Look up what player is associated with this local player.
    byte playerIndex = (byte)gamer.Tag;

    if (prevPlayer != currentPlayer)
    {
        if (gamer.IsHost)
        {
            packetWriter.Write((byte)MessageType.Go);
            packetWriter.Write(currentPlayer);

            //Send the data to everyone in the session
            gamer.SendData(packetWriter, SendDataOptions.ReliableInOrder);
        }

        prevPlayer = currentPlayer;
    }

    //check to see if we should have each player check their card
    if (waitTime == 0 && ReadyToCheckCards)
    {
        waitTime = gameTime.TotalGameTime.TotalMilliseconds;
    }

    //still waiting to check cards and enough time has elapsed?
    if (ReadyToCheckCards && gameTime.TotalGameTime.TotalMilliseconds >
                                        waitTime + millisecondsToShowCards)
    {
        CheckCards(gamer.IsHost);
    }

    if (selectionChanged)
    {
        packetWriter.Write((byte)MessageType.SelectedCards);
        packetWriter.Write(selectedCards);

        gamer.SendData(packetWriter, SendDataOptions.ReliableInOrder);
        selectionChanged = false;
    }

    //For concentration we disable input if not our turn
    if (players[playerIndex].Enabled)
    {
        //Only send data if something actually changed
        byte currHighlightedCard = players[playerIndex].HandleInput();
```

```
        if (prevHighlightedCard != currHighlightedCard)
        {
            //Write the player state into a network packet
            packetWriter.Write((byte)MessageType.HighlightedCard);
            packetWriter.Write(currHighlightedCard);

            //Send the data to everyone in the session
            gamer.SendData(packetWriter, SendDataOptions.InOrder);

            prevHighlightedCard = currHighlightedCard;
        }
    }
}
```

We start the method by storing the index of our player collection. We collect this value from the Tag property of the gamer object passed in. We then check to see if the currentPlayer is different from the prevPlayer. If it is and the player is the host (server), we prepare a network message. We set the first byte to be our message type Go. We then send the data, making sure that it is not only reliable but is in order. We do not want to send data this way very often, but in this case we need to make sure that everyone knows whose turn it is. We then set our next byte to the currentPlayer, which is the new player that needs to go. We then set the prevPlayer value to the currentPlayer, regardless if the player is the host or not.

We then check to see if the cards are ready to be checked for a match. If the wait time is zero, we know that two cards were just selected. We store the total milliseconds in our wait time, just like we did for the single-player mode. We then check to see if 2 seconds have passed. When the condition is true, we call the CheckCards method to perform the same logic we did in the single-player game.

We are passing in a boolean stating whether the person calling the CheckCards method is a host. In a single-player game, we always call GetNextPlayer, but in a multiplayer game we only want one machine controlling who gets to go next. We need to modify the CheckCards method to accept a boolean parameter called isHost, and we need to check to see if that parameter is true before we end the player's turn, get next player, and start the next player's turn. The code to do that is as follows:

```
//No match
Cards[selectedCards[0]].IsFaceUp = false;
Cards[selectedCards[1]].IsFaceUp = false;

if (isHost)
{
    //End this players Turn
    players[currentPlayer].Enabled = false;
    players[currentPlayer].Visible = false;
```

28

```
    GetNextPlayer();

    //Start next players Turn
    players[currentPlayer].Enabled = true;
    players[currentPlayer].Visible = true;
}
```

Before we continue to discuss the UpdateLocalGamer method, we need to replace the "no match" code in the CheckCards method with the preceding code. Then in our Update method where we call CheckCards in single-player mode, we need to pass in true because the single player acts like a host.

Back inside of the UpdateLocalGamer method, after we call the newly modified CheckCards method, our next condition checks to see if the card selection has changed. If the selectionChanged flag is true, we let all the other players know that a card has been selected. You saw this flag get set to true in our SelectCard method, which is called by the player whose turn it is. Finally, we set the selectionChanged flag to false so we don't kick off the selectionChanged condition because we just sent the selectedCards.

The final section of the UpdateLocalGamer method checks to see if the gamer who is passed in (playerIndex contains gamer.Tag data) is actually enabled. If he or she is the current player, we check the player's input by calling the HandleInput method on the player object. It returns the currently highlighted card index. If this has changed since the last time we checked for a highlighted card, we send a network message with a message type of HighlightedCard. We add in the actual card index that is highlighted and then send this data in order. It is not the end of the world if one of these packets does not make it to its destination. The next time a card is highlighted, a new message will be sent, and the game instances will be in sync then. Finally, we set the previously stored highlighted card index to the current highlighted card index.

The UpdateLocalGamer method checks the states of several items in the game and then sends the appropriate network messages. It also updates anything it needs to locally. The counterpart to the UpdateLocalGamer method is the ReadIncomingPackets method. We called this method at the end of our UpdateNetworkSession method. This is where local gamers can process any network messages they were sent.

We can add the following ReadIncomingPackets method:

```
private void ReadIncomingPackets(LocalNetworkGamer gamer, GameTime gameTime)
{
    while (gamer.IsDataAvailable)
    {
        NetworkGamer sender;
        gamer.ReceiveData(packetReader, out sender);

        //Ignore packets sent by local gamers
        //since we already know their state
```

```
if (sender.IsLocal)
    continue;

//Get the player index
byte playerIndex = (byte)gamer.Tag;

//Determine the type of message this is
byte header = packetReader.ReadByte();

if (header == (byte)MessageType.StartGame)
{
    for (int p = 0; p < NumberOfCards; p++)
    {
        Cards[p].Value = packetReader.ReadByte();
        Cards[p].Location.PackedValue = packetReader.ReadUInt32();
    }

    //Make sure everyone has the right starting player
    currentPlayer = packetReader.ReadByte();
    prevPlayer = currentPlayer;
}
else if (header == (byte)MessageType.DeclareWinner)
{
    byte numberOfHighScores = packetReader.ReadByte();
    List<int> highScoreIndices = new List<int>(numberOfHighScores);
    for (byte i = 0; i < numberOfHighScores; i++)
        highScoreIndices.Add(packetReader.ReadByte());

    bool localIsAWinner = false;
    foreach (NetworkGamer g in OurGame.NetworkSession.AllGamers)
    {
        if (g.IsLocal)
        {
            //Did this local machine win?
            //check to see if this players index is
            //in the high score index list
            if (highScoreIndices.Contains((byte)gamer.Tag))
            {
                localIsAWinner = true;

                OurGame.WonGameState.Gamertag = gamer.Gamertag;
                break;
            }
        }
    }
```

28

```
            if (localIsAWinner)
                GameManager.ChangeState(OurGame.WonGameState.Value, null);
            else
                GameManager.ChangeState(OurGame.LostGameState.Value, null);
        }
        else if (header == (byte)MessageType.RequestToJoinInProgressGame)
        {   //Sent by person joining game in progress
            if (gamer.IsHost)
            {
                packetWriter.Write((byte)MessageType.JoinedInProgressGame);

                for (int p = 0; p < NumberOfCards; p++)
                {
                    packetWriter.Write(Cards[p].Value);
                    packetWriter.Write(Cards[p].Location.PackedValue);
                    packetWriter.Write(Cards[p].IsFaceUp);
                    packetWriter.Write(Cards[p].IsVisible);
                }

                for (int i = 0; i < players.Count; i++)
                {
                    packetWriter.Write((byte)players[i].Score);
                }

                packetWriter.Write(selectedCards);

                packetWriter.Write(currentPlayer);

                gamer.SendData(packetWriter, SendDataOptions.Reliable, sender);
            }
        }
        else if (header == (byte)MessageType.JoinedInProgressGame)
        {   //received by person joining game in progress
            for (int p = 0; p < NumberOfCards; p++)
            {
                Cards[p].Value = packetReader.ReadByte();
                Cards[p].Location.PackedValue = packetReader.ReadUInt32();
                Cards[p].IsFaceUp = packetReader.ReadBoolean();
                Cards[p].IsVisible = packetReader.ReadBoolean();
            }

            for (int i = 0; i < players.Count; i++)
            {
                players[i].Score = packetReader.ReadByte();
            }
```

```
        selectedCards = packetReader.ReadBytes(2);
        waitTime = 0;

        currentPlayer = packetReader.ReadByte();
}
else if (header == (byte)MessageType.HighlightedCard)
{
    players[currentPlayer].HighlightedCard = packetReader.ReadByte();
    players[currentPlayer].Visible = true;
}
else if (header == (byte)MessageType.SelectedCards)
{
    byte[] selected = new byte[2];
    selected = packetReader.ReadBytes(2);

    if (selectedCards[0] != 255 && selected[0] != selectedCards[0])
    {
        if (selectedCards[1] != 255 && selected[1] != selectedCards[1])
        {
            //below should only happen on really bad network connections
            //timer hasn't ran out yet, force a call to Check Cards
            // after waiting up to 2 seconds
            while (gameTime.TotalGameTime.TotalMilliseconds > waitTime +
                                              millisecondsToShowCards)
                waitTime = gameTime.TotalGameTime.TotalMilliseconds;

            //we are not the host since we were just
            //told about Card Selection
            CheckCards(false);
        }
    }

    selectedCards = selected;

    if (selectedCards[0] != 255)
        Cards[selectedCards[0]].IsFaceUp = true;
    if (selectedCards[1] != 255)
    {
        Cards[selectedCards[1]].IsFaceUp = true;
        players[currentPlayer].Visible = false;

        //both cards selected, reset timer
        waitTime = 0;
    }

    //don't do selection Change logic in UpdateLocalGamer
```

28

```
                    selectionChanged = false;
              }
              else if (header == (byte)MessageType.Go)
              {
                    //below should only happen on bad network connections
                    //timer hasn't ran out yet, force a call to Check Cards
                    if (ReadyToCheckCards && gameTime.TotalGameTime.TotalMilliseconds <
                                                 waitTime + millisecondsToShowCards)
                    {
                        // just wait up to 2 seconds
                        while (gameTime.TotalGameTime.TotalMilliseconds >
                                             waitTime + millisecondsToShowCards)
                            waitTime = gameTime.TotalGameTime.TotalMilliseconds;

                        //we are not the host since we were just told to Go
                        CheckCards(false);
                    }

                    //make currentPlayer (before we change it) to not be enabled or drawn
                    players[currentPlayer].Enabled = false;
                    players[currentPlayer].Visible = false;

                    //highlight the player who is now going
                    currentPlayer = packetReader.ReadByte();

                    //make prevPlayer the same so we don't kick off our own Go event!
                    prevPlayer = currentPlayer;

                    players[currentPlayer].Enabled = true;
                    players[currentPlayer].Visible = true;
              }
        }
    }
}
```

Although network data is available for the gamer that was passed into this method, we call ReceiveData on the gamer object. This method returns the number of bytes read from the network packet. We are not capturing the return value. This method also outputs the sender of the network packet. Thus, we have the gamer this packet was sent to (passed in to the method), and we have the gamer this packet was sent from.

If the packet was sent from a local gamer, we just continue in our while loop. We do not need to process any of the data because we already handled it locally in our UpdateLocalGamer method. Assuming the sender is a remote player, we store the index of our player collection from the Tag property of our gamer object. Every piece of network data we send has a one-byte header. We store that byte by calling the ReadByte method on the packetReader object. We then have several if then else conditions to determine which network message we need to process. We could have used a switch statement instead. However, the extra indentions would have caused the code lines to not fit as nicely on these pages.

In the first condition, we are checking to see if the message type is StartGame. We sent this message from our StartGame method. We sent each card value followed by the card location. We retrieve the data in a similar way by reading the card value followed by the card location for all 20 cards. Because the Location is stored as a HalfVector2, we read it from the packetReader with the ReadUInt32 method. We populate the PackedValue with the unsigned integer value. We are compressing our data pretty nicely and not sending very much across the wire.

In the next condition, we are checking to see if we received a message that has declared the winner. We have not written the code that sends this data yet. We can do that now by adding in the following FindWinner method:

```
private void FindWinner()
{
    int highScore = players[0].Score;

    //Find most pairs
    for (int i = 1; i < numberOfPlayers; i++)
    {
        if (players[i].Score > highScore)
            highScore = players[i].Score;
    }

    //check for any players that have same as highest player
    List<int> highScoreIndices = new List<int>();
    for (int i = 0; i < numberOfPlayers; i++)
    {
        if (players[i].Score == highScore)
            highScoreIndices.Add(i);
    }

    //Make sure our gamertag is set to empty so it will have
    //the right value ("You") for check
    OurGame.WonGameState.Gamertag = string.Empty;

    bool localIsAWinner = false;
    foreach (NetworkGamer gamer in OurGame.NetworkSession.AllGamers)
    {
        if (gamer.IsLocal)
        {
            //Did this local machine win?
            //check to see if this players index is in the high score index list
            if (highScoreIndices.Contains((byte)gamer.Tag))
            {
```

28

```
        localIsAWinner = true;

        //It is possible to have more than one winner on a local
        // multiplayer for network multiplayer, each screen will
        //get own gamer tag "won"
        //but with a shared screen, we need to display ".. and .."
        if (OurGame.WonGameState.Gamertag == "You")
            OurGame.WonGameState.Gamertag = gamer.Gamertag;
        else
            OurGame.WonGameState.Gamertag += " and " + gamer.Gamertag;
    }
  }
}


foreach (LocalNetworkGamer gamer in OurGame.NetworkSession.LocalGamers)
{
    packetWriter.Write((byte)MessageType.DeclareWinner);
    packetWriter.Write((byte)highScoreIndices.Count);
    foreach (int i in highScoreIndices)
        packetWriter.Write((byte)i);

    //Send the data to everyone in the session
    gamer.SendData(packetWriter, SendDataOptions.Reliable);
}

//Force Network Update to send winning information packets
OurGame.NetworkSession.Update();

if (localIsAWinner)
    GameManager.PushState(OurGame.WonGameState.Value, null);
else
    GameManager.PushState(OurGame.LostGameState.Value, null);
}
```

The first thing the FindWinner method does is iterate through each player's score and then store the highest score it found. It then loops through all the players again, adding each index of the player collection in a collection of high score indices. It is possible to have a tie, so we are storing all the winners in this collection. We need to update WonGameState and the IWonGameState interface. We are going to display the gamer tag of the player(s) who won. We currently just show "You Won!!!" We can add the following property signature to our IWonGameState interface in the GameStateInterfaces.cs file:

```
string Gamertag { get; set; }
```

Then in the actual `WonGameState` class, we can add a private string called `gamertag`, and we can add the following `Gamertag` property:

```
public string Gamertag
{
    get
    {
        if (string.IsNullOrEmpty(gamertag))
            return ("You");
        else
            return (gamertag);
    }

    set { gamertag = value; }
}
```

We check to see if `gamertag` is null or empty. If it is, we simply keep the original functionality and display "You." Otherwise, we actually return the gamer tag. We can change the two instances inside the `Draw` method where we draw the string `"You Won!!!"` to `Gamertag + " Won!!!"`. We could also set presence data at the bottom of our `StateChanged` method:

```
foreach (SignedInGamer signedInGamer in SignedInGamer.SignedInGamers)
{
    //since the gamertag in this state, we check with contains
    if (Gamertag.Contains(signedInGamer.Gamertag))
        signedInGamer.Presence.PresenceMode = GamerPresenceMode.WonTheGame;
    else //could be other local gamers didn't win
        signedInGamer.Presence.PresenceMode = GamerPresenceMode.GameOver;
}
```

Back to our `FindWinner` state, we actually clear out the `Gamertag` on the `WonGameState`. This ensures that even if other games are played, the value is initialized and will actually return "You" the first time it is queried. We loop through all the gamers in our network session, and if the gamer is local we check to see if he or she is in the high score list. If so, we set the `Gamertag` property on the `WonGameState` class appropriately.

Next we loop through all the local gamers in our network session and send out a network message with a message type of `DeclareWinner`. We pass in the total number of high scores (because there can be a tie) we are sending. We then send each high score we stored. We want to make sure all the players know when the game is over, so we set `Reliable` when sending the data. After sending the `DeclareWinner` message, we force a network session update. We do this because the very next thing our local player will do is push either `WonGameState` or `LostGameState` onto the stack. When the state is changed, the network session will be ended shortly thereafter. We want to make sure everyone gets notified of who won the game.

28

Now that you have seen how we send the winner information, we can get back to the `ReadIncomingPackets` method, where we actually read in this message. If a `DeclareWinner` message type was received, we read in the number of high scores and then create a local high score indices collection and add each index we read from the network packet into this collection. We then process the same logic we did in the `FindWinner` method. If a local winner is found, we set the `Gamertag` and change the state to `WonGameState`. If a local player did not win, we change the state to `LostGameState`.

The next message type we are checking in the `ReadIncomingPackets` method is `RequestToJoinInProgressGame`. We ignore this message unless the player is the host. If the player is the host, we create a new packet with a message type of `JoinedInProgressGame`. We then iterate through all the cards and write the card data to the packet. We then loop through all the players and write out each player's score to the packet. We also write out the current `selectedCards` values. Finally, we write out the current player index. We send this packet with the `Reliable` send data option. We only send this packet to the player who just joined by sending it right back to the person who sent the request to join the game.

The next condition is where we process the `JoinedInProgressGame` message that the host just created. The player who just joined will read all the values and set his or her card data. This player will also set each player's score. The player will set the `selectedCards` byte array passed in from the host and set the `waitTime` variable in case both cards were selected already. Finally, the current player will be set with the last byte read from the packet. The gamer who just joined the game is now in synch with everyone else in the game.

The next message type we check for is the `HighlightedCard` message. We simply set the current player's `HighlightedCard` index to the value we retrieved from the packet. We then set the `Visible` property to true so the highlighted card will be displayed.

The next message type we check for is the `SelectedCards` message. We read in the two bytes into our new array. We have created a new array because each machine has its own timer to determine when to stop displaying the selected cards. It is possible on bad network connections to get a new selection before the time has run out. We want to make sure the player has enough time to see the previously selected cards. We check the values of the current `selectedCards` byte array and if they do not equal either the default value of 255 or the bytes we just read in, we wait until the timer runs down and force a call to `CheckCards` before continuing to select the cards just passed in.

We then check to see if they have actual values. If they are not the initial 255 value, we change the `IsFaceUp` property to true. If the second card has a value, we also set the current player's visibility to false. We also reset the `waitTime` so `CheckCards` will get called as soon as it can. Finally, we set the `selectionChanged` flag to false. We do not want to kick off the section change event because we just responded to a selection changed event.

The final message type we check is the `Go` message. Before we read any data, we make sure that if we're waiting to check cards from a previous player's turn that we wait and then call `CheckCards`. This is in case we have a bad network connection.

We make sure the current player is disabled and not visible. Then we read in the current player from the packet and set that player to be enabled and visible. We also set the prevPlayer equal to the currentPlayer so we do not kick off the Go event. That completes the ReadIncomingPackets method.

Handling Players Leaving and Joining the Game

The core of our multiplayer game logic is complete. The only problem is that we set the network session to AllowJoinInProgress and AllowHostMigration when we created the network session in the NetworkMenuState. Because we did this, we need to make sure we can handle those cases.

When we created the network template, we put comments in a couple places because it was dependent on game-specific functionality. One of the places we need to modify is the PlayerLeft method. This gets called whenever a player leaves the game. In the last chapter, we set the SessionLobbyState to hook in to the GamerLeft event and set it to call the playing state's PlayerLeft method.

Our updated PlayerLeft method is as follows:

```
public void PlayerLeft(byte gamerId)
{
    if (OurGame.NetworkSession != null)
    {
        NetworkGamer gamer = OurGame.NetworkSession.FindGamerById(gamerId);

        int playerThatLeft = 0;
        //possible to return null if gamer was there,
        //but isn't by the time we call this
        if (gamer != null)
        {
            //Handle the player leaving our game
            playerThatLeft = (int)gamer.Tag;
        }
        else
        {
            //We need to determine which gamer left
            byte[] playersRemaining = new byte[players.Count + 1];

            //populate a list of all players we currently have
            for (int i = 0; i < players.Count; i++)
                playersRemaining[i] = (byte)i;
```

```
        //now loop through and remove all people that still exists

        //We don't have the actual gamer that left, so let's find it
        foreach (NetworkGamer g in OurGame.NetworkSession.AllGamers)
        {
            for (int i = 0; i < playersRemaining.Length; i++)
            {
                //this player still exists so "clear" out the value
                if (playersRemaining[i] == (byte)g.Tag)
                    playersRemaining[i] = 255;
            }
        }

        //now only one non 255 value exists, find it
        //and set that as playerThatLeft
        for (int i = 0; i < playersRemaining.Length; i++)
        {
            if (playersRemaining[i] != 255)
            {
                //we found the gamer that left
                playerThatLeft = playersRemaining[i];
                break;
            }
        }
    }

    //Finally remove the player from our list
    players.RemoveAt(playerThatLeft);

    //Reset each gamer's player Index
    byte playerIndex = 0;
    foreach (NetworkGamer g in OurGame.NetworkSession.AllGamers)
    {
        g.Tag = playerIndex;
        playerIndex++;
    }

    //If the player that left was the current player, then
    //change the selected cards to no values and pick next player
    if (currentPlayer == playerThatLeft)
    {
        //selectedCards[0] = selectedCards[1] = 255;
        //selectionChanged = true;

        //Let the host determine who should go next
        foreach (LocalNetworkGamer localGamer in
```

```
                                OurGame.NetworkSession.LocalGamers)
    {
        if (localGamer.IsHost)
        {

            packetWriter.Write((byte)MessageType.StartGame);
            for (int p = 0; p < NumberOfCards; p++)
            {
                packetWriter.Write(Cards[p].Value);
                packetWriter.Write(Cards[p].Location.PackedValue);
            }

            //Determine who goes next
            GetNextPlayer();

            packetWriter.Write(currentPlayer);

            localGamer.SendData(packetWriter,
                SendDataOptions.ReliableInOrder);

            players[currentPlayer].Enabled = true;
            players[currentPlayer].Visible = true;

            break;
        }
    }
}

    //set number of players
    numberOfPlayers = players.Count;
    }
}
```

The code that was already present from our network game template tried to find the
gamer by the ID passed in. It called the NetworkSession.FindGamerById method. The original method just returned if we did not have a valid gamer object. If we do get a valid
gamer object, we use the return value and store the Tag property of the gamer in the
playerThatLeft variable. If we do not get a valid gamer object, our job is a little more
difficult. We have quite a bit of code to simply determine which player actually left the
game. We go through all the players that were in the game and initialize their index. We
then loop through all the gamers we actually have, checking to see if the stored player
index matches the ones we just set. If they match, we replace the index we set to 255
because that player is still in the game. Now the only valid index in the list is the player
who left the game. So we iterate through the playersRemaining list, ignoring all the
values that were just set to 255. Once we find the index of the player who just left the

game, we set the same variable we set previously if the XNA Framework told us which gamer left.

Now we remove the player who just left from the player collection. We loop through all the gamers and reset their Tag property with the newly calculated player index.

We then compare the playerThatLeft with the currentPlayer. If they are a match, we know that the person who left the game is the current player (who was actively taking his or her turn). We then check to see if the player is a host by iterating through the LocalGamers collection. Because the player was in the middle of his or her turn, the host will send all the card information to everyone again by issuing a StartGame message. Before issuing which player should go, the host calls the GetNextPlayer method to determine who should go next. The last thing we do is update the numberOfPlayers value with the new number of players. We did not do this earlier because the GetNextPlayer method would not get the correct player if all players except the new host left.

Because we are removing a player from the list before we call GetNextPlayer, we need to put the first statements of the GetNextPlayer method in a condition to make sure we are not trying to access an index that is out of range:

```
if (currentPlayer <= players.Count)
{
    players[currentPlayer].Enabled = false;
    players[currentPlayer].Visible = false;
}
```

The next method we need to modify is the JoinInProgressGame method. We can replace the comment //TODO: Handle local player joining with the following code:

```
//We need to set the player's controller index if they are local
players[(byte)gamer.Tag].PlayerIndex =
    ((LocalNetworkGamer)gamer).SignedInGamer.PlayerIndex;

packetWriter.Write((byte)MessageType.RequestToJoinInProgressGame);

((LocalNetworkGamer)gamer).SendData(packetWriter, SendDataOptions.ReliableInOrder);
```

The method updates the new numberOfPlayers value since a new player join. We then check to see if the player is local; if so we call our SetupGame method to initialize everything for ourselves. We then set PlayerIndex on the Player object to the PlayerIndex associated with the signed-in gamer. We then write our first packet, which only consists of the RequestToJoinInProgressGame message type. We then send the data, making sure to mark the packet as Reliable because it is important that everyone know a new player just joined the game.

Now we can replace the comment TODO: Handle remote player joining with the following code:

```
players.Add(new Player(Game));
```

```
players[(byte)gamer.Tag].Enabled = false;
players[(byte)gamer.Tag].Visible = false;
```

If the gamer who just joined is not local gamer, we need to create a new `Player` object and add it to the players collection. We also set the `Enabled` and `Visible` flags on the player object to false. We know that the remote gamer will always have his or her `Tag` property populated with his or her index because this is done by `SessionLobbyState`.

Wrapping Up the Game

We can run our game and have several modes available to us. We can play single player, local multiplayer, multiplayer over a system link, and multiplayer over LIVE. We have used a lot of the knowledge gained through the course of this book to create a fully functional multiplayer game.

However, we need to tie up a couple of loose ends. Switching from one mode to another can cause some issues. For example, if we start a multiplayer game and then hit the Back button to bring up the start menu, we can select a single-player game. The problem is that our network session is not null, so all the logic that relies on it being null for a single-player game will not work. Fortunately, we can easily correct this by adding the following code to the `MenuSelected` method under the first case of menu item 0:

```
//Clear out network session
if (OurGame.NetworkSession != null)
{
    OurGame.NetworkSession.Dispose();
    OurGame.NetworkSession = null;

    GameManager.ChangeState(OurGame.PlayingState.Value, PlayerIndexInControl);
    OurGame.PlayingState.StartGame(1);

}
else if (GameManager.ContainsState(OurGame.PlayingState.Value))
    GameManager.PopState();
else
{
    GameManager.ChangeState(OurGame.PlayingState.Value, PlayerIndexInControl);
    OurGame.PlayingState.StartGame(1);
}
break;
```

Now whenever a single-player game is selected, the network session will be cleared out if it wasn't already.

The final piece we can clean up is the HighScoresState.cs code file. Currently, the high scores state determines whether or not the high scores should be displayed. But it does not take into account that the high scores shouldn't be displayed when a multiplayer

28

game finishes. We are not storing any high scores for a multiplayer game because the scores are simply there to determine who had the most matches of card pairs. The high scores are only valid for the single-player mode when the player is racing against the clock. In the `StateChanged` method of the `HighScoresState` class, we need to add the following code inside the condition that checks if the current state is `HighScoresState`:

```
//If we have a network session then
//we don't need to do anything with a high score
if (OurGame.NetworkSession != null)
{
    GameManager.PopState();
    return;
}
```

As soon as we come into the state, we check to see whether the network session is not null. If it is not null, we pop `HighScoresState` off the stack and then return out of the method.

There are a couple of things that could be done to improve the game. We could allow better selection of the cards. We currently restrict movement to horizontal. We could let the player move vertically to select the cards. We could create an options menu state that allows the gamer to pick the design of the cards he or she wants to use. The `HelpState` could be populated to display helpful information about the game, such as the rules and how to select other card designs. The `CreditsState` could be populated to scroll the different people who worked on the game. Actual card animations of matches could be used to rotate and move the cards from the table to the player's hands. The actual gamer pictures could be displayed along with the pile of cards they have accumulated. Music and sound effects could also be added to the game.

Summary

In this chapter, we took the existing NetworkGameTemplate project we created from the last chapter and built a full game that includes the following modes: single player, local multiplayer, multiplayer over system link, and multiplayer over LIVE. We were able to put into practice what you have learned over the last few chapters concerning how we send data across the wire. We utilized client/server and peer-to-peer strategies when creating this game. You saw how data can be sent to just one player and how data can be ignored by the player who sent it. You saw how to create different message types for the different types of data we want to send in our game and how to pack the data in a way that can be transmitted efficiently over the wire. We have successfully created a full-featured multiplayer turn-based game that can even be played over Xbox LIVE!

CHAPTER 29

Creating a Real-time Multiplayer Game

In this chapter, we are going to take the networking skeleton we created in the Chapter 27, "Creating a Networking Game Skeleton," and create a real-time multiplayer game. A real-time game (also known as a twitch-based game) is one where all the players are actively playing at the same time. It is the opposite of a turn-based game. Most AAA titles are real-time games.

Game Design

Just like with the last game, before we actually create this game we need to think about what the game will do. We need to map this out so we can determine where we should use the various networking strategies.

For this game we are using the logic from the AIDemo we created in Chapter 18, "AI Algorithms." We will create a real game with a timer and scoring. We will also utilize the networking template from Chapter 27.

We want to allow two players on the same console, so we will have to create a split screen like we did in Chapter 5, "Handling Input to Move Our Camera." We will be using 720p HD settings, so we will split the screen horizontally instead of vertically. We definitely want to have single-player capabilities, and the majority of that logic is in place already from the initial AI demo. Finally, we want to allow both system link and LIVE network games. We will allow up to four players total, with a maximum of two on the same console.

Each player will have his or her own unique color. It is important that each player's color is the same across the games. We will have the host keep track of which players have which colors assigned to them. We also need one machine to control all the enemies and their corresponding AI states. We will use the host machine to maintain the AI state. The rest of the data will be simply sent and received in a peer-to-peer fashion. This will include items such as the score. When a player captures an enemy, the player will send a message stating so. The message will include the enemy's new location. This will kick off code on each machine to add 100 points to that player's score. The same is true if a player is captured by an enemy: 50 points are deducted by each peer. The player's new position is sent along with the WasCaptured message.

Using the Networking Template

We will start by using the template we made in Chapter 27. We can copy the XELibrary folder from the last chapter. We need to change the names of the folders, projects, and solutions from NetworkGameTemplate to ChaseAndEvade.

We can open up the Windows solution and rename the namespace, changing it from NetworkGameTemplate to ChaseAndEvade. We can open the Game1.cs file and change the class name to ChaseAndEvade. As we rename both the namespace and the class, we can let Visual Studio replace all instances for us by right-clicking the newly changed name and selecting Replace All Instances. We can also change the AssemblyName and Default Namespace in the project properties to ChaseAndEvade. Double-clicking the Properties node in the Solution Explorer window is a quick way to bring up the properties window.

We need to open up the AssemblyInfo.cs file and change the Guid so the games can find each other during network play. We can also change the AssemblyTitle so the title will show up correctly on the Xbox 360. At this point we should be able to compile our newly created ChaseAndEvade game successfully.

We need to replace the TitleIntro.png file with the one from the CD. If we want to change any of the other default textures (session list, session lobby, and so on), we could do that as well. For this game we can use the same textures we used for the networking game template.

Finally, we need to change the containerName value inside the HighScoreState.cs file from NetworkGameTemplate to ChaseAndEvade. We can also change the scores in the InitializeDefaultHighScores method to the highest score being 800 and the rest in increments of 50 or 100.

Adding in Game-Specific Functionality

The core code in this chapter will be the logic we created with the AI demo back in Chapter 18. We will be modifying the PlayingState.cs code file mainly because that is where the majority of the game logic resides. We need to add the following private member fields:

```
private Model sphere;
private Skybox skybox;

private Camera camera;

private const int MaxEnemies = 10;
private Enemy[] enemies = new Enemy[MaxEnemies];

private Player singlePlayer;

private const float ArenaSize = 500;

public bool RestrictToXY = true;

private float moveUnit = 20;

private Random rand = new Random();

private const float SeekRadius = 75.0f;
private const float EvadeRadius = 75.0f;
```

We can now add our camera to our constructor:

```
camera = new Camera(game);
game.Components.Add(camera);
```

In the AI demo, all the game code was inside the Game1.cs code file. We will be putting some of the code into different files. Most of the logic will be placed in the PlayingState.cs file, but we also need to create Player.cs and Enemy.cs blank code files. Enemy.cs can be found in Listing 29.1.

LISTING 29.1   Enemy.cs

```
using System;
using Microsoft.Xna.Framework;
using Microsoft.Xna.Framework.Graphics;

namespace ChaseAndEvade
{
    public class Enemy
    {
        public enum AIState { Attack, Retreat, Search }

        public AIState State;
        public Vector3 Position;
        public Vector3 Velocity;
        public Color Color;
```

29

```
        public float ChangeDirectionTimer;
        public Vector3 RandomVelocity;
        public int RandomSeconds;
        public int Health;
    }
```

The enemy-specific code did not change from the AIDemo project other than we removed the World matrix property. We will calculate this on the fly when we draw the sphere in the DrawModel method that we add to the PlayingState code later. Player.cs, on the other hand, changes drastically. The code can be found in Listing 29.2.

LISTING 29.2   Player.cs

```
using System;
using Microsoft.Xna.Framework;
using Microsoft.Xna.Framework.Graphics;

using XELibrary;

namespace ChaseAndEvade
{
    public class Player
    {
        private InputHandler input;
        private PlayingState playingState;

        private Vector3 playerInput;

        public int Score = 0;
        public byte Id;

        private float playerMoveUnit = 25;

        public PlayerIndex PlayerIndex;

        public float CurrentZ = 0;

        private PlayerState simulationState;

        Random rand = new Random();

        public Player(Game game)
        {
            input = (InputHandler)game.Services.GetService(
                typeof(IInputHandler));
```

```
        playingState = (PlayingState)game.Services.GetService(
            typeof(IPlayingState));

        ResetPosition();
    }

    public Color Color;

    private struct PlayerState
    {
        public Vector3 Position;
        public Vector3 Velocity;
    }

    public Vector3 HandleInput(PlayerIndex playerIndex)
    {
        PlayerIndex = playerIndex;

        playerInput = new Vector3(input.GamePads[
                                  (int)playerIndex].ThumbSticks.Left, 0);

        //restrict to 2D?
        if (!playingState.RestrictToXY)
        {
            if (input.GamePads[(int)playerIndex].Triggers.Right > 0)
                playerInput.Z--;
            else if (input.GamePads[(int)playerIndex].Triggers.Left > 0)
                playerInput.Z++;
        }

        if (input.GamePads[(int)playerIndex].Triggers.Right > 0)
            CurrentZ--;
        else if (input.GamePads[(int)playerIndex].Triggers.Left > 0)
            CurrentZ++;

        //Normalize our vector so we don't go faster
        //when heading in multiple directions
        if (playerInput.LengthSquared() != 0)
            playerInput.Normalize();

        return (playerInput);
    }

    public void ResetPosition()
    {
        simulationState.Position = new Vector3(-rand.Next(300), 0, -300);
```

```
        }

        public void SetPosition(Vector3 position)
        {
            simulationState.Position = position;
        }

        public Vector3 Position
        {
            get { return (simulationState.Position); }
        }

        public Vector3 Velocity
        {
            get { return (simulationState.Velocity); }
        }

        public void Update(Vector3 playerInput)
        {
            this.playerInput = playerInput;

            // Update the master simulation state.
            UpdateState(ref simulationState);
        }

        private void UpdateState(ref PlayerState state)
        {
            state.Velocity = playerInput;

            state.Velocity *= playerMoveUnit;

            // Update the position and velocity.
            state.Position += state.Velocity;

            playingState.KeepWithinBounds(ref state.Position, ref state.Velocity);
        }
    }
}
```

The Player class is brand new. In our original AIDemo, the Player class simply consisted of Position, Velocity, World, and Color. Our new class does not have the World matrix property because we will calculate that when we need it in the DrawModel method, which we will add shortly to our PlayingState.

The Position and Velocity properties are now embedded inside a struct called PlayerState. We did this because we want to use prediction and smoothing in this network game. You know from Chapter 25, "Networking Basics," that we need to store multiple states of our object to determine a guess as to where we should draw the object. For now, we are just storing one state called simulationState. We are treating it just as if we had the properties directly exposed. In fact, we are returning the simulationState's Position and Velocity values in the player's corresponding properties.

We brought over the playerMoveUnit member field from the AIDemo. We refactored code from the AIDemo's Update and UpdatePlayer methods in our new UpdateState method. We first set the player's velocity to a new variable, playerInput. You will see how this vector is populated shortly. We then take our updated velocity and factor in the playerMoveUnit, just like we did at the bottom of the UpdatePlayer method in the AIDemo project. We finish the UpdateState method by adding our velocity to our position and then calling the KeepWithinBounds method, just like we did at the end of the Update method in the AIDemo.

We can now add the KeepWithinBounds method to our PlayingState code:

```
public void KeepWithinBounds(ref Vector3 position, ref Vector3 velocity)
{
    if ((position.X < -OurGame.ArenaSize) || (position.X > OurGame.ArenaSize))
        velocity.X = -velocity.X;
    if ((position.Y < -OurGame.ArenaSize) || (position.Y > OurGame.ArenaSize))
        velocity.Y = -velocity.Y;
    if ((position.Z < -OurGame.ArenaSize) || (position.Z > OurGame.ArenaSize))
        velocity.Z = -velocity.Z;

    position += velocity;
}
```

The KeepWithinBounds method did not change from the original AIDemo. We are simply making sure the position being passed in stays within the arena. We can add the ArenaSize float to our Game1 class:

```
public readonly float ArenaSize = 500;
```

Inside the PlayingState class, we can also add in the DrawModel method we will use to draw both the player and enemy models:

```
public void DrawModel(ref Model m, Camera cam, Color color, Vector3 position)
{
    Matrix world = Matrix.CreateTranslation(position);

    Matrix[] transforms = new Matrix[m.Bones.Count];
    m.CopyAbsoluteBoneTransformsTo(transforms);

    foreach (ModelMesh mesh in m.Meshes)
    {
        foreach (BasicEffect be in mesh.Effects)
```

29

```
    {
        be.EnableDefaultLighting();

        be.AmbientLightColor = Color.Silver.ToVector3();
        be.DiffuseColor = color.ToVector3();
        be.Projection = cam.Projection;
        be.View = cam.View;
        be.World = world * mesh.ParentBone.Transform;
    }

    mesh.Draw();
    }
}
```

The `DrawModel` method is very similar to how it existed in the AIDemo. However, instead of passing in the world matrix, we are passing in a position. Because we know we want to allow multiple viewports to support split-screen gaming, we are also passing in a camera. We are setting our ambient light color to silver and setting a diffuse color on the model to get a little better coloring than we had before.

Back inside of our `Player` class, the `UpdateState` method utilizes a variable called `playerInput`. This variable gets populated in the `HandleInput` method. This method takes in the `playerIndex` from which we should be accepting input. It then sets the `playerInput` vector to the current value of the left thumbstick. The thumbstick returns a value between –1 and 1 on both the X and Y axis. Because the thumbstick only has two dimensions, we provide the Z value 0 in our `playerInput` vector. We have left the check in place to see if we are restricting movement to only along the X and Y axes.

The next section is new. We check the left and right trigger values and set the `CurrentZ` float appropriately. This is utilized by our `PlayingState` code to zoom the camera in and out. We finish the method by normalizing the input and returning the latest values we retrieved from the controller. Thus, we see the `UpdateState` method is simply reading the input from the controller and updating the velocity and position of the player appropriately.

We can create two new methods in our PlayingState.cs file called `UpdateSinglePlayer` and `UpdateEnemyPosition`:

```
private void UpdateSinglePlayer(GameTime gameTime)
{
    Vector3 playerInput = singlePlayer.HandleInput(PlayerIndexInControl.Value);

    float elapsedTime = (float)gameTime.ElapsedGameTime.TotalSeconds;

    playerInput *= elapsedTime;

    singlePlayer.Update(playerInput);
```

```
    for (int i = 0; i < enemies.Length; i++)
    {
        Enemy enemy = enemies[i];

        UpdateEnemyPosition(i, gameTime, elapsedTime, enemy);

        //reset player or enemy if collided
        if ((enemy.Position - singlePlayer.Position).Length() <
            (sphere.Meshes[0].BoundingSphere.Radius * 2))
        {
            if (enemy.State == Enemy.AIState.Attack)
            {
                singlePlayer.ResetPosition();
                singlePlayer.Score -= 50;
            }
            else
            {
                //enemy.Position.X = enemy.Position.Y = 0;
                enemy.Position = new Vector3((i * 50) + 50, (i * 25) - 50, -300);
                singlePlayer.Score += 100;
            }
        }
    }
}

private void UpdateEnemyPosition(int enemyIndex, GameTime gameTime,
    float elapsedTime, Enemy enemy)
{
    switch (enemy.State)
    {
        case Enemy.AIState.Search:
            {
                MoveRandomly(enemyIndex, gameTime);
                break;
            }
        case Enemy.AIState.Attack:
            {
                TrackPlayer(enemyIndex);
                break;
            }
        case Enemy.AIState.Retreat:
            {
                EvadePlayer(enemyIndex);
                break;
            }
```

29

```
    default:
        {
            throw (new ApplicationException("Unknown State: " +
                enemy.State.ToString()));
        }
    }
}

    enemy.Velocity *= elapsedTime;
    enemy.Position += enemy.Velocity;
    KeepWithinBounds(ref enemy.Position, ref enemy.Velocity);
}
```

We will be calling this method from our Update method. The first task we complete is
grabbing the player input from the HandleInput method we just looked at in the Player
object. We then apply the elapsedTime to the value as usual. Next, we call Update on our
Player object, which simply calls the UpdateState method we recently looked at.

At this point we know the player's velocity and position have been updated, and we
know the player is still within the arena walls. The last part of the UpdateSinglePlayer
method loops through all the enemies and processes the appropriate AI state the enemy
is in. UpdateEnemyPosition updates each enemy's velocity and position and makes sure
it stays in the arena. Finally, UpdateSinglePlayer checks to see if the player collided
with any enemies, and depending on the enemy's state the player's score will either
increase or decrease. If the player has captured a fleeing AI enemy, the enemy's position
will be reset randomly. If the player was captured, the player's position will be reset
randomly. Other than the scoring, this is basically the same code we had in the Update
method of the AIDemo.

UpdateSinglePlayer called one of three methods, depending on which state an enemy
was in. We are going to add those methods now and discuss the differences between our
new versions and the original ones created in the AIDemo in Chapter 18. The first
method we can add is the MoveRandomly method:

```
private void MoveRandomly(int enemyIndex, GameTime gameTime)
{
    Enemy enemy = enemies[enemyIndex];

    if (enemy.ChangeDirectionTimer == 0)
        enemy.ChangeDirectionTimer =
            (float)gameTime.TotalGameTime.TotalMilliseconds;

    //has the appropriate amount of time passed?
    if (gameTime.TotalGameTime.TotalMilliseconds >
        enemy.ChangeDirectionTimer + enemy.RandomSeconds * 1000)
    {
        enemy.RandomVelocity = Vector3.Zero;
        enemy.RandomVelocity.X = rand.Next(-1, 2);
```

```
        enemy.RandomVelocity.Y = rand.Next(-1, 2);
        //restrict to 2D?
        if (!RestrictToXY)
            enemy.RandomVelocity.Z = rand.Next(-1, 2);

        enemy.ChangeDirectionTimer = 0;
    }

    enemy.Velocity = enemy.RandomVelocity;

    enemy.Velocity *= moveUnit;

    if (enemy.Health < 5)
        enemy.Color = Color.LightBlue;
    else
        enemy.Color = Color.Pink;

    float distance = 0;
    Vector3 tv = Vector3.Zero;
    if (OurGame.NetworkSession == null)
    {
        tv = singlePlayer.Position - enemy.Position;
        distance = tv.Length();
    }
    else
    {
        //Handle Multiple players
    }

    if (distance < EvadeRadius)
        if (enemy.Health < 5)
            enemy.State = Enemy.AIState.Retreat;

    if (distance < SeekRadius)
        if (enemy.Health >= 5)
            enemy.State = Enemy.AIState.Attack;
}
```

The first thing that is different between the two methods is the parameters we are passing in. Instead of passing in the enemy object itself, we are passing in an index where we will retrieve enemy from our array of enemies. From there, the code is identical until we set the color of the enemy. Originally we just set the enemies to orange when they were moving randomly. In order to improve game play, we now set them to a light color that indicates what they will do once they are close enough to a player. If they are in attack mode when they are close to a player, they are assigned a pink color. If they will flee from the player, they are assigned a light blue color. This helps the gamer know whether or not he or she should stay away from the enemy. Of course, this is optional and can easily be changed so that all enemies are the same color when they are randomly searching for the player.

The final difference between this updated version and the original in the AIDemo is that we are preparing for handling multiple players. For now, when the game is in single-player mode, we simply set the `distance` variable to the distance between the enemy and the `singlePlayer` variable representing the player.

The `TrackPlayer` method is shown next:

```
private void TrackPlayer(int enemyIndex)
{
    Enemy enemy = enemies[enemyIndex];

    Vector3 tv = Vector3.Zero;
    float distance = 0;

    if (OurGame.NetworkSession == null)
    {
        tv = singlePlayer.Position - enemy.Position;
        distance = tv.Length();
    }
    else
    {
        //Handle Multiple Players
    }

    //after all vectors are checked, we need to normalize for velocity
    tv.Normalize();
    enemy.Velocity = tv * moveUnit;

    enemy.Color = Color.Red;

    if (distance > SeekRadius * 1.25f)
        enemy.State = Enemy.AIState.Search;
}
```

Other than preparing for multiple players (via the placeholder), this method functions identically to the original. The next method we can add is the `EvadePlayer` method:

```
private void EvadePlayer(int enemyIndex)
{
    Enemy enemy = enemies[enemyIndex];

    float distance = 0;
    Vector3 tv = Vector3.Zero;
```

```
    if (OurGame.NetworkSession == null)
    {
        tv = enemy.Position - singlePlayer.Position;
        distance = tv.Length();
    }
    else
    {
        //Handle Multiple Players
    }

    //after all vectors are checked, we need to normalize for velocity
    tv.Normalize();
    enemy.Velocity = tv * moveUnit;

    enemy.Color = Color.Navy;

    if (distance > EvadeRadius * 1.25f)
        enemy.State = Enemy.AIState.Search;
}
```

Just like the `TrackPlayer` method, the `EvadePlayer` method functions identically to the original version created in the AIDemo. It now has a placeholder for when we need to add in multiplayer support.

Now we need to create the list of enemies. We can create the following `CreateEnemies` method:

```
private void CreateEnemies()
{
    for (int i = 0; i < MaxEnemies; i++)
    {
        enemies[i] = new Enemy();
        enemies[i].Position = new Vector3((i * 50) + 50, (i * 25) - 50, -300);
        enemies[i].Velocity = Vector3.Zero;
        enemies[i].ChangeDirectionTimer = 0;
        enemies[i].RandomVelocity = Vector3.Left;
        enemies[i].RandomSeconds = (i + 2) / 2;
        enemies[i].State = Enemy.AIState.Search;
        //alternate every other enemy to either attack or evade (based on health)
        if (i % 2 == 0)
            enemies[i].Health = 1;
        else
            enemies[i].Health = 10;
    }
}
```

29

This method is new, but the contents of the method were taken directly from the Initialize method in the AIDemo. The only difference is that we no longer need to set the enemy's World matrix because we are calculating it on the fly in the DrawModel method.

We will actually call the CreateEnemies method inside the StartGame method. Therefore, we need to add the following code to the end of the StartGame method:

```
if (numberOfPlayers == 1)
{
    //Do Game Initialization tasks
    //i.e. Shuffling cards, setting up enemies
    CreateEnemies();
}
else
{
    //Handle Multiplayer
}


SetPresenceInformation();
```

We do not need to modify the SetPresenceInformation method already present in this network game template. However, because we have our own player object complete with its own Score property, we can remove the singlePlayerScore private member field from the PlayingState. We can remove the reference to this variable from the SetupGame method. Finally, we can change the Score property to return singlePlayer.Score.

At the end of the SetupGame method, we can add the following code:

```
if (OurGame.NetworkSession == null) //single player mode
{
    singlePlayer = new Player(Game);
    singlePlayer.Color = Color.Black;
}
else
{
    //Handle Multiplayer
}
```

When we start a new game, we initialize our single player and set its color to black. We have also put in a placeholder in our initialization code for handling multiple players.

Because we know we want to draw our scene twice if we have multiple players on the same machine, we will go ahead and modify the Draw method to handle this now. We should replace the current Draw method provided to us by the network template with the following two methods:

```
public override void Draw(GameTime gameTime)
{
```

```
    GraphicsDevice.Clear(Color.Black);

    DrawScene(gameTime, camera);

    base.Draw(gameTime);
}

private void DrawScene(GameTime gameTime, Camera cam)
{
    OurGame.SpriteBatch.Begin();

    skybox.Draw(cam.View, cam.Projection, Matrix.CreateScale(OurGame.ArenaSize));

    //Draw enemies
    for (int i = 0; i < MaxEnemies; i++)
    {
        Enemy enemy = enemies[i];
        if (enemy != null)
            DrawModel(ref sphere, cam, enemy.Color, enemy.Position);
    }

    if (OurGame.NetworkSession == null)
    {
        //Draw single player
        if (singlePlayer != null)
        {
            SetCameraProperties(cam, singlePlayer);

            DrawModel(ref sphere, cam, singlePlayer.Color, singlePlayer.Position);

            string gamertag = SignedInGamer.SignedInGamers[
                                        PlayerIndexInControl.Value].Gamertag;
            OurGame.SpriteBatch.DrawString(OurGame.Font, gamertag + ": " +
                singlePlayer.Score.ToString(), new Vector2(151, 201),
                Color.Black);
            OurGame.SpriteBatch.DrawString(OurGame.Font, gamertag + ": " +
                singlePlayer.Score.ToString(), new Vector2(150, 200),
                singlePlayer.Color);
        }
    }
    else
    {
        //Handle Multiple Players
    }
    //Show the timer
    string timeText;
```

```
    if (currentTime.Seconds < 0) //show negative total seconds
        timeText = "Time: " + currentTime.TotalSeconds.ToString("00");
    else  //show time in minute : seconds when positive
        timeText = "Time: " + currentTime.Minutes.ToString("0") + ":" +
            currentTime.Seconds.ToString("00");

    timeTextShadowPosition = new Vector2(TitleSafeArea.X, TitleSafeArea.Y +
        OurGame.Font.LineSpacing * 2);
    timeTextPosition = new Vector2(TitleSafeArea.X + 1.0f, TitleSafeArea.Y +
        OurGame.Font.LineSpacing * 2 + 1.0f);

    OurGame.SpriteBatch.DrawString(OurGame.Font, timeText,
        timeTextShadowPosition, Color.Black);
    OurGame.SpriteBatch.DrawString(OurGame.Font, timeText,
        timeTextPosition, Color.Firebrick);

    OurGame.SpriteBatch.End();
}
```

The Draw method is very straightforward. We are clearing our device and then calling the DrawScene method, passing in the game time and the default camera. The DrawScene method starts the sprite batch and then draws the skybox. It then loops through all the enemies and draws each one. Then it checks to see if the game is in single-player mode. If so, it makes sure the single-player object has been initialized already. Once we have a valid player object, we call a new method called SetCameraProperties. We knew when we made the original AIDemo that we were not going to win any awards for the way the camera worked. Although we still will not win any awards, we are going to be modifying the Camera object shortly. After setting the camera properties so it is focused on the player, we then draw the player object on the screen. We then draw the gamer tag along with the score of the player. Finally, we draw the time remaining on the screen before ending the sprite batch.

The SetCameraProperties method is as follows:

```
private void SetCameraProperties(Camera cam, Player player)
{
    cam.Position.X = player.Position.X;
    cam.Position.Y = player.Position.Y + 10;
    cam.Position.Z = player.CurrentZ;

    if (cam.Position.X >= OurGame.ArenaSize - 20)
        cam.Position.X = OurGame.ArenaSize - 20;
    if (cam.Position.X <= -OurGame.ArenaSize + 20)
        cam.Position.X = -OurGame.ArenaSize + 20;

    if (cam.Position.Y >= OurGame.ArenaSize - 20)
        cam.Position.Y = OurGame.ArenaSize - 20;
```

```
    if (cam.Position.Y <= -OurGame.ArenaSize + 20)
        cam.Position.Y = -OurGame.ArenaSize + 20;

    if (cam.Position.Z >= OurGame.ArenaSize - 20)
        cam.Position.Z = OurGame.ArenaSize - 20;
    if (cam.Position.Z <= player.Position.Z + 20)
        cam.Position.Z = player.Position.Z + 20;

    player.CurrentZ = cam.Position.Z;

    cam.Target = player.Position;
}
```

We start the method by setting the camera position based on the player position passed in. We have no offset for the X axis. We have a positive offset of 10 for the Y axis. For the Z axis, we utilize the CurrentZ value associated to the player. This value is populated when the player pulls the left or right trigger. This allows us to zoom in on (or away from) the sphere that represents the player. The next three sets of conditions simply keep the camera from getting too close to the arena edge. If we go too far, the walls will be clipped, and we will lose the illusion of being in a large room. Because we clamp the camera position, we go ahead and reset the CurrentZ zoom factor to the newly clamped value. Finally, we set the camera's target to the player's position. This will cause the camera to always look at the player's sphere. In order for this method to work, we will need to modify the existing Camera object in the XELibrary.

In the Camera.cs class we need to remove the Position property. We then need to rename the cameraPosition private member field to Position. We also need to change the modifier to public. Finally, we need to replace all instances of cameraPosition in Camera.cs to Position.

We do not want to allow the gamer to be able to move the camera. Instead, the camera should follow the player's sphere on the screen. Because we are setting the Target property on the camera, it should force the camera to look at the target. The problem is that our camera class is always overwriting the value of the target vector in its Update method. To correct this, we need to add the following code right after the UpdateInput condition:

```
if (targetSet)
{
    Matrix.CreateLookAt(ref Position, ref cameraTarget, ref cameraUpVector,
        out view);

    base.Update(gameTime);
    return;
}
```

With this code we are bypassing all of the Update method if the target has been set by an outside source. We tell the camera to look at the target passed in instead of determining where to look based on the input read from the controller. We need to create a private boolean variable called `targetSet` that is initialized to false. We then need to modify the `Target` property to set this flag:

```
public Vector3 Target
{
    get { return (cameraTarget); }
    set
    {
        cameraTarget = value;
        targetSet = true;
    }
}
```

We need to load the sphere model and the skybox. We also need to add the following code to the `LoadContent` method:

```
sphere = Content.Load<Model>(@"Models\sphere0");
skybox = Content.Load<Skybox>(@"Skyboxes\skybox2");
```

The sphere0.x and skybox2.tga files can be found in this chapter's folder on the CD. The sphere can be added to the Models folder. The skybox2 texture can be added to the Skyboxes folder. The SkyboxPipeline assembly will need to be referenced inside the Content project. The skybox2 texture will need to have the Content Processor value changed to SkyboxProcessor in the properties window.

In the playing state's `Update` method, we need to call the `UpdateSinglePlayer` method we created earlier. We can replace the code where we set the `currentTime` with the following code:

```
if (OurGame.NetworkSession == null)
    UpdateSinglePlayer(gameTime);


currentTime = currentStopTime.Subtract(DateTime.Now);
if (currentTime.Seconds < 0)
{
    GameManager.ChangeState(OurGame.WonGameState.Value, null);
    currentTime = TimeSpan.Zero;
}
```

If the game is in single-player mode, we call the `UpdateSinglePlayer` method. We also set the `currentTime` just like before. However, now when the timer reaches zero, instead of just keeping the value at zero, we also change the state to the `WonGameState`.

At this point we can compile and run our game. We can start up a single-player game and have the same demo we had running in Chapter 18. It now runs within our Networking framework, complete with scoring and a timer. Whereas before it was a demo, now it really is a game.

Making It Multiplayer

Now we can think about networking. We know we want to send messages to each player for when we capture an enemy and when we are captured. The multiplayer game will still run in a timed mode, unlike our Concentration game from the last chapter. Once the timer expires, the person with the most points wins.

Each of the players needs to know what the other players are doing. We know we shouldn't actually pass the model over the network because that can be looked up locally. In our case, our model is always a sphere, but it could easily be any 3D model. We could have a byte ID (assuming we had fewer than 255 models the player could pick from) and then simply send the ID to the other players so they know which model to load up with the game. That seems pretty obvious, but we can use this same logic and make sure we are not passing any information over the wire that can be determined on each machine.

In our game, each player will have his or her own color. We could pass around the `PackedValue` of `Color`. However, we will use the same logic and have a list of colors available. We only pass around a single byte, and each client can look up the color from a predefined list.

We need to know what input the other players are giving. We can then take the input and do the calculation on each player's object on the client. So we update our position locally and then take the latest information we have for the other players and update them as well by calling their `HandleInput` method, passing in the input we received from the incoming network packets.

We also know that because this is a real-time game, we will need to handle smoothing and prediction because our network packets will be delayed coming over the wire. Therefore, we want to store the state a player is in and compare it to previous and new states to determine where we need to move the player. However, before we implement prediction and smoothing for the game, we need to update our code to handle multiple players.

When we set up the networking template, we simply set the gamer's `Tag` object to the player index value. For a real-time game we will not be storing a list of players. The `SessionLobbyState` needs to be modified to update the `Tag` property correctly. In the `Update` method of the `SessionLobbyState` class, we need to change the condition where we check to see if this machine is the host. We need to replace the condition with the following code:

```
if (OurGame.NetworkSession.IsHost)
{
    if (OurGame.NetworkSession.IsEveryoneReady &&
        OurGame.NetworkSession.SessionState == NetworkSessionState.Lobby)
            OurGame.NetworkSession.StartGame();
}
```

We removed the code that keeps track of an index. We simply call `StartGame` on the network session when everyone is ready. The second place we need to modify the

SessionLobbyState is in the GamerJoinedEventHandler method. We need to replace the first two statements with the following code:

```
Player player = new Player(Game);
player.PlayerIndex = PlayerIndexInControl.Value;
e.Gamer.Tag = player;
```

We create a new player object for the player who just joined the game, and we set the PlayerIndex value so we know which controller we should check for input. We finally set the Tag property to the newly created player object.

Now we can update our Update method in the playing state. The very first condition in the Update method checks to see if the network session is null. We want to create a false portion to that condition to handle when we do have a network session and therefore have a multiplayer (local, system link, or LIVE) game. We need to add the following false condition:

```
else
    UpdateNetworkSession(gameTime);
```

Therefore, when the Update method is called in a multiplayer game, we will call the following UpdateNetworkSession method:

```
private void UpdateNetworkSession(GameTime gameTime)
{
    bool sendPacketThisFrame = false;

    framesSinceLastSend++;
    if (framesSinceLastSend >= framesBetweenPackets)
    {
        sendPacketThisFrame = true;
        framesSinceLastSend = 0;
    }

    //Update our locally controlled player, and
    //send their latest position to everyone else
    foreach (LocalNetworkGamer gamer in OurGame.NetworkSession.LocalGamers)
    {
        UpdateLocalGamer(gamer, gameTime, sendPacketThisFrame);
    }

    //We Do actual sending and receiving of network packets
    try
    {
        OurGame.NetworkSession.Update();
    }
    catch (Exception e)
    {
```

```
        OurGame.MessageDialogState.Message = e.Message;
        OurGame.MessageDialogState.IsError = true;
        GameManager.PushState(OurGame.MessageDialogState.Value,
            PlayerIndexInControl);

        OurGame.NetworkSession.Dispose();
        OurGame.NetworkSession = null;
    }

    //Make sure the session has not ended
    if (OurGame.NetworkSession == null)
        return;

    //Get packets that contain data of remote players
    foreach (LocalNetworkGamer gamer in OurGame.NetworkSession.LocalGamers)
    {
        ReadIncomingPackets(gamer, gameTime);
    }
}
```

The method is basically identical to what we had in the last chapter. The main difference
is that we are pumping the XNA Framework's network session object every frame, but we
are only sending data based on the framesBetweenPackets value. We need to create two
private member fields to help us determine if we should send network data:

```
private int framesBetweenPackets = 6;
private int framesSinceLastSend;
```

The UpdateLocalGamer method contains a lot of the logic that determines which network
messages we need to send. We need to add the following UpdateLocalGamer method to
our playing state:

```
private void UpdateLocalGamer(LocalNetworkGamer gamer, GameTime gameTime,
    bool sendPacketThisFrame)
{
    //Get player from local network gamer
    Player player = gamer.Tag as Player;

    float elapsedTime = (float)gameTime.ElapsedGameTime.TotalSeconds;

    //get player index
    PlayerIndex playerIndex = gamer.SignedInGamer.PlayerIndex;

    Vector3 playerInput = player.HandleInput(playerIndex);

    playerInput *= elapsedTime;
```

29

```
    player.UpdateLocal(playerInput);

    for (int i = 0; i < enemies.Length; i++)
    {
        if (gamer.IsHost)
        {
            //Host Updates the Enemy States
            UpdateEnemy(i, gameTime);

            //if we are to send a packet, do so
            if (sendPacketThisFrame)
            {
                SendEnemyData(i, gamer);
            }
        }

        //Only check collisions against local gamers
        //even though as the host we are processing the enemies
        //we are not specifying when we think an enemy collided with someone else
        //it is up to the individual players to let us know when that happens
        CheckForCollisions(i, gamer);
    }

    // Periodically send our state to everyone in the session.
    if (sendPacketThisFrame)
    {
        packetWriter.Write((byte)MessageType.PlayerMove);
        player.WriteNetworkPacket(packetWriter, gameTime);
        gamer.SendData(packetWriter, SendDataOptions.InOrder);
    }
}
```

We extract the player object from the gamers' Tag property. We then retrieve the correct player index for this signed-in gamer so we know from which controller we should check for input. We pass the player index into the HandleInput method of the player object. We have the same logic in place we used in the UpdateSinglePlayer method. However, to try and make the code clearer, instead of simply calling player.Update, we are calling player.UpdateLocal. We need to rename the Update method in our Player class to UpdateLocal. And we need to make sure we change it in the UpdateSinglePlayer method as well.

After updating the local player, we loop through all the enemies. If the local player is the host, we call UpdateEnemy on each enemy. We then check to see if we should send any network packets. If so, we call SendEnemyData. We will see both of these methods shortly. Regardless of whether or not the local player is the host, we call the CheckForCollision method to see if this local gamer collided with the enemy. The host maintains all the enemies' state and passes it around, but each individual gamer determines if he or she has collided with an enemy.

The last task the UpdateLocalGamer method performs is checking to see if packets should be sent. If packets should be sent, the method creates a PlayerMove message by calling a WriteNetworkPacket method on the player object. The player object will write and read different pieces of information to handle movement. We will review that method in a moment.

The UpdateEnemy method is shown here:

```
private void UpdateEnemy(int enemyIndex, GameTime gameTime)
{
    //loop through all gamers to determine what we should do
    float elapsedTime = (float)gameTime.ElapsedGameTime.TotalSeconds;

    Enemy enemy = enemies[enemyIndex];

    UpdateEnemyPosition(enemyIndex, gameTime, elapsedTime, enemy);
}
```

We already have the code for the UpdateEnemyPosition because we called the method from the UpdateSinglePlayer method. It simply checks the state of the enemy and determines the correct velocity and position, making sure the enemy stays within the walls of the arena.

The CheckForCollisions method is as follows:

```
private void CheckForCollisions(int enemyIndex, LocalNetworkGamer gamer)
{
    Enemy enemy = enemies[enemyIndex];
    //Enemy initialized yet?
    if (enemy == null)
        return;

    Player player = gamer.Tag as Player;

    //reset player or enemy if collided
    if ((enemy.Position - player.Position).Length() <
        (sphere.Meshes[0].BoundingSphere.Radius * 2))
    {
        if (enemy.State == Enemy.AIState.Attack)
        {
            player.ResetPosition();
            player.Score -= 50;
```

```
        //Send player position
        //send player score
        packetWriter.Write((byte)MessageType.WasCaptured);
        packetWriter.Write(player.Score);
        packetWriter.Write(player.Position);

        gamer.SendData(packetWriter, SendDataOptions.ReliableInOrder);
    }
    else
    {
        enemy.Position = new Vector3(-rand.Next(300), -rand.Next(300), -300);
        player.Score += 100;

        //send enemy position
        //send player score
        packetWriter.Write((byte)MessageType.CapturedEnemy);
        packetWriter.Write(player.Score);
        packetWriter.Write((byte)enemyIndex);
        packetWriter.Write(enemy.Position);

        gamer.SendData(packetWriter, SendDataOptions.ReliableInOrder);
    }
  }
}
```

We retrieve the player object from the gamer Tag property, and then we check to see if the player has collided with the enemy. If a collision occurred, we have the same logic we put in place for single-player mode, but this time we also send out network packets to let everyone else know what happened.

We can add in the packetWriter and packetReader private member fields to our playing state:

```
private PacketWriter packetWriter = new PacketWriter();
private PacketReader packetReader = new PacketReader();
```

UpdateLocalGamer calls the following SendEnemyData method:

```
private void SendEnemyData(int enemyIndex, LocalNetworkGamer gamer)
{
    Enemy enemy = enemies[enemyIndex];
    packetWriter.Write((byte)MessageType.EnemyState);

    packetWriter.Write((byte)enemyIndex); //set index

    packetWriter.Write((byte)enemy.State);
    packetWriter.Write(enemy.Position);
```

```
packetWriter.Write(enemy.Velocity);
packetWriter.Write((byte)enemy.Health);

gamer.SendData(packetWriter, SendDataOptions.InOrder);
}
```

The method is straightforward—it takes in the enemy index and retrieves the enemy from the array. It then creates a EnemyState message and populates the packet with the enemy's index, state, position, velocity, and health. The code to retrieve these values can be found in the ReadEnemyData method:

```
private Enemy ReadEnemyData(out byte enemyIndex)
{
    enemyIndex = packetReader.ReadByte();
    Enemy enemy = enemies[enemyIndex]; //read index
    if (enemy == null)
        enemy = new Enemy();

    enemy.State = (Enemy.AIState)packetReader.ReadByte();
    enemy.Position = packetReader.ReadVector3();
    enemy.Velocity = packetReader.ReadVector3();
    enemy.Health = packetReader.ReadByte();

    //No need to pass around color because we know what color
    //we should be based on the state we are in
    if (enemy.State == Enemy.AIState.Search)
    {
        if (enemy.Health < 5)
            enemy.Color = Color.LightBlue;
        else
            enemy.Color = Color.Pink;
    }
    else if (enemy.State == Enemy.AIState.Attack)
        enemy.Color = Color.Red;
    else if (enemy.State == Enemy.AIState.Retreat)
        enemy.Color = Color.Blue;
    else
        enemy.Color = Color.Black; //shouldn't get here

    return (enemy);
}
```

Besides reading in all the values in the packet, this method also determines what the color of the enemy should be based on the health passed in. It also will create an instance of the enemy if one does not already exist.

The following MessageType enum needs to be added to our PlayingState class:

```
private enum MessageType : byte { RequestToJoinInProgressGame, Color,
    JoinedInProgressGame, PlayerMove, EnemyState, CapturedEnemy, WasCaptured };
```

UpdateLocalGamer calls the player's WriteNetworkPacket method:

```
public void WriteNetworkPacket(PacketWriter packetWriter, GameTime gameTime)
{
    // Send our current time.
    packetWriter.Write((float)gameTime.TotalGameTime.TotalSeconds);

    // Send the current state of the player.
    packetWriter.Write(simulationState.Position);
    packetWriter.Write(simulationState.Velocity);
    packetWriter.Write(Score);

    // Also send our current inputs. These can be used to more accurately
    // predict how the player is likely to move in the future.
    packetWriter.Write(playerInput);
}
```

The player object writes out the total seconds of the game. This will be used later when we dig into prediction and smoothing. We then write out the position of the player as well as the velocity and score. Finally, we write out the input vector we obtained from reading the game pad.

We put in several placeholders to handle multiplayer game play. The first placeholder appears in the false condition inside the StartGame method. We need to add the following code:

```
if (OurGame.NetworkSession.IsHost)
    CreateEnemies();
```

If we have more than one player in this game, we check to see if this machine is the host machine. If it is, we call CreateEnemies to create and populate the enemies array.

The next placeholder appears in our SetupGame method. If our network session is not null, we need to add the following code inside the false part of the condition of the SetupGame method:

```
foreach (NetworkGamer gamer in OurGame.NetworkSession.AllGamers)
{
    Player player = new Player(Game);

    if (gamer.IsLocal)
        player.PlayerIndex = ((LocalNetworkGamer)gamer).SignedInGamer.PlayerIndex;

    gamer.Tag = player;
}
```

```
//Find host and tell players their color
if (OurGame.NetworkSession.IsHost)
{
    foreach (NetworkGamer gamer in OurGame.NetworkSession.AllGamers)
    {
        Player player = gamer.Tag as Player;

        byte assignedColorIndex = SetPlayerColor(player, gamer);

        packetWriter.Write((byte)MessageType.Color);
        packetWriter.Write(gamer.Id);
        packetWriter.Write(assignedColorIndex);

        ((LocalNetworkGamer)OurGame.NetworkSession.Host).SendData(
            packetWriter, SendDataOptions.Reliable);
    }
}
```

We loop through all the gamers, initializing the new player. If the gamer is local, we also set the correct controller index. Because we require the gamer to be signed in, we get the value from the SignedInGamer property on the gamer. We then set the Tag property with the newly created player object.

Then we check to see if this machine is the host. If so, we loop through all the gamers in the network session. We retrieve each player from the gamer.Tag property. We then make a call to SetPlayerColor to determine which color this player should be. Finally, we write out the MessageType.Color message, which includes the gamer's ID and the color we assigned to the player.

The SetPlayerColor method is shown here:

```
private byte SetPlayerColor(Player player, NetworkGamer gamer)
{
    //color already set?
    if (colors.ContainsKey(gamer.Id))
    {
        Color c = colors[gamer.Id];

        byte index = GetIndexFromColor(c);

        return (index);
    }

    Color color;

    do
```

29

```
        {
            color = defaultColors[(byte)++colorIndex];

            if (colorIndex > 3)
                colorIndex = 0;

        } while (colors.ContainsValue(color));

        player.Color = color;

        colors.Add(gamer.Id, player.Color);

        return ((byte)colorIndex);
    }
```

Before we dig into the SetPlayerColor method, we need to create the colors dictionary, a variable to hold our current index, and a list of default colors we can assign the players. We can create these private member fields in our playing game state:

```
private Dictionary<byte, Color> colors;
private int colorIndex = 0;
private Color[] defaultColors;
```

We also need to initialize them in our SetupGame method:

```
colorIndex = 0;
colors = new Dictionary<byte, Color>(4);

defaultColors = new Color[4];
defaultColors[0] = Color.Green;
defaultColors[1] = Color.Purple;
defaultColors[2] = Color.OliveDrab;
defaultColors[3] = Color.Black;
```

We always initialize the current color index to 0. We clear out the color dictionary as well. Finally, we set the default colors our players' spheres can be. Because there are a maximum of four players, we only create four default colors.

In the SetPlayerColor method, we check the colors dictionary to see if the gamer passed in is already in the collection. If he or she is already in the collection, we return the player's color by making a call to the GetIndexFromColor method:

```
private byte GetIndexFromColor(Color c)
{
    for (byte i = 0; i < defaultColors.Length; i++)
    {
        if (defaultColors[i] == c)
            return (i);
```

```
    }

    throw new ApplicationException("Color " + c.ToString() +
        " is not a valid default color.");
}
```

The `GetIndexFromColor` method retrieves a known index of the color passed in. Instead of passing around a `PackedValue`, which is four bytes, we are going to pass around a single-byte index.

Back in our `SetPlayerColor` method, we continue to access the `defaultColors` array until we find a color that is not already associated with a gamer. We then assign that color to the player and store the color and the gamer in the colors dictionary. We also return the color index that was assigned to the player.

The `UpdateNetworkSession` method calls the `ReadIncomingPackets` method. The code for the method is shown here:

```
private void ReadIncomingPackets(LocalNetworkGamer gamer, GameTime gameTime)
{
    while (gamer.IsDataAvailable)
    {
        NetworkGamer sender;
        gamer.ReceiveData(packetReader, out sender);

        //Ignore packets sent by local gamers
        //since we already know their state
        if (sender.IsLocal)
            continue;

        //Get up the player index
        Player player = gamer.Tag as Player;

        //Determine the type of packet this is
        byte header = packetReader.ReadByte();

        if (header == (byte)MessageType.RequestToJoinInProgressGame)
        { //Sent by person joining game in progress
            if (gamer.IsHost)
            {
                //Set color for player that just joined (sender of this message)
                Player p;

                packetWriter.Write((byte)MessageType.JoinedInProgressGame);

                //pass in number of ticks left in the game
                packetWriter.Write(currentTime.Ticks);
```

```
            //Now write all the player's colors
            foreach (NetworkGamer g in OurGame.NetworkSession.AllGamers)
            {
                packetWriter.Write(g.Id);
                p = g.Tag as Player;

                if (p.Color == Color.TransparentBlack)
                    SetPlayerColor(p, g);

                packetWriter.Write(GetIndexFromColor(p.Color));
            }

            gamer.SendData(packetWriter, SendDataOptions.Reliable, sender);

            //Time sensitive info - send now.
            OurGame.NetworkSession.Update();
        }
    }
    else if (header == (byte)MessageType.JoinedInProgressGame)
    {   //received by person joining game in progress

        //retrieve amount of time left in play
        //read in number of ticks left in the game
        currentTime = new TimeSpan(packetReader.ReadInt64());
        //calculate our stop time based on how much time is left
        //we do not pass this in since different machines can have
        //different date times. (Not just time zones, but actually
        //have a few seconds or minutes difference)
        currentStopTime = DateTime.Now.Add(currentTime);

        //Set each player's color
        //loops through each enemy in the packet
        while (packetReader.Position < packetReader.Length)
        {
            NetworkGamer g = OurGame.NetworkSession.FindGamerById(
                                                packetReader.ReadByte());
            Player p = g.Tag as Player;
            p.Color = defaultColors[packetReader.ReadByte()];
        }
    }
    //Add in other conditions for Game specific MessageTypes
    else if (header == (byte)MessageType.EnemyState)
    {
        byte enemyIndex;
```

```
        //loops through each enemy in the packet
        while (packetReader.Position < packetReader.Length)
        {
            //Read this enemy's info
            Enemy enemy = ReadEnemyData(out enemyIndex);

            //see if we collided with this enemy
            CheckForCollisions(enemyIndex, gamer);

            //store the enemy in our list
            enemies[enemyIndex] = enemy;
        }
    }
    else if (header == (byte)MessageType.Color)
    {
        NetworkGamer g = OurGame.NetworkSession.FindGamerById(
                                            packetReader.ReadByte());
        Player p = g.Tag as Player;
        p.Color = defaultColors[packetReader.ReadByte()];
    }
    else if (header == (byte)MessageType.PlayerMove)
    {
        //The player object we want to update is the sender
        player = sender.Tag as Player;

        player.ReadNetworkPacket(packetReader, gameTime);
    }
    else if (header == (byte)MessageType.CapturedEnemy)
    {
        //This player just told us they captured an enemy
        player = sender.Tag as Player;

        player.Score = packetReader.ReadInt32();
        byte enemyIndex = packetReader.ReadByte();
        enemies[enemyIndex].Position = packetReader.ReadVector3();
    }
    else if (header == (byte)MessageType.WasCaptured)
    {
        //This player just told us they were captured
        player = sender.Tag as Player;

        player.Score = packetReader.ReadInt32();
        player.SetPosition(packetReader.ReadVector3());
    }
    }
}
```

29

The first message in the ReadIncomingPackets method is the RequestToJoinInProgressGame message type. Remember this is the message that is generated when a gamer joins a game that is in progress. The player who wants to join the game is the one who sends this message. Everyone except the host ignores the request. The host retrieves the player object from the sender's (the gamer wanting to join the game) Tag property. The host then generates its own network message that is sent directly to the player who joined. This message includes the current time left in the game (in ticks). The message also includes every gamer ID along with his or her associated color. Because the packet contains time-sensitive information, the Update method on the network session is called immediately. Before the color is written to the message, we make sure the player actually has a color assigned. We check to see if the default value of TransparentBlack is still associated with the color of the player. If it is, we call SetPlayerColor to get the next available color and assign it to the new player.

The second message is JoinedInProgressGame. This is the message the host just sent in the previous paragraph. The player who just joined the in-progress game receives this message and extracts out the remaining amount of time in the game. The player then calculates his or her local stop time based on how much time is left. This way, if there are a few seconds difference between the two machine clocks, there is no issue. It also avoids issues with time zones and daylight savings time. Finally, each remaining byte is read from the packet, and each player is assigned the color passed in from the host.

While we are discussing joining an in-progress game, we need to write the code that tells us a player has just joined. The SessionLobbyState calls the PlayingState.JoinInProgress method. We have two placeholders in this method to handle when a local player joins as well as when a remote player joins. We do not care if a remote player joins, but we do care when a local player has joined because we need to kick off the RequestToJoinInProgressGame message. We need to add the following code in place of the Handle local player joining placeholder inside the JoinInProgressGame method:

```
Player player = gamer.Tag as Player;
packetWriter.Write((byte)MessageType.RequestToJoinInProgressGame);
((LocalNetworkGamer)gamer).SendData(packetWriter, SendDataOptions.Reliable);
```

The false part of the condition that contains the remote player joining placeholder can be removed altogether because we do not need to do any special processing for a remote player joining our game.

The next message in the ReadIncomingPackets method is the EnemyState message. As long as data is present, we iterate through the packet, retrieving the enemy index and then checking for a collision between the gamer and the enemy associated to that index. We then store the enemy in our local list.

The next message is MessageType.Color, which tells us the color of a particular gamer. This gets sent by the SetupGame method. Because the gamer ID is the first byte in the packet, we call FindGamerById to retrieve the correct gamer. From there, we get the player object and finally set the player's color by passing in the index we read from the packet into the defaultColors array.

The PlayerMove message is populated by the UpdateLocalGamer method. This is the message we receive that constantly updates the player's positions in the world. We obtain the player object from the sender's Tag property. Once we had the player object, we called the player's ReadNetworkPacket method. The ReadNetworkPacket method on the Player object is shown next:

```
public void ReadNetworkPacket(PacketReader packetReader,
                              GameTime gameTime)
{
    // Read what time this packet was sent.
    float packetSendTime = packetReader.ReadSingle();

    // Read simulation state from the network packet.
    simulationState.Position = packetReader.ReadVector3();
    simulationState.Velocity = packetReader.ReadVector3();
    Score = packetReader.ReadInt32();

    // Read remote inputs from the network packet.
    playerInput = packetReader.ReadVector3();
}
```

As expected (based on what the WriteNetworkPacket method we looked at earlier did), the reader method extracts the total seconds value and the position, velocity, and score. Finally, it retrieves the playerInput vector. When we add in prediction and smoothing, we will be modifying this method.

The last two messages we read in the ReadIncomingPackets method are the CapturedEnemy and WasCaptured messages. Each reads in the player's score. The CapturedEnemy condition also reads in the new position of the enemy, whereas the WasCaptured condition reads in the new position of the player.

We have not actually drawn the player sphere on the screen when in multiplayer mode. We need to add the following code under the Handle Multiple Players placeholder in the DrawScene method:

```
int y = 0;
//draw all players
foreach (NetworkGamer gamer in OurGame.NetworkSession.AllGamers)
{
    Player player = gamer.Tag as Player;

    // Draw the player.
```

29

```
   if (gamer.IsLocal)
     if (((LocalNetworkGamer)gamer).SignedInGamer.PlayerIndex == cam.PlayerIndex)
       SetCameraProperties(cam, player);

   DrawModel(ref sphere, cam, player.Color, player.Position);

   OurGame.SpriteBatch.DrawString(OurGame.Font, gamer.Gamertag + ": " +
       player.Score.ToString(), new Vector2(151, 201 + (y * 60)), Color.Black);
   OurGame.SpriteBatch.DrawString(OurGame.Font, gamer.Gamertag + ": " +
       player.Score.ToString(), new Vector2(150, 200 + (y * 60)), player.Color);
   y++;
}
```

We are simply iterating through all the gamers; if the current gamer is local and the player index associated with the camera matches the player index of the gamer we are currently on, we call the SetCameraProperties method. Regardless of whether or not this gamer is local, we actually draw the model, passing in the appropriate camera, color, and position. Finally, we draw the player's gamer tag along with his or her score on the screen in a vertical list.

If we currently run our game and start a system link network game, we would see all the players nicely displayed. However, we would briefly see the enemies, which would then disappear because we have not populated the three core enemy methods for a multiplayer game. We will do that now by starting with the MoveRandomly method. We need to add the following code in the condition where the Handle Multiple Players placeholder appears:

```
Vector3 closestTrackingVector = Vector3.Zero;
foreach (NetworkGamer g in OurGame.NetworkSession.AllGamers)
{
    Player player = g.Tag as Player;

    tv = player.Position - enemy.Position;

    if (closestTrackingVector == Vector3.Zero)
        closestTrackingVector = tv;
    else
    {
        //may be backwards? need to check
        if (tv.Length() < closestTrackingVector.Length())
            closestTrackingVector = tv;
    }
}

tv = closestTrackingVector;
distance = tv.Length();
```

When the game is in single-player mode, we assign our tracking vector (tv) to the singlePlayer position minus the enemy position. We then set the distance to the length of this vector. To save some page flipping, here is the code snippet for the single-player mode:

```
tv = singlePlayer.Position - enemy.Position;
distance = tv.Length();
```

At the end of the method we simply check to see if the distance is less than the seek or evade radius. If so, the enemy changes it's AI state because it can now "see" the player.

We want to do the same thing with the multiplayer version, except we have to take into account that we can have more than one player close by. Therefore, we initialize a tracking vector called closestTrackingVector. We then loop through all our gamers and check their positions, storing each one in the tracking vector variable (tv) just like we did in the single-player mode. We then check to see which vector length is smaller. If the newly calculated tracking vector is smaller than the current closest tracking vector, we reset the closest tracking vector to the new tracking vector. This way, by the time we are done iterating through all the gamers, the closest tracking vector will be just that—the vector that is closest to the enemy. We set the tracking vector variable to be the closestTrackingVector and set the distance variable to be the length of that vector. This way, the logic we already have in place for the single-player game will continue to function as expected.

Next, we look at the TrackPlayer method. We insert the following code under the Handle Multiple Players placeholder:

```
Vector3 closestTrackingVector = Vector3.Zero;
foreach (NetworkGamer g in OurGame.NetworkSession.AllGamers)
{
    Player player = g.Tag as Player;

    tv = player.Position - enemy.Position;

    if (closestTrackingVector == Vector3.Zero)
        closestTrackingVector = tv;
    else
    {
        //may be backwards? need to check
        if (tv.Length() < closestTrackingVector.Length())
            closestTrackingVector = tv;
    }
}

tv = closestTrackingVector;
distance = tv.Length();
```

29

This code is identical to the code we just added to the `MoveRandomly` method. The exact same logic applies. The final method we need to update is the `EvadePlayer` method. We need to add the following code under the `Handle Multiple Players` placeholder:

```
Vector3 closestTrackingVector = Vector3.Zero;
foreach (NetworkGamer g in OurGame.NetworkSession.AllGamers)
{
    Player player = g.Tag as Player;

    tv = enemy.Position - player.Position;

    if (closestTrackingVector == Vector3.Zero)
        closestTrackingVector = tv;
    else
    {
        if (tv.Length() < closestTrackingVector.Length())
            closestTrackingVector = tv;
    }

}
tv = closestTrackingVector;
distance = tv.Length();
```

You can see this is also very similar. The only difference is that we are subtracting the player position from the enemy position instead of the other way around. The overall logic is identical. Now when we have multiple players near an enemy, they will track the one that is closest to them.

Now when we run the game we not only see the enemies, but they are tracking all the players as expected.

If we complete the game in multiplayer mode, we are greeted with an error. The `HighScoresState` is trying to call the `Score` property of the `PlayingState`. However, because this is a multiplayer game, the `singlePlayer` variable was never set, and we receive a null reference exception. To fix this, we need to update the `HighScoresState` just like we did in the last chapter.

Currently, the high scores state determines whether or not the high scores should be displayed. However, it does not take into account that the high scores shouldn't be displayed when a multiplayer game finishes. In the `StateChanged` method of the `HighScoresState` class, we need to add the following code inside the condition that checks whether the current state is `HighScoresState`:

```
//If we have a network session then
//we don't need to do anything with a high score
if (OurGame.NetworkSession != null)
{
    GameManager.PopState();
```

```
    return;
}
```

As soon as we come into the state, we check to see if the network session is not null. If it is not null, we pop `HighScoresState` off the stack and then return out of the method.

With the Concentration game we made in the last chapter, we did not have to worry about two different views of our cards for the different players when they were on the same local machine. For this game we definitely need to provide two different viewports for both players on the same machine. We are only allowing a maximum of two local players, but we could allow up to four local players. If we did this, we would want to modify the multiple viewport code we are able to create to accommodate four views instead of just two.

To start, we need to store our general full-screen viewport. In our Game1.cs code file we can create a new public variable:

```
public Viewport FullscreenViewport;
```

Then inside the `ChaseAndEvade` constructor we can add in the following statements right after we set the preferred backbuffer width and height:

```
graphics.ApplyChanges();
FullscreenViewport = GraphicsDevice.Viewport;
```

Then at the very top of our `Draw` method we can make sure our graphics device viewport is always set to full screen by adding the following line:

```
GraphicsDevice.Viewport = FullscreenViewport;
```

Now in our `PlayingState` we can actually create the split-screen viewports. We need to add the following private member fields:

```
//Local Multiplayer
private Viewport leftViewport;
private Viewport rightViewport;
private Camera camera2;
```

We will initialize these fields in our `StateChanged` method. We need to add the following code to the end of the false condition inside the `StateChanged` method:

```
if (camera2 != null)
{
    Game.Components.Remove(camera2);
    camera2 = null;
}

if (OurGame.NetworkSession != null)
{
```

29

```
if (OurGame.NetworkSession.LocalGamers.Count > 1)
{
    leftViewport = OurGame.FullscreenViewport;
    rightViewport = OurGame.FullscreenViewport;

    leftViewport.Width = leftViewport.Width / 2;

    rightViewport.X = leftViewport.Width + 1;
    rightViewport.Width = (rightViewport.Width / 2) - 1;

    graphicsDevice.Viewport = leftViewport;
    camera.Viewport = leftViewport;
    camera.PlayerIndex = SignedInGamer.SignedInGamers[0].PlayerIndex;

    camera2 = new Camera(Game);
    graphicsDevice.Viewport = rightViewport;
    camera2.Viewport = rightViewport;
    camera2.Position = camera.Position;
    camera2.Orientation = camera.Orientation;
    camera2.PlayerIndex = SignedInGamer.SignedInGamers[1].PlayerIndex;
    Game.Components.Add(camera2);
}
```

The first thing we check is whether or not the second camera is initialized. If it is already initialized, we remove it from our game components and set it to null. In the second condition we are simply checking for a multiplayer game by seeing whether the network session is not null. If we are in a multiplayer game, we check to see how many local gamers we have playing. If we have more than one local player, we know we need to split the screen. We are splitting the screen with a vertical bar, so one player will play on the left side of the screen while the other player will play on the right side of the screen.

TIP

If we wanted to have four players, we could modify our code to handle more than just the left and right viewports. We could create `topleft`, `topright`, `bottomleft`, and `bottomright`. If only three people join the game, we could simply black out one of the viewports. Typically, games will black out the bottom-right viewport.

We first initialize both the left and right viewports with our full-screen viewport information. We then cut the left viewport width in half. We slide the right viewport over by modifying its X property, and we also cut the width in half. We set the default camera's viewport to be the left viewport after setting the graphics device viewport. This is needed because the `Camera` class is setting its projection based on the graphics device viewport. We also set the first camera's index to the first player signed in.

Next, we initialize the second camera and set the graphics device viewport. We also set the second camera's position, orientation, and player index values. We then add the second camera to our game component collection.

To actually draw to both viewports, we need to add the following code right after we clear the device in the Draw method:

```
if ((OurGame.NetworkSession != null) &&
    (OurGame.NetworkSession.LocalGamers.Count > 1))
{
    GraphicsDevice.Viewport = camera2.Viewport;
    DrawScene(gameTime, camera2);

    //prepare viewport for main camera
    GraphicsDevice.Viewport = camera.Viewport;
}
```

As long as we are in a multiplayer mode and have more than one local gamer, we first set our graphics device viewport to match our second camera's viewport. We then draw the scene, passing in the second camera. We then set the graphics device viewport to the original camera's viewport.

While we are in the Draw method, we need to reset the graphics device viewport to be full screen in case another state is being drawn over top of the playing state. We need to add the following code right before we call base.Draw in our Draw method:

```
GraphicsDevice.Viewport = OurGame.FullscreenViewport;
```

Now we can have multiple players on the same machine. In the next section, we will implement prediction and smoothing for the other players in the game.

Prediction and Smoothing

In this last section of the chapter, we are going to update the code to handle prediction of the other players as well as smoothing. We discussed these concepts in Chapter 25, and now we are going to put them into practice.

We need to add in two more states to keep track of:

```
private PlayerState previousState;
private PlayerState displayState;
```

We need to initialize all the states to the same value in our Player constructor:

```
previousState = displayState = simulationState;
```

Both the Position and Velocity properties in the Player class should return the displayState values instead of the simulationState values. Because local gamers do not need prediction or smoothing, we can simply copy the simulation state directly into the display state at the end of our UpdateLocal method:

```
displayState = simulationState;
```

However, for remote players, we do need to apply our prediction algorithms as well as smooth out the movements of those players. The ReadNetworkPacket method needs to have the signature changed. A new TimeSpan parameter called latency needs to be added:

```
public void ReadNetworkPacket(PacketReader packetReader,
                              GameTime gameTime, TimeSpan latency)
```

Then, to apply smoothing, we need to add the following code to the beginning of the ReadNetworkPacket method:

```
previousState = displayState;
currentSmoothing = 1;
```

The currentSmoothing variable is a private float that can be added to the Player class. It is used to interpolate the displayState from the previousState toward the simulationState. At the end of the ReadNetworkPacket method, we need to add the following line of code:

```
ApplyPrediction(gameTime, latency, packetSendTime);
```

As the name implies, the following method will actually apply the prediction algorithm to the Player object:

```
private void ApplyPrediction(GameTime gameTime, TimeSpan latency,
    float packetSendTime)
{
    float localTime = (float)gameTime.TotalGameTime.TotalSeconds;

    float timeDelta = localTime - packetSendTime;

    // Maintain a rolling average of time deltas from the last 100 packets.
    clockDelta.AddValue(timeDelta);

    float timeDeviation = timeDelta - clockDelta.AverageValue;

    latency += TimeSpan.FromSeconds(timeDeviation);

    TimeSpan oneFrame = TimeSpan.FromSeconds(1.0 / 60.0);

    // Apply prediction by updating our simulation state however
    // many times is necessary to catch up to the current time.
    while (latency >= oneFrame)
    {
```

```
        UpdateState(ref simulationState);

        latency -= oneFrame;
    }
}
```

The first two lines determine the difference between the current local time and the remote time the packet was sent. The difference is stored in `timeDelta`. This time difference is added in the `clockDelta` collection. The collection is a special type we will create shortly. It will store the values and have a special method that returns the average of all the time deltas stored. The next statement stores the difference between the `timeDelta` and the average value of the added time deltas in the `timeDeviation` variable.

The `timeDeviation` value is then added to the latency value that was passed in. We then check to see if the latency is greater than or equal to one frame. We need to declare the following private member field:

```
TimeSpan oneFrame = TimeSpan.FromSeconds(1.0 / 60.0);
```

One frame is one-sixtieth of a second. While the latency is greater than or equal to the time of one frame, we continually call the `UpdateState` method, passing in our `simulationState`. The `simulationState` is our true state. Before we started the journey of adding in smoothing and prediction, our player object only had the simulation state. After we update our simulation state, we subtract the `oneFrame` amount from the latency amount so we can exit the `while` loop when we are caught up.

The `clockDelta` member field is of the type `RollingAverage`. `RollingAverage` is a class that Microsoft created in its own Network Prediction sample. The code in this section is based on that sample and is distributed in source code form under the Microsoft Permissive License (Ms-PL). The license is included on the CD in this chapter's folder. The code for the RollingAverage.cs file can be seen in Listing 29.3.

LISTING 29.3   RollingAverage.cs

```
private class RollingAverage
{
    float[] sampleValues;
    int sampleCount;
    float valueSum;

    int currentPosition;

    public RollingAverage(int sampleCount)
    {
        sampleValues = new float[sampleCount];
    }

    public void AddValue(float newValue)
```

```
    {
        valueSum -= sampleValues[currentPosition];
        valueSum += newValue;

        sampleValues[currentPosition] = newValue;

        currentPosition++;

        if (currentPosition > sampleCount)
            sampleCount = currentPosition;

        if (currentPosition >= sampleValues.Length)
        {
            currentPosition = 0;

            valueSum = 0;

            foreach (float value in sampleValues)
            {
                valueSum += value;
            }
        }
    }

    public float AverageValue
    {
        get
        {
            if (sampleCount == 0)
                return 0;

            return valueSum / sampleCount;
        }
    }
}
}
```

To keep the listing short, the comments have been removed. The file on the CD remains unaffected. The purpose of this class is to keep track of a certain number of values and provide an average on those values when asked. That really is the extent of it. To accomplish this, a float array, the number of values stored (sampleCount), the value sum, and the current position of the array are declared at the beginning of the class. The constructor takes in the number of samples we will store in our collection. We can actually create our clockDelta private member field back in the Player class now. We want to store 100 samples of time differences between the local machine and the remote machine that sent the packet:

```
private RollingAverage clockDelta = new RollingAverage(100);
```

The RollingAverage class has only one method—it allows us to add the value to the array the constructor just initialized. In order to keep from having to loop through all the entries in the array to keep the valueSum up to date, it simply deducts the current value we are replacing from the valueSum before adding in the new value. This is a nice little optimization. It increments the current position and checks to see if the position is greater than the number of samples we have stored. This is important when we calculate the average if we have not filled up the samples array. The last check the AddValue method does is to determine whether the current position is greater than or equal to the size of our samples array. If it is, the method resets the position to 0 so the next value added will overwrite the first position. It could end there, but because of rounding errors that could occur over time with the shortcut taken earlier, a full recalculation of the samples is done here by zeroing out the valueSum variable and iterating through all the sample values, adding each one to the valueSum.

The last piece of the RollingAverage class is the AverageValue property. It first checks to make sure some samples exist so it does not get a divide-by-zero error. It calculates the average by quickly dividing the sum of the samples by the value of the samples.

Because we changed the signature of the ReadNetworkPacket method of the Player class, we need to modify the ReadIncomingPackets method in the PlayingState class. Inside the condition where we check to see if the message type is PlayerMove, we need to calculate the latency by dividing the number of ticks the roundtrip took to receive this message from the sender:

```
TimeSpan latency = OurGame.NetworkSession.SimulatedLatency +
    TimeSpan.FromTicks(sender.RoundtripTime.Ticks / 2);
```

We also make sure we take into account the latency we are simulating, if any. This way, when we play a system link game and modify our simulation latency and packet loss values in the main game class, we can correctly calculate our prediction algorithms. We need to actually pass our newly calculated latency value into the player.ReadNetworkPacket method.

At the very bottom of UpdateNetwork inside the PlayingState class, we need to add the following code:

```
foreach (NetworkGamer gamer in OurGame.NetworkSession.RemoteGamers)
{
    Player player = gamer.Tag as Player;

    player.UpdateRemote(framesBetweenPackets);
}
```

This code iterates through all the remote players in the game and calls the UpdateRemote method for each of them, passing in the framesBetweenPackets variable, which signifies we are only sending network data every six frames (or 10 times a second).

29

Here's the code for the UpdateRemote method we need to add to the Player class:

```
public void UpdateRemote(int framesBetweenPackets)
{
    float smoothingDecay = 1.0f / framesBetweenPackets;

    currentSmoothing -= smoothingDecay;

    if (currentSmoothing < 0)
        currentSmoothing = 0;

    UpdateState(ref simulationState);

    if (currentSmoothing > 0)
    {
        UpdateState(ref previousState);
        ApplySmoothing();
    }
    else
    {
        //No smoothing required, just do a straight copy
        displayState = simulationState;
    }
}
```

We start by calculating how much we need to smooth our movement. This is based on the framesBetweenPackets passed in. We want to complete our smoothing operation at the same time the next packet should arrive.

We deduct the calculated smoothingDecay from our currentSmoothing value. We initialized currentSmoothing to 1 in our ReadNetworkPacket method. If we were sending a packet every frame, there would be no need for smoothing. We make sure the newly calculated currentSmoothing value is not less than zero. We then update the state on this remote player. As long as we need to smooth the results, we also update the previous state of this remote player so our calculations will work. Finally, we call the ApplySmoothing method, which we will discuss shortly. If there is no need to smooth the movements, we simply overwrite our display state with the simulation state. We were just returning the simulation state's Position and Velocity values before but we changed it to return the display state when we started to add in our prediction and smoothing algorithms.

The ApplySmoothing method is as follows:

```
private void ApplySmoothing()
{
    displayState.Position = Vector3.Lerp(simulationState.Position,
                                previousState.Position,
                                currentSmoothing);
```

```
displayState.Velocity = Vector3.Lerp(simulationState.Velocity,
                                     previousState.Velocity,
                                     currentSmoothing);
}
```

For both of the values in our state, we perform a linear interpolating calculation. You have seen this term a couple of times before. For our purposes, *interpolating* simply means we have a starting vector and an ending vector, along with a weight value that we can use to determine a new vector somewhere between the two. The XNA Framework provides the Lerp method on certain types, including Vector3. It takes in two Vector3 values and a float. The float should be a value between 0 and 1; it signifies the weight of the second vector over the first. By passing in our simulation state's position first and our previous state's position second, we can utilize the currentSmoothing float value we calculated to get a newly calculated vector where we will actually draw the player. We do the exact same calculation for the velocity of the player.

We can modify the values in the SetSimulatedValues method in our ChaseAndEvade game class to include some latency and packet loss to see the code works over a system link. Just remember to reset these values to zero when shipping a real game!

We did not apply prediction or smoothing to the enemies, but that would be an excellent exercise to complete. We also left the WonGameState simply stating "You Won!!!" to everyone. Instead, we should put in logic similar what we used in the last chapter to display the exact players who won (including if there was a tie).

We need to tie up a few loose ends before we complete the chapter. We need to make sure we do not allow someone to pause a multiplayer game. In the Update method of the PlayingState class, we need to wrap the entire contents of the condition that checks to see if the Start button was pressed with the following condition:

```
if (OurGame.NetworkSession == null ||
    OurGame.NetworkSession.AllGamers.Count ==
    OurGame.NetworkSession.LocalGamers.Count)
```

In the preceding condition where we check whether the Back button was pressed, we need to wrap the assignment of storedTime with the same condition. This will prevent the player from pausing the game or stopping his or her timer when bringing up the menu.

Although we will not do so here, it would be beneficial to create a separate menu to bring up while the game is being played. The new menu should restrict the options because the gamer was in a certain game. We discuss trial modes in the next part of the book; however, our menu items should have an option to buy the game, which should only be visible if the game is running in trial mode.

Another task that should be completed is to trim down the amount of data we are passing across the wire. To keep the code a little more simple, we have been passing around Vector3 types for the position and velocity values. Chapter 25 explained a way to trim the size of the data we need to send across the wire. Although we trimmed some of the other types, it would be a good idea to also trim down the amount of bytes we are passing around for the position and velocity.

Summary

This completes a very comprehensive look at writing networking games. In this part of the book, we have discussed the theory behind creating network games. We talked about ways to condense the amount of data we need to send across the Internet. We created a simple network demo for the Zune that also ran on Windows and the Xbox 360. We created a template we can use as a starting point for our network games. We created a turn-based game in the last chapter and a fully functional real-time game in this chapter.

We have written a lot of reusable networking code. We created two games that allow multiple players to play locally and remotely. Our games even allow multiple people to play locally while playing against multiple people at a different location. Many games out don't even tackle networking. It is not easy to get right, but we made great progress in getting two complete games working successfully across the Internet.

In the next part of the book, we will look at some best practices for creating Xbox LIVE Community Games. We round out the book discussing ways we can make money by selling the games we make. Congratulations on getting through the hardest part of the book!

PART XI

Xbox LIVE Community Games

CHAPTER 30

Best Practices for Creating an Xbox LIVE Community Game

Xbox LIVE Community Games (XBLCG) are games we can upload to the Xbox LIVE servers and sell to any Xbox LIVE member. We have spent the entire book seeing what it takes to create a game. We have covered a lot of material that should help us create a great game. In this last part of the book, we will look at making sure our masterpieces are using the best practices for community games and discussing what it takes to sell games on Xbox LIVE.

This chapter discusses the best practices you should be aware of when developing Xbox LIVE Community Games. When gamers play AAA titles as well as Xbox LIVE Arcade games, they expect certain things to work consistently. For example, they expect to be able to cancel out of a menu item by pressing the B button. We will discuss some of these best practices we want to incorporate to make our games as great as they can be so we do not frustrate any potential gamers.

Handling Any Display

Regardless of whether our game is being played on a 15" monitor, a 21" TV, or a 200" projector screen, we need to make sure the game is displayed correctly. Different displays may have different resolutions, aspect ratios, and overscan areas. We discussed using the TitleSafeArea, which is extremely important to make sure any critical data shows up on the display.

We should set our game's resolution to 1280×720. By using 720p native resolution, we can be sure the game will work on all televisions. By targeting this resolution, we have a consistent way to manage our textures.

When displaying text, we should always use at least a 14-point font. This ensures that the text can be read on smaller standard-definition televisions. We want to draw the sprite fonts at their full size and not scale them down.

Game Artwork

When creating artwork assets for our games, we want to make sure we do not use the same artwork for our Windows games and our Xbox 360 games. For example, if we have a help texture that displays the controller and what each button does, it does not look good to have a keyboard and a mouse on the same graphic. This hurts the Xbox 360 console experience.

Consistent Controls

Our games should always support the Xbox 360 controller. Even if we are expecting the gamer to have a steering wheel, guitar, big button controller, or any other type of controller, we need to make sure the game is playable with a normal controller.

Also we should not hard-code the game to only use player index 0 (PlayerIndex.One). Gamers expect that any controller they pick up will be the one the game recognizes for the input. Perhaps they have a guitar in the first player controller slot and want to use a regular controller for the game. Also once the player starts using the controller, the game should not allow input from any other controllers. It would not be fun for the player if someone were to pick up a second controller and mess up the game play with any actions taken with that controller.

We determine which controller to use by checking input from any controller on our start screen (TitleIntroState). As soon as the Start button is pressed, we pass in the corresponding player index to the next game state. This keeps any other controllers from affecting the game after the start page is passed.

Even though we should always support the Xbox 360 controller, we also should handle multiple controller types. If our game is well-suited for the racing wheel, for example, we should definitely work to make sure it handles that type of controller correctly. There are many types of controllers that the XNA Framework supports. Not only does it support the Xbox 360 controller, but it also supports flight sticks, arcade sticks, dance pads, steering wheels, big button controllers, guitars (and alternate guitars), and drum kits. To determine what controller our player is using, we can call the GamePad.GetCapabilities method to check the GamePadCapabilities.GamePadType return value.

If the user presses the Guide button, we should make sure the game goes into a paused state if it is currently playing in a single-player mode. It would not be very nice to let the gamer be obliterated by the enemies while he or she is using the Guide. We can check to see if the game is active by checking the IsActive property on the Game object. The game should also pause automatically if the controller becomes disconnected from the system. We can poll to see if the controller is connected in our Update method. For multiplayer games, however, bringing up the Guide or an unconnected controller should not pause the game. We can check the IsConnected property on the game pad state to determine if a controller was connected but then became disconnected. We simply store the previous and current states and compare the two.

Handling Menus Appropriately

We have created some menus in our games. These menus need a little work to behave in an appropriate manner. Menus should allow navigation with the left thumbstick as well as the D-pad. Menu operations should notify the user of both valid and invalid actions. The user should be able to see and hear whether or not an action was successful. Pressing A should select the menu item. Pressing B should cancel out of the menu and return to the previous state.

When displaying an active menu item, we need to use graphical items such as pulsating text for gamers who cannot easily discern the color differences between the selected menu item and the unselected items. If an invalid selection is made, the gamer needs to be made aware of the error, and it should be obvious what the gamer should do next.

We definitely want to make sure we remove the default code in the game's Update method that exits the game without warning when the controller's Back button is pressed. We have been allowing gamers to exit after they get all the way back to the title screen. We could even add in a confirmation message here.

Trial Mode Experience

Our Xbox LIVE Community Game gets a trial mode out of the box. When a gamer downloads a demo of our game, the XNA Framework runs the game in trial mode. This is a timed mode that allows the gamer to play the game for a short time and encourages him or her to purchase the game. For trial games there is no Xbox LIVE matchmaking. We should disable any menu items to Xbox LIVE multiplayer games—or we could bring up the marketplace if the user has selected the entry. You will see how to bring up the marketplace shortly.

We can check to see if our game is running in trial mode by querying the Guide.IsTrialMode property. If the property returns true, the game is in trial mode. This property is initialized to true and can be changed when the gamer purchases the game or signs in, or it can change on its own shortly after the game starts up. Because of this, we should not simply check the value once at startup. Instead, we should check on every frame. It would be wise to create a menu entry for purchasing the game if the game is in trial mode. We want to make it as easy as possible for the gamer to purchase our game.

Because trial mode only runs our game for a small amount of time, we need to determine ways to give the player a great sampling of our game play. This may mean we want to skip certain intro screens and just jump to game play. It may be we want to ignore any story information typically displayed when the game starts. At the time of this writing, the trial mode time is set to 4 minutes. This may be changed at a later date. As you design your games, you need to think about how you can get potential buyers hooked on your game idea and game play in just a few minutes. This can be challenging.

If, for some reason, we wanted to end the trial mode before the time is up, we can call the `Guide.ShowMarketplace` method. This will activate the purchase screen. When the purchase screen is opened, the `Game.IsActive` flag is set to false. If we followed earlier advice, we will pause the game. This is important because the gamer may purchase the game. If the player purchases the game, we want to make sure he or she can continue the game where it left off. This means we need to be able to handle the fact that `IsTrialMode` can change in the middle of game play. We should not require a restart of the game to take advantage of the fact that the player bought the game. We may need to stop the game play and reload the game data. It would be best to change anything we need immediately without losing the game state.

When the player exits our game in trial mode, we may want to display a state that gives the gamer the option to go to the Marketplace to purchase the game by using the `Guide.ShowMarketplace` method.

We can simulate trial mode by setting the aptly named `Guide.SimulateTrialMode` property to true. We can also select the "Play Trial Game" option on the Xbox 360 Dashboard to launch our game, which sets the `IsTrialMode` property to true. In order to simulate a player purchasing our game, we can set the `Guide.SimulateTrialMode` property to false in the middle of trial game play via a non-used button on the controller being pressed. It is important to make sure our game continues to run without requiring a restart.

Handling Any Audio System

Just like we want our game to work on any display, we want our game's sound to be right on any audio system. Perhaps the game is being played with a device that only produces mono sound—it might be played on a 5.1 surround sound system or just on a normal stereo system. The gamer could also be using headphones.

The main goal we want to achieve is keeping all our sound assets at the same volume. We do not want to make the player change volume because the songs and sound effects are at different volume levels. A good way to make sure our sounds are at a good level is by listening to the Xbox 360 startup sound. We should set our volume so that when we turn on the Xbox 360, the startup sound is loud but not overbearing. We should then match our game sounds to that sound level.

We also want to allow the gamer to turn down the music or the sound effects. We should allow the gamer to mute the music as well. We want to make sure the music in our game is set to the music category (either in XACT or by setting the appropriate music content processor). This way, gamers can utilize their own music.

Using the Gamer Profile

Gamer profiles are used to identify the different gamers. They are used to store saved games, to identify a user to store a high score in the high score list, and to determine what the game defaults are (such as the Y axis being inverted). We used the `Gamertag` in our games as well as the gamer profile picture. These can really add to the game play.

We can check the `Gamer.SignedInGamers` list, passing in our active controller to determine which gamer is signed in. We can handle `SignedInGamer.SignedOut` even on our active controller player index and return to the `TitleIntroState` (main menu) if appropriate. We could also just ignore this and continue with game play.

Networking Games

We spent a good portion of time creating networking games. Multiplayer games are not trivial, and having the ability to play other gamers around the world is a great feature. We need to make sure the gaming experience is user friendly.

Our multiplayer games should support invites. Allowing other gamers to join a game is a great way for interest in our game to spread. A gamer can send invites to his or her friends. Alternatively, those friends can see what the gamer is playing and join in.

If possible, our games should allow joining in progress. At the very least, we should allow some kind of observation mode if the game does not lend itself to changing the number of players midstream.

If we have a full-featured session list that can be customized by game type, we should still have a Quick Match feature so a player can quickly find a game and get into the action. Quick Match should be the default. This helps gamers find other players via Xbox LIVE more successfully.

If we create a Custom Match session with certain criteria, we should limit the number of sessions returned. This will make it easier for the player to pick a session. Our session lobby should display all the game match settings so the gamer knows what he or she is about to get into once the game starts.

It is very important to make sure our network games run successfully over the Internet. We should simulate latency and packet loss. We discussed these topics in detail in Part X, "XNA Framework Networking."

Some accounts cannot host or join multiplayer games on the Xbox LIVE. For example, some child accounts and all Xbox LIVE Silver accounts cannot host or join a network game, even if the game is purchased. We can verify whether a gamer is eligible to host or join a network game by checking the `Privileges.AllowOnlineSessions` flag in the `SignedInGamer` class.

Using Rich Presence

It is a good idea to set the rich presence data. This lets other players know what game the current gamer is playing. Not only is the game title broadcasted, but the values can be set with the predefined list of rich presence strings. Because the rich presence text can be viewed by anyone on Xbox LIVE, the text needs to be "E" rated. To ensure this, Xbox LIVE Community Games cannot set their own custom presence text. As we develop our games, the rich presence text would appear as follows:

> XNA Creators Club
>
> creators.xna.com
>
> PresenceMode Predefined String Here

Once a game has gone through peer review, we know the name of the game is clean. Because this is the case, an XBLCG shows the name of the game in place of the creators.xna.com text:

> XNA Creators Club
>
> Game Title
>
> PresenceMode Predefined String Here

Setting presence data is not required, but setting appropriate values in the presence mode is helpful.

Handling the Storage Device Correctly

When we save high scores, we need to ensure we pick the storage device appropriately. Either we can ask the player to select a storage device as soon as the game is launched, or if we do not need the storage device immediately, we can defer asking until we need it. When we saved the high score data in the TunnelVision, Concentration, and Chase and Evade games, we made sure we knew the storage device in which we were storing the file. We could have required the game to ask for this as soon as the game started. If a player wants to load a previously saved game, this would need to be done earlier. For the examples we used in this book, we didn't force the gamer to pick a storage device unless he or she was sent to the high score screen. We definitely do not want to ask the gamer to select a storage device more than once. The only exception to this would be if the player has disconnected his or her storage device. We can check the IsConnected property of the storage device to determine whether this is the case.

Marketing the Game

It is important that we use a nice thumbnail for our game. This is simply done by replacing the GameThumbnail.png file at the root of our game project. This way, as the gamer is scrolling through the list of games, he or she can see the game thumbnail to quickly identify our game.

Microsoft can put the game on a featured list. This list displays the box art and adds a nice polished look to our game. This way, a prospective buyer can see the box the game comes in. It is also important to take screenshots of our games as well as create videos. These items give the gamer a reason to download our game to try it out in the first place. The screenshots and videos can be thought of as the resume, whereas the trial mode can be thought of as the interview. We want to put our best foot forward so the gamer will be compelled to purchase our game. Figure 30.1 shows the images and details panes of an Xbox LIVE Community Game.

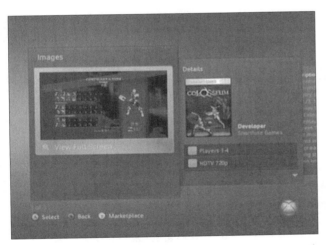

FIGURE 30.1   Community Games under Game Marketplace displays the screenshots taken of the game as well as the box art associated with the game.

Not only is this information displayed on Xbox LIVE, but it is also displayed on Xbox.com. Gamers can go to Xbox.com and browse to the Xbox LIVE Marketplace. They can purchase games directly from the e-commerce site and have the game downloads queue up on their Xbox 360. The screenshots and box art are all displayed on the website, as can be seen in Figure 30.2.

30

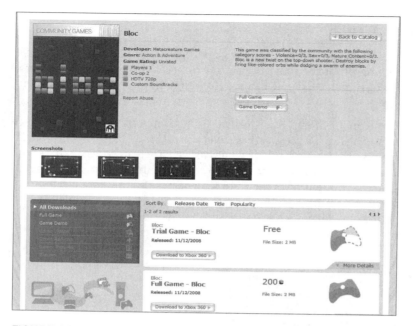

FIGURE 30.2   Xbox LIVE Marketplace on Xbox.com allows the gamer to see the box art and screenshots on the product detail page.

Summary

After those long networking chapters, we finally had a nice short chapter to discuss some best practices when developing games to sell on Xbox LIVE. Players expect games to behave in a certain way. This chapter is a reminder of some of the things we need to take care of in order to provide a great gaming experience. This chapter also provided some additional information that can help us market our game. We will spend the next chapter discussing what it takes to sell our game on Xbox LIVE.

CHAPTER 31

Selling the Game on Xbox LIVE Marketplace

Microsoft has provided a way for us to take the games we create and sell them on the Xbox LIVE Marketplace. We discussed some things to keep in mind when getting our games ready for the wild. In this chapter we will discuss how to utilize the Creators Club website for doing peer reviews of other developer projects as well as how to set up play testing, peer review, and final submission for our games. We will also discuss what Microsoft requires in order to pay us and how frequently we will get paid by Microsoft. All the information in this chapter is only applicable if you have a Creators Club Premium Membership. None of the items discussed in this chapter are available to non-Premium members. Trial memberships allow development on the Xbox 360, but none of these features are accessible to the trial membership.

Reviewing Other Creators' Games

To start off, we are going to see what it takes to review other peoples' games. This is important so we can see what will happen when we submit our games. Games in peer review should be considered finished games. This is not the place to test out games. That is done in the peer testing process, which we discuss a little later. This is the place we make sure there are no critical issues that cause the game to function improperly. We need to check specific things when reviewing a game. Obviously these are the same things we want to make sure our game is compliant with.

For a game to pass peer review, it needs to run without problems. It is not acceptable to release a game that does not work. Although our games can have a wide variety of content, some content is never acceptable. We then classify the game, which simply means we go through a list of settings and set the scale as to how much of the various content the game has. For example, Offensive Language can be set to 0 (which means there was no offensive or potentially offensive language), 1 (which means there is mean-spirited or demeaning language during game play but no vulgarity or profanity), 2 (which means there is occasional profanity or vulgarity in the game but it isn't a common experience), or 3 (which means there is mild swearing or expletives are present in the game). We will see a full list of unacceptable content shortly.

The Games Catalog on the Creators Club website can be seen in Figure 31.1. This is where we look for any games that need to be reviewed. For any game that says "In Review," we can click the "review this game" link to review the game.

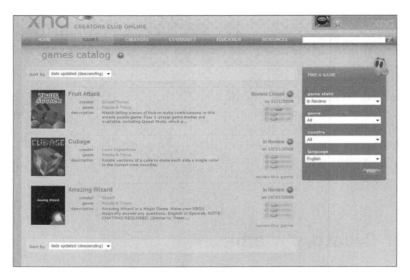

FIGURE 31.1   The Games Catalog on the Creators Club website is where Premium members can review any games waiting for evaluation.

If this is the first time we are reviewing the game, we are presented with a Peer Review Terms and Conditions page. It is important to read this carefully. If we are in agreement with the terms, we can click the Accept the Terms and Conditions check box and then click the Start Review button (see Figure 31.2).

We are presented with the actual game information page (see Figure 31.3). On this page we need to click the Download button to download the .ccgame file. While waiting for the game to download, we should read the description and make note of the capabilities so that when we play the game we can make sure they match up. We need to look at all the screenshots and watch the video in its entirety to make sure the material is appropriate. We can then unpack the .ccgame file, which will deploy the game to the Xbox 360.

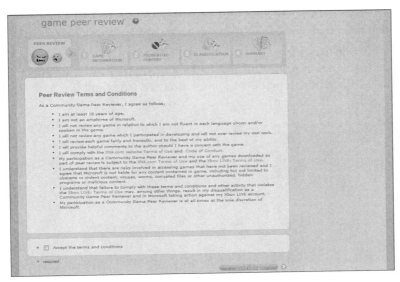

FIGURE 31.2 The first time we review a game, we are presented with the Peer Review Terms and Conditions page.

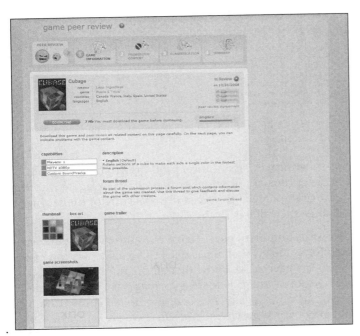

FIGURE 31.3 The first part of the Game Information page allows us to download the page and view the screenshots, description, capabilities, and videos for the game.

We need to make sure we have XNA Game Studio Connect running so it can deploy successfully. We then play the game, checking for any game defects or prohibited content.

We can then check any boxes where the game has defects or prohibited content on the second half of the Game Information page. This can be seen in Figure 31.4. If we check any of the boxes, we need to describe in detail what we witnessed (the limit is 1,024 characters).

FIGURE 31.4   The second part of the Game Information page allows us to check any boxes noting any game defects or prohibited content.

After we click Next, we are presented with the Classification page shown in Figure 31.5. The sliders are preset to whatever the creator of the game set them to. If we agree with the creator of the game, we do not change the sliders. However, if we feel any of the settings need to be different, we simply change the value with the slider.

The last step of the review process is the Summary page. Figure 31.6 shows the Summary page. This page should be checked for accuracy. If changes need to be made, we can click the Previous button to return to the last page. If we know that all the information is accurate, we can check the box at the bottom of the page for the languages we reviewed the game in. If any boxes were checked, signaling a game defect of prohibited content, we will see a rejection summary as well that contains our comments. Once we are satisfied, we can click the Submit Review button to submit the review and send feedback to the creator of the game.

Now that we have seen what it takes to review someone else's game, we can look at what it takes to submit our game to be reviewed by others.

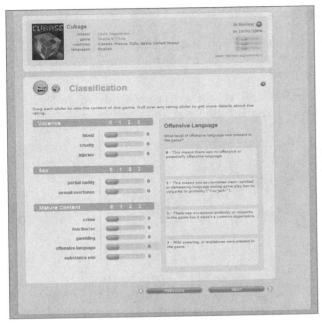

FIGURE 31.5   The Classification page allows us to change the values of any of the classification settings.

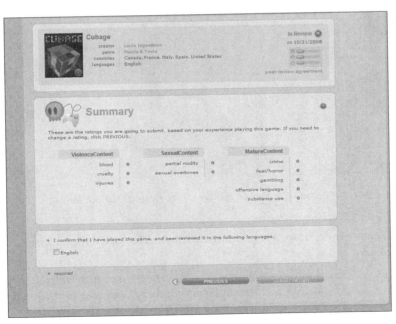

FIGURE 31.6   The Summary page allows us to see all the information we entered about the game before we submit.

Submitting Our Games

To begin, we select the Submit Game dropdown menu under Games on the Creators Club website. This brings us to the My Game Submission page shown in Figure 31.7. We simply enter the name of our game and click Done.

After some processing, the page will refresh, and we will see the screen shown in Figure 31.8. We can edit or delete the project. We can also click the Add Game button.

FIGURE 31.7   We start the process of submitting a game by adding a project to our profile. We enter the game title and click Done.

FIGURE 31.8   After we enter the game title, the project is in the system. To actually add the game, we click the Add Game button.

When we click the Add Game button, we are presented with the General Information page, shown in Figure 31.9.

At the top of the General Information page, we need to select the game genre from the dropdown list. We then need to specify how many players can play our game and whether it offers cooperative play. We can specify the maximum HDTV mode as well as whether we have a custom soundtrack. We also specify whether our game will run over Xbox LIVE, how many players the game supports, and whether cooperative play is allowed over LIVE.

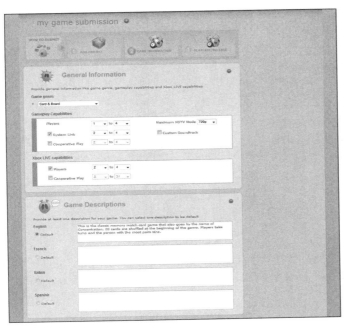

FIGURE 31.9   We need to enter general information about the game, including the genre, capabilities, and game description.

The next piece of information we need to add is the game description. Boxes are available for us to enter descriptions in different languages. We specify which language is the default by selecting the appropriate radio button. We can scroll down the page to see the same classification information we saw when we reviewed a game, as shown in Figure 31.10. We need to be as accurate as possible about the content of our game. If enough peer reviewers disagree with our classification, the game will be rejected.

The final part of the page is where we upload all the different images for our game. You can see this portion of the page in Figure 31.11. We need to include a 64×64 JPEG thumbnail that represents our game. We also need to provide a 584×700 JPEG gamebox that represents our game. We need to upload at least one 1000×562 JPEG screenshot. If we have a video, we can provide a link to MSN Soapbox. After we have provided all the information on our game, we can click the Done button.

After finishing entering the game information, we are presented with the Playtest and Game Release page. The top portion of this page can be seen in Figure 31.12. The description (from the default language) along with our classification and the thumbnail are displayed at the top of the page. The next section allows us to upload our new game binary. This is the actual .ccgame file we get by packaging our game file in Visual Studio. Simply right-click our project and select Package as XNA Creators Club Game from the menu. This will create the .ccgame file for us, which we can upload to this page.

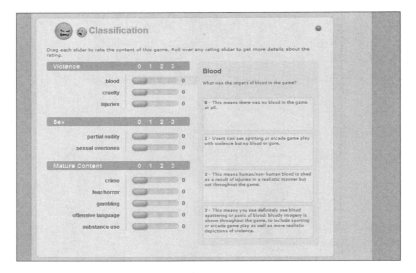

FIGURE 31.10   When we submit our game, we have to specify the classification of the game.

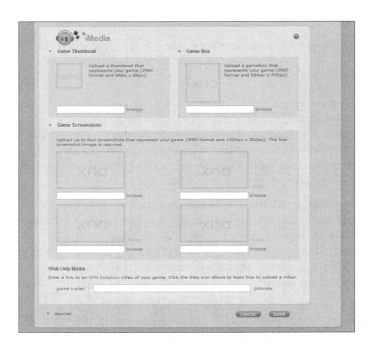

FIGURE 31.11   We need to add different images that represent our game. We can also associate an MSN Soapbox video to our game.

31

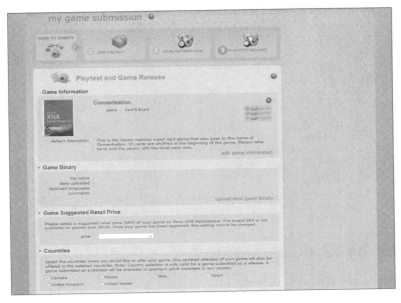

FIGURE 31.12   The final page of the submission process is where we actually upload our .ccgame file and set the price.

The actual location of the .ccgame file is under the bin/Xbox 360/Release folder. It is important to compile the game in release mode when we want to put our game up for peer review. After we upload our game, we can see what price options are available to us. If the game is over 50MB, then the lowest suggested retail price will not be available to select. We cannot submit a game that is over 150MB. This is the compressed size of the .ccgame file. If we are submitting the game for peer review, we can select the countries where we would like to offer our game. If we are submitting the game for playtesting, all countries will have access to the game.

When we submit our game to be playtested or peer reviewed, a forum entry will be created automatically. As we create the game submission, we can set the text that the first post in the thread will contain. This should include any important information on what should be tested or reviewed. The last section we see at the bottom of this page contains two radio buttons, where we pick whether we are submitting this game to be playtested or as a release to be peer reviewed (see Figure 31.13). Once we have picked the correct option, we can click the Submit button.

After we submit the game we should monitor the forum to check to see what kind of feedback we get so we can improve our game. Remember, we need to send our game to playtest before sending it to peer review.

FIGURE 31.13   We have to choose if the submission is a playtest submission or a release to be peer reviewed.

Making Money by Making Games

Any games you submit have the potential of being sold on Xbox LIVE, assuming they pass peer review. Because of the business side to this, you have to make sure you give Microsoft your tax information so that everything can be handled correctly. Under the Creators menu item on the Creators Club website is a dropdown menu item called My Business. When you click this item, you see a link where you can enter your personal tax information. The link takes you away from the Creators Club website and to an external payment provider.

The following personal information will be collected:

First name

Last name

Country

Account type

Street address

City

State/province

ZIP/postal code

Primary telephone number

Email address

U.S. tax identifier

The following bank information will be collected:

Routing number

Swift code

Account number

International bank account number

Account holder name

Bank name

Street address

City

State

ZIP/postal code

You have to enter all this information within 5 minutes. This is done for security purposes, so you need to make sure you have all your information ready. The web page displays a timer to show you how much time you have.

After you go through this process, you will be set up with Microsoft to get paid. You can make up to 70% on the sale of your games. If Microsoft places your game on the featured items list on the Xbox LIVE Marketplace, an additional 10% to 30% will be retained by Microsoft. This amount is not fixed. There is no way to ask Microsoft to not put your game on the featured list. It is expected to dramatically increase sales when a game is in a featured list. All royalties are calculated in U.S. dollars, and once you have obtained a minimum payout limit you get paid in your local currency. Creators will be paid every quarter. It will take no longer than 45 days after the end of the quarter to actually receive the funds. The minimum payout limit per quarter is $150.

If creating the game was a team effort, you will need to look into filing as a team (that is, as a business). If you do not file as a business, the team member that submits the game is responsible for the taxes associated with the revenue. It is always wise to consult a tax professional.

Summary

In this chapter, you have seen what is required to review other creators' games and what it takes to submit a game for review. You also learned the information you need to provide in order to get paid. It is a great thing to be able to take the knowledge you have and create an enjoyable game that you can distribute to all the Xbox LIVE members. There is nothing else like this. Although you could always create Windows games, there has never been a great distribution model for the indie game developer before now. The potential of selling games through the Xbox LIVE Marketplace is very great.

We have covered a lot of material in this book. We discussed many concepts and many techniques that can aid in making great games. You can take this knowledge and apply your own creativity and hard work to create some really amazing games!

Index

Numerics

E

F

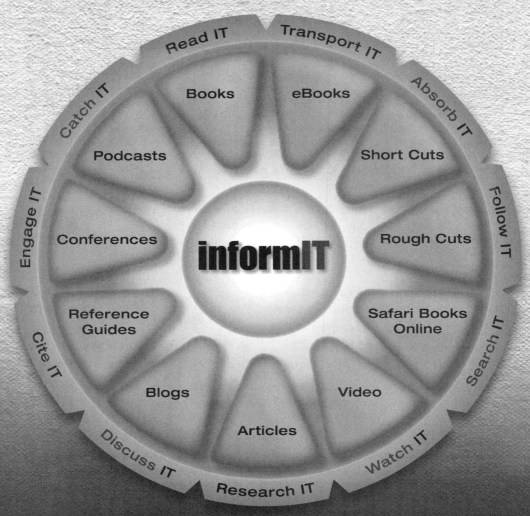

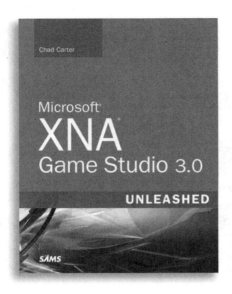

FREE Online
Edition

Your purchase of **Microsoft XNA Game Studio 3.0 Unleashed** includes access to a free online edition for 120 days through the Safari Books Online subscription service. Nearly every Sams book is available online through Safari Books Online, along with more than 5,000 other technical books and videos from publishers such as Addison-Wesley Professional, Cisco Press, Exam Cram, IBM Press, O'Reilly, Prentice Hall, and Que.

SAFARI BOOKS ONLINE allows you to search for a specific answer, cut and paste code, download chapters, and stay current with emerging technologies.

Activate your FREE Online Edition at www.informit.com/safarifree

> **STEP 1:** Enter the coupon code: UXOGKEH.

> **STEP 2:** New Safari users, complete the brief registration form.
> Safari subscribers, just log in.

If you have difficulty registering on Safari or accessing the online edition, please e-mail customer-service@safaribooksonline.com